THE WILEY BICENTENNIAL–KNOWLEDGE FOR GENERATIONS

Each generation has its unique needs and aspirations. When Charles Wiley first opened his small printing shop in lower Manhattan in 1807, it was a generation of boundless potential searching for an identity. And we were there, helping to define a new American literary tradition. Over half a century later, in the midst of the Second Industrial Revolution, it was a generation focused on building the future. Once again, we were there, supplying the critical scientific, technical, and engineering knowledge that helped frame the world. Throughout the 20th Century, and into the new millennium, nations began to reach out beyond their own borders and a new international community was born. Wiley was there, expanding its operations around the world to enable a global exchange of ideas, opinions, and know-how.

For 200 years, Wiley has been an integral part of each generation's journey, enabling the flow of information and understanding necessary to meet their needs and fulfill their aspirations. Today, bold new technologies are changing the way we live and learn. Wiley will be there, providing you the must-have knowledge you need to imagine new worlds, new possibilities, and new opportunities.

Generations come and go, but you can always count on Wiley to provide you the knowledge you need, when and where you need it!

William J. Pesce
WILLIAM J. PESCE
PRESIDENT AND CHIEF EXECUTIVE OFFICER

Peter Booth Wiley
PETER BOOTH WILEY
CHAIRMAN OF THE BOARD

www.wiley.com/college/microsoft ***or***
call the MOAC Toll-Free Number: 1+(888) 764-7001 (U.S. & Canada only)

www.wiley.com/college/microsoft *or*
call the MOAC Toll-Free Number: 1+(888) 764-7001 (U.S. & Canada only)

Microsoft Certified Application Specialist (MCAS)

Approved Courseware

▪ What does this logo mean?

It means this courseware has been approved by the Microsoft® Certified Application Specialist program to be among the finest available for learning Microsoft® Office Word 2007, Microsoft® Office Excel 2007, Microsoft® Office PowerPoint 2007, Microsoft® Office Access 2007, Microsoft® Office Outlook 2007, or Microsoft® Windows Vista™. It also means that upon completion of this courseware, you may be prepared to take an exam for Microsoft Certified Application Specialist qualification.

▪ What is a Microsoft Certified Application Specialist?

A Microsoft Certified Application Specialist is an individual who has passed exams for certifying his or her skills in one or more of the Microsoft Office desktop applications such as Microsoft Word, Microsoft Excel, Microsoft PowerPoint, Microsoft Outlook, Microsoft Access or on the Microsoft Windows Vista operating system. The Microsoft Certified Application Specialist program is the only program approved by Microsoft for testing proficiency in Microsoft Office desktop applications or the Microsoft Windows operating system. This testing program can be a valuable asset in any job search or career development.

▪ More Information

To learn more about becoming a Microsoft Certified Application Specialist and exam availability, visit www.microsoft.com/learning/msbc.

Microsoft® Official Academic Course

Microsoft® Windows Vista™

Credits

EXECUTIVE EDITOR	John Kane
SENIOR EDITOR	Gary Schwartz
DIRECTOR OF MARKETING AND SALES	Mitchell Beaton
MICROSOFT STRATEGIC RELATIONSHIPS MANAGER	Merrick Van Dongen of Microsoft Learning
GLOBAL MOAC MANAGER	Laura McKenna
DEVELOPMENT AND PRODUCTION	Custom Editorial Productions, Inc
EDITORIAL ASSISTANT	Jennifer Lartz
PRODUCTION MANAGER	Kelly Tavares
CREATIVE DIRECTOR/COVER DESIGNER	Harry Nolan
TECHNOLOGY AND MEDIA	Lauren Supira/Elena Santa Maria
COVER PHOTO	Corbis

Wiley 200th Anniversary logo designed by: Richard J. Pacifico

This book was set in Garamond by Aptara, Inc. and printed and bound by Bind Rite Graphics.
The covers were printed by Phoenix Color.

ISBN-13 978-0-47006956–1

Printed in the United States of America

10 9 8 7 6 5 4 3 2

Foreword from the Publisher

Wiley's publishing vision for the Microsoft Official Academic Course series is to provide students and instructors with the skills and knowledge they need to use Microsoft technology effectively in all aspects of their personal and professional lives. Quality instruction is required to help both educators and students get the most from Microsoft's software tools and to become more productive. Thus our mission is to make our instructional programs trusted educational companions for life.

To accomplish this mission, Wiley and Microsoft have partnered to develop the highest quality educational programs for Information Workers, IT Professionals, and Developers. Materials created by this partnership carry the brand name "Microsoft Official Academic Course," assuring instructors and students alike that the content of these textbooks is fully endorsed by Microsoft, and that they provide the highest quality information and instruction on Microsoft products. The Microsoft Official Academic Course textbooks are "Official" in still one more way—they are the officially sanctioned courseware for Microsoft IT Academy members.

The Microsoft Official Academic Course series focuses on *workforce development.* These programs are aimed at those students seeking to enter the workforce, change jobs, or embark on new careers as information workers, IT professionals, and developers. Microsoft Official Academic Course programs address their needs by emphasizing authentic workplace scenarios with an abundance of projects, exercises, cases, and assessments.

The Microsoft Official Academic Courses are mapped to Microsoft's extensive research and job-task analysis, the same research and analysis used to create the Microsoft Certified Application Specialist (MCAS) and Microsoft Certified Application Professional (MCAP) exams. The textbooks focus on real skills for real jobs. As students work through the projects and exercises in the textbooks they enhance their level of knowledge and their ability to apply the latest Microsoft technology to everyday tasks. These students also gain resume-building credentials that can assist them in finding a job, keeping their current job, or in furthering their education.

The concept of life-long learning is today an utmost necessity. Job roles, and even whole job categories, are changing so quickly that none of us can stay competitive and productive without continuously updating our skills and capabilities. The Microsoft Official Academic Course offerings, and their focus on Microsoft certification exam preparation, provide a means for people to acquire and effectively update their skills and knowledge. Wiley supports students in this endeavor through the development and distribution of these courses as Microsoft's official academic publisher.

Today educational publishing requires attention to providing quality print and robust electronic content. By integrating Microsoft Official Academic Course products, Wiley*PLUS*, and Microsoft certifications, we are better able to deliver efficient learning solutions for students and teachers alike.

Bonnie Lieberman
General Manager and Senior Vice President

www.wiley.com/college/microsoft *or*
call the MOAC Toll-Free Number: 1+(888) 764-7001 (U.S. & Canada only)

Preface

Welcome to the Microsoft Official Academic Course (MOAC) program for Microsoft Windows Vista. MOAC represents the collaboration between Microsoft Learning and John Wiley & Sons, Inc. publishing company. Microsoft and Wiley teamed up to produce a series of textbooks that deliver compelling and innovative teaching solutions to instructors and superior learning experiences for students. Infused and informed by in-depth knowledge from the creators of Microsoft Office and Windows Vista™, and crafted by a publisher known worldwide for the pedagogical quality of its products, these textbooks maximize skills transfer in minimum time. With MOAC, students are hands on right away—there are no superfluous text passages to get in the way of learning and using the software. Students are challenged to reach their potential by using their new technical skills as highly productive members of the workforce.

Because this knowledgebase comes directly from Microsoft, architect of the Microsoft 2007 Office System and the Windows Vista operating system and creator of the Microsoft Certified Application Specialist (MCAS) exams, you are sure to receive the topical coverage that is most relevant to students' personal and professional success. Microsoft's direct participation not only assures you that MOAC textbook content is accurate and current; it also means that students will receive the best instruction possible to enable their success on certification exams and in the workplace.

■ The Microsoft Official Academic Course Program

The *Microsoft Official Academic Course* series is a complete program for instructors and institutions to prepare and deliver great courses on Microsoft software technologies. With MOAC, we recognize that, because of the rapid pace of change in the technology and curriculum developed by Microsoft, there is an ongoing set of needs beyond classroom instruction tools for an instructor to be ready to teach the course. The MOAC program endeavors to provide solutions for all these needs in a systematic manner in order to ensure a successful and rewarding course experience for both instructor and student—technical and curriculum training for instructor readiness with new software releases; the software itself for student use at home for building hands-on skills, assessment, and validation of skill development; and a great set of tools for delivering instruction in the classroom and lab. All are important to the smooth delivery of an interesting course on Microsoft software, and all are provided with the MOAC program. We think about the model below as a gauge for ensuring that we completely support you in your goal of teaching a great course. As you evaluate your instructional materials options, you may wish to use the model for comparison purposes with available products.

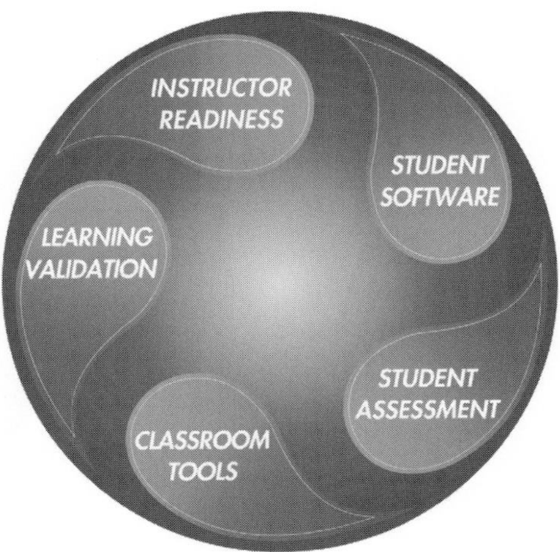

www.wiley.com/college/microsoft ***or***
call the MOAC Toll-Free Number: 1+(888) 764-7001 (U.S. & Canada only)

Illustrated Book Tour

■ Pedagogical Features

MOAC for Windows Vista is designed to cover all the learning objectives in the MCAS exams, referred to as "objective domains." The Microsoft Certified Application Specialist (MCAS) exam objectives are highlighted throughout the textbooks. Many pedagogical features have been developed specifically for *Microsoft Official Academic Course* programs. Unique features of our task-based approach include a Lesson Skill Matrix that correlates skills taught in each lesson to the MCAS objectives; Certification, Workplace, and Internet Ready exercises; and three levels of increasingly rigorous lesson-ending activities: Competency, Proficiency, and Mastery Assessment.

Presenting the extensive procedural information and technical concepts woven throughout the textbook raises challenges for the student and instructor alike. The Illustrated Book Tour that follows provides a guide to the rich features contributing to *Microsoft Official Academic Course* program's pedagogical plan. Following is a list of key features in each lesson designed to prepare students for success on the certification exams and in the workplace:

- Each lesson begins with a **Lesson Skill Matrix.** More than a standard list of learning objectives, the Skill Matrix correlates each software skill covered in the lesson to the specific MCAS "objective domain."
- Every lesson features a real-world **Business Case** scenario that places the software skills and knowledge to be acquired in a real-world setting.
- Every lesson opens with a **Software Orientation.** This feature provides an overview of the software features students will be working with in the lesson. The orientation will detail the general properties of the software or specific features, such as a ribbon or dialog box; and it includes a large, labeled screen image.
- Concise and frequent **Step-by-Step** instructions teach students new features and provide an opportunity for hands-on practice. Numbered steps give detailed, step-by-step instructions to help students learn software skills. The steps also show results and screen images to match what students should see on their computer screens.
- **Illustrations:** Screen images provide visual feedback as students work through the exercises. The images reinforce key concepts, provide visual clues about the steps, and allow students to check their progress.
- **Button images:** When the text instructs a student to click a particular toolbar button, an image of the button is shown in the margin.
- **Key Terms:** Important technical vocabulary is listed at the beginning of the lesson. When these terms are used later in the lesson, they appear in bold italic type and are defined. The Glossary contains all of the key terms and their definitions.
- Engaging point-of-use **Reader aids,** located throughout the lessons, tell students why this topic is relevant (*The Bottom Line*), provide students with helpful hints (*Take Note*), show alternate ways to accomplish tasks (*Another Way*), or point out things to watch out for or avoid (*Troubleshooting*). Reader aids also provide additional relevant or background information that adds value to the lesson.

- **Certification Ready?** features throughout the text signal students where a specific certification objective is covered. They provide students with a chance to check their understanding of that particular MCAS objective and, if necessary, review the section of the lesson where it is covered. MOAC offers complete preparation for MCAS certification.
- **New Feature:** The New Feature icon appears near any software feature that is new to Office 2007.
- **Competency, Proficiency, and Mastery Assessments** provide three progressively more challenging lesson-ending activities.
- **Internet Ready** projects combine the knowledge students acquire in a lesson with a Web-based research task.
- **Circling Back.** These integrated projects provide students with an opportunity to review and practice skills learned in previous lessons.
- **Workplace Ready.** These features preview how Microsoft Windows Vista is used in real-world situations.
- **Student CD:** The companion CD contains the data files needed for each lesson. These files are indicated by the CD icon in the margin of the textbook.

■ Lesson Features

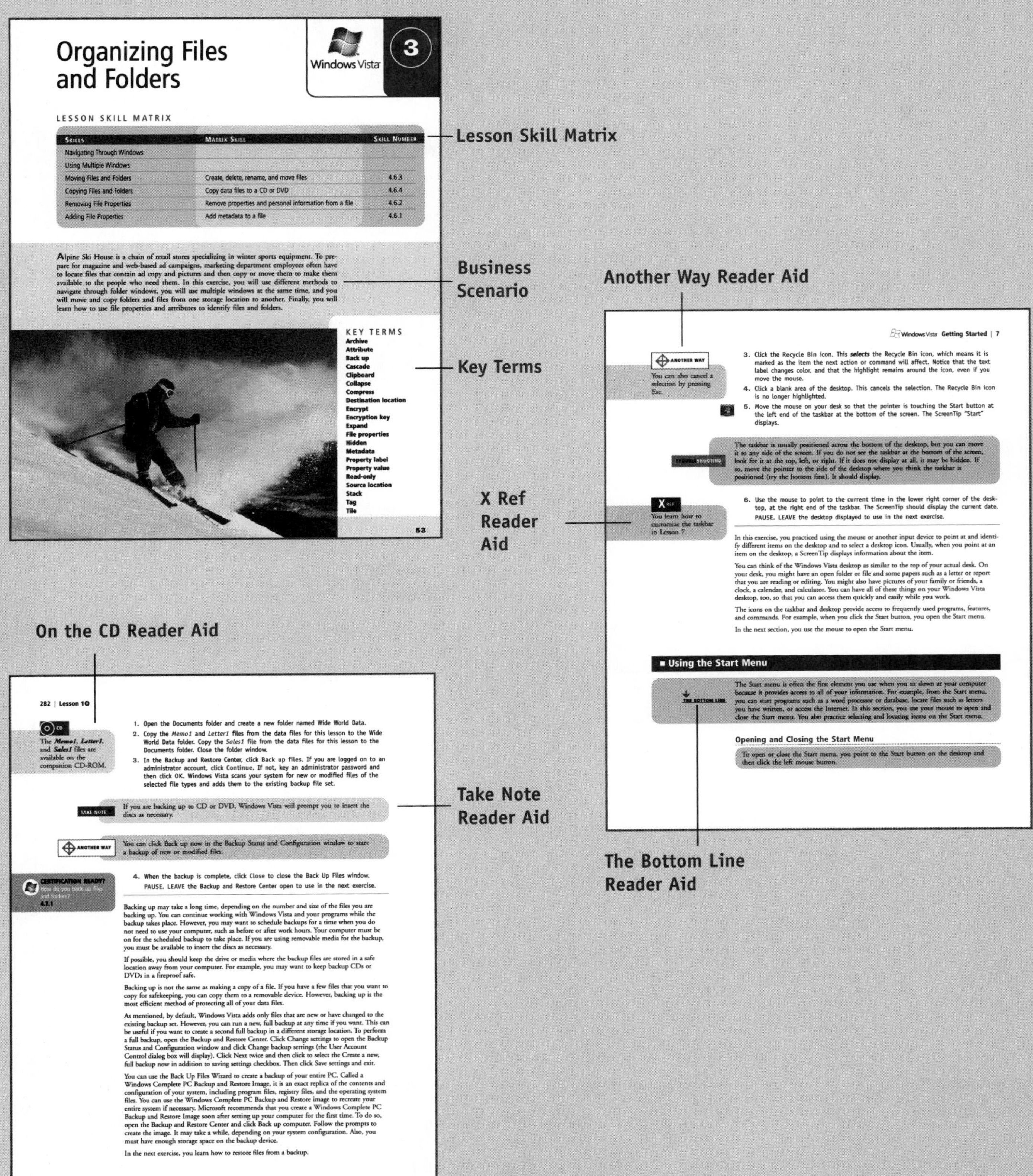

www.wiley.com/college/microsoft ***or***
call the MOAC Toll-Free Number: 1+(888) 764-7001 (U.S. & Canada only)

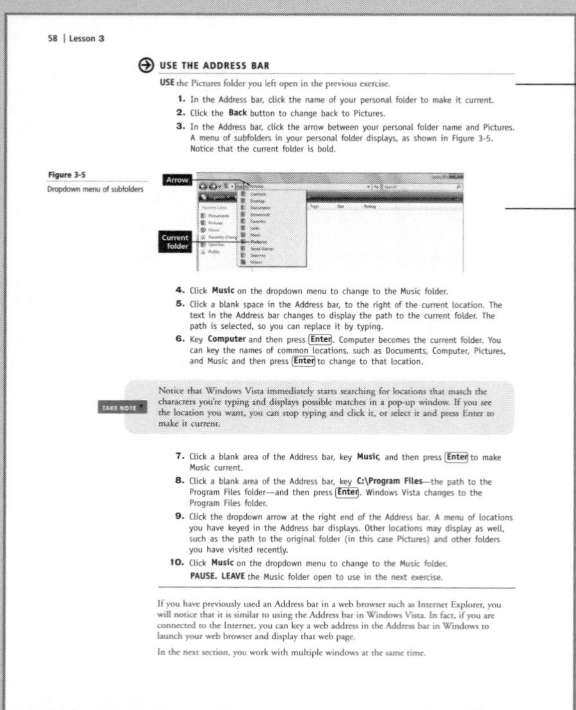

58 | Lesson 3

USE THE ADDRESS BAR

USE the Pictures folder you left open in the previous exercise.

1. In the Address bar, click the name of your personal folder to make it current.
2. Click the **Back** button to change back to Pictures.
3. In the Address bar, click the arrow between your personal folder name and Pictures. A menu of subfolders in your personal folder displays, as shown in Figure 3-5. Notice that the current folder is bold.

Figure 3-5
Dropdown menu of subfolders

4. Click **Music** on the dropdown menu to change to the Music folder.
5. Click a blank space in the Address bar, to the right of the current location. The text in the Address bar changes to display the path to the current folder. The path is selected, so you can replace it by typing.
6. Key **Computer** and then press Enter. Computer becomes the current folder. You can key the names of common locations, such as Documents, Computer, Pictures, and Music and then press Enter to change to that location.

TAKE NOTE: Notice that Windows Vista immediately starts searching for locations that match the characters you're typing and displays possible matches in a pop-up window. If you see the location you want, you can stop typing and click it, or select it and press Enter to make it current.

7. Click a blank area of the Address bar, key **Music**, and then press Enter to make Music current.
8. Click a blank area of the Address bar, key **C:\Program Files**—the path to the Program Files folder—and then press Enter. Windows Vista changes to the Program Files folder.
9. Click the dropdown arrow at the right end of the Address bar. A menu of locations you have keyed in the Address bar displays. Other locations may display as well, such as the path to the original folder (in this case Pictures) and other folders you have visited recently.
10. Click **Music** on the dropdown menu to change to the Music folder.

PAUSE. LEAVE the Music folder open to use in the next exercise.

If you have previously used an Address bar in a web browser such as Internet Explorer, you will notice that it is similar to using the Address bar in Windows Vista. In fact, if you are connected to the Internet, you can key a web address in the Address bar in Windows to launch your web browser and display that web page.

In the next section, you work with multiple windows at the same time.

Hands-On Practice

Screen Images with Callouts

Troubleshooting Reader Aid

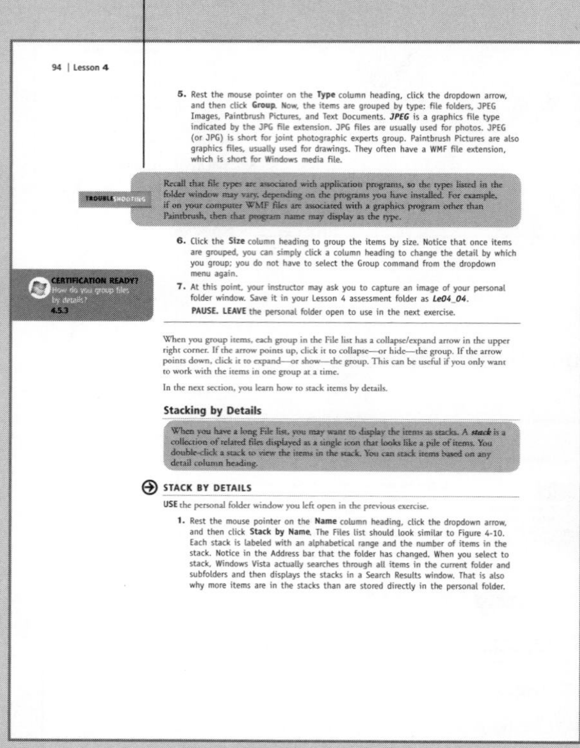

94 | Lesson 4

5. Rest the mouse pointer on the **Type** column heading, click the dropdown arrow, and then click **Group**. Now, the items are grouped by type: file folders, JPEG Images, Paintbrush Pictures, and Text Documents. ***JPEG*** is a graphics file type indicated by the JPG file extension. JPG files are usually used for photos. JPEG (or JPG) is short for joint photographic experts group. Paintbrush Pictures are also graphics files, usually used for drawings. They often have a WMF file extension, which is short for Windows media file.

TROUBLESHOOTING: Recall that file types are associated with application programs, so the types listed in the folder window may vary, depending on the programs you have installed. For example, if on your computer WMF files are associated with a graphics program other than Paintbrush, then that program name may display as the type.

6. Click the **Size** column heading to group the items by size. Notice that once items are grouped, you can simply click a column heading to change the detail by which you group; you do not have to select the Group command from the dropdown menu again.
7. At this point, your instructor may ask you to capture an image of your personal folder window. Save it in your Lesson 4 assessment folder as ***Le04_04***.

PAUSE. LEAVE the personal folder open to use in the next exercise.

CERTIFICATION READY? How do you group files by details? 4.5.3

When you group items, each group in the File list has a collapse/expand arrow in the upper right corner. If the arrow points up, click it to collapse—or hide—the group. If the arrow points down, click it to expand—or show—the group. This can be useful if you only want to work with the items in one group at a time.

In the next section, you learn how to stack items by details.

Stacking by Details

When you have a long File list, you may want to display the items as stacks. A ***stack*** is a collection of related files displayed as a single icon that looks like a pile of items. You double-click a stack to view the items in the stack. You can stack items based on any detail column heading.

STACK BY DETAILS

USE the personal folder window you left open in the previous exercise.

1. Rest the mouse pointer on the **Name** column heading, click the dropdown arrow, and then click **Stack by Name**. The Files list should look similar to Figure 4-10. Each stack is labeled with an alphabetical range and the number of items in the stack. Notice in the Address bar that the folder has changed. When you select to stack, Windows Vista actually searches through all items in the current folder and subfolders and then displays the stacks in a Search Results window. That is also why more items are in the stacks than are stored directly in the personal folder.

Easy-to-Read Tables

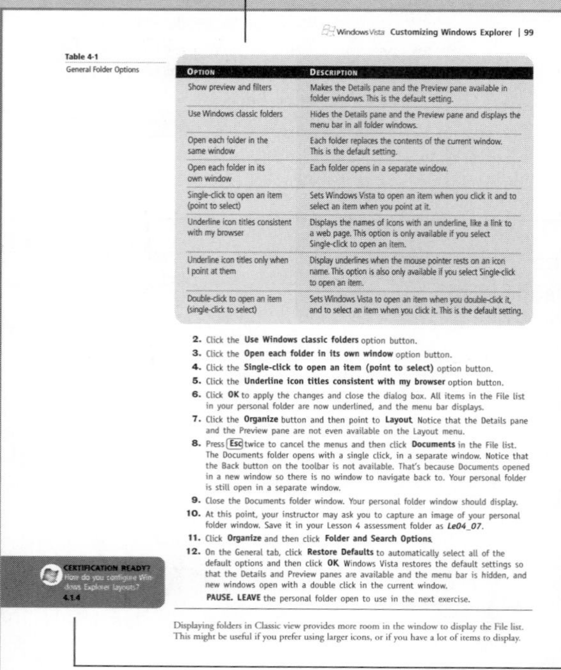

Windows Vista Customizing Windows Explorer | 99

Table 4-1
General Folder Options

Option	Description
Show preview and filters	Makes the Details pane and the Preview pane available in folder windows. This is the default setting.
Use Windows classic folders	Hides the Details pane and the Preview pane and displays the menu bar in all folder windows.
Open each folder in the same window	Each folder replaces the contents of the current window. This is the default setting.
Open each folder in its own window	Each folder opens in a separate window.
Single-click to open an item (point to select)	Sets Windows Vista to open an item when you click it and to select an item when you point at it.
Underline icon titles consistent with my browser	Displays the names of icons with an underline, like a link to a web page. This option is only available if you select Single-click to open an item.
Underline icon titles only when I point at them	Display underlines when the mouse pointer rests on an icon name. This option is also only available if you select Single-click to open an item.
Double-click to open an item (single-click to select)	Sets Windows Vista to open an item when you double-click it, and to select an item when you click it. This is the default setting.

2. Click the **Use Windows classic folders** option button.
3. Click the **Open each folder in its own window** option button.
4. Click the **Single-click to open an item (point to select)** option button.
5. Click the **Underline icon titles consistent with my browser** option button.
6. Click **OK** to apply the changes and close the dialog box. All items in the File list in your personal folder are now underlined, and the menu bar displays.
7. Click the **Organize** button and then point to **Layout**. Notice that the Details pane and the Preview pane are not even available on the Layout menu.
8. Press Esc twice to cancel the menus and then click **Documents** in the File list. The Documents folder opens with a single click, in a separate window. Notice that the Back button on the toolbar is not available. That's because Documents opened in a new window so there is no window to navigate back to. Your personal folder is still open in a separate window.
9. Close the Documents folder window. Your personal folder window should display.
10. At this point, your instructor may ask you to capture an image of your personal folder window. Save it in your Lesson 4 assessment folder as ***Le04_07***.
11. Click **Organize** and then click **Folder and Search Options**.
12. On the General tab, click **Restore Defaults** to automatically select all of the default options and then click **OK**. Windows Vista restores the default settings so that the Details and Preview panes are available and the menu bar is hidden, and new windows open with a double click in the current window.

PAUSE. LEAVE the personal folder open to use in the next exercise.

CERTIFICATION READY? How do you configure Windows Explorer layouts? 4.1.4

Displaying folders in Classic view provides more room in the window to display the File list. This might be useful if you prefer using larger icons, or if you have a lot of items to display.

Microsoft Certified Application Specialist (MCAS) Certification Objective Alert

www.wiley.com/college/microsoft *or*
call the MOAC Toll-Free Number: 1+(888) 764-7001 (U.S. & Canada only)

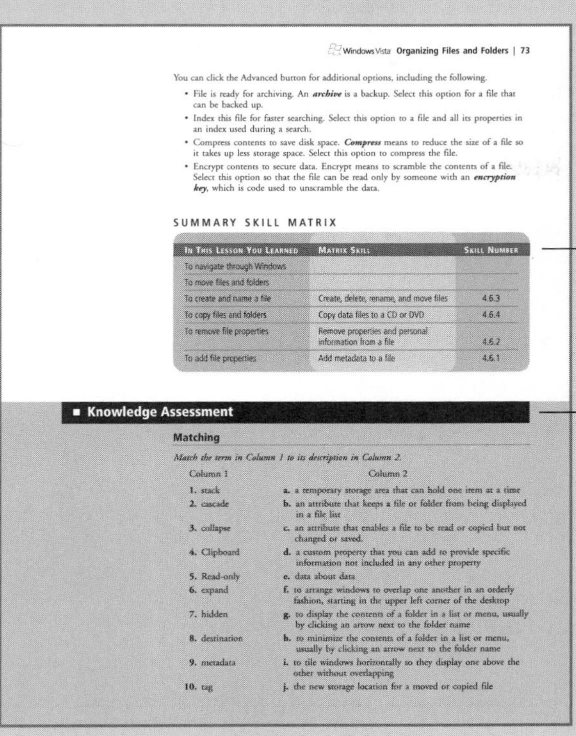

Windows Vista Organizing Files and Folders | 73

You can click the Advanced button for additional options, including the following.

- File is ready for archiving. An ***archive*** is a backup. Select this option for a file that can be backed up.
- Index this file for faster searching. Select this option to a file and all its properties in an index used during a search.
- Compress contents to save disk space. ***Compress*** means to reduce the size of a file so it takes up less storage space. Select this option to compress the file.
- Encrypt contents to secure data. Encrypt means to scramble the contents of a file. Select this option so that the file can be read only by someone with an ***encryption key***, which is code used to unscramble the data.

SUMMARY SKILL MATRIX

In This Lesson You Learned	Matrix Skill	Skill Number
To navigate through Windows		
To move files and folders		
To create and name a file	Create, delete, rename, and move files	4.6.3
To copy files and folders	Copy data files to a CD or DVD	4.6.4
To remove file properties	Remove properties and personal information from a file	4.6.2
To add file properties	Add metadata to a file	4.6.1

■ Knowledge Assessment

Matching

Match the term in Column 1 to its description in Column 2.

Column 1	Column 2
1. stack	**a.** a temporary storage area that can hold one item at a time
2. cascade	**b.** an attribute that keeps a file or folder from being displayed in a file list
3. collapse	**c.** an attribute that enables a file to be read or copied but not changed or saved.
4. Clipboard	**d.** a custom property that you can add to provide specific information not included in any other property
5. Read-only	**e.** data about data
6. expand	**f.** to arrange windows to overlap one another in an orderly fashion, starting in the upper left corner of the desktop
7. hidden	**g.** to display the contents of a folder in a list or menu, usually by clicking an arrow next to the folder name
8. destination	**h.** to minimize the contents of a folder in a list or menu, usually by clicking an arrow next to the folder name
9. metadata	**i.** to tile windows horizontally so they display one above the other without overlapping
10. tag	**j.** the new storage location for a moved or copied file

Summary Skill Matrix

Knowledge Assessment Questions

Proficiency Assessment Projects

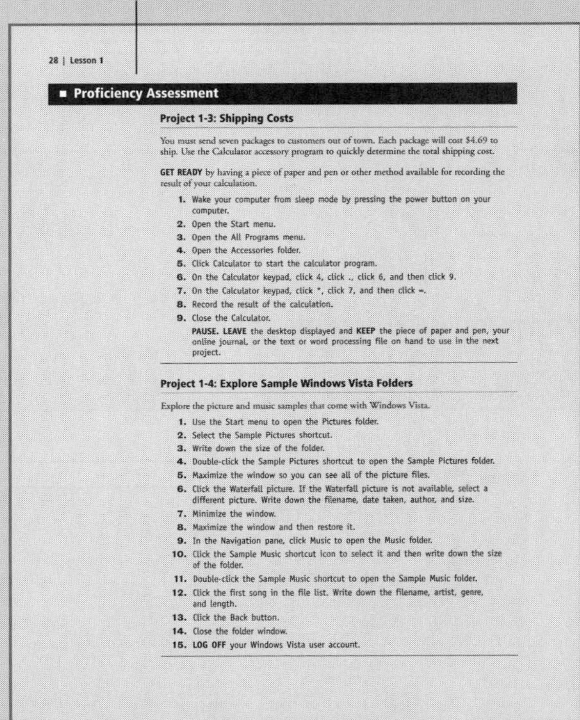

28 | Lesson 1

■ Proficiency Assessment

Project 1-3: Shipping Costs

You must send seven packages to customers out of town. Each package will cost $4.69 to ship. Use the Calculator accessory program to quickly determine the total shipping cost.

GET READY by having a piece of paper and pen or other method available for recording the result of your calculation.

1. Wake your computer from sleep mode by pressing the power button on your computer.
2. Open the Start menu.
3. Open the All Programs menu.
4. Open the Accessories folder.
5. Click Calculator to start the calculator program.
6. On the Calculator keypad, click 4, click ., click 6, and then click 9.
7. On the Calculator keypad, click *, click 7, and then click =.
8. Record the result of the calculation.
9. Close the Calculator.

   PAUSE. LEAVE the desktop displayed and **KEEP** the piece of paper and pen, your online journal, or the text or word processing file on hand to use in the next project.

Project 1-4: Explore Sample Windows Vista Folders

Explore the picture and music samples that come with Windows Vista.

1. Use the Start menu to open the Pictures folder.
2. Select the Sample Pictures shortcut.
3. Write down the size of the folder.
4. Double-click the Sample Pictures shortcut to open the Sample Pictures folder.
5. Maximize the window so you can see all of the picture files.
6. Click the Waterfall picture. If the Waterfall picture is not available, select a different picture. Write down the filename, date taken, author, and size.
7. Minimize the window.
8. Maximize the window and then restore it.
9. In the Navigation pane, click Music to open the Music folder.
10. Click the Sample Music shortcut icon to select it and then write down the size of the folder.
11. Double-click the Sample Music shortcut to open the Sample Music folder.
12. Click the first song in the file list. Write down the filename, artist, genre, and length.
13. Click the Back button.
14. Close the folder window.
15. **LOG OFF** your Windows Vista user account.

Competency Assessment Projects

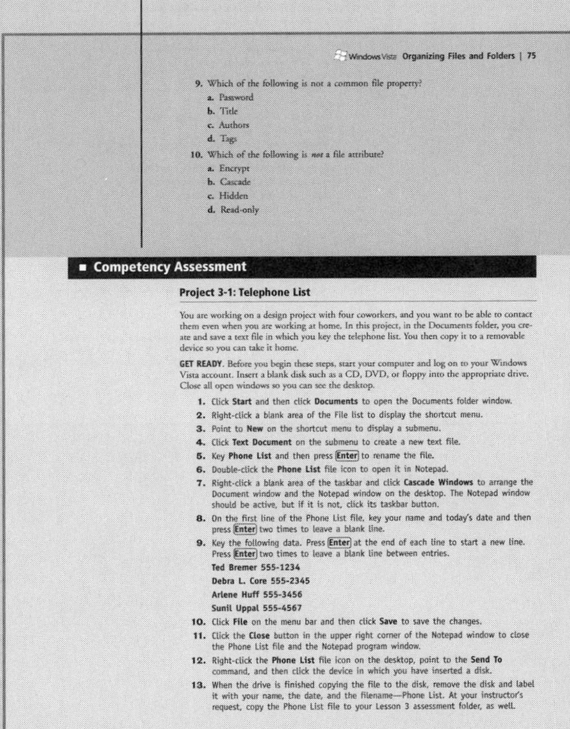

Windows Vista Organizing Files and Folders | 75

9. Which of the following is not a common file property?
   a. Password
   b. Title
   c. Authors
   d. Tags
10. Which of the following is *not* a file attribute?
   a. Encrypt
   b. Cascade
   c. Hidden
   d. Read-only

■ Competency Assessment

Project 3-1: Telephone List

You are working on a design project with four coworkers, and you want to be able to contact them even when you are working at home. In this project, in the Documents folder, you create and save a text file in which you key the telephone list. You then copy it to a removable device so you can take it home.

GET READY. Before you begin these steps, start your computer and log on to your Windows Vista account. Insert a blank disk such as a CD, DVD, or floppy into the appropriate drive. Close all open windows so you can see the desktop.

1. Click **Start** and then click **Documents** to open the Documents folder window.
2. Right-click a blank area of the File list to display the shortcut menu.
3. Point to **New** on the shortcut menu to display a submenu.
4. Click **Text Document** on the submenu to create a new text file.
5. Key **Phone List** and then press Enter to rename the file.
6. Double-click the **Phone List** file icon to open it in Notepad.
7. Right-click a blank area of the taskbar and click **Cascade Windows** to arrange the Document window and the Notepad window on the desktop. The Notepad window should be active, but if it is not, click its taskbar button.
8. On the first line of the Phone List file, key your name and today's date and then press Enter two times to leave a blank line.
9. Key the following data. Press Enter at the end of each line to start a new line. Press Enter two times to leave a blank line between entries.

   Ted Bremer 555-1234
   Debra L. Core 555-2345
   Arlene Huff 555-3456
   Sunil Uppal 555-4567
10. Click **File** on the menu bar and then click **Save** to save the changes.
11. Click the **Close** button in the upper right corner of the Notepad window to close the Phone List file and the Notepad program window.
12. Right-click the **Phone List** file icon on the desktop, point to the **Send To** command, and then click the device in which you have inserted a disk.
13. When the drive is finished copying the file to the disk, remove the disk and label it with your name, the date, and the filename—Phone List. At your instructor's request, copy the Phone List file to your Lesson 3 assessment folder, as well.

www.wiley.com/college/microsoft *or*
call the MOAC Toll-Free Number: 1+(888) 764-7001 (U.S. & Canada only)

Mastery Assessment

Mastery Assessment Projects

Project 1-5: Show Off Windows Vista

You recently hired an assistant who has never used a personal computer before. In this project, give him a tour of some of the basic features of Windows Vista.

1. Start your computer and log on to your account.
2. Using ScreenTips, locate the icon on the Quick Launch toolbar that displays the desktop.
3. Open your personal folder and select all items in the file list at the same time.
4. Maximize and then minimize the window.
5. Open the window and then restore it.
6. Move the window to the upper right corner of the desktop and then close it.
7. Open the Computer window and identify the different types of disk drives.
8. From the Computer window, open the Documents window.
9. Close the Documents window.
10. Open the Recycle Bin window and then close it.
11. Log off and then log back on.
12. Lock the computer.

PAUSE. LEAVE your computer locked until the next project.

Project 1-6: Windows Vista and Printers

Because you are working in a small office, you must be able to solve problems on your own. You are getting a new printer and want to learn how to set it up with your computer before it arrives. In this project, use Windows Help and Support to find out how to set up a printer for use with Windows Vista.

1. Unlock the computer and log on to your user account.
2. Open Windows Help and Support and display the Table of Contents.
3. Locate and click the link to information about Printers and printing.
4. Locate and click the link to information about Printers.
5. Open and read the information about adding or removing a printer.
6. When you are finished, close the Help and Support window.

LOG OFF your Windows Vista user account.

INTERNET READY

As was mentioned at the beginning of this lesson, Northwind Traders is a small, growing company that helps Inuit artists in Alaska market their work to customers around the globe. To prepare for a press release announcing the company's expansion, use Internet search tools to locate information about the history of Inuit art. For example, you might find out the types of traditional Inuit art created over the years, as well as the type of art created by contemporary artists. Use the information you find to write a paragraph that you can include in the press release that summarizes the evolution of Inuit art from the past to the present.

Internet Ready Project

Circling Back

The Baldwin Museum of Science is sponsoring a series of four seminars for high school science teachers. The manager of special events has hired you as a temporary assistant to help with the planning and organization of the seminars. In particular, you will be responsible for organizing information for seminar participants. Your manager has already given you a list of tasks that she needs completed quickly, including calculating the cost of lunch for the participants and organizing files for the seminar handbook.

Circling Back Projects

Project 1: Lunch Costs

Use the Calculator program to calculate the total cost of lunch for 57 participants. Insert the information into a text document, print the document, copy it to your CB1 assessment folder, and then delete it.

GET READY. Before you begin these steps, make sure your computer is connected to a printer, or to a network that has a printer. Verify that the printer has paper and that the printer is active, or turned on.

1. Start your computer and log on to your Windows Vista account.
2. Open the **Start** menu and then click **Documents**.
3. Create a new folder in Documents and rename it **Seminars**.
4. Open the **Seminars** folder and create a new text document named **Lunch**.
5. In the **Seminars** folder, create a folder named **Memos**.
6. Move the **Lunch** document into the **Memos** folder.
7. Open the **Lunch** document in Notepad.
8. Minimize the **Memos** folder window.
9. On the first line, key **Memorandum** and then press Enter twice.
10. Key today's date and then press Enter.
11. Key **To: Manager of Special Projects** and then press Enter.
12. Key **From:** and then key your name.
13. Press Enter twice and then key the following text, pressing Enter at the end of each line to start a new line:
    Based on the estimated cost of $9.85 per person,
    I have calculated that the total cost of lunch for the
    57 teachers attending the first seminar is
14. Save the changes to the file.
15. Open the **Start** menu and click **All Programs**.
16. Click **Accessories** and then click **Calculator**.
17. On the Calculator keypad, click 5, click 7, and then click *.
18. On the Calculator keypad, click 9, click the decimal point, click 8, click 5, and then click =.
19. Arrange the open windows side by side and make the **Lunch** document active.
20. Move the insertion point to the end of the file, press Spacebar, and key the result of the calculation, as a dollar value, followed by a period to end the sentence.
21. Press Enter twice and key **Please let me know if you have any questions.** Your desktop should look similar to Figure 1. At this point, your instructor may ask you to capture an image of the screen. Save it in your CB1 assessment folder as *CB1_01*.

Workplace Ready Scenario

Workplace Ready

Archiving with Windows Vista

Even the most organized personal computer becomes cluttered with files over time. A good plan for making sure you can find the most current files when you need them includes creating an archive. An archive is simply a place to store older files that you no longer use on a daily basis. Windows Vista is an ideal tool to use to set up an archive.

Suppose you are a sales assistant at an insurance agency. Much of the business is organized around the calendar. For example, you prepare monthly sales reports, quarterly commission statements, and annual renewal letters. Documents for each new cycle replace the documents from the last cycle. You don't want to delete the older files, because you may need to reference them in the future. What should you do with the older files?

With Windows Vista, you can create a folder named Archive where you can store the outdated files. You can keep the Archive folder in Documents so that if you need to look back or reference a file, you can get to it quickly. Within the Archive folder, you can use a structure based on date and file type to organize the files into subfolders that clearly identify the file content, as shown in the figure.

By archiving older files, you keep your computer uncluttered so you can locate and identify active file information. You still have access to the older files if you need them, but they are stored out of the way. After a while, when the Archive folder starts to get too big, you can move the archived files off of your local disk to an external device, using the file and folder naming tools provided by Windows Vista to label them based on date and type.

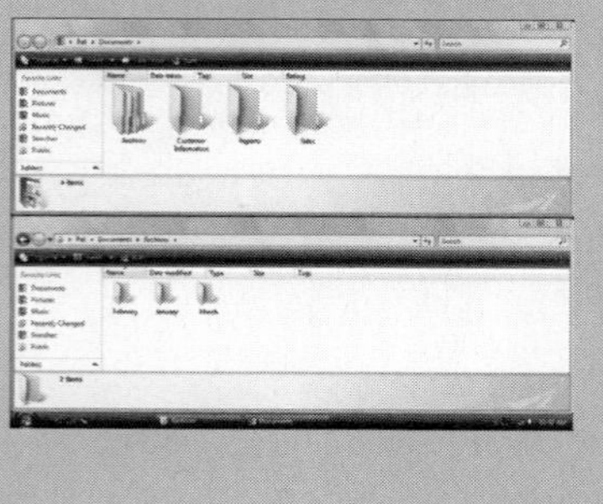

Conventions and Features Used in This Book

This book uses particular fonts, symbols, and heading conventions to highlight important information or to call your attention to special steps. For more information about the features in each lesson, refer to the Illustrated Book Tour section.

CONVENTION	MEANING
NEW FEATURE	This icon indicates a new or greatly improved Windows feature in this version of the software.
THE BOTTOM LINE	This feature provides a brief summary of the material to be covered in the section that follows.
CLOSE	Words in all capital letters and in a different font color than the rest of the text indicate instructions for opening, saving, or closing files or programs. They also point out items you should check or actions you should take.
CERTIFICATION READY?	This feature signals the point in the text where a specific certification objective is covered. It provides you with a chance to check your understanding of that particular MCAS objective and, if necessary, review the section of the lesson where it is covered.
CD	This indicates a file that is available on the student CD.
TAKE NOTE*	Reader aids appear in shaded boxes found in your text. *Take Note* provides helpful hints related to particular tasks or topics.
ANOTHER WAY	*Another Way* provides an alternative procedure for accomplishing a particular task.
TROUBLESHOOTING	*Troubleshooting* covers common problems and pitfalls.
X REF	These notes provide pointers to information discussed elsewhere in the textbook or describe interesting features of Windows Vista that are not directly addressed in the current topic or exercise.
SAVE	When a toolbar button is referenced in an exercise, the button's picture is shown in the margin.
Alt+Tab	A plus sign (+) between two key names means that you must press both keys at the same time. Keys that you are instructed to press in an exercise will appear in the font shown here.
A ***cell*** is the area where data is entered.	Key terms appear in bold italic.
Key **My Name is.**	Any text you are asked to key appears in color.
Click **OK.**	Any button on the screen you are supposed to click on or select will also appear in color.
OPEN *FitnessClasses*.	The names of data files will appear in bold, italic, and color for easy identification.

Instructor Support Program

The *Microsoft Official Academic Course* programs are accompanied by a rich array of resources that incorporate the extensive textbook visuals to form a pedagogically cohesive package. These resources provide all the materials instructors need to deploy and deliver their courses. Resources available online for download include:

- The **MSDN Academic Alliance** is designed to provide the easiest and most inexpensive developer tools, products, and technologies available to faculty and students in labs, classrooms, and on student PCs. A free 1-year membership is available to qualified MOAC adopters.
- The **Instructor's Guide** contains Solutions to all the textbook exercises, Syllabi for various term lengths, and Data Files for all the documents students need to work the exercises. The Instructor's Guide also includes chapter summaries and lecture notes. The Instructor's Guide is available from the Book Companion site (http://www.wiley.com/college/microsoft) and from Wiley*PLUS*.
- The **Test Bank** contains hundreds of multiple-choice, true-false, and short answer questions and is available to download from the Instructor's Book Companion site (http://www.wiley.com/college/microsoft) and from Wiley*PLUS*. A complete answer key is provided. It is available in Microsoft Word format. The easy-to-use test-generation program fully supports graphics, print tests, student answer sheets, and answer keys. The software's advanced features allow you to create an exam to meet your exact specifications. The computerized test bank provides:
    - Varied question types to test a variety of comprehension levels—multiple-choice, true-false, and short answer.
    - Allows instructors to edit, randomize, and create questions freely.
    - Allows instructors to create and print different versions of a quiz or exam.
- **PowerPoint Presentations and Images.** A complete set of PowerPoint presentations is available on the Instructor's Book Companion site (http://www.wiley.com/college/microsoft) and in Wiley*PLUS* to enhance classroom presentations. Approximately 50 PowerPoint slides are provided for each lesson. Tailored to the text's topical coverage and Skills Matrix, these presentations are designed to convey key Windows Vista concepts addressed in the text.

  All figures from the text are on the Instructor's Book Companion site (http://www.wiley.com/college/microsoft) and in Wiley*PLUS*. You can incorporate them into your PowerPoint presentations, or create your own overhead transparencies and handouts.

  By using these visuals in class discussions, you can help focus students' attention on key elements of Windows Vista and help them understand how to use it effectively in the workplace.
- **Microsoft Business Certification Pre-Test and Exams (U.S. & Canada only).** With each MOAC textbook, students receive information allowing them to access a Pre-Test, Score Report, and Learning Plan, either directly from Certiport, one of Microsoft's exam delivery partners, or through links from Wiley*PLUS* Premium. They also receive a code and information for taking the certification exams.

- **The Wiley Faculty Network** lets you tap into a large community of your peers effortlessly. Wiley Faculty Network mentors are faculty like you, from educational institutions around the country, who are passionate about enhancing instructional efficiency and effectiveness through best practices. Faculty Network activities include technology training and tutorials, virtual seminars, peer-to-peer exchanges of experience and ideas, personal consulting, and sharing of resources. To register for a seminar, go to www.wherefacultyconnect.com or phone 1-866-4FACULTY (U.S. and Canada only).

Wiley*PLUS*

Broad developments in education over the past decade have influenced the instructional approach taken in the Microsoft Official Academic Course programs. The way that students learn, especially about new technologies, has changed dramatically in the Internet era. Electronic learning materials and Internet-based instruction is now as much a part of classroom instruction as printed textbooks. Wiley*PLUS* provides the technology to create an environment where students reach their full potential and experience academic success that will last them a lifetime!

Wiley*PLUS* is a powerful and highly-integrated suite of teaching and learning resources designed to bridge the gap between what happens in the classroom and what happens at home and on the job. Wiley*PLUS* provides instructors with the resources to teach their students new technologies and guide them to reach their goals of getting ahead in the job market by having the skills to become certified and advance in the workforce. For students, Wiley*PLUS* provides the tools for study and practice that are available to them 24/7, wherever and whenever they want to study. Wiley*PLUS* includes a complete online version of the student textbook; PowerPoint presentations; homework and practice assignments and quizzes; links to Microsoft's Pre-Test, Learning Plan, and a code for taking the certification exam (in Wiley*PLUS* Premium); image galleries; test-bank questions; gradebook; and all the instructor resources in one easy-to-use website.

Organized around the everyday activities you and your students perform in the class, Wiley*PLUS* helps you:

- **Prepare & Present** outstanding class presentations using relevant PowerPoint slides and other Wiley*PLUS* materials—and you can easily upload and add your own.
- **Create Assignments** by choosing from questions organized by lesson, level of difficulty, and source—and add your own questions. Students' homework and quizzes are automatically graded, and the results are recorded in your gradebook.
- **Offer context-sensitive help to students, 24/7.** When you assign homework or quizzes, you decide if and when students get access to hints, solutions, or answers where appropriate—or they can be linked to relevant sections of their complete, online text for additional help whenever—and wherever they need it most.
- **Track Student Progress:** Analyze students' results and assess their level of understanding on an individual and class level using the Wiley*PLUS* gradebook, or export data to your own personal gradebook.
- **Administer Your Course:** Wiley*PLUS* can easily be integrated with another course management system, gradebook, or other resources you are using in your class, providing you with the flexibility to build your course, your way.
- **Seamlessly integrate all of the rich Wiley*PLUS* content and resources with WebCT and Blackboard**—with a single sign-on.

Please view our online demo at **www.wiley.com/college/wileyplus.** Here you will find additional information about the features and benefits of Wiley*PLUS*, how to request a "test drive" of Wiley*PLUS* for this title, and how to adopt it for class use.

MICROSOFT BUSINESS CERTIFICATION PRE-TEST AND EXAMS AVAILABLE THROUGH WILEY*PLUS* PREMIUM (US & CANADA ONLY)

Enhance your students' knowledge and skills and increase their performance on Microsoft Business Certification exams with adoption of the Microsoft Official Academic Course program for Windows Vista.

With the majority of the workforce classified as *information workers*, certification on the 2007 Microsoft Office system and Windows Vista is a critical tool in terms of validating the desktop computing knowledge and skills required to be more productive in the workplace. Certification is the primary tool companies use to validate the proficiency of desktop computing skills among employees. It gives organizations the ability to help assess employees' actual computer skills and select job candidates based on verifiable skills applying the latest productivity tools and technology.

Microsoft Pre-tests, delivered by Certiport, provide a simple, low-cost way for individuals to identify their desktop computing skill level. Pre-Tests are taken online, making the first step towards certification easy and convenient. Through the Pre-Tests, individuals can receive a custom learning path with recommended training.

To help students to study for and pass the Microsoft Certified Application Specialist, or MCAS exam, each MOAC textbook includes information allowing students to access a Pre-Test, Score Report, and Learning Plan, either directly from Certiport or through links from the Wiley*PLUS* Premium course. Students also receive a code and information for taking the certification exams. Students who do not have access to Wiley*PLUS* Premium can find information on how to purchase access to the Pre-Test and a code for taking the certification exams by clicking on their textbook at:

http://www.wiley.com/college/microsoft.

The Pre-Test can only be taken once. It provides a simple, low-cost way for students to evaluate and identify their skill level. Through the Pre-Test, students receive a recommended study plan that they can print out to help them prepare for the live certification exams. The Pre-Test is comprised of a variety of selected response questions, including matching, sequencing exercises, "hot spots" where students must identify an item or function, and traditional multiple-choice questions. After students have mastered all the certification objectives, they can use their code to take the actual Microsoft Certified Application Specialist (MCAS) exams for Office 2007 and Windows Vista.

Wiley*PLUS* Premium includes a complete online version of the student textbook, PowerPoint® presentations, homework and practice assignments and quizzes, links to Microsoft's Pre-Test, Learning Plan and a certification voucher, image galleries, test bank questions, gradebook, and all the instructor resources in one, easy-to-use website. Together, with Wiley*PLUS* and the MCAS Pre-Test and exams delivered by Certiport, we are creating the best of both worlds in academic learning and performance based validation in preparation for a great career and a globally recognized Microsoft certification—the higher education learning management system that accesses the industry-leading certification pre-test.

Contact your Wiley rep today about this special offer.

MSDN ACADEMIC ALLIANCE—FREE 1-YEAR MEMBERSHIP AVAILABLE TO QUALIFIED ADOPTERS!

MSDN Academic Alliance (MSDN AA) is designed to provide the easiest and most inexpensive way for universities to make the latest Microsoft developer tools, products, and technologies available in labs, classrooms, and on student PCs. MSDN AA is an annual membership program for departments teaching Science, Technology, Engineering, and Mathematics (STEM) courses. The membership provides a complete solution to keep academic labs, faculty, and students on the leading edge of technology.

Software available in the MSDN AA program is provided at no charge to adopting departments through the Wiley and Microsoft publishing partnership.

As a bonus to this free offer, faculty will be introduced to Microsoft's Faculty Connection and Academic Resource Center. It takes time and preparation to keep students engaged while giving them a fundamental understanding of theory, and the Microsoft Faculty Connection is designed to help STEM professors with this preparation by providing articles, curriculum, and tools that professors can use to engage and inspire today's technology students.

* Contact your Wiley rep for details.

For more information about the MSDN Academic Alliance program, go to:

http://msdn.microsoft.com/academic/

Important Web Addresses and Phone Numbers

To locate the Wiley Higher Education Rep in your area, go to the following Web address and click on the "*Who's My Rep?*" link at the top of the page.

http://www.wiley.com/college

Or Call the MOAC Toll Free Number: 1 + (888) 764-7001 (U.S. & Canada only).

To learn more about becoming a Microsoft Certified Application Specialist and exam availability, visit www.microsoft.com/learning/msbc.

Student Support Program

Book Companion Website (www.wiley.com/college/microsoft)

The book companion site for the MOAC series includes the Instructor Resources, the student CD files, and Web links to important information for students and instructors.

Wiley*PLUS*

Wiley*PLUS* is a powerful and highly-integrated suite of teaching and learning resources designed to bridge the gap between what happens in the classroom and what happens at home and on the job. For students, Wiley*PLUS* provides the tools for study and practice that are available 24/7, wherever and whenever they want to study. Wiley*PLUS* includes a complete online version of the student textbook; PowerPoint presentations; homework and practice assignments and quizzes; links to Microsoft's Pre-Test, Learning Plan, and a code for taking the certification exam (in Wiley*PLUS* Premium); image galleries; test bank questions; gradebook; and all the instructor resources in one easy-to-use website.

Wiley*PLUS* provides immediate feedback on student assignments and a wealth of support materials. This powerful study tool will help your students develop their conceptual understanding of the class material and increase their ability to answer questions.

- A **Study and Practice** area links directly to text content, allowing students to review the text while they study and answer. Access to Microsoft's Pre-Test, Learning Plan, and a code for taking the MCAS certification exam is available in Study and Practice. Additional Practice Questions tied to the MCAS certification that can be re-taken as many times as necessary, are also available.
- An **Assignment** area keeps all the work you want your students to complete in one location, making it easy for them to stay on task. Students have access to a variety of interactive self-assessment tools, as well as other resources for building their confidence and understanding. In addition, all of the assignments and quizzes contain a link to the relevant section of the multimedia book, providing students with context-sensitive help that allows them to conquer obstacles as they arise.
- A **Personal Gradebook** for each student allows students to view their results from past assignments at any time.

Please view our online demo at www.wiley.com/college/wileyplus. Here you will find additional information about the features and benefits of Wiley*PLUS*, how to request a "test drive" of Wiley*PLUS* for this title, and how to adopt it for class use.

Student CD

The CD-ROM included with this book contains the practice files that you will use as you perform the exercises in the book. By using the practice files, you will not waste time creating the samples used in the lessons, and you can concentrate on learning how to use Microsoft Windows Vista. With the files and the step-by-step instructions in the lessons, you will learn by doing, which is an easy and effective way to acquire and remember new skills.

Copying the Practice Files

Your instructor might already have copied the practice files before you arrive in class. However, your instructor might ask you to copy the practice files on your own at the start of class. Also, if you want to work through any of the exercises in this book on your own at home or at your place of business, you may want to copy the practice files. Note that you can also open the files directly from the CD-ROM, but you should be cautious about carrying the CD-ROM around with you as it could become damaged.

1. Insert the CD-ROM in the CD-ROM drive of your computer.
2. Start Windows Explorer.
3. In the left pane of Explorer, locate the icon for your CD-ROM and click on this icon. The folders and files contained on the CD will appear listed on the right.
4. Locate and select the **Data** folder. This is the folder that contains all of the practice files, separated by Lesson folders.
5. Right-click on the **Data** folder and choose **Copy** from the menu.
6. In the left pane of Windows Explorer, choose the location to which you would like to copy the practice files. This can be a drive on your local PC or an external drive.
7. Right-click on the drive/location to which you want to copy the practice files and choose **Paste.** This will copy the entire Data folder to your chosen location.
8. Close Windows Explorer.

If you only want to copy the files for one lesson, you can open the Data folder and right-click the desired Lesson folder within the Data folder.

Deleting the Practice Files

Use the following steps when you want to delete the practice files from your hard disk or other drive. Your instructor might ask you to perform these steps at the end of class. Also, you should perform these steps if you have worked through the exercises at home or at your place of business and want to work through the exercises again. Deleting the practice files and then reinstalling them ensures that all files and folders are in their original condition if you decide to work through the exercises again.

1. Start Windows Explorer.
2. Browse through the drives and folders to locate the practice files.
3. Select the **Data** folder.
4. Right-click on the **Data** folder and choose **Delete** from the menu.
5. Close Windows Explorer.

Wiley Desktop Editions

Wiley MOAC Desktop Editions are innovative, electronic versions of printed textbooks. Students buy the desktop version for 60% off the U.S. price of the printed text, and get the added value of permanence and portability. Wiley Desktop Editions provide students with numerous additional benefits that are not available with other e-text solutions.

Wiley Desktop Editions are NOT subscriptions; students download the Wiley Desktop Edition to their computer desktops. Students own the content they buy to keep for as long as they want. Once a Wiley Desktop Edition is downloaded to the computer desktop, students have instant access to all of the content without being online. Students can also print out the sections they prefer to read in hard copy. Students also have access to fully integrated resources within their Wiley Desktop Edition. From highlighting their e-text to taking and sharing notes, students can easily personalize their Wiley Desktop Edition as they are reading or following along in class.

You can use the Search function in the Open dialog box to quickly find the specific file for which you are looking.

Preparing to Take the Microsoft Certified Application Specialist (MCAS) Exam

The Microsoft Certified Application Specialist program is part of the new and enhanced Microsoft Business Certifications. It is easily attainable through a series of verifications that provide a simple and convenient framework for skills assessment and validation.

For organizations, the new certification program provides better skills verification tools that help with assessing not only in-demand skills on the 2007 Microsoft Office system and Windows Vista, but also the ability to quickly complete on-the-job tasks. Individuals will find it easier to identify and work towards the certification credential that meets their personal and professional goals.

To learn more about becoming a Microsoft Certified Application Specialist and exam availability, visit www.microsoft.com/learning/msbc.

Microsoft Certified Application Specialist (MCAS) Program

The core Microsoft Office Specialist credential has been upgraded to validate skills with the 2007 Microsoft Office system as well as the new Windows Vista operating system. The Application Specialist certifications target information workers and cover the most popular business applications such as Word 2007, PowerPoint 2007, Excel 2007, Access 2007, Outlook 2007 and Windows Vista.

By becoming certified, you demonstrate to employers that you have achieved a predictable level of skill in the use of a particular Office application or the Windows operating system. Employers often require certification either as a condition of employment or as a condition of advancement within the company or other organization. The certification examinations are sponsored by Microsoft but administered through exam delivery partners like Certiport.

Preparing to Take an Exam

Unless you are a very experienced user, you will need to use a test preparation course to prepare to complete the test correctly and within the time allowed. The *Microsoft Official Academic Course* series is designed to prepare you with a strong knowledge of all exam topics, and with some additional review and practice on your own. You should feel confident in your ability to pass the appropriate exam.

After you decide which exam to take, review the list of objectives for the exam. This list can be found in the MCAS Objectives Appendix at the back of this book. You can also easily identify tasks that are included in the objective list by locating the Lesson Skill Matrix at the start of each lesson and the Certification Ready sidebars in the margin of the lessons in this book.

To take the MCAS test, visit *www.microsoft.com/learning/msbc* to locate your nearest testing center. Then call the testing center directly to schedule your test. The amount of advance notice you should provide will vary for different testing centers, and it typically depends on the number of computers available at the testing center, the number of other testers who have already been scheduled for the day on which you want to take the test, and the number of times per week that the testing center offers MCAS testing. In general, you should call to schedule your test at least two weeks prior to the date on which you want to take the test.

When you arrive at the testing center, you might be asked for proof of identity. A driver's license or passport is an acceptable form of identification. If you do not have either of these items of documentation, call your testing center and ask what alternative forms of identification will be accepted. If you are retaking a test, bring your MCAS identification number, which will have been given to you when you previously took the test. If you have not prepaid or if your organization has not already arranged to make payment for you, you will need to pay the test-taking fee when you arrive.

Test Format

All MCAS certification tests are live, performance-based tests. There are no true/false or short-answer questions. Instructions are general: you are told the basic tasks to perform on the computer, but you aren't given any help in figuring out how to perform them. You are not permitted to use reference material.

As you complete the tasks stated in a particular test question, the testing software monitors your actions. An example question might be:

Open the file named *Wiley Guests* and select the word *Welcome* in the first paragraph. Change the font to 12 point, and apply bold formatting. Select the words *at your convenience* in the second paragraph, move them to the end of the first paragraph using drag and drop, and then center the first paragraph.

When the test administrator seats you at a computer, you will see an online form that you use to enter information about yourself (name, address, and other information required to process your exam results). While you complete the form, the software will generate the test from a master test bank and then prompt you to continue. The first test question will appear in a window. Read the question carefully, and then perform all the tasks stated in the test question. When you have finished completing all tasks for a question, click the Next Question button.

You have 45 to 50 minutes to complete all questions, depending on the test that you are taking. The testing software assesses your results as soon as you complete the test, and the test administrator can print the results of the test so that you will have a record of any tasks that you performed incorrectly. If you pass, you will receive a certificate in the mail within two to four weeks. If you do not pass, you can study and practice the skills that you missed and then schedule to retake the test at a later date.

Tips for Successfully Completing the Test

The following tips and suggestions are the result of feedback received from many individuals who have taken one or more MCAS tests:

- Make sure that you are thoroughly prepared. If you have extensively used the application for which you are being tested, you might feel confident that you are prepared for the test. However, the test might include questions that involve tasks that you rarely or never perform when you use the application at your place of business, at school, or at home. You must be knowledgeable in all the MCAS objectives for the test that you will take.
- Read each exam question carefully. An exam question might include several tasks that you are to perform. A partially correct response to a test question is counted as an incorrect response. In the example question on the previous page, you might apply bold formatting and move the words *at your convenience* to the correct location, but forget to center the first paragraph. This would count as an incorrect response and would result in a lower test score.
- You are not allowed to use the application's Help system. The Help function is always disabled for all exams.
- The test does display the amount of time that you have left. The test program also displays the number of items that you have completed along with the total number of test items (for example, "35 of 40 items have been completed"). Use this information to gauge your pace.
- If you skip a question, you can return to it later.

If You Do Not Pass the Test

If you do not pass, you can use the assessment printout as a guide to practice the items that you missed. There is no limit to the number of times that you can retake a test; however, you must pay the fee each time that you take the test. When you retake the test, expect to see some of the same test items on the subsequent test; the test software randomly generates the test items from a master test bank before you begin the test. Also expect to see several questions that did not appear on the previous test.

Acknowledgments

MOAC Instructor Advisory Board

We would like to thank our Instructor Advisory Board, an elite group of educators who has assisted us every step of the way in building these products. Advisory Board members have acted as our sounding board on key pedagogical and design decisions leading to the development of these compelling and innovative textbooks for future Information Workers. Their dedication to technology education is truly appreciated.

Catherine Binder, Strayer University & Katharine Gibbs School–Philadelphia

Catherine currently works at both Katharine Gibbs School in Norristown, PA and Strayer University in King of Prussia, PA. Catherine has been at Katharine Gibbs School for 4 years. Catherine is currently the Department Chair/Lead instructor for PC Networking at Gibbs and the founder/advisor of the TEK Masters Society. Since joining Strayer University a year and a half ago she has risen in the ranks from adjunct to DIT/Assistant Campus Dean.

Catherine has brought her 10+ year's industry experience as Network Administrator, Network Supervisor, Professor, Bench Tech, Manager and CTO from such places as Foster Wheeler Corp, KidsPeace Inc., Victoria Vogue, TESST College, AMC Theatres, Blue Mountain Publishing and many more to her teaching venue.

Catherine began as an adjunct in the PC Networking department and quickly became a full-time instructor. At both schools she is in charge of scheduling, curricula and departmental duties. She happily advises about 80+ students and is committed to Gibbs/Strayer life, her students, and continuing technology education every day.

Penny Gudgeon, CDI College

Penny is the Program Manager for IT curriculum at Corinthian Colleges, Inc. Until January 2006, Penny was responsible for all Canadian programming and web curriculum for five years. During that time, Corinthian Colleges, Inc. acquired CDI College of Business and Technology in 2004. Before 2000 she spent four years as IT instructor at one of the campuses. Penny joined CDI College in 1997 after her working for 10 years first in programming and later in software productivity education. Penny previously has worked in the fields of advertising, sales, engineering technology and programming. When not working from her home office or indulging her passion for life long learning, and the possibilities of what might be, Penny likes to read mysteries, garden and relax at home in Hamilton, Ontario, with her Shih-Tzu, Gracie, and husband, Al.

Jana Hambruch, School District of Lee County

Ms. Hambruch currently serves as Director for the Information Technology Magnet Programs at The School District of Lee County in Ft Myers, Florida. She is responsible for the implementation and direction of three schools that fall under this grant program. This program has been recognized as one of the top 15 most innovative technology programs in the nation. She is also co-author of the grant proposal for the IT Magnet Grant prior to taking on the role of Director.

Ms. Hambruch has over ten years experience directing the technical certification training programs at many Colleges and Universities, including Barry University, the University of South Florida, Broward Community College, and at Florida Gulf Coast University, where she served as the Director for the Center for Technology Education. She excels at developing alternative training models that focus on the tie between the education provider and the community in which it serves.

Ms. Hambruch is a past board member and treasurer of the Human Resources Management Association of SW Florida, graduate of Leadership Lee County Class of 2002, Steering Committee Member for Leadership Lee County Class of 2004 and a former board member of the Career Coalition of Southwest Florida. She has frequently lectured for organizations such as Microsoft, American Society of Training and Development, Florida Gulf Coast University, Florida State University, University of Nevada at Las Vegas, University of Wisconsin at Milwaukee, Canada's McGill University, and Florida's State Workforce Summit.

Dee Hobson, Richland College

Dee Hobson is currently a faculty member of the Business Office Systems and Support Division at Richland College. Richland is one of seven colleges in the Dallas County Community College District and has the distinction of being the first community college to receive the Malcolm Baldrige National Quality Award in 2005. Richland also received the Texas Award for Performance Excellence in 2005.

The Business Office Systems and Support Division at Richland is also a Certiport Authorized Microsoft Office testing center. All students enrolling in one of Microsoft's application software courses (Word, Excel, PowerPoint, and Access) are required to take the respective Microsoft certification exam at the end of the semester.

Dee has taught computer and business courses in K-12 public schools and at a proprietary career college in Dallas. She has also been involved with several corporate training companies and with adult education programs in the Dallas area. She began her computer career as an employee of IBM Corporation in St. Louis, Missouri. During her ten-year IBM employment, she moved to Memphis, Tennessee, to accept a managerial position and to Dallas, Texas, to work in a national sales and marketing technical support center.

Keith Hoell, Katharine Gibbs School–New York

Keith has worked in both non-profit and proprietary education for over 10 years, initially at St. John's University in New York, and then as full-time faculty, Chairperson and currently Dean of Information Systems at the Katharine Gibbs School in New York City. He also worked for General Electric in the late 80's and early 90's as the Sysop of a popular bulletin board dedicated to ASCII-Art on GE's pioneering GEnie on-line service before the advent of the World Wide Web. He has taught courses and workshops dealing with many mainstream IT issues and varied technology, especially those related to computer hardware and operating system software, networking, software applications, IT project management and ethics, and relational database technology. An avid runner and a member of The New York Road Runners, he won the Footlocker Five Borough Challenge representing Queens at the 2005 ING New York City Marathon while competing against the 4 other borough reps. He currently resides in Queens, New York.

Michael Taylor, Seattle Central Community College

Michael worked in education and training for the last 20 years in both the public and private sector. He currently teaches and coordinates the applications support program at Seattle Central Community College and also administers the Microsoft IT Academy. His experience outside the educational world is in Travel and Tourism with wholesale tour operations and cruise lines.

Interests outside of work include greyhound rescue. (He adopted 3 x-racers who bring him great joy.) He also enjoys the arts and is fortunate to live in downtown Seattle where there is much to see and do.

MOAC Office 2007 and Windows Vista Reviewers

We also thank the many reviewers who pored over the manuscript, providing invaluable feedback in the service of quality instructional materials.

Access

Susan Fry, Boise State University
Leslie Jernberg, Eastern Idaho Technical College
Dr. Deborah Jones, South Georgia Technical College
Suzanne Marks, Bellevue Community College
Kim Styles, Tri-County Technical College & Anderson School District 5
Fred Usmani, Conestoga College

Excel

Bob Gunderson, TriOS College
Christie Hovey, Lincoln Land Community College
Barbara Lave, Portland Community College
Trevor McIvor, Bow Valley College
Donna Madsen, Kirkwood Community College
James M. Veneziano, Davenport University—Caro
Dorothy Weiner, Manchester Community College

PowerPoint

Barbara Gillespie, Cuyamaca College
Caroline de Gruchy, Conestoga College
Tatyana Pashnyak, Bainbridge College
Michelle Poertner, Northwestern Michigan College
Janet Sebesy, Cuyahoga Community College

Outlook

Julie Boyles, Portland Community College
Joe LaMontagne, Davenport University—Grand Rapids
Randy Nordell, American River College
Echo Rantanen, Spokane Community College
Lyndsey Webster, TriOS College

Project

Janis DeHaven, Central Community College
Dr. Susan Jennings, Stephen F. Austin State University
Jack Maronowski, Curriculum Director, CDI College
Diane D. Mickey, Northern Virginia Community College
Linda Nutter, Peninsula College
Marika Reinke, Bellevue Community College

Vista

Gary Genereaux, Fanshawe College
Debi Griggs, Bellevue Community College
Katherine James, Seneca College
Diane Mickey, Northern Virginia Community College
Sue Miner, Lehigh Carbon Community College

Word

Diana Anderson, Big Sandy Community & Technical College
Donna Hendricks, South Arkansas Community College
Dr. Donna McGill-Cameron, Yuba Community College—Woodland Campus
Patricia McMahon, South Suburban College
Jack Maronowski, Curriculum Director, CDI College
Nancy Noe, Linn-Benton Community College
Teresa Roberts, Wilson Technical Community College

Focus Group and Survey Participants

Finally, we thank the hundreds of instructors who participated in our focus groups and surveys to ensure that the Microsoft Official Academic Courses best met the needs of our customers.

Jean Aguilar, Mt. Hood Community College
Konrad Akens, Zane State College
Michael Albers, University of Memphis
Diana Anderson, Big Sandy Community & Technical College
Phyllis Anderson, Delaware County Community College
Judith Andrews, Feather River College
Damon Antos, American River College
Bridget Archer, Oakton Community College
Linda Arnold, Harrisburg Area Community College–Lebanon Campus
Neha Arya, Fullerton College
Mohammad Bajwa, Katharine Gibbs School–New York
Virginia Baker, University of Alaska Fairbanks
Carla Bannick, Pima Community College
Rita Barkley, Northeast Alabama Community College
Elsa Barr, Central Community College – Hastings
Ronald W. Barry, Ventura County Community College District
Elizabeth Bastedo, Central Carolina Technical College
Karen Baston, Waubonsee Community College
Karen Bean, Blinn College
Scott Beckstrand, Community College of Southern Nevada
Paulette Bell, Santa Rosa Junior College
Liz Bennett, Southeast Technical Institute
Nancy Bermea, Olympic College
Lucy Betz, Milwaukee Area Technical College
Meral Binbasioglu, Hofstra University
Catherine Binder, Strayer University & Katharine Gibbs School–Philadelphia
Terrel Blair, El Centro College
Ruth Blalock, Alamance Community College
Beverly Bohner, Reading Area Community College
Henry Bojack, Farmingdale State University
Matthew Bowie, Luna Community College
Julie Boyles, Portland Community College
Karen Brandt, College of the Albemarle
Stephen Brown, College of San Mateo
Jared Bruckner, Southern Adventist University
Pam Brune, Chattanooga State Technical Community College
Sue Buchholz, Georgia Perimeter College
Roberta Buczyna, Edison College
Angela Butler, Mississippi Gulf Coast Community College
Rebecca Byrd, Augusta Technical College
Kristen Callahan, Mercer County Community College
Judy Cameron, Spokane Community College
Dianne Campbell, Athens Technical College
Gena Casas, Florida Community College at Jacksonville
Jesus Castrejon, Latin Technologies
Gail Chambers, Southwest Tennessee Community College
Jacques Chansavang, Indiana University–Purdue University Fort Wayne
Nancy Chapko, Milwaukee Area Technical College
Rebecca Chavez, Yavapai College
Sanjiv Chopra, Thomas Nelson Community College
Greg Clements, Midland Lutheran College
Dayna Coker, Southwestern Oklahoma State University–Sayre Campus
Tamra Collins, Otero Junior College
Janet Conrey, Gavilan Community College
Carol Cornforth, West Virginia Northern Community College
Gary Cotton, American River College
Edie Cox, Chattahoochee Technical College
Rollie Cox, Madison Area Technical College
David Crawford, Northwestern Michigan College
J.K. Crowley, Victor Valley College
Rosalyn Culver, Washtenaw Community College
Sharon Custer, Huntington University
Sandra Daniels, New River Community College
Anila Das, Cedar Valley College
Brad Davis, Santa Rosa Junior College
Susan Davis, Green River Community College
Mark Dawdy, Lincoln Land Community College
Jennifer Day, Sinclair Community College
Carol Deane, Eastern Idaho Technical College
Julie DeBuhr, Lewis-Clark State College
Janis DeHaven, Central Community College
Drew Dekreon, University of Alaska–Anchorage
Joy DePover, Central Lakes College
Salli DiBartolo, Brevard Community College
Melissa Diegnau, Riverland Community College
Al Dillard, Lansdale School of Business
Marjorie Duffy, Cosumnes River College
Sarah Dunn, Southwest Tennessee Community College
Shahla Durany, Tarrant County College–South Campus
Kay Durden, University of Tennessee at Martin
Dineen Ebert, St. Louis Community College–Meramec
Donna Ehrhart, State University of New York–Brockport
Larry Elias, Montgomery County Community College
Glenda Elser, New Mexico State University at Alamogordo
Angela Evangelinos, Monroe County Community College
Angie Evans, Ivy Tech Community College of Indiana
Linda Farrington, Indian Hills Community College
Dana Fladhammer, Phoenix College
Richard Flores, Citrus College
Connie Fox, Community and Technical College at Institute of Technology West Virginia University
Wanda Freeman, Okefenokee Technical College
Brenda Freeman, Augusta Technical College

Susan Fry, Boise State University
Roger Fulk, Wright State University–Lake Campus
Sue Furnas, Collin County Community College District
Sandy Gabel, Vernon College
Laura Galvan, Fayetteville Technical Community College
Candace Garrod, Red Rocks Community College
Sherrie Geitgey, Northwest State Community College
Chris Gerig, Chattahoochee Technical College
Barb Gillespie, Cuyamaca College
Jessica Gilmore, Highline Community College
Pamela Gilmore, Reedley College
Debbie Glinert, Queensborough Community College
Steven Goldman, Polk Community College
Bettie Goodman, C.S. Mott Community College
Mike Grabill, Katharine Gibbs School–Philadelphia
Francis Green, Penn State University
Walter Griffin, Blinn College
Fillmore Guinn, Odessa College
Helen Haasch, Milwaukee Area Technical College
John Habal, Ventura College
Joy Haerens, Chaffey College
Norman Hahn, Thomas Nelson Community College
Kathy Hall, Alamance Community College
Teri Harbacheck, Boise State University
Linda Harper, Richland Community College
Maureen Harper, Indian Hills Community College
Steve Harris, Katharine Gibbs School–New York
Robyn Hart, Fresno City College
Darien Hartman, Boise State University
Gina Hatcher, Tacoma Community College
Winona T. Hatcher, Aiken Technical College
BJ Hathaway, Northeast Wisconsin Tech College
Cynthia Hauki, West Hills College – Coalinga
Mary L. Haynes, Wayne County Community College
Marcie Hawkins, Zane State College
Steve Hebrock, Ohio State University Agricultural Technical Institute
Sue Heistand, Iowa Central Community College
Heith Hennel, Valencia Community College
Donna Hendricks, South Arkansas Community College
Judy Hendrix, Dyersburg State Community College
Gloria Hensel, Matanuska-Susitna College University of Alaska Anchorage
Gwendolyn Hester, Richland College
Tammarra Holmes, Laramie County Community College
Dee Hobson, Richland College
Keith Hoell, Katharine Gibbs School–New York
Pashia Hogan, Northeast State Technical Community College
Susan Hoggard, Tulsa Community College
Kathleen Holliman, Wallace Community College Selma
Chastity Honchul, Brown Mackie College/Wright State University
Christie Hovey, Lincoln Land Community College
Peggy Hughes, Allegany College of Maryland
Sandra Hume, Chippewa Valley Technical College
John Hutson, Aims Community College
Celia Ing, Sacramento City College
Joan Ivey, Lanier Technical College
Barbara Jaffari, College of the Redwoods
Penny Jakes, University of Montana College of Technology
Eduardo Jaramillo, Peninsula College
Barbara Jauken, Southeast Community College
Susan Jennings, Stephen F. Austin State University
Leslie Jernberg, Eastern Idaho Technical College
Linda Johns, Georgia Perimeter College
Brent Johnson, Okefenokee Technical College
Mary Johnson, Mt. San Antonio College
Shirley Johnson, Trinidad State Junior College–Valley Campus
Sandra M. Jolley, Tarrant County College
Teresa Jolly, South Georgia Technical College
Dr. Deborah Jones, South Georgia Technical College
Margie Jones, Central Virginia Community College
Randall Jones, Marshall Community and Technical College
Diane Karlsbraaten, Lake Region State College
Teresa Keller, Ivy Tech Community College of Indiana
Charles Kemnitz, Pennsylvania College of Technology
Sandra Kinghorn, Ventura College
Bill Klein, Katharine Gibbs School–Philadelphia
Bea Knaapen, Fresno City College
Kit Kofoed, Western Wyoming Community College
Maria Kolatis, County College of Morris
Barry Kolb, Ocean County College
Karen Kuralt, University of Arkansas at Little Rock
Belva-Carole Lamb, Rogue Community College
Betty Lambert, Des Moines Area Community College
Anita Lande, Cabrillo College
Junnae Landry, Pratt Community College
Karen Lankisch, UC Clermont
David Lanzilla, Central Florida Community College
Nora Laredo, Cerritos Community College
Jennifer Larrabee, Chippewa Valley Technical College
Debra Larson, Idaho State University
Barb Lave, Portland Community College
Audrey Lawrence, Tidewater Community College
Deborah Layton, Eastern Oklahoma State College
Larry LeBlanc, Owen Graduate School–Vanderbilt University
Philip Lee, Nashville State Community College
Michael Lehrfeld, Brevard Community College
Vasant Limaye, Southwest Collegiate Institute for the Deaf – Howard College
Anne C. Lewis, Edgecombe Community College
Stephen Linkin, Houston Community College
Peggy Linston, Athens Technical College
Hugh Lofton, Moultrie Technical College
Donna Lohn, Lakeland Community College
Jackie Lou, Lake Tahoe Community College
Donna Love, Gaston College

Curt Lynch, Ozarks Technical Community College
Sheilah Lynn, Florida Community College–Jacksonville
Pat R. Lyon, Tomball College
Bill Madden, Bergen Community College
Heather Madden, Delaware Technical & Community College
Donna Madsen, Kirkwood Community College
Jane Maringer-Cantu, Gavilan College
Suzanne Marks, Bellevue Community College
Carol Martin, Louisiana State University–Alexandria
Cheryl Martucci, Diablo Valley College
Roberta Marvel, Eastern Wyoming College
Tom Mason, Brookdale Community College
Mindy Mass, Santa Barbara City College
Dixie Massaro, Irvine Valley College
Rebekah May, Ashland Community & Technical College
Emma Mays-Reynolds, Dyersburg State Community College
Timothy Mayes, Metropolitan State College of Denver
Reggie McCarthy, Central Lakes College
Matt McCaskill, Brevard Community College
Kevin McFarlane, Front Range Community College
Donna McGill, Yuba Community College
Terri McKeever, Ozarks Technical Community College
Patricia McMahon, South Suburban College
Sally McMillin, Katharine Gibbs School–Philadelphia
Charles McNerney, Bergen Community College
Lisa Mears, Palm Beach Community College
Imran Mehmood, ITT Technical Institute–King of Prussia Campus
Virginia Melvin, Southwest Tennessee Community College
Jeanne Mercer, Texas State Technical College
Denise Merrell, Jefferson Community & Technical College
Catherine Merrikin, Pearl River Community College
Diane D. Mickey, Northern Virginia Community College
Darrelyn Miller, Grays Harbor College
Sue Mitchell, Calhoun Community College
Jacquie Moldenhauer, Front Range Community College
Linda Motonaga, Los Angeles City College
Sam Mryyan, Allen County Community College
Cindy Murphy, Southeastern Community College
Ryan Murphy, Sinclair Community College
Sharon E. Nastav, Johnson County Community College
Christine Naylor, Kent State University Ashtabula
Haji Nazarian, Seattle Central Community College
Nancy Noe, Linn-Benton Community College
Jennie Noriega, San Joaquin Delta College
Linda Nutter, Peninsula College
Thomas Omerza, Middle Bucks Institute of Technology
Edith Orozco, St. Philip's College
Dona Orr, Boise State University
Joanne Osgood, Chaffey College
Janice Owens, Kishwaukee College
Tatyana Pashnyak, Bainbridge College
John Partacz, College of DuPage
Tim Paul, Montana State University–Great Falls
Joseph Perez, South Texas College
Mike Peterson, Chemeketa Community College
Dr. Karen R. Petitto, West Virginia Wesleyan College
Terry Pierce, Onandaga Community College
Ashlee Pieris, Raritan Valley Community College
Jamie Pinchot, Thiel College
Michelle Poertner, Northwestern Michigan College
Betty Posta, University of Toledo
Deborah Powell, West Central Technical College
Mark Pranger, Rogers State University
Carolyn Rainey, Southeast Missouri State University
Linda Raskovich, Hibbing Community College
Leslie Ratliff, Griffin Technical College
Mar-Sue Ratzke, Rio Hondo Community College
Roxy Reissen, Southeastern Community College
Silvio Reyes, Technical Career Institutes
Patricia Rishavy, Anoka Technical College
Jean Robbins, Southeast Technical Institute
Carol Roberts, Eastern Maine Community College and University of Maine
Teresa Roberts, Wilson Technical Community College
Vicki Robertson, Southwest Tennessee Community College
Betty Rogge, Ohio State Agricultural Technical Institute
Lynne Rusley, Missouri Southern State University
Claude Russo, Brevard Community College
Ginger Sabine, Northwestern Technical College
Steven Sachs, Los Angeles Valley College
Joanne Salas, Olympic College
Lloyd Sandmann, Pima Community College–Desert Vista Campus
Beverly Santillo, Georgia Perimeter College
Theresa Savarese, San Diego City College
Sharolyn Sayers, Milwaukee Area Technical College
Judith Scheeren, Westmoreland County Community College
Adolph Scheiwe, Joliet Junior College
Marilyn Schmid, Asheville-Buncombe Technical Community College
Janet Sebesy, Cuyahoga Community College
Phyllis T. Shafer, Brookdale Community College
Ralph Shafer, Truckee Meadows Community College
Anne Marie Shanley, County College of Morris
Shelia Shelton, Surry Community College
Merilyn Shepherd, Danville Area Community College
Susan Sinele, Aims Community College
Beth Sindt, Hawkeye Community College
Andrew Smith, Marian College
Brenda Smith, Southwest Tennessee Community College
Lynne Smith, State University of New York–Delhi
Rob Smith, Katharine Gibbs School–Philadelphia
Tonya Smith, Arkansas State University–Mountain Home
Del Spencer – Trinity Valley Community College

Jeri Spinner, Idaho State University
Eric Stadnik, Santa Rosa Junior College
Karen Stanton, Los Medanos College
Meg Stoner, Santa Rosa Junior College
Beverly Stowers, Ivy Tech Community College of Indiana
Marcia Stranix, Yuba College
Kim Styles, Tri-County Technical College
Sylvia Summers, Tacoma Community College
Beverly Swann, Delaware Technical & Community College
Ann Taff, Tulsa Community College
Mike Theiss, University of Wisconsin–Marathon Campus
Romy Thiele, Cañada College
Sharron Thompson, Portland Community College
Ingrid Thompson-Sellers, Georgia Perimeter College
Barbara Tietsort, University of Cincinnati–Raymond Walters College
Janine Tiffany, Reading Area Community College
Denise Tillery, University of Nevada Las Vegas
Susan Trebelhorn, Normandale Community College
Noel Trout, Santiago Canyon College
Cheryl Turgeon, Asnuntuck Community College
Steve Turner, Ventura College
Sylvia Unwin, Bellevue Community College
Lilly Vigil, Colorado Mountain College
Sabrina Vincent, College of the Mainland
Mary Vitrano, Palm Beach Community College
Brad Vogt, Northeast Community College
Cozell Wagner, Southeastern Community College
Carolyn Walker, Tri-County Technical College
Sherry Walker, Tulsa Community College
Qi Wang, Tacoma Community College
Betty Wanielista, Valencia Community College
Marge Warber, Lanier Technical College–Forsyth Campus
Marjorie Webster, Bergen Community College
Linda Wenn, Central Community College
Mark Westlund, Olympic College
Carolyn Whited, Roane State Community College
Winona Whited, Richland College
Jerry Wilkerson, Scott Community College
Joel Willenbring, Fullerton College
Barbara Williams, WITC Superior
Charlotte Williams, Jones County Junior College
Bonnie Willy, Ivy Tech Community College of Indiana
Diane Wilson, J. Sargeant Reynolds Community College
James Wolfe, Metropolitan Community College
Marjory Wooten, Lanier Technical College
Mark Yanko, Hocking College
Alexis Yusov, Pace University
Naeem Zaman, San Joaquin Delta College
Kathleen Zimmerman, Des Moines Area Community College

We would also like to thank Lutz Ziob, Sanjay Advani, Jim DiIanni, Merrick Van Dongen, Jim LeValley, Bruce Curling, Joe Wilson, and Naman Kahn at Microsoft for their encouragement and support in making the Microsoft Official Academic Course programs the finest instructional materials for mastering the newest Microsoft technologies for both students and instructors.

www.wiley.com/college/microsoft *or*
call the MOAC Toll-Free Number: 1+(888) 764-7001 (U.S. & Canada only)

Brief Contents

www.wiley.com/college/microsoft *or*
call the MOAC Toll-Free Number: 1+(888) 764-7001 (U.S. & Canada only)

Contents

Lesson 14: Collaborating with Others 381

Lesson 15: Customizing Your Computing Environment 424

FOR INSTRUCTORS

Wiley***PLUS*** is built around the activities you perform in your class each day. With Wiley***PLUS*** you can:

Prepare & Present

Create outstanding class presentations using a wealth of resources such as PowerPoint™ slides, image galleries, interactive simulations, and more. You can even add materials you have created yourself.

Create Assignments

Automate the assigning and grading of homework or quizzes by using the provided question banks, or by writing your own.

Track Student Progress

Keep track of your students' progress and analyze individual and overall class results.

Now Available with WebCT and Blackboard!

"It has been a great help, and I believe it has helped me to achieve a better grade."

Michael Morris,
Columbia Basin College

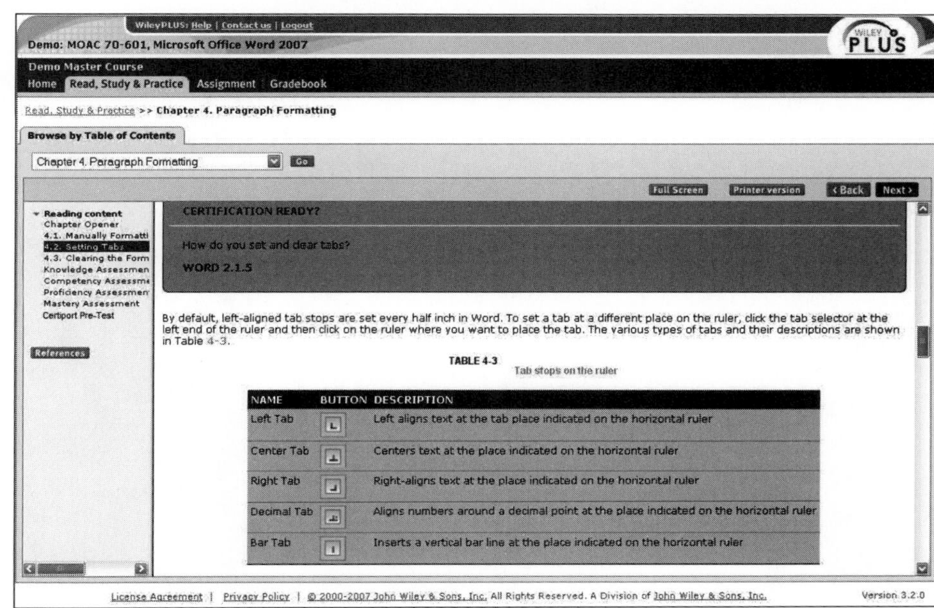

FOR STUDENTS

You have the potential to make a difference!

Wiley*PLUS* is a powerful online system packed with features to help you make the most of your potential and get the best grade you can!

With Wiley***PLUS*** you get:

A complete online version of your text and other study resources.

•

Problem-solving help, instant grading, and feedback on your homework and quizzes.

•

The ability to track your progress and grades throughout the term.

•

Access to Microsoft's Assessment, Learning Plan, and MCAS examination voucher.

For more information on what Wiley*PLUS* can do to help you and your students reach their potential, please visit www.wiley.com/college/*wileyplus*.

76% of students surveyed said it made them better prepared for tests.*

*Based on a survey of 972 student users of Wiley*PLUS*

www.wiley.com/college/microsoft *or*
call the MOAC Toll-Free Number: 1+(888) 764-7001 (U.S. & Canada only)

www.wiley.com/college/microsoft *or*
call the MOAC Toll-Free Number: 1+(888) 764-7001 (U.S. & Canada only)

Microsoft® Official Academic Course

Microsoft® Windows Vista™

Getting Started

LESSON SKILL MATRIX

Skills	Matrix Skill	Skill Number
Getting Started with Windows Vista		
Using the Start Menu		
Using a Folder Window		
Accessing Help and Support	Locate information in Windows Help and Support	7.2.1
Locking the Computer	Manually lock a computer	1.4.2

Northwind Traders is a small company that helps Inuit artists in Alaska market their work to customers around the globe. Originally, the owner was able to use a paper filing system for tasks such as invoicing and storing information about artists and buyers. Now that the business has grown, however, the owner has invested in a personal computer running the Windows Vista operating system. Two employees will share the system: the owner and the assistant. In this lesson, you will learn how to start your computer and log on to Windows Vista, identify screen elements, open and manipulate windows, get help while using Windows Vista, and log off and shut down the computer.

KEY TERMS

Background
Button
Desktop
File
Folder
Gadgets
Icon
Maximize
Menu
Minimize
Mouse
Pane
Path
Pointer
Recycle Bin
Restore Down
ScreenTip
Scrollbar
Select

■ Getting Started with Windows Vista

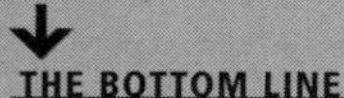

THE BOTTOM LINE

To use your computer, you must be able to use Windows Vista. Windows Vista is an operating system, which is the software that controls the way your computer communicates with you—the user—and with the other parts of the computer, such as the screen, the keyboard, and the printer. Once you log on to Vista, you can use it to access and manage information. In this section, you will start your computer, log on, and practice using the mouse.

Starting the Computer

Windows Vista loads into your computer's memory and starts automatically when you turn on your computer. The on/off switch is usually located on the front of the computer system, and the monitor may have an on/off switch as well. In some cases, such as in a computer lab, you may not have access to an on/off switch. In that case, skip to the next section.

START THE COMPUTER

TAKE NOTE*

When the computer first start it performs a procedure called the Power On Self Test, or POST, during which it checks to make sure components are working properly.

GET READY. Before you begin these steps, if your computer is already on, you should turn it off by clicking the Start button in the lower left corner of the screen, then clicking the right-pointing arrow in the lower right corner of the Start menu, and then clicking the Shut Down command. For more information, refer to the section "Shutting Down Windows Vista," later in this lesson. Click the Start button in the lower left corner of the screen and then click the Power button.

1. Press the power switch on your computer. You will hear sounds such as a beep and whirring as the system starts.
2. Press the power switch on your monitor to turn it on, if necessary. As Windows Vista starts, it checks your computer components to make sure everything is working, and you may see information about your system flash on the screen. Finally, a user account login screen displays. The login screen varies, depending on your system configuration. It may list the names of the people authorized to use the computer. It should look similar to Figure 1-1.

Figure 1-1

Windows Vista Welcome screen

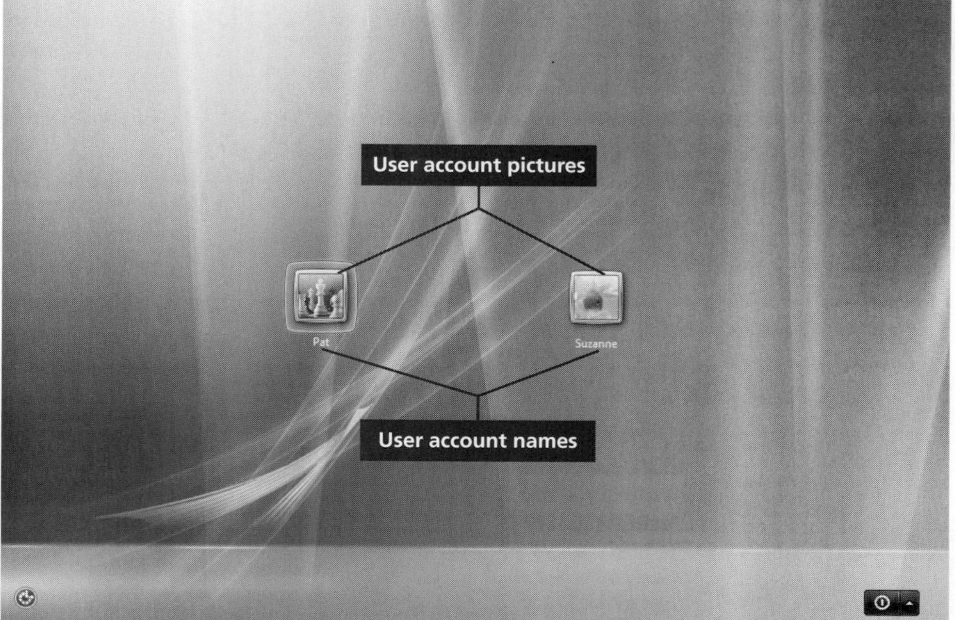

TROUBLESHOOTING

Your user account login screen may not look exactly the same as the Welcome screen in Figure 1-1.

PAUSE. LEAVE the user account login screen displayed to use in the next exercise.

You have just turned on your computer and started Windows Vista. This is sometimes called "booting" or "booting up." The Welcome screen displays the names of the system users, who are the people authorized to use the computer.

Each user has his or her own account. An account is a collection of settings that defines which tasks a user may perform and which system resources a user may access. User accounts make it possible for multiple users to share the same computer while keeping their files separate and maintaining security. This is very useful in a small business that may not have many computers, as well as for a family or in a computer lab. There are different editions of Windows Vista, and each edition offers slightly different features. Windows Vista Ultimate is used for the steps and figures in this book. You might have a different edition installed. For example, if you work in a small business, you might have Windows Vista Business. In an educational environment, you might have Windows Vista Enterprise. On a home computer, you might have Windows Vista Home Basic or Home Premium. You can find more information about the different editions in Windows Help and Support, which is covered later in this lesson. In the next section, you will log on to your account.

TAKE NOTE*

There are two types of user accounts: Administrator and Standard. Administrators can make system-wide changes, such as installing new programs or hardware, while Standard users can usually only access their own files. At times while you work in Windows Vista, you may see a message advising you that you need Administrative authorization to continue. If you have an Administrator account, you can click the Continue button to go forward. If you have a Standard account, you may need to supply a password to continue.

X REF

You select a picture when you create a new account, but you can change it at any time. Creating an account, selecting a picture, and setting up a password are covered in Lesson 11, "Monitoring the Windows Vista Environment."

Logging On

To access the information on your computer, you must log on to your account.

LOG ON

USE the user account login screen you left open in the previous exercise.

1. Move the mouse—or other input device—so that the pointer touches your name on the Welcome screen. If your system has a different user account login screen, move the pointer to the box where you enter your user name. The ***mouse*** is a device attached to your computer that lets you select commands. The ***pointer*** is an icon that moves on the screen when you move the mouse or other input device. On the Windows Vista desktop, the pointer usually looks like an arrow pointing up and to the left.
2. Press and release the left mouse button one time. This is called a click. When you click your account picture, the Windows desktop or the Password screen displays. If you click a user name box, key your user name and then press Enter on your keyboard to display the Windows desktop or the Password screen.
3. If the Password screen displays, click in the password box, key your password, and then press **Enter**. A password is a string of characters such as a word or phrase that protects your account from unauthorized access. When you key the password, black dots display in the password box to hide the actual password from anyone who might be looking over your shoulder. The Windows Vista ***desktop*** displays. The desktop is the main work area that displays when Windows Vista is running. It should look similar to Figure 1-2.

TROUBLESHOOTING

Some computers, such as a notebook or other mobile device, might not have a mouse. They use other input devices such as a touchpad, trackball, or stylus to move the pointer and select items on the screen. If your computer does not have a mouse, use the available input device to move the pointer and select items.

TROUBLESHOOTING If the Welcome Center window displays, click the Close button (the white X on the red background) in the upper right corner of the window to close it so you can get a clear view of the desktop.

TROUBLESHOOTING If you do not know your password, consult your instructor or your system administrator.

4. Take a moment to identify the elements of the desktop that are shown in Figure 1-2. Refer to Table 1-1 for a description of each element.

Table1-1

Common desktop elements

ELEMENT	DESCRIPTION
Taskbar	The ***taskbar*** usually runs across the bottom of the desktop (although it can be moved to the top, left side, or right side). It displays buttons and icons to let you access the features that you use most frequently. A ***button*** is an element that you can click to select a command or action.
Start button	The ***Start button*** is a round button with the Microsoft Windows logo on it. You click the Start button to open the ***Start menu***, which provides access to everything stored on your computer. A ***menu*** is a list of choices.
Sidebar	The ***Sidebar*** is a vertical bar usually located along the right side of the desktop. It displays ***gadgets***, which are programs or tools designed to provide information at a glance. A clock, a slide show, and an Internet news feed are the default gadgets. You learn more about the Sidebar and gadgets in Lesson 7, "Personalizing the Windows Vista Workspace."
Quick Launch toolbar	The Quick Launch toolbar is an area of the taskbar that displays ***shortcuts*** to frequently used programs. A shortcut is a link to a program, feature, or command.
Recycle Bin icon	The Recycle Bin icon represents the ***Recycle Bin***, a folder where deleted items are stored until you remove them permanently or restore them to their original location. You learn more about using the Recycle Bin in Lesson 2, "Working with Files and Folders."
Shortcut icons	Shortcut icons on the desktop let you quickly access programs, folders, and files that you use most often. The arrow in the lower left corner indicates that the icon is a shortcut. The shortcut icons on your desktop depend on how your computer is set up. Many programs create icons on the desktop during installation, or you can create your own shortcut icons on the desktop, on the taskbar, and in folders. You learn more about working with shortcuts in Lesson 7.
Background	The ***background*** is the broad, empty area where windows open and display content. By default, the background displays a picture that you select when you first set up your user account, but you can change it at any time to a different picture, or to a solid color like the one shown in Figure 1-2.
Notification area	At the right end of the taskbar is the notification area, where the time and information about the programs running on your computer displays. You learn more about the notification area in Lesson 7.

Figure 1-2

Windows Vista desktop

TROUBLESHOOTING As you will discover, Windows Vista can be easily customized and changed. Therefore, it is likely that the way your screen looks will often be different from the figures used throughout this book. For example, your Windows Vista desktop may not look the same as the desktop shown in Figure 1-2. It may display a different background, different colors, or different desktop icons.

PAUSE. LEAVE the Windows Vista desktop displayed to use in the next exercise.

As you have seen, in Windows Vista, the logon procedure always starts from a user account login screen. However, the actual steps may vary depending on the way your system is set up.

- On some systems, you simply click your user name to log on.
- If your account has a password, you must key it when you reach the password screen to log on.

Also, log on procedures vary depending on the computing environment. For example, if you are working on a small business or home network, you probably log on to a workgroup account. A workgroup is a group of connected computers that share resources such as printers. In a workgroup, your user account is usually set up on a particular computer, and you must log on to that computer. The same is true if you are using a standalone computer.
In a larger business or educational environment, you probably log on to a domain. A domain is a group of connected computers that have a common set of rules and procedures and can be administered from a central location. If your user account is on a domain, you can log on to any computer that is part of the domain.Because it is easy to customize Windows Vista, you are finding out that your screen may frequently look different from the screens used to illustrate this book. In the next section, you will practice using the mouse while you familiarize yourself with the main components of the Windows Vista desktop.

Using the Mouse to Identify Desktop Items

In Windows Vista, you use a mouse or other input device to point to and select items. The pointer moves on the screen in response to the movement of the device.

USE THE MOUSE TO IDENTIFY DESKTOP ITEMS

TROUBLESHOOTING

If you are using a different type of input device, practice using it in place of a mouse to identify desktop items.

1. Move the mouse on your desk or on a mouse pad on your desk so that the pointer moves on the desktop. If you move the mouse to the left or right, the mouse pointer moves to the left or right. If you move the mouse away from yourself toward the back of your desk, the pointer moves toward the top of the desktop. If you move the mouse toward yourself, the pointer moves toward the bottom of the desktop.

2. Move the pointer so that it is touching the **Recycle Bin** icon. This is called pointing to the Recycle Bin. Notice that the icon is highlighted, and that a ***ScreenTip*** displays information about the Recycle Bin, as shown in Figure 1-3. An ***icon*** is a small picture that represents an item or command. A ScreenTip is a pop-up balloon that displays information about the item you are pointing at on the screen.

Figure 1-3

Point to the Recycle Bin icon

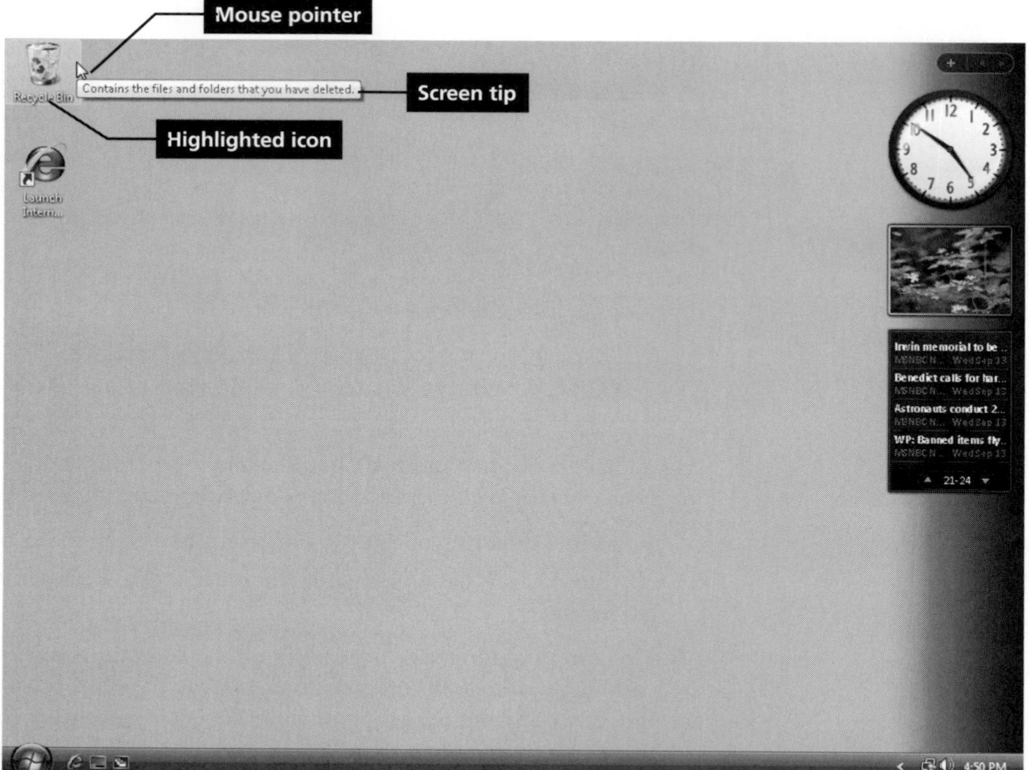

TAKE NOTE*

If the mouse reaches the edge of your desk or mouse pad before the pointer is in the correct spot on the desktop, you can pick up the mouse and reposition it without moving the pointer on the screen.

TROUBLESHOOTING

If the pointer changes to a hand with a pointing finger and the text label is underlined when you point to the Recycle Bin icon, it means your computer has been set to enable single-click launching of icons. If so, when you point at an icon, it becomes selected, and when you click it, it opens. If pointing selects the Recycle Bin icon, skip step 3. If you accidentally click the Recycle Bin icon, the folder window opens. Click the Close button in the upper right corner to close it, and continue with step 4. You learn how to change the folder options in Lesson 4, "Customizing Windows Explorer."

You can also cancel a selection by pressing Esc.

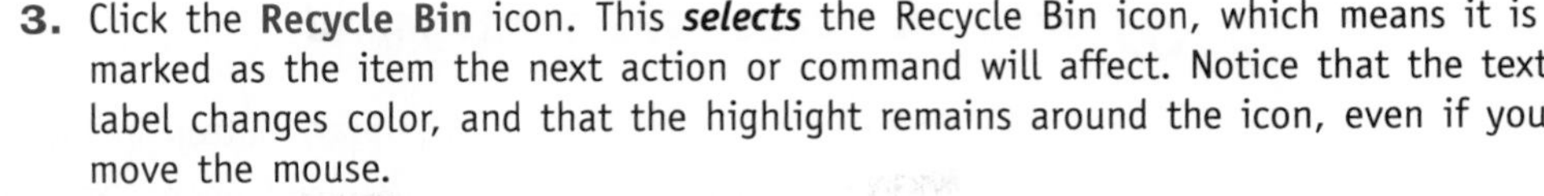

3. Click the **Recycle Bin** icon. This ***selects*** the Recycle Bin icon, which means it is marked as the item the next action or command will affect. Notice that the text label changes color, and that the highlight remains around the icon, even if you move the mouse.
4. Click a blank area of the desktop. This cancels the selection. The Recycle Bin icon is no longer highlighted.

5. Move the mouse on your desk so that the pointer is touching the Start button at the left end of the taskbar at the bottom of the screen. The ScreenTip "Start" displays.

TROUBLESHOOTING

The taskbar is usually positioned across the bottom of the desktop, but you can move it to any side of the screen. If you do not see the taskbar at the bottom of the screen, look for it at the top, left, or right. If it does not display at all, it may be hidden. If so, move the pointer to the side of the desktop where you think the taskbar is positioned (try the bottom first). It should display.

XREF

You learn how to customize the taskbar in Lesson 7.

6. Use the mouse to point to the **current time** in the lower right corner of the desktop, at the right end of the taskbar. The ScreenTip should display the current date.

PAUSE. LEAVE the desktop displayed to use in the next exercise.

In this exercise, you practiced using the mouse or another input device to point at and identify different items on the desktop and to select a desktop icon. Usually, when you point at an item on the desktop, a ScreenTip displays information about the item.

You can think of the Windows Vista desktop as similar to the top of your actual desk. On your desk, you might have an open folder or file and some papers such as a letter or report that you are reading or editing. You might also have pictures of your family or friends, a clock, a calendar, and calculator. You can have all of these things on your Windows Vista desktop, too, so that you can access them quickly and easily while you work.

The icons on the taskbar and desktop provide access to frequently used programs, features, and commands. For example, when you click the Start button, you open the Start menu.

In the next section, you use the mouse to open the Start menu.

Using the Start Menu

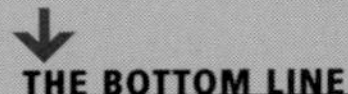

The Start menu is often the first element you use when you sit down at your computer because it provides access to all of your information. For example, from the Start menu, you can start programs such as a word processor or database, locate files such as letters you have written, or access the Internet. In this section, you use your mouse to open and close the Start menu. You also practice selecting and locating items on the Start menu.

Opening and Closing the Start Menu

To open or close the Start menu, you point to the Start button on the desktop and then click the left mouse button.

OPEN AND CLOSE THE START MENU

1. Use your mouse to point to the **Start** button in the lower left corner of the desktop.
2. Click the **Start** button. The Start menu opens, as show in Figure 1-4. Take a moment to use the figure to locate the parts of the Start menu on your screen. (Of course, because Windows Vista is easily customized, your Start menu probably does not look exactly the same as the one in the figure.)

Figure 1-4

Windows Vista Start menu

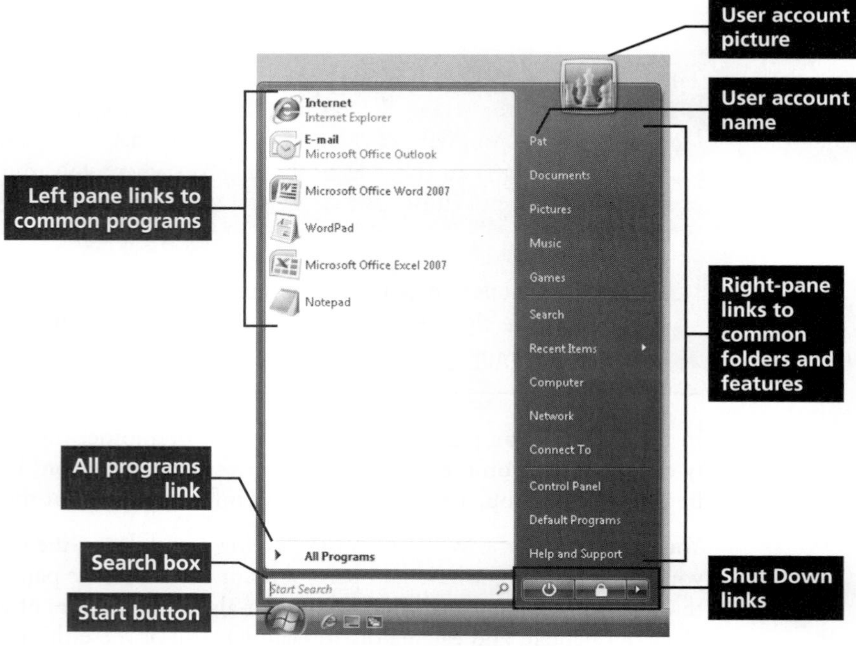

ANOTHER WAY

You can also open the Start menu by pressing the Windows logo key on your keyboard, and close it by pressing Esc.

3. Click the **Start** button again. The Start menu closes.

PAUSE. LEAVE the desktop displayed to use in the next exercise.

You may have noticed that the Start menu is divided into two main sections, which are called ***panes***. The left pane is a menu of links to commonly used programs, and the right pane is a menu of links to commonly used features and ***folders***. Your user account name and picture display at the top of the right pane. A folder is a place where you can store items such as ***files*** and other folders. A file is a set of information stored with a single name. The tools you need to end your Windows session and shut off your computer are at the bottom of the right pane, and the tools you need to search your computer to find information are at the bottom of the left pane.

Identifying Items on the Start Menu

Most items on the Start menu are links to the programs, folders, and files that you use most often. Simply click a link to access the feature you need.

IDENTIFY ITEMS ON THE START MENU

1. Click the **Start** button to open the Start menu.
2. Point to the word **Documents** near the top of the right pane. It should highlight, and a ScreenTip should display. The highlighted item is often called the current or active item, which means it is the item that the next command will affect.

3. Point to the word **Computer** in the right pane. You might notice that the picture at the top of the pane changes depending on the current item. When you point at Computer, the picture shows a computer system.
4. Click **All Programs** at the bottom of the left pane. A menu of all the programs installed on your computer displays in the left pane, as shown in Figure 1-5. (The programs on your computer are probably different from the ones shown in the figure.) Notice that each program on the menu has an icon next to it to represent the program type. If an item on the menu is a folder, it has a folder icon instead.

Figure 1-5

All Programs menu

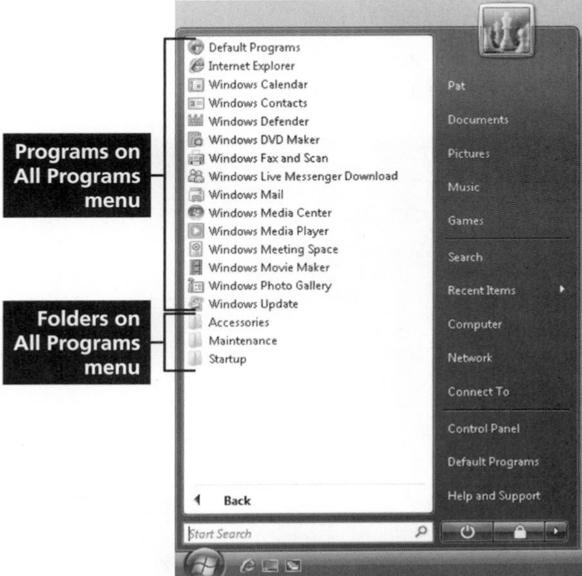

5. Click the **Accessories** folder on the All Programs menu. The folder opens—or expands—to display its contents, as shown in Figure 1-6.

Figure 1-6

Expand the Accessories folder

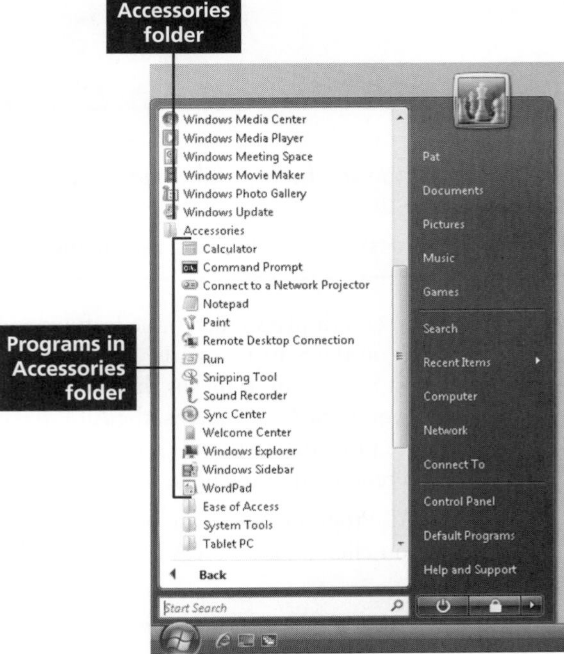

TROUBLESHOOTING

Sometimes there are too many items on the All Programs menu to display within the Start menu pane. In that case, a scrollbar displays along the right edge of the pane. You can drag the scrollbar up or down to see additional items on the menu. You learn more about using scrollbars in the next section.

6. Click **Calculator** on the Accessories menu. The Calculator displays on the desktop and the Start menu closes. (Notice that a button representing the window displays on the taskbar.) The Calculator is one of the accessory tools that come with Windows to help make your work easier. You can use the calculator to perform basic mathematical functions.
7. On the Calculator keypad, click **5**, click *, click **3**, and then click =. The result—15—shows in the Calculator display, as shown in Figure 1-7.

Figure 1-7

Calculator

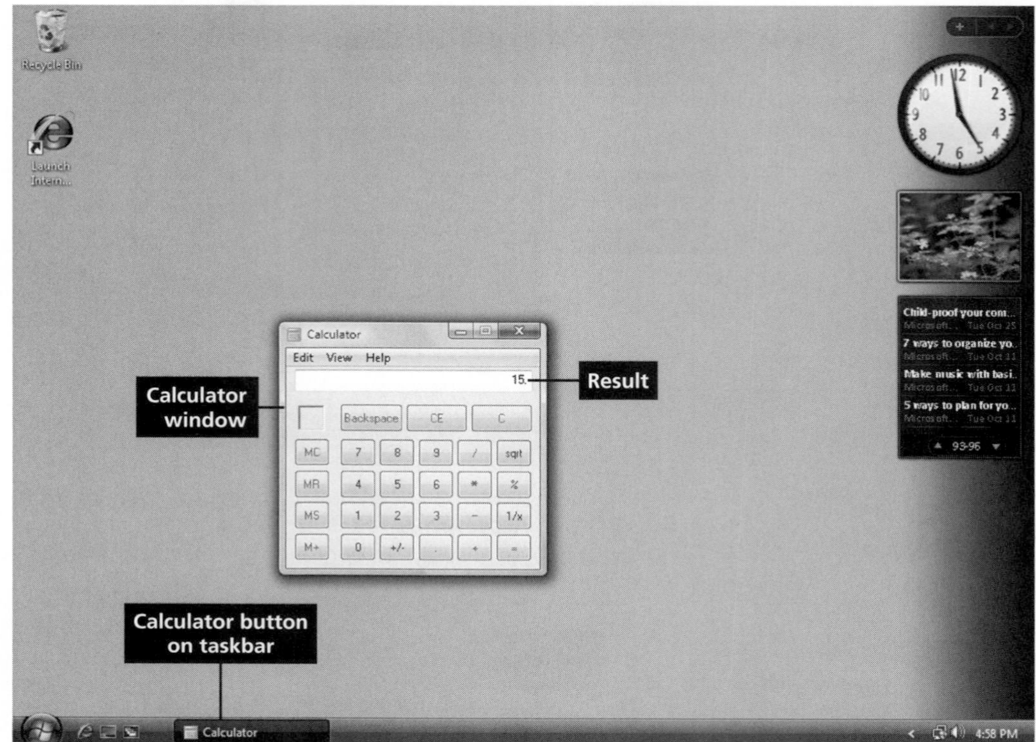

8. Click the **Close** button in the top right corner of the Calculator (the white X on a red background).

PAUSE. LEAVE the desktop displayed to use in the next exercise.

As you have seen, the Start menu displays links to the features and folders that you use most often. When you click a link on the Start menu, the feature starts, or the folder opens. If there is a right-pointing arrow next to an item, it means that when you click the item, a menu will display. For example, when you click All Programs, the All Programs menu displays. When you click a program icon, the program starts and displays in its program window, and the Start menu closes. A button representing the open window displays on the taskbar.

X REF

Lesson 7 covers customizing the Start menu.

Some of the items on the All Programs menu are organized into folders, such as Accessories and Maintenance. When you click a folder on All Programs, the folder expands on the menu so you can see its contents.

The Accessories folder stores useful tools and programs that come with Windows Vista. In addition to the Calculator, Windows Accessories usually include WordPad, a basic word processing program, and Paint, a graphics editing program. Other accessory programs may be available as well.

In the next section, you open folder windows.

■ Using a Folder Window

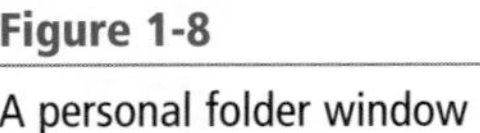

Imagine an office without file folders or desk drawers. Letters, reports, telephone lists, and other printed information might be strewn willy-nilly on the desk, chair, and even the floor! You'd never be able to find anything when you needed it. With Windows Vista, you organize your electronic data in much the same way as you'd organize an office. You create folders on your computer in which you can store information. When you open a folder, its contents display in a window that also has elements designed to help you manage your data and navigate in Windows. In this section, you open and close folders that come with Windows Vista and practice identifying and using the folder elements.

Opening and Closing a Folder Window

You can easily open a folder that is listed on the Start menu by clicking it. If the icon is on the desktop, you double-click to open it. To close a window, click its Close button.

OPEN AND CLOSE A FOLDER WINDOW

1. Click the **Start** button to open the Start menu.
2. Click your user account name at the top of the right pane of the Start menu. Your personal folder window opens. It should look similar to the one in Figure 1-8, although the name and the contents may be different, depending on your user name and the items stored in the folder. Notice that a button representing the window displays on the taskbar.
3. Take a moment to identify the elements of a folder window, as shown in Figure 1-8. Refer to Table 1-2 for descriptions of each element.

Figure 1-8

A personal folder window

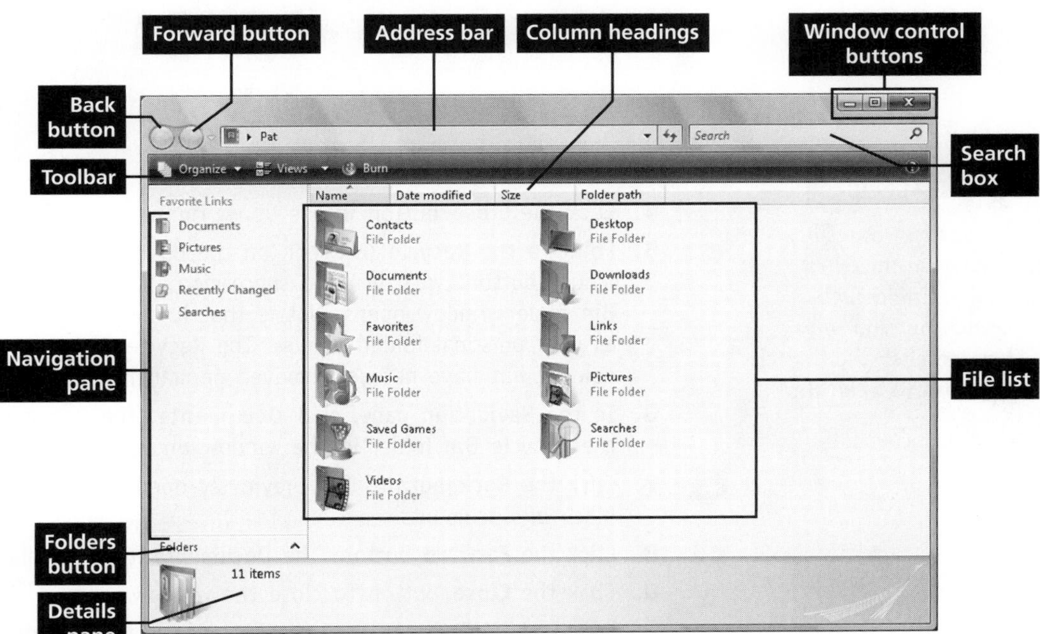

Table1-2

Common window elements

ELEMENT	DESCRIPTION
File list	The file list displays the contents of the current folder, including programs, files, subfolders, and links to other locations. Double-click an item to open it.
Navigation pane	The Navigation pane displays links to other locations. Click a link to display that location.
Back and Forward buttons	Click the Back and Forward buttons to navigate to folders that you have been viewing.
Toolbar	The toolbar displays buttons for common tasks, such as organizing the contents of a folder, or changing the way the file list displays.
Address bar	The Address bar displays the name of the current folder. It may also display the complete ***path*** to the location, with each part of the path separated by arrows. The path is the route Windows takes from a storage device through folders and subfolders to a specific destination. For example, the Address bar might display the name of your personal folder, an arrow, and then the name of the current folder. You can key a path in the Address bar to go to that location.
Headings	The column headings label the details displayed in the file list.
Search box	Key a word or phrase in the Search box to quickly locate a file in the current folder or its subfolders.
Details pane	The Details pane displays properties of the selected item, which are details or characteristics such as name, size, and type.
Window control buttons	The three window control buttons let you control the size and position of the window on the desktop. Click the Minimize button to reduce the window to a button on the taskbar. Click the Maximize button to expand the window to fill the desktop. When the window is maximized, the Restore Down button displays. Click the Restore Down button to return the window to its previous size and location on the desktop. Click the Close button to close the window.
Folders button	Click the Folders button to display a hierarchical list of the contents of your computer system. Click it again to hide the list.

TROUBLESHOOTING

If your computer has been customized to enable single-click launching, you only have to click the Recycle Bin icon to open the folder window.

4. Click the **Close** button in the upper right corner of the window. The window closes.
5. Point to the **Recycle Bin** icon on the desktop and then press and release the left mouse button twice in rapid succession. This is called a double-click. The Recycle Bin folder window opens. Notice that it has many of the same common elements as your personal folder window. The Recycle Bin folder contains items you have deleted but have not yet removed permanently.
6. In the Navigation pane, click **Documents**. The Documents folder opens, replacing the Recycle Bin folder in the window on your desktop.
7. Click the **Back** button. The previously opened folder—the Recycle Bin—displays in place of Documents.
8. Click the **Forward** button. The Documents folder displays.
9. Click the **Close** button to close the window.

PAUSE. LEAVE the desktop displayed to use in the next exercise.

Find out more about navigating in Windows in Lesson 3, "Organizing Files and Folders."

Recall that a folder is a storage location where you can keep files, subfolders—which are folders stored within other folders—and links. Most folder windows have the same common elements so that once you learn how to work in one folder, you can work in any folder.

Windows Vista comes with a few special folders already set up to help you get started and to organize system information. Table 1-3 describes some of the special folders.

Table1-3

Vista folders

ELEMENT	DESCRIPTION
Personal	Each user account has a personal folder, named with the user name assigned to the account. It displays at the top of the right pane on the Start menu. The personal folder contains files that belong only to the assigned user and that are not shared with other people using the same computer. By default, it displays frequently used folders so that you can quickly access your stored data, including documents, pictures, and music.
Documents	The Documents folder is the default folder for storing document files, such as letters, presentations, reports, and spreadsheets. Many programs use Documents as the default storage location for new documents, which means they automatically store new files in Documents unless you specify a different location. Documents is called My Documents in previous versions of Windows.
Computer	The Computer folder provides access to drives and other storage devices as well as to network locations connected to your computer. Computer is called My Computer in previous versions of Windows.
Pictures	The Pictures folder is set up to store and display digital pictures. Many graphics and photo editing programs use Pictures as the default storage location for picture files. Pictures is called My Pictures in previous versions of Windows.
Music	The Music folder is set up to store and organize digital music. Many digital music players use Music as the default storage location for music files. Music is called My Music in previous versions of Windows.
Recycle Bin	The Recycle Bin folder stores items you have deleted but have not yet removed permanently from your computer. You can restore items from the Recycle Bin if you realize you deleted them in error, or you can empty the Recycle Bin to remove the items permanently.

Selecting Items in a Folder

To perform any type of command or action on an item, you must first select it. For example, you must select a file to move it. You can select one or more items by using your mouse.

SELECT ITEMS IN A FOLDER

1. Click the **Start** button and then click your personal folder to open it.

2. In the file list, click the **Documents** folder to select it. Select means to mark an item to indicate that it will be affected by the next action or command. The selected item is highlighted and has a selection box around it, as shown in Figure 1-9. A description of the item displays in the Details pane.

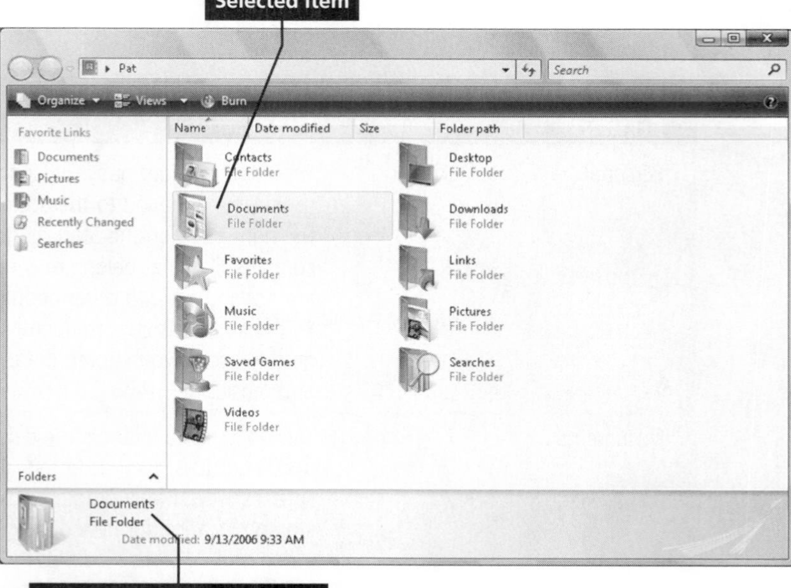

Figure 1-9

Select an item

TROUBLESHOOTING

If your computer has been customized to enable single-click launching, you only have to point at an item to select it.

3. In the file list, click the **Pictures** file folder to select it. Notice that Documents is no longer selected.
4. Press and hold down **Ctrl** on your keyboard and then click the **Documents** file folder. Now both items are selected, as shown in Figure 1-10. You can select multiple items anywhere in the list by holding down **Ctrl** while you click.

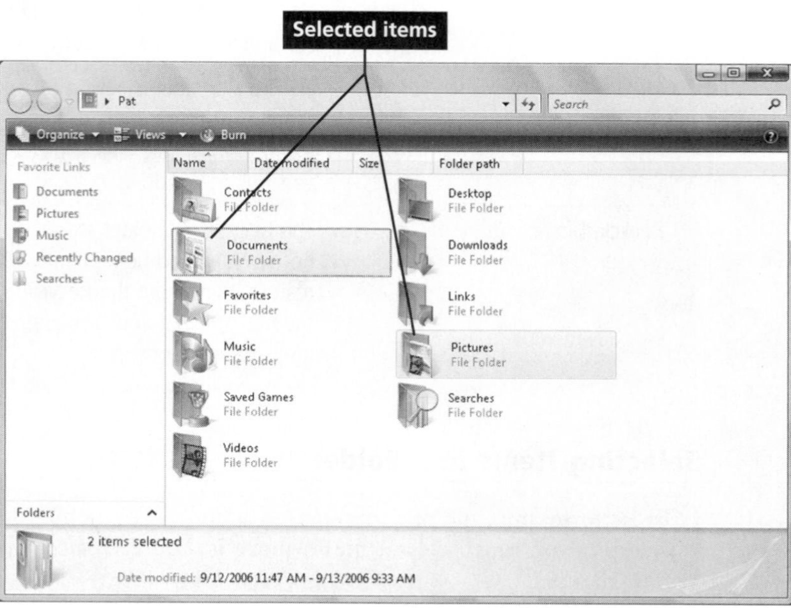

Figure 1-10

Select multiple items

5. Click the first item in the file list—it may be the Contacts file folder—press and hold down **Shift** on your keyboard, and then click the last item in the file list—it may be Videos. All items in the list are selected. You can select multiple items that are adjacent in a list by holding down Shift while you click.

ANOTHER WAY

You can also drag the pointer around items to select them.

6. Click any blank area in the file list to deselect the items.
7. Double-click the **Documents** folder icon. The Documents folder opens, replacing your personal folder in the open window.
8. Click the **Back** button to return to your personal folder.
9. Click the **Close** button to close the window.

PAUSE. LEAVE the desktop displayed to use in the next exercise.

When you select an item, you make it current, or active. Recall that the current item is the one on which the next action or command will occur. For example, you select a file before you move it or print it.

The easiest way to select an item is to click it. When you want to select more than one item, you combine the click with a key press.

- Press and hold Ctrl while you click to select items that are not adjacent to one another.
- Press and hold Shift while you click to select items that are adjacent to one another.

To cancel a selection, click a blank area in the window or press Esc.

Minimizing, Maximizing, and Restoring a Window

Sometimes you need to quickly change the size or position of a window on the desktop. Minimize the window to temporarily remove it from the desktop, maximize it to increase its size to fill the desktop, and then restore it back to its original size and position.

MINIMIZE, MAXIMIZE, AND RESTORE A WINDOW

1. Click the **Start** button and then click **Computer** in the right pane of the Start menu. The Computer folder window opens. It displays the components of your computer system, including disk drives. Notice the common window elements.
2. Click the **Minimize** button in the upper right corner of the window. The window is reduced to a button on the taskbar, as shown in Figure 1-11.

Figure 1-11

Minimize a window

3. Click the **Computer** taskbar button. The window opens.
4. Click the **Maximize** button in the upper right corner of the window. The window expands to fill the desktop, as shown in Figure 1-12. Notice that some of the colors in the window change to indicate it is maximized, and that the Maximize button is now replaced by the Restore Down button.

Figure 1-12
Maximize a window

5. Click the **Minimize** button to once again reduce the window to a taskbar button.
6. Click the taskbar button to return the window to its previous size and position—in this case, maximized.
7. Click the **Restore Down** button in the upper right corner of the window. The window returns to the size and position it had before you maximized it in step 4.
8. Click the Close button to close the Computer window.

PAUSE. LEAVE the desktop displayed to use in the next exercise.

When you ***minimize*** a window, you reduce it to a taskbar button. A minimized window is not closed. It remains running on your computer in a minimized state. When you ***maximize*** a window, you expand it to fill the desktop. You cannot see other items on the desktop behind it, but they are still there. When you ***restore down*** a window, it returns to its previous size and position. These commands become more and more useful as you start working with multiple windows at the same time, because they enable you to juggle many tasks at once. For example, you might be writing a letter with a word processing program in one window and need to look up a name and address in your contacts list at the same time. You can easily manipulate the windows so that you can access the information you need, when you need it.

You may have noticed that the Computer folder was divided into two sections.

- Hard Disk Drives, which lists the hard disks that are fixed inside your computer or attached externally.
- Devices with Removable Storage, which shows devices such as digital video disk (DVD) or compact disk (CD) drives, as well as universal serial bus (USB) devices such as flash drives, scanners, or cameras that are currently connected to your computer.

A drive is a device that reads and writes data on storage media, such as a CD or DVD. In Windows Vista, each drive is assigned a drive letter to help you identify it as part of your computer system. For example, the main hard disk drive is called drive C:, or Local Disk C:. See Table 1-4 for information about different types of storage devices.

Table1-4

Disk drives and storage devices

Element	Description
Hard disk	A hard disk is a device that contains one or more inflexible platters coated with material in which data can be recorded magnetically. Most personal computers have at least one primary hard disk fixed inside the computer. It is usually called drive C: or Local Disk C: and is the location where files and programs are typically stored. Some hard disks are attached externally to a computer. External drives can be removed and stored in a different location to safeguard data, or attached to a different computer to transfer data.
Hard disk drive	A hard disk drive is the device that reads data from and writes data to a hard disk.
DVD drive	A DVD drive is a drive that reads data on DVDs or CDs. If the drive is a DVD burner, it can also write data on a DVD or CD. DVD burners may be labeled RW, which stands for read and write. DVDs can store a large amount of data, making them suitable for storing videos, pictures, and music as well as data.
CD drive	A CD drive reads data on a compact disk. If the drive is a CD burner, it can write data on a CD. A CD burner may be labeled RW, which stands for read and write. Although they do not have as large a capacity as DVDs, CDs are suitable for storing music and pictures as well as data.
Flash drive	A flash drive is a small storage device that plugs into a USB port on the computer. Flash drives can be moved from one computer to another, making it easy to share and transport information. Flash drives may also be called memory keys, key drives, pen drives, or thumb drives.
Network drive	A network drive is any type of drive that is connected to a network and that can be accessed by users on the network. A network drive makes it possible for people to share files and folders stored on that drive.
Other	Other types of storage devices include scanners, digital cameras, and digital video camcorders, which can be attached to a USB port. Data from the attached device can be transferred to the computer. A scanner is a device that converts a printed image to a digital file. A digital camera is a camera that records and stores pictures in digital format. A digital video camcorder records and stores video in digital format.

Moving a Window

You can use the mouse to drag a window to any position on the desktop.

MOVE A WINDOW

1. Click the **Start** button and then click your personal folder to open it.
2. Move the pointer so it is touching the blank area of the window above the Address bar, to the left of the window control buttons.
3. Press and hold the left mouse button and then move the mouse up and to the left. Notice that the window moves with the mouse. This action is called click and drag, or just drag.
4. Release the mouse button when the upper left corner of the window is in the upper left corner of the desktop. This action is called drop. Dropping is usually combined with dragging in order to move or copy items.
5. Move the pointer so it is touching the blank area of the window above the Address bar again, then drag the window down and to the right.
6. Drop the window when its lower right corner is in the lower right corner of the desktop.

PAUSE. LEAVE your personal folder open to use in the next exercise.

In this section, you used different mouse actions to move a window on the desktop. There are five common mouse actions.

- Click — A click is when you press and release the left mouse button. This action is commonly used for selecting.
- Double-click — A double-click is when you press and release the left mouse button twice in rapid succession. A double-click is often used to start a program or open a subfolder.
- Right-click — A right-click is when you press and release the right mouse button. When you right-click an item, a shortcut menu usually displays, offering you a list of frequently used commands.
- Drag — Drag, which may be called click and drag, is when you press and hold the left mouse button and then drag the mouse to a different location. Drag is used to select multiple items, or, when combined with drop, to move items.
- Drop — Drop is when you release the mouse button after a drag.

TROUBLESHOOTING

If you are left-handed, you may have trouble clicking and right-clicking with your right hand. You can switch the mouse buttons so that you can use the mouse comfortably with your left hand. Ask your instructor for more information, or consult Lesson 15, "Customizing Your Computing Environment."

Resizing and Scrolling a Window

You can use the mouse to change the height and width of a window on the desktop. If there are too many items in the file list to display in the window, you can scroll the window up and down or left and right.

RESIZE AND SCROLL A WINDOW

USE the personal folder window you left open in the previous exercise.

1. Position the pointer over the top border of the window. It should change shape to a vertical double-headed pointer, as shown in Figure 1-13.

Figure 1-13
Resize a window

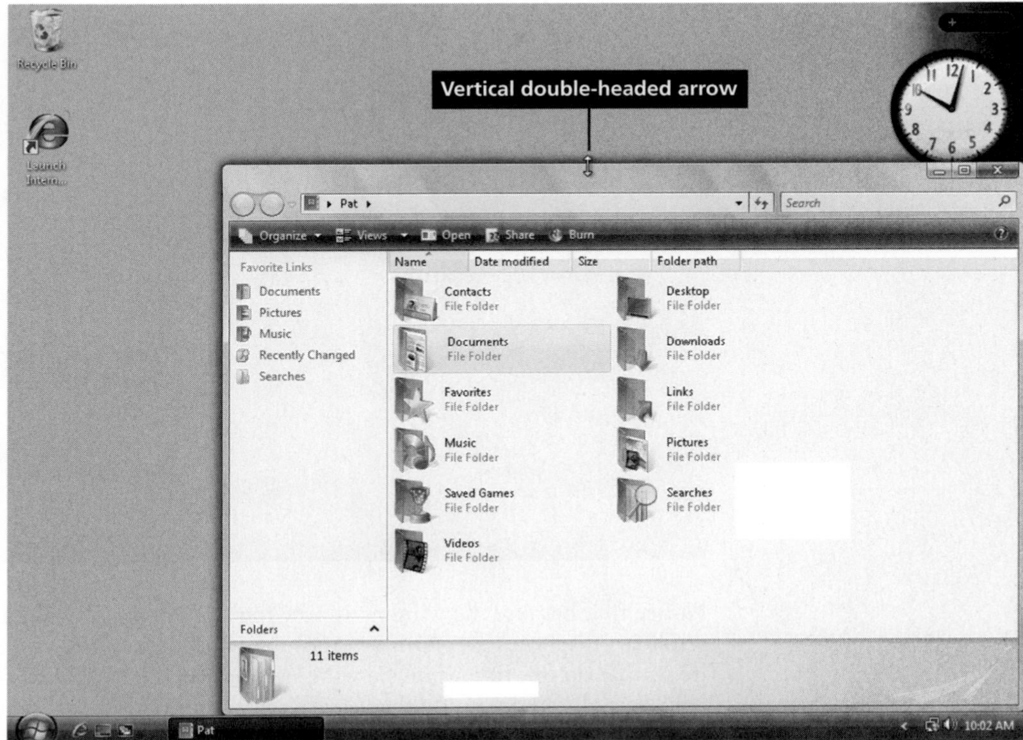

2. Drag up to the top of the desktop and then release the mouse button. The window height increases.
3. Position the pointer over the left border of the window so it resembles a horizontal double-headed pointer. Then drag to the left. Release the mouse button at the left edge of the desktop. The width of the window increases.
4. Position the pointer over the top left corner of the window so it resembles a diagonal double-headed pointer. Then drag down and to the right to decrease the size of the window. Release the mouse button when the window is approximately three inches square, as shown in Figure 1-14. When you drag a window corner, both the height and width change at the same time.

Figure 1-14

Scrollbars display when needed

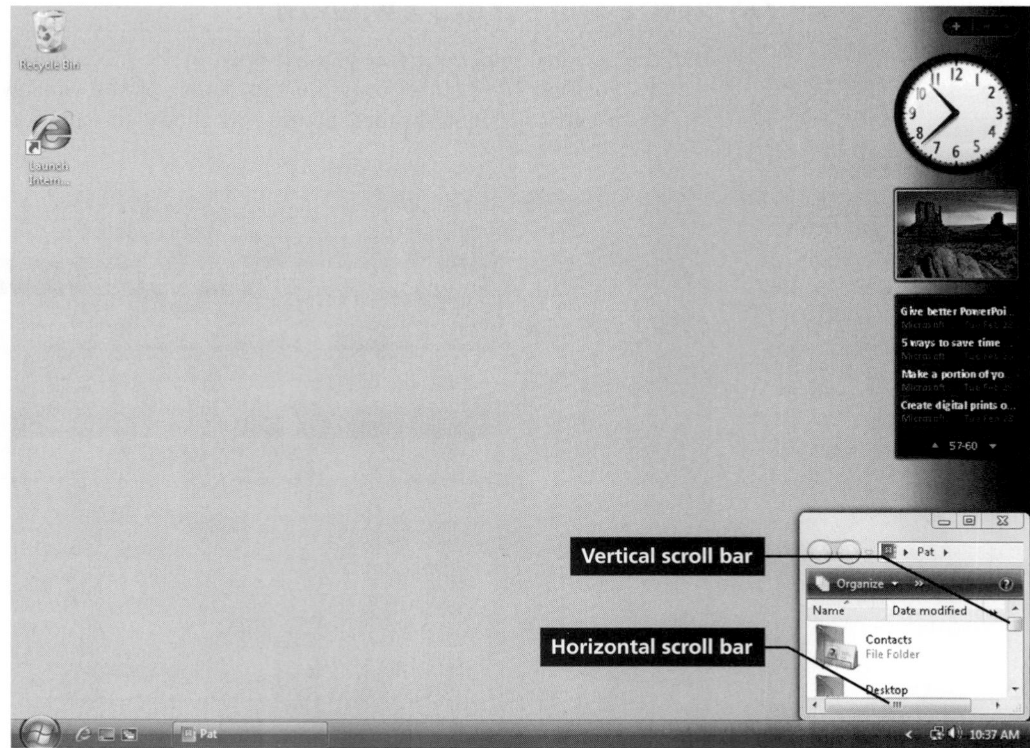

Notice that because the window is now too small to display all of the items in the file list, scrollbars display. A ***scrollbar*** is a tool that you use to scroll—or shift—the display to show items that do not fit within the window. You use the horizontal scrollbar to shift the display left and right, and you use the vertical scrollbar to shift the display up and down. A scrollbar has three main parts—a scroll box, which is a box on the scrollbar that you can drag to quickly shift the display, and two arrows that you can click to shift the display one space or line a time in either direction.

TAKE NOTE*

The size of the scroll box on a scrollbar indicates the amount of content that displays in the window relative to the entire content of the folder. So, a small scroll box means a small percentage of the total content displays, and a large scroll box means that most of the content displays.

5. Click the **down scroll arrow** on the vertical scrollbar. The content in the window scrolls so you can see additional items.
6. Click the **down scroll arrow** three or four times.
7. Drag the **scroll box** all the way to the bottom of the vertical scrollbar. Now the items at the bottom of the file list display in the window. You should see the icon of the last folder in the list—possibly the Videos folder icon.
8. Click the **right scroll arrow** on the horizontal scrollbar to shift the display horizontally. The window should look similar to Figure 1-15.

Figure 1-15

Scroll a window

9. Position the pointer over the upper left corner of the window so it resembles a diagonal double-headed arrow. Then drag to increase the size of the window, so that the entire file list displays. Notice that the scrollbars disappear when they are not needed.
10. Close your personal folder window.

PAUSE. LEAVE the desktop displayed to use in the next exercise.

Keep in mind that content that does not fit within the borders of a window is not missing or deleted—you just can't see it. It is like text printed on a page in a book—just because you don't have the book open to that page doesn't mean the text is not there. Scrolling is like turning the pages of the book so that you can view additional information.

■ Accessing Help and Support

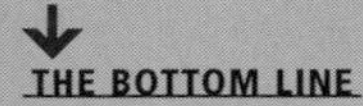

When you have a question about a feature in Windows Vista, you can find useful information in Windows Help and Support. Access Help and Support from the Start menu and use the home page to locate basic information about your computer or Windows Vista.

1. Click the **Start** button and then click **Help and Support** near the bottom of the right pane on the Start menu. The Windows Help and Support home page displays in a window, as shown in Figure 1-16. Notice that some elements in the window are the same as in a folder window, including the Back and Forward buttons, the Search box, and a toolbar.

Figure 1-16

Windows Help and Support home page

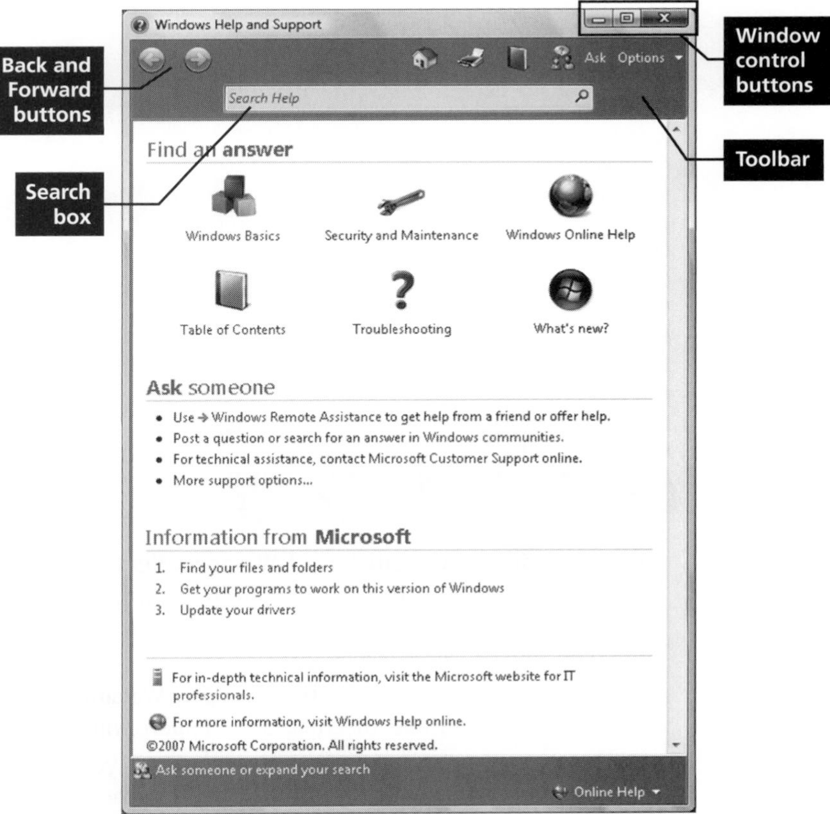

2. Click **Windows Basics** under the heading Find an answer. A page listing all of the Windows Basics topics displays. The topics are grouped under headings, and each topic is a link to a page of specific help information.

You can also open Help and Support from many locations in Windows Vista, simply by clicking the Help button. For example, in the Documents window, click Help to open the Working with the Documents folder Help and Support topic page.

TROUBLESHOOTING

Microsoft updates the Help and Support content on a regular basis, so it is possible that the links used in these steps and in the figures are not the same as those on your screen. If necessary, use different links to complete the exercise.

3. Click **The Start menu (overview)** under the heading Desktop fundamentals. A page of information about the Start menu displays.
4. Drag the vertical scroll box down slowly so you can review the information about the Start menu.
5. Click the **Back** button to return to the previous page and then click **Working with windows**. A page of information about how to work with windows displays. You can also scroll down in this page.
6. Click the **Help and Support home** button on the toolbar. The home page displays. The Help and Support home button is available on all pages within Help and Support.
7. Click **Table of contents** to display the Contents page. Each item on the page is a link to a main topic.
8. Click **Getting Started** to display the Getting Started topic, as shown in Figure 1-17. Items that have a question mark icon are links to specific topics, and items that have books are links to subtopics.

Figure 1-17

Getting Started Help topic

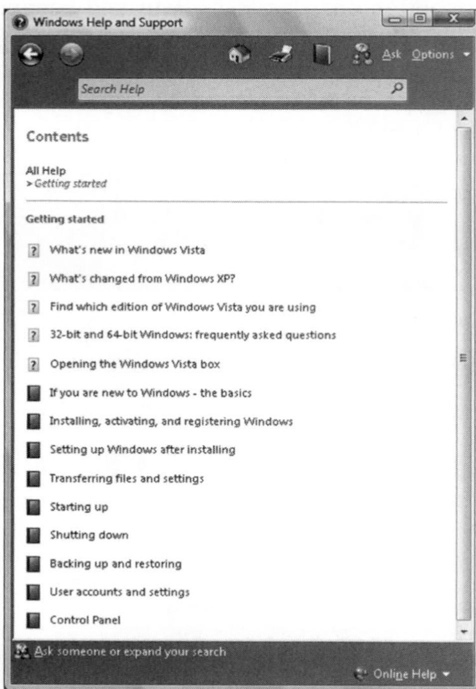

9. Click **Find which edition of Windows Vista you are using**. The topic page displays. Some pages provide specific instructions for performing tasks. This page walks you through the steps for locating information about your version of Windows Vista.
10. On the help page, click **Click to open Welcome Center**. The Welcome Center window opens, and the Help and Support window stays open as well.
11. Next to the picture of the computer under your user name, locate the name of the Windows Vista edition you are using and then click the **Close** button to close the Welcome Center window.
12. Click the **Close** button in the Help and Support window.

PAUSE. LEAVE your desktop displayed to use in the next exercise.

CERTIFICATION READY
How do you locate information in Windows Help and Support?
7.2.1

Windows Help and Support is full of information to help you accomplish any Windows task. It is organized as a series of linked pages that you can browse through in any order. Some pages provide information, and some walk you through specific steps. The color of text helps identify the type of link.

- Blue text links to another topic or to a specific task. The link may go to a location on a different page, on the same page, or in a different window. It may even go to a location on the Internet.
- Green text links to a definition. When you click the link, a definition displays in a ScreenTip.
- Violet text indicates a link that has already been used at least once. This can help you identify pages you have already accessed.

For a more in-depth look at how to use the Help and Support Center, refer to Lesson 8, "Getting Help and Support."

■ Shutting Down Windows Vista

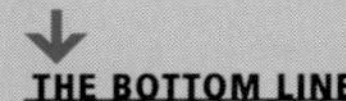

When you are finished using your computer, you should shut it down. Shutting down insures that your data is saved and your computer system is secure. It also saves energy. Windows Vista provides a few options for shutting down, including locking the computer, logging off, entering sleep mode, or turning off your computer. In this section, you learn how to use the different options for shutting down Windows Vista.

Locking the Computer

When you need to leave your computer for a short time, but want to be sure no one else can access your files, you can lock the computer.

LOCK THE COMPUTER

1. Click the **Start** button and then click the **Lock this computer** button at the bottom of the right pane. The computer is locked, and your user account login screen displays. The computer remains locked until you log back on.
2. Follow the correct procedure to log on. For example, key your password and then press **Enter**. Any windows you were using before you locked the computer remain open so you can continue working.

You can also lock your computer by pressing Ctrl+Alt+Del and then clicking Lock this computer, or by clicking the menu arrow to the right of the Lock button on the Start menu and then clicking Lock.

PAUSE. LEAVE your desktop displayed to use in the next exercise.

Locking your computer is a good way to maintain security when you have to step away from your system for any length of time but you do not want to shut it down, or log off. However, when you lock the computer, only you or a system administrator can unlock it.
If you share the computer with other users, you should not lock it.

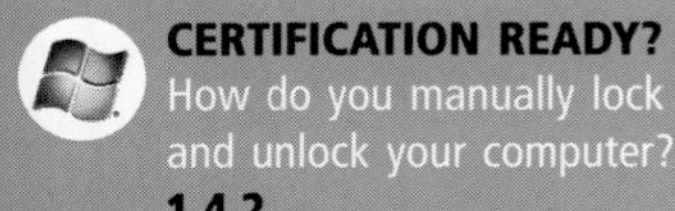

CERTIFICATION READY?
How do you manually lock and unlock your computer?
1.4.2

Note that to unlock the computer you use the procedure you usually use to log on to your Windows Vista user account. For example, you may click your account picture, or key your user account password. That means that anyone who knows your password can unlock the computer.

Logging Off

Log off when you want to end your Windows Vista session, but also want to leave the computer running. Logging off makes it easy for your or someone else to quickly log on without having to wait for the computer to start up again.

LOG OFF

1. Click the **Start** button and then click the arrow to the right of the Lock button to display a menu of options related to shutting down, as shown in Figure 1-18.

Figure 1-18

Menu of shutdown options

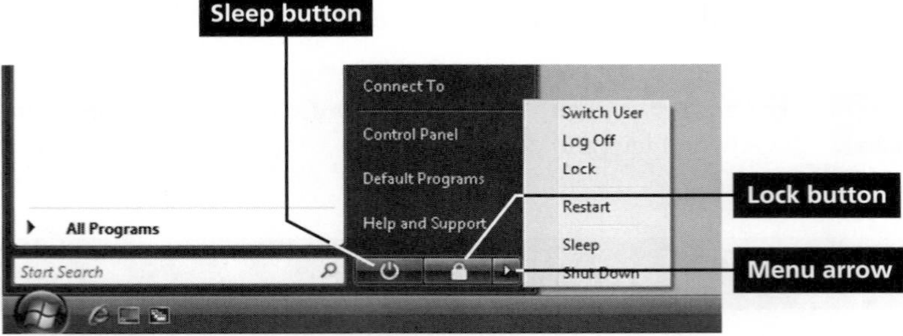

2. Click **Log Off** on the menu. Your session ends, closing all open windows. The user account login screen displays so that any user may log on.
3. Log on to your user account. Close the Welcome Center window, if necessary.

PAUSE. LEAVE your desktop displayed to use in the next exercise.

Logging off is useful if someone else needs to access his or her account. You can end your Windows session but leave the computer running so that someone else can easily log on. Your data is saved when you log off, so even if someone else shuts off the computer, your information remains stored for future use.

Entering Sleep Mode

You can put your computer to sleep to conserve power and then bring it back to life in a matter of seconds when you need it.

ENTER SLEEP MODE

1. Click the **Start** button and then click the **Sleep** button. The computer saves your data and then enters ***sleep mode***, which is a state of low power consumption. Usually, the display and the fan turn off. The computer remains in sleep mode until you turn it back on.

If you do not have a Sleep button on your Start menu, your computer may not support sleep mode, or your system administrator may have disabled it. In its place there is probably a Shut Down button. You learn how to shut down the computer in the next section.

2. Press the power button on your computer. The computer wakes from sleep mode and displays your user account login screen.

TROUBLESHOOTING

If pressing the power button does not wake your computer, try clicking the mouse button or pressing any key on the keyboard. If you are using a notebook computer, open the lid. If the system still does not wake, consult the documentation that came with the system.

3. Log on to your user account.

PAUSE. LEAVE your desktop displayed to use in the next exercise.

Sleep mode is useful for saving power when you are not using your computer. When your computer goes into sleep mode, Windows Vista saves all of your open documents and programs but does not shut off, or even log you off your user account. You can quickly resume full power operation at any time. By default, if you don't use your computer for a predetermined amount of time, it automatically goes to sleep. This conserves power and also keeps the system and your data secure. Sleep mode is particularly useful for mobile devices such as notebook computers that may rely on a battery. In fact, your notebook computer may automatically go into sleep mode when you close the lid.

Turning Off Your Computer

When you want to shut down Windows and turn off all of your computer components, use the Shut Down command.

TURN OFF YOUR COMPUTER

1. Close all open windows.
2. Click the **Start** button and then click the arrow to the right of the Lock button
3. Click **Shut Down** on the menu. Your session ends, closing all open windows, and your computer turns off. If necessary, manually turn off your display.

Managing power options, such as changing the sleep mode settings, are covered in Lesson 9, "Managing System Resources."

Because sleep mode is an effective way to conserve power but keep your computer ready to respond quickly, you may not need to shut down very often. You should shut down your computer, however, if you need to repair the computer or install new hardware components such as memory. As you have seen, Windows Vista provides many options for shutting down windows. In addition to those covered in this section, you may find two other options on the Shut Down menu useful.

- Restart lets you shut down, closing all open windows, and then restart your computer. Restarting is sometimes necessary when you install or uninstall new programs or devices, or if you are having a problem with your system.
- Switch Users lets you remain logged on to the system, but the user account login screen displays so that another user can log on. Switching users is useful if someone else who uses the computer needs to check something quickly in his or her files while you are working.

You can use the Power button on the Welcome screen to shut down, restart, or enter sleep mode. Click the button to shut off, or click the arrow next to the button to display a menu of shutdown options.

SUMMARY SKILL MATRIX

In This Lesson You Learned	Matrix Skill	Skill Number
To get started with Windows Vista		
To use the Start menu		
To use a folder window		
To access help and support	Locate information in Windows Help and Support.	7.2.1
To lock the computer	Manually lock the computer	1.4.2

■ Knowledge Assessment

Fill in the Blank

Complete the following sentences by writing the correct word or words in the blanks provided.

1. The ______________ screen lists the names of all of the people authorized to use the computer.
2. A(n) ______________ is a link to a program, feature, or command.
3. The ______________ is the main work area that displays when Windows Vista is running.
4. A(n) ______________ is a list of options.
5. ______________ an item to indicate that it will be affected by the next action or command.
6. ______________ a window to return it to its previous size and position.
7. ______________ a window to reduce it to a button on the taskbar.
8. ______________ a window to increase its size to fill the desktop.
9. A(n) ______________ is a tool that you use to shift the display to show items that do not fit within a window.
10. ______________ mode is a state of low power consumption.

True/False

Circle T if the statement is true or F if the statement is false.

T | F 1. Only one person can have a user account on a computer running Windows Vista.

T | F 2. An icon is a small picture that represents an item or command.

T | F 3. You can only select one item at a time in a file list.

T | F 4. The Address bar displays the name of the current folder.

T | F 5. The Restore Down button only displays when a window is maximized.

T | F 6. To select items that are not adjacent to one another, press and hold Shift while you click each item.

T | F 7. The main hard disk drive is called drive C: or Local Disk C:.

T | F 8. If there is not enough room in a window to display all content, the extra content is deleted.

T | F 9. The only way to get help and support for Windows Vista tasks is to call Microsoft on the telephone.

T | F 10. Locking your computer is a good way to maintain security when you have to step away from your system for any length of time.

■ Competency Assessment

Project 1-1: Identify Disk Drives

Use Windows Vista to learn about your computer system.

GET READY by having a piece of paper and pen on hand to write down information about your computer. Alternatively, your instructor may ask you to start an online journal or create a text or word processing file in which you can record the information in this and the remaining projects.

1. Turn on your computer and monitor.
2. On the user account login screen, click or key your **user name**.
3. If necessary, key your password in the Password box and then press Enter to display the desktop.
4. If necessary, click the **Close** button to close the Welcome Center.
5. Click the **Start** button to open the Start menu.
6. Click **Computer** on the right pane of the Start menu to display the Computer folder window.
7. Click to select the icon representing your hard disk drive, which is usually named Local Disk(C:).
8. Determine the total size of the disk and the amount of free space on the disk. Then write the information on a piece of paper, or record it in your online journal or text or word processing file.
9. Count how many devices with removable storage you have and write the number on a piece of paper. If you can identify the type of drive, record that information as well. For example, record the letter of the CD drive, DVD drive, or network drive.
10. Click the **Close** button to close the Computer window.
11. Click the **Start** button to open the Start menu.
12. Click the **Lock** button to lock your computer.
13. Log on to your Windows Vista user account in order to unlock the computer.

PAUSE. LEAVE the Windows Vista screen displayed and **KEEP** the piece of paper and pen on hand, if necessary, to use in the next project.

Project 1-2: Proper Shutdown

Use Help and Support to find out how to turn off your computer properly.

1. On the user account login screen, click or key your **user name**.
2. If necessary, key your password in the Password box and then press Enter.
3. Click the **Start** button to open the Start menu.
4. Click **Help and Support** to open the Help and Support home page.
5. Click **Windows Basics** to display the list of topics.
6. Click **Turning off your computer properly** to display the help topic.
7. Read the information on the help page.
8. Drag the **vertical scroll box** down so you can continue reading the help topic.
9. At the end of the help topic, under the heading See also, click **Turning off a computer: frequently asked questions.**
10. Click **Is my data safe while my computer is asleep.** Read the answer and then record the explanation in your own words on the piece of paper, in your online journal, or in the text or word processing file.
11. Click the **Close** button to close the Help and Support window.
12. Click the **Start** button to open the Start menu.
13. Click the **Sleep** button to put your computer into sleep mode.

PAUSE. LEAVE your computer in sleep mode for the next project.

■ Proficiency Assessment

Project 1-3: Shipping Costs

You must send seven packages to customers out of town. Each package will cost $4.69 to ship. Use the Calculator accessory program to quickly determine the total shipping cost.

GET READY by having a piece of paper and pen or other method available for recording the result of your calculation.

1. Wake your computer from sleep mode by pressing the power button on your computer.
2. Open the Start menu.
3. Open the All Programs menu.
4. Open the Accessories folder.
5. Click Calculator to start the calculator program.
6. On the Calculator keypad, click 4, click ., click 6, and then click 9.
7. On the Calculator keypad, click *, click 7, and then click =.
8. Record the result of the calculation.
9. Close the Calculator.

PAUSE. LEAVE the desktop displayed and **KEEP** the piece of paper and pen, your online journal, or the text or word processing file on hand to use in the next project.

Project 1-4: Explore Sample Windows Vista Folders

Explore the picture and music samples that come with Windows Vista.

1. Use the Start menu to open the Pictures folder.
2. Select the Sample Pictures shortcut.
3. Write down the size of the folder.
4. Double-click the Sample Pictures shortcut to open the Sample Pictures folder.
5. Maximize the window so you can see all of the picture files.
6. Click the Waterfall picture. If the Waterfall picture is not available, select a different picture. Write down the filename, date taken, author, and size.
7. Minimize the window.
8. Maximize the window and then restore it.
9. In the Navigation pane, click Music to open the Music folder.
10. Click the Sample Music shortcut icon to select it and then write down the size of the folder.
11. Double-click the Sample Music shortcut to open the Sample Music folder.
12. Click the first song in the file list. Write down the filename, artist, genre, and length.
13. Click the Back button.
14. Close the folder window.
15. **LOG OFF** your Windows Vista user account.

■ Mastery Assessment

Project 1-5: Show Off Windows Vista

You recently hired an assistant who has never used a personal computer before. In this project, give him a tour of some of the basic features of Windows Vista.

1. Start your computer and log on to your account.
2. Using ScreenTips, locate the icon on the Quick Launch toolbar that displays the desktop.
3. Open your personal folder and select all items in the file list at the same time.
4. Maximize and then minimize the window.
5. Open the window and then restore it.
6. Move the window to the upper right corner of the desktop and then close it.
7. Open the Computer window and identify the different types of disk drives.
8. From the Computer window, open the Documents window.
9. Close the Documents window.
10. Open the Recycle Bin window and then close it.
11. Log off and then log back on.
12. Lock the computer.

PAUSE. LEAVE your computer locked until the next project.

Project 1-6: Windows Vista and Printers

Because you are working in a small office, you must be able to solve problems on your own. You are getting a new printer and want to learn how to set it up with your computer before it arrives. In this project, use Windows Help and Support to find out how to set up a printer for use with Windows Vista.

1. Unlock the computer and log on to your user account.
2. Open Windows Help and Support and display the Table of Contents.
3. Locate and click the link to information about Printers and printing.
4. Locate and click the link to information about Printers.
5. Open and read the information about adding or removing a printer.
6. When you are finished, close the Help and Support window.

LOG OFF your Windows Vista user account.

INTERNET READY

As was mentioned at the beginning of this lesson, Northwind Traders is a small, growing company that helps Inuit artists in Alaska market their work to customers around the globe. To prepare for a press release announcing the company's expansion, use Internet search tools to locate information about the history of Inuit art. For example, you might find out the types of traditional Inuit art created over the years, as well as the type of art created by contemporary artists. Use the information you find to write a paragraph that you can include in the press release that summarizes the evolution of Inuit art from the past to the present.

Working with Files and Folders

SKILL MATRIX

Skills	Matrix Skill	Skill Number
Creating and Renaming a Folder	Create and rename a folder	4.2.1, 4.2.2
Working with Files		
Creating and Naming a File	Create, delete, rename, and move files	4.6.3
Using Undo and Redo		
Capturing a Screen Image		
Deleting Files and Folders	Create, delete, rename, and move files	4.6.3
Using the Recycle Bin		

Southridge Video is a video production company that develops and produces training videos and webcasts for a variety of clients. Whenever the company adds a new client, the account manager uses Windows Vista to set up a folder so there is a place to store all files and other information related to the client. In this lesson, you will learn how to work with files and folders. You will use Windows Vista to create and rename folders and files, enter data into a file, and then save, print, and close the file. You will use the Undo and Redo commands to reverse the previous action. Finally, you will learn how to delete files and folders and how to use the Recycle Bin so you can restore or permanently remove deleted items.

KEY TERMS

Compatible program
Dialog box
Filename extension
File type
Format
Insertion point
Program
Redo
Shortcut menu
Submenu
Text editor
Undo

Creating and Renaming a Folder

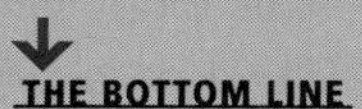

You use folders in Windows Vista to store your computer files just as you use folders to store printed files in a filing cabinet. Every file on your computer is stored in a folder, so it is important to know how to create and name folders. By giving each folder a unique and descriptive name, you can quickly recognize it and know what files it contains. In this exercise, you create a new folder on the desktop, name it, and then rename it.

CREATE AND RENAME A FOLDER

GET READY. Before you begin these steps, start your computer and log on to your Windows Vista account. Close all open windows so you can see the desktop.

1. Point to any blank area of the desktop and then press and release the right mouse button. Recall that this is called right-clicking. A ***shortcut menu*** displays. A shortcut menu is a list of commands or options relevant to the current task that displays when you right-click an item.

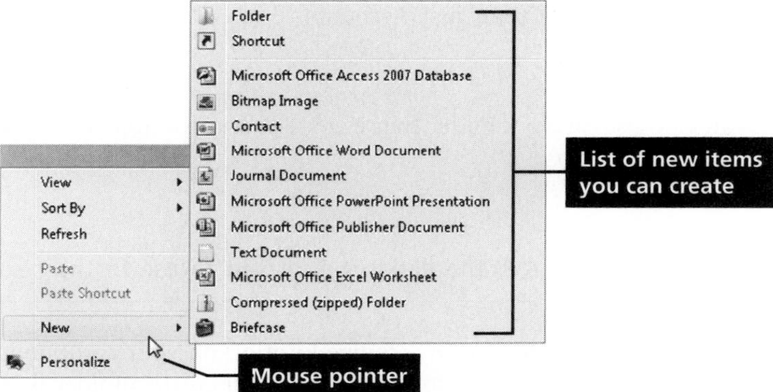

Figure 2-1
Shortcut menu

TROUBLESHOOTING

If you are using a computer without a mouse, use the available input device, such as a touchpad or trackball, in place of the mouse.

2. Point to **New** on the shortcut menu to display a ***submenu***, as shown in Figure 2-1. A submenu is a menu that opens off of another menu. The New submenu displays a list of the types of files, folders, and other items that you can create. The list depends on the programs you have installed on your computer, so the one you see on your desktop is probably not the same as the one in the figure. Each ***program*** is a set of instructions that a computer uses to perform a task, such as word processing or photo editing. Programs are sometimes called applications.

To display a shortcut menu by using the keyboard, select an item and then press Shift+F10.

3. Click **Folder** at the top of the New submenu. Windows Vista creates a new folder on the desktop, as shown in Figure 2-2. The default name—New Folder—is selected. In Windows Vista, and most programs that run on Windows Vista, selected text is replaced when you key new text.

Figure 2-2
New folder with default name

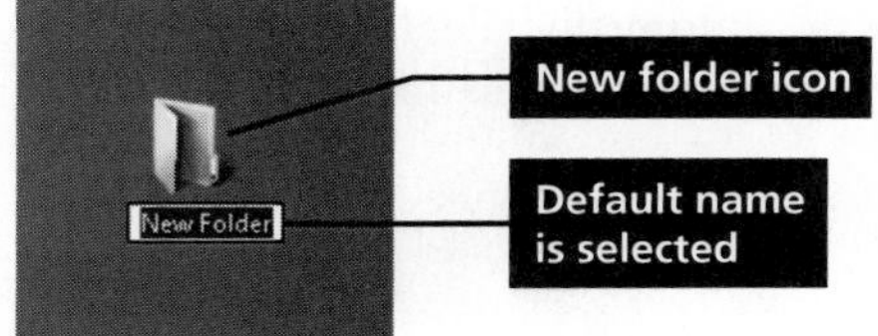

4. Key **Accounts** and then press Enter. The new folder is renamed Accounts.
5. Right-click the **Accounts** folder icon and then click **Rename** on the shortcut menu. The folder name—Accounts—is selected.
6. Move the pointer to the left of the first character in the name—*A*—and click. The text is deselected and an insertion point displays to the left of the folder name, as shown in Figure 2-3. An ***insertion point*** is a blinking vertical bar that indicates the location where text will be inserted.

Figure 2-3

Renaming a folder

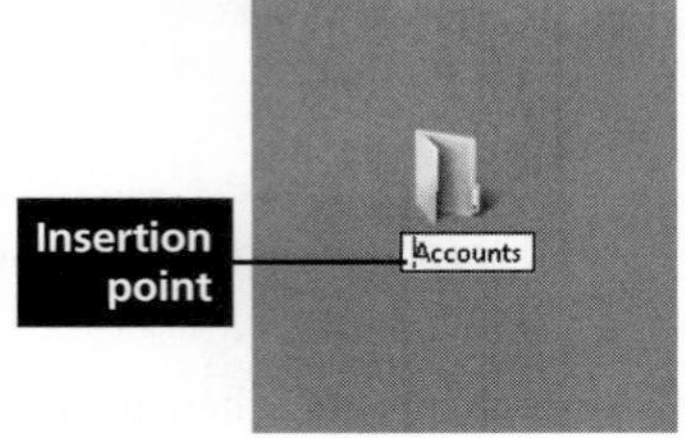

7. Key **Active**, press the spacebar to insert a space, and then press Enter. The text is inserted and the folder name changes to Active Accounts. This name is more descriptive than just Accounts.

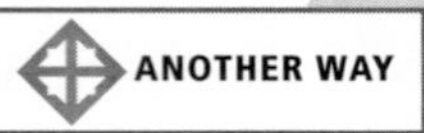

You can also select a folder name by selecting the folder icon and then clicking the folder name.

PAUSE. LEAVE the desktop displayed to use in the next exercise.

TAKE NOTE*

Your instructor may want you to create an assessment folder where you can store files that you create while using this book. You can create subfolders for each lesson in the main folder.

You can create folders in any storage location on your computer, including disk drives, removable devices, and in other folders. Where you create a folder is important, because it helps you stay organized. If you use a folder often, you may want it on the desktop so you can access it quickly at any time. Sometimes, you might create a subfolder, or a folder within another folder. For example, if you work for a company that has many clients, you might have a folder for each client. In a client's folder, you might have a folder for storing correspondence and a folder for storing invoices.

Using a descriptive name for a folder helps you identify the folder contents at a glance. For example, if you name a folder Information, you cannot tell what information it contains. If you name the folder Regional Sales Information, you know exactly what the folder contains.

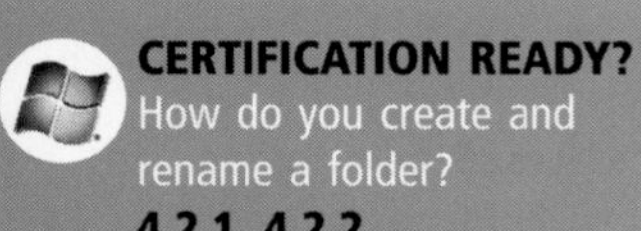

A folder name can have up to 260 characters, but that includes the complete path to the folder. (In Lesson 1 "Getting Started with Windows Vista", you learned that a path is the route Windows Vista takes from a storage device through folders and subfolders to a specific destination.) There are nine characters that you cannot use in a folder name: \ / ? : * " > < |. If you try to key these characters in a folder name, Windows Vista displays a ScreenTip to remind you that they are unavailable.

In the next section, you work with files.

In Lesson 5, "Working with Multimedia Files," you learn how to create different types of folders for storing different types of information, including pictures, music, and video.

■ Working with Files

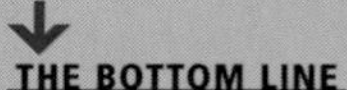

The data on your computer is stored in individual files. Each file has a unique name so that Windows Vista can distinguish one set of data from another. In addition, each file has a file type, or format, which identifies the specific kind of data. For example, plain text is stored in a text file, and pictures are stored in a graphics file. You use Windows Vista to manage and organize files, but you use application programs to work with the data in the file. In this section, you use Windows Vista to create and name a file and then you use the Notepad text editor program that comes with Windows Vista to enter, save, and print a text file.

Creating and Naming a File

Creating and naming a file using Windows Vista is similar to creating and naming a folder. You use the New command on the shortcut menu to select the type of file you want to create and then you replace the default filename with a descriptive filename.

CREATE AND NAME A FILE

1. Right-click a blank area of the desktop and then point to **New** on the shortcut menu to display the New submenu. The New submenu displays types of files you can create as well as programs for which you can create a new file. The ***file type***, which may be called file format, determines the way the file is saved. It is usually associated with a program that can read and manipulate the data in the file. The list depends on the programs you have installed on your computer, but one of the options should be Text Document.
2. Click **Text Document** on the New submenu. Windows Vista creates a new text document on the desktop, as shown in Figure 2-4. As with a new folder, the default name—New Text Document—is selected, so you can replace it simply by keying a new name.

Figure 2-4

New text document

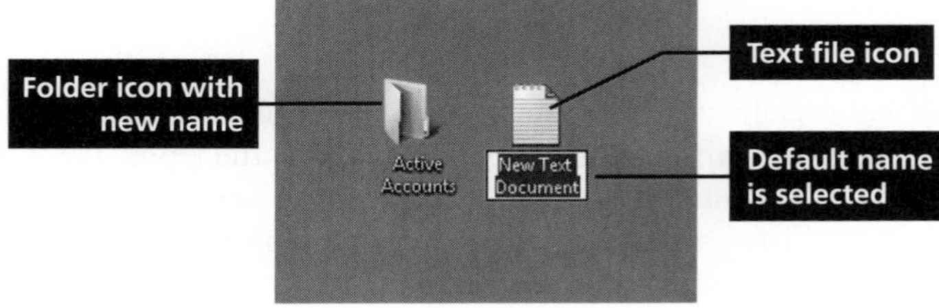

TAKE NOTE*

Different file icons identify different file types and the default associated programs. Notice that the text document icon is a simple notebook because it is associated with a text editing program.

3. Key **Names** and then press **Enter**. The new file is renamed Names.
4. Right-click the **Names** file icon and then click **Rename** on the shortcut menu. Key **Contact Data**—a more descriptive filename—and then press **Enter** to rename the file.

PAUSE. LEAVE the desktop displayed to use in the next exercise.

Many of the rules for creating and naming files are the same as those for creating and naming folders.

- You can create a file in any storage location.
- You should use a descriptive filename so that you can identify the contents of the file at a glance.
- A filename can have up to 260 characters, including the path.
- You cannot use the characters \ / ? : * " > < | in a filename.

In addition, filenames generally have a ***filename extension***, which is a set of characters added to the end of a filename to identify the file type. Most filename extensions are three or four characters separated from the filename by a period, which may be called a dot. For example, the filename extension for the text file you just created is .txt, so the complete filename is Contact Data.txt. By default, the file extension does not display in Windows Vista. Table 2-1 describes some common file types and their filename extensions.

Table 2-1

Common file types

FILENAME EXTENSION	FILE TYPE
.txt	Text
.rtf	Rich text format
.doc or .docx	Word document
.bmp	Bitmap image
.gif	Graphics interchange format, usually used for drawings or cartoons
.jpg or .jpeg	Joint photographic experts group, usually used for digital photographs
.xls or .xlsx	Excel spreadsheet
.html or .htm	Hypertext markup language file, usually used for web pages
.pdf	Portable document format
.ppt or .pptx	PowerPoint presentation

X REF

Lesson 4, "Customizing Windows Explorer," covers how to show or hide file extensions.

You will usually use a program to create a file. For example, if you are writing a report, you will use your word processor program to create the report file. Or if you are designing a marketing brochure, you will use your desktop publishing program to create the file. Most Windows Vista programs start with a new, blank file open, and then you use the File > Save As command to save and name the file.

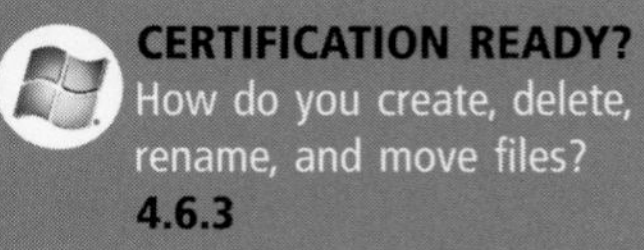

CERTIFICATION READY?
How do you create, delete, rename, and move files?
4.6.3

There may be times when you want to use Windows Vista to create and name files before you start working with a program. For example, you may want to set up a storage filing system for a new project, or you may be preparing files for someone else. For example, if you are in charge of a team organizing a sales meeting, you may want to set up folders and files in a specific structure with specific names. Then other team members can locate and access the files. They can use the necessary programs to enter the data.

Opening and Closing a File

When you open a file, the program associated with the file type opens as well. The contents of the file display in the program window along with the tools you need to edit and manipulate the data using that program. You can close a file by closing the program window.

OPEN AND CLOSE A FILE

1. Double-click the **Contact Data** file icon on the desktop. The file opens in a Notepad program window, as shown in Figure 2-5. Notepad is the default program that Windows Vista associates with text files. Notice that the program window has some elements in common with a folder window, such as the Window Control buttons for minimizing, maximizing, and closing the window. Also notice that a taskbar button for the window displays on the taskbar. The file is blank because you have not yet entered any text.

Figure 2-5

File open in Notepad

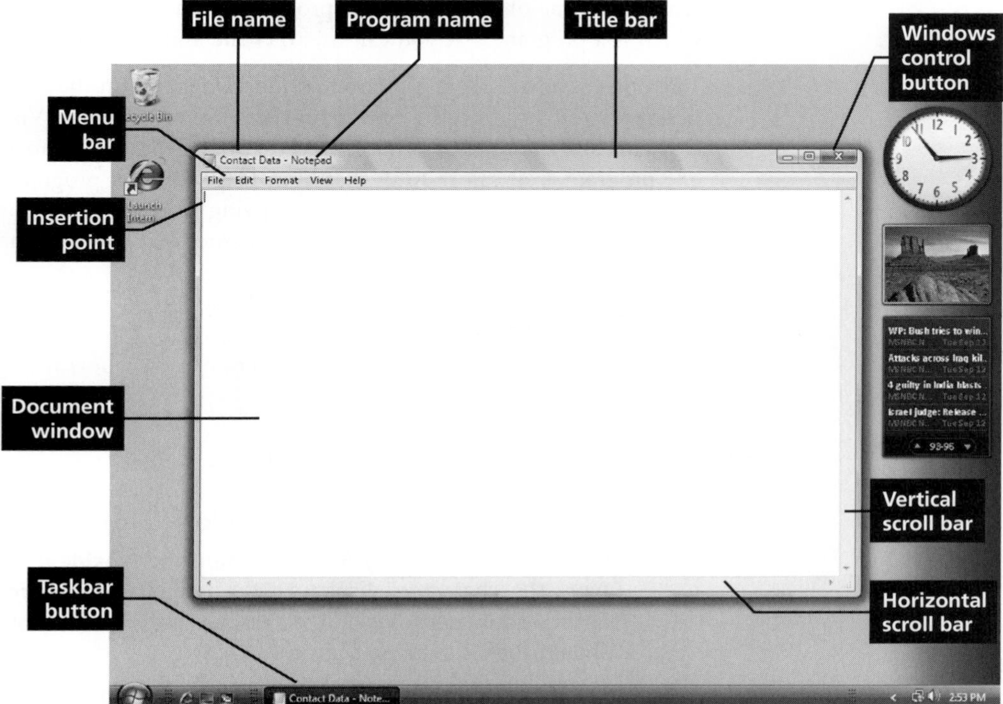

2. Take a moment to identify the elements of the Notepad program window, as shown in Figure 2-5.
3. Click the **Close** button in the program window's upper right corner. The window closes.

TROUBLESHOOTING

If the program displays a dialog box asking if you want to save the changes to the file, it means you made changes to the file content. Click Don't Save to close the program and the file without saving the changes.

ANOTHER WAY

You can also right-click a file icon and then click Open on the shortcut menu to open a file.

ANOTHER WAY

You can also close the Notepad program window by clicking File on the menu bar and then clicking Exit.

TAKE NOTE

As you have seen, Windows Vista uses the default associated program to open a file. You can open a file using a different ***compatible program***, which is any program that can read the file type, by using the Open With command. Right-click the file icon and point to Open With on the shortcut menu to display a menu of compatible programs. Then just click the program you want to use.

PAUSE. LEAVE the desktop displayed to use in the next exercise.

Notepad is one of the Accessories programs found in Windows Vista. It is a basic ***text editor***, which is a program that you can use to create and edit text-based files.

The options and tools in a program window depend on the tasks for which the program is designed. You will find that programs that run on Windows Vista all share some common elements and commands. That means that once you learn how to perform certain tasks in one program, you can transfer that knowledge to other programs. Some common commands include saving, closing, printing, and copying. You also use common keystrokes for entering and editing data. In the next exercise, you enter text and save the file.

Entering and Editing Text in a File

To enter text, simply key the characters on your keyboard. You can make changes by inserting and replacing existing text.

ENTER AND EDIT TEXT IN A FILE

1. Double-click the **Contact Data** file icon to open the file in Notepad.
2. On your keyboard, key **Mr. Mark Hanson, President** and then press **Enter**. As you type, the characters display to the left of the insertion point. When you press **Enter**, the insertion point moves to the beginning of the next line. The file should look similar to Figure 2-6.

Figure 2-6

Key text in a Notepad file

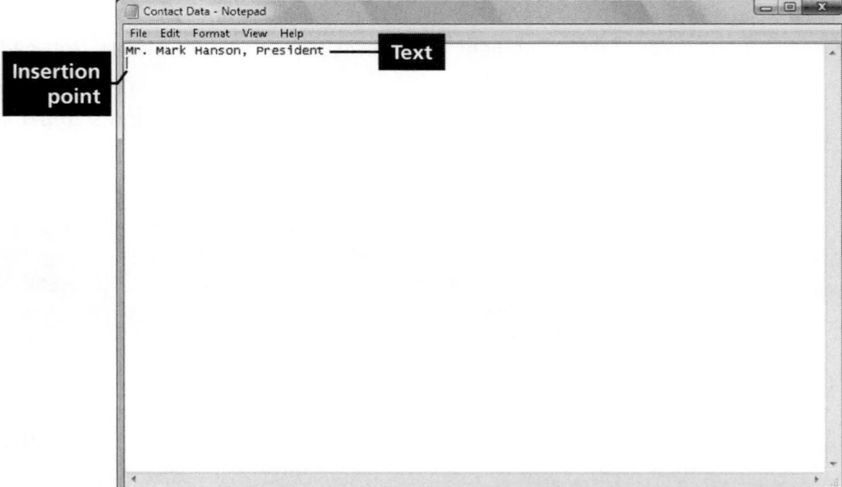

3. Key **m_hanson@tailspintoys.com** and then press **Enter** twice.
4. Key **Ms. Sandra I. Martines.**
5. Press **Backspace**. The insertion point moves to the left, deleting the previous character.

TAKE NOTE*

To delete a character to the right of the insertion point, press Delete.

6. Key z, **Vice President**, press Enter, and then key **s_i_martinez@tailspintoys.com**. Press Enter twice.
7. Move your pointer to the left of the *M* at the beginning of the first line of text and click the left mouse button. This positions the insertion point to the beginning of the file. You can move the insertion point anywhere within the text by clicking the new location.

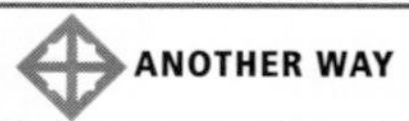

To quickly move the insertion point to the beginning of a file, press Ctrl+Home.

8. Key your name. The characters are inserted into the text, and the existing text shifts to the right. By default, new text is inserted to the left of the insertion point.
9. Press Enter, key today's date, and then press Enter three times to insert blank lines.
10. Position the pointer to the left of the *V* at the beginning of the word *Vice*. Then drag to the right to select the text **Vice President**. The file should look similar to Figure 2-7. As with file and folder names, when the text is selected, you can key replacement text.

Figure 2-7

Select text to replace it

To select a single word, double-click it.

To select text using the keyboard, position the insertion point to the beginning of the selection, press and hold Shift, then move the insertion point to the end of the selection.

11. Key **Product Manager**. The new text replaces the selected text.

PAUSE. LEAVE the Contact Data file open in Notepad to use in the next exercise.

As mentioned earlier, many of the commands and actions you use in one Windows Vista program can be used in other programs as well. Most programs use the same keystrokes for entering and editing text, as well as for moving the insertion point around in text. Table 2-2 describes some common keystrokes for moving the insertion point in text.

Table 2-2

Common keystrokes

PRESS THIS	TO DO THIS
Right arrow	Move insertion point one space to the right
Left arrow	Move insertion point one space to the left
Up arrow	Move insertion point one line up
Down arrow	Move insertion point one line down
Home	Move insertion point to beginning of line
End	Move insertion point to end of line
Ctrl+Home	Move insertion point to beginning of file
Ctrl+End	Move insertion point to end of file
Ctrl+right arrow	Move insertion point to beginning of next word
Ctrl+left arrow	Move insertion point to beginning of previous word
Backspace	Delete character to left of insertion point
Delete	Delete character to right of insertion point
Enter	Start a new line or paragraph

Notepad, and other basic text editors, are useful for editing plain text files, including system files that provide instructions to programs such as Windows Vista. However, the options for editing text in Notepad are limited to very basic tasks, such as inserting and replacing text. To create more sophisticated text-based documents in which you can ***format*** text and pages, you should use a word processor, such as Microsoft Office Word, or the WordPad program that comes with Windows Vista. Format means to apply features to change the appearance of data or an element. For example, you can format text using color or styles such as bold or italics. You can format a page by changing the width of margins or spacing.

In the next section, you save the changes to the file.

Saving a File

To make sure the data you enter in a file is available for use in the future, you must save it. Saving writes all changes you have made to the file on the storage disk. If you do not save the file, the changes will be lost, and you may have to spend time recreating them.

SAVE A FILE

USE the Contact Data file you left open in Notepad in the previous exercise.

1. In the Notepad window, click **File** on the menu bar. The File menu commands drop down, as shown in Figure 2-8.

Figure 2-8

File menu

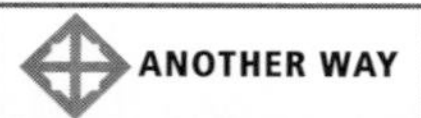

To quickly save changes to a file, press Ctrl+S.

2. On the File menu, click **Save.** The program saves the changes to the file and keeps the file open so you can continue working.
3. Click the **Close** button to close the file and the program.
4. Double-click the **Contact Data** file icon on the desktop. The file opens in Notepad. Now the file contains data.

PAUSE. LEAVE the Contact Data file open in Notepad to use in the next exercise.

While you work, your computer saves the data in its memory, but when you close a file or shut down the computer, the data in memory is not retained unless you save the file first. To make sure you do not lose work in the event of a power failure or other catastrophe, you should get in the habit of saving frequently.

In the next section, you learn how to save a copy of a file with a different name.

Saving a File with a Different Name

To save a file with a different name you use the File > Save As command. Save As creates a copy of the original file with the new name, leaving the original unchanged.

SAVE A FILE WITH A DIFFERENT NAME

USE the Contact Data file you left open in Notepad in the previous exercise.

1. Click **File** on the menu bar and then click Save As. The Save As ***dialog box*** displays, as shown in Figure 2-9. A dialog box is a window in which you select options or enter data to control the way a program executes a command. In this case, you want to change the filename before saving the file. Notice that the current filename is already selected.

Figure 2-9

Save As dialog box

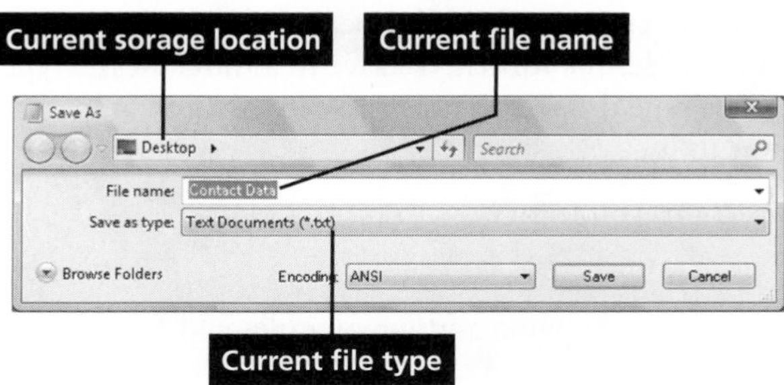

2. Key **New Contact Data** to replace the old filename and then click the **Save** button. The program saves the file with the new name and keeps the new file open. The original file remains unchanged.
3. On your keyboard, press Ctrl + End. This moves the insertion point to the end of the file.
4. Key **Ms Diane Tibbott, Assistant Product Manager**, press Enter, and then key **d_tibbott@tailspintoys.com**.
5. Click **File** > **Save** to save the changes to the file. It should look similar to Figure 2-10.

Figure 2-10

File with saved changes

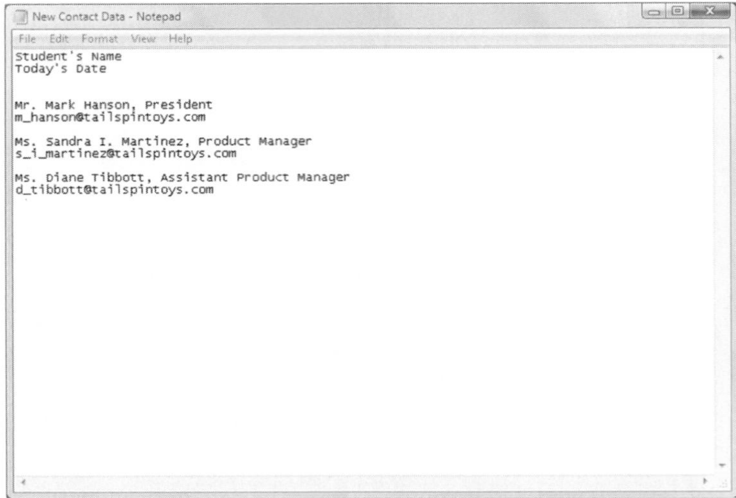

6. Click the **Close** button to close the file and the program. Notice that two text document files are on the desktop now—Contact Data and New Contact Data.

PAUSE. LEAVE the desktop displayed to use in the next exercise.

It is a good idea to become familiar with the differences between the Save and the Save As commands. While you are working in a file, use the Save command to save changes. Use the Save As command to quickly create a copy of the existing file. If you create a new file using a program, you also use the Save As command to save the file for the first time.

In addition to saving a file with a different name, you can use the Save As command to save a file in a different storage location. This is useful for creating a copy of a file on a removable device, such as a flash drive or floppy disk, or for making a copy of a file available on a network drive so others can access it. To save a file in a different location, simply select or key the location in the Address bar in the Save As dialog box. For example, if your instructor wants you to save copies of the files you create in this lesson in an assessment folder on a network drive, a Web site, or a removable device such as a Flash drive, click File>Save As, then select or key the storage location in the Address bar in the Save As dialog box.

Sometimes you can also use the Save As command to save a file as a different file type. You may want to do this so that you can open the file using a different program. For example, if you have an older version of a word processor on your home computer, you can save a copy of the file in the older file format. To save in a different file type, in the Save As dialog box, click the Save as type dropdown arrow to see a list of compatible file types and then click the type you want to use.

In the next section, you learn how to print a file.

You learn more about copying and moving files and folders in Lesson 3, "Organizing Files and Folders."

Printing a File

Print a file when you want a hard copy for your files, or to distribute to other people. You can print a file using a program's File > Print command, or you can print directly from Windows Vista. In this exercise, you print from Windows Vista.

PRINT A FILE

GET READY. Before you begin these steps, make sure your computer is connected to a printer, or to a network that has a printer. Verify that paper is in the printer and that the printer is active, or turned on.

X REF

You learn more about printing and printers in Lesson 9, "Managing System Resources."

1. Right-click the **New Contact Data** icon on the desktop.
2. Click **Print.** Windows Vista prints one copy of the file on the default printer.
3. Right-click the **Contact Data** icon on the desktop, and then click Print. Windows Vista prints one copy of the file.

PAUSE. LEAVE the desktop displayed to use in the next exercise.

When you print with Windows Vista, you quickly print a single copy of the file using the default print settings. Most programs let you select options such as the number of copies to print, specific pages, and even to use a different printer. To change print options, open the file in its associated program and click File > Print to display a Print dialog box. Select the options you want to use and then click Print.

In the next section, you use the Undo and Redo commands to reverse the previous action.

■ Using Undo and Redo

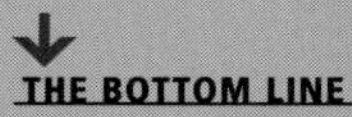

If you perform an action or command accidentally, you can easily reverse it by using the ***Undo*** command. You can use ***Redo*** to reverse an Undo action. In Windows Vista, Undo works only on the most recent action, and Redo works only on the most recent Undo action. Undo and Redo are usually available as menu commands or—in some programs—toolbar buttons. In this section, you will rename a folder and use Undo and Redo to reverse the actions.

USE UNDO AND REDO

1. On the desktop, right-click the **Active Accounts** folder icon and then click **Rename**. Then key **Tailspin Toys Account** and press **Enter**.
2. Right-click a blank area of the desktop and then click **Undo Rename**. Windows Vista reverses the previous action, renaming the folder. Notice that the filename is again Active Accounts.
3. Right-click a blank area of the desktop and then click **Redo Rename**. Windows Vista reverses the Undo action, and the filename is now Tailspin Toys Account.

PAUSE. LEAVE the desktop displayed to use in the next exercise.

To quickly undo the previous action, press Ctrl+Z. To quickly redo the previous action, press Ctrl+Y. If you are working in a folder window, the Undo and Redo commands are available on the Organize dropdown menu.

Undo and Redo can come in handy for reversing actions you make by mistake and also for letting you try a command and then change your mind. It is important to remember, however, that in Windows Vista, Undo and Redo affect the most recent actions only.

You may have noticed that both the Undo and Redo commands take on the name of the action that they will affect. When you rename a folder, you see Undo Rename or Redo Rename on the shortcut menu. If you deleted the folder, the commands would display as Undo Delete or Redo Delete. This helps you keep track of the action that will be reversed.

In the next section, you learn how to capture an image of the screen.

■ Capturing a Screen Image

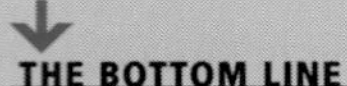

THE BOTTOM LINE

You can capture a picture of the image on your screen using the Print Screen key on your keyboard. You can then insert the image into a file so you can save it, print it, or even edit it. Capturing a screen image may be useful if you want someone to see how the screen should look at any given time, or during a certain procedure. For example, a computer administrator might provide employees with instructions for logging on to the company's computer system, and illustrate the instructions with an image of the user login screen. In this exercise, you capture an image of your desktop and of a folder window which you insert into graphics files.

CAPTURE A SCREEN IMAGE

1. Press **Print Screen** on your keyboard. Windows Vista captures a picture of your desktop. The picture is stored on the Windows Clipboard—a temporary storage area in your computer's memory.

TROUBLESHOOTING

If you cannot find a Print Screen key on your keyboard, look for a key labeled Prt Scr or Prnt Scrn.

2. Right-click a blank area of the desktop, click **New** on the shortcut menu, and then click **Bitmap Image** to create a new graphics file.
3. Key **Desktop Capture** and press Enter to rename the file.
4. Right-click the **Desktop Capture** file icon, click **Open** on the shortcut menu, and then click **Paint**. The file opens in the Paint graphics program. Currently, there is no data stored in the file.
5. Click **Edit** on the menu bar and then click **Paste** on the Edit menu. The image of the desktop is pasted into the Desktop Capture file. It should look similar to Figure 2-11, although the position of the icons on the desktop may vary. Paste is the command that copies the item from the Office Clipboard into the current file. If the image is larger than the document area, you can scroll to view the hidden parts.

Figure 2-11

Picture of the desktop in a Paint file

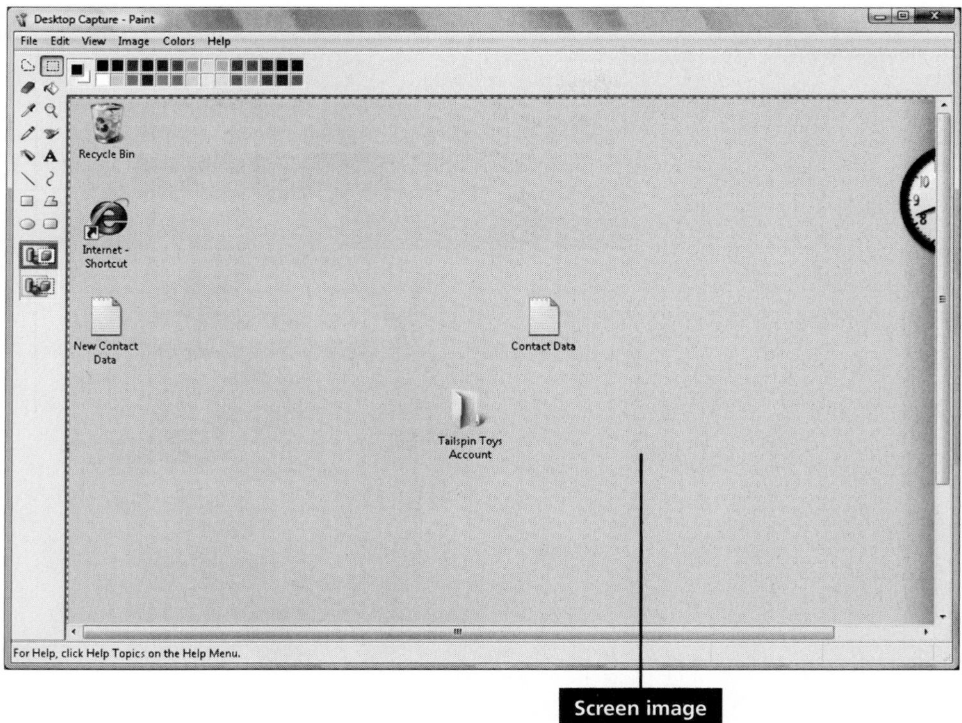

6. Click **File** > **Save** to save the Desktop Capture file, and then click the **Close** button in the upper right corner of the Paint window to close the window.

TAKE NOTE* If your instructor wants you to save a copy of the file in a different location—such as a removable device or a network drive—use the File > Save As command.

7. Right-click a blank area of the desktop, click **New** on the shortcut menu, and then click **Bitmap Image** to create a new graphics file. Key **Window Capture** and press **Enter** to rename the file.
8. Click the **Start** button and then click your user account name to open your personal folder window.
9. Press and hold down **Alt** on your keyboard and then press **Print Screen**. When you press Alt and Print Screen at the same time, Windows Vista captures an image of the active window only.
10. Close your personal folder window.

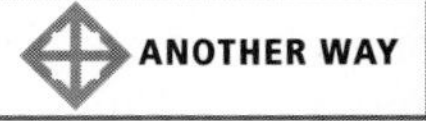
ANOTHER WAY Some programs have a Paste button you can click to paste the contents of the Clipboard into a file.

11. Right-click the **Window Capture** file icon, click **Open** on the shortcut menu, and then click Paint. The file opens in Paint.
12. Click **Edit** on the menu bar and then click **Paste** on the Edit menu. The image of the personal folder window is pasted into the Window Capture file. It should look similar to Figure 2-12.

Figure 2-12

Picture of the window in a Paint file

13. Click **File** > **Save** to save the Window Capture file, and then click the **Close** button in the upper right corner of the Paint window to close the window.

    PAUSE. LEAVE the desktop displayed to use in the next exercise.

As mentioned, the Windows Clipboard is a temporary storage area in your computer's memory. It can only store one item or selection at a time. You learn more about the Clipboard in Lesson 3, "Organizing Files and Folders," when you copy and move files and folders.

You can insert a screen capture picture into different types of files, including graphics files, word processing files, some online journals, or Web pages. Usually, the image will be larger than the document area. In most programs you can resize an image by dragging a sizing handle—a small rectangle in the corners and on the sides of the image—or by using a command such as Image > Resize or Format > Picture.

Your instructor may want you to save screen captures as assessment tools for this book. Ask what type of files to use and where to save them. For example, your instructor may want you to create a folder named with your own name on a Flash drive, external hard drive, network drive, or on a Web site or other online storage location set up for use with this book. You can then create subfolders for each lesson where you can store the files you create in each lesson. For example, your instructor may want you to store the Desktop Capture and Window Capture files in a subfolder named Lesson 2. Use the File > Save As command to save a copy of the file in the specified location.

In the next section you delete files and folders.

Deleting Files and Folders

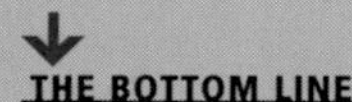

Over time, you will accumulate many files and folders on your computer. Some may continue to be useful while others you may not need any more. To keep your computer from getting cluttered with unnecessary information, you can delete the files and folders that you no longer need. Deleting sends an item to the Recycle Bin. In this section, you delete a file and a folder.

DELETE FILES AND FOLDERS

GET READY. Before you begin these steps, ask your instructor if you should save copies of the Contact Data, New Contact Data, Desktop Capture, and Window Capture files in a different location, such as an assessment folder on a removable device or network location. If so, open each file and use the File > Save As command to save a copy in the specified location.

1. On the desktop, right-click the **Contact Data** file icon and then click **Delete** on the shortcut menu. Windows Vista displays a confirmation dialog box, as shown in Figure 2-13, asking if you are sure you want to move the file to the Recycle Bin.

Figure 2-13

Delete confirmation dialog box

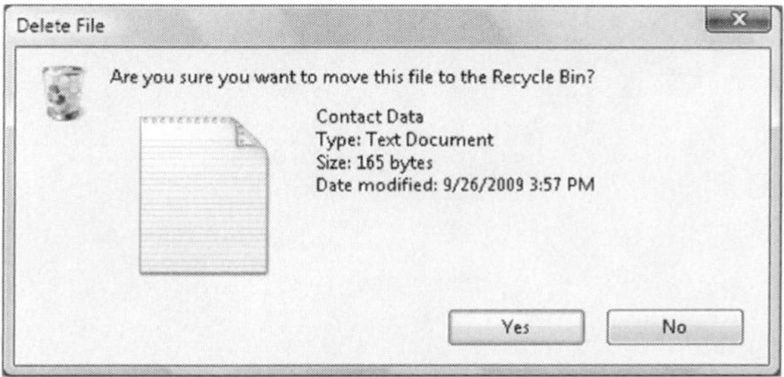

TROUBLESHOOTING

If the confirmation dialog box does not display, someone customized the Recycle Bin settings on your computer so that deleted items are automatically moved to the bin without confirmation. To change the setting, right-click the Recycle Bin icon on the desktop and click Properties. In the Recycle Bin Properties dialog box, click to select the Display delete conformation dialog check box and then click OK.

2. Click **Yes** to delete the file. Windows Vista deletes the Contact Data file from the desktop.
3. Click the **Tailspin Toys Account** folder to select it.
4. Press **Delete** on your keyboard. This is an alternative method of deleting an item. Windows Vista displays the confirmation dialog box.

TAKE NOTE*

You can delete more than one item at a time. Simply select all the items to delete and then press Delete on your keyboard. Or right-click the selection and click Delete. The confirmation dialog box lists the number of items you have selected.

5. Click **Yes** to delete the folder.

PAUSE. LEAVE the desktop displayed to use in the next exercise.

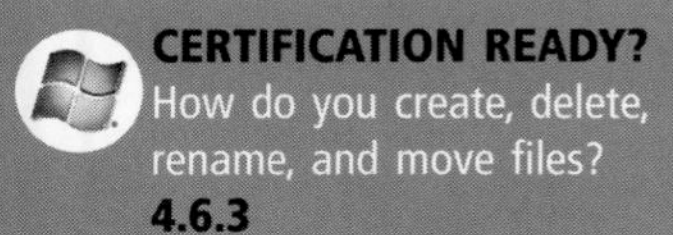

When you delete a folder, note that all items in the folder are deleted as well. For that reason, it is a good idea to open and check the contents of a folder before you delete it.

In the next section, you use the Recycle Bin to permanently delete a file and to restore a folder.

■ Using the Recycle Bin

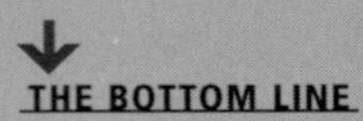

The Recycle Bin folder that comes with Windows Vista is the storage location for items that you delete. Items stay in the Recycle Bin until you remove them permanently or restore them to their original location. In this section, you open the Recycle Bin and restore a deleted folder. You then permanently remove a deleted file.

USE THE RECYCLE BIN

1. On the desktop, double-click the **Recycle Bin** icon to open the Recycle Bin folder window. It should look similar to Figure 2-14. If you or someone else using your computer has deleted other items, they may be listed in the Recycle Bin as well.

Figure 2-14

Items in the Recycle Bin

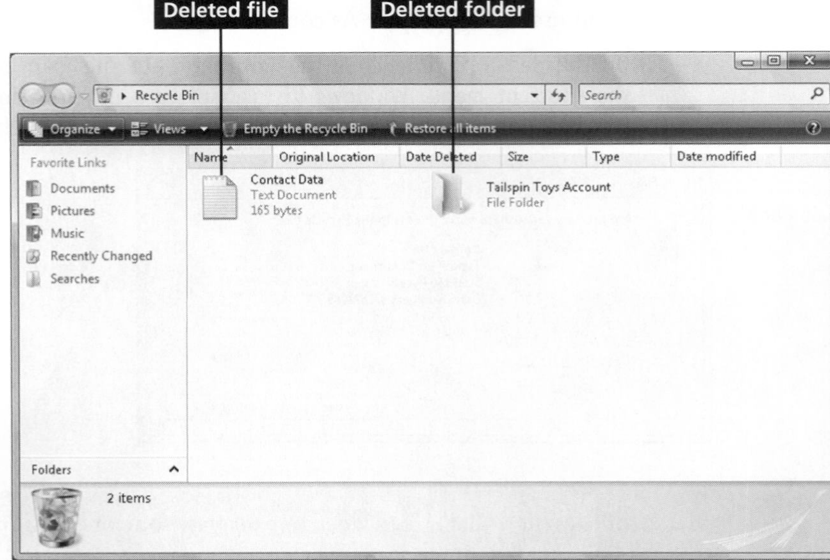

TROUBLESHOOTING

If you see the button Restore all items instead of Restore this item, it means you did not select an item to restore.

2. Click the **Tailspin Toys Account** folder to select it.
3. On the Recycle Bin window toolbar, click **Restore this item**. Windows Vista removes the folder from the Recycle Bin and restores it to its original storage location—in this case, the desktop.
4. Click the **Minimize** button in the Recycle Bin window. The Tailspin Toys Account folder should display on the desktop.
5. Delete the Tailspin Toys Account folder to send it back to the Recycle Bin.
6. Also delete the New Contact Data, Desktop Capture, and Window Capture files from the desktop.
7. Click the **Recycle Bin** window taskbar button to restore the window.
8. On the Recycle Bin window toolbar, click **Empty the Recycle Bin**. Windows Vista displays a confirmation dialog box, as shown in Figure 2-15, asking if you are sure you want to permanently delete the items.

TROUBLESHOOTING

The restored folder icon may not display in the same place on the desktop where it displayed before it was deleted. If you don't see it right away, look for it in a line with other icons.

Figure 2-15

Delete confirmation dialog box

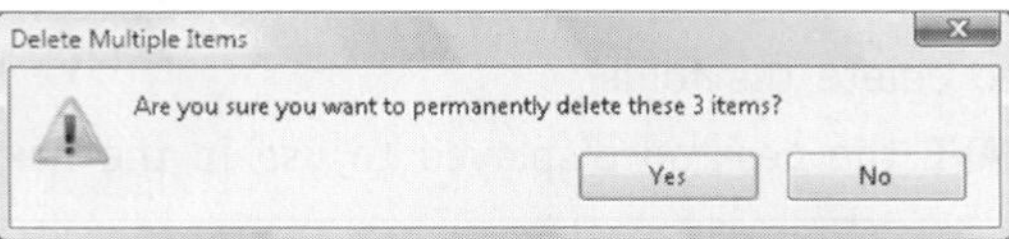

9. Click **Yes** to permanently delete the items. The Recycle Bin folder is now empty.

CLOSE the Recycle Bin folder window and LOG OFF your Windows Vista user account.

TAKE NOTE*

To permanently delete an item without emptying the entire bin, right-click the item in the Recycle Bin and click Delete on the shortcut menu.

The Recycle Bin can save you from many an errant deletion, because you can always locate a file or folder and restore it. Note that when you restore a folder, all of the items in the folder that were deleted are restored as well.

You may be tempted to leave every deleted item in your Recycle Bin forever, just in case you need it in the future. However, items in the Recycle Bin take up storage space on your disk drive. If you never empty the Recycle Bin, some day space will run low. Once you are certain you no longer need the items in the bin, you should empty it to free up space.

X REF

Determining free disk space and making more space available are covered in Lesson 9.

You may have noticed that the Recycle Bin icon on the desktop changes depending on whether it contains items or is empty. If it is empty, the icon resembles an empty basket. If it contains items, paper is in the basket.

You can empty the bin without opening the folder window by right-clicking the icon on the desktop and clicking Empty Recycle Bin, but you must open the window to restore items.

You can permanently delete or restore individual items using shortcut menus. Just right-click the item to affect and then select the desired command.

SUMMARY SKILL MATRIX

In This Lesson You Learned	Matrix Skill	Skill Number
To create and rename a folder	Create and rename a folder	4.2.1, 4.2.2
To work with files		
To create and name a file	Create, delete, rename, and move files	4.6.3
To use Undo and Redo		
To capture a screen image		
To delete files and folders	Create, delete, rename, and move files	4.6.3
To use the Recycle Bin		

■ Knowledge Assessment

Fill in the Blank

Complete the following sentences by writing the correct word or words in the blanks provided.

1. A(n) _______________ menu is a list of commands or options relevant to the current task that displays when you right-click and item.
2. A menu that opens off of another menu is called a(n) _______________.
3. A(n) _______________ is a set of instructions that a computer uses to perform a task, such as word processing or photo editing.
4. The blinking vertical bar that indicates the location where text will be inserted is called the insertion _______________.
5. The file _______________ determines the way the file is saved.
6. The filename _______________ is a set of characters added to the end of a filename.
7. Press _______________ to start a new line of text.
8. A window in which you select options or enter data to control the way a program executes a command is called a(n) _______________ box.
9. A text _______________ is a program that you can use to create text-based files.
10. Use the _______________ command to reverse the most recent action.

True/False

Circle T if the statement is true or F if the statement is false.

T | F 1. There is no limit to the length of a file or folder name.

T | F 2. In Windows Vista, and most programs that run on Windows Vista, selected text is replaced when you key new text.

T | F 3. You cannot use a question mark in a file or folder name.

T | F 4. You can only create text files with Windows Vista.

T | F 5. Notepad is the default program that Windows Vista associates with text files.

T | F 6. Press Backspace to move the insertion one space to the left.

T | F 7. Use the File > Save As command to quickly save changes you make to a file.

T | F 8. On a menu, Undo and Redo take on the name of the action that they will affect.

T | F 9. When you delete a file, it is permanently erased from your computer.

T | F 10. Items in the Recycle Bin are stored in your computer's memory, so they do not take up any storage space on your disk drive.

■ Competency Assessment

Project 2-1: Prepare for Family Photos

A relative plans to send you family photos in digital format so you can select one to use for a New Year's Card. In this exercise, you will prepare a folder for storing the digital files and create a text document that you can use to key descriptions of the files. When the relative fails to send the photos, you delete the folder and the file.

GET READY. Before you begin these steps, start your computer and log on to your Windows Vista account. Close all open windows so you can see the desktop. At your instructor's request, create an assessment folder where you can store the files you create in the projects for this lesson.

1. Right-click a blank area of the desktop to display the shortcut menu.
2. Point to **New** on the shortcut menu to display a submenu.
3. Click **Folder** on the submenu to create a new folder.
4. Key **Card Photos** and then press Enter to rename the folder.
5. Right-click the **Card Photos** folder icon and then click **Rename**.
6. Key **NY Card Photos** and then press Enter.
7. Right-click a blank area of the desktop and then click **Undo Rename** to restore the name to Card Photos.
8. Double-click the **Card Photos** folder to open it.
9. Right-click a blank area in the folder window, point to **New** on the shortcut menu, and then click **Text Document** on the New submenu to create a new text document in the Card Photos folder.
10. Key **Photo Descriptions** and press Enter to rename the file.
11. Right-click a blank area in the folder window, point to **New** on the shortcut menu, and then click **Bitmap Image** on the New submenu to create a new graphics file.
12. Key **Photo Capture** and press Enter to rename the file.
13. Press the Print Screen key on your keyboard to capture an image of the desktop.
14. Right-click the Photo Capture file, click **Open with**, and then click **Paint** to open the file in the Paint graphics program.
15. Click **Edit** on the menu bar and then click **Paste** to paste the image from the Clipboard into the file.

16. Click **File** on the menu bar and then click **Save** to save the changes to the Photo Capture file in the Card Photos folder on your desktop. At your instructor's request, click **File > Save As** and save a copy of the file in your assessment folder.
17. Click the **Close** button in the Paint program window to close it.
18. Right-click the **Photo Descriptions** file and then click **Delete** . Click **Yes** in the confirmation dialog box.
19. Close the Card Photos folder and then press Delete. Click **Yes** in the confirmation dialog box.
20. Double-click the **Recycle Bin** icon on the desktop to open it.
21. Click **Empty the Recycle Bin** on the toolbar and then click **Yes** in the confirmation dialog box to permanently delete all items.
22. Close the Recycle Bin folder window.

PAUSE. LEAVE the desktop displayed to use in the next project.

Project 2-2: Policy Memo

You are planning a meeting to discuss overtime policies with employees at Southridge Video. In this exercise, you create a text file and key a memo announcing the meeting. You will save the memo and then save a copy with a different name. You will edit the second memo for a meeting on sick day policies. You will save and print the second menu and then delete both files.

GET READY. Before you begin these steps, make sure your computer is connected to a printer or to a network that has a printer. Verify that paper is in the printer and that the printer is active, or turned on.

1. Right-click a blank area of the desktop and then point to **New** on the shortcut menu. Click **Text Document** on the New submenu to create a new text document.
2. Key **Overtime Memo** and press Enter to rename the file.
3. Double-click the **Overtime Memo** file icon to open it in Notepad.
4. Key **Memo** and then press Enter twice. Key **Date:**, press spacebar, key today's date, and then press Enter twice. Key **From:**, press spacebar, key your name, and then press Enter twice. Key **Re:**, press spacebar, key **Overtime Policies**, and then press Enter twice.
5. Key the following lines. Press Enter at the end of the first line to start the second line.

   There will be a meeting at 10 a.m. on Monday to discuss these policies.

   I expect everyone to attend.
6. Click **File** on the menu bar and then click **Save** to save the changes to the file. At your instructor's request, click **File > Save As** and save a copy of the file in your assessment folder.
7. Click **File** and then click **Save As** to display the Save As dialog box.
8. Key **Sick Day Memo**. At your instructor's request, select a different storage location, such as your assessment folder on a removable device or network drive, and then click **Save** to save the file with a new name.
9. In the **Sick Day Memo** file, move the insertion point to the left of the *O* in *Overtime* (on the line beginning *Re:*), drag to select the entire word, and then key **Sick Day** to replace the selected text.
10. Click **File** on the menu bar and then click **Save** to save the changes.
11. Close the **Sick Day Memo** file.
12. Right-click the **Sick Day Memo** file icon on the desktop and then click **Print** to print one copy using the default settings.
13. Click the **Sick Day Memo** file icon to select it, press and hold Ctrl, and then click the **Overtime memo** file icon to select it as well. Press Delete and then click **Yes** in the confirmation dialog box.

14. Double-click the **Recycle Bin** icon on the desktop to open it. Click **Empty the Recycle Bin** on the toolbar, and then click **Yes** in the confirmation dialog box to permanently delete all items.
15. Close the Recycle Bin folder window.

PAUSE. LEAVE the desktop displayed to use in the next project.

■ Proficiency Assessment

Project 2-3: Potential Clients

Your manager asks you to prepare folders for storing information about two potential clients. The clients never sign a contract, so you must then delete the folders.

1. Right-click a blank area of the desktop, point to **New** on the shortcut menu, and then click **Folder**.
2. Key **Potential Clients**and then press Enter.
3. Open the Potential Clients folder.
4. Right-click a blank area of the folder window, point to **New**, and then click **Folder**.
5. Key **Trey Research** and then press Enter.
6. Right-click a blank area of the folder window, point to **New**, and then click **Folder**.
7. Key **Contoso, Inc.** and then press Enter.
8. Right-click the **Contoso, Inc.** folder icon and then click **Rename**.
9. Key **Contoso, Ltd.** and then press Enter.
10. Right-click the **Trey Research** folder icon and then click **Delete**. Click **Yes** in the confirmation dialog box to send the folder to the Recycle Bin.
11. Right-click the **Contoso, Ltd.** folder icon and then click **Delete**. Click **Yes** in the confirmation dialog box to send the folder to the Recycle Bin.
12. Close the Potential Clients folder.
13. Right-click the **Potential Clients** folder icon on the desktop and then click **Delete**. Click **Yes** in the confirmation dialog box to send the folder to the Recycle Bin.
14. Double-click the **Recycle Bin** icon on the desktop to open it. Click **Empty the Recycle Bin** on the toolbar and then click **Yes** in the confirmation dialog box to permanently delete all items.
15. Close the Recycle Bin folder window.

PAUSE. LEAVE the desktop displayed to use in the next project.

Project 2-4: Introducing New Executives

You must read a short speech introducing new executives to two different corporate divisions. In this exercise, you will create a text file and key a short paragraph introducing the executive to one division. After saving the changes, you will close it and print it. You will then open it, save it with a new name, edit it for the other division, save it, and print it. After printing, you will delete both files.

GET READY. Before you begin these steps, make sure your computer is connected to a printer or to a network that has a printer. Verify that paper is in the printer and that the printer is active, or turned on.

1. Right-click a blank area of the desktop, point to **New**, and then click **Text Document**.
2. Key **Manufacturing** and press Enter.
3. Double-click the **Manufacturing** file icon.

4. Key your name, press Enter, key today's date, and then press Enter twice. Key the following lines. Press Enter at the end of each line to start a new line.

   I am pleased to be here at the manufacturing division's annual luncheon.

   As many of you already know, we have a new vice president of manufacturing who would like to say a few words.

   Please join me in welcoming Ms. Annette Hill.

5. Click **File** on the menu bar and then click **Save** to save the changes to the file. At your instructor's request, save a copy of the file in your assessment folder.
6. Close the file. Then right-click the file icon on the desktop and click **Print**.
7. After the file prints, double-click the file icon to open the file.
8. Click **File** and then click **Save As**. Key **Accounting** and, at your instructor's request, select a different storage location, such as your assessment folder on a removable device or network drive. Then click **Save** to save the file with a new name.
9. Select the first occurrence of the word *manufacturing* on the first line and then key **accounting** to replace the selected text. Select the second occurrence of the word *manufacturing* on the second line and then key **accounting**.
10. Select the name *Ms. Annette Hill* and then key **Mr. Jay Fleugel** to replace the selection.
11. Click **File** and then click **Save** to save the changes.
12. Close the file. Then right-click the file icon on the desktop and click **Print**.
13. Click the **Accounting** file icon, press and hold Shift, and then click the **Manufacturing** file icon. Press Delete and then click **Yes** in the confirmation dialog box.
14. Double-click the **Recycle Bin** icon on the desktop to open it. Click **Empty the Recycle Bin** on the toolbar and then click **Yes** in the confirmation dialog box to permanently delete all items.
15. Close the Recycle Bin folder window.

    PAUSE. LEAVE the desktop displayed to use in the next project.

Mastery Assessment

Project 2-5: Second Interview

You have called back a candidate for a second job interview. You will not be present, and you want the other interviewer to have access to your notes from the first interview. In this project, you will set up a folder in which you will create a text file. You will key some notes about the candidate, save the file, and then print it. You will delete the file and folder when you are finished.

GET READY. Before you begin these steps, make sure your computer is connected to a printer or to a network that has a printer. Verify that paper is in the printer and that the printer is active, or turned on.

1. Create a new folder on the desktop and name it **Candidate 1**.
2. Open the folder and in it create a new text document file named **Kathie Flood**.
3. Open the text document file in Notepad.
4. Key your name and today's date at the top of the file.
5. Key the following lines of text:

   Self-assured

   Experienced

   Pleasant

   Intelligent

   Possibly over-qualified?

6. Save the file, close it, and then print one copy.
7. At your instructor's request, save a copy of the file in your assessment folder, and then delete the original text document.
8. Delete the folder.
9. Empty the Recycle Bin.

   PAUSE. LEAVE the desktop displayed to use in the next project.

Project 2-6: Marketing Brochure

You have been asked to assist the marketing manager in preparing a cover for a new brochure. You will start by setting up a folder for the project. In the folder, you will create a text file and questions that you will print for the manager. You will then create a bitmap image file that can be used for artwork. But because the project is cancelled, you delete all items

GET READY. Before you begin these steps, make sure your computer is connected to a printer, or to a network that has a printer. Verify that there is paper in the printer and that the printer is active, or turned on.

1. Create a new folder on the desktop and name it **Cover**.
2. Rename the folder Marketing Brochure Cover.
3. Create a new text document in the **Marketing Brochure Cover** folder and name it **Brochure Cover Notes**.
4. Open the text document in Notepad and key your name and today's date at the top of the file.
5. Key the following lines of text in the file:

   Photo or drawing?

   Color or black and white?

   Size?

   Commercial printer or in-house?
6. Save the file, close it, and then print it. At your instructor's request, save a copy of the file in your assessment folder.
7. In the Marketing Brochure Cover folder, create a bitmap image file. Name the file Cover Art.
8. Capture an image of the Marketing Brochure Cover folder window.
9. Open the Cover Art file in Paint, and paste the image from the Clipboard into the file.
10. Save the file. At your instructor's request, save a copy of the file in your assessment folder.
11. Close the Marketing Brochure Cover folder and then delete it.
12. Empty the Recycle Bin.

    LOG OFF your Windows Vista user account.

INTERNET READY

Southridge Video develops and produces digital videos. The technical director wants all employees to understand the different types of digital video file formats that might be used. In this exercise, use web search tools to locate definitions for at least five digital video formats. Create a text file and use Notepad to record the file format names, extensions, and definitions. Save the file with a descriptive filename.

Organizing Files and Folders

LESSON SKILL MATRIX

Skills	Matrix Skill	Skill Number
Navigating Through Windows		
Using Multiple Windows		
Moving Files and Folders	Create, delete, rename, and move files	4.6.3
Copying Files and Folders	Copy data files to a CD or DVD	4.6.4
Removing File Properties	Remove properties and personal information from a file	4.6.2
Adding File Properties	Add metadata to a file	4.6.1

Alpine Ski House is a chain of retail stores specializing in winter sports equipment. To prepare for magazine and web-based ad campaigns, marketing department employees often have to locate files that contain ad copy and pictures and then copy or move them to make them available to the people who need them. In this exercise, you will use different methods to navigate through folder windows, you will use multiple windows at the same time, and you will move and copy folders and files from one storage location to another. Finally, you will learn how to use file properties and attributes to identify files and folders.

KEY TERMS

Archive
Attribute
Back up
Cascade
Clipboard
Collapse
Compress
Destination location
Encrypt
Encryption key
Expand
File properties
Hidden
Metadata
Property label
Property value
Read-only
Source location
Stack
Tag
Tile

■ Navigating Through Windows

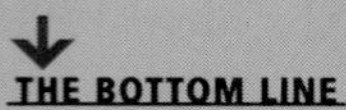

To locate and organize the data you have stored on your computer system, it is important to know how to navigate from one storage location to another. You can use the many navigational tools that Windows Vista provides to browse forward and back through folders or jump directly to a specific location.

Browsing Through Recently Opened Windows

Use the Forward and Back buttons on a window's toolbar to browse through windows you have opened recently. Click the Back button to view the previous window. Click the Forward button to return to the window that was open before you clicked Back. Use the Recent Pages dropdown menu to select from a list of recently opened windows.

BROWSE THROUGH RECENTLY OPENED WINDOWS

GET READY. Before you begin these steps, start your computer and log on to your Windows Vista account. Close all open windows so you can see the desktop. If necessary, create a new folder named Lesson 3 in a storage location specified by your instructor, where you can store assessment files and folders that you create during this lesson.

1. Click **Start** and then click **Computer** to open the Computer folder window. Recall that the Computer window displays components of your computer system, such as disk drives and other devices.

TROUBLESHOOTING

By default, Windows Vista replaces the contents of the current window with the next folder that you open, but it can be customized to open each folder in a separate window. If the Local Disk (C:) folder opens in a new, separate window, your system has been customized. To restore the default settings, click Organize on the window's toolbar, click Folder and Search options, click the Restore Defaults button, and then click OK. You learn more about customizing folder windows in Lesson 4, "Customizing Windows Explorer."

2. In the file list, double-click the **Local Disk (C:)** icon to change to the folder that displays the contents of your hard disk drive.
3. In the file list, double-click the **Program Files** folder to change to the Program Files folder. The Program Files folder is where Windows Vista stores the files for the programs installed on your computer. It should look similar to Figure 3-1, although the specific contents depend on the programs you have installed.

Figure 3-1

Program Files folder

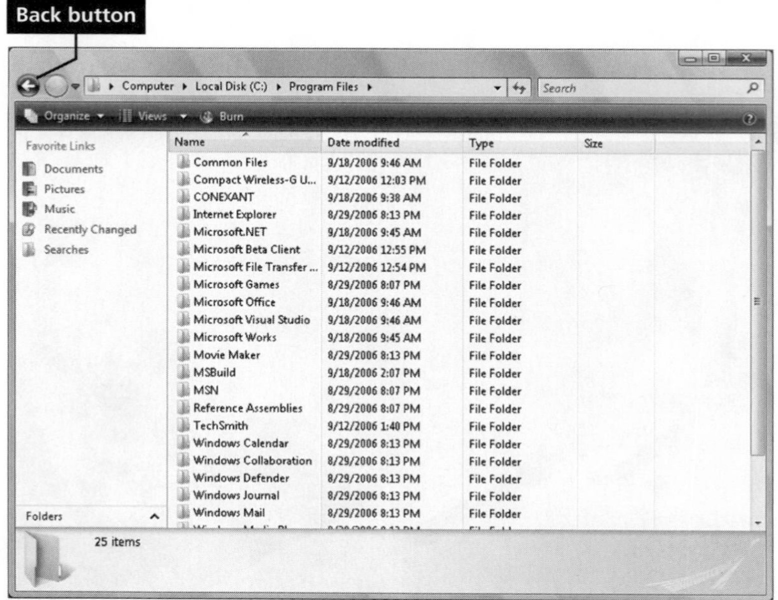

4. Click the **Back** button on the Program Files window toolbar. The previous folder displays—in this case, the Local Disk (C:) window. Notice that once you click Back, the Forward button becomes available as well.

5. Click the **Forward** button on the window toolbar. The folder that was open before you clicked Back displays again— in this case, Program Files. Now only the Back button is available because there are no other folders to go forward to.
6. Double-click the **Windows Photo Gallery** folder icon to change to the folder where the files for the Windows Photo Gallery program are stored. (You may have to scroll down the file list to locate the folder.) Windows Photo Gallery comes with Windows Vista. It is a program for viewing and organizing pictures.
7. Click the **Back** button on the window toolbar to return to the previous folder (Program Files) and then click the **Back** button again to return to folder open prior to that—Local Disk (C:).
8. Click the **Forward** button to change to the Program Files folder and then click the **Forward** button again to change to the Windows Photo Gallery folder.
9. Click the **Recent Pages** dropdown arrow to the right of the Forward button. A menu of all the locations you have viewed during the current session displays, as shown in Figure 3-2. A checkmark indicates the current location.

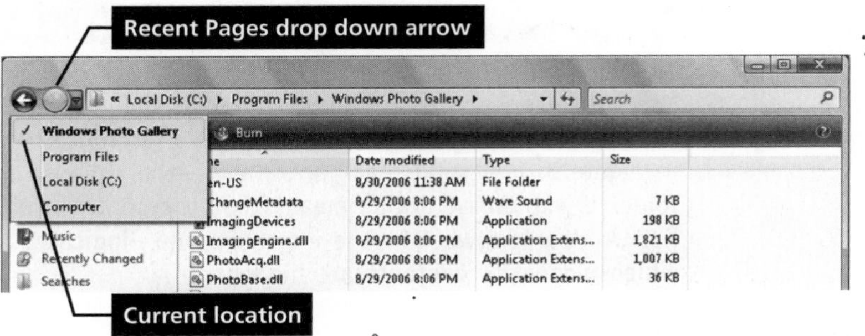

Figure 3-2
Recent Pages menu

> **TAKE NOTE*** You can use ScreenTips to help identify buttons on the window toolbar, including the Recent Pages dropdown arrow. You'll notice that the ScreenTip for the Back and Forward buttons changes to indicate the window that will display when you click the button. For example, the ScreenTip for the Back button might say Back to Computer, if the previous window was Computer.

10. Click **Computer** on the Recent Pages menu to change to the Computer folder. When you click a location on the Recent Pages menu, you go directly to that folder instead of browsing through all previously opened folders.

PAUSE. LEAVE the Computer folder open to use in the next exercise.

Browsing lets you easily move back and forth among the folders you have been using. However, it may not be convenient when you need to access a completely different storage location. In the next section, you practice navigating using the options in the Navigation pane.

Using the Navigation Pane

> The Favorite Links in the Navigation pane let you quickly open common folders, such as Documents or Pictures. You can expand the Folders list to access any location on your system.

USE THE NAVIGATION PANE

USE the Computer folder you left open in the previous exercise.

1. In the Favorite Links list in the Navigation pane, click **Pictures** to change to the Pictures folder.
2. Click **Music** to change to the Music folder.
3. Click **Documents** to change to the Documents folder.

You learn how to add Favorite links to the Navigation pane in Lesson 4 and how to store searches in Lesson 6, "Searching for Files and Folders."

4. To expand the Folders list, click **Folders**, or the up arrow icon to the right of the word Folders, at the bottom of the Navigation pane. The Folders list displays the contents of your computer as a hierarchical, or tree, diagram. At the top is the root folder, which is the desktop. All folders and subfolders branch off the root.

TROUBLESHOOTING

To see more items in the Folders list, increase the height of the current window by dragging a top or bottom window border, or by maximizing the window. For more information on resizing windows, refer to Lesson 1, "Getting Started."

5. Move the mouse pointer over your personal folder near the top of the Folders list. Arrowheads display to the left of items that contain subfolders or files, as shown in Figure 3-3. A solid black arrowhead—the collapse arrow—indicates that the folder is ***expanded***, which means that the contents of the folder display in the list. A clear arrowhead—the expand arrow—indicates that the folder is ***collapsed***, which means its contents are hidden.

Figure 3-3

Folders list

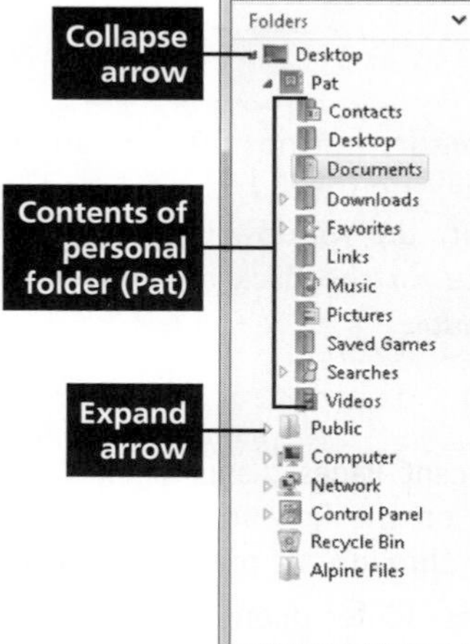

6. Click your personal folder in the Folders list. Clicking an item in the Folders list makes that item current. The contents display in the File list area of the window.
7. Click the collapse arrow to the left of your personal folder in the Folders list. The folder collapses in the Folders list to hide its subfolders, but it is still current, and its contents still display in the window's File list. Once the folder is collapsed, the arrow changes to an expand arrow.
8. Click the expand arrow to the left of Computer in the Folders list. The Folders list expands to display the contents of the Computer folder, and the arrow changes to a collapse arrow, as shown in Figure 3-4. Notice that clicking the arrowhead does not make the Computer folder current. The contents of your personal folder still display in the File list.

Figure 3-4

Collapse and expand the Folders list

TAKE NOTE * You can change the width of the Navigation pane by dragging the border between the pane and the File list. For example, to make the pane wider, drag the border to the right. To make the pane narrower, drag the border to the left.

9. Click **Local Disk (C:)** in the Folders list to make it current.
10. Click the expand arrow to the left of your personal folder and then click the expand arrow to the left of Favorites. (You may have to scroll the Folders list to locate the items.) The Folders list expands, but the current folder is still Local Disk (C:).
11. Click the collapse arrow to the left of Favorites and then click **Pictures.** Pictures is now the current folder.
12. Click **Folders**, or the down arrow icon to the right of Folders, to collapse the entire Folders list.

PAUSE. LEAVE the Pictures folder open to use in the next exercise.

The Folders list in the Navigation pane is useful because you can see the entire storage system of your computer while working with the contents of a specific folder. You can easily move among the many storage locations without browsing through multiple folders, simply by expanding the folder list and then clicking the location you want to make current.

You can also work with folders in the Navigation pane in much the same way you work with them in their storage locations. For example, you can rename a folder or delete it. Simply right-click the folder in the Folders list to display a shortcut menu and then select the command you want to use.

In the next section, you practice using the Address Bar to navigate.

Using the Address Bar

The Address bar displays your current location as a series of links separated by arrows. Click a link to go directly to that location. If you want to open a subfolder of one of the displayed links, click the arrow to the left of the folder in the Address bar and click the subfolder. You can also key the name of a location in the Address bar to go directly to that location.

USE THE ADDRESS BAR

USE the Pictures folder you left open in the previous exercise.

1. In the Address bar, click the name of your personal folder to make it current.
2. Click the **Back** button to change back to Pictures.
3. In the Address bar, click the arrow between your personal folder name and Pictures. A menu of subfolders in your personal folder displays, as shown in Figure 3-5. Notice that the current folder is bold.

Figure 3-5
Dropdown menu of subfolders

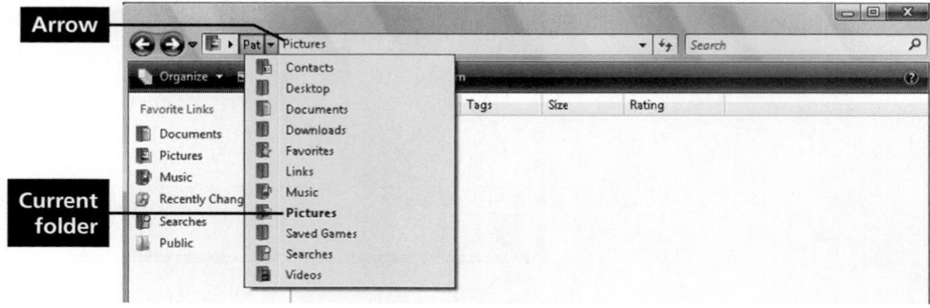

4. Click **Music** on the dropdown menu to change to the Music folder.
5. Click a blank space in the Address bar, to the right of the current location. The text in the Address bar changes to display the path to the current folder. The path is selected, so you can replace it by typing.
6. Key **Computer** and then press **Enter**. Computer becomes the current folder. You can key the names of common locations, such as Documents, Computer, Pictures, and Music and then press **Enter** to change to that location.

TAKE NOTE* Notice that Windows Vista immediately starts searching for locations that match the characters you're typing and displays possible matches in a pop-up window. If you see the location you want, you can stop typing and click it, or select it and press Enter to make it current.

7. Click a blank area of the Address bar, key **Music**, and then press **Enter** to make Music current.
8. Click a blank area of the Address bar, key **C:\Program Files**—the path to the Program Files folder—and then press **Enter**. Windows Vista changes to the Program Files folder.
9. Click the dropdown arrow at the right end of the Address bar. A menu of locations you have keyed in the Address bar displays. Other locations may display as well, such as the path to the original folder (in this case Pictures) and other folders you have visited recently.
10. Click **Music** on the dropdown menu to change to the Music folder.

PAUSE. LEAVE the Music folder open to use in the next exercise.

If you have previously used an Address bar in a web browser such as Internet Explorer, you will notice that it is similar to using the Address bar in Windows Vista. In fact, if you are connected to the Internet, you can key a web address in the Address bar in Windows to launch your web browser and display that web page.

In the next section, you work with multiple windows at the same time.

■ Using Multiple Windows

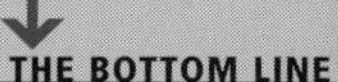

THE BOTTOM LINE

Although by default each folder opens in the same window, there may be times when you want to work with more than one window at once. For example, you may want to compare the contents of two folders, or copy or move an item from one folder to another or from a folder to a removable device. Or, you might want to use the Calculator while you view an invoice document. You can open a new window at any time. In this section, you open multiple windows, arrange windows on the desktop, and change the active window.

Opening and Arranging Multiple Windows

There is no limit to the number of windows you can have open at once. To open additional windows, simply click the Start button and select the window you want to open. You can arrange multiple windows in a variety of ways on the desktop, including overlapped evenly or side by side. In this section, you practice arranging multiple windows.

OPEN AND ARRANGE MULTIPLE WINDOWS

USE the Music folder you left open in the previous exercise.

1. Click the **Start** button and then click your personal folder. It opens in a new window, overlapping the Music window, which was already open.
2. Click the **Start** button again and then click **Computer** to open the Computer folder in a new window. Now three windows are open, as shown in Figure 3-6. (The size and position of the three windows on your screen may be different from the illustration.)

Figure 3-6

Three windows open at once

3. Right-click a blank area of the Windows taskbar. A shortcut menu displays.
4. Click **Cascade Windows** on the shortcut menu. Windows Vista ***cascades*** the open windows, which means that they overlap one another in an orderly fashion, starting in the upper left corner of the desktop, as shown in Figure 3-7. You can see the active window on top, but only portions of the other windows are visible.

Figure 3-7

Cascading windows overlap

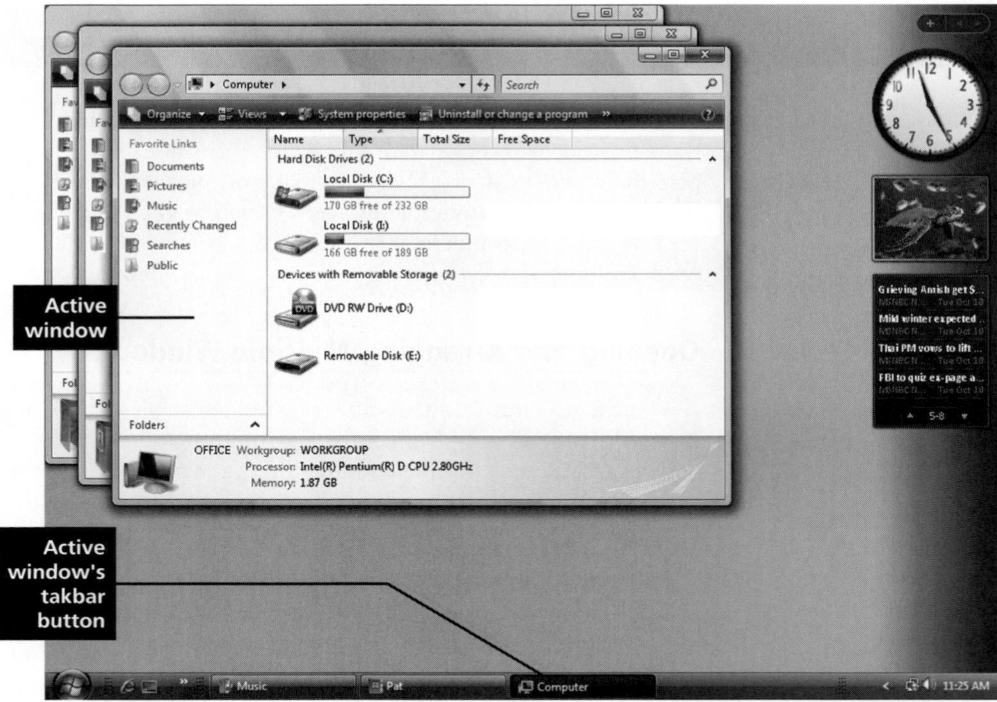

5. Right-click a blank area of the taskbar and click **Show Windows Stacked.** Windows Vista ***stacks*** the windows, which means they are tiled horizontally, as shown in Figure 3-8. The windows are automatically sized to display one above the other without overlapping.

Figure 3-8

Stacked windows are tiled horizontally

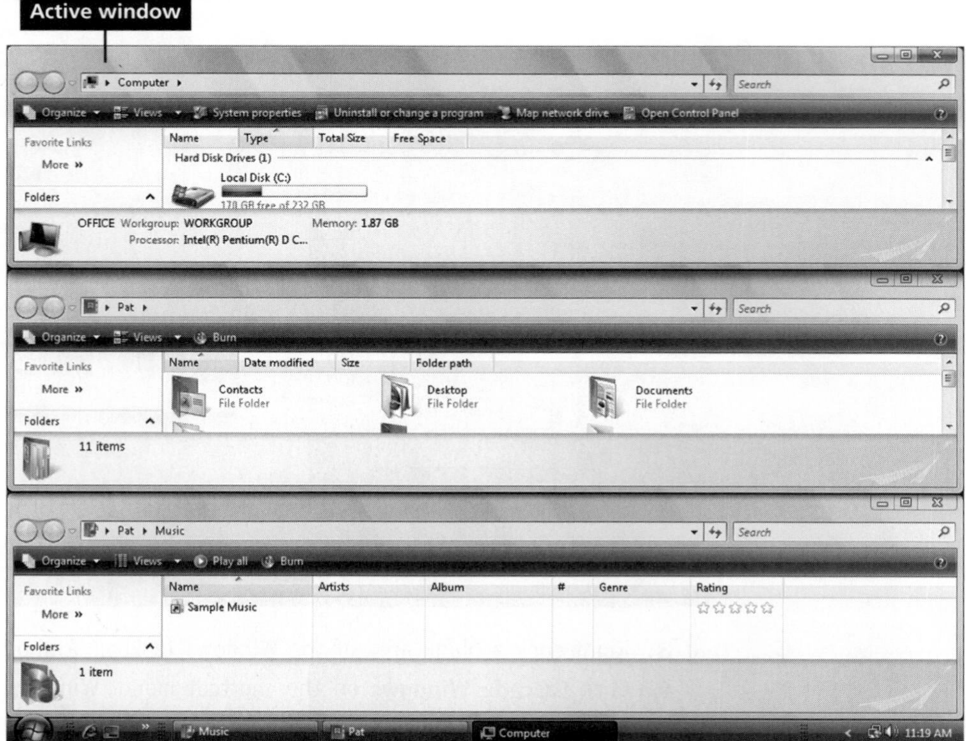

6. Right-click a blank area of the taskbar and click **Show Windows Side by Side**. Windows Vista tiles the window vertically, which means they are arranged vertically on the desktop and sized to display next to each other without overlapping, as shown in Figure 3-9.

Figure 3-9

Side by side windows are tiled vertically

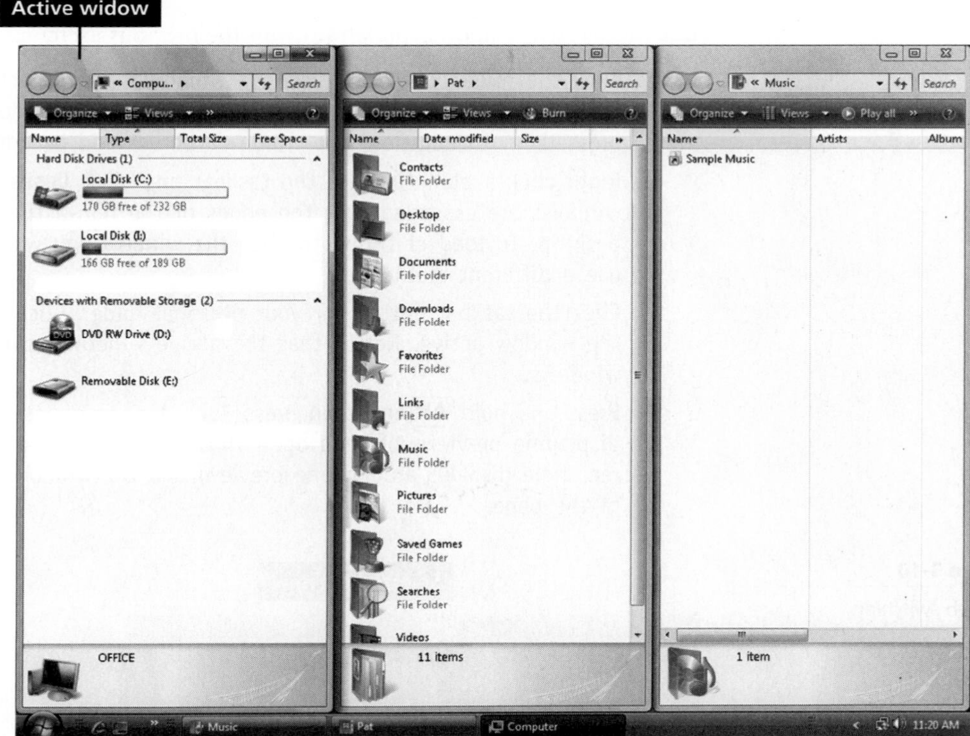

7. Right-click a blank area of the taskbar and click **Undo Show Side by Side**. Windows Vista restores the windows to the previous arrangement, in this case stacked horizontally.

   PAUSE. LEAVE the three windows stacked vertically to use in the next exercise.

There are three basic options for arranging windows on the desktop.

- Cascade, which overlaps the windows evenly, with the active window on top.
- Stack, which tiles the windows horizontally one above the other. If there are only two or three windows, each window extends across the width of the screen. If there are more than three windows, they are sized to fit so that none of them overlap.
- Side by side, which tiles the windows vertically next to each other. Each window displays in its entirety, extending from the top of the screen to the bottom.

Keep in mind that the more windows you have open, the smaller each one displays when tiled or stacked. You can exclude a window from an arrangement by minimizing it before selecting the command to cascade, stack, or arrange side by side.

The next time you open a window, it displays in its previous size and position on the desktop, even if it is the only open window. You can move or resize the window, or maximize it, if you want.

In the next section, you practice changing the active window.

Changing the Active Window

No matter how many windows are open, only one can be active, or current. You can easily change the active window.

CHANGE THE ACTIVE WINDOW

USE the stacked windows you left open in the previous exercise.

1. Click the **Music** window. Clicking a window makes it active. Notice that the Close button in the active window is red, and that the window's taskbar button appears pressed in. In addition, the window's border and background are brighter.
2. Right-click a blank area of the taskbar and click **Cascade Windows.** When the windows are cascaded only the edges of the non-active windows are visible on the desktop. Instead of trying to click the window you want to make active, you can use a different method.
3. Click the taskbar button for your personal folder. Clicking a taskbar button makes the window active. Notice that the active window moves in front of the other open windows.
4. Press and hold **Alt** and then press **Tab**. A pane opens in the middle of the desktop, displaying previews of each open window, as shown in Figure 3-10. A selection rectangle displays around one preview, and the window name displays at the top of the pane.

Figure 3-10

Alt+Tab switching

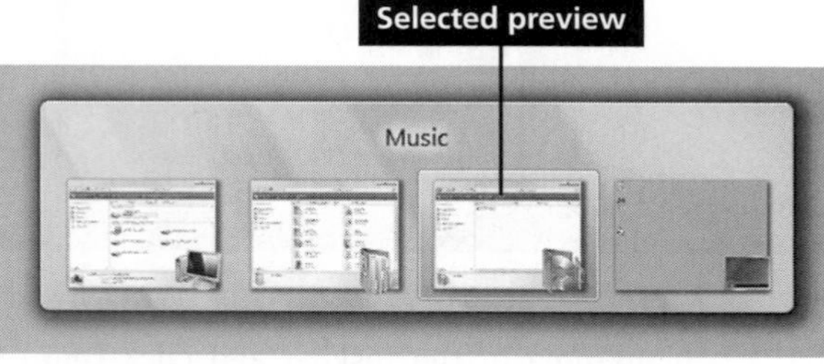

5. While continuing to hold down **Alt**, press **Tab** again, and the selection rectangle moves to the next preview. Press **Tab** until the selection rectangle is around Computer, then release **Tab** and **Alt**. Computer becomes active. This procedure is called Alt+Tab switching, and you can use it to cycle through all open windows.
6. Close the Computer window. Make your personal folder active and then close it. Make Music active and then close it.

PAUSE. LEAVE the desktop displayed to use in the next exercise.

You can only work in the active window, no matter how many windows are open at the same time. Windows Vista provides many tools for changing the active window.

- The easiest way to make a window active is to click in it.
- You can click a taskbar button to make its window active.
- Use Alt+Tab switching to cycle through all open windows. Release both the Alt key and the Tab key when the window you want to make active is selected.

TAKE NOTE* On some systems, the Quick Launch toolbar on the taskbar displays a Switch Between Windows button. When you click the button, Windows Vista displays a 3-D view of all open windows. You can click a window to make it active.

In the next section, you learn how to move files and folders from one storage location to another.

■ Moving Files and Folders

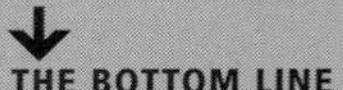

You can move a file or folder from one storage location to another. This is useful for reorganizing your storage system. In addition, you can move a file or folder to a removable disk to give to someone else or to take to a different computer, or you can move a file or folder to a network drive so others can access it. When you move a file, it is deleted from the original location and is stored in the new location, only. You can move items by using the Cut and Paste commands, or by dragging them to the new location.

MOVE FILES AND FOLDERS

1. Click **Start** and then click **Documents** to open the Documents folder. Click the Minimize button to minimize the Documents window.
2. Right-click a blank area of the desktop, point to **New** on the shortcut menu, and then click **Folder.**
3. Key **Alpine Files** and then press Enter to rename the new folder.
4. Right-click the **Alpine Files** folder and click **Cut** on the shortcut menu. The Cut command moves an item from its source location and places it in the Clipboard. A ***source location*** is the location where the item was originally stored. The ***Clipboard*** is a temporary storage area that can hold one item at a time.
5. Click the **Documents** taskbar button to restore the window.
6. Right-click a blank area of the File list in the Documents window and click **Paste** on the shortcut menu. The Paste command copies the item from the Clipboard to its ***destination location***, which is the new storage location. (The destination is sometimes called the target.) In this case, Windows Vista pastes the Alpine Files folder into the Documents window.

TAKE NOTE * Note that only one item can be stored on the Clipboard at a time. Each item that you cut—or copy—replaces the item currently on the Clipboard.

TAKE NOTE * When you move a folder, any items stored in the folder are also moved.

7. Right-click a blank area of the File list, point to **New**, and then click **Text Document**. Key **Ad Text** and press Enter to rename the new text document.
8. Drag the **Ad Text** file icon onto the Alpine Files folder icon, as shown in Figure 3-11. Notice that when you drag the item over a potential destination, it displays an arrow and the message Move to *destination name*.

Figure 3-11

Drag an item to move it

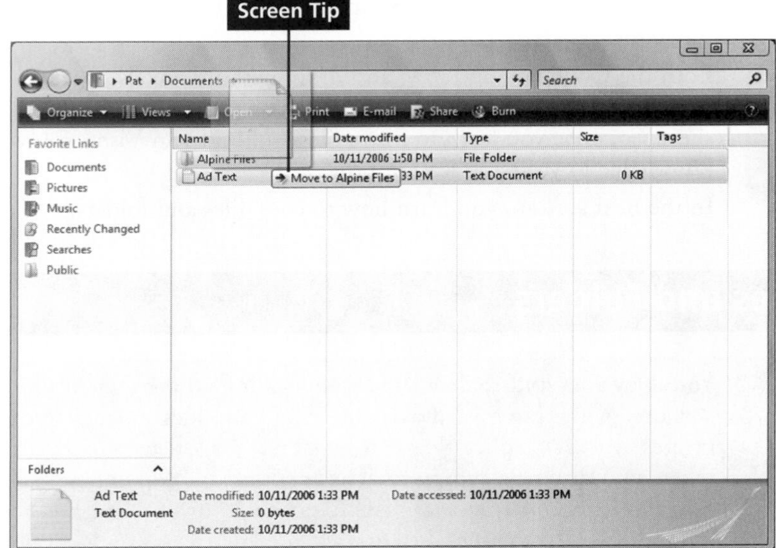

9. When the ScreenTip message is Move to Alpine Files, release the mouse button. Windows Vista moves the file. Notice that the Ad Text file icon no longer displays in the Documents file list. That is because it has been deleted from the Documents folder and is now stored only in the Alpine Files folder.
10. Double-click the **Alpine Files** folder icon to open it. The Ad Text file displays in the File list.
11. At this point, your instructor may ask you to capture an image of the Alpine Files window to save in your Lesson 3 assessment folder. If so, press the **Alt** key and the **Print Screen** key at the same time, open a graphics or word processing file, and click **Edit** > **Paste**. Save the file as ***Le03_01*** in your assessment folder. (Refer to Lesson 2 if you need a refresher on capturing images.)

You can use the Folders list in the Navigation pane to move folders. Expand the Folders list so you can see both the original location and the destination, then drag the item from the original location to the destination. You can also drag items from the File list to a folder in the Folders list, and vice versa. Alternatively, right-click the item that you want to move and then click Cut. Then right-click the destination and click Paste.

PAUSE. LEAVE the Alpine Files folder open to use in the next exercise.

As you have just seen, moving an item deletes it from its original source location and places it in a new destination location. As with most tasks, Windows Vista provides multiple options for moving files and folders. Each has benefits for use in different situations. As you become more comfortable working with Windows Vista, you will be able to select the method that works best for you.

The Cut and Paste commands provide a versatile method for moving files and folders, because once an item is cut to the Clipboard, you can navigate away from the source to locate the destination. Each item stays on the Clipboard until you cut—or copy—another item. That means that you can paste an item from the Clipboard as many times as you want, into many different locations. In addition, Cut and Paste are available on shortcut menus, so they are easily accessible from any location.

The drag and drop method is useful when you can see both the source and the destination locations on the screen at the same time. For example, you can move an item to a subfolder in the same folder you used in the previous exercise. You can also stack or arrange windows side by side so you can drag items from one window to another, or use the Folders list in the Navigation pane. Dragging is quick and easy and does not require any menus or commands.

You can move multiple items at the same time using either the Cut and Paste commands or the drag and drop methods. Simply select all of the items you want to move and then move the items.

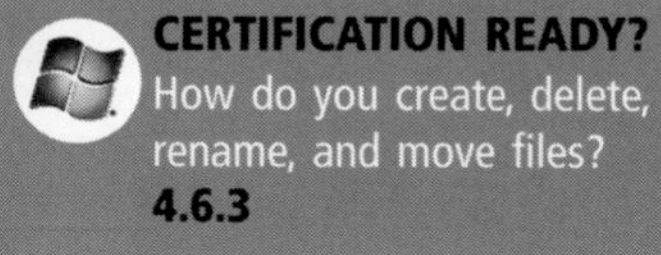

Both the Clipboard and drag and drop methods are also used in programs that run on Windows Vista to move selected data, such as text, graphics, and even formulas in a spreadsheet. So, once you learn to move files and folder in Vista, you will be able to transfer that knowledge to your application programs.

In the next section, you learn how to copy files and folders.

■ Copying Files and Folders

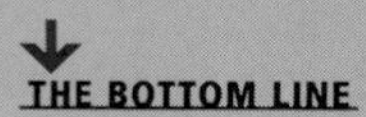

You copy files and folders from one location to another in order to have multiple versions of the same item available. Copying does not delete the original file—it simply creates an exact replica that can be stored for safekeeping, shared with someone else, or taken to a different computer. The methods for copying are similar to those for moving. You can use the Copy and Paste commands, or you can press and hold Ctrl while dragging an item to the new location.

Copying to a Different Folder

You can easily copy a file or folder to a different folder on your computer. You—or others—can edit the copy while the original remains unchanged in its original location. In this exercise, you will copy a file—supplied with this book—from the data files storage location to the Alpine Files folder. You will then create a new folder and copy two files into it.

COPY TO A DIFFERENT FOLDER

USE the Alpine Files folder you left open in the previous exercise.

The Alpine_Photo1 file is available on the companion CD-ROM.

1. Navigate to the ***Alpine_Photo1*** file in the data files for this lesson.
2. Right-click the ***Alpine_Photo1*** file icon and then click **Copy** on the shortcut menu. This copies the item to the Clipboard, leaving the original file in its source location.
3. Navigate to the Alpine Files folder.
4. Right-click a blank area of the File list and then click **Paste** on the shortcut menu. Windows Vista pastes a copy of the ***Alpine_Photo1*** file into the Alpine Files folder.
5. In the Alpine Files folder, create a new folder named Files for Review.
6. Right-click the **Ad Text** file in the Alpine Files folder and then click **Copy** on the shortcut menu.
7. Right-click the **Files for Review** folder icon and then click **Paste** on the shortcut menu. Windows Vista pastes a copy of the Ad Text file into the Files for Review folder.
8. Double-click the **Files for Review** folder to open it.
9. Click **Start**, click **Documents**, and then double-click the **Alpine Files** folder to open it.
10. Right-click a blank area of the taskbar and click **Show Windows Stacked** on the shortcut menu. With the windows stacked on the screen, you can see both copies of the Ad Text file, as shown in Figure 3-12.

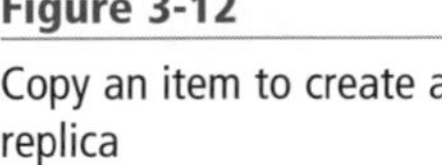

Figure 3-12

Copy an item to create a replica

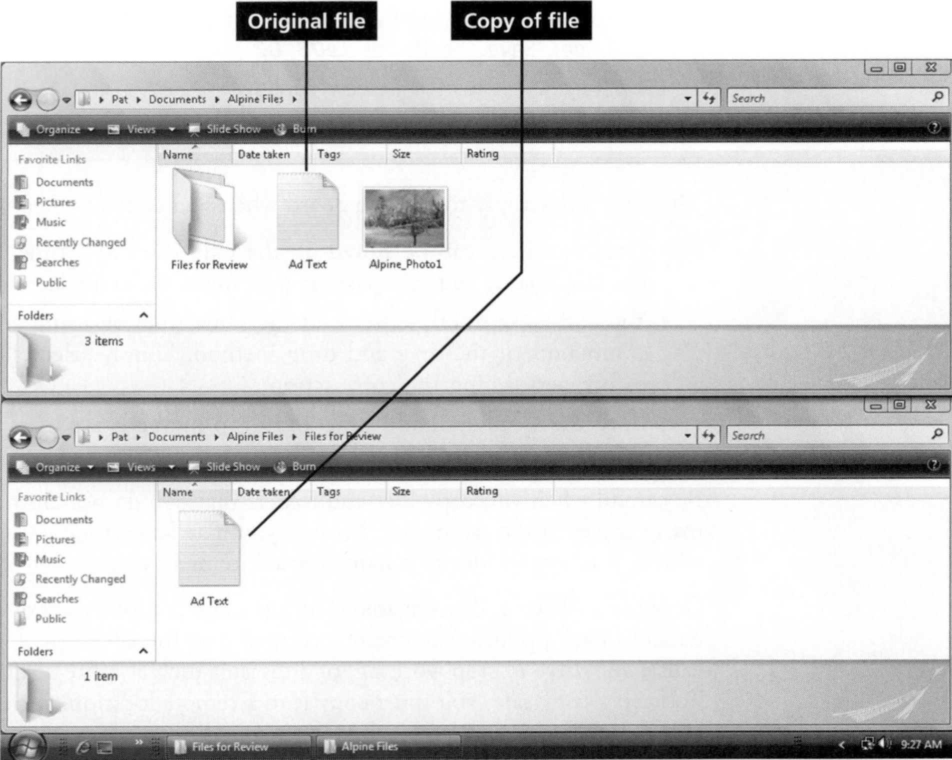

11. Press and hold Ctrl and drag the ***Alpine_Photo1*** file from the Alpine Files folder window to the Files for Review folder window, as shown in Figure 3-13. Notice that a plus sign displays with the icon as you drag, and the ScreenTip indicates that you are copying—not moving—the item. Also, a vertical bar indicates the location where the copied file will be inserted.

Figure 3-13

Drag to copy an item

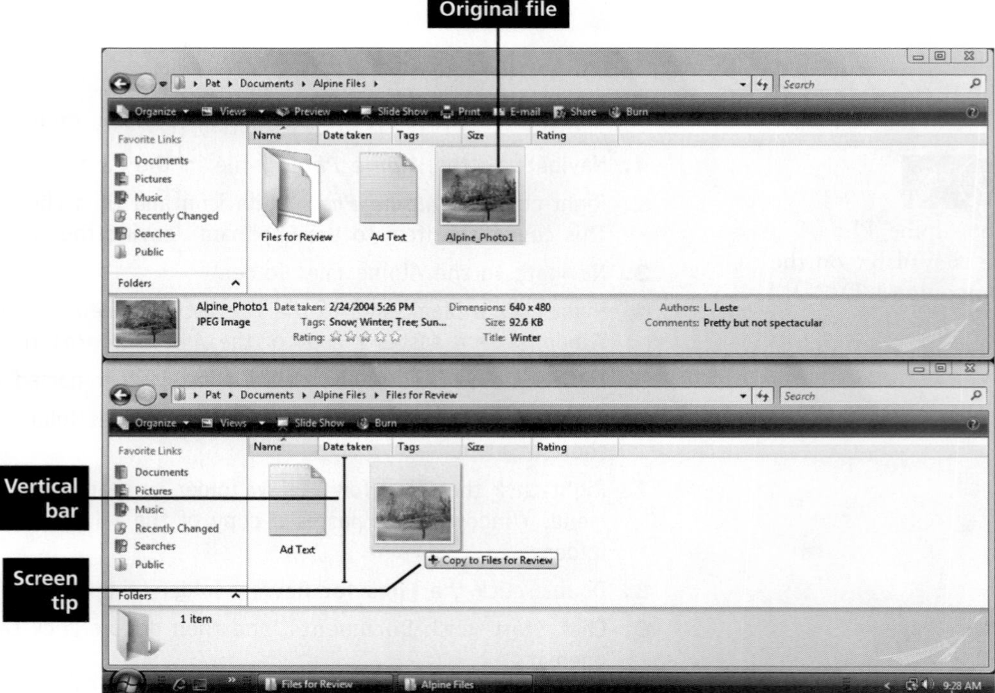

12. Release the mouse button to copy the file into the Files for Review folder. Now both the Ad Text and ***Alpine_Photo1*** files are stored in the Alpine Files folder and in the Files for Review folder. (At this point, your instructor may ask you to capture an image of the screen for you to save in your Lesson 3 assessment folder. Save the file as ***Le03_02***.)
13. Close the Files for Review window.

PAUSE. LEAVE the Alpine Files folder open to use in the next exercise.

The same rules apply to the Clipboard when you copy as when you cut.

- Only one item can be stored on the Clipboard at a time. As long as the item is on the Clipboard, you can paste it into many different locations.
- You can copy multiple items at the same time by using either the Cut and Paste commands or the drag and drop method. Simply select all items you want to copy before performing the copy action.
- Both the Clipboard and drag and drop methods are used in programs that run on Windows Vista to copy selected data

Be careful when you copy files and folders that you do not clutter your computer with too many copies of the same item, because you may have trouble keeping track of which item is which. It is a good idea to rename copied items so you can tell them apart.

Copying a file to a different folder on the same computer is not a good way to ***back up*** your data. To back up means to create a copy of data for safekeeping. A mechanical failure that causes the drive to stop working, or a disaster such as a fire or flood, would affect both files. To keep a copy safe, you must copy it to a remote location, such as a network, or to a removable device so you can physically take it to a different location, such as a safe. In the next section, you copy items to a removable storage device.

The best way to keep copies of data safe is to create a backup. Backing up is covered in Lesson 10, "Managing Software."

Copying to a Storage Device

When you want to create a copy of a file or folder that you physically take away from your computer, you can copy it to a removable storage device. This is useful for keeping a copy safe in a different location, creating a copy you can use on your home computer, or giving a copy to someone else. Use the Send to command to quickly copy an item to a storage device.

COPY TO A STORAGE DEVICE

GET READY. Before you begin these steps, insert a removable storage device into your computer. For example, insert a CD or DVD into a compatible drive, or plug a flash drive into a USB port. You may also use an external hard drive attached to a USB port, or a network drive. If an AutoPlay window displays, click the Close button.

USE the Alpine Files folder you left open in the previous exercise.

1. Right-click the **Files for Review** folder in the Alpine Files folder window.
2. Point to **Send To** on the shortcut menu. A menu of available locations displays, as shown in Figure 3-14. (The locations on your computer will be different from those in the illustration, depending on the number and type of devices you have available.)

Figure 3-14
Send To menu

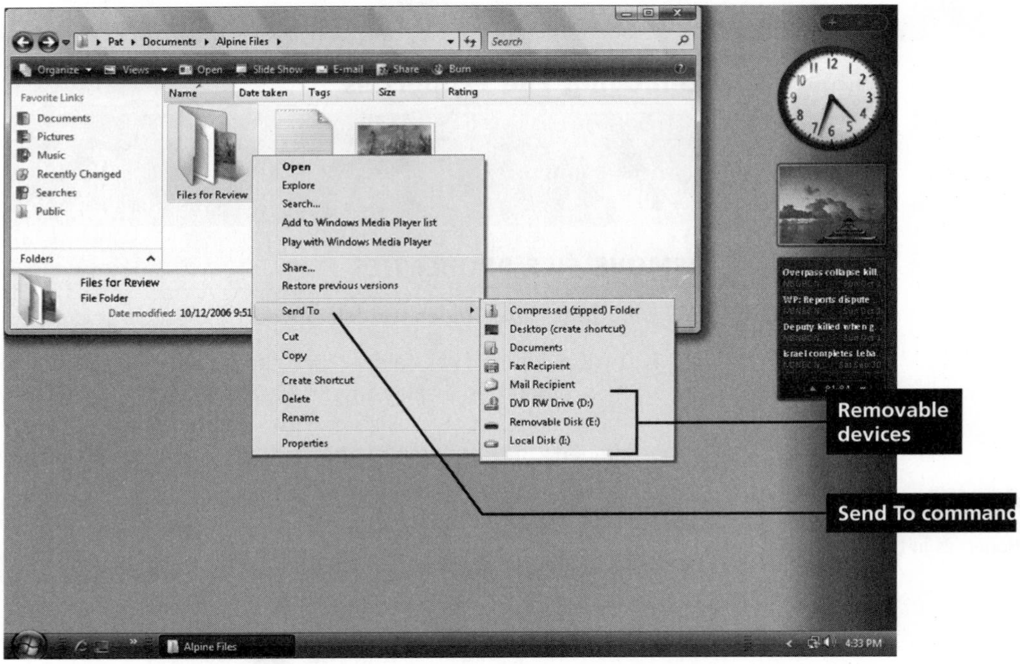

3. On the menu, click the drive to which you have attached a removable device, or in which you have inserted the removable media. Windows Vista copies the folder to the selected location. If you are copying to a CD or DVD drive, Windows Vista may automatically open a window to display the drive's contents. If so, you may skip step 4.

TROUBLESHOOTING

Some devices, such as CD and DVD drives, may prompt you to prepare or format the disk before copying the items. Click OK or Next, or press Enter to continue.

Lesson 5, "Working with Multimedia Files," covers copying pictures, music, and videos to CDs and DVDs.

4. Click the **Start** button and click **Computer** to open the Computer window. Double-click the drive to which you attached the removable device, or in which you inserted the removable media. A window for the drive opens so you can see the items stored there. The name of the window depends on the drive or attached device.
5. In the device window, double-click the **Files for Review** folder to open it. Notice that when you copy a folder, all items in the folder are copied as well.
6. Close the device window. If you used removable media such as a CD or DVD, remove the media from the drive and label it **Files for Review**, with your name.

PAUSE. LEAVE the Alpine Files folder open to use in the next exercise.

CERTIFICATION READY? How do you copy data files to a CD or DVD? **4.6.4**

You can also use the Copy and Paste commands and drag and drop method to copy or move items to a removable or network device. Also, most CD and DVD drives come with their own software programs that you can use to transfer data —including music, pictures, and videos—onto a disk.

In the next section, you work with file and folder properties.

■ Using File Properties

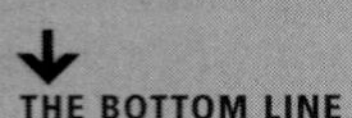

THE BOTTOM LINE

File properties are details that identify a file, such as the filename, file type, and date of creation. Some general properties are applied automatically and cannot be modified, but other more specific properties can easily be added, edited, or removed. The more you individualize the file properties, the easier it is to identify a particular file. By removing properties, you can keep certain information private when you share a file with others. In this section, you remove, add, and edit file properties.

Removing File Properties

You can remove a single property, selected properties, or all properties. To work with a single, common property, use the Details pane of the folder window where the file is stored. To work with all file properties, use the File Properties dialog box.

REMOVE FILE PROPERTIES

USE the Alpine Files folder you left open in the previous exercise.

1. In the Alpine Files folder, click the ***Alpine_Photo1*** file to select it. Some of the common properties display in the Details pane, as shown in Figure 3-15. Each property has a label, such as Size or Title, and a value. The ***property label*** is the name of the property. The ***property value*** is the variable data that is specific to each file.

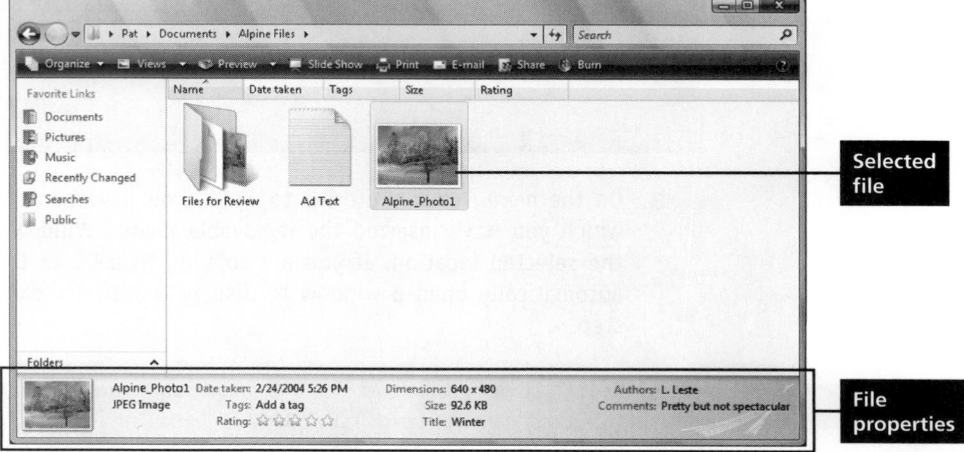

Figure 3-15

Properties in the Details pane

TROUBLESHOOTING

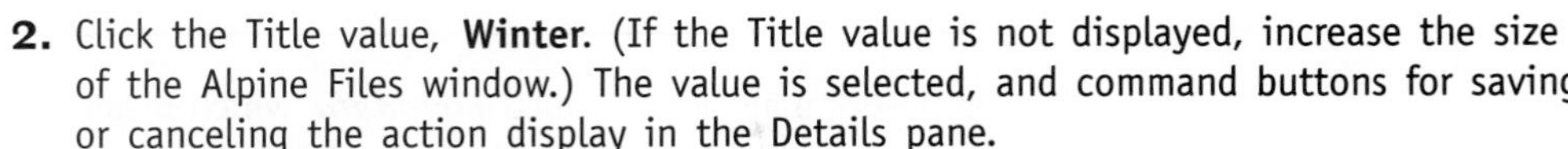
If necessary, increase the size of the Alpine Files window on your screen by dragging a window border or maximizing the window. The number of properties you can see depends on the size of the window. The more room in the Details pane, the more properties display.

TROUBLESHOOTING

If the value is not selected, you are not clicking in the right place. Be sure to click the value, not the property label.

2. Click the Title value, **Winter**. (If the Title value is not displayed, increase the size of the Alpine Files window.) The value is selected, and command buttons for saving or canceling the action display in the Details pane.
3. Press **Delete** to remove the title and then click the **Save** button. The Title property is removed.
4. Right-click the ***Alpine_Photo1*** file in the File list and then click **Properties** to display the General tab of the file's Properties dialog box. The properties on the General tab are added automatically by Windows Vista, and you cannot edit or remove them.
5. Click the **Details** tab to display the Details page. It should look similar to Figure 3-16. The property labels display in the left column, and the property values display in the right column.

Figure 3-16

Details in a file's Properties dialog box

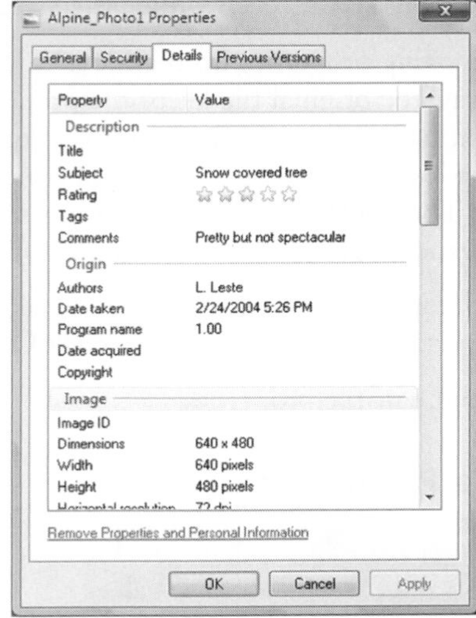

6. Click the link **Remove Properties and Personal Information** at the bottom of the dialog box. A Remove Properties dialog box displays so you can select the specific properties you want to remove.
7. Click the **Remove the following properties from this file** option button and then click the **Subject**, **Comments**, **Authors**, and **Date taken** checkboxes to select them. These are the properties you will remove, leaving the unchecked properties intact. The dialog box should look similar to the one shown in Figure 3-17.

Figure 3-17

Remove Properties dialog box

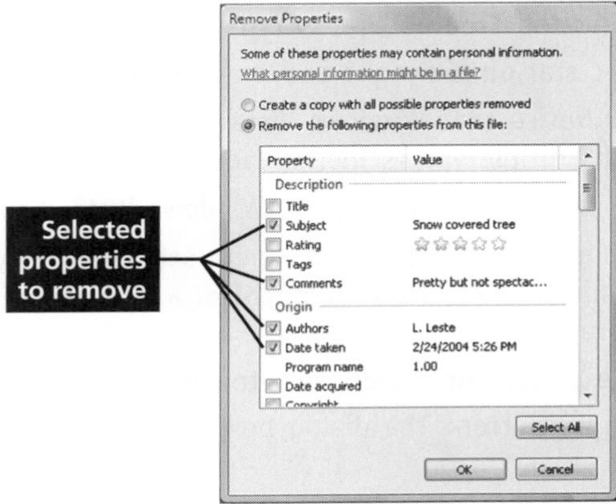

8. Click **OK**. The properties are removed and the Remove Properties dialog box closes. The file's Properties dialog box is still open, but the selected properties have been removed.

   PAUSE. LEAVE the Alpine_Photo1 Properties dialog box open to use in the next exercise.

File properties may also be called ***metadata***, which means data about data. Each type of file has different properties associated with it. For example, a photo file has properties specific to photographs, including information about the camera, lens, and settings; a word processing file has properties such as word count, line count, and number of pages. Folders, disks, and drives also have associated properties.

Some file types do not have any variable properties at all. For example, you cannot remove, add, or edit properties for text files or rich text files.

Removing properties is particularly useful when you need to give the file to someone else. You may have personal or private information stored in the properties, such as authors' names, company codes, or comments you would rather not share. By removing properties, you can insure that your private data remains secure, even while others are working with the file.

One option available when removing properties from a file is to create a copy of the file with all properties removed. That way, the original file keeps the properties so you can use them, and you can share the copy that has no properties. To create a copy with the properties removed, click the Create a copy with all possible properties removed option button in the Remove Properties dialog box. Then click OK. Windows Vista creates the copy in the same storage location as the original and adds *-Copy* to the filename.

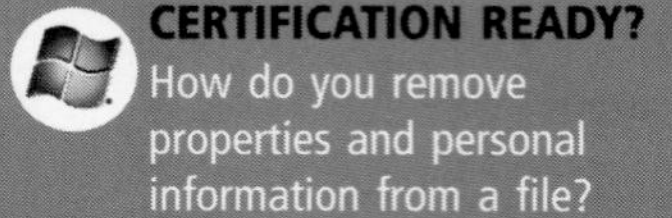

CERTIFICATION READY?
How do you remove properties and personal information from a file?
4.6.2

When you want to remove all properties from a file without making a copy, click the Select All button in the Remove Properties dialog box and then click OK.

In the next exercise, you add and edit file properties.

Adding and Editing File Properties

You can easily customize properties to differentiate one file from another. For example, add properties where there are no values, or edit existing values to be more specific or correct.

ADD AND EDIT FILE PROPERTIES

USE the Alpine_Photo1 Properties dialog box you left open in the previous exercise.

1. On the Details page of the Alpine_Photo1 Properties dialog box, move the mouse pointer over the Value column of the Title property. A text box displays with the prompt Add a title.
2. Click the **Add a title** text box, key **Brochure Cover**, and then press Tab to move to the next property, Subject.
3. Key **Snow Covered Tree** and press Tab to select the Ratings property.
4. Click the last star on the right and press Tab to move to the Tags property.
5. Key **Winter**. Notice that Windows Vista adds a semicolon after the text, because you can add multiple values in the Tags property.
6. Click to the right of the semicolon. Windows Vista displays the prompt Add a tag.
7. Key **Snow**, click to the right of the next semicolon, key **Tree**, click to the right of the next semicolon, key **New Hampshire**, and then press Tab to move to the Comments property.
8. Key **Suitable photo for inside, but too plain for cover.**
9. Click the **Apply** button. The dialog box should look similar to Figure 3-18.

TROUBLESHOOTING

If pressing Tab does not move the selector to the Tags property, click the Tags value box.

Figure 3-18

Add file properties

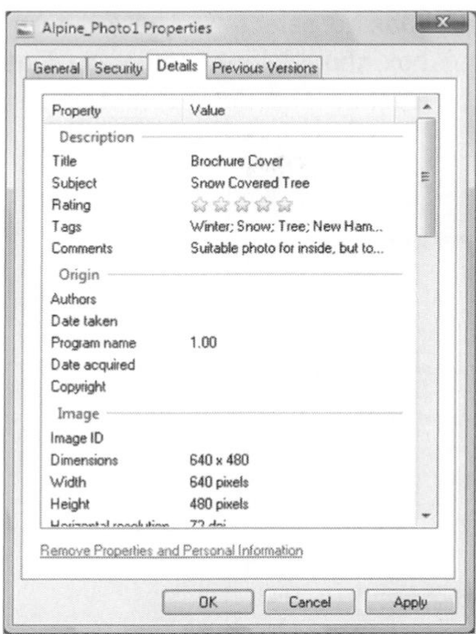

10. Click the **Title value**—Brochure Cover—to select it, key **Page 3 Illustration**, and then press **Enter** to change the text. Editing a file property is as simple as clicking the existing value and keying the new value.
11. Click **Apply** to save the change to the Title property.

You can add or edit common properties in the Details pane of a folder window. Select the file to display its properties in the Details pane, then click the value to the right of the property. Key the new or edited data and then press Enter or click the Save button.

You learn more about searching in Lesson 6.

PAUSE. LEAVE the Alpine_Photo1 Properties dialog box open to use in the next exercise.

One of the most useful properties is a ***tag***. A tag is a custom property that you can add to provide specific information not included in any other property. A tag may include any data that you can type, such as words, phrases, or even codes. You can add many tags.

CERTIFICATION READY?
How do you add metadata to a file?
4.6.1

Properties become very useful when you start searching for files. Windows Vista can search based on the property values, which can help narrow a search considerably. For example, you can search for all files that were created on a certain day, or by a certain author.

In the next exercise, you set file attributes.

Setting File and Folder Attributes

Most files and folders have two basic ***attributes***: Read-only and Hidden. An attribute is a setting that determines how a file or folder can be viewed or edited. The ***Read-only*** attribute allows a file to be read or copied but not changed or saved. The ***Hidden*** attribute keeps a file from being displayed in a file list. You can select or deselect the attributes on the General page of the item's Properties dialog box. Folder attributes can also be applied to all items stored in the folder.

SET FILE AND FOLDER ATTRIBUTES

USE the Alpine_Photo1 Properties dialog box that you left open in the previous exercise.

1. In the Alpine_Photo1 Properties dialog box, click the **General** tab to display the General page. The Attributes checkboxes are at the bottom of the page.

2. Click the **Read-only** checkbox to select it. The Read-only attribute protects the file from editing. The dialog box should look similar to Figure 3-19. When Read-only is selected, the file can be opened and viewed, but it cannot be changed.

Figure 3-19

Set file attributes

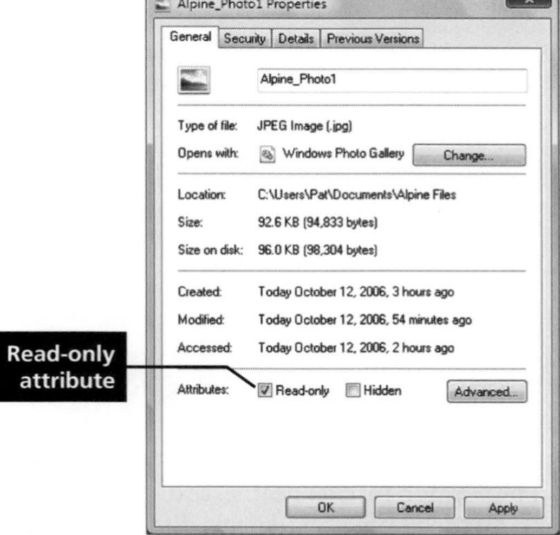

TAKE NOTE

Notice that the Read-only checkbox is filled, not checked. That's because some items in the folder are Read-only, while others are not.

3. Click **OK** to close the dialog box.
4. Right-click the **Files for Review** folder and then click **Properties.** The folder's Properties dialog box displays.
5. Click the **Hidden** checkbox to select it. The Hidden attribute sets the folder so that it will not display in the file list.
6. Click **OK** to apply the change and close the dialog box. A Confirm Attribute Changes dialog box displays, asking if you want the change to affect this folder only, or to items stored in the folder as well.
7. Click the **Apply changes to this folder only** button and then click **OK.** Notice that the folder appears dimmed in the Alpine Files file list, but that it is still visible. The item is not hidden until the next time you open the location where it is stored.
8. In the Files for Review Properties dialog box, click the **Hidden** checkbox to deselect it, and then click **OK.**
9. In the Confirm Attribute Changes dialog box, click the **Apply changes to this folder only** button, and then click **OK.** Now, the folder is no longer marked with the Hidden attribute.
10. Navigate to the Documents folder.
11. At your instructor's request, copy or move the Alpine Files folder and its contents to your Lesson 3 assessment folder. Then, delete the Alpine Files folder from the Documents folder.
12. Close the Documents folder.

LOG OFF your Windows Vista user account.

X REF

Setting folder options to show or hide hidden files is covered in Lesson 4.

In this exercise you learned about two of the most common file and folder attributes: Read only and hidden.

- Read-only allows a file to be read or copied but not changed or saved. Use it to protect files from unauthorized editing. When a file is marked as read-only, you cannot edit, remove, or add file properties.
- Hidden keeps a file from being displayed in a file list. Hidden files are not deleted, but they cannot be viewed unless you modify folder options to display hidden files.

You can click the Advanced button for additional options, including the following.

- File is ready for archiving. An ***archive*** is a backup. Select this option for a file that can be backed up.
- Index this file for faster searching. Select this option to a file and all its properties in an index used during a search.
- Compress contents to save disk space. ***Compress*** means to reduce the size of a file so it takes up less storage space. Select this option to compress the file.
- Encrypt contents to secure data. Encrypt means to scramble the contents of a file. Select this option so that the file can be read only by someone with an ***encryption key***, which is code used to unscramble the data.

SUMMARY SKILL MATRIX

In This Lesson You Learned	Matrix Skill	Skill Number
To navigate through Windows		
To move files and folders		
To create and name a file	Create, delete, rename, and move files	4.6.3
To copy files and folders	Copy data files to a CD or DVD	4.6.4
To remove file properties	Remove properties and personal information from a file	4.6.2
To add file properties	Add metadata to a file	4.6.1

■ Knowledge Assessment

Matching

Match the term in Column 1 to its description in Column 2.

Column 1	Column 2
1. stack	**a.** a temporary storage area that can hold one item at a time
2. cascade	**b.** an attribute that keeps a file or folder from being displayed in a file list
3. collapse	**c.** an attribute that enables a file to be read or copied but not changed or saved.
4. Clipboard	**d.** a custom property that you can add to provide specific information not included in any other property
5. Read-only	**e.** data about data
6. expand	**f.** to arrange windows to overlap one another in an orderly fashion, starting in the upper left corner of the desktop
7. hidden	**g.** to display the contents of a folder in a list or menu, usually by clicking an arrow next to the folder name
8. destination	**h.** to minimize the contents of a folder in a list or menu, usually by clicking an arrow next to the folder name
9. metadata	**i.** to tile windows horizontally so they display one above the other without overlapping
10. tag	**j.** the new storage location for a moved or copied file

Multiple-Choice

Select the best response for the following questions.

1. Which button should you click to display the previously viewed folder?
   a. OK
   b. Previous
   c. Back
   d. Recent Pages

2. How many windows can you have open at the same time?
   a. as many as you want.
   b. one
   c. two
   d. ten

3. How many windows can be active at the same time?
   a. as many as you want
   b. one
   c. two
   d. ten

4. Which of the following is not a method of changing the active window?
   a. Alt+Tab switching
   b. clicking in the window
   c. clicking the window's taskbar button
   d. stacking the window

5. How many items can be stored on the Clipboard at one time?
   a. as many as you want
   b. one
   c. two
   d. ten

6. Which key do you press and hold when you want to copy a file by dragging?
   a. Alt
   b. Esc
   c. Shift
   d. Ctrl

7. Which command places an item from the Clipboard in a new location?
   a. Cut
   b. Copy
   c. Paste
   d. Stack

8. On which page of a file's Properties dialog box will you find the properties that you can remove, add, or edit?
   a. General
   b. Details
   c. Remove
   d. Attributes

9. Which of the following is not a common file property?
   a. Password
   b. Title
   c. Authors
   d. Tags
10. Which of the following is *not* a file attribute?
    a. Encrypt
    b. Cascade
    c. Hidden
    d. Read-only

■ Competency Assessment

Project 3-1: Telephone List

You are working on a design project with four coworkers, and you want to be able to contact them even when you are working at home. In this project, in the Documents folder, you create and save a text file in which you key the telephone list. You then copy it to a removable device so you can take it home.

GET READY. Before you begin these steps, start your computer and log on to your Windows Vista account. Insert a blank disk such as a CD, DVD, or floppy into the appropriate drive. Close all open windows so you can see the desktop.

1. Click **Start** and then click **Documents** to open the Documents folder window.
2. Right-click a blank area of the File list to display the shortcut menu.
3. Point to **New** on the shortcut menu to display a submenu.
4. Click **Text Document** on the submenu to create a new text file.
5. Key **Phone List** and then press Enter to rename the file.
6. Double-click the **Phone List** file icon to open it in Notepad.
7. Right-click a blank area of the taskbar and click **Cascade Windows** to arrange the Document window and the Notepad window on the desktop. The Notepad window should be active, but if it is not, click its taskbar button.
8. On the first line of the Phone List file, key your name and today's date and then press Enter two times to leave a blank line.
9. Key the following data. Press Enter at the end of each line to start a new line. Press Enter two times to leave a blank line between entries.

   Ted Bremer 555-1234

   Debra L. Core 555-2345

   Arlene Huff 555-3456

   Sunil Uppal 555-4567
10. Click **File** on the menu bar and then click **Save** to save the changes.
11. Click the **Close** button in the upper right corner of the Notepad window to close the Phone List file and the Notepad program window.
12. Right-click the **Phone List** file icon on the desktop, point to the **Send To** command, and then click the device in which you have inserted a disk.
13. When the drive is finished copying the file to the disk, remove the disk and label it with your name, the date, and the filename—Phone List. At your instructor's request, copy the Phone List file to your Lesson 3 assessment folder, as well.

14. Click the **Close** button in the upper right corner of the Documents window to close it.

PAUSE. LEAVE the desktop displayed to use in the next project.

Project 3-2: Catalog Photo

An equipment manufacturer has submitted a picture for use in an Alpine Ski House catalog. In this project, you must locate the picture in the data files and copy it to the Documents folder. You will then remove all file properties and add new properties. You will also set the file attributes so that no one can edit the file.

The Catalog_Photo1 file is available on the companion CD-ROM.

1. Navigate to the ***Catalog_Photo1*** file in the data files for this lesson, right-click it, and then click **Copy** on the shortcut menu.
2. In the Navigation pane of the folder window, click **Folders** to display the Folders list.
3. Click the **expand arrow** next to your personal folder in the Folders list and then click **Documents** to display the contents of the Documents folder in the File list.
4. Right-click a blank area of the File list and then click **Paste** on the shortcut menu to paste the ***Catalog_Photo1*** file into the Documents folder.
5. Right-click the ***Catalog_Photo1*** file and then click **Properties** to open its Properties dialog box. Click the **Details** page tab.
6. Click **Remove Properties and Personal Information** to open the Remove Properties dialog box.
7. Click the **Remove the following properties from this file** option button.
8. Click to select the **Title** and the **Comments** checkboxes and then click **OK** to remove the selected properties.
9. In the Properties dialog box, click the **Title** property value box and key **Ski Boots, Inc. photo**.
10. Click the **Comments** property value box and key **Place beside product in catalog**.
11. Click the **Apply** button to add the properties to the file, keeping the dialog box open.
12. Click the **General** tab and then click the **Read-only** attributes checkbox.
13. Click **OK** to apply the changes and close the dialog box.
14. At your instructor's request, copy the ***Catalog_Photo1*** file to your Lesson 3 assessment folder, and then delete it from the Documents folder.
15. Click the **Close** button in the upper right corner of the Documents window to close it.

PAUSE. LEAVE the desktop open to use in the next project.

■ Proficiency Assessment

Project 3-3: Organize Project Files

To keep your design project organized, you must keep all files in the same storage location. In this project you create a folder for storing the files, and move it to your Documents folder. You also locate and copy the Phone List text file into the folder, and then move the entire folder to your Documents folder.

USE the Phone List file you created in Project 3-1, which is stored in your Documents folder, or use the ***Phone_List1*** file from the data files for this lesson.

The ***Phone_List1*** file is available on the companion CD-ROM.

1. If necessary, navigate to the data files for this lesson, right-click the ***Phone_List1*** text file, and click **Copy.** Then, to paste the file into the Documents folder, navigate to your Documents folder, right-click the Files list area, and click Paste. Close the Documents folder window.

2. Right-click a blank area of the desktop, point to **New** on the shortcut menu, and then click **Folder** on the submenu to create a new folder.
3. Key **Design Project** and then press **Enter** to rename the folder.
4. Right-click the **Design Project** icon on the desktop and then click **Cut** on the shortcut menu to move the folder to the Clipboard.
5. Click the **Start** button and then click **Documents.**
6. Right-click a blank area of the File list in the Documents window and then click **Paste** on the shortcut menu to paste the Design Project folder from the Clipboard into the Documents folder.
7. Double-click the **Design Project** folder icon to open it.
8. Click the **Start** button and then click **Documents** to open the Documents folder window.
9. Right-click a blank area of the taskbar and click **Show Windows Stacked** to tile the Documents window and the Design Project window horizontally on the desktop.
10. Click the **Phone List** file icon in the Documents window, drag it to the **Design Project** window, and then drop it in the File list area. At this point, your instructor may ask you to capture an image of the screen for assessment. If so, capture the image, paste it into a graphics or word processing file named Proj3_3, and save or copy the file to your Lesson 3 assessment folder.
11. Click the **Close** button in the upper right corner of the Documents window to close it.
12. Click the **Close** button in the upper right corner of the Design Project window to close it.

PAUSE. LEAVE the Windows Vista desktop displayed to use in the next project.

Project 3-4: Publicity Photo

Your local newspaper is writing an article about some high school students. The reporter has asked you for a photo of one of the students to use with the article. In this project, you will copy the photo to a new folder and remove all properties that might disclose personal or private information. You will then copy the entire folder to a removable device so you can give it to the reporter.

GET READY. Before you begin these steps, insert a blank disk such as a CD or DVD into the appropriate drive, or attach a removable device such as a Flash drive to a USB port. If necessary, close the AutoPlay window.

The ***Student_Photo1*** file is available on the companion CD-ROM.

1. Click **Start** and then click **Documents** to open the Documents window.
2. Right-click a blank area of the File list, point to **New**, and then click **Folder**. Key **News Photo** and then press **Enter** to rename the folder.
3. Navigate to the location where the data files for this lesson are stored and open the folder window.
4. Locate ***Student_Photo1*** from the data files for this lesson, right-click it, and then click **Copy** on the shortcut menu.
5. Click the **Recent Pages** dropdown arrow on the window's toolbar and then click **News Photo** to change to the News Photo folder.
6. Right-click a blank area of the File list and then click **Paste** on the shortcut menu to paste the ***Student_Photo1*** file into the News Photo folder.
7. Right-click the ***Student_Photo1*** file and then click **Properties** to open its Properties dialog box. Click the **Details** tab.
8. Click **Remove Properties and Personal Information** to open the Remove Properties dialog box.
9. Click the **Remove the following properties from this file** button.

10. Click the **Select All** button and then click **OK** to remove all properties.
11. In the Properties dialog box, click **OK** to apply the change and close the dialog box.
12. In the Navigation pane, click **Documents** to change to the Document folder.
13. Right-click the **News Photo** folder icon, point to the **Send To** command, and then click the drive or device to which you want to copy the folder.
14. If you used a removable disk such as a CD or DVD, when the drive is finished copying the file to the disk, remove the disk and label it with your name, the date, and the folder name—News Photo.
15. If your instructor requests, copy the News Photo folder to your Lesson 3 assessment folder, as well, and then delete it from the Documents folder. Click the **Close** button in the upper right corner of the Documents window to close it.

PAUSE. LEAVE the desktop displayed to use in the next project.

■ Mastery Assessment

Project 3-5: Corporate Visit

Members of the design team are traveling to the corporate office to discuss the project and want to take all of the files you have organized with them. In this project, you will add a document file to the Design Project folder, set the folder attributes so it is read-only, and then copy it to a removable device.

GET READY. Before you begin these steps, insert a blank disk such as a CD or DVD into the appropriate drive, or attach a removable device such as a Flash drive to a USB port. If necessary, close the AutoPlay window.

USE the Design Project folder containing the phone list files you created in Projects 3-1 and 3-3, or create a new Design Project folder and use the ***Phone_List2*** file from the data files for this lesson.

The ***Design_Report1***, ***Phone_List2***, and ***Catalog_Photo2*** files are available on the companion CD-ROM.

1. If necessary, open **Documents** and create a new folder named Design Project and copy the Phone_List2 file from the data files for this lesson to the Design Project folder.
2. Copy the document file ***Design_Report1*** from the data files for this lesson.
3. Paste the file into the Design Project folder.
4. Copy the ***Phone_List2*** and ***Catalog_Photo2*** files from the data files for this lesson to the Design Project folder. There should now be three files in the Design Project folder: ***Phone_List1*** or ***Phone_List2***, ***Design_Report1***, and ***Catalog_Photo2***.
5. Navigate to the Documents folder.
6. Right-click the **Design Project** folder and then click **Properties** to open its Properties dialog box.
7. Select the **Read-only** attribute and then close the dialog box, applying the change to the folder and all its subfolders and files.
8. Copy the **Design Project** folder to the removable device. Your instructor may ask you to copy it to your Lesson 3 assessment folder, as well.
9. If you used a removable device such as a CD or DVD, remove the device from the drive and label it with your name, the date, and the folder name.
10. Delete the Design Project folder from the Documents folder. Close the **Documents** window.

PAUSE. LEAVE the desktop displayed to use in the next project.

Project 3-6: Fundraising Files

You have assumed responsibility for fundraising for a local homeless shelter. There are several files on the organization's office computer that you need to work with at home, including an expense spreadsheet, a list of donors, and a drawing that a child made of the shelter. In this project, you will locate the three files and copy them to the Documents folder. You will then create a new folder and move all three files into it. You will remove all properties from all three files and then send the entire folder to a removable device.

The ***Expenses, Donors,*** and ***Shelter*** files are available on the companion CD-ROM.

GET READY. Before you begin these steps, insert a blank disk such as a CD, DVD, or floppy into the appropriate drive. If necessary, close the AutoPlay window.

1. Locate the files ***Expenses, Donors,*** and ***Shelter*** in the data files for this lesson. Copy them to the Documents folder.
2. In the **Documents** folder, create a new folder named **Shelter Fundraiser.**
3. Open both the **Documents** folder window and the **Shelter Fundraiser** folder window at the same time. **Stack** them on the desktop so you can see both.
4. Move the ***Expenses, Donors,*** and ***Shelter*** files from the Documents folder into the Shelter Fundraiser folder.
5. Remove all properties from the ***Expenses, Donors,*** and ***Shelter*** files.
6. Copy the **Shelter Fundraiser** folder to a removable device.
7. At your instructor's request, copy the Shelter Fundraiser folder to your Lesson 3 assessment folder, as well.
8. Delete the Shelter Fundraiser folder, and then close all open windows.
9. **LOG OFF** your Windows Vista user account.

INTERNET READY

Alpine Ski House is a chain of retail stores specializing in winter sports equipment. The manager of a store in Franconia, New Hampshire wants to plan an outing to a local ski area for the staff. In this exercise, use Internet search tools to locate a ski area near Franconia. Create a text file and use Notepad to record information about the ski area, such as the name, the number of trails, and the available facilities. See if you can find information about how far the area is from your home town. Save the file with a descriptive filename and then copy it to a removable disk.

Workplace Ready

Archiving with Windows Vista

Even the most organized personal computer becomes cluttered with files over time. A good plan for making sure you can find the most current files when you need them includes creating an archive. An archive is simply a place to store older files that you no longer use on a daily basis. Windows Vista is an ideal tool to use to set up an archive.

Suppose you are a sales assistant at an insurance agency. Much of the business is organized around the calendar. For example, you prepare monthly sales reports, quarterly commission statements, and annual renewal letters. Documents for each new cycle replace the documents from the last cycle. You don't want to delete the older files, because you may need to reference them in the future. What should you do with the older files?

With Windows Vista, you can create a folder named Archive where you can store the outdated files. You can keep the Archive folder in Documents so that if you need to look back or reference a file, you can get to it quickly. Within the Archive folder, you can use a structure based on date and file type to organize the files into subfolders that clearly identify the file content, as shown in the figure.

By archiving older files, you keep your computer uncluttered so you can locate and identify active file information. You still have access to the older files if you need them, but they are stored out of the way. After a while, when the Archive folder starts to get too big, you can move the archived files off of your local disk to an external device, using the file and folder naming tools provided by Windows Vista to label them based on date and type.

Circling Back

The Baldwin Museum of Science is sponsoring a series of four seminars for high school science teachers. The manager of special events has hired you as a temporary assistant to help with the planning and organization of the seminars. In particular, you will be responsible for organizing information for seminar participants. Your manager has already given you a list of tasks that she needs completed quickly, including calculating the cost of lunch for the participants and organizing files for the seminar handbook.

Project 1: Lunch Costs

Use the Calculator program to calculate the total cost of lunch for 57 participants. Insert the information into a text document, print the document, copy it to your CB1 assessment folder, and then delete it.

GET READY. Before you begin these steps, make sure your computer is connected to a printer, or to a network that has a printer. Verify that the printer has paper and that the printer is active, or turned on.

1. Start your computer and log on to your Windows Vista account.
2. Open the **Start** menu and then click **Documents**.
3. Create a new folder in Documents and rename it **Seminars**.
4. Open the **Seminars** folder and create a new text document named **Lunch**.
5. In the **Seminars** folder, create a folder named **Memos**.
6. Move the **Lunch** document into the **Memos** folder.
7. Open the **Lunch** document in Notepad.
8. Minimize the **Memos** folder window.
9. On the first line, key **Memorandum** and then press Enter twice.
10. Key today's date and then press Enter.
11. Key **To: Manager of Special Projects** and then press Enter.
12. Key **From:** and then key your name.
13. Press Enter twice and then key the following text, pressing Enter at the end of each line to start a new line:

    Based on the estimated cost of $9.85 per person,

    I have calculated that the total cost of lunch for the

    57 teachers attending the first seminar is
14. Save the changes to the file.
15. Open the **Start** menu and click **All Programs**.
16. Click **Accessories** and then click **Calculator**.
17. On the Calculator keypad, click **5**, click **7**, and then click *.
18. On the Calculator keypad, click **9**, click the decimal point, click **8**, click **5**, and then click =.
19. Arrange the open windows side by side and make the **Lunch** document active.
20. Move the insertion point to the end of the file, press spacebar, and key the result of the calculation, as a dollar value, followed by a period to end the sentence.
21. Press Enter twice and key **Please let me know if you have any questions.** Your desktop should look similar to Figure 1. At this point, your instructor may ask you to capture an image of the screen. Save it in your CB1 assessment folder as ***CB1_01***.

Figure 1

Open windows side by side

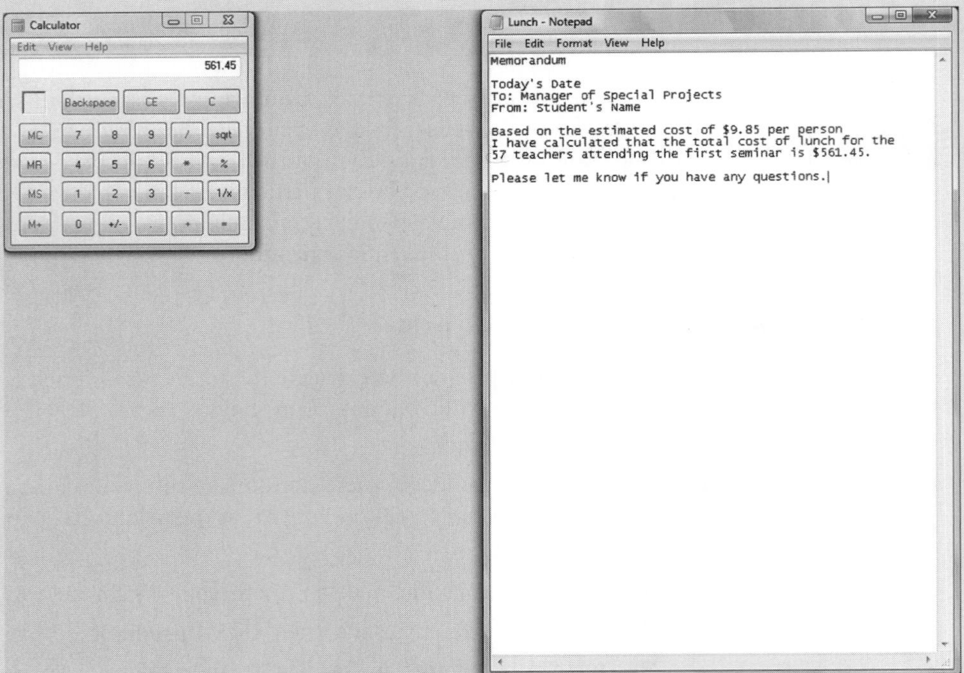

22. Save the changes to the **Lunch** document and then close it.
23. Close the **Calculator** window.
24. Maximize the **Memos** folder window.
25. Print the **Lunch** text document.
26. At your instructor's request, copy the Lunch text document to your CB1 assessment folder.
27. Delete the **Lunch** text document.
28. Restore the **Memos** folder window and then close it.

PAUSE. LEAVE the Windows Vista desktop open to use in the next project.

Project 2: Handbook Files

Set up a folder for the seminar handbook files and then create a text file in the folder, listing the topics and dates of each seminar. You will locate two picture files that might be suitable for the handbook cover and then copy them into the folder. You will enter file properties for the picture files and set file attributes.

1. **OPEN** the **Documents** folder and then open the **Seminars** folder.
2. Create a new folder named **Handbook**.
3. Open the **Handbook** folder, create a new text document file, and name it **Schedule**.
4. Open the **Schedule** text document in **Notepad**.
5. On the first line, key your name and then press **Enter**.
6. Key today's date and then press **Enter** twice.
7. Key the following list, pressing **Enter** once to start a new line, or twice to leave a blank line:

   Seminar 1, October 15

   Our Changing Climate

   Seminar 2, January 10

   Exploring Space

Seminar 3, March 12
Animal Habitats

Seminar 4, June 7
Everyday Physics

8. Save the changes to the file. It should look similar to Figure 2.

Figure 2

Schedule Notepad document

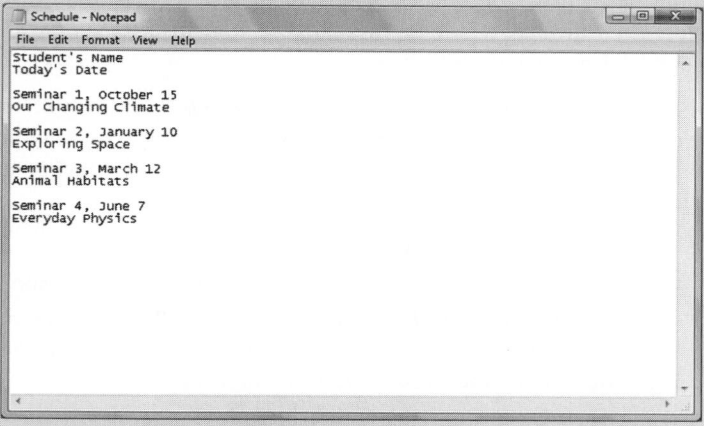

The ***Handbook_Picture1*** and ***Handbook_Picture2*** files are available on the companion CD-ROM.

9. Close the **Schedule** file and then print it. At your instructor's request, copy it to your CB1 assessment folder.
10. Navigate to the data files for this lesson and locate ***Handbook_Picture1***.
11. Right-click the ***Handbook_Picture1*** picture file and click **Copy**. Then navigate to your Handbook folder, right-click the Files list area, and click Paste, to paste the file into the folder.
12. Locate the ***Handbook_Picture2*** file in the data files and copy it to the Handbook folder.
13. Right-click the ***Handbook_Picture1*** file and click **Properties**. Make the **Details** tab active.
14. Key the following file properties:
    Title: **Chemistry Set**
    Subject: **Seminar Handbook**
    Rating: ***
    Tags: **Science; Beakers; Chemistry**
    Comments: **May be suitable for cover, or somewhere inside.**
15. Click **OK** to save the properties and close the dialog box.
16. Open the Properties dialog box for the ***Handbook_Picture2*** file and make the **Details** tab active.
17. Key the following file properties:
    Title: **Microscope**
    Subject: **Seminar Handbook**
    Rating: **
    Tags: **Science; Microscope**
    Comments: **May be suitable for cover, or somewhere inside.**
18. Click **OK** to save the properties and close the dialog box.
19. Open the **Properties** dialog box for the ***Handbook_Picture1*** file.
20. Set the file attribute to **Read-only.**
21. Set the file attribute for the ***Handbook_Picture2*** file to **Read-only.**

PAUSE. LEAVE the Handbook folder open to use in the next project.

Project 3: Removable Files

The manager of special events is leaving on a brief business trip and wants to review the handbook files you have been working on. In this project, you will remove the read-only attributes and all of the file properties and personal information from the picture files and then copy the entire Handbook folder to a removable device.

GET READY. Before you begin these steps, insert a blank disk such as a CD or DVD into the appropriate drive, or attach a removable device such as Flash drive to a USB port. If necessary, close the AutoPlay window. Alternatively, your instructor may ask you to copy the folder to your CB1 assessment folder.

USE the Handbook folder containing the ***Schedule*** text document, the ***Handbook_Picture1*** file, and the ***Handbook_Picture2*** file that you created in Project 2, or create a new Handbook folder and use the ***Schedule, Handbook_Picture3*** and ***Handbook_Picture4*** files from the data files for this Lesson.

The ***Schedule, Handbook_Picture3***, and ***Handbook_Picture4*** files are available on the companion CD-ROM.

TROUBLESHOOTING

If Windows Vista displays a User Account Control dialog box, click Continue. If necessary, ask your instructor for an administrator's password, key it in the text box, and then click OK.

1. Open the **Handbook** folder.
2. If necessary, navigate to the data files for this lesson and then copy the ***Schedule*** text file and the ***Handbook_Picture3*** and ***Handbook_Picture4*** picture files to the **Handbook** folder. Rename ***Handbook_Picture3*** to **Handbook_Picture1**. Rename ***Handbook_Picture4*** to **Handbook_Picture2**.
3. Open the **Properties** dialog box for ***Handbook_Picture1***.
4. Remove the **Read-only** file attribute, and click **Apply**.
5. Make the **Details** tab active.
6. Click **Remove Properties and Personal Information**.
7. In the Remove Properties dialog box, select the **Remove the following properties from this file** option button and then click **Select All**.
8. Click **OK** to remove the properties and close the dialog box.
9. Click **OK** to close the **Properties** dialog box.
10. Open the **Properties** dialog box for ***Handbook_Picture2***.
11. Remove the **Read-only** file attribute and click **Apply**.
12. Make the **Details** tab active.
13. Click **Remove Properties and Personal Information**.
14. In the Remove Properties dialog box, select the **Remove the following properties from this file** option button and then click **Select All**.
15. Click **OK** to remove the properties and close the dialog box.
16. Click **OK** to close the Properties dialog box.
17. Close the **Handbook** folder window.
18. Right-click the **Handbook** folder icon on the desktop, point to the **Send To** command, and then click the device in which you have inserted a disk or attached a drive.
19. When the drive is finished copying the folder to the disk, remove the disk and label it with your name, the date, and the folder name **Handbook**.
20. Navigate to the Documents folder. At the request of your instructor, copy the Seminars folder to your CB1 assessment folder.
21. Delete the Seminars folder and its contents from the Documents folder.
22. Navigate to the Recycle Bin.
23. Empty the Recycle Bin.
24. Close all open windows.

LOG OFF your Windows Vista user account and shut down your computer.

Customizing Windows Explorer

LESSON SKILL MATRIX

Skills	Matrix Skill	Skill Number
Changing the Icon Size	Change the way files are displayed within folders	4.5.1
Displaying or Hiding Details	Display or hide file and folder details	4.5.2
Sorting by Details	Sort files by details	4.5.4
Grouping by Details	Group files by details	4.5.3
Stacking by Details	Stack files by details	4.5.5
Changing a Folder Window Layout	Configure Windows Explorer layouts	4.1.4
Setting General Folder Options	Configure Windows Explorer layouts	4.1.4
Setting Advanced Folder Options	Show and hide file extensions; Show and hide protected operating system files; Show hidden files and folders	4.1.1 4.1.2 4.1.3
Adding and Removing Favorite Links	Add folders to the Favorite Links list	4.2.4

Consolidated Messenger is a bicycle delivery service in a large urban community. The dispatchers must be prepared to respond quickly to orders and requests at any moment of the day, so it is important to have immediate access to all of the necessary files, tools, and information available on the company's computers. In this lesson, you will learn how to customize the Windows Explorer file management system in Windows Vista to organize and display the files and folders for quick and easy access. Specifically, you will learn to change the folder view by changing the way files are displayed in the folder list; organize the file list by details such as name, size, or creation date; configure the elements displayed in a folder window; and select advanced folder settings such as showing hidden or protected files or file extensions and adding or removing Favorite links.

KEY TERMS

ascending order
byte
chronologically
descending order
details
gigabyte
jpg
kilobyte
megabyte
stack
tiles
wmf

Changing the File List View

THE BOTTOM LINE

Windows Vista is designed to help you locate the files and folders you need quickly and easily. Usually, the contents of the current folder display as icons in the File list. You can customize the File list to change the size of the icons, or to display ***details*** about each item. Details are specific information about a file or folder, similar to properties. If you choose to display details, you can use the details to arrange the items into an order that is most useful to you. For example you can sort items by date to locate files modified most recently, or group them according to type to find graphics file. In this section, you learn how to change the size of icons in the File list and to display details. You also learn how to select the details you want to display, and how to group, sort, and stack items based on details.

Changing the Icon Size

In most folders, items in the File list display as ***tiles***, which are medium-sized icons with a label to the right. The label displays the item name and type, and may also include additional information such as file size. You can select from a variety of icon sizes, or display the items in a list with or without details.

CHANGE THE ICON SIZE

GET READY. Before you begin these steps, start your computer and log on to your Windows Vista account. Close all open windows so you can see the desktop. Create a new folder named Lesson 4 in a storage location specified by your instructor, where you can store assessment files and folders that you create during this lesson.

1. Click the **Start** button and then click your personal folder.

2. Click the dropdown arrow to the right of the Views button on the window's toolbar. A menu displays, as shown in Figure 4-1. The slider along the left side of the menu indicates the current icon view. In the figure, it is Tiles. At the top of the menu are four icon sizes: Small, Medium, Large, and Extra Large.

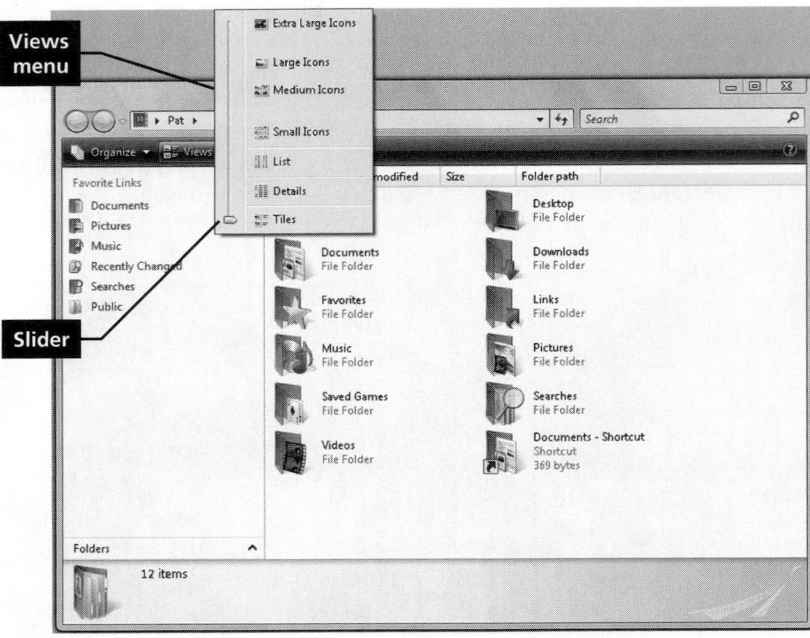

Figure 4-1

The Views dropdown menu

TROUBLESHOOTING

Don't worry if your personal folder does not open in Tiles view. The views on your computer may have been customized.

3. Click **Large Icons** on the menu. Each item displays as a large icon above the item's name, as shown in Figure 4-2.

Figure 4-2

Large Icons view

4. Click the dropdown arrow to the right of the Views button again and then click **Extra Large Icons** on the dropdown menu to increase the size of the icons even more.
5. Click the Views button dropdown arrow and then click **Small Icons.**
6. Click the Views button dropdown arrow and then click **Medium Icons.**
7. Click the Views button dropdown arrow and then click **Tiles.** In Tiles view, the icon size is medium, but the name and type of the item display to the right of the icon.
8. Click the Views button dropdown arrow and then click **List.** In List view, the icon size is small, but the items display in a single list along the left side of the File list pane.

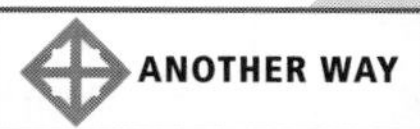

You can also use a shortcut menu to change the File list view. Right-click a blank area of the File list and then click View. Click the option you want to use.

9. Click the Views button dropdown arrow and then click **Details.** The File list should look similar to Figure 4-3. In Details view, information about each item displays in columns in the File list. (Your File list may have been customized to show different information than displays in the figure.)
10. At your instructor's request, capture an image of your personal folder window at this point. Paste it into a graphics or word processing file and save it in the Lesson 4 assessment folder as ***Le04_01***.

Figure 4-3

Details view

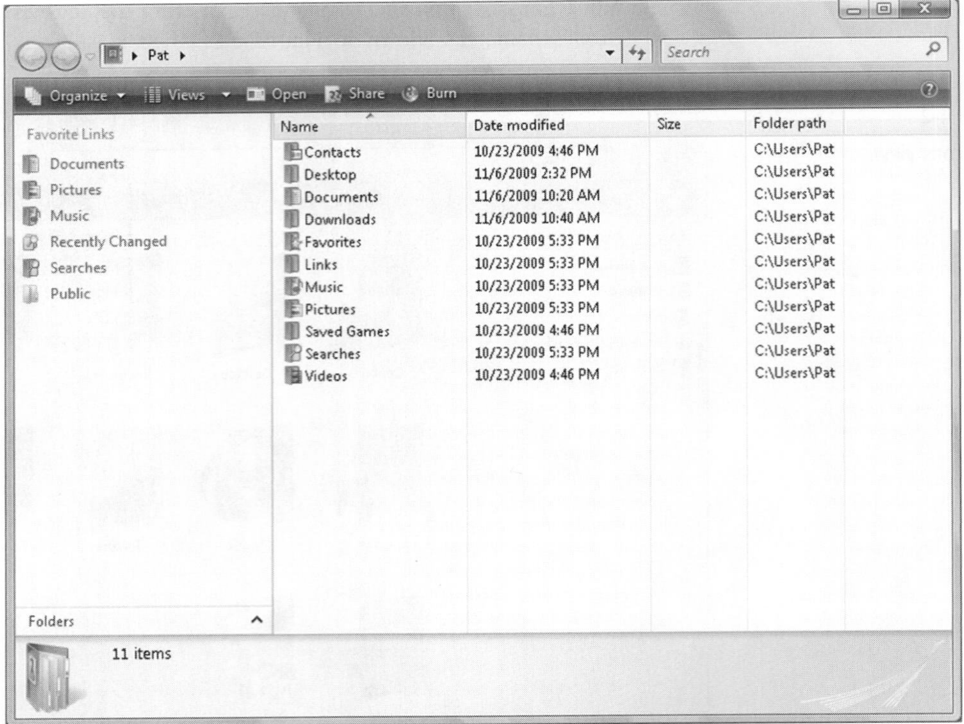

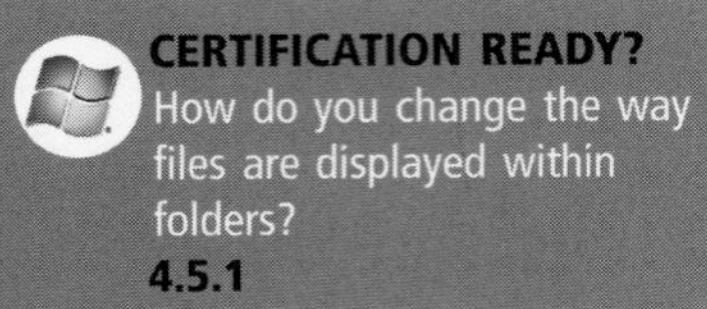

CERTIFICATION READY?
How do you change the way files are displayed within folders?
4.5.1

PAUSE. LEAVE the personal folder window open to use in the next exercise.

The icon size you select is basically a matter of personal choice, although it may affect the number of items you can view in a window. For example, you might find it easier to see and identify icons when they are large. But, in Large Icons or Extra Large Icons view, fewer items fit within the window. You may have to scroll to find the item you need.

You can cycle through the four most commonly used views by clicking the Views button. Click to change to Tiles, Large Icons, List, or Details.

In the next section, you learn how to select the details you want to display in Details view.

Displaying or Hiding Details

By default, the item name, date modified, size, and path display in Details view, but it is easy to customize details to display other information. You can customize the specific information that you want displayed or hidden in the File list.

DISPLAY OR HIDE DETAILS

USE the personal folder window you left open in the previous exercise.

1. Right-click any column heading in the File list. For example, right-click **Name.** A shortcut menu displays common details, with checkmarks next to the ones that are currently displayed.

TROUBLESHOOTING If different details are displayed in your personal folder window, right-click any column heading and click to select Size, Date Modified, and Folder path. Then, click to deselect any other details that may be selected. Click OK to apply the changes, and begin again with step 1.

TAKE NOTE* Notice that Name is not available on the shortcut menu. A menu item that is grayed out is not available. In this case, Name is not available because you cannot hide the Name detail.

2. Click **Date modified** to deselect it. The column is removed from the File list pane, as shown in Figure 4-4.

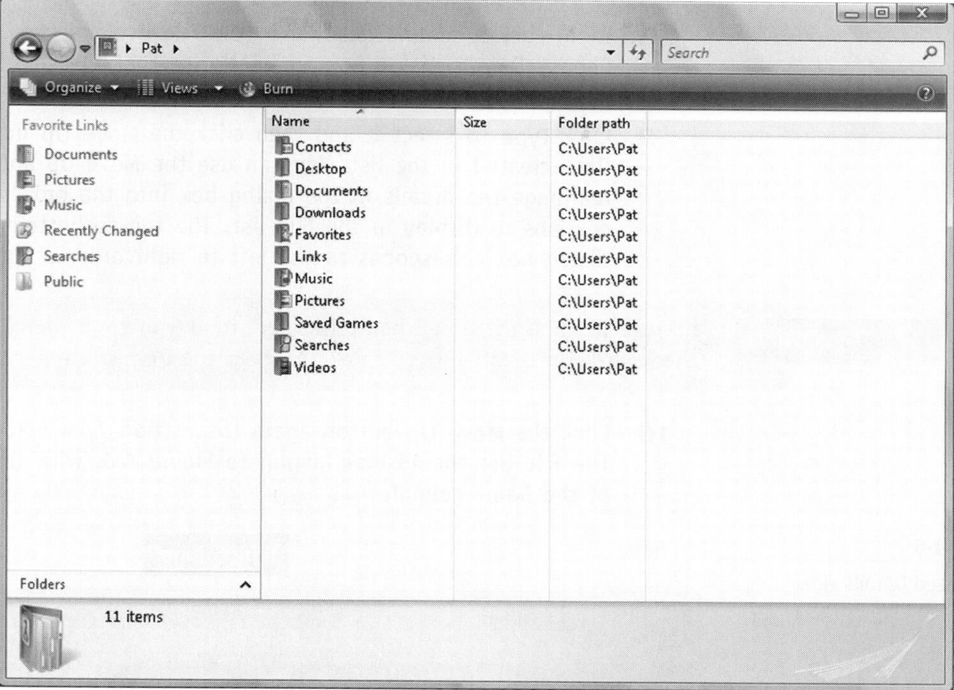

Figure 4-4

The Date modified column is hidden

3. Right-click a column heading in the File list again and then click **More...**. The Choose Details dialog box displays, as shown in Figure 4-5. In this dialog box, you can select and deselect any detail, and you can rearrange the order in which they display in the File list. The details that are currently displayed are listed at the top of the Details list and are checked.

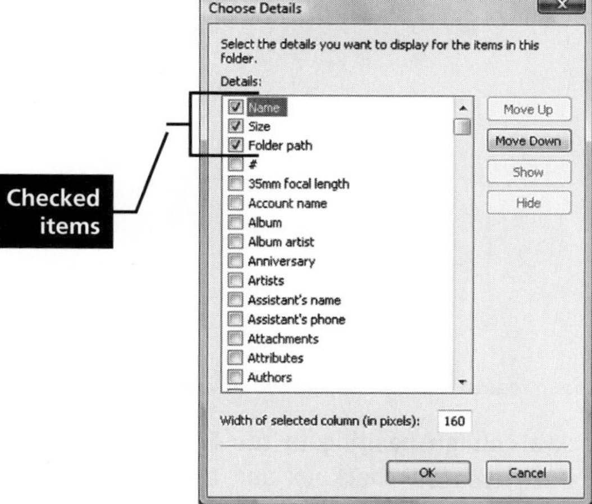

Figure 4-5

The Choose Details dialog box

4. Click to deselect the Size checkbox.
5. Scroll down the list and click to select the **Date created** checkbox. (The details are listed in alphabetical order.)
6. Continue scrolling down and click to select the **Type** checkbox.
7. Click **OK**. The Date created and Type columns are added to the File list view.

TAKE NOTE* You can adjust the width of a details column by dragging or double-clicking the border of the column heading.

8. Right-click a column heading in the File list and then click **More...** to open the Choose Details dialog box again. Notice that the selected details are at the top of the list.
9. Click **Type** to select it and then click the **Move Up** button. Type moves above Date created in the list. You can use the Move Up and Move Down buttons to rearrange the details in the dialog box into the order in which you want the columns to display in the File list. The top to bottom order of items in the dialog box corresponds to the left to right order of columns in the File list.

TROUBLESHOOTING Be sure to click the detail name to select it. If you click the checkbox, you toggle the checkmark on or off but you do not select the item itself.

10. Click the **Move Up** button again to position Type below Name and then click **OK**. The File list should look similar to Figure 4-6, with the Type column to the right of the Name column.

Figure 4-6

Customized Details view

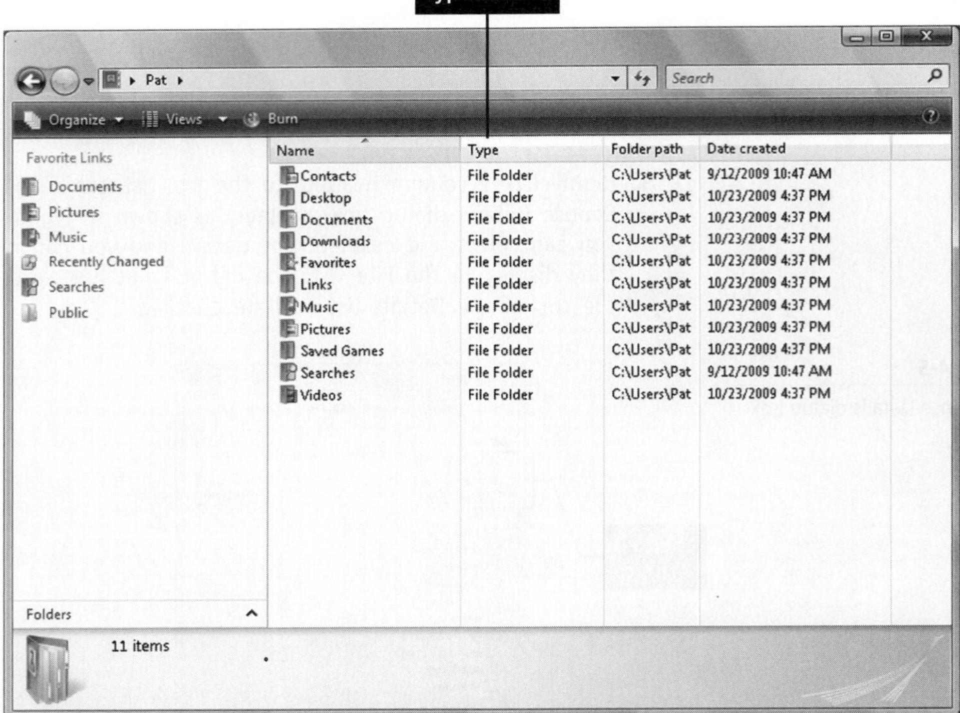

11. Right-click a column heading in the File list and then click **More....** Click to deselect the **Date created** checkbox and then click to select the **Date modified** and **Size** checkboxes. Click **OK**. The Name, Type, Folder path, Date modified, and Size columns should display in Details view.
12. At this point, your instructor may ask you to capture an image of your personal folder window and paste it in a file. Save the file in your Lesson 4 assessment folder as ***Le04_02***.

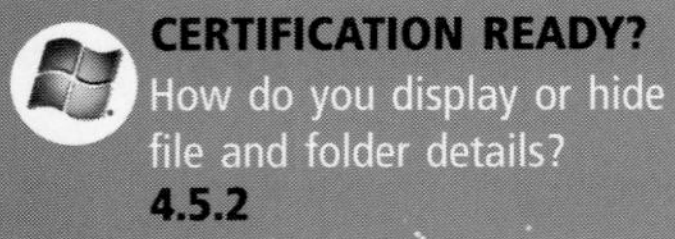

PAUSE. LEAVE the personal folder open to use in the next exercise.

Some of the information that displays in the details columns is generated automatically by Windows Vista, such as the Date modified, Type, and Size details. Other information is stored as part of the item's properties, such as Tags and Comments.

Properties are covered in Lesson 3, "Organizing Files and Folders."

Details can help you identify a folder or file, or distinguish it from a similar item. For example, you can use the Date modified information to identify a file that has been edited more recently than one with a similar name. Other details can help you manage your files and folders. For example, you can use the Size detail to determine if a file is too large to fit on a CD or to transmit via e-mail. Note that size is usually measured in bytes, kilobytes, megabytes, or gigabytes. A ***byte*** is a unit of data representing one character. A ***kilobyte*** is 1,024 bytes. A ***megabyte*** is about one million bytes. A ***gigabyte*** is about one billion bytes.

You may have noticed that the list of items in the Choose Details dialog box is quite long. Many of the details are appropriate for a specific file type, such as 35mm focal length, which is for pictures, and Album artist, which is for music.

Next, you learn how to arrange the file list based on details.

Sorting by Details

You can sort the File list based on the details in any column heading, in either ascending or descending order. ***Ascending order*** means items are sorted alphabetically from A to Z, numerically from 0 to 9, or ***chronologically***—by date—from oldest to newest. ***Descending order*** is the opposite: alphabetically from Z to A, numerically from 9 to 0, or chronologically from newest to oldest. The quickest way to sort the File list is to click the heading by which you want to sort. Each time you click, the sort order is reversed.

SORT BY DETAILS

GET READY. Before you begin these steps, copy the files ***Bike1***, ***Rider1***, ***Messenger1***, ***Messenger2***, and ***Dispatch_Note1*** from the data files for this lesson to your personal folder.

The ***Bike1***, ***Rider1***, ***Messenger1***, ***Messenger2***, and ***Dispatch_Note1*** files are available on the companion CD-ROM.

USE the personal folder window you left open in the previous exercise.

1. Click the **Name** column heading in the File list. Windows Vista arranges the File list into descending alphabetical order by name, sorting the files at the top of the list, followed by the folders. It should look similar to the one in Figure 4-7. Notice that there is a small arrowhead at the top of the Name column. The arrowhead displays in the column that is used for the sort. The arrow points down when the sort is descending and up when the sort is ascending.

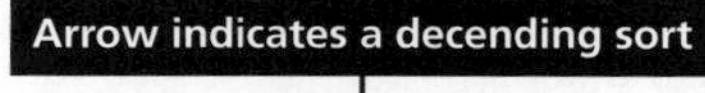

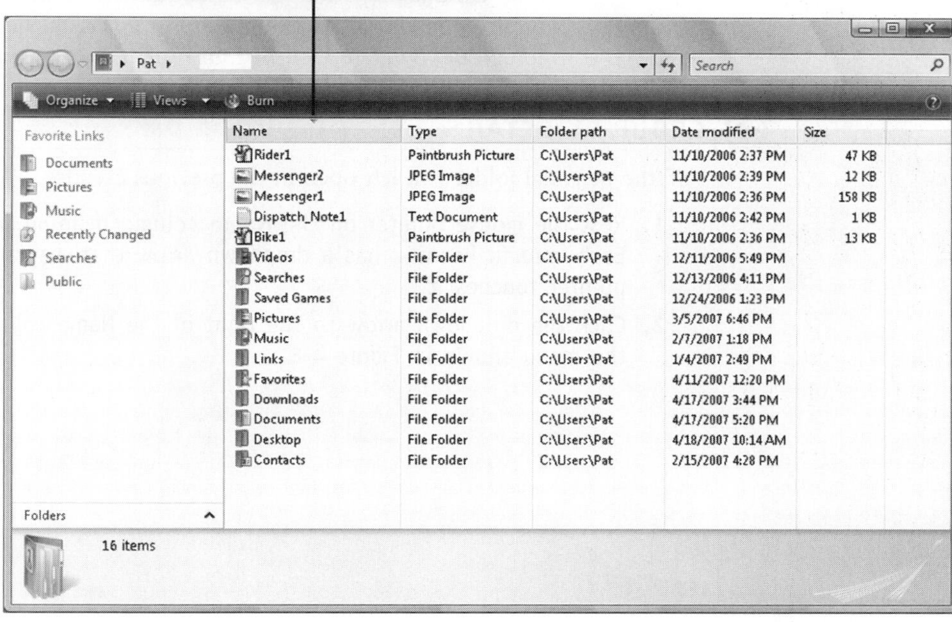

Figure 4-7

Descending alphabetical sort order by Name

If the arrow points up, the list is in ascending order. Click the heading again to reverse the sort into descending order.

2. Click the **Name** column heading again. Windows Vista reverses the sort into ascending order. Notice that the folders are sorted alphabetically at the top, followed by the files. Also, notice that the arrowhead now points up, indicating the sort is ascending.

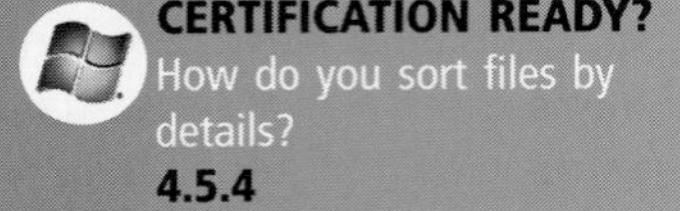

When you rest the mouse pointer on a column heading, a dropdown arrow displays. Click the arrow to display a menu, then click Sort to sort the File list by that column.

3. Click the **Date modified** column heading. Windows Vista sorts the columns chronologically by date modified, in descending order.
4. Click the **Type** column heading to sort the list by Type, alphabetically in ascending order. Notice that each time you sort, the sort order is reversed, even if you are sorting by a different detail.
5. Click the **Size** column heading to sort the list by Size in descending order, then click it again to reverse the sort into ascending order.
6. At this point your instructor may ask you to capture an image of your personal folder. Save it as ***Le04_03*** in your Lesson 4 assessment folder.

CERTIFICATION READY?
How do you sort files by details?
4.5.4

PAUSE. LEAVE the personal folder open to use in the next exercise.

You may have noticed that column headings display even when you select a File list view other than Details. Therefore, you can use the column headings to sort the File list in any view. Simply click a column heading to sort the list and then click it again to reverse the sort order.

In the next section, you learn how to group items by details.

Grouping by Details

If a folder contains many items, grouping can help you organize them into smaller, more manageable lists. Groups may be alphabetical, numerical, or chronological, depending on the detail by which you choose to group. For example, you can group alphabetically by Name, chronologically by Date modified, or numerically by Size.

GROUP BY DETAILS

USE the personal folder you left open in the previous exercise.

1. Rest the mouse pointer on the **Name** column heading. A dropdown arrow displays. Each column heading has a dropdown arrow that displays only when the mouse pointer touches it.
2. Click the dropdown arrow to the right of the Name column heading to display the menu shown in Figure 4-8.

Figure 4-8

Dropdown menu

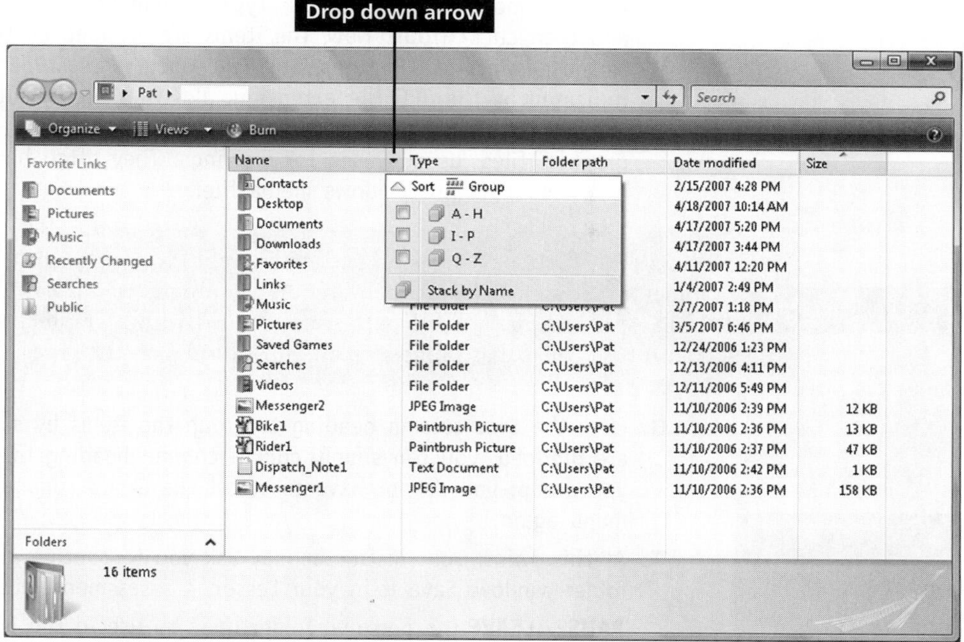

3. Click **Group** on the dropdown menu. Windows Vista arranges the items into alphabetical groups, as shown in Figure 4-9.

Figure 4-9

Items grouped alphabetically by Name

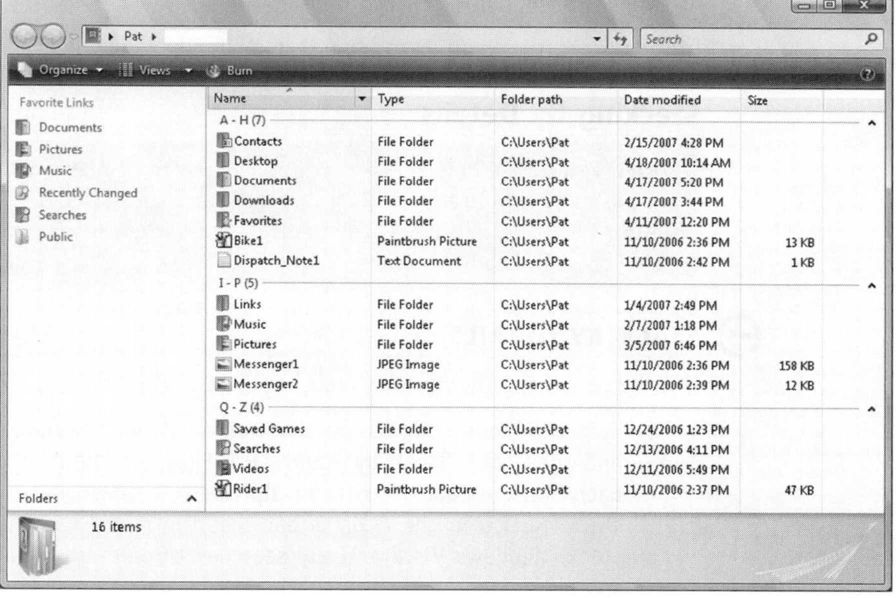

4. Rest the mouse pointer on the **Name** column heading, click the dropdown arrow, and then click **Sort**. Windows Vista removes the groups and sorts the list alphabetically by Name.

5. Rest the mouse pointer on the **Type** column heading, click the dropdown arrow, and then click **Group.** Now, the items are grouped by type: file folders, JPEG Images, Paintbrush Pictures, and Text Documents. ***JPEG*** is a graphics file type indicated by the JPG file extension. JPG files are usually used for photos. JPEG (or JPG) is short for joint photographic experts group. Paintbrush Pictures are also graphics files, usually used for drawings. They often have a WMF file extension, which is short for Windows media file.

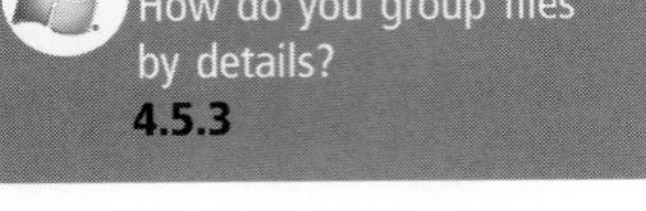

Recall that file types are associated with application programs, so the types listed in the folder window may vary, depending on the programs you have installed. For example, if on your computer WMF files are associated with a graphics program other than Paintbrush, then that program name may display as the type.

6. Click the **Size** column heading to group the items by size. Notice that once items are grouped, you can simply click a column heading to change the detail by which you group; you do not have to select the Group command from the dropdown menu again.

CERTIFICATION READY?
How do you group files by details?
4.5.3

7. At this point, your instructor may ask you to capture an image of your personal folder window. Save it in your Lesson 4 assessment folder as ***Le04_04***.

PAUSE. LEAVE the personal folder open to use in the next exercise.

When you group items, each group in the File list has a collapse/expand arrow in the upper right corner. If the arrow points up, click it to collapse—or hide—the group. If the arrow points down, click it to expand—or show—the group. This can be useful if you only want to work with the items in one group at a time.

In the next section, you learn how to stack items by details.

Stacking by Details

When you have a long File list, you may want to display the items as stacks. A ***stack*** is a collection of related files displayed as a single icon that looks like a pile of items. You double-click a stack to view the items in the stack. You can stack items based on any detail column heading.

STACK BY DETAILS

USE the personal folder window you left open in the previous exercise.

1. Rest the mouse pointer on the **Name** column heading, click the dropdown arrow, and then click **Stack by Name.** The Files list should look similar to Figure 4-10. Each stack is labeled with an alphabetical range and the number of items in the stack. Notice in the Address bar that the folder has changed. When you select to stack, Windows Vista actually searches through all items in the current folder and subfolders and then displays the stacks in a Search Results window. That is also why more items are in the stacks than are stored directly in the personal folder.

Figure 4-10

Items stacked by Name

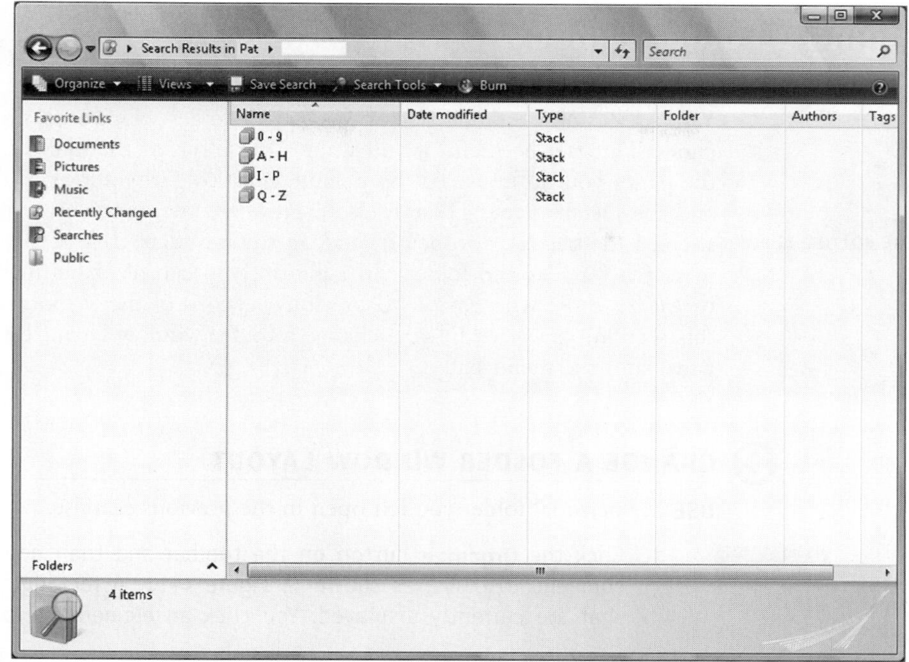

TROUBLESHOOTING The stacked items in your personal folder may not be exactly the same as those in the figure, depending on the files and folders you have stored in your personal folder.

2. Click the **Type** column heading to stack by Type. As with groups, once the list is stacked, you can just click a column heading to change the detail.
3. Scroll down and locate the Paintbrush Picture stack.

TROUBLESHOOTING If WMF files are associated with a different program on your computer, locate the stack for that program's files, or locate the WMF File stack.

4. Double-click the **Paintbrush Picture** stack to display the stacked items individually. The Bike1 and Rider1 files should be included in the File list. (You may have other Paintbrush Picture files as well.) At this point your instructor may ask you to capture an image of the Paintbrush Picture folder window. Save it in your Lesson 4 assessment folder as ***Le04_05***.
5. Click the **Back** button on the window's toolbar three times to navigate back to your personal folder. It should be sorted alphabetically by name.

PAUSE. LEAVE the personal folder open to use in the next exercise.

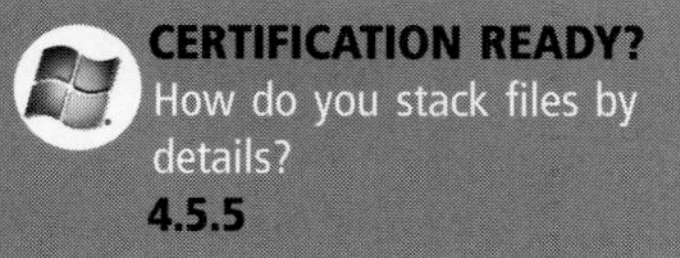
CERTIFICATION READY? How do you stack files by details?
4.5.5

Learn more about working with search folders in Lesson 6, "Searching for Files and Folders."

In the next section, you learn how to change the layout of a folder window.

■ Changing a Folder Window Layout

THE BOTTOM LINE

You can customize the layout of the current folder window by showing or hiding different panes. This can be useful if you want more room in the File list, because you can hide the panes you do not need. By default, most folder windows display the Navigation Pane and the Details Pane. There is also a Preview Pane, which you can use to preview a selected file before you open it, and, in some folders, a Search Pane, which you can use to search for files and folders. In addition, you can display a menu bar, which may be useful for those who have used previous versions of the Windows operating system. In this section, you learn how to change a folder window layout by showing and hiding panes and the menu bar.

CHANGE A FOLDER WINDOW LAYOUT

USE the personal folder you left open in the previous exercise.

1. Click the **Organize** button on the toolbar and then point to **Layout**. The Layout submenu displays, as shown in Figure 4-11. A rectangle is around the elements that are currently displayed. You click an element to toggle it off or on.

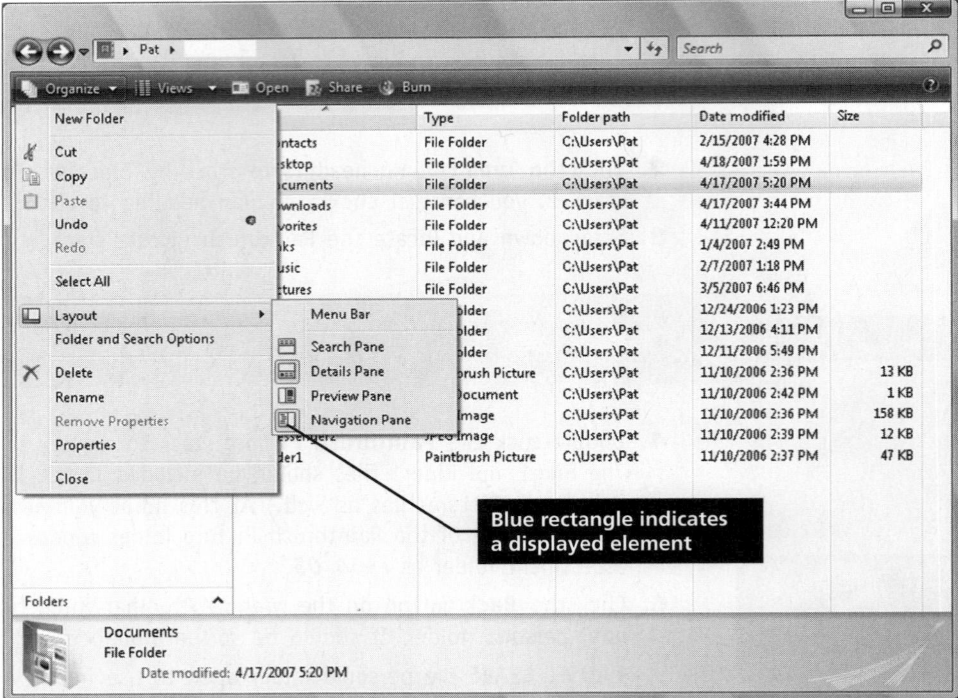

Figure 4-11
Layout submenu

2. Click **Details Pane**. The Details pane is hidden and no longer displays in the personal folder window.
3. Click the **Organize** button, point to **Layout**, and then click **Search Pane**. The Search pane displays between the Address bar and the toolbar.
4. Click **Organize**, point to **Layout**, and then click **Preview Pane**. The Preview pane displays, but no preview displays in it. You must select a file to see it in the Preview pane.
5. In the File list, click the ***Messenger1*** file. A preview of the file displays in the Preview pane, as shown in Figure 4-12.

Figure 4-12

Preview a file in the Preview pane

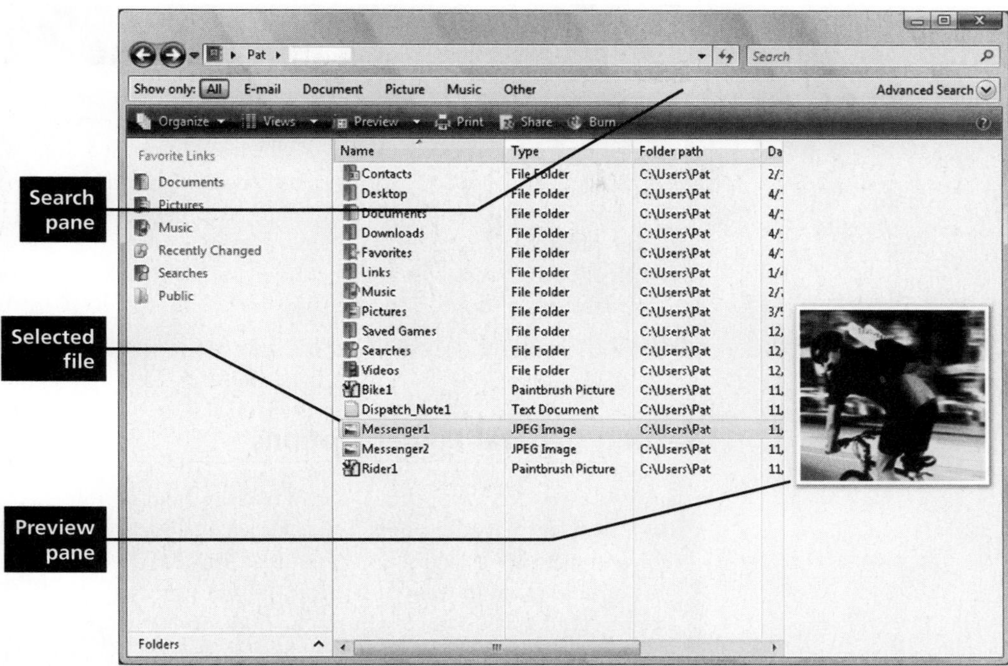

6. Click **Organize**, point to **Layout**, and then click **Menu Bar**. The menu bar displays above the toolbar. If you are familiar with versions of Windows prior to Windows Vista, you may feel comfortable using menu commands to control your folder windows.
7. Click **Documents** in the Navigation bar (or double-click it in the File list) to open the Documents folder. Notice that the changes you made to the layout of the panes in the personal folder window do not affect the Document window, but that the menu bar remains displayed.
8. Navigate back to your personal folder. At this point, your instructor may ask you to capture an image of your personal folder window. Save it in your lesson 4 assessment folder as ***Le04_06***.
9. Click **Organize**, point to **Layout**, and then click **Menu Bar** to hide the menu bar.
10. Click **Organize**, point to **Layout**, and then click **Preview Pane** to hide the Preview pane.
11. Click **Organize**, point to **Layout**, and then click **Search Pane** to hide the Search pane.
12. Click **Organize**, point to **Layout**, and then click **Details Pane** to display the Details pane.

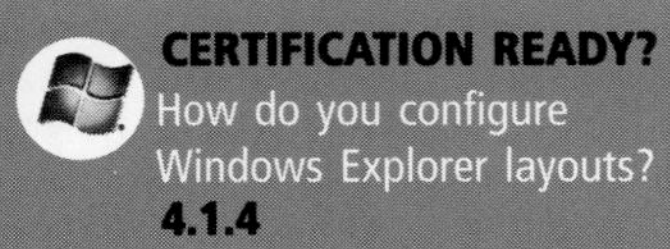

PAUSE. LEAVE the personal folder open to use in the next exercise.

The Search pane is not available in all folder windows. For example, it is available in your personal folder and in Computer, but not in Documents, Pictures, or Music.

As you saw in this exercise, the layout you configure in one folder window does not affect the layout of other windows. However, the configured folder retains the new layout until you change it again, even if you close the window.

Windows Vista frequently provides different ways to accomplish a single task. For example, you can view details about a file in the Details pane, or by using Details view. If you like Details view, you may decide you can keep the Details pane hidden, to make more room available in the File list area. Likewise, if you are working with Small Icons or Details view, you may find you need the Preview pane to preview a file. But, if you change to Large Icons, you may be able to preview the file on the icon itself.

In the next section, you learn how to manage folder options.

■ Managing Folder Options

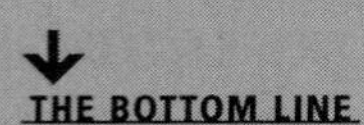

THE BOTTOM LINE

Folder options in Windows Vista let you manage the way all folder windows open and display. The folder options that you select apply to all folder windows. Folder options are organized into two categories: general options and advanced options.You can set general options to control basic features such as how many clicks it takes to open a folder, and you can set advanced options to control features such as whether to display hidden files and file extensions. In this section, you learn how to set general folder options and advanced folder options, and you also learn how to revert to the default Windows Vista folder option settings.

Setting General Folder Options

Instead of customizing the layout of each individual folder, you can use general folder options to display all folders in Classic view, which means that the Details pane and the Preview pane are hidden. You can also control how a folder window opens. By default, you double-click an item to open it, but you can set Windows Vista to open an item with a single click, which you might find more convenient. By default, each folder that you open replaces the contents of the current window. You can set Windows Vista to open each folder in a separate window.

SET GENERAL FOLDER OPTIONS

USE the personal folder you left open in the previous exercise.

1. Click the **Organize** button and then click **Folder and Search Options**. The General tab of the Folder Options dialog box displays, as shown in Figure 4-13. Table 4-1 describes the options on the General tab.

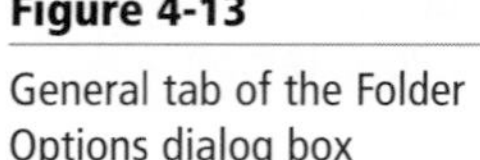

Figure 4-13

General tab of the Folder Options dialog box

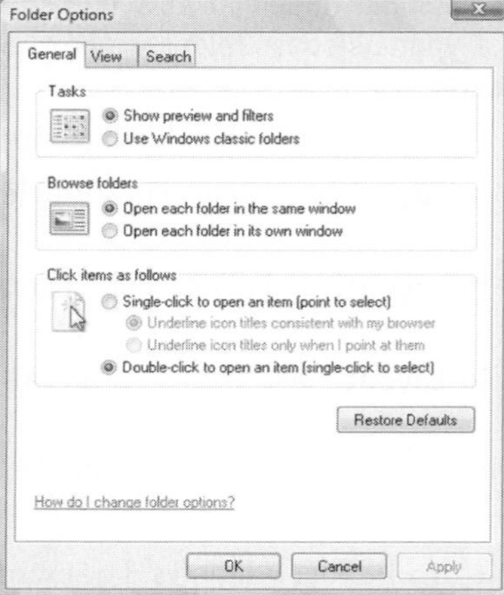

Table 4-1

General Folder Options

OPTION	DESCRIPTION
Show preview and filters	Makes the Details pane and the Preview pane available in folder windows. This is the default setting.
Use Windows classic folders	Hides the Details pane and the Preview pane and displays the menu bar in all folder windows.
Open each folder in the same window	Each folder replaces the contents of the current window. This is the default setting.
Open each folder in its own window	Each folder opens in a separate window.
Single-click to open an item (point to select)	Sets Windows Vista to open an item when you click it and to select an item when you point at it.
Underline icon titles consistent with my browser	Displays the names of icons with an underline, like a link to a web page. This option is only available if you select Single-click to open an item.
Underline icon titles only when I point at them	Display underlines when the mouse pointer rests on an icon name. This option is also only available if you select Single-click to open an item.
Double-click to open an item (single-click to select)	Sets Windows Vista to open an item when you double-click it, and to select an item when you click it. This is the default setting.

2. Click the **Use Windows classic folders** option button.
3. Click the **Open each folder in its own window** option button.
4. Click the **Single-click to open an item (point to select)** option button.
5. Click the **Underline icon titles consistent with my browser** option button.
6. Click **OK** to apply the changes and close the dialog box. All items in the File list in your personal folder are now underlined, and the menu bar displays.
7. Click the **Organize** button and then point to **Layout**. Notice that the Details pane and the Preview pane are not even available on the Layout menu.
8. Press **Esc** twice to cancel the menus and then click **Documents** in the File list. The Documents folder opens with a single click, in a separate window. Notice that the Back button on the toolbar is not available. That's because Documents opened in a new window so there is no window to navigate back to. Your personal folder is still open in a separate window.
9. Close the Documents folder window. Your personal folder window should display.
10. At this point, your instructor may ask you to capture an image of your personal folder window. Save it in your Lesson 4 assessment folder as ***Le04_07***.
11. Click **Organize** and then click **Folder and Search Options**.
12. On the General tab, click **Restore Defaults** to automatically select all of the default options and then click **OK**. Windows Vista restores the default settings so that the Details and Preview panes are available and the menu bar is hidden, and new windows open with a double click in the current window.

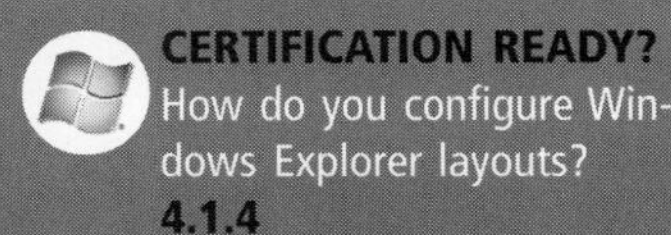

PAUSE. LEAVE the personal folder open to use in the next exercise.

Displaying folders in Classic view provides more room in the window to display the File list. This might be useful if you prefer using larger icons, or if you have a lot of items to display.

You might prefer opening each folder in a separate window if you are working with more than one folder at a time, because it lets you see multiple folder windows on your screen at once. However, the desktop can quickly become crowded with open windows.

In the next section, you learn how to set advanced folder options.

Setting Advanced Folder Options

Though the general folder options are mostly a matter of personal preference and convenience, you can also select advanced folder options to customize and control the information that displays in all folder windows. There is a long list of advanced settings, ranging from what information to show in ScreenTips to whether to show ScreenTips at all. In this section, you learn how to use the advanced settings to display file extensions, protected operating system files, and hidden files and folders. You also learn how to restore the default settings.

SET ADVANCED FOLDER OPTIONS

USE the personal folder you left open in the previous exercise.

1. Click the **Type** column heading dropdown arrow and then click **Group** to group the File list items by Type.
2. If necessary, click the **Type** column heading to sort the list in descending order.
3. Click the **Organize** button and then click **Folder and Search Options** to open the Folder Options dialog box.
4. Click the **View** tab. It should look similar to Figure 4-14. Under Advanced settings is a long list of available options.

Figure 4-14

View tab of the Folder Options dialog box

XREF

For information on setting the Hidden file attribute, refer to Lesson 3, "Organizing Files and Folders."

5. Scroll through the list to read the available options. Note which options are selected and which are not.
6. In the Advanced settings list, click to select the **Show hidden files and folders** option button. Selecting this option sets Windows Vista to display files and folders that have the Hidden file attribute selected.
7. Click to clear the **Hide extensions for known file types** checkbox. Clearing this option sets Windows Vista to display file extensions with filenames.
8. Click to clear the **Hide protected operating system files** checkbox. Clearing this option sets Windows Vista to display files that are part of the operating system. Windows Vista displays a Warning dialog box, asking if you are sure you want to display the protected operating system files.

9. Click **Yes** and then click **OK** in the dialog box to apply the changes and close the dialog box. The File list should look similar to Figure 4-15. Notice that there are more types and more items in the list, because hidden items are now displayed. Also, you can see the file extensions for each file in the list.

Figure 4-15

Hidden files and file extensions display in the File list

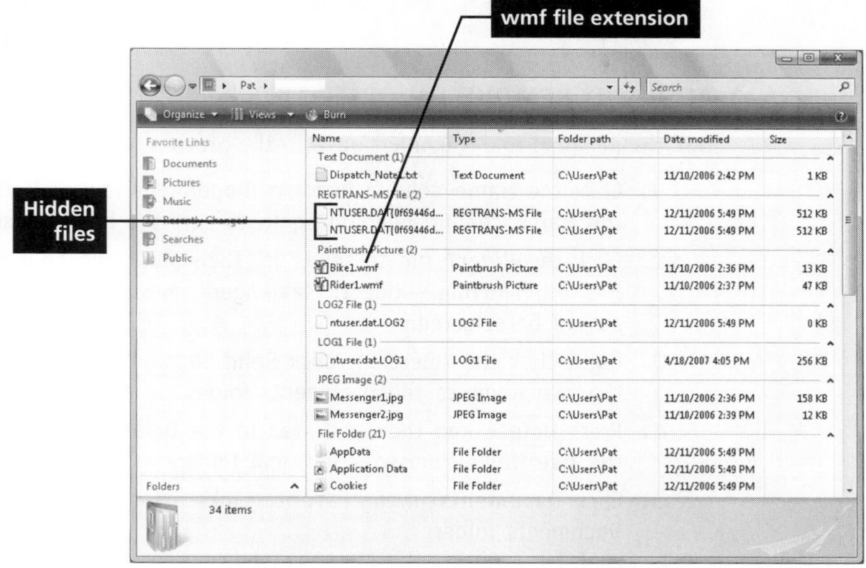

10. Click the **Organize** button and then click **Folder and Search Options**. Click the **View** tab.
11. Below the Advanced settings list, click **Restore Defaults** and then click **OK**. Windows Vista restores the default advanced settings. The hidden files, protected operating system files, and file extensions are now hidden.

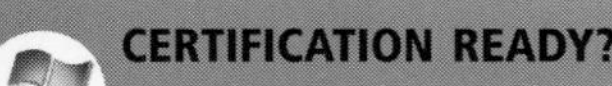

TAKE NOTE*

When hidden files and folders are displayed, their icons are dimmer than the icons of items that are not hidden.

CERTIFICATION READY?
How do you show and hide file extensions?
4.1.1
How do you show and hide protected operating system files?
4.1.2
How do you show hidden files and folders?
4.1.3

PAUSE. LEAVE the personal folder open to use in the next exercise.

Some of the advanced folder options can improve your computer's performance. For example, select the Always show icons, never thumbnails option to prohibit use of live previews. Live previews require more system resources and may slow down your computer, so if you prohibit them, your computer may run faster. If your system crashes frequently, you may want to select the Launch folder windows in a separate process option. It increases the stability of Windows Vista by opening every folder in a separate part of memory. However, there is a trade-off. Launching folder windows in a separate process requires more system resources, so it may slow down your computer's performance.

You may have noticed that at the top of the View tab in the Folder Options dialog box there are two buttons that you can use to customize folder views:

- Apply to Folders. Click this button to apply the current view settings to all folders of the same type. For example, if you want all picture folders to display in Tiles view, you can set any picture folder to display Tiles, open the Folder Options dialog box, and then click the Apply to Folders button.
- Reset Folders. Click this button to reset all folders to the default view settings.

In the next section, you learn how to add and remove items to the Favorite Links list.

■ Adding and Removing Favorite Links

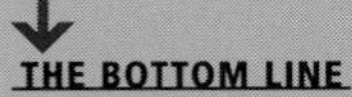

THE BOTTOM LINE

The Favorite Links list displays links to common locations, such as Documents, Pictures, and Music. You can add your own links to the list so that you can quickly and easily access the places you use most often. In this section, you learn how to add and remove Favorite links.

ADD AND REMOVE FAVORITE LINKS

USE the personal folder you left open in the previous exercise.

1. Click the **Name** column heading dropdown arrow and click **Sort.** If necessary, click the **Name** column heading again to sort the list in descending order.
2. Click the ***Rider1*** file to select it. Then press and hold **Shift** and click the ***Bike1*** file. All five files—Rider1, Messenger2, Messenger1, Dispatch_Note1, and Bike1—should be selected.
3. Right-click the selection, click **Send To**, and then click **Documents.** This copies the five items to the Documents folder.
4. Press **Delete** and then click **Yes** in the Delete Confirmation dialog box to delete the five items from your personal folder.
5. Click **Documents** in the Favorite Links list in the Navigation bar to open the Documents folder.
6. Click the **Views** button dropdown arrow and then click **Details** to change to Details view.
7. Right-click a blank area of the File list, click **New**, and then click **Folder**. Key **Consolidated** and press **Enter** to rename the new folder.
8. Select the five files—***Rider1***, ***Messenger2***, ***Messenger1***, ***Dispatch_Note1***, and ***Bike1***—and move them into the Consolidated folder.
9. Rest the mouse pointer on the **Consolidated** folder icon and then press and hold the left mouse button.
10. Drag the folder icon to the Favorite Links list. Release the mouse button when the ScreenTip displays **Create link in Links**, and a horizontal bar displays at the bottom of the list, as shown in Figure 4-16. When you release the mouse button, Windows Vista adds the folder to the Favorite Links list.

TROUBLESHOOTING

You can use the Cut and Paste or Drag and Drop method to move the files. Moving files is covered in Lesson 3.

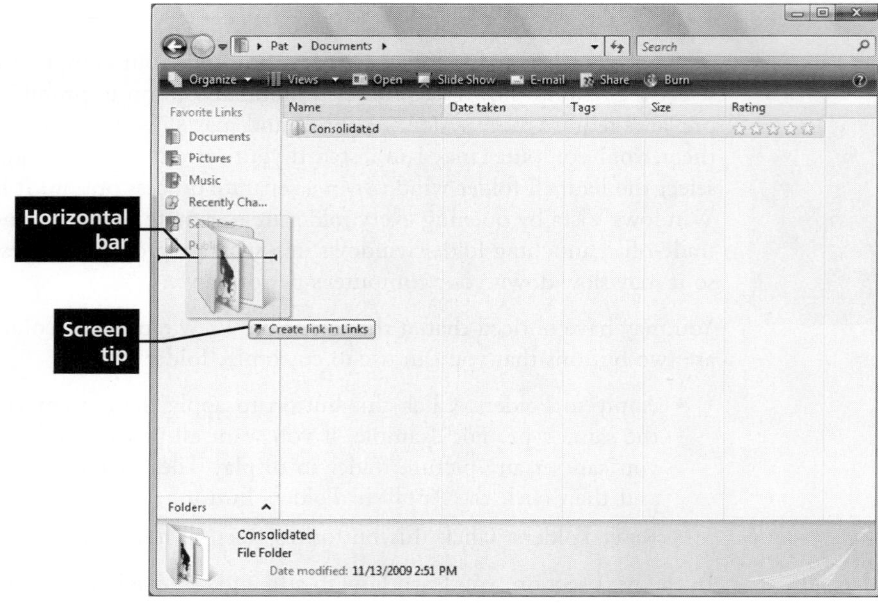

Figure 4-16

Drag an item to the Favorite Links list

11. Navigate back to your personal folder. Notice that the link to the Consolidated folder displays in the Favorite Links list, as shown in Figure 4-17.

Figure 4-17

New item in the Favorites Links list

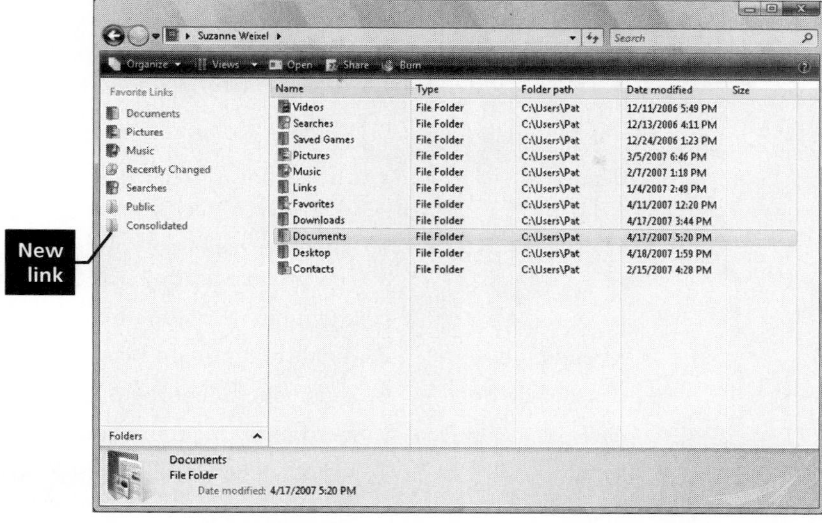

12. Click **Consolidated** in the Favorite Links list to open the Consolidated folder.
13. At this point, your instructor may ask you to capture an image of the Consolidated folder window. Save it in your Lesson 4 assessment folder as ***Le04_08***.
14. Navigate back to your personal folder.
15. Right-click **Consolidated** in the Favorite Links list and then click **Remove Link** on the shortcut menu. Click **Yes** in the Delete File confirmation dialog box. Consolidated is removed from the Favorite Links list, but the Consolidated folder remains stored in Documents.
16. Navigate to the Documents folder and delete the Consolidated folder.
17. **CLOSE** the Documents folder window.

LOG OFF your Windows Vista account.

CERTIFICATION READY?
How do you add folders to the Favorite Links list?
4.2.4

You can rearrange items in the list by dragging them up or down. You can also drag items from the Folders list to the Favorite Links list.

Removing an item from the Favorites list does not delete the original item, just the link to the item.

SUMMARY SKILL MATRIX

In This Lesson You Learned	Matrix Skill	Skill Number
To change the icon size	Change the way files are displayed within folders	4.5.1
To display or hide details	Display or hide file and folder details	4.5.2
To sort by details	Sort files by details	4.5.4
To group by details	Group files by details	4.5.3
To stack by details	Stack files by details	4.5.5
To change a folder window layout	Configure Windows Explorer layouts	4.1.4
To set general folder options	Configure Windows Explorer layouts	4.1.4
To set advanced folder options	Show and hide file extensions; Show and hide protected operating system files; Show hidden files and folders	4.1.1 4.1.2 4.1.3
To add and remove Favorite links	Add folders to the Favorite Links list	4.2.4

■ Knowledge Assessment

Matching

Match the term in Column 1 to its description in Column 2.

Column 1	Column 2
1. details	**a.** a collection of related files displayed as a single icon that looks like a pile of items
2. tiles	**b.** sorted alphabetically from A to Z, numerically from 0 to 9, or chronologically from oldest to newest
3. byte	**c.** a graphics file type often used for photos
4. ascending order	**d.** about one million bytes
5. descending order	**e.** about one billion bytes
6. chronologically	**f.** specific information about a file or folder
7. stack	**g.** sorted alphabetically from Z to A, numerically from 9 to 0, or chronologically from newest to oldest
8. JPG	**h.** a unit of data representing one character
9. gigabyte	**i.** by date
10. megabyte	**j.** medium-sized icons with a label displaying the item name and type

True/False

Circle T if the statement is true or F if the statement is false.

T | F **1.** You cannot change the size of icons in the File list.

T | F **2.** Some details are for specific types of files.

T | F **3.** You cannot rearrange the order of the details columns in the File list.

T | F **4.** You can sort the File list based on the details in any column heading.

T | F **5.** Each time you click a column heading, the sort order is reversed.

T | F **6.** When you stack items, Windows Vista displays the stacks in a Search Results window.

T | F **7.** In Windows classic folders, the Details pane and the Preview pane are hidden, and the menu bar displays.

T | F **8.** By default, you single-click a folder icon to open the folder window.

T | F **9.** By default, file extensions display in all File lists.

T | F **10.** When you delete a folder from the Favorite Links list, you delete the folder from its original storage location as well.

■ Competency Assessment

Project 4-1: Locate the Most Recent Financial Information

You work as an account assistant at an insurance company. Your manager is attending a meeting at corporate headquarters, but she forgot to bring along the most recent financial information. In this exercise, you organize a list of files so that you can identify the most recent spreadsheet and send her the information she needs.

GET READY. Before you begin these steps, start your computer and log on to your Windows Vista account. Close all open windows so you can see the desktop. In addition, have on hand a piece of paper and a pen or pencil, or create a file or online journal where you can record information.

1. Click the **Start** button and then click **Documents**.
2. Right-click a blank area of the File list, click **New**, and then click **Folder**.
3. Key **Financial Data** and press **Enter** to rename the folder.
4. Copy the files ***Financial_Memo***, ***Sales_Letter***, ***Monthly_Sales***, ***Monthly_Data***, ***Monthly_Info***, and ***Updated_Info*** from the data files for this lesson to the Financial Data folder. Then open the Financial Data folder window.
5. Click the arrow to the right of the Views button on the window's toolbar.
6. Click **Details** to change the File list view.
7. Rest the mouse pointer on the **Type** column heading.
8. Click the dropdown arrow and then click **Group** to group the items by type.
9. Right-click any column heading and then click **More...** to display the Choose Details dialog box.
10. Scroll down the Details list and then click to select the **Date created** checkbox.
11. Click to select the **Date created** detail and then click the **Move Up** button as many times as necessary to position the detail below Name and above Date modified in the list.
12. Scroll down the list and then click to select the **Subject** checkbox.
13. Click **OK**.
14. If necessary, maximize the window to display all detail columns.
15. Rest the mouse pointer on the Date modified column heading, click the dropdown arrow, and then click **Sort** to sort the items by date modified.
16. If necessary, click the **Date modified** column heading to sort the list into descending order. The most recently modified file should display at the top of the list.
17. Record the name of the most recently modified file on a piece of paper, in a file, or in an online journal along with the date modified, date created, and subject details.
18. If requested by your instructor, capture an image of the Financial Data folder window. Save it in your Lesson 4 assessment folder as ***Proj04_01***.
19. **CLOSE** the Financial Data folder window.

PAUSE. LEAVE the desktop displayed and keep the piece of paper and pen or pencil or file or online journal handy to use in upcoming projects.

The ***Financial_Memo***, ***Sales_Letter***, ***Monthly_Sales***, ***Monthly_Data***, ***Monthly_Info***, and ***Updated_Info*** files are available on the companion CD-ROM.

Project 4-2: Experiment with Layouts and Views

You have recently started a new job at an advertising agency, and you have a brand new Windows Vista computer. During your lunch hour, you want to spend some time experimenting with different settings to find the ones that you are most comfortable with. In this project, you will use your personal folder to try out different layouts and views, and to practice arranging items in the File list.

1. Click the **Start** button and then click your personal folder.
2. Click the arrow to the right of the Views button on the window's toolbar to see the dropdown Views menu and then click **Extra Large Icons** to increase the size of the icons in the File list.
3. Click the arrow to the right of the Views button again and then click **Small Icons** on the dropdown menu to decrease the size of the icons in the File list.
4. Click the **Name** column heading to sort the File list in ascending alphabetical order. If the list is in descending order, click the column heading again to reverse the sort.

5. Rest the mouse pointer on the Name column heading so that a dropdown arrow displays. Click the dropdown arrow and then click **Group** to group the items alphabetically by name.
6. Rest the mouse pointer on the Name column heading again, click the dropdown arrow, and then click **Stack by Name** to stack the items alphabetically by name.
7. Double-click the **Q-Z** stack to open it.
8. Navigate back to the personal folder window.
9. Click the **Organize** button, point to **Layout**, and then click **Details Pane** to hide the Details pane.
10. Click the **Organize** button, point to **Layout**, and then click **Navigation Pane** to hide the Navigation pane.
11. Click the arrow to the right of the Views button and click **Large Icons**.
12. Click the **Organize** button, point to **Layout**, and then click **Navigation Pane** to display the Navigation pane.
13. Drag the **Videos** icon from the File list to the bottom of the Favorite Links list in the Navigation pane.
14. Click the **Organize** button and then click **Folder and Search Options** to open the Folder Options dialog box.
15. Click to select the **Open each folder in its own window** option button.
16. Click the **View** tab.
17. Click to select the **Show hidden files and folders** options button and then click **OK**.
18. Double-click the **Documents** folder icon in the File list. Documents should open in a separate folder window.
19. Close the Documents folder window.
20. At this point your instructor may ask you to capture an image of your personal folder window. Save it in your Lesson 4 assessment folder as ***Proj04_02***.
21. Click the arrow to the right of the Views button on the window's toolbar and click **Tiles** on the dropdown menu.
22. Click the **Organize** button, point to **Layout**, and then click **Details Pane** to display the Details pane.
23. Click the **Organize** button and then click **Folder and Search Options**. Click the **Restore Defaults** button.
24. Click the **View** tab, click the **Restore Defaults** button, and then click **OK**.
25. Right-click **Videos in the Favorite Links list**, click **Remove Link**, and then click **Yes**.
26. **CLOSE** your personal folder window.

PAUSE. LEAVE the desktop displayed to use in the next project.

■ Proficiency Assessment

Project 4-3: Classic Windows

The regional sales manager for the insurance company is scheduled to visit your office and will need to use your computer to review the financial files. He is accustomed to using a previous version of Windows. In this project, you prepare your computer for him by configuring Windows Explorer to use classic folders and to open items using a single click. You also add a link to the Financial Data folder to the Favorite Links list so he can access it easily from any folder location. When he cancels the visit, you revert all settings to the defaults.

1. **OPEN** the **Documents** folder.
2. Click the **Organize** button and then click **Folder and Search Options** to display the Folder Options dialog box.

3. Click to select the **Use Windows classic folders** option button.
4. Click to select the **Single-click to open an item (point to select)** and then **Underline icon titles only when I point at them** option buttons. Then click **OK**.
5. Drag the **Financial Data** folder icon to the bottom of the Favorite Links list in the Navigation bar.
6. Click **Financial Data** in the Favorite Links list to open the folder.
7. At this point your instructor may ask you to capture an image of the Financial Data folder window. Save it in your Lesson 4 assessment folder as ***Proj04_03***.
8. Click the **Organize** button and then click **Folder and Search Options**.
9. Click the **Restore Defaults** button and then click **OK**.
10. Right-click **Financial Data** in the Favorite Links list and then click **Remove Link** on the shortcut menu.
11. Click **Yes** in the confirmation dialog box to remove the link
12. **CLOSE** the **Financial Data** folder.

PAUSE. LEAVE the desktop displayed to use in the next project.

Project 4-4: Yard Sale Pictures

You are preparing a flyer announcing a yard sale, and you want to include a picture. A friend gave you a group of picture files, but the filenames are not descriptive, and you are not sure what graphics file type they are. In this project, you will change the folder layout so that you can preview the files without opening them. You will also select to display file extensions so you can identify the file types.

The ***Yard_Sale1***, ***Yard_Sale2***, ***Yard_Sale3***, and ***Yard_Sale4*** files are available on the companion CD-ROM.

1. Click the **Start** button and then click **Documents**.
2. Right-click a blank area of the File list, click **New**, and then click **Folder**. Key **Yard Sale Pictures** and press Enter to rename the folder.
3. Copy the files ***Yard_Sale1***, ***Yard_Sale2***, ***Yard_Sale3***, and ***Yard_Sale4*** from the data files for this lesson to the Yard Sale Pictures folder. Then open the Yard Sale Pictures folder window.
4. Click the arrow to the right of the Views button on the window's toolbar and then click **Details** to change the File list view.
5. Click the **Organize** button, click **Folder and Search Options**, and then click the **View** tab.
6. Click to clear the **Hide extensions for known file types** checkbox and then click **OK**.
7. In the Yard Sale Pictures folder window, click the **Organize** button, click **Layout**, and then click **Preview Pane** to display the Preview pane.
8. Click the ***Yard_Sale1*** file to select it. A preview should display in the Preview pane.
9. Click the ***Yard_Sale2*** file to select it and see its preview.
10. Click the ***Yard_Sale3*** file to preview it.
11. Click the ***Yard_Sale4*** file to preview it.
12. At this point your instructor may ask you to capture an image of the Yard Sale Pictures folder window. Save it in your Lesson 4 assessment folder as ***Proj04_04***.
13. On your piece of paper in a file, or in an online journal, record the full filename and extension of all four picture files. Then indicate which picture you think would look best in the flyer.
14. In the Yard Sale Pictures folder window, click the **Organize** button, click **Layout**, and then click **Preview Pane** to hide the Preview pane.

15. Click the **Organize** button, click **Folder and Search Options**, and then click the **View** tab.
16. Click to select the **Hide extensions for known file types** checkbox and then click **OK**.
17. **CLOSE** the **Yard Sale Pictures** folder window.

PAUSE. LEAVE the desktop displayed and keep the piece of paper and pen or pencil, or file or online journal handy to use in the next project.

■ Mastery Assessment

Project 4-5: Copy Spreadsheet Files

The account manager you work with came back from corporate headquarters with additional financial data files. She wants you to put all of the spreadsheet files on a removable device so she can take them with her when she travels to visit clients. In this project, you copy the additional files into the Financial Data folder and then organize them by type. You then copy all of the spreadsheet files to a removable device.

GET READY. Before you begin these steps, insert a blank disk such as a CD or DVD into the appropriate drive, or attach a device such as a Flash drive to a USB port. If necessary, close the AutoPlay window.

The ***Northeast_Sales***, ***Midatlantic_Sales***, ***Sale_Tips***, and ***Pie_Chart*** files are available on the companion CD-ROM.

1. Copy the files ***Northeast_Sales***, ***Midatlantic_Sales***, ***Sale_Tips***, and ***Pie_Chart*** from the data files for this lesson to the Financial Data folder. Then open the Financial Data folder window.
2. Change to Details view, if necessary.
3. Select to show only the following details: Name, Date modified, Type, Size, and Tags.
4. Sort the items chronologically in ascending order by Date modified.
5. Group the items by type.
6. Select all Excel Worksheet files and copy them to the removable device. Alternatively, your instructor may ask you to copy them to a subfolder named Spreadsheets in your Lesson 4 assessment folder.
7. If you are using a CD or DVD, when the device is finished copying the files, remove the disk and label it with your name, the date, and the title, Spreadsheets.
8. Sort the items in the Financial Data folder in ascending alphabetical order by Name.
9. Navigate to the Documents folder.
10. Delete the Financial Data folder.
11. **CLOSE** the Documents folder.

PAUSE. LEAVE the desktop displayed to use in the next project.

Project 4-6: Select a Picture by Size

A friend was inspired by your yard sale to hold one of her own. She would like to create a flyer similar to yours and has asked you to copy one of your picture files to a removable disk for her to use. She does not care what the picture looks like, but she wants it to be a bitmap image and she needs a small file size. In this project, you organize the yard sale pictures so that you can identify the smallest bitmap image picture file, which you then copy to a removable device.

GET READY. Before you begin these steps, insert a blank disk such as a CD into the appropriate drive, or attach a device such as a Flash drive to a USB port. If necessary, close the AutoPlay window.

1. Open the **Yard Sale Pictures** folder window.
2. Change the view to Details, if necessary.
3. Sort the items by Size, in ascending order.
4. Display the Type detail.
5. Group the items by type. You should be able to identify the smallest bitmap image file.
6. Copy the smallest bitmap image file to the removable device. Alternatively, your instructor may ask you to copy it to a subfolder named Yard Sale Picture in your Lesson 4 assessment folder.
7. If you are using a CD or DVD, when the device is finished copying the files, remove the disk and label it with your name, the date, and the title, Yard Sale Picture.
8. At this point your instructor may ask you to capture an image of the Yard Sale Pictures folder. Save it in your Lesson 4 assessment folder with the name ***Proj04_06***.
9. Navigate to the Documents folder.
10. Delete the Yard Sale Pictures folder.

LOG OFF your Windows Vista user account.

INTERNET READY

Consolidated Messenger is a bicycle delivery service in a large urban community. In this exercise, use Internet search tools to locate information about the equipment a bike messenger might need, such as a bike, a helmet, and a bag. Additional equipment might include specialized apparel such as shoes and rain gear. Once you have identified the equipment, create a budget detailing how much someone might expect to spend to get started as a bike messenger. You can set up the budget in a spreadsheet, such as an Excel worksheet file, or write it out on paper.

Working with Multimedia Files

LESSON SKILL MATRIX

Skills	Matrix Skill	Skill Number
Previewing Media Files		
Customizing Folders for Specific File Types	Set the folder type	4.2.6
Managing Multimedia Files		
Burning Files to a CD or DVD	Copy data files to a CD or DVD	4.6.4

The School of Fine Art offers classes in visual and performing arts to people of all ages. Its marketing department is preparing a multimedia presentation to promote the school's programs. The presentation will incorporate graphics, music, sound, and video. The multimedia files are all in digital format so they can be stored and organized using Windows Vista. In this lesson, you will learn how to work with multimedia files in the Windows Vista environment. Specifically, you will learn how to view graphics files and how to play music, sound, and video files. You will learn how to create folders customized for a specific multimedia file type, how to acquire multimedia files, and how to copy multimedia files to a CD or DVD.

KEY TERMS

AutoPlay
burn
Controller toolbar
frame
Live File System
loop
mastered
multimedia
playlist
shuffle
sound card
template
WMA
WMV

■ Previewing Media Files

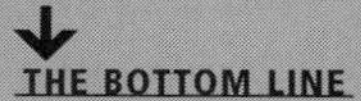

Windows Vista includes tools that help you organize and manage your multimedia files. ***Multimedia*** files store audio, graphics, animation, and video in digital format. In this section, you learn how to use Windows Vista to preview picture files and to play audio and video files in a media player program. You use the sample pictures, music, and video files that come with Windows Vista.

Previewing Picture Files

A picture file contains graphics such as photographs, drawings, or cartoons. By default, pictures display in Large Icons view, but you can change the view in a folder by using the same views you use for other files, such as Details. You can also use the Preview pane to preview a picture file before opening it. In addition, if a folder stores picture files, Windows Vista offers a Slide Show view, which you can use to display full-screen sized pictures.

PREVIEW PICTURE FILES

Refer to Table 2-1 in Lesson 2, "Working with Files and Folders," for information about other graphics file types.

Refer to Lesson 4, "Customizing Windows Explorer," for information about folder views.

GET READY. Before you begin these steps, start your computer and log on to your Windows Vista account. Close all open windows so you can see the desktop. Create a new folder named Lesson 5 in a storage location specified by your instructor, where you can store assessment files and folders that you create during this lesson.

1. Click the **Start** button and then click **Pictures** to open the Pictures folder.
2. Double-click the **Sample Pictures** shortcut in the File list to open the Sample Pictures folder. This folder stores sample picture files that come with Windows Vista. By default, the items display in Large Icons view, so you can see the content of each file. The files are all in JPG format, which is a common graphics file format for digital photographs.
3. Click the **Autumn Leaves** picture file. The folder window should look similar to Figure 5-1. Notice that the Details pane displays information specific to a picture file, such as the Date taken and the Dimensions. Also notice that the toolbar displays buttons useful for managing picture files.

Figure 5-1

The Sample Pictures folder

TROUBLESHOOTING

If the Details pane is not displayed, click the Organize button, point to Layout, and then click Details Pane.

4. Click the dropdown arrow to the right of the Views button on the window's toolbar and then click **Small Icons**. In Small Icons view, there is no preview of the image on the icon, so you cannot see the file's content.
5. Click the **Organize** button, point to **Layout**, and then click **Preview Pane** to display the Preview pane in the folder window. Now you can see a larger preview of the selected picture file.

TAKE NOTE

To make the preview larger, you can drag the border between the File list and the Preview pane to the left. As the width of the Preview pane increases, so does the size of the preview itself.

6. Click the **Slide Show** button on the window's toolbar to start displaying the pictures in the current folder as a Photo Gallery slide show. Recall that Windows Photo Gallery is a photo management program that comes with Windows Vista. In a slide show, each picture in the folder displays for a set amount of time, sized to fill the desktop. By default, the pictures ***loop*** in consecutive order. When pictures loop, they display continuously from beginning to end and back to the beginning again, without stopping.
7. Right-click the desktop. A shortcut menu displays commands for controlling the slide show, as shown in Figure 5-2. You can pause or exit the slide show, change the speed, view the next picture or the previous picture, or select to ***shuffle*** the pictures. Shuffle means to display the pictures in random order. You can also toggle off the loop command so that the slide show stops after the last picture displays.

Figure 5-2

Slide show shortcut menu

8. Click **Pause** on the shortcut menu. The slide show pauses.
9. Right-click the desktop and click **Slide Show Speed - Fast**. The slide show resumes playing at a faster speed.
10. Right-click the desktop and click **Shuffle**. The slide show continues, but now the pictures display in random order.
11. Right-click the desktop and click **Shuffle**. Right-click the desktop and click **Slide Show Speed - Medium**. This resets the slide show to the default settings.

TAKE NOTE* You can make any picture the desktop background. Simply open the folder where the picture file is stored, right-click the file in the File list, and then click Set as Desktop Background. You learn more about backgrounds in Lesson 7, "Personalizing the Windows Vista Workspace."

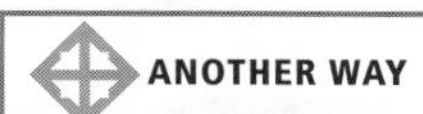

ANOTHER WAY

You can also cancel the slide show by pressing Esc on your keyboard.

12. Right-click the desktop and click **Exit**. The slide show closes. The Sample Pictures folder window still displays on the desktop.

PAUSE. LEAVE the Sample Pictures folder window open to use in the next exercise.

Windows Photo Gallery, which comes with Windows Vista, is a useful program for organizing picture files. You can use it to find and view files, as well as to add properties such as tags and ratings. You can even perform some basic modifications, such as rotating or cropping the picture content. For more information, consult Windows Help and Support.

You may have other graphics programs installed on your computer that you can use instead of Windows Photo Gallery. For example, you might have Microsoft Office Picture Manager, or Paint, or a program from a different manufacturer. Some graphics programs, such as Adobe's Fireworks or Photoshop, provide sophisticated picture creation and editing tools.

When you double-click a picture file in a File list, it opens in the graphics program that is set as the default on your computer. Alternatively, you can select the picture file, click the Open button dropdown arrow on the window's toolbar, and then click the name of the program you want to use to open the file.

In the next section, you learn how preview audio and video files.

Previewing Audio and Video Files

An audio file stores music or sound in digital format, and a video file stores video in digital format. A video file may store audio, as well. Audio and video files play using a media player program, such as Windows Media Player, which comes with Windows Vista. You can preview audio and video files in a folder by using the Preview pane.

PREVIEW AUDIO AND VIDEO FILES

GET READY. Before you begin these steps, make sure speakers are connected to your computer and turned on. If you do not have speakers, you will not be able to hear the audio.

USE the Sample Pictures folder window you left open in the previous exercise.

1. Click **Music** in the Favorite Links list in the Navigation pane of the Sample Pictures folder and then double-click the **Sample Music** shortcut in the File list. The Sample Music folder stores sample music files that come with Windows Vista. The files are all in ***WMA*** file format. WMA stands for Windows Media Audio file, which is a format commonly used for audio that will be played on a Windows-based computer. Table 5-1, located at the end of this exercise, describes some common audio and video file formats.
2. Display the Preview pane, if necessary, and then click the file named **Amanda** in the File list to select it. The folder window should look similar to Figure 5-3. Notice that the Details pane displays details specific to music files, such as the

artist and album names, the genre, and the length. The album cover art may display as well. In the Preview pane, the album cover displays with a ***controller toolbar***. A controller toolbar has buttons for playing, pausing, stopping, and sometimes rewinding or fast-forwarding a media file. In this case, it has a Play/Pause button, a Stop button, and a Switch to fill mode button, which you can use to play the file in the default media player program.

Figure 5-3

The Sample Music folder

TROUBLESHOOTING If Windows Media Player is not the default media player program on your computer, the folder window may display differently. The same functions should be available, however.

3. Click the **Play** button on the controller toolbar in the Preview pane. The music file plays, and the Play button changes to a Pause button.

TROUBLESHOOTING If the music does not play, check to be sure you have speakers connected correctly to your computer. If the speakers are connected, you may need to adjust the volume. Click the volume icon in the Notification area on the Taskbar and drag the slider up. If the slider is not available, click the Mute button.

4. Click the **Pause** button on the controller toolbar to pause the audio.
5. Click the **Play** button on the controller toolbar again. The music resumes playing from the point where it left off.
6. Click the **Stop** button on the controller toolbar to stop the audio.
7. Navigate to the Public Videos folder. For example, expand the Folders list in the Navigation pane, and click Public Videos, or click your personal folder and double-click Videos. In the Videos window, double-click the **Sample Videos** shortcut in the File list. The Sample Videos folder stores sample video files that come with Windows Vista. The files are all in ***WMV*** file format, which stands for Windows Media Video.

TAKE NOTE The sample video and music files that come with Windows Vista may be stored in the Public folder. Items stored in the Public folder are available to all people using the same computer or who have access to the computer on a network. You learn more about the Public folder in Lesson 14, "Collaborating with Others."

8. Click the **Bear** file to select it. The video file details display in the Details pane, and the last frame of the video displays in the Preview pane, above the controller toolbar, as shown in Figure 5-4. A ***frame*** is a single image in a video.
9. Click the **Play** button on the controller toolbar in the Preview pane. The video starts playing in the Preview pane. Because the video includes audio, you can hear the audio through your computer speakers as well.
10. When the video clip ends, close the Sample Videos folder window.

Figure 5-4

The Sample Videos folder

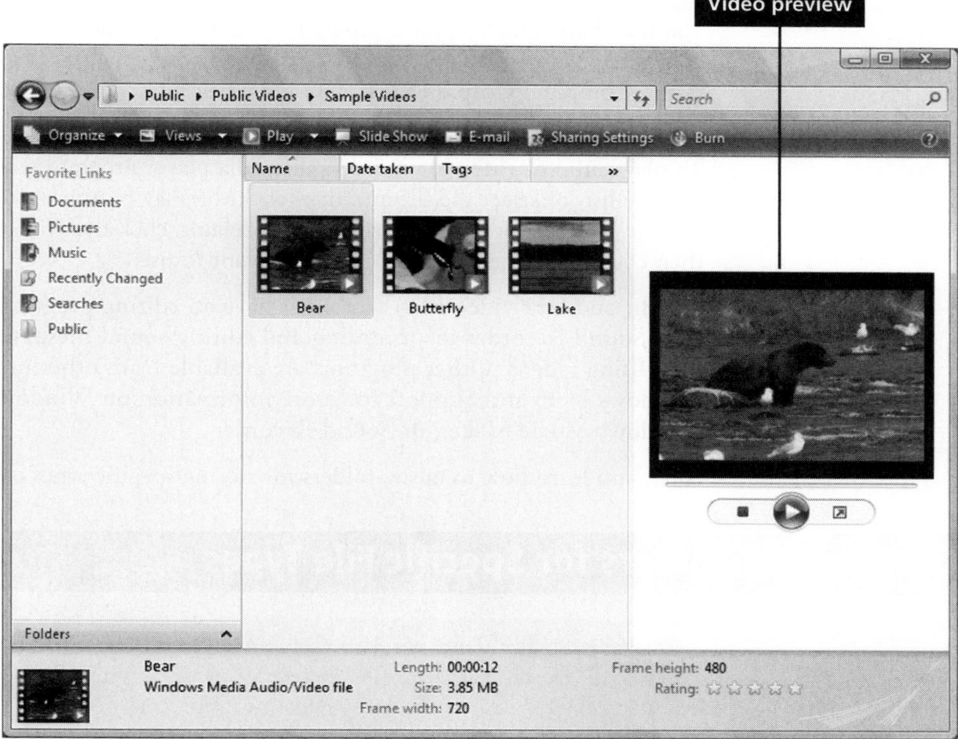

PAUSE. LEAVE the Windows Vista desktop displayed to use in the next exercise.

Table 5-1

Common audio and video file types

Filename extension	File type
.wma	Windows Media Audio file
.wav	Waveform sound file
.aiff	Audio Interchange File Format file
.cda	Compact Disk Digital Audio file
.midi	Musical Instrument Digital Interface file
.mp3, .mpg	Moving Pictures Experts Group file (used for both audio and video)
.wmv	Windows Media Video file
.avi	Audio Video Interleaved file
.mov	Apple QuickTime Movie file

To play audio, your computer must be equipped with a sound card and speakers. A ***sound card*** is a hardware device installed inside your computer that lets your computer input, process, and output sound. Some systems have built-in speakers, or you can attach speakers to a port on the outside of your computer.

In addition, you must have a media player program, such as Windows Media Player. Most media player programs let you play and organize audio and video files. For example, you can create ***playlists***, which are groups of audio or video files stored together for convenient playback; access the Internet to locate information about a song or artist; and copy files to a CD or DVD.

You may have a media player program other than Windows Media Player installed on your computer. Many media players are available for free, such as RealNetworks RealPlayer and Apple Computer Corp.'s QuickTime. However, not all audio and video file types are compatible with all media players.

To play audio or video in your default media player program, you can double-click the file in the File list, or select the file and then click the Play button on the storage folder window's toolbar. To use a program other than the default, click the Play button dropdown arrow and then click the name of the program you want to use.

To edit audio or video files, you must have an editing program. Windows Vista comes with Sound Recorder for recording and editing sound files, and Windows Movie Maker for editing videos. Other programs are available from other manufacturers. Consult Windows Help and Support for more information on Windows Media Player, Windows Movie Maker, or Sound Recorder.

Next, you learn how to create folders for storing specific types of multimedia files.

■ Customizing Folders for Specific File Types

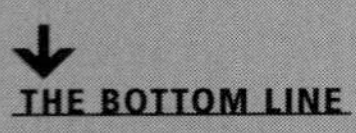

By default, a new folder is set to store any type of file, but you can customize folders for storing specific types of files including pictures and video, music, or documents. You can customize a new folder or an existing folder using options in the folder's Properties dialog box. Once you customize a folder, commands and features for managing the specified type of file become available. In this section, you learn how to customize folders for different types of files.

CUSTOMIZE FOLDERS FOR SPECIFIC FILE TYPES

1. Right-click a blank area of the desktop, point to **New** on the shortcut menu, and then click **Folder**. Key **Presentation** and press Enter to rename the folder.
2. Right-click the **Presentation** folder and click **Properties** to open the Presentation Files Properties dialog box. Click the **Customize** tab. In the Use this folder type as a template: box, you can see that the folder is set to the default All Items, which means it is not customized for any particular type of file. A ***template*** is a model that has certain characteristics or features that you may want to recreate.
3. Click the dropdown arrow in the Use this folder type as a template: box to display a list of available folder templates, as shown in Figure 5-5. You can select to customize the folder for All Items, Documents, Pictures and Videos, Music Details, or Music Icons.

Figure 5-5

Customize a folder

4. Click **Pictures and Videos** to customize the folder for storing picture and video files and then click **OK** to apply the change and close the dialog box.
5. Double-click the **Presentation** folder to open it.
6. Click **Start**, click **Pictures**, and then double-click the **Sample Pictures** shortcut.
7. Select the **Garden** and **Winter Leaves** files and then copy them to the Clipboard. (Recall that to select multiple files, you select the first, press and hold **Ctrl**, and then select the next.) Switch to the **Presentation** folder and paste the two files. Notice that the default folder view is Large Icons, and that the Slide Show button is available on the toolbar. In addition, the Preview Pane is still displayed. (At this point, your instructor may ask you to capture an image of the Presentation folder window. Save it in your Lesson 5 assessment folder as ***Le05_01***.)
8. Switch back to the **Sample Pictures** folder, click **Music** in the Navigation pane, and then double-click the **Sample Music** shortcut.
9. Select the **Amanda** and **Despertar** files and copy them to the Clipboard. Switch to the **Presentation** folder and paste the two files. Click a blank area of the File list to deselect the pasted files. Even though the files are music files, you can store them in the folder customized for pictures and video. Alternatively, you can create a folder customized for music.
10. Right-click a blank area of the File list, point to **New**, and then click **Folder**. Key **Songs** and press **Enter** to rename the new folder.
11. Right-click the **Songs** folder, click **Properties**, and then click the **Customize** tab.
12. Click the dropdown arrow in the Use this folder type as a template: box and then click **Music Details** on the dropdown list. Music Details customizes the folder to display details useful for managing music files. Click **OK** to apply the change and close the dialog box.
13. Move the two music files into the **Songs** folder and then open the Songs folder. The files display in Details view, and the commands on the toolbar are customized for music files, as shown in Figure 5-6.

Figure 5-6

Songs folder displaying Music Details

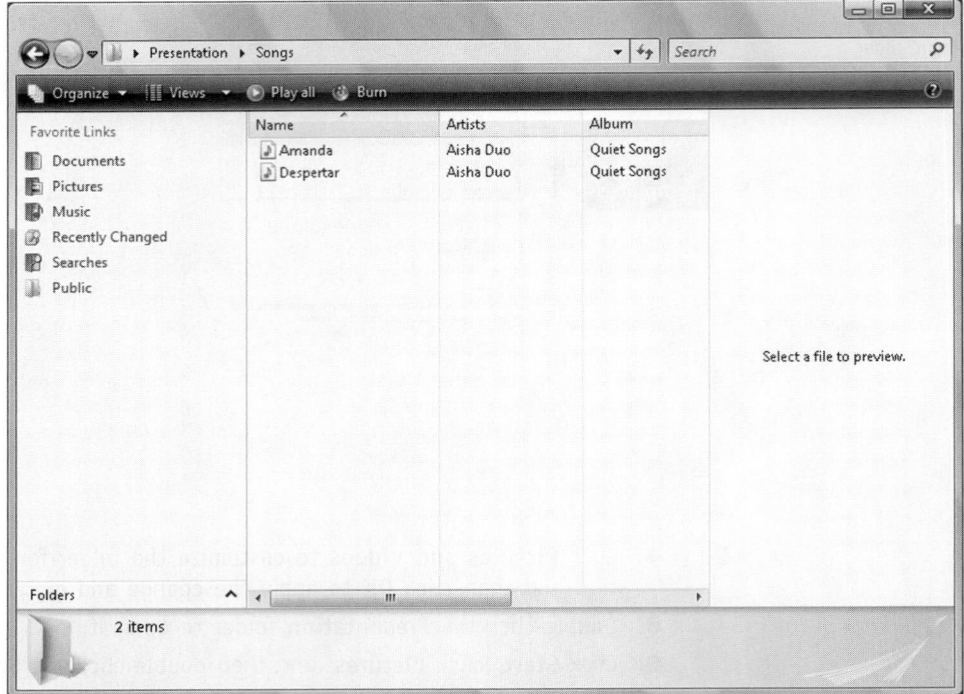

14. Click the **Back** button to return to the Presentation folder. Right-click the **Songs** folder, click **Properties**, and then click the **Customize** tab.
15. Click the dropdown arrow in the Use this folder type as a template: box and then click **Music Icons** on the dropdown list. Music Icons customizes the folder to open in Large Icons view. Click **OK** to apply the change and close the dialog box.
16. Open the **Songs** folder. It should look similar to Figure 5-7. Notice the view is Large Icons, and the Preview Pane does not display. (At this point, your instructor may ask you to capture an image of the Songs folder window. Save it in your Lesson 5 assessment folder as ***Le05_02***.

Figure 5-7

Songs folder displaying Music Icons

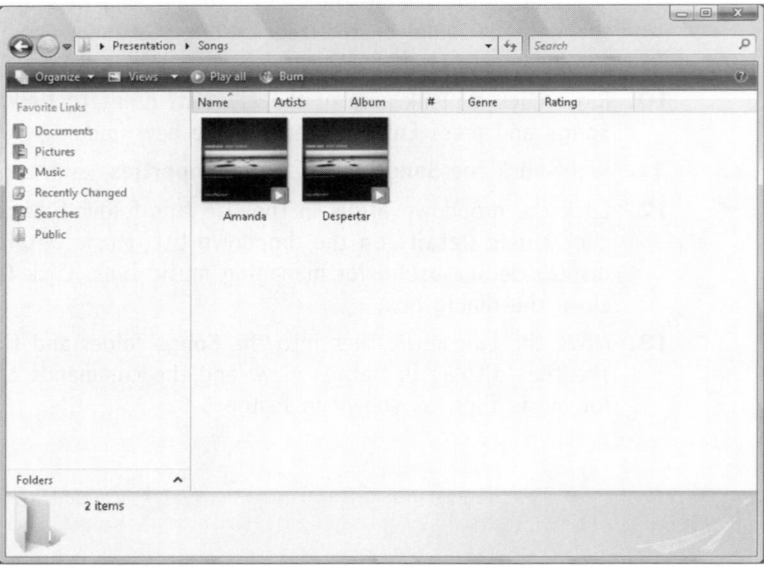

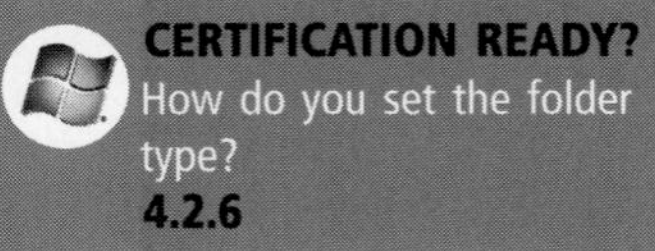

CERTIFICATION READY?
How do you set the folder type?
4.2.6

17. Navigate from the Songs folder back to the Presentation folder.

PAUSE. LEAVE the Presentation folder open to use in the next exercise.

In addition to the Pictures and Videos, Music Details, and Music Icons templates, you can select to customize a folder based on the Documents template. When you customize a folder for documents, it displays details useful for managing document files, such as Date modified, Type, and Size.

You can change the view and layout in a customized folder, and you can set folder options. If you change the view and want all folders of the same type to use that view, click Organize, Folder and Search Options, and click the View tab. At the top of the tab, click the Apply to Folders button and then click Yes. The view is applied to all folders of the same type.

You may have noticed that Windows Vista automatically customizes certain folders for specific file types. For example, Documents is customized for document files, Pictures is customized for picture files, Music for music files, and so on. When you create a sub folder in a customized folder, the sub folder assumes the same customization. That means that if you create a sub folder in Pictures, it is customized for picture files.

In addition, there are certain situations in which Windows Vista assumes that you are creating a folder for a specific file type. For example, if you store only video files in a folder, Windows Vista automatically applies the Pictures and Video template. If you store only music files in a folder, Windows Vista applies the Music Details template. Also, if you create a folder that includes the word *Pictures* in the folder name, Windows Vista applies the Pictures and Video template to customize the folder for pictures.

You can also customize the way the folder icon displays in a File list by using the options on the Customize tab of the folder's Properties dialog box. Click the Choose File button to select a file stored in the folder to display it on the folder icon. This can help you identify the contents of the folder. You can also change the icon itself. If you don't want to use the default folder icon, click the Change Icon button to select from a list of available icons.

In the next section, you learn how to acquire and manage multimedia files.

■ Managing Multimedia Files

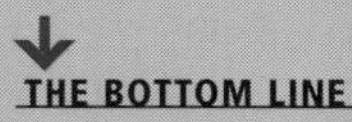

Many tasks associated with multimedia files are the same as for other types of files. For example, you can use the Copy, Cut, and Paste commands to copy or move them, and you can use the Delete command to send them to the Recycle Bin. However, there are also some unique tasks for managing multimedia files, such as importing pictures from a digital camera, creating a video DVD or a music CD, or printing photo-quality pictures. In this section, you will learn how to use Windows Vista to accomplish these tasks.

Importing Pictures

To be able to work with digital pictures, you must be able to import them from your digital camera. When you connect your camera to your computer — either using a cable or wireless connection — Windows Vista recognizes it and automatically starts the tools you need to import the pictures. In this section, you learn how to import pictures from your camera.

IMPORT PICTURES

TAKE NOTE

The first time you connect the camera, Windows Vista will automatically install the necessary device driver.

GET READY. Before you begin these steps, make sure you have a Windows Vista—compatible digital camera that contains pictures available for use, as well as the USB cord that you need to connect the camera to your computer. If you do not have a digital camera, you cannot complete the steps in this section. Skip ahead to the next section, "Printing a Picture."

USE the Presentation folder you left open in the previous exercise.

1. Plug the USB cord into the camera and then into the computer. Then turn on the camera. Windows Vista recognizes the camera and displays the AutoPlay dialog box

with options for managing the digital camera. It should look similar to Figure 5-8, although the name of the camera depends on the actual camera you have connected. ***AutoPlay*** is a feature of Windows Vista that selects a program or action to use whenever you work with digital media.

Figure 5-8

AutoPlay dialog box

TROUBLESHOOTING If the AutoPlay dialog box does not display, it may be turned off or set to display the contents of the camera in a folder window. In either case, navigate to the Computer folder, right-click your camera's icon, and click Import pictures on the shortcut menu.

2. In the AutoPlay dialog box, click **Import pictures**. The Importing Pictures and Videos dialog box displays, prompting you to add a tag to the pictures. This step is optional, but it can be useful if the pictures you are importing have a common characteristic. Windows Vista will use the tag to name the imported files and the folder in which they are stored, and the tag is added to the files' properties.

TAKE NOTE If you do not key a tag, the files will have the name assigned by the camera, which is usually a series of letters and numbers.

TAKE NOTE If you want to erase the pictures from your camera's storage device after importing, click to select the Erase after importing checkbox.

3. Click the **Tag these pictures (optional):** text box, key **Presentation**, and then click the **Import** button. Windows Vista begins importing the pictures. This may take a while, depending on the number of pictures you have to import. When the pictures are imported, Windows Vista displays them in the Windows Photo Gallery.
4. Close the Windows Photo Gallery window.
5. In the Presentation folder window, click **Pictures** in the Navigation pane to navigate to the Pictures folder. A new folder named with the current date and the tag you keyed in step 3 displays in the File list, as shown in Figure 5-9. This folder contains the picture files imported from the camera.

Figure 5-9

Imported pictures are stored in the Pictures folder

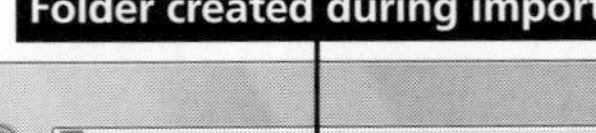

6. Double-click the new folder to open it. The files display in Large Icons view. Windows Vista automatically named them using the tag you keyed in step 3 and consecutive numbers. The window should look similar to Figure 5-10, although the pictures will be the ones imported from your camera.

Figure 5-10

Imported pictures

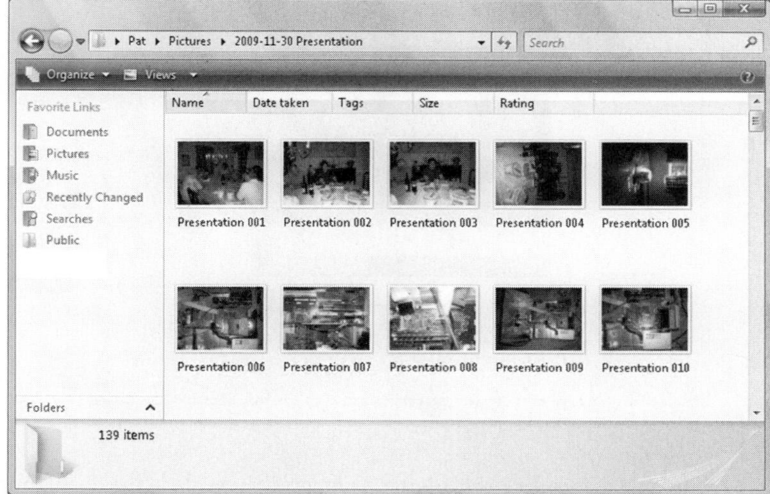

7. Turn off your camera and disconnect it from your computer,

   PAUSE. LEAVE the folder storing the imported pictures open to use in the next exercise.

Your camera may have come with software for importing and managing pictures. If so, this software may start automatically when you connect your camera to your computer. You can use it, or close it and use Windows Vista.

You can also import pictures from sources other than a digital camera. For example, you can use a scanner to import a printed picture into digital format, you can insert the camera's memory card directly into a drive or slot in your computer, or you can download them from the Internet.

In the next section, you learn how to print a picture.

Printing a Picture

Windows Vista also provides the tools you need to print a photograph directly from your computer. In this section, you print a photo.

PRINT A PICTURE

GET READY. Before you begin these steps, make sure your printer is correctly set up and connected to your computer, and that paper is loaded into the printer. If you have a photo-quality printer and photo paper, the result will be a photo-quality print. If not, you can still print the picture on a standard printer, using standard paper. You may use any picture imported from your camera to complete the following steps. If you did not import pictures from a camera, copy the ***Camel*** file from the data files for this lesson to the Presentation folder and then print it.

The ***Camel*** file is available on the companion CD-ROM.

USE the folder you left open in the previous exercise.

1. Right-click the picture you want to print and click **Print** on the shortcut menu. Windows Vista displays the first page of the Print Pictures wizard, as shown in Figure 5-11. A wizard is a series of dialog boxes that prompt you through the steps to complete a procedure.

Figure 5-11

Print Pictures wizard

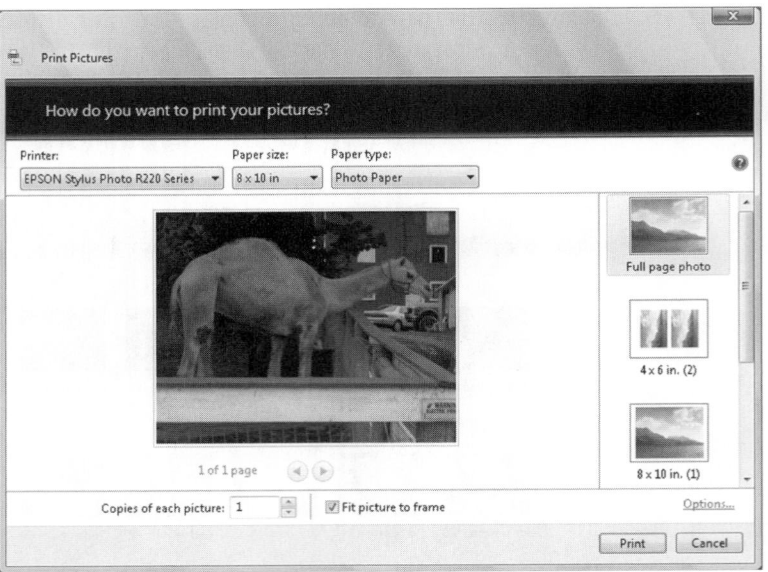

You can also select the file to print and then click the Print button on the window's toolbar to open the Print Pictures wizard.

2. Click the **Printer:** box dropdown arrow and click the printer you want to use.
3. Click the **Paper size:** box dropdown arrow and click the paper size you want to use.
4. Click the **Paper type**: box dropdown arrow and click the type of paper you want to use.
5. Click a layout in the Layout pane on the right side of the window.
6. Click the **Copies of each picture:** box and key the number of copies you want to print.
7. Click **Print** to print the picture. The Print Pictures wizard closes.
8. Navigate back to the Presentation folder, if necessary.

PAUSE. LEAVE the Presentation folder open to use in the next exercise.

Digital pictures are often sized differently from standard paper sizes, and therefore may print with a border around them. Select the Fit picture to frame option in the Print Pictures dialog box to resize the picture to fit the exact size of the paper.

In the printer's properties dialog box, you may be able to select additional options specific to your printer. For example, you may be able to view a preview or select a print quality. Click the Options link in the Print Pictures dialog box and then click Printer Properties to display properties specific to your printer.

In the next section, you learn how to copy pictures to a CD or DVD.

Burning Files to a CD or DVD

You can burn any type of file including pictures, music, and video to a CD or DVD so that you can view the files on a different computer, or even using a DVD player. ***Burn*** is simply another term for copying files to a disc. In this section, you learn how to burn files to a CD or DVD. The steps are the same for both types of disc.

BURN FILES TO A CD OR DVD

GET READY. To complete these steps, you must have a CD or DVD recorder drive installed for use with your computer, as well as a blank, writeable CD or DVD.

USE the Presentation folder you left open in the previous exercise.

1. Insert the CD or DVD into the appropriate recorder drive. The AutoPlay dialog box should display options for managing a blank CD or DVD.
2. Click **Burn files to disc**. The Burn a Disc dialog box displays, prompting you to key a title for the disc.

TAKE NOTE

Keep in mind that most music, pictures, and video are copyrighted, which means you cannot copy or duplicate them without permission or authorization from the owner or artist.

3. Key **Presentation Disc** and then click **Next**. Windows Vista begins formatting the disc. This may take a few minutes, depending on the type of disc you are using and your recorder. When the process is complete, Windows Vista opens a folder window for the disc. Notice that the text in the File list area prompts you to drag files to the folder window to add them to the disc.
4. Right-click the Taskbar and click **Show Windows Side by Side** to arrange the two windows so you can see them both on the desktop.
5. In the Presentation window, select the **Garden** and **Winter Leaves** files and drag them to the Presentation Disc window, as shown in Figure 5-12. Release the mouse button to drop them into the Pictures window. Windows Vista copies them to the disc. You can repeat the process to add other files to the disc as well.

Figure 5-12

Drag files to the disc

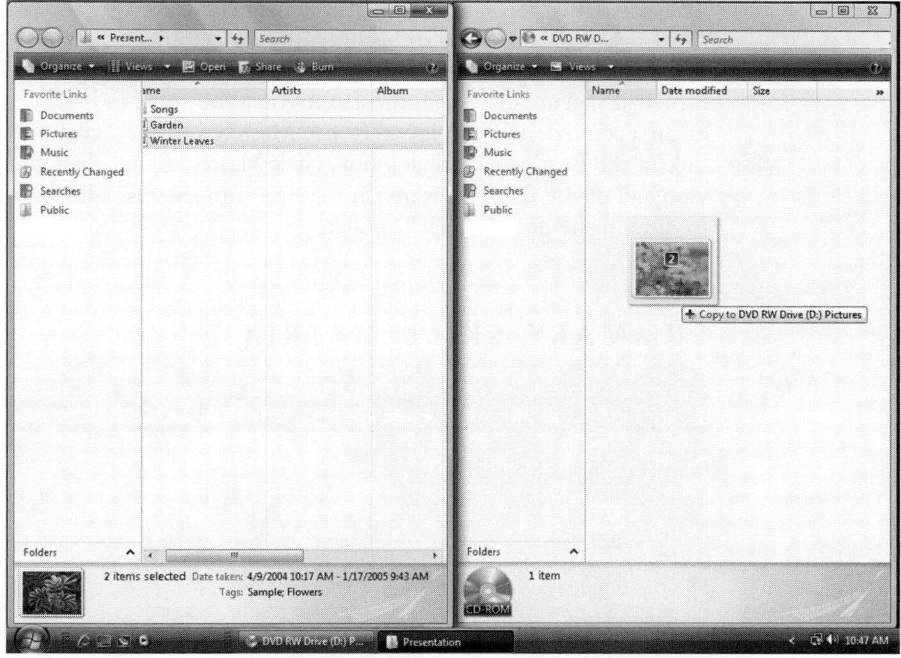

ANOTHER WAY

You can also copy files to a disc by using the Send to command. Right-click a file, click Send to, and then click the drive in which the disc is located.

6. In the Presentation window, double-click the **Songs** folder to open it.

7. Select the **Amanda** music file and then click the **Burn** button on the window's toolbar. Windows Vista copies the file to the disc. This is another convenient method of sending files to a writeable disc.
8. Eject the disc from the drive. Windows Vista completes the burn process by closing the CD and then ejecting it. Closing prepares the disc for use in a computer or other device. Label the disc with your name and the current date.
9. Close the Songs folder window. At your instructor's request, copy the Presentation folder to your Lesson 5 assessment folder, and then delete it from the desktop.

TAKE NOTE

Your instructor may also ask you to delete the folder in which the files imported from your camera are stored, or to move it to your Lesson 5 assessment folder.

LOG OFF your Windows Vista account.

Windows Vista closes a disc automatically when you select to eject it after burning. You can manually close a disc by right-clicking the drive in the Computer window and clicking Close session on the shortcut menu. You can add files to a closed disc, but you must close it again to prepare it for use.

Windows Vista uses two types of formatting for blank CDs or DVDs. The default format is called ***Live File System***, which enables you to copy multiple files to the disc at any time, instead of copying them all at once. Live File System is new to Windows Vista and is not compatible with some computers running older versions of the operating system. That means that discs burned using Live File System may not play in older computers. In addition, they may not play in all CD or DVD players.

The alternative format is called ***Mastered***. Mastered format requires you to burn all files to the disc at the same time. It is compatible with older versions of Windows as well as with Windows Vista, and with most CD and DVD players. You may want to use the Mastered format if you are creating a music CD that you want to be able to play in an older computer or on a standalone CD player. To use Mastered format, click the Show formatting options link in the Burn a Disc dialog box, click Mastered, and then click Next to format the disc. Copy all of the files you want on the disk into the disc's folder window and then click Burn to disc on the disc window's toolbar.

SUMMARY SKILL MATRIX

In This Lesson You Learned	Matrix Skill	Skill Number
To preview media files		
To customize folders for specific file types	Set the folder type	4.2.6
To manage multimedia files		
To burn files to a CD or DVD	Copy data files to a CD or DVD	4.6.4

■ Knowledge Assessment

Fill in the Blank

Complete the following sentences by writing the correct word or words in the blanks provided.

1. _______________ files store audio, graphics, animations, and video in digital format.
2. A(n) _______________ toolbar has buttons for playing, pausing, stopping, and sometimes rewinding or fast-forwarding a media file.
3. A(n) _______________ is a single image in a video.
4. A(n) _______________ is a group of audio or video files stored together for convenient playback.
5. A(n) _______________ is a model that has certain characteristics or features that you may want to recreate.
6. _______________ is a feature of Windows Vista that you use to select a program or action to use whenever you work with digital media.
7. _______________ is another term for copying files to a DVD or CD.
8. _______________ File System is the default formatting that Windows Vista uses for CDs and DVDs.
9. An alternative format for CDs and DVDs is _______________, which requires you to burn all files to the disc at the same time.
10. Pictures _______________ in a slide show so that they display continuously from beginning to end and back to the beginning again, without stopping.

True/False

Circle T if the statement is true or F if the statement is false.

T | F 1. In Slide Show view, pictures are sized to fill the desktop.
T | F 2. The Windows Photo Gallery program is useful for managing audio files.
T | F 3. Video files may store audio as well.
T | F 4. You can preview audio and video files in the Preview pane of a folder window.
T | F 5. All computers have built-in speakers so you can hear audio and music files.
T | F 6. The default folder type is All Items.
T | F 7. You can select the Music and Videos template to customize a folder for storing music or video files.
T | F 8. Select the Music Icons template to customize a folder to display in Large Icons view.
T | F 9. You cannot change the view and layout in a customized folder.
T | F 10. You must have a CD or DVD recorder drive to burn files to a disc.

Competency Assessment

Project 5-1: Slide Show Pictures

You are a member of a community garden club and you are preparing a slide show for the annual banquet. You must organize the pictures that you want to use. In this project, you will create a new folder and customize it for storing pictures. You will copy the pictures into the folder and then preview them. You will select one picture to print as a gift for the outgoing president.

GET READY. Before you begin these steps, start your computer and log on to your Windows Vista account. Close all open windows so you can see the desktop. Make sure you have a printer connected to your computer and loaded with paper.

1. Right-click a blank area of the desktop, click **New**, and then click **Folder**.
2. Key **Banquet** and press Enter to rename the folder.
3. Right-click the **Banquet** folder, click **Properties** to open the Properties dialog box, and then click the **Customize** tab.
4. Click the **Use this folder type as a template:** dropdown arrow and click **Pictures and Video**. Click **OK** to apply the change and close the dialog box.
5. Copy the files ***Flower1***, ***Flower2***, ***Flower3***, ***Flower4***, and ***Flower5*** from the data files for this lesson to the Banquet folder.
6. Make the Banquet folder window active and display the Preview pane, if necessary.
7. Click the ***Flower4*** file to select it and display it in the Preview pane.
8. Click the ***Flower1*** file.
9. Click the **Slide Show** button on the window's toolbar to change to Slide Show view. Watch the five pictures loop through the slide show. If necessary, minimize the Banquet window.

The ***Flower1, Flower2, Flower3, Flower4,*** and ***Flower5*** files are available on the companion CD-ROM.

TROUBLESHOOTING

If the Slide Show button is not available, repeat steps 3 and 4 to be sure you customized the folder for Pictures and Video.

10. Right-click the desktop and click **Slide Show Speed - Fast** to increase the speed with which the pictures change.
11. Right-click the desktop and click **Shuffle** to display the pictures in a random order.
12. Right-click the desktop and click **Loop** to turn the looping feature off so that the slide show stops after each picture has displayed once.
13. When the slide show stops, right-click the desktop and click **Loop** to turn the feature back on.
14. Right-click the desktop and click **Shuffle** to turn the feature off.
15. Right-click the desktop and click **Slide Show Speed - Medium**.
16. Right-click the desktop and click **Exit** to end the slide show.
17. Right-click the ***Flower3*** file and click **Print** on the shortcut menu.
18. Click the **Printer:** dropdown arrow and click your printer.
19. Click the **Paper size:** dropdown arrow and click the size of paper you are using.
20. Click the **Paper type:** dropdown arrow and click the type of paper you are using.
21. In the Layout pane, click the layout that you want to use.
22. Click **Print** to print the picture.
23. When the printing is finished, your instructor may ask you to capture an image of the Banquet folder window. Save it in your Lesson 5 assessment folder as ***Proj05_01***.
24. Close the Banquet folder window.

PAUSE. LEAVE the Windows Vista desktop displayed to use in the next project.

Project 5-2: Sound Effects

As a marketing assistant at the School of Fine Art, you are responsible for collecting digital sound effects to use in the multimedia presentation. In this project, you will create a folder customized for storing music files. You will copy the sound files into the folder and preview them. You will then burn them onto a CD or DVD.

GET READY. Before you begin these steps, make sure that you have a CD or DVD available to use in the recorder drive connected to your computer. Also, make sure your speakers are correctly connected to your computer so that you can hear the sounds.

1. Right-click a blank area of the desktop, click **New**, and then click **Folder**.
2. Key **Sounds** and press Enter to rename the folder.
3. Right-click the **Sounds** folder, click **Properties** to open the Properties dialog box, and then click the **Customize** tab.
4. Click the **Use this folder type as a template**: dropdown arrow and click **Music Icons**. Click **OK** to apply the change and close the dialog box.
5. Copy the files ***Sound1***, ***Sound2***, ***Sound3***, ***Sound4***, and ***Sound5*** from the data files for this lesson to the Sounds folder. These files are in the WAV format.
6. Make the Sounds folder window active and display the Preview pane, if necessary.
7. Click the ***Sounds1*** file to select it and display it in the Preview pane.
8. Click the **Play** button on the controller toolbar in the Preview pane to play the sound. (It should sound like marching.)
9. Click to select the ***Sounds2*** file and then click the **Play** button on the controller toolbar to play the sound.
10. Repeat step 9 for the remaining files to preview each sound.
11. Insert a blank CD or DVD into your recordable drive.
12. In the AutoPlay dialog box, click **Burn files to disc**.
13. Key **Sound Effects** and then click **Next**. Windows Vista formats the disk using the Live File System. When the formatting is complete, Windows Vista opens a folder window for the Sound Effects disc.
14. Right-click the Taskbar and click **Show Windows Side by Side** so that you can see both the Sounds window and the Sound Effects window.
15. In the Sounds window, select all five of the sound files.
16. Drag the files to the Sound Effects window and then release the left mouse button. Windows Vista copies the files to the disc.
17. When the copying is finished, eject the disc. Windows Vista closes the disc and then ejects it.
18. Remove the disc from the drive and label it with your name and the current date.
19. At this point, your instructor may ask you to capture an image of the Sounds folder window. Save it in your Lesson 5 assessment folder as ***Proj05_02***.
20. Close the Sounds folder window.

PAUSE. LEAVE the Windows Vista desktop displayed to use in the next project.

CD

The ***Sound1***, ***Sound2***, ***Sound3***, ***Sound4***, and ***Sound5*** files are available on the companion CD-ROM.

■ Proficiency Assessment

Project 5-3: More Flowers

The garden club has asked you to expand the slide show. In this project, you will import pictures from a digital camera and then copy them into the Banquet folder. (If you do not have a digital camera, you can use the files provided on the companion CD.) You will preview the new pictures and print one to give to the new president.

The ***Flower6***, ***Flower7***, ***Flower8***, ***Flower9***, and ***Flower10*** files are available on the companion CD-ROM.

GET READY. Before you begin, make sure you have a printer connected to your computer and loaded with paper. Have on hand your digital camera and its USB cord for connecting the camera to your computer. If you do not have a digital camera, copy the files ***Flower6***, ***Flower7***, ***Flower8***, ***Flower9***, and ***Flower10*** from the data files for this lesson to the Banquet folder, open the Banquet folder, and then skip ahead to step 9.

1. Connect the **USB cord** to your camera and then to your computer and turn on the camera.
2. In the **AutoPlay** dialog box, click **Import pictures**.
3. Click the **Tag these pictures (optional):** text box, key **Garden Club**, and then click the **Import** button.
4. When the importing is complete, close the Windows Photo Gallery window.
5. Click **Start** and then click **Pictures**. Double-click the **Garden Club** folder to open it (the name of the folder will also include today's date).
6. Select five of the pictures, right-click the selection, and then click **Copy** on the shortcut menu.
7. Close the folder window and then open the Banquet folder.
8. Paste the five pictures into the Banquet folder.
9. Click the ***Flower6*** file to select it and display it in the Preview pane.
10. Click the **Slide Show** button on the window's toolbar and watch pictures loop through the slide show.
11. Right-click the desktop and click **Slide Show Speed - Slow** to decrease the speed with which the pictures change.
12. Right-click the desktop and click **Loop** to turn the loop feature off so that the slide show stops after each picture has displayed once.
13. When the slide show stops, right-click the desktop and click **Loop** to turn the feature back on.
14. Right-click the desktop and click **Slide Show Speed - Medium** to revert to the default speed.
15. Right-click the desktop and click **Exit** to end the slide show.
16. Right-click the ***Flower6*** file and click **Print** on the shortcut menu.
17. Click the **Printer:** dropdown arrow and click your printer option.
18. Click the **Paper size:** dropdown arrow and click the size of paper you are using.
19. Click the **Paper type:** dropdown arrow and click the type of paper you are using.
20. In the Layout pane, click the layout that you want to use.
21. Click **Print** to print the picture.
22. When the printing is finished, your instructor may ask you to capture an image of the Banquet folder window. Save it in your Lesson 5 assessment folder as ***Proj05_03***. Alternatively, your instructor may ask you to copy the Banquet folder to your Lesson 5 assessment folder.
23. Close the Banquet folder window and then delete it from your desktop.

PAUSE. LEAVE the Windows Vista desktop displayed to use in the next project.

Project 5-4: Background Music

The marketing director at the School of Fine Art has asked you to provide three music files that might be suitable to play during the credits of the multimedia presentation. In this project, you will change the folder type of the Sounds folder to Music Details, and you will copy three music files from the Sample Music folder to the Sounds folder. You will preview the music files and then burn them to a disc that you can give to the marketing director.

GET READY. Before you begin these steps, make sure that you have a CD or DVD available to use in the recorder drive connected to your computer.

1. From the desktop, right-click the **Sounds** folder, click **Properties**, and then click the **Customize** tab.
2. Click the **Use this folder type as a template**: dropdown arrow and click **Music Details**. Click **OK** to apply the change and close the dialog box.
3. Click **Start** and then click **Music**. Double-click the **Sample Music** folder.
4. Select the files ***Muita Bobeira***, ***OAM's Blues***, and ***Symphony No. 3 in E-flat major***.
5. Right-click the selection and click **Copy** on the shortcut menu.
6. Close the Sample Music folder and open the Sounds folder. Display the Preview pane, if necessary.
7. Paste the three files you copied into the Sounds folder.
8. Click the ***Muita Bobeira*** file to select it and display it in the Preview pane.
9. Click the **Play** button on the controller toolbar in the Preview pane to play the song. (If you do not want to listen to the entire song, click the Stop button on the controller toolbar.)
10. Repeat step 9 to preview the other two music files.
11. Insert a CD or DVD into your recordable drive. In the AutoPlay dialog box, click **Burn files to disc**.
12. Key **Background Music** and then click **Next** to format the disc.
13. Close the Background Music window.
14. In the Sounds window, select the three music files you pasted in step 7 and then click the Burn button on the window's toolbar to copy the files to the disc.
15. When the copying is finished, eject the disc. Windows Vista closes the disc and ejects it.
16. Remove the disc from the drive and label it with your name and the current date.
17. Close the Sounds folder window. At your instructor's request, copy it to your Lesson 5 assessment folder and then delete it from the desktop.

PAUSE. LEAVE the Windows Vista desktop displayed to use in the next project.

Mastery Assessment

Project 5-5: Financial Analysis

As a financial analyst at a consulting firm, you are responsible for delivering presentations about current financial situations. You believe it will help hold the audience's attention if you add sound effects to the presentations. You decide to organize some digital sound files to have on hand to use whenever you create a presentation. In this project, you will create a folder customized for storing music files, and you will copy some sound files to it. You will preview the sound files and then burn them onto a CD or DVD.

GET READY. Before you begin these steps, make sure that you have a CD or DVD available to use in the recorder drive connected to your computer.

1. On the desktop, create a new folder named **Financial Sounds**.
2. Customize the folder for storing music details.
3. Copy the files ***Sound6***, ***Sound7***, ***Sound8***, ***Sound9***, and ***Sound10*** from the data files for this lesson to the Financial Sounds folder.
4. Preview each of the sounds in the Financial Sounds folder.
5. Insert a CD or DVD into your recordable drive.
6. Name the disc **More Sounds** and format it using the Live File System.
7. Burn the ***Sound6***, ***Sound7***, ***Sound8***, ***Sound9***, and ***Sound10*** files to the disc.
8. Eject the disc and label it with your name and the current date.

The ***Sound6***, ***Sound7***, ***Sound8***, ***Sound9***, and ***Sound10*** files are available on the companion CD-ROM.

9. Close the Financial Sounds folder window. At your instructor's request, copy it to your Lesson 5 assessment folder, and then delete it from your desktop.

   PAUSE. LEAVE the Windows Vista desktop displayed to use in the next project.

Project 5-6: Annual Report Cover

You are an assistant in the publications department of a large manufacturing company, and you are involved in preparing the annual report that will be sent out to all shareholders and potential investors. You must organize the pictures that will be used throughout the report and suggest one photo to use on the report cover. In this project, you will create a new folder and customize it for storing pictures. You will either import pictures from a digital camera, or copy pictures from the Sample Pictures folder into the new folder. You will preview the pictures as a slide show, select one to print, and then burn all of them to a disc to give to your supervisor for approval.

GET READY. Before you begin these steps, make sure you have a printer connected to your computer and loaded with paper. You should also have a CD or DVD available to use in the recordable drive in your computer. If you plan to import pictures from a digital camera, have the camera and its USB port ready. If you are not importing pictures from a digital camera, skip steps 3–7 and copy five files from the Sample Pictures folder into the Report Photos folder.

1. Create a new folder on the desktop and name it **Report Photos**.
2. Customize the Report Photos folder for storing pictures and videos.
3. Connect the USB cord to your camera and then to your computer. Turn on the camera.
4. Import the pictures from the camera, using the tag **Annual Report**.
5. When the importing is complete, close the Windows Photo Gallery window and navigate to the Pictures folder.
6. Open the Annual Report folder (the name of the folder will also include today's date) and select five of the pictures.
7. Copy the selected files and paste them into the Report Photos folder.
8. Preview the pictures in the Report Photos folder as a slide show.
9. Select one of the pictures and print it.
10. Insert a blank CD or DVD into your recordable drive.
11. Name the disc **Annual Report** and format it using the Live File System.
12. Burn all of the files from the Report Photos folder onto the disc.
13. Eject the disc and label it with your name and the current date.
14. Close all open windows.
15. At your instructor's request, copy the Report Photos folder to your Lesson 5 assessment folder, and then delete it from your desktop. If you imported pictures from a digital camera, your instructor may ask you to copy it to your Lesson 5 assessment folder, as well, and then delete it.

    LOG OFF your Windows Vista user account.

INTERNET READY

Students at the School of Fine Art often make their work available for viewing on the Internet. Copyright laws protect their rights as artists so that others cannot recreate or use their work without permission. Conversely, they cannot use others' work in their original projects. It is important for the school to maintain a clear policy on copyright infringement and to make sure all students understand the policy. In this exercise, use web search tools to locate information about copyright laws. Try to find a clear and concise explanation about the rights of artists. Once you have located the information, use a word processor or pen and paper to write a copyright policy for the School of Fine Art. Remember to cite the Internet sources you used to find the information.

Searching for Files and Folders

LESSON SKILL MATRIX

Skills	Matrix Skill	Skill Number
Using a Search Box		
Searching from the Start Menu	Search by using keywords	4.4.4
Searching in a Folder	Search by using wildcards	4.4.3
Using a Search Folder	Search by using a virtual folder	4.4.2
Conducting an Advanced Search	Filter results of a search	4.4.6
Reusing a Search	Redisplay the results of a previous search	4.4.5
Using Search Tools		
Customizing the Index	Specify whether a folder should be indexed	4.4.1

Contoso, Ltd. is a construction and land development company. The legal department is responsible for obtaining information about local zoning ordinances, obtaining permits, and tracking correspondence with local authorities, clients, and others. Many documents pass through the department on a daily basis, and the assistants must be able to find each one at any time. In this lesson, you will learn how to use Windows Vista Search tools to locate files. You will learn to search from the Start menu, from any folder, and using the Search folder. You will learn to save the results of a search to use again. You will learn to use the search index to improve the speed of a search.

KEY TERMS

Boolean filter
Filter
Index
Indexed location
Keyword
Offline files
Search box
Search folder
Search results
Search text
Syntax
Virtual folder
Wildcard characters

■ Using a Search Box

THE BOTTOM LINE

You may not always remember where you store a file or folder. Instead of browsing aimlessly through the contents of your computer to find it, you can use the Search tools Windows Vista provides to quickly find the item you need. One of the easiest ways to start a search is by using a Search box. A ***Search box*** is an area where you can key ***search text***, which is the text that Windows Vista will look for to locate programs, files, and folders stored on your computer. You can key up to 30 characters of text in the Search box, from a single character, to a ***keyword*** or phrase. A keyword is a word that relates to a particular topic. You can even use ***wildcard characters***, which are characters that substitute for one or more actual characters. Windows Vista will search for the text in an item's name, contents, and properties. In this section, you learn how to use a Search box to find a file or folder.

Searching from the Start Menu

The Search box on the Start menu is a quick tool to use to find a program, file, or folder when you are not sure where the item is stored. From the Start menu, Windows Vista searches the indexed locations on your computer. An ***indexed location*** is one that is included in the Windows Vista ***index***, which is a collection of information about the items stored on your computer. Windows Vista uses the index to increase the speed and accuracy of a search. In this exercise, you learn how to search from the Start menu using text and keywords.

SEARCH FROM THE START MENU

GET READY. Before you begin these steps, start your computer and log on to your Windows Vista account. Close all open windows so you can see the desktop. Create a new folder named Lesson 6 in a storage location specified by your instructor, where you can store assessment files and folders that you create during this lesson.

CD

The ***Bobcat1***, ***Bobcat2***, ***Barb***, and ***Financials*** files are available on the companion CD-ROM.

1. Click the **Start** button and then click **Documents** to open the Documents folder.
2. Create a new folder and name it **Company Info**.
3. Open the **Company Info** folder and create another new folder. Name the new folder **Contoso** and then open it.
4. Create a new, blank text file in the Contoso folder and name it **Client List**. Then, copy the ***Bobcat1*** and ***Bobcat2*** graphics files and the ***Financials*** and ***Barb*** document files from the data files for this lesson to the **Contoso** folder.
5. Close all open windows.
6. Click the **Start** button to display the Start menu. In the Search box at the bottom of the left pane, key **C**. As soon as you start keying characters in the Search box, Windows Vista starts looking for matching items. In this case, it starts searching for any item that is named with a word starting with the letter C. The text you type does not have to be the name of an item; it can be in the contents of the item, or in a property. Windows Vista displays the search results in the left pane of the Start menu, organized by type. The ***search results*** are all of the items that match the criteria that you are looking for, which in this case, is the text in the Search box. Your Start menu should look similar to Figure 6-1, although the search results depend on the contents of your computer, so you may not have the exact items in the figure.

TROUBLESHOOTING

If a search is taking a very long time, it may be because you have a lot of email items saved. To exclude email, open any folder window, click Start>Control Panel>System and Maintenance. Under Indexing Options, click Change how Windows searches. Click the Modify button. Click to deselect the checkbox next to your email program, and then click OK. Click Close in the Indexing Options dialog box. Close the Control Panel window. You learn more about indexing options later in this lesson.

Figure 6-1

Search from the Start menu

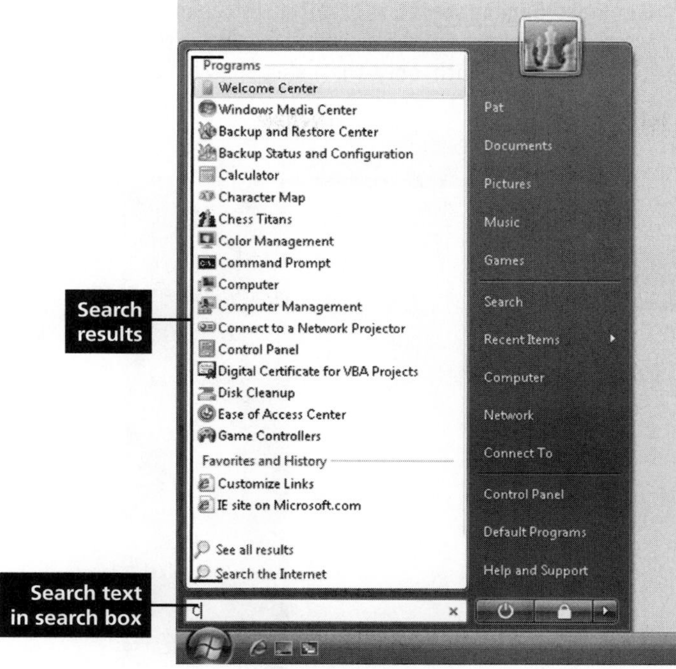

X REF

Refer to Lesson 3, "Organizing Files and Folders," for information about properties.

7. Key the letters **om**, so the text Com displays in the Search box. Windows Vista filters the search to find items with the text Com in the name, contents, or properties. To ***filter*** means to find items that meet certain criteria and exclude items that do not. In this case, the criteria are the text Com. Now, the search results listed should include the Company Info folder, as shown in Figure 6-2, along with other items that match the search text. (Remember, the items on your computer will not be exactly the same as those in the Figure.)

Figure 6-2

Filter the search to Co

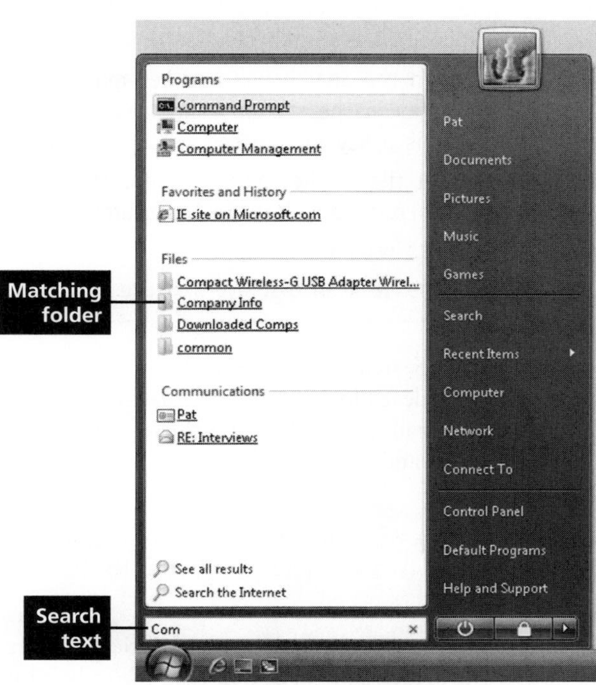

8. Press **Backspace** to delete the letter m, and then key **ntoso** to complete the word Contoso in the Search box. Now, the search results should look similar to Figure 6-3, with only the exact match Contoso and its contents displayed.

Figure 6-3

Filter the search to Contoso

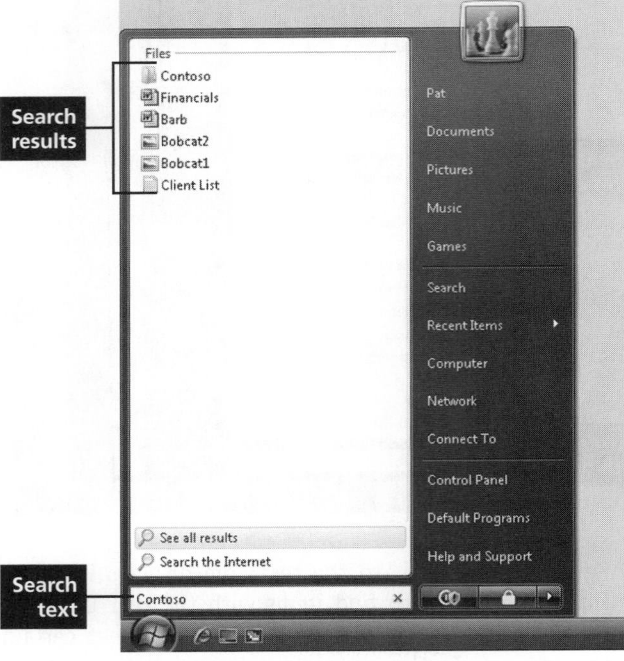

TAKE NOTE*

You can open the Financials and Barb documents in a word processor such as WordPad or Microsoft Office Word to see the contents.

TAKE NOTE*

To see a file's properties, right-click the file, click Properties, and then click the Details tab.

9. Press **Backspace** to delete the text in the Search box and then key **Dear**. The ***Financials*** and ***Barb*** documents should display in the search results. The text Dear is not part of either file's name or properties, but since both are letters, it is in the file contents as part of the salutation. You may have other letter documents that also display in the search results.
10. Delete the text in the Search box and key **machinery**. The ***Bobcat1*** and ***Bobcat2*** files should display in the search results. Machinery is not in either file's name or contents, but it is a keyword in the Tags property of both files.
11. Click the Bobcat1 file in the search results. The file opens in your default graphics program. You can open any item in the search results list by clicking it.
12. Close the graphics program window.

PAUSE. LEAVE the desktop displayed to use in the next exercise.

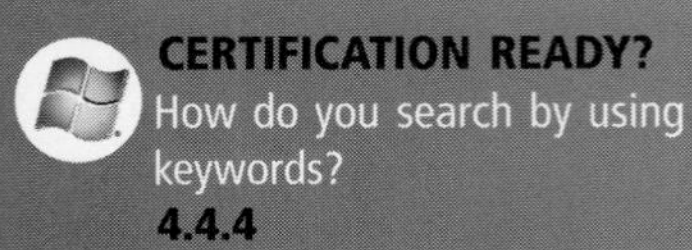

CERTIFICATION READY?
How do you search by using keywords?
4.4.4

As mentioned earlier, the Search box on the Start menu is a quick tool to use to find a program or an item stored in an indexed location. By default, indexed locations include your personal folder and its contents, email, ***offline files***, which are copies of network files that you store locally on your computer, and websites stored in your web browser's history.

XREF

Lesson 14, "Collaborating with Others," covers working with offline files. You learn how to add indexed locations later in this lesson.

When you search for items, Windows Vista automatically filters the search results based on the information you provide. Using a Search box, the only information you can provide is text. As you have seen, if you know the item's name, you can type it and quickly locate the item wherever it is stored. If you don't know the item's name, you can use text that is in the contents of the item. If you are not sure of the item's contents, you can key text that is in a property, such as a keyword in the Tags or Comments property. You can also use wildcard characters, which you learn about in the next exercise.

When you search using text other than the item's name, Windows Vista may not be able to find the exact item you need, but it will narrow down the search results so you can find the item more easily.

You can also use standard search syntax to instruct Windows Vista to look for the search text in a particular property only. ***Syntax*** is the way words are arranged. To specify a property, key the property, a colon, and then the search text. So, to look for files named March, key Name:March in the Search box. To look for files with a tag March, key Tag:March. You learn more about specifying criteria in the "Conducting an Advanced Search" section, later in this lesson.

Sometimes, more than one copy of the same item will display in the search results list because it may be stored in more than one location. You can right-click the item and click Properties to see the path to the item, or click Open file location to open the folder in which the item is stored. In addition, if Windows Vista finds more items than can fit within the search pane on the Start menu, you can click Show all results to open a Search folder window displaying all found items. You learn about using a Search folder later in this lesson.

In the next section, you learn how to start a search in a folder.

Searching in a Folder

When you know that a file or folder is stored in a particular location, you can start your search in that location. Starting in a particular folder narrows down the search right from the start, so Windows Vista can find the item faster. In addition, you can use the Search pane in a folder window to select a category of items to search. In this section, you learn how to search in a folder using text, wildcard characters, and the Search pane.

SEARCH IN A FOLDER

1. Click **Start** and then click **Documents**. If necessary, change the View to Details.
2. Click in the **Search** box in the upper right corner of the window and key **B**. Windows Vista filters the contents of the current folder and displays the search results in the File list. It should look similar to Figure 6-4. (You may have additional items that contain the letter B stored in Documents, and you may have different details displayed.) Notice that the location in the Address bar is now Search Results in Documents. This is not an actual folder on your computer, but a ***virtual folder***, which is a temporary location used to store the results of a search. Also, tools you might need for searching display on the window's toolbar.

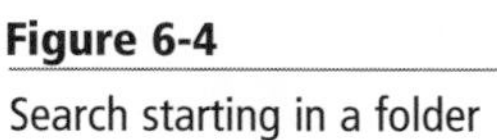

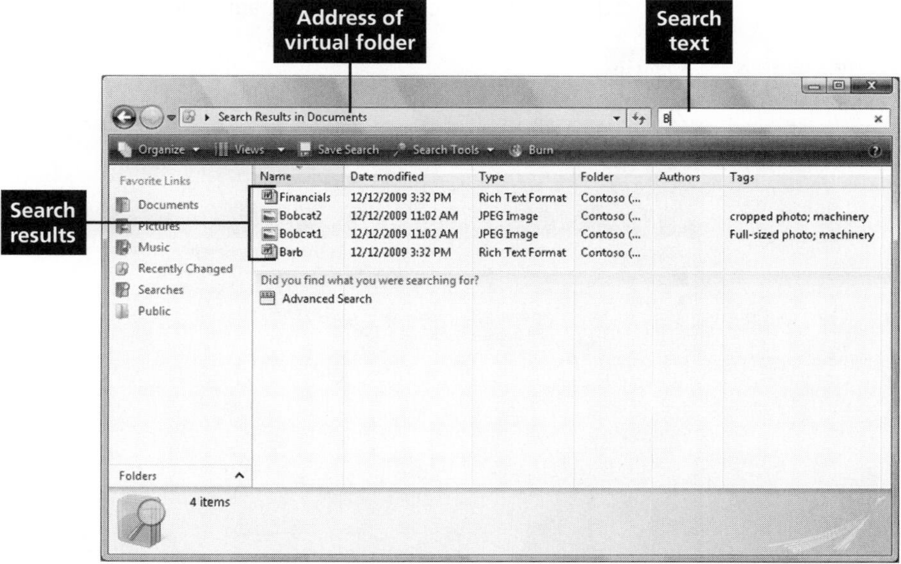

Figure 6-4

Search starting in a folder

3. In the Search box, key **?b** so that B?b displays. ? is the wildcard character that represents any single character. Windows Vista filters the search results to display items that include the text B, any other single character, and then another B. In this case, the two Bobcat files display.
4. Press **Backspace** twice to delete the final b and the question mark and then key ***b** so that B*b displays. * is the wildcard character that represents one or more characters. Windows Vista filters the search results to display items that have text starting and ending with the letter B, with one or more characters in between. In this case, that includes the two Bobcat files and the Rich Text Format file named Barb, as shown in Figure 6-5.

Figure 6-5

Search using wildcards

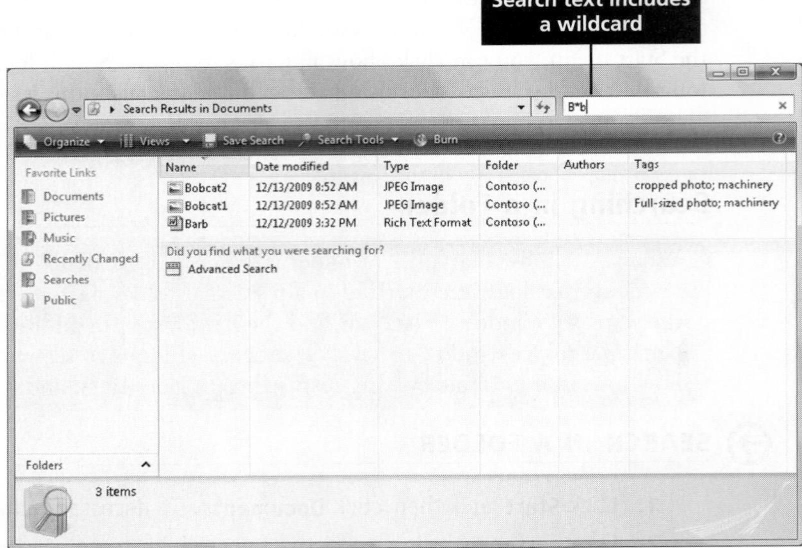

5. Delete the text B*b from the Search box and key **jpg**. The two JPEG Image files—Bobcat1 and Bobcat2—display in the search results. You can type a filename extension to filter the search results to a particular file type.

6. Click the **Search Tools** button on the window's toolbar to display a dropdown menu of options.
7. Click **Search Pane** on the menu to display the Search pane. The window should look similar to Figure 6-6. The buttons in the Search pane let you quickly filter the file list by category. By default, all types of items are included in the search.

Figure 6-6

Display the Search pane

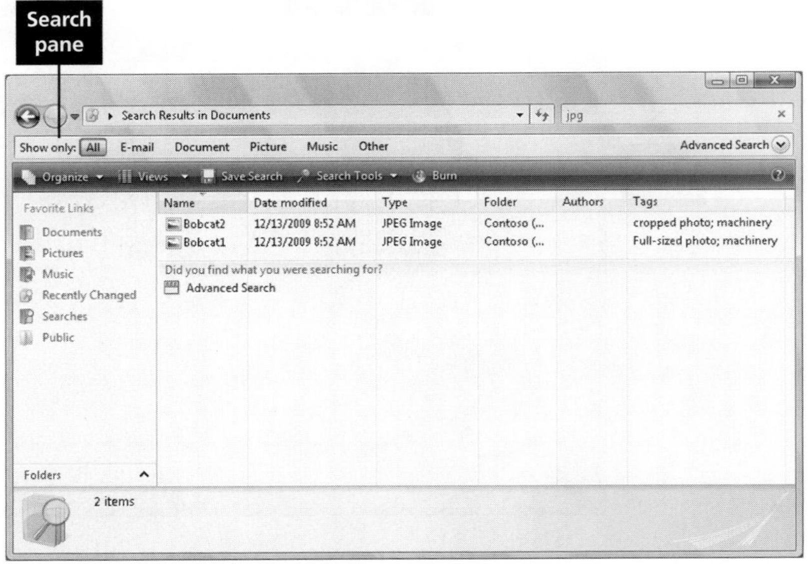

8. Click the **Document** button in the Search pane and then delete the text jpg from the Search box. The Client List text file and the two Rich Text Format files display in the File list. The Document category includes most files that you create with an application, such as word processing files, spreadsheets, and presentations.
9. In the Search pane, click **Picture**. The two JPEG Image files display. Use the Picture filter when you want to displays graphics files, such as photos and drawings.

TAKE NOTE* You can use file details, sorting, grouping, and stacking to arrange items in the search results file list so that they are easier to identify. Refer to Lesson 4, "Customizing Windows Explorer," for more information.

10. In the Search pane, click **Other**. The two folders display. The Other filter displays all items that are not included in the other categories, such as shortcuts and folders, and other types of files such as audio files.
11. Click in the **Search** box and key **machinery**. No items in the Other category match this keyword.
12. Click the **All** button in the Search pane. Windows Vista identifies both Bobcat pictures as matches, because they both have the keyword machinery as a tag.
13. At this point, your instructor may ask you to capture an image of the Search Results window. Save it in your Lesson 6 assessment folder as ***Le06_01***.
14. **CLOSE** the **Search Results** window.

PAUSE. LEAVE the desktop displayed to use in the next exercise.

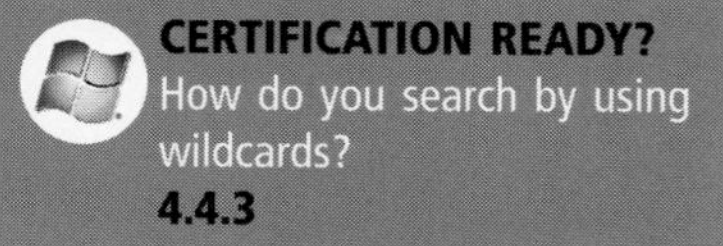

CERTIFICATION READY?
How do you search by using wildcards?
4.4.3

Windows Vista applies the same filtering process to text that you key in a Search box in a folder to text that you key in the Search box on the Start menu. It looks for the text in the item's name, the contents of the file, and the file properties. The search is faster than from the Start menu because instead of searching all indexed locations, Windows Vista searches just the current folder and all subfolders. You can make the search even faster by selecting a category in the Search pane. Selecting a category reduces the number of items Windows Vista searches.

As mentioned, a question mark is the wildcard for any single character, and an asterisk is the wildcard for one or more characters. If you key Invoice? in the Search box, Windows Vista will locate files with names such as Invoice1, Invoice2, and Invoice3, but not Invoice25. If you key Invoice*, it will locate Invoice1 and Invoice25, as well as a file named Invoices or Invoice_List. You can use wildcard characters in any Search box.

Next, you learn how to use a Search folder.

Using a Search Folder

When you do not know where a file is stored, you can start your search using a ***Search folder***, which is a virtual folder designed specifically for searching. When you start in a Search folder, Windows Vista will search all indexed locations, so you can search more than one location at a time. In addition, in a Search folder, you can access Search tools such as the Search pane, which can help you narrow the search, as well as file management tools such as detail column headings that can help you organize the search results. In this section, you learn to use a Search Folder to start a search.

USE A SEARCH FOLDER

USE the desktop you left displayed in the previous exercise.

1. Click **Start** and then click **Search**. A new, blank Search folder displays, as shown in Figure 6-7.

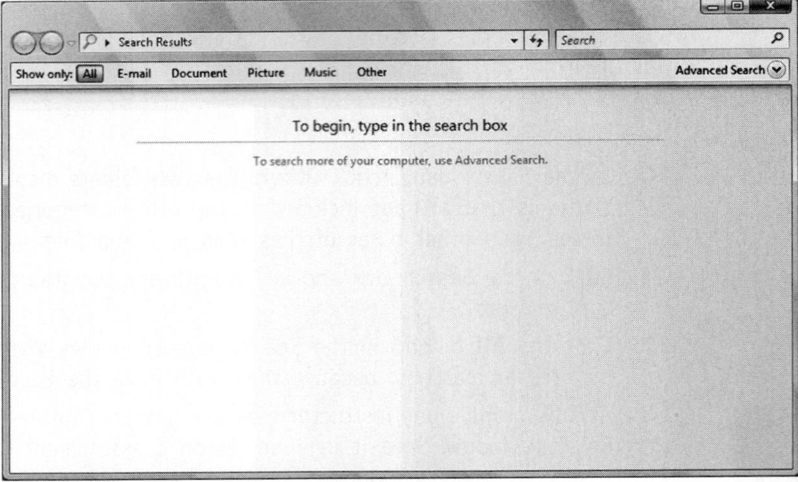

Figure 6-7
A Search folder

2. Click in the **Search** box and key **B**. Windows Vista searches all indexed locations and displays the search results in the File list. The list is very long, and the search may take a long time, because it includes all items in all indexed locations that have the letter B in the name, contents, or properties.
3. Click the **Picture** button in the Search pane. This filters the search to display only graphics files. The ***Bobcat1*** and ***Bobcat2*** files are included, but there are probably other graphics files that have B in the name, contents, or properties that display as well.
4. If the File list is not in Details view, click the **Views** button on the window's toolbar and click **Details**.
5. Click the **Date taken** column heading to sort the File list into descending order by Date taken. Although no items have been removed from the search results, the two Bobcat files should be near the top, making them easier to find.

TROUBLESHOOTING

Each of the Bobcat files may display more than once in the search results. That's because Windows Vista may locate them in the data files for this lesson as well as in the Contoso folder. If you have opened the files, the Recent Items folder may contain shortcut links to them as well.

6. Click in the **Search box** and key **ob** so the text Bob displays. Now, the two Bobcat pictures should be the only files in the list—unless you have other graphics files that have the text Bob in the name, contents, or properties.
7. Click the **Document** button in the Search pane to change the search results to only Document files. The ***Financials*** file displays in the File list, as shown in Figure 6-8. Although the text Bob is not part of the filename or properties, it is in the contents of the document, so Windows Vista identifies it as a match.

Figure 6-8

Search for documents in a Search folder

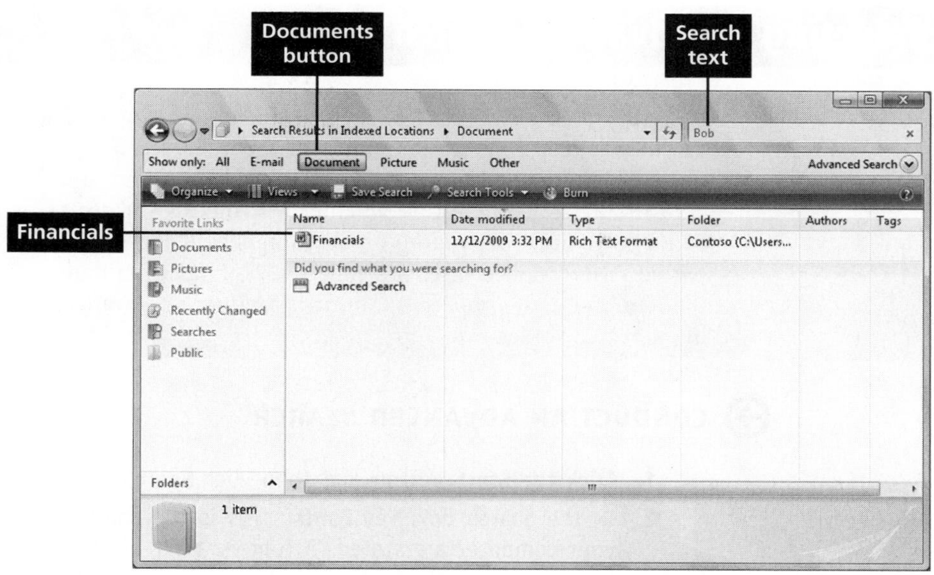

CERTIFICATION READY?
How do you search by using a virtual folder?
4.4.2

8. At this point, your instructor may ask you to capture an image of the Search folder window. Save it in your Lesson 6 assessment folder as ***Le06_02***.
9. **CLOSE** the Search folder.

PAUSE. LEAVE the desktop displayed to use in the next exercise.

A Search folder is a virtual folder, which means it does not actually exist on a storage device. Rather, it is a temporary location in your computer's memory, used only to organize and display the results of the current search.

Note that you can use keywords and wildcard characters while searching in a Search folder, just as you can from the Start menu or in a folder window.

Another way to filter a search is to use Boolean filters. A ***Boolean filter*** is a filter that uses common logical phrases, such as AND, OR, and NOT, as well as marks such as quotations and parentheses to combine words in the search text. For example, if you want to find a file that has the text March and April, you can key March AND April in the Search box. To find a file that has the text March or the text April, you can key March OR April. (Boolean filters must be typed in all uppercase letters.) Table 6-1 describes common Boolean filters.

Table 6-1

Common Boolean Filters

FILTER	RESULT
word1 AND word2	Finds items that contain both words.
word1 OR word2	Finds items that contain either of the words
word1 NOT word2	Finds items that contain word1, but not word2
"word1 word2"	Finds items that contain the exact text within the quotation marks
(word1 word2)	Finds items that contain all words within the parentheses in any order

In the next section, you learn how to conduct an advanced search.

■ Conducting an Advanced Search

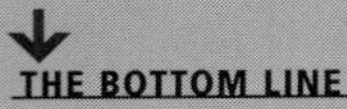

THE BOTTOM LINE

Using a search box to find an item is quick and easy as long as you know text that is part of the item's name, contents, or properties. If not, you can use an advanced search to locate an item based on other criteria. Using an advanced search you can look for an item in any storage location whether it is indexed or not. This means the search may take a long time, depending on the number of non-indexed locations you have on your system. You can also filter the search results based on date and file size, as well as text in the item name or properties. You can conduct an advanced search in any folder, including a Search folder.

CONDUCT AN ADVANCED SEARCH

1. Click the **Start** button and then click **Search** to display a new Search folder.
2. In the Search box, key **Fonts**. This is the name of the folder where all fonts on your computer are stored. A font is a set of characters in a particular typeface. Because the Fonts folder is not in an indexed location, Windows Vista does not identify it as a match.

TROUBLESHOOTING

Indexed locations on your system may contain items that match the text Fonts. Windows Vista will locate and display those items in the File list.

3. Click the **Advanced Search** expand arrow at the right end of the Search pane to display the Advanced Search options. The window should look similar to Figure 6-9.

Figure 6-9

Advanced Search options

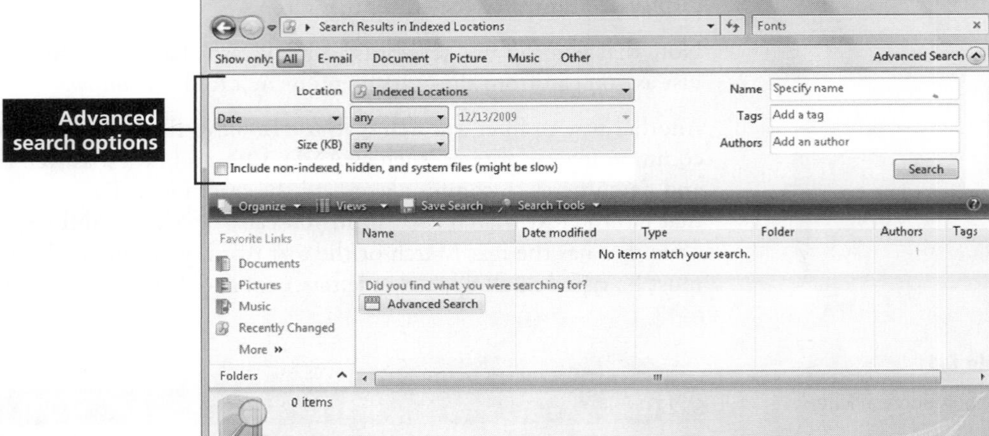

ANOTHER WAY

You can also click the Advanced Search button in the File list to display the Advanced Search options.

4. Click the **Location** dropdown arrow to display a list of available locations and then click **Everywhere**. This option specifies that Windows Vista should search all locations, whether they are indexed or not. You can also select to search your computer, a drive, or specific folders.

5. Click the **Search** button. Windows starts searching every location on your system, displaying matches as it finds them. Color gradually moves across the Address bar from left to right indicating the progress of the Search, as shown in Figure 6-10. You can click the Stop button as soon as you see the item you are looking for, or you can let the search continue to the end. Keep in mind that searching all locations—indexed and not—may take a very long time.

Figure 6-10

Search everywhere

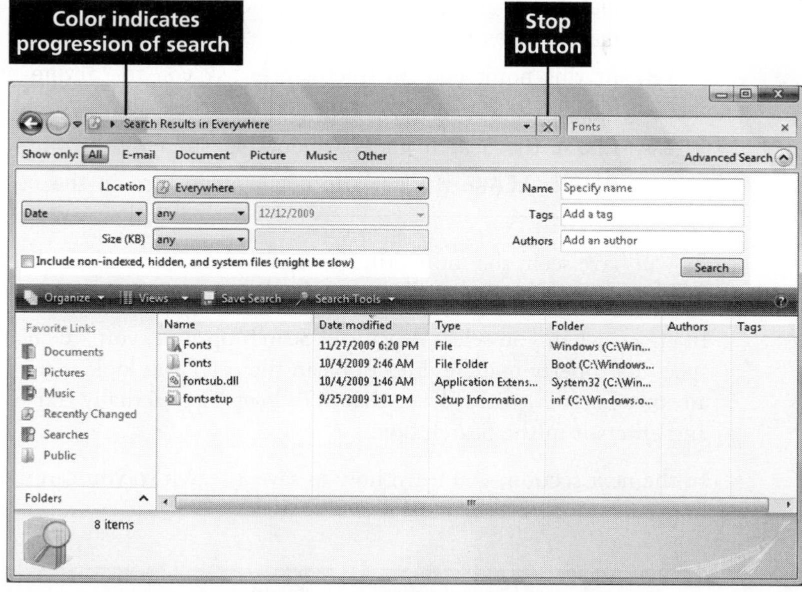

6. As soon as you see any folder named Fonts in the search results, click the **Stop** button to the right of the Address bar to stop the search.

7. Delete the text **Fonts** from the Search box. Click the **Location** dropdown arrow and click **Indexed Locations**.

8. Click the **Date** dropdown arrow and click **Date created**. You can select to search based on a specific date, on the date created, or on the date modified.

9. Click the dropdown arrow to the right of the date box and click **is**. This specifies that you want to match the date exactly. You can also choose a date before or after a particular date. Today's date should display on the date button.

10. Click the **Search** button. Windows Vista searches indexed locations for items created today. It should find the Company Info and Contoso folders and the Client List text file. It may find other items as well. The window should look similar to Figure 6-11.

TROUBLESHOOTING

If you work on a network, or if you store a large number of email items, the search for a Fonts folder may take too long. Click the Stop button to stop the search and then continue with step 7.

Figure 6-11

Search by date

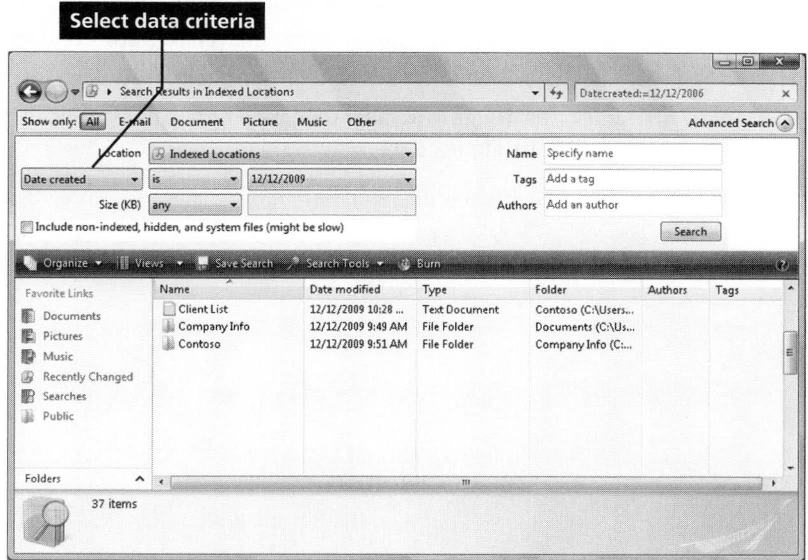

11. Click the dropdown arrow to the right of Size (KB) and click **is greater than**. You can search based on any size, a specific size, or items greater than or less than the specified size.
12. Click the **Add a file size** text box and key **5**. Then click the **Search** button. Windows Vista searches for items created today, that are greater than 5KB in size. Neither the Company Info nor Contoso folders nor the Client List text file matches these criteria, so they no longer display in the search results. There may be files that do match the criteria displayed.

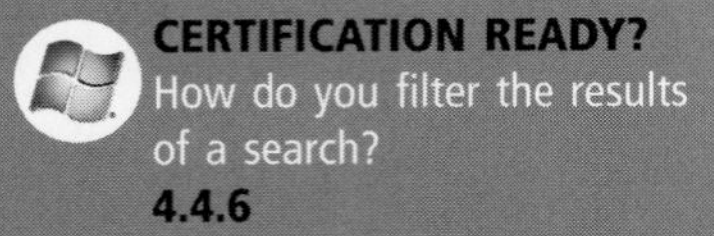

13. At this point your instructor may ask you to capture an image of the Search Results folder window. Save it in your Lesson 6 assessment folder as ***Le06_03***.
14. **CLOSE** the Search folder window.

PAUSE. LEAVE the desktop displayed to use in the next section.

As you have seen, the more criteria you can include in a search, the greater the chance you will locate the file you need.

In effect, when you select Advanced Search options, you are creating search text that includes specific property matches and Boolean filters. If you look at the Search box during an advanced search, you will see that Windows Vista actually translates your selections into text and enters it in the Search box.

In the next section, you learn how to save a search so you can use it again later.

■ Reusing a Search

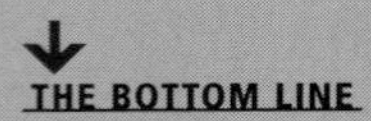

If you frequently search for the same items using the same filters, you may want to save the search. Saving a search means that you can reuse it again and again at any time without having to reenter search text and select criteria. You can save a search that you start from any folder window, including a Search folder. Saved searches are saved in the Searches folder, which you can access from your personal folder or from the Favorite Links list in the Navigation pane of any folder window. In this section, you learn how to save and reuse a search.

REUSE A SEARCH

1. Click the **Start** button and then click **Search** to open a Search folder.
2. Click the **Advanced Search** expand arrow to display the Advanced Search options.
3. Click the **Date** dropdown arrow and click **Date created**.
4. Click the dropdown arrow to the right of the date box and click **is**.
5. Click the **Name** box and then key **Co***. The Advanced Search options should look similar to Figure 6-12.

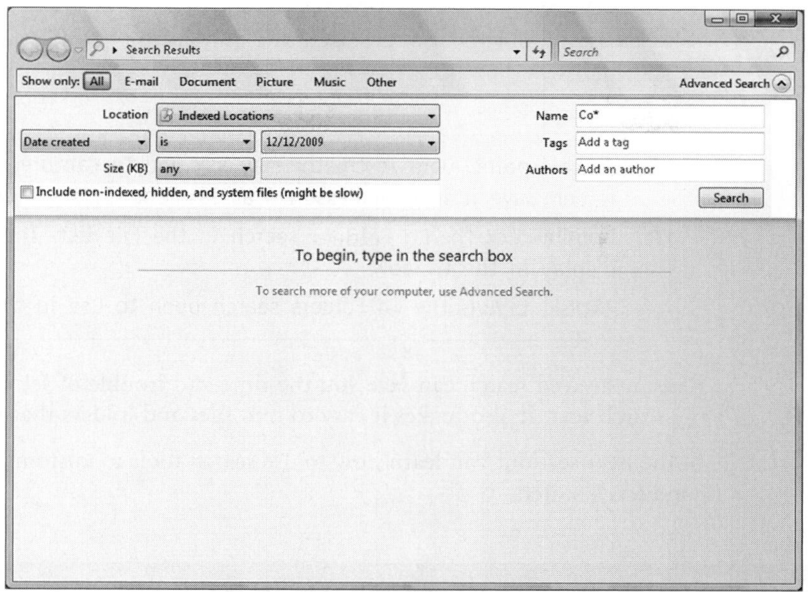

Figure 6-12

Set up an advanced search

6. Click the **Search** button. Windows Vista searches for items created today, with the text Co followed by any other characters in the name. The Company Info and Contoso folders should display in the search results.
7. Click the **Save Search** button on the window's toolbar. A Save As dialog box displays.
8. In the **File name** box, key **Co Folders**. The dialog box should look similar to Figure 6-13.

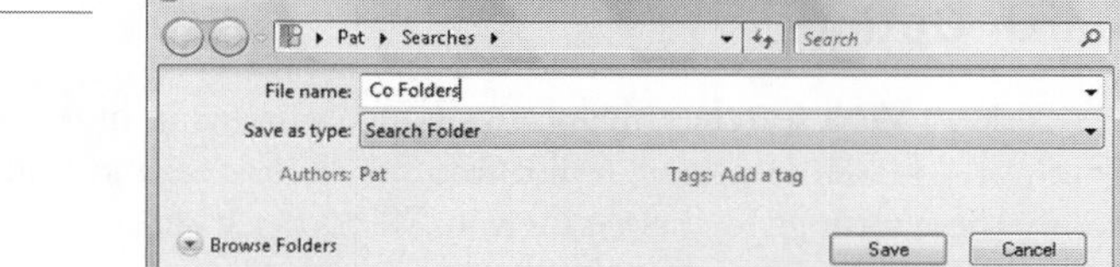

Figure 6-13

Save As dialog box

9. Click **Save** to save the search. Then close the Search folder window.
10. Click the **Start** button and then click your personal folder.
11. In the Favorite Links list in the Navigation pane, click **Searches** to open the Searches folder. The saved Co Folders search should be in the File list, along with built-in searches that come with Windows Vista, as shown in Figure 6-14.

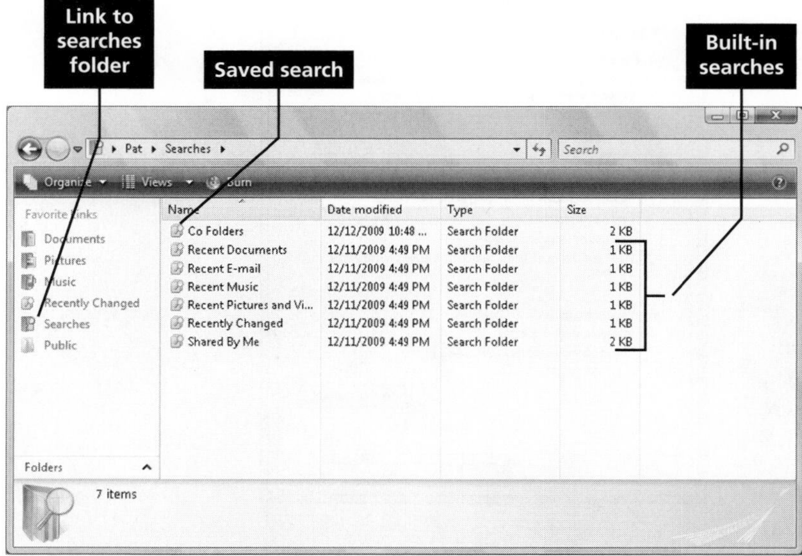

Figure 6-14

Saved searches

ANOTHER WAY

You can also double-click the Searches folder icon in the File list to open the Searches folder window.

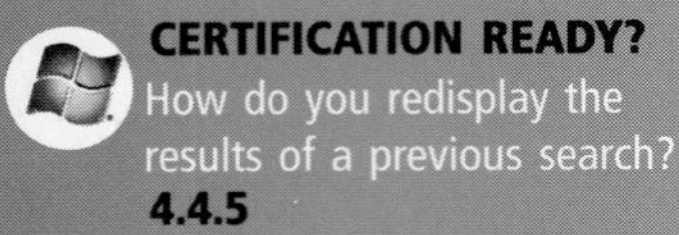

CERTIFICATION READY?
How do you redisplay the results of a previous search?
4.4.5

12. At this point, your instructor may ask you to capture an image of the Searches folder. Save it in your Lesson 6 assessment folder as ***Le06_04***.
13. Double-click the **Co Folders** search in the File list. The results of the search display in the window.

PAUSE. LEAVE the Co Folders search open to use in the next exercise.

Reusing a saved search can save you the time and trouble of selecting the criteria and keying the search text. It also makes it easy to find files and folders that you use frequently.

In the next section, you learn how to use search tools to customize the way Windows Vista conducts a search.

■ Using Search Tools

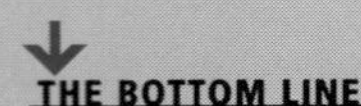

THE BOTTOM LINE

You can use the search tools provided by Windows Vista to customize the way a search takes place. For example, you can change settings on the Search tab of the Folder Options dialog box to specify what to search and how to search. You can also add or remove locations from the index. In this section, you learn how to change search options and how to modify indexed locations.

Setting Search Options

By default, Windows Vista searches file locations and contents in indexed locations, and file-names only in non-indexed locations. It also searches subfolders and finds partial matches. You can modify these settings to change the way Windows Vista conducts a search.

SET SEARCH OPTIONS

USE the Co Folders search you left open in the previous exercise.

1. Click the **Search Tools** button on the window's toolbar and click **Search options**. The Search tab of the Folder Options dialog box displays, as shown in Figure 6-15.

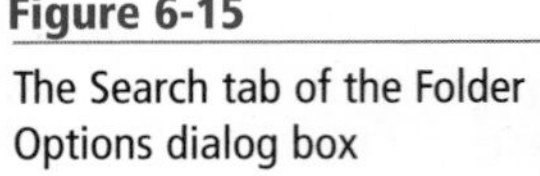

Figure 6-15

The Search tab of the Folder Options dialog box

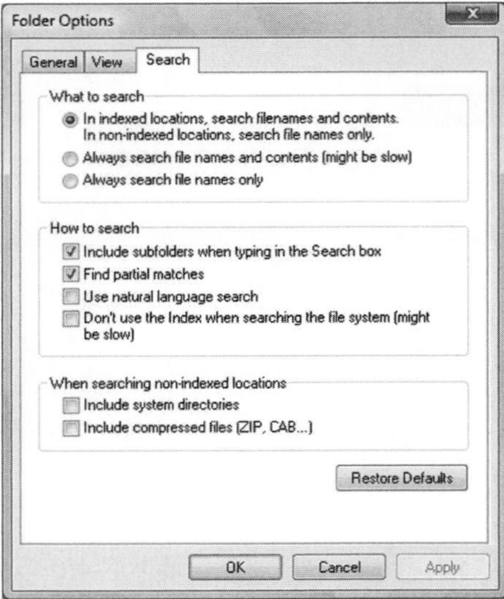

ANOTHER WAY

You can also click the Organize button on a folder window's toolbar, click Folder and Search Options, and then click the Search tab.

For more information on the Folder Options dialog box, refer to Lesson 4.

2. Under **How to search**, click to deselect all checkboxes. This deselects the options for searching subfolders and finding partial matches.
3. Click **OK**.
4. From the Co Folders window, navigate to the Documents folder.
5. In the **Search** box, key **Client List**. No matches display because Windows Vista is no longer set to search subfolders.
6. Click the **Start** button to display the Start menu and then key **Cl** in the Search box. No matches display because Windows Vista is no longer set to find partial matches.
7. Key **ient** to complete the word *Client*, and the Client List file should display in the search results.
8. Press Esc to close the Start menu.
9. Click the **Search Tools** button in the Search Results window toolbar and then click **Search options**.
10. Click the **Restore Defaults** button and then click **OK**.

PAUSE. LEAVE the Search Results window open to use in the next exercise.

The Use natural language search option on the Search tab of the Folder Options dialog box controls whether Windows Vista will understand standard sentences and phrases keyed in a Search box. By default, natural language is off, so you must use Boolean filters and specify properties to filter a search. If you turn natural language on, you can use search text the way you would speak. For example, if you want to find picture files with the words Red and Rose in the name, you could key the search text: Pictures named Red Rose. Without natural language, you would have to key: *kind: picture name: Red AND Rose.*

In the next section, you learn how to customize the index.

Customizing the Index

As mentioned, by default, Windows Vista searches file locations and contents in indexed locations and filenames only in non-indexed locations. It also searches subfolders and finds partial matches. You can customize the index to add or remove locations. For example, you can remove locations to speed up a search, or add a location if you frequently use it to store files and folders you might need to find.

CUSTOMIZE THE INDEX

USE the Search Results window you left open in the previous exercise.

1. Click the **Search Tools** button on the window's toolbar and click **Modify Index Locations**. The Indexing Options dialog box displays, as shown in Figure 6-16. (The items in your Indexing Options dialog box may not be the same as those in the figure.)

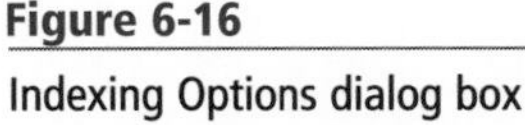

Figure 6-16

Indexing Options dialog box

2. Click the **Modify** button to display the locations that you are authorized to change. This should include Offline Files and may include other locations such as the program you use to organize your email. A checkmark next to a location indicates that it is included in the index.

TAKE NOTE*

If you have an administrator account, you may click the Show all locations button. Windows Vista will ask for permission to continue and may prompt you to enter a password. It will then include your local disk in the list of available locations so you can select or deselect individual folders on your computer.

3. Click to deselect the **Offline Files** checkbox. This removes Offline files from the Index.
4. Click **OK** and then click **Close** in the Indexing Options dialog box.
5. Click the **Search Tools** button on the window's toolbar and click **Modify Index Locations** to once again open the Indexing Options dialog box.
6. Click the **Modify** button and then click to select the **Offline Files** checkbox.
7. Click **OK** and then click **Close** in the Indexing Options dialog box.
8. In the **Search Results** window, click Searches in the navigation pane to open the Searches folder. At your instructor's request, copy the Co Folders search to your Lesson 6 assessment folder, and then delete it.
9. Navigate to the Documents folder and delete the Company Info folder.

LOG OFF your Windows Vista account.

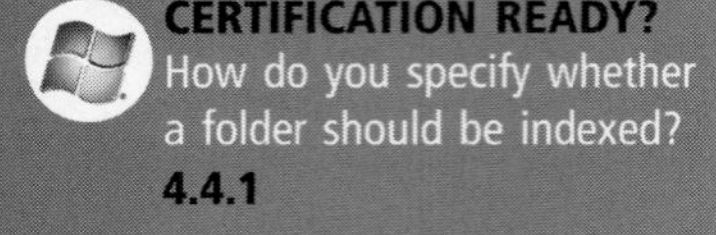

You can also specify whether to index a folder using its Properties dialog box. Right-click the folder and click Properties. Click the Advanced button in the Attributes section to display the Advanced Attributes dialog box. Select the Index this folder for faster searching checkbox to include the folder in the index, or deselect the checkbox to exclude it from the index. Click OK and then click OK in the Properties dialog box.

The Windows Vista index stores information such as the filename, size, and other properties. Its sole purpose is to make searching faster, more efficient, and more accurate. By default, system files and program files are not indexed, because you rarely need to find them. Your personal folders and files, which you may need to find using a search, are included in the index.

Although you can add locations to the index, if you add too many and the index becomes too large, it will start taking longer for Windows Vista to complete a search. If you remove locations, you may find that Windows Vista is not finding the items you need.

SUMMARY SKILL MATRIX

In this lesson you learned	Matrix Skill	Skill Number
To use a search box		
To search from the Start menu	Search by using keywords	4.4.4
To search in a folder	Search by using wildcards	4.4.3
To use a Search folder	Search by using a virtual folder	4.4.2
To conduct an Advanced Search	Filter results of a search	4.4.6
To reuse a search	Redisplay the results of a pervious search	4.4.5
To use search tools		
To customize the index	Specify whether a folder should be indexed	4.4.1

■ Knowledge Assessment

Matching

Match the term in Column 1 to its description in Column 2.

Column 1	Column 2
1. Search box	**a.** a temporary location used to store information, such as the results of a search
2. search text	**b.** a word that relates to a particular topic
3. search results	**c.** an area where you can key search text
4. search folder	**d.** the text that Windows Vista will look for to locate programs, files, and folders stored on your computer
5. wildcard	**e.** a collection of information about items stored on a computer, used to increase the speed and accuracy of a search
6. keyword	**f.** the way words are arranged
7. index	**g.** the items that match the specified criteria
8. filter	**h.** a virtual folder designed specifically for searching
9. virtual folder	**i.** to find items that meet certain criteria while excluding items that do not meet the criteria
10. syntax	**j.** characters that substitute for one or more actual characters

True/False

Circle T if the statement is true or F if the statement is false.

T F 1. A question mark is the Boolean filter for OR.
T F 2. An asterisk is the wildcard character that stands for one or more characters.
T F 3. By default, Windows Vista searches subfolders.
T F 4. System files are included in indexed locations.
T F 5. You can start an advanced search from the Start menu.
T F 6. You can save a search to use it again.
T F 7. A virtual folder exists in memory, not on a storage device.
T F 8. Boolean filters must be keyed in all uppercase letters.
T F 9. You must add a location to the index to include it in a search.
T F 10. Use the buttons in the Search pane to filter the search results by category.

■ Competency Assessment

Project 6-1: Find Program Files

While you were on vacation, a temporary worker deleted all of the program shortcuts from your desktop. In this project, you will search from the Start menu for the Notepad, WordPad, and Paint programs and create new desktop shortcut icons.

GET READY. Before you begin these steps, start your computer and log on to your Windows Vista account. Close all open windows so you can see the desktop.

1. Click **Start** to open the Start menu.

2. In the Search box at the bottom of the left pane of the Start menu, key **WordPad**. The program name should display in the search results in the left pane of the Start menu.
3. Right-click the **WordPad** program name in the search results, point to **Send To** on the shortcut menu, and then click **Desktop (create shortcut)**.
4. Delete the text **WordPad** from the Search box and key **Notepad**.
5. Right-click the **Notepad** program name in the search results, point to **Send To** on the shortcut menu, and then click **Desktop (create shortcut)**.
6. Delete the text **Notepad** from the Search box and key **Paint**.
7. Right-click the **Paint** program name in the search results, point to **Send To** on the shortcut menu, and then click **Desktop (create shortcut)**.
8. Press Esc to close the Start menu.
9. Delete the WordPad, Notepad, and Paint shortcuts from the desktop.

PAUSE. LEAVE the Windows Vista desktop displayed to use in the next project.

Project 6-2: Find Waterfront Files

As an assistant in the legal department of Contoso, Ltd., you must keep track of a lot of paperwork such as permits, permit applications, and correspondence with community administrators. You have many different types of files pertaining to your Waterfront project stored in different folders. In this project, you will locate all of the files pertaining to the Waterfront project and move them into the same folder.

The ***Zoning1***, ***Waterfront1***, and ***Walter1*** files are available on the companion CD-ROM.

1. From the desktop, click the **Start** button and then click **Documents**.
2. Right-click a blank area of the File list, click **New**, and then click **Folder**.
3. Key **Letters** and press Enter to rename the folder.
4. Copy the ***Walter1*** file from the data files for this lesson to the Letters folder.
5. In the Documents folder, create another new folder and name it **Regulations**. Copy the ***Zoning1*** file from the data files for this lesson to the **Regulations** folder.
6. In the Documents folder, create another new folder and name it **Site Photos**. Copy the ***Waterfront1*** file from the data files for this lesson to the Site Photos folder.
7. In the Documents folder, create another new folder and name it **Waterfront Project**.
8. Open the Letters folder and right-click a blank area of the File list, click **New** on the shortcut menu, and then click **Text Document**.
9. Key **Waterfront2** and then press Enter.
10. Navigate to the Documents window.
11. Click in the **Search** box and key **Waterfront**. Four items should display in the search results: the Waterfront Project folder and the ***Zoning1***, ***Waterfront1***, and ***Waterfront2*** files.
12. At this point, your instructor may ask you to capture an image of the Search Results window. Save it in your Lesson 6 assessment folder as ***Proj06_02***.
13. Select all three files (click the first file, press and hold Ctrl, and then click the other two files).
14. Right-click the selection and click **Cut**.
15. Double-click the **Waterfront Project** folder to open it.
16. Right-click a blank area of the File list and then click **Paste** to paste the three files into the folder.
17. **CLOSE** the Waterfront Project folder window.

PAUSE. LEAVE the desktop displayed to use in the next project.

■ Proficiency Assessment

Project 6-3: Find Fonts

You work at a stationery store where customers can order personalized invitations, cards, and other items. The store owner wants to print out a sample of Times New Roman font and Garamond font so people can see the difference. In this project, you will use an advanced search to find the Fonts folder. You will then search the Fonts folder to find the Times New Roman font file, which you will print, and then to find the Garamond font file, which you will print.

GET READY. Before you begin, make sure your printer is correctly connected to your computer and loaded with paper.

1. From the desktop, click **Start** and then click **Search** to display a Search folder.
2. Click the **Advanced Search** expand arrow to display the Advanced Search options.
3. Click the **Location** dropdown arrow and click **Everywhere**.
4. Click the **Name** box and key **Fonts**. Then click the **Search** button to begin the search. (If the search is taking too long, click the **Stop** button and try the following: Click the **Location** dropdown arrow, click **Local Hard Drives (C:)** and then click the **Search** button. If the Windows Vista system files are stored on a network, click the **Location** dropdown arrow, click **Choose search locations**, click **Expand Network**, and then click the location where the Windows files are stored. Click the **Search** button to start the Search.)
5. As soon as you see a Fonts folder in the search results, click the **Stop** button to stop the Search.
6. In the search results list, double-click the **Fonts** folder to open it. If there are multiple Fonts folders, double-click the one stored in the Windows folder.
7. Click in the **Search** box and key **Times**. All of the Times New Roman font files should display in the File list. At this point, your instructor may ask you to capture an image of the Fonts folder window. Save it in your Lesson 6 assessment folder as ***Proj06_03***.
8. Right-click the file named **Times New Roman** (not Times New Roman Bold or Italic) and click **Print** on the shortcut menu.
9. Click **Print** in the Print dialog box to print the file.
10. In the **Fonts** folder window, click in the **Search** box and delete the text **Times**.
11. Key **Garamond** to display the Garamond font files in the File list.
12. Right-click the file named **Garamond** (not Garamond Bold or Italic) and click **Print** on the shortcut menu.
13. Click **Print** in the Print dialog box to print the file.
14. **CLOSE** the Fonts folder window.

PAUSE. LEAVE the desktop displayed to use in the next project.

Project 6-4: More Waterfront Files

Another legal assistant at Contoso keeps sending you files but does not tell you which ones relate to the Waterfront project. None of the filenames indicate the content. In this project, you will create a folder for files from the other assistant and copy new files into it. You will search the folder for the Waterfront files and then save the search so you can use it again when she sends you additional files. You will use the saved search to locate Waterfront files, which you will copy into the Waterfront folder.

1. From the desktop, click **Start** and then click **Documents**.
2. Create a new folder and name it **A's Files**.

The ***Zoning2***, ***Photo1***, and ***Walter2*** files are available on the companion CD-ROM.

3. Copy the ***Zoning2***, ***Photo1***, and ***Walter2*** files from the data files for this lesson to the A's Files folder.
4. Close all open windows.
5. Click **Start** and then click **Search** to open a Search folder.
6. Click the **Advanced Search** expand arrow to display the Advanced Search options.
7. Click the **Location** dropdown arrow and click **Choose search locations** to open the Choose Search Locations dialog box.
8. Click the expand arrow next to your personal folder to expand it.
9. Click the expand arrow next to the Documents folder to expand it.
10. Click to select the checkbox to the left of the **A's Files** folder.
11. Click **OK**.
12. Click in the **Search** box and key **Waterfront**. Two files—***Photo1*** and ***Walter2***—should display in the search results. Your instructor may ask you to capture an image of the Search folder. Save it in your Lesson 6 assessment folder as ***Proj06_04***.
13. Click the **Save Search** button on the window's toolbar to display the Save As dialog box.
14. Click in the **File name** box and key **A's Waterfront Files**. Then click **Save**. Close the folder window.

The ***Photo2*** and ***Walter3*** files are available on the companion CD-ROM.

15. Copy the files ***Photo2*** and ***Walter3*** from the data files for this lesson to the A's Files folder in Documents.
16. Click **Searches** in the Favorite Links list in the Navigation pane to open the Searches folder.
17. In the File list of the Searches folder, double-click the **A's Waterfront Files** search. Windows Vista runs the search and this time finds three files—***Walter2***, ***Walter3***, and ***Photo1***.
18. Select all three files, right-click the selection, and click **Cut** on the shortcut menu.
19. Navigate to the Documents folder, right-click the **Waterfront Project** folder, and click **Paste** on the shortcut menu.
20. Open the Waterfront Project folder. It should contain six files.
21. **CLOSE** the Waterfront Project folder window.

PAUSE. LEAVE the desktop displayed to use in the next project.

■ Mastery Assessment

Project 6-5: Picture Files

The hard drive on your home computer has become full. As a result, your computer is performing slowly, and you have no storage space for new files. You know that picture files take up a lot of space, so you decide to move the largest of your picture files to an external drive. In this project, you will search your local hard drive for picture files that are larger than 100KB. You will save the search so that when you purchase an external drive in the future, you can open the saved search, locate the files, and move them to the new drive.

1. From the desktop, open a new Search folder.
2. In the Search pane, click **Picture** to limit the search to picture files.
3. Display the **Advanced Search** options and select to search your **local hard drive**.
4. Select to search for files that are **greater than 100KB** in size.
5. Run the search. It may take a while, depending on how many picture files are stored on your local drive.
6. When the search is complete, save it with a name such as Large Picture Files.

7. At your instructor's request, open the Searches folder and copy the Large Picture Files search to your Lesson 6 assessment folder.
8. Close all open windows.
9. If you want, run the search and copy the results to a removable device, such as a DVD or external drive. Then, delete the saved search from the Searches folder.

PAUSE. LEAVE the desktop displayed to use in the next project.

Project 6-6: Customize a Search

As a legal assistant at Contoso, Ltd., you think you can make your search for files related to the Waterfront project more efficient. For example, because you know that the Waterfront Project folder contains Waterfront files, you do not need to keep searching it. You also think you could search faster user natural language search text. In this project, you will change the Search options to allow natural language searches, and you will exclude the Waterfront Project folder from the index. You will then search for photo files using wildcard characters, and then using natural language search text.

The ***Photo3***, ***Photo4***, and ***Photo5*** files are available on the companion CD-ROM.

1. Copy the files ***Photo3***, ***Photo4***, and ***Photo5*** from the data files for this lesson to the A's Files folder.
2. Open the Documents folder, open the Searches folder, and then open the A's Waterfront Files saved search.
3. Display the Search tab of the Folder Options dialog box.
4. Select the option to **Use natural language search**.
5. Modify the **Index** to exclude the **Waterfront Project** folder. If you are not authorized to modify all locations in the index, use the folder's Properties dialog box.
6. Navigate to the Documents folder and key the search text **Photo?** to search for any file that starts with the text Photo followed by any single character. The search results should display ***Photo2***, ***Photo3***, ***Photo4***, and ***Photo5***. ***Photo1***, which is in the Waterfront Project folder, should be excluded. If your instructor asks you to capture an image of the folder window, save in your Lesson 6 assessment folder as ***Proj06_06***.
7. Navigate to the Documents folder and key the search text **pictures of the Waterfront Site**. The search results should display ***Photo3*** and ***Photo5***.
8. Restore the default Search options.
9. Copy the A's Waterfront Files search to your Lesson 6 assessment folder, and then delete it from the Searches folder.
10. Delete the A's Files, Letters, Site Photos, Regulations, and Waterfront Project folders from Documents.
11. **CLOSE** all open windows.

LOG OFF your Windows Vista user account.

INTERNET READY

At Contoso, Ltd., assistants in the legal department often have to search the Internet to find information. Most web browsers come with search tools, such as Live Search in Microsoft Internet Explorer, or you can use a search site, such as Google or Yahoo. In this exercise, test at least three different web search tools to see how they compare. Key the same search text in each search tool. Then, compare the results to see which search tool is more effective for your needs. For example, you might compare the number of results, the type of results, and the relevance of the results to the search text. You might consider whether the search tool is easy or difficult to use. You might also note how many advertisements there are on the search results page, or whether there are pop-up ads. Record the results in a spreadsheet or word processing file.

Personalizing the Vista Workspace

LESSON SKILL MATRIX

Skills	Matrix Skill	Skill Number
Customizing the Start Menu		
Selecting Start Menu Settings	Customize the Start menu	6.1.1
Pinning, Unpinning, and Removing Start Menu Items	Pin and unpin items from the Start menu; Add a program to the Start menu	6.1.2, 6.1.4
Managing the Taskbar		
Moving and Sizing the Taskbar	Move the Taskbar to the right side of the screen	6.2.3
Hiding the Taskbar	Automatically hide the Taskbar when not in use	6.2.4
Displaying and Hiding the Quick Launch Toolbar	Display the Quick Launch toolbar on the Taskbar	6.2.1
Adding a Toolbar to the Taskbar	Add a toolbar to the Taskbar	6.2.2
Customizing the Notification Area	Customize the notification area	6.2.5
Working with shortcuts		
Adding a Folder Shortcut to the Start Menu	Add a folder shortcut to the Start menu	4.2.3
Configuring a Program to Start Automatically	Configure a program to start automatically	6.1.3
Managing the Windows Sidebar		
Hiding and Displaying the Sidebar	Display the Windows Sidebar	6.4.1
Configuring the Sidebar	Configure the Windows Sidebar	6.4.2
Adding Gadgets to the Sidebar	Add gadgets to the Windows Sidebar	6.4.3
Customizing the Desktop		
Selecting a Desktop Background	Change the appearance of a computer	6.3.1
Customizing Window Colors	Change the appearance of a computer	6.3.1
Adjusting Display Settings	Adjust your display resolution; Adjust the display refresh rate; Select the display color depth setting	3.4.1, 3.4.2, 3.4.3
Selecting a Screen Saver	Change the screen saver; Change the screen saver delay time	6.3.4, 1.4.1
Controlling Desktop Icons	Arrange desktop icons; Adjust icon size	6.3.2 3.4.4

Woodgrove Bank prides itself on developing personal relationships with customers. Branches are designed with an open floor plan, so managers' desks are available to anyone at any time. That means computer screens are visible throughout the bank. The company wants to develop desktop settings that represent the company and that can be applied to all PCs to project a uniform image. In this lesson, you will learn how to personalize the Windows Vista workspace. Specifically, you will learn to customize the Start menu, manage the Taskbar and the Sidebar, customize the desktop, and work with shortcuts.

KEY TERMS
Active information
color depth
color scheme
Context menu
Gadget Gallery
inactive
Live preview
notifications
pin
pixel
refresh rate
resolution
screen saver
toolbar sizing handle
wallpaper

■ Customizing the Start Menu

THE BOTTOM LINE

The Start menu is your entry point into the programs and features installed on your computer. The default settings are designed to meet the needs of most people, by providing access to the most commonly used items. You can customize the Start menu so that the items you use most often are always easily available. In this section, you will learn how to select Start menu settings and to place program shortcuts on the Start menu.

Selecting Start Menu Settings

The default Start menu settings make the most commonly used items available. In the Customize Start Menu dialog box, you can select the way links, icons, and menus display and behave. You can also set the number of recent programs you want on the menu and choose whether to display a link to your Internet browser and your email program.

SELECT START MENU SETTINGS

GET READY. Before you begin these steps, start your computer and log on to your Windows Vista account. Close all open windows so you can see the desktop. Create a new folder named Lesson 7 in a storage location specified by your instructor, where you can store assessment files and folders that you create during this lesson.

1. Right-click a blank area of the Taskbar to display a shortcut menu and then click **Properties**. The Taskbar and Start Menu Properties dialog box displays.
2. Click the **Start Menu** tab and then click the **Customize** button. The Customize Start Menu dialog box displays, as shown in Figure 7-1. The list at the top of the dialog box includes items such as links, icons, and programs that are available to display in the right pane of the Start menu, as well as options that control how each item opens. Other elements in the dialog box let you set the number of recently used programs that will display in the left pane and select the Internet and E-mail programs to display. There is also a button that restores the default settings.

Figure 7-1

Customize Start Menu dialog box

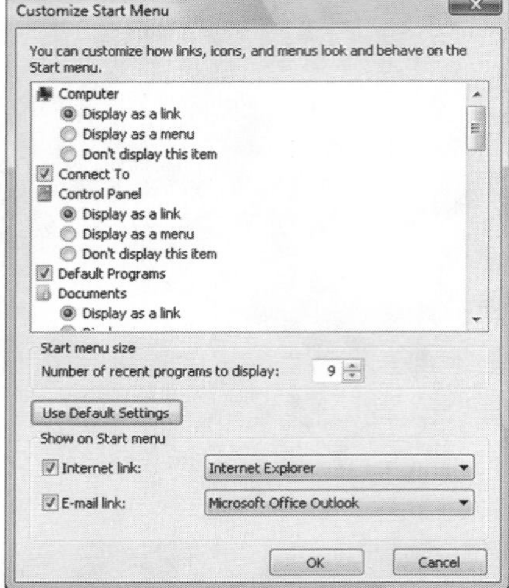

TROUBLESHOOTING

If the Customize Classic Start Menu dialog box displays, click Cancel to return to the Taskbar and Start Menu Properties dialog box, click the Start menu option button, and then click the Customize button.

To open the Taskbar and Start Menu dialog box with the Start Menu tab active, click the Start button, right-click a blank area of the Start menu, and click Properties.

3. Click the **Use Default Settings** button to restore the defaults. If necessary, click to select the **Internet link** and **E-mail link** checkboxes and then click **OK** to return to the Start Menu tab of the Taskbar and Start Menu Properties dialog box. Recall that when a checkbox is selected, it has a checkmark in it; when it is not selected, it is blank.
4. If necessary, click to select the Store and display a list of recently opened files checkbox and the Store and display a list of recently opened programs checkbox.
5. Click **OK** in the Taskbar and Start Menu Properties dialog box.
6. Click the **Start** button to display the Start menu with the default settings. It should look similar to Figure 7-2, although the specific programs and item names on your computer may be different from the ones in the figure. Notice that nine recently used programs and an Internet and email program are listed in the left pane, and links to standard folders are in the right pane. In the right pane, all but Recent Items are set to display as links, which means when you click the item, the folder window opens. Recent Items is set to display as a menu, which means when you point to it or click it, a menu or list of recently used items displays.

Figure 7-2

Default Start menu

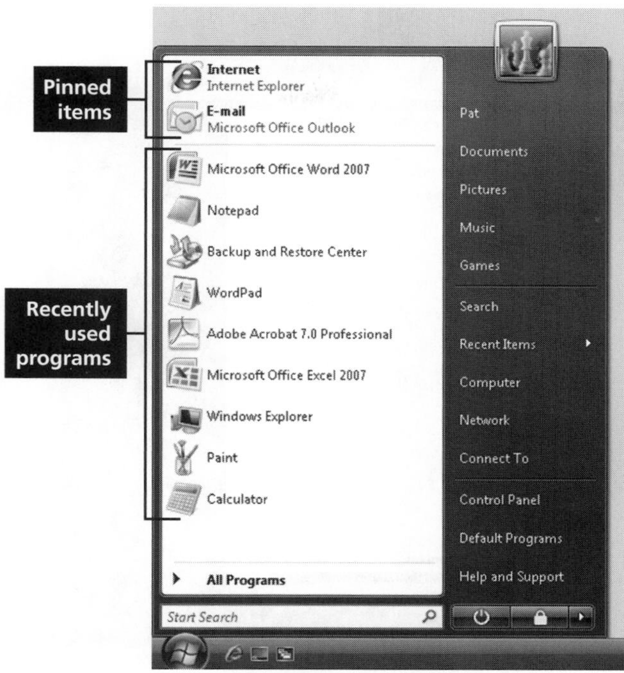

7. Right-click a blank area of the Taskbar and then click **Properties**. Click the **Start Menu** tab and then click the **Customize** button to display the Customize Start Menu dialog box again. In the list at the top of the dialog box, you can select which items to display in the right pane, and how you want the items to behave.
8. Under Computer, click the **Display as a menu** option button. Selecting this option changes the way the item opens from a link to a menu.
9. Click to clear the **Connect To** and **Default Programs** checkboxes. Deselecting these items removes them from the right pane of the Start menu.
10. Scroll down the list, noting the available options. At the bottom of the list, click to deselect the **Use Large Icons** checkbox.
11. Under Start menu size, click the down increment arrow to change the number of recent programs to display to four.
12. Under Show on Start menu, click to clear the **Internet link** and **E-mail link** checkboxes.
13. Click **OK** and then click **Apply** in the Taskbar and Start Menu Properties dialog box.

TAKE NOTE*

Using smaller icons lets you fit more items on the Start menu.

TAKE NOTE*

Clicking an Apply button in a dialog box applies the current options but leaves the dialog box open so that you can make additional changes.

14. Click the **Start** button. The Start menu should look similar to Figure 7-3. In the left pane, notice that only four recently used programs are listed, and that the icons are smaller. The Internet and email links do not display. In the right pane, notice that the Connect To and Default Programs items do not display, and that Computer is now a menu. If you point to it, a menu of computer components, such as storage devices, displays.

Figure 7-3

Customized Start menu

15. At this point, your instructor may ask you to capture an image of the screen showing the Start menu. (Use Alt+Print Screen to capture just the Start menu, or Print Screen to capture the full desktop.) Save it in your Lesson 7 assessment folder as ***Le07_01***.
16. Press Esc to cancel the Start menu and click the **Customize** button on the Start Menu tab of the Taskbar and Start Menu Properties dialog box.
17. Click the **Use Default Settings** button to restore the default settings, click to select the **Internet link** and **E-mail link** checkboxes, and then click **OK.** Click **OK** in the Taskbar and Start Menu Properties dialog box to apply the changes and close the dialog box.

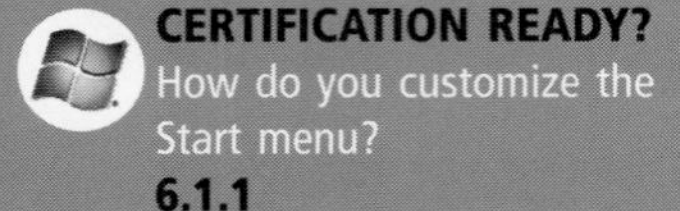
CERTIFICATION READY?
How do you customize the Start menu?
6.1.1

PAUSE. LEAVE the Windows Vista desktop displayed to use in the next exercise.

You can easily use the options in the Customize Start Menu dialog box to control the items that display in both the left and right panes of the Start menu. As you have seen, you can also select to display items in the right pane as menus instead of as links.

You might prefer using a menu if you want to go directly to an item stored in the main folder rather than having to navigate through folder windows. For example, if you frequently access a particular storage device, such as a flash drive, you can set Computer to display as a menu. Then, instead of opening the Computer folder and navigating to the flash drive, you can just select the flash drive from the Computer menu.

In addition to selecting items to display in the right pane, you may have noticed options for controlling general Start menu behavior, including the following:

- Enable context menus and dragging and dropping. ***Context menu*** is another term for shortcut menu. This option is selected by default. If you deselect this option, no shortcut menus display when you right-click a Start menu item, and you cannot drag an item to pin or unpin it to the Start menu.
- Highlight newly installed programs. This option is selected by default, so that when a new program is installed on your computer, the All Programs menu and the item on the All Programs menu are highlighted. If you deselect this option, newly installed programs are not highlighted.
- Open submenus when I pause on them with the mouse pointer. This option is selected by default. If you deselect this option, you must click an item to open a menu.

- Sort All Programs menu by name. This option is selected by default. Deselect this option if you want to arrange items on the All Programs menu in a different order, not alphabetically by name. You can drag the items to reposition them on the menu.

Finally, in addition to selecting to display links to your Internet browser and email program, you can select the specific program to display. This is useful if you have more than one browser or email program installed. Simply click the dropdown arrow and click the program to use.

In the next section, you learn how pin, unpin, and remove Start menu items.

Pinning, Unpinning, and Removing Start Menu Items

To make programs always available on the Start menu, you can add them to the pinned items list at the top of the left pane. You can easily unpin them when you no longer need them. You can also remove any item from the list of recently used programs.

PIN, UNPIN, AND REMOVE START MENU ITEMS

1. Click the **Start** button, click **All Programs**, and then click **Accessories** to expand the Accessories folder.
2. Right-click **Calculator** to display a shortcut menu.
3. On the shortcut menu, click **Pin to Start Menu**. To ***pin*** means to place a shortcut to the program in the pinned items list, which is at the top of the left pane of the Start menu.
4. Press Esc to close the All Programs menu. Notice that Calculator now displays in the list of pinned items at the top of the left pane.
5. Click **All Programs** on the Start menu, click **Accessories** to expand it, if necessary, and then click **Notepad** to launch the Notepad program. Click the **Close** button to exit Notepad.
6. Click the **Start** button. Notepad should display in the list of recently used programs. Right-click it and click **Pin to Start Menu** on the shortcut menu. Notepad moves up to the list of pinned items, as shown in Figure 7-4.

TROUBLESHOOTING

If the Start menu closes when you press Esc, click the Start button to display it again.

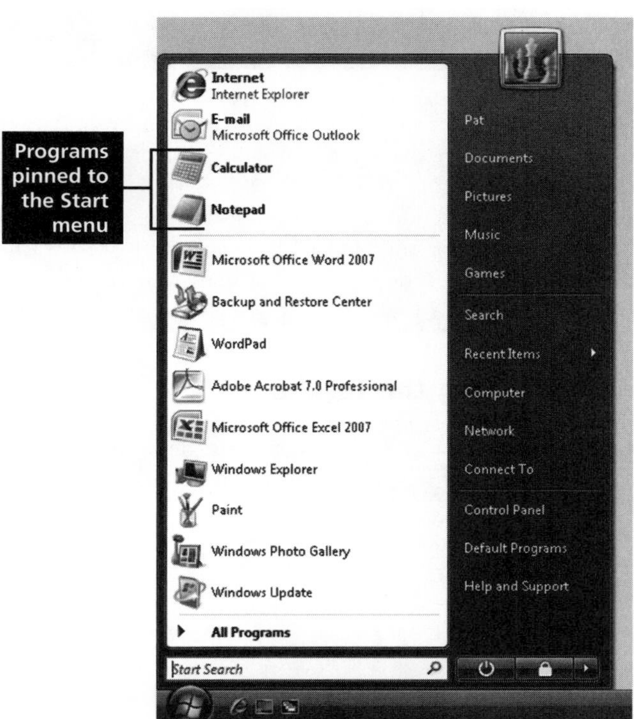

Figure 7-4
Pinned items on the Start menu

TROUBLESHOOTING

If Notepad does not display in the list of recently used programs, make sure you have selected the Store and display a list of recently opened programs checkbox on the Start Menu tab of the Taskbar and Start Menu Properties dialog box. Then, try repeating step 5 to open Notepad again. If it still does not display, try using WordPad in place of Notepad.

7. At this point, your instructor may ask you to capture an image of the screen with the Start menu displayed. Save it in your Lesson 7 assessment folder as ***Le07_02***.
8. Right-click **Calculator** in the list of pinned items and then click **Unpin from Start Menu**. It is removed from the list and no longer displays on the Start menu.
9. Right-click **Notepad** and click **Unpin from Start Menu**. It is removed from the list of pinned items and moves back to the list of recently used programs.
10. Right-click **Notepad** in the list of recently used programs and click **Remove from this list**. Notepad no longer displays on the Start menu.
11. Press Esc to close the Start menu.

PAUSE. LEAVE the desktop displayed to use in the next exercise.

CERTIFICATION READY?
How do you pin and unpin items from the Start menu?
6.1.2
How do you add a program to the Start menu?
6.1.4

When you pin a program to the Start menu, you create a shortcut to the program so you do not have to open the All Programs list to find it. Unpinning or removing a program does not delete the program or remove the program from the All Programs list.

Note that you can use a different procedure to pin folders and files to the Start menu. Adding a folder shortcut to the Start menu is covered later in this lesson.

If you have a lot of items pinned to the Start menu, you may run out of room for recently used programs, and Windows Vista may display a message indicating that all items cannot be displayed. You can decrease the number of items in your recently used programs list, or you can deselect the option for using large icons on the Start menu. Both of these options leave more room on the Start menu for pinned items.

Next, you learn how to customize the Taskbar.

■ Managing the Taskbar

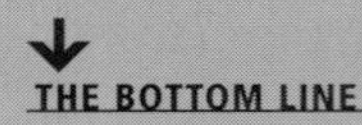

The Taskbar provides access to the Start menu and all open windows. It also displays the notification area and the Quick Launch Toolbar. By default, it always displays along the bottom of the desktop. You can customize the Taskbar to suit your working style. For example, you might want it positioned on the side of the desktop, or you might not want it to display unless you need it. In this section, you learn how to resize and move the Taskbar and how to hide it. You also learn how to show or hide the Quick Launch Toolbar, create your own toolbars on the Taskbar, and customize the notification area.

Moving and Sizing the Taskbar

You can move the Taskbar to any side of the desktop. You can also make the Taskbar wider to display larger icons or more Taskbar buttons.

MOVE AND SIZE THE TASKBAR

GET READY. Before you begin these steps, make sure the Taskbar is not locked. Right-click a blank area of the Taskbar to display a shortcut menu and then locate the Lock the Taskbar command. If it has a checkmark next to it, click it to unlock the Taskbar.

1. Position the mouse pointer so that it is touching a blank area of the Taskbar.
2. Press and hold the left mouse button and then drag the Taskbar toward the right side of the desktop.
3. When the Taskbar displays on the right, release the left mouse button. Your desktop should look similar to Figure 7-5.

Figure 7-5

Move the Taskbar to the right side of the screen

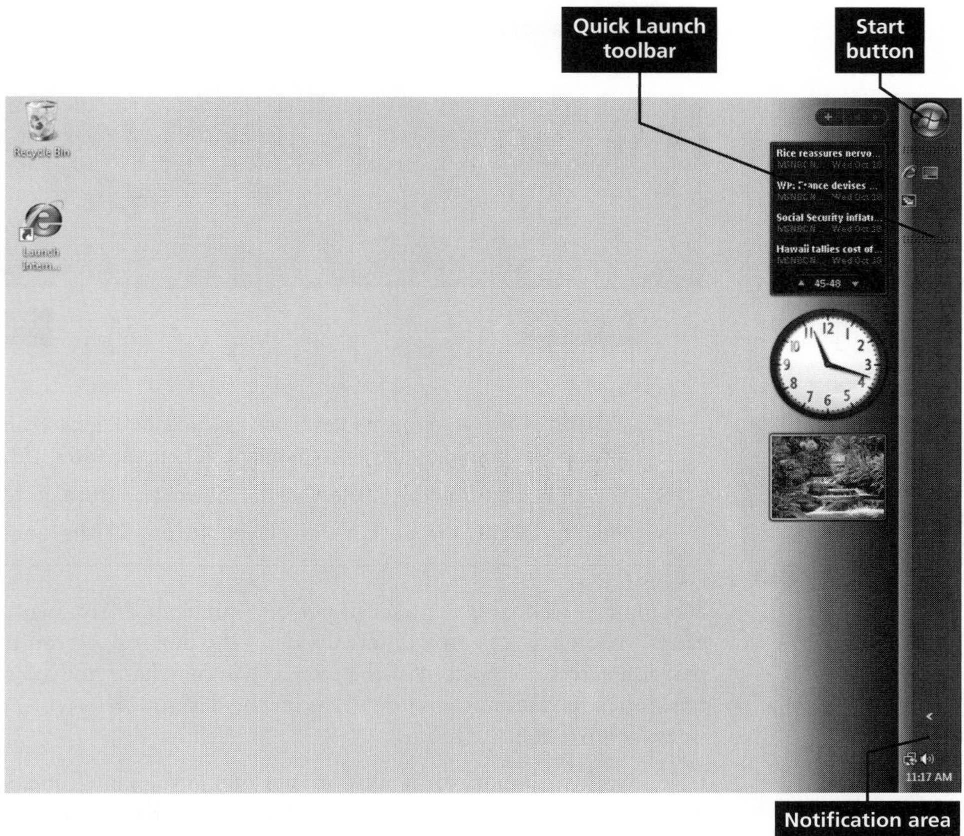

4. Drag the Taskbar to the top of the desktop, to the left side, and then back to the bottom.
5. Position the mouse pointer so that it is touching the top border of the Taskbar. It should change to resemble a vertical double-headed arrow.
6. Press and hold the left mouse button and drag up. As you drag, the height of the Taskbar increases in increments of approximately .5 inches.
7. When the Taskbar is about 4 inches high, release the left mouse button. Your desktop should look similar to Figure 7-6.

Figure 7-6

Resize the Taskbar

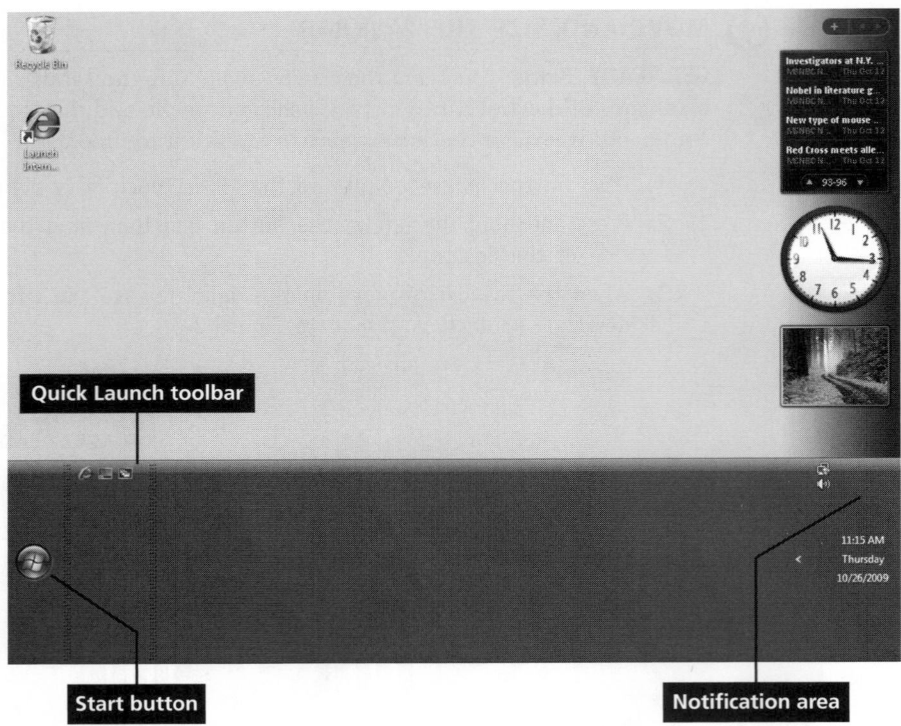

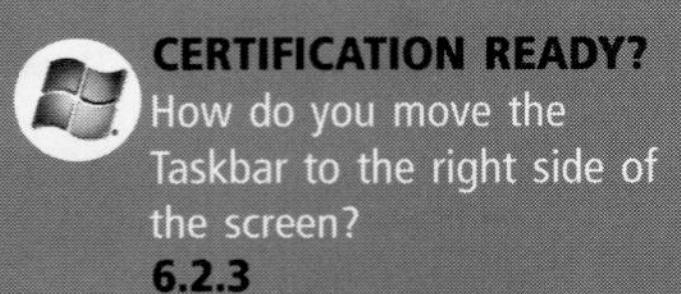

CERTIFICATION READY?
How do you move the Taskbar to the right side of the screen?
6.2.3

8. At this point your instructor may ask you to capture an image of the screen. Save it in your Lesson 7 assessment folder as ***Le07_03***.
9. Drag the top border of the Taskbar down to return it to its default size.

PAUSE. LEAVE the desktop displayed to use in the next exercise.

Moving the Taskbar is a matter of personal preference. You may find it less distracting or easier to access if it is on a different side of the desktop, or you may like it in its default position across the bottom of the screen. You may have noticed that no matter where it is positioned, it does not obscure items on the desktop. Shortcuts, open windows, and the sidebar move to make room.

If you work with many programs or windows at the same time, you may want to resize your Taskbar so that you can see every Taskbar button. Keep in mind, however, that a larger Taskbar leaves less space to view programs and other content on the desktop.

Note that you cannot move or resize the Taskbar if it is locked. Locking keeps it anchored in its current position.

In the next section, you learn how to hide the Taskbar.

Hiding the Taskbar

You can control whether the Taskbar displays by using options on the Taskbar tab of the Taskbar and Start Menu Properties dialog box.

HIDE THE TASKBAR

1. Click the **Start** button and then click your personal folder to open it. Click the **Maximize** button in the folder window to increase its size to fill the desktop. Notice that you can see the Taskbar along the bottom of the screen, because in its default setting, it always displays on top of open windows
2. Right-click a blank area of the Taskbar and click **Properties** on the shortcut menu. The Taskbar tab of the Taskbar and Start Menu Properties dialog box displays.
3. Click to select the **Auto-hide the taskbar** checkbox. Notice that the preview area shows how the change will affect the display.
4. Click **Apply**. Immediately, the Taskbar is hidden so that it no longer displays across the bottom of the screen.
5. Move the mouse pointer to the bottom of the screen, where the Taskbar was. The Taskbar displays.
6. In the Taskbar and Start Menu Properties dialog box, click to deselect the **Auto-hide the taskbar** checkbox and then click **Apply**. The Taskbar displays again.
7. In the Taskbar and Start Menu Properties dialog box, click to deselect the **Keep the taskbar on top of other windows** checkbox and then click **Apply**. This option does not hide the Taskbar, but lets the active window display in front.
8. Click your personal folder's Taskbar button to make the window active. The window moves to the front, on top of the Taskbar. This makes more space available for viewing the contents of the window.
9. Move the mouse pointer to the bottom of the screen, where the Taskbar was. It does not display, because it is not hidden, just obscured by your personal folder window.
10. Minimize your personal folder window. Now, you can see the Taskbar.
11. In the Taskbar and Start Menu Properties dialog box, click to select the **Keep the taskbar on top of other windows** checkbox and then click **OK** to apply the changes and close the dialog box.
12. Right-click your personal folder's Taskbar button and click **Close** on the shortcut menu.

PAUSE. LEAVE the desktop displayed to use in the next exercise.

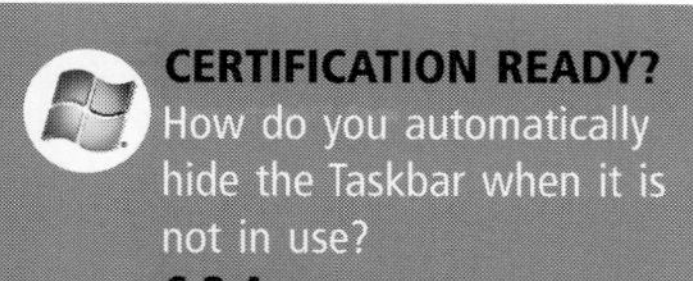
CERTIFICATION READY?
How do you automatically hide the Taskbar when it is not in use?
6.2.4

Hiding the Taskbar makes more space available on the desktop. You may prefer it hidden if you spend a lot of time working in the same window, but if you frequently change windows, or need to access other programs and features, you may want the Taskbar displayed at all times.

The Taskbar tab of the Taskbar and Start Menu Properties dialog box provides other options that you might find useful:

- Lock the taskbar. Select this option to keep the Taskbar locked in its current position and size. Recall that you can quickly toggle this option by right-clicking the Taskbar and clicking Lock the Taskbar on the shortcut menu.
- Group similar taskbar buttons. Deselect this option to show a separate Taskbar button for each open window. If you use many open windows at a time, this could result in an overcrowded Taskbar, with very small buttons.
- Show Quick Launch. Use this option to toggle the display of the Quick Launch Toolbar off and on.

- Show window previews (thumbnails). Use this option to toggle the display of ***live previews*** for your Taskbar buttons. A live preview is a thumbnail sized replica of the window, showing the actual window content. When live preview is off, only a ScreenTip displays. (Live preview is only available if you are using the Aero version of Windows Vista.)

In the next section, you learn how to control the Quick Launch Toolbar.

Displaying and Hiding the Quick Launch Toolbar

The Quick Launch Toolbar is a toolbar of shortcuts that displays to the right of the Start button on the Taskbar. You can select whether you want to display the Quick Launch Toolbar, and you can make it larger or smaller as necessary.

DISPLAY AND HIDE THE QUICK LAUNCH TOOLBAR

1. Right-click a blank area of the Taskbar and click **Properties** on the shortcut menu. The Taskbar tab of the Taskbar and Start Menu Properties dialog box displays.
2. Click to deselect the **Show Quick Launch** checkbox. Notice that the preview area shows how the change will affect the display.
3. Click **Apply**. Immediately, the Quick Launch Toolbar is hidden.
4. In the Taskbar and Start Menu Properties dialog box, click to select the **Show Quick Launch** checkbox and then click **OK**. The dialog box closes, and the toolbar displays on the Taskbar again.

You can also toggle the Quick Launch Toolbar off and on using the Taskbar shortcut menu. Right-click the Taskbar, point to Toolbars on the shortcut menu, and then click Quick Launch. A checkmark indicates that the toolbar is displayed.

5. Position the mouse pointer over the toolbar sizing handle to the right of the Quick Launch Toolbar. A ***toolbar sizing handle*** is an element that displays at one end of Taskbar toolbar, comprised of three columns of dots. Drag the handle to change the width of the toolbar.
6. Press and hold the left mouse button. The mouse pointer should change to a double vertical line with a two-headed arrow.
7. Drag the handle to the left until only one icon displays on the Quick Launch Toolbar. Then release the mouse button. Now, the toolbar is not wide enough for all of its icons, so a double chevron displays. A double chevron looks like two right angle brackets side by side.
8. Click the **double chevron**. A menu of hidden toolbar icons displays, as shown in Figure 7-7. You can click any icon on the menu to select it.

X REF

You learn how to add shortcuts to the Quick Launch Toolbar later in this lesson.

Figure 7-7
Customize the Quick Launch Toolbar

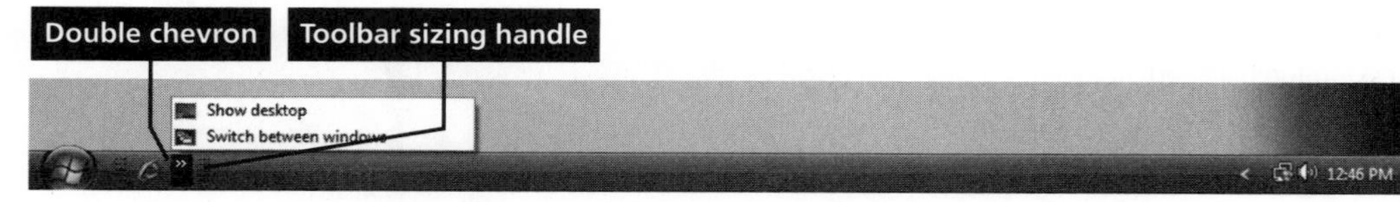

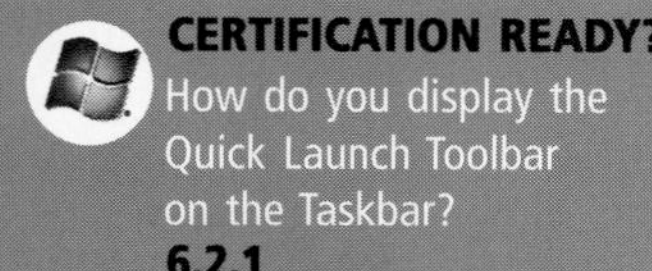

CERTIFICATION READY?
How do you display the Quick Launch Toolbar on the Taskbar?
6.2.1

9. Click a blank area of the desktop to close the menu and then drag the Quick Launch Toolbar sizing handle to the right until all icons display.

   PAUSE. LEAVE the desktop displayed to use in the next exercise.

The Quick Launch Toolbar is just one more tool providing quick access to the programs you use most often. It's easy to start a program because the Quick Launch Toolbar displays on the Taskbar, and you can single-click an icon to select it.

In the next section, you learn about the other toolbars you can display on the Taskbar.

Adding a Toolbar to the Taskbar

In addition to the Quick Launch Toolbar, Windows Vista has other toolbars you can display on the Taskbar. To toggle Taskbar toolbars off and on, use the Taskbar shortcut menu. You can also control the way a toolbar displays on the Taskbar, including the size of the icons, and whether text labels are visible.

ADD A TOOLBAR TO THE TASKBAR

1. Right-click a blank area of the Taskbar and then point to **Toolbars** on the shortcut menu. A list of available toolbars displays, including the Quick Launch Toolbar, and an option to create a new toolbar.

TAKE NOTE*

Recall that a checkmark next to an item on a menu indicates that the item is selected, or toggled on. In this case, a checkmark means that the toolbar is displayed.

2. Click **Desktop** on the Toolbars menu. The Desktop toolbar displays on the Taskbar, to the left of the notification area. The double chevron indicates that icons are hidden.

ANOTHER WAY

You can also use the Toolbars tab of the Taskbar and Start Menu dialog box to display toolbars on the Taskbar. Right-click a blank area of the Taskbar, click Properties, and then click the Toolbars tab. Click to select the toolbars you want to display and then click OK.

3. Drag the **Desktop** toolbar sizing handle to the left to increase the width of the toolbar. Stop dragging when you can see an icon for your personal folder.
4. Click the icon for your personal folder. A single click opens the folder window. Close the window.
5. Right-click the **Desktop** toolbar on the Taskbar. At the top of the shortcut menu are options for controlling the display of the toolbar, as shown in Figure 7-8.

Figure 7-8

Desktop toolbar shortcut menu

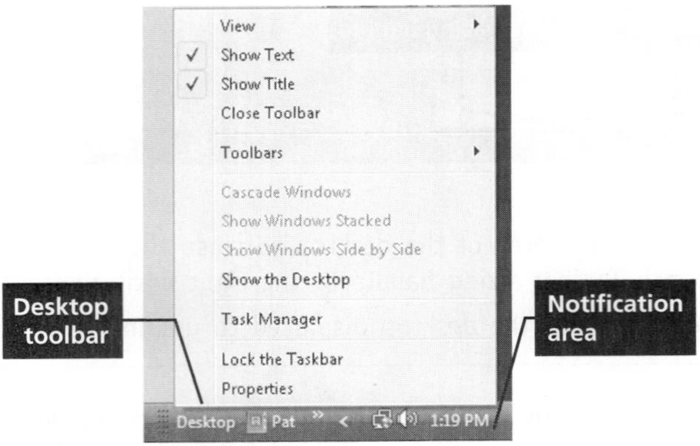

TROUBLESHOOTING If a menu of options for a program or feature displays instead of options for the Desktop toolbar, you right-clicked the icon in the Notification area. To display a toolbar's menu, be sure to right-click a blank area of the toolbar or the toolbar name.

6. Point to **View** on the shortcut menu and then click **Large Icons**. The size of the icons on the Desktop toolbar increases, and the height of the Taskbar increases as well. Notice that the icons on the Quick Launch Toolbar do not change, because the command affects only the current toolbar.
7. Right-click the **Desktop** toolbar again and then click to deselect **Show Text**. This toggles the command to hide the names of icons on the toolbar. When the names are off, you can identify the icons by using ScreenTips.
8. Right-click the **Desktop** toolbar again and then click to deselect **Show Title**. This toggles the command to hide the name of the toolbar. At this point, your instructor may ask you to capture an image of the screen showing the Desktop toolbar on the Taskbar. Save it in your Lesson 7 assessment folder as ***Le07_04***.
9. Right-click the **Desktop** toolbar and click **Show Title** to toggle the toolbar name on. Then right-click the Desktop toolbar and click **Show Text** to toggle the icon names on.
10. Right-click the **Desktop** toolbar, point to **View**, and then click **Small Icons** to return to the default small icon display.
11. Right-click the **Desktop** toolbar and click **Close Toolbar** on the shortcut menu. The Confirm Toolbar Close dialog box displays.

TROUBLESHOOTING If the Confirm Toolbar Close dialog box does not display, someone customized your system so the toolbar would be hidden without the extra step.

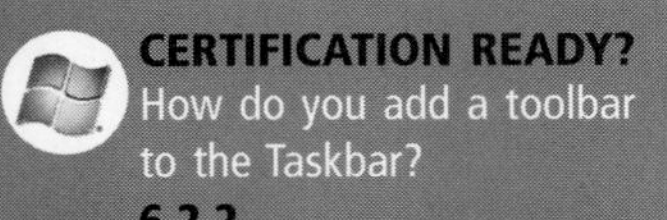

CERTIFICATION READY?
How do you add a toolbar to the Taskbar?
6.2.2

12. Click **OK** to hide the toolbar.

PAUSE. LEAVE the desktop displayed to use in the next exercise.

As mentioned, the toolbar shortcut menu options affect only the current toolbar, no matter how many toolbars are displayed on the Taskbar. If you want to change the display of a different toolbar, such as the Quick Launch Toolbar, right-click that toolbar and select the desired options.

You can easily create a Taskbar toolbar for any folder on your computer by right-clicking the Taskbar, pointing to Toolbars, and clicking New Toolbar. In the New Toolbar - Choose a folder window, navigate to the folder you want to use and then click Select Folder. Windows Vista creates a custom toolbar and displays it on the Taskbar.

In the next section, you customize the notification area.

Customizing the Notification Area

The notification area displays icons for programs, pop-up messages about the status or progress of programs and devices, and system icons, such as the clock. You can customize the area to show or hide icons.

CUSTOMIZE THE NOTIFICATION AREA

ANOTHER WAY

To open the Taskbar and Start Menu Properties dialog box with the Notification Area tab active, right-click a blank area of the notification area and click Properties.

1. Right-click a blank area of the Taskbar and then click **Properties** to display the Taskbar and Start Menu Properties dialog box.
2. Click the **Notification Area** tab.
3. Under Icons, click to deselect the **Hide inactive icons** checkbox. Under System icons, click to deselect the **Clock** checkbox. Notice that the preview displays how the change will affect the notification area.
4. Click the **Apply** button. The clock is removed from the notification area, and all icons—even those that are inactive—display. By default, Windows Vista hides inactive icons. ***Inactive*** means that the program is not running, or the feature is not in use.
5. In the Taskbar and Start Menu Properties dialog box, click to select the **Clock** checkbox and the **Hide inactive icons** checkbox. Then click **Apply**. The clock displays, and inactive icons are hidden.
6. Click the left-pointing arrow to the right of the notification area. The area temporarily expands to show all of the hidden icons.

TAKE NOTE*

Although the notification area will automatically hide the icons momentarily, you can click the right-pointing arrowhead to hide them immediately.

7. In the Taskbar and Start Menu Properties dialog box, click the **Customize** button. The Customize Notification Icons dialog box displays. It includes a list of all icons that are currently in the notification area as well as icons that have been in that area in the past. By default, all icons are set to be hidden when inactive.

TROUBLESHOOTING

The items in your notification area depend on the programs installed on your system and the way your system is set up. They may not be the same as the items on a different computer.

8. Click the first item in the list to select it. A dropdown arrow becomes available.
9. Click the dropdown arrow to display a menu of choices. If you click Hide, the icon will always be hidden, even when it is active. If you click Show, the icon will always show, even when it is inactive.
10. Click **Show** and then click **OK**. In the Taskbar and Start Menu Properties dialog box, click **Apply**. The icon that you selected to show should display in the notification area, even if it is inactive.
11. Click **Customize** again and then click the **Default Settings** button to restore the default settings.
12. Click **OK** and then click **OK** in the Taskbar and Start Menu Properties dialog box.

PAUSE. LEAVE the desktop displayed to use in the next exercise.

CERTIFICATION READY?
How do you customize the notification area?
6.2.5

In addition to the Clock, you can select to show or hide an icon for your system Volume and one for your Network. On some systems, you can display a Power icon as well.

Usually, you can click an icon in the notification area to display options or controls for that program or feature. For example, if you click the Volume icon, you display a slider that lets you adjust the volume higher or lower. You can usually double-click an icon to launch the program, or to open a window where you can select options and settings for that program.

Sometimes, Windows Vista displays ***notifications*** in the notification area, which are pop-up windows that provide information about the status of a program, or prompt you to take action. For example, Windows Update may display a notification when updates are ready for downloading or installing.

In the next section, you learn how to work with shortcuts.

■ Working with Shortcuts

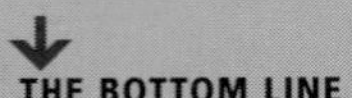

Shortcuts are the icons that let you quickly launch programs, open folders, and access features from any Windows Vista location at any time. Some shortcuts come built into Windows Vista, such as the items on the Start menu or the Quick Launch Toolbar, but you can create your own shortcuts to programs and folders that you use a lot. In this section, you learn how to create a shortcut on the desktop and in a folder window. You also learn how to add a shortcut to the Quick Launch Toolbar or the Start menu, and how to use a shortcut to configure a program to start automatically. You also learn how to delete shortcuts.

Creating a Shortcut on the Desktop

A shortcut on the desktop gives you instant access to a program, folder, or file that you use frequently.

CREATE A SHORTCUT ON THE DESKTOP

1. Click **Start**, click **All Programs**, and then click **Accessories**.
2. Right-click **Calculator** on the Accessories menu and then click **Send To**. On the Send To submenu, click **Desktop (create shortcut)**. Windows Vista creates a desktop shortcut to the Calculator program. Recall that an arrow in the lower left corner of an icon indicates that it is a shortcut.
3. Click **Start** to open the Start menu if it is not already open and then click your personal folder to open it.
4. Right-click the **Documents** folder, click **Send To**, and then click **Desktop (create shortcut)**. Windows Vista creates a shortcut to the Documents folder on the desktop.
5. Navigate to the Computer folder. Right-click the **Local Disk (C:)** icon and click **Create Shortcut**. Windows Vista creates a desktop shortcut to the drive. If an item does not have the Send To command available, you can usually use the Create Shortcut command to create a shortcut.

TAKE NOTE*

Usually, the Create Shortcut command creates a shortcut in the same location as the original item. Creating a shortcut to a storage device is different, because you cannot create a shortcut in the Computer folder.

6. Close the folder window so you can see the desktop. The new shortcuts display as shown in Figure 7-9, along with other items that may have already been on the desktop.

Figure 7-9

Create shortcuts on the desktop

7. At this point, your instructor may ask you to capture an image of the screen. Save it in your Lesson 7 assessment folder as ***Le07_05***.
8. Right-click the **Calculator** shortcut icon and click **Delete** on the shortcut menu. A delete file confirmation dialog box displays.
9. Click **Yes** to delete the icon.
10. Right-click the **Documents** folder shortcut icon, click **Delete**, and then click **Yes** to delete the icon.
11. Right-click the **Local Disk (C) - Shortcut** icon, click **Delete**, and then click **Yes** to delete the icon.

PAUSE. LEAVE the desktop displayed to use in the next exercise.

The desktop is a handy place to keep shortcuts to items you use frequently because you can get to them easily. In addition, it is a good idea to store shortcuts instead of actual items on the desktop, because it saves disk space. Finally, when you delete a shortcut, it has no affect on the actual item itself. You delete the shortcut icon only, leaving the original item intact in its original storage location.

The Send To> Desktop (shortcut) command is available on virtually every shortcut menu that displays when you click a program, folder, or file. Alternatively, you can use the Create Shortcut command. That makes it easy to create a Desktop shortcut for any item.

In the next section, you create a shortcut on the Quick Launch Toolbar.

Creating a Shortcut on the Quick Launch Toolbar

You can easily add any item to the Quick Launch Toolbar, creating a shortcut that you can use to access that item with a single click.

CREATE A SHORTCUT ON THE QUICK LAUNCH TOOLBAR

1. Click **Start**, click **All Programs**, and then click **Accessories**.
2. Right-click **Calculator** and then click **Add to Quick Launch**. Notice that a shortcut to the Calculator program now displays on the Quick Launch Toolbar.
3. Open your personal folder window.
4. Drag the **Documents** folder icon from the folder window to the Quick Launch Toolbar. A vertical bar indicates where the shortcut will be placed.
5. Release the left mouse button when the ScreenTip displays Move to Quick Launch. Windows Vista creates a shortcut to the Documents folder on the Quick Launch Toolbar. The Quick Launch Toolbar should look similar to Figure 7-10.

Figure 7-10

Create shortcuts on the Quick Launch Toolbar

6. At this point your instructor may ask you to capture an image of the screen showing the Quick Launch Toolbar. Save it your Lesson 7 assessment folder as ***Le07_06***.
7. Right-click the **Calculator** shortcut icon, click **Delete** on the shortcut menu, and then click Yes in the confirmation dialog box.
8. Right-click the **Documents** folder shortcut icon, click **Delete**, and then click **Yes** to delete the icon.

PAUSE. LEAVE your personal folder window open to use in the next exercise.

Shortcuts on the Quick Launch Toolbar are convenient because you can keep the Quick Launch Toolbar displayed at all times, even when the desktop is hidden by open windows. Also, you single-click to launch an item from the Quick Launch Toolbar, rather than double-click, which you do to launch an item from the desktop.

Note that only programs have the Add to Quick Launch command on their shortcut menus. To add a file, folder, or device to the Quick Launch Toolbar, you must use the drag and drop method.

Adding an item to the Quick Launch Toolbar creates a shortcut only—it does not affect the original item, which remains stored in its original location. Likewise, deleting an icon from the Quick Launch Toolbar does not delete the actual item.

In the next section, you add a shortcut to a folder to the Start menu.

Adding a Folder Shortcut to the Start Menu

Previously, you learned how to customize the Start menu to display shortcuts to programs you use all the time. You can also pin a shortcut to a folder to the Start menu.

ADD A FOLDER SHORTCUT TO THE START MENU

USE your personal folder that you left open in the previous exercise.

1. In your personal folder window, double-click **Documents** to open the Documents folder.
2. Right-click a blank area, point to **New**, and then click **Folder** to create a new folder. Key **Woodgrove Info** and press **Enter** to rename the folder.
3. Drag the **Woodgrove Info** folder onto the **Start** button. Release the left mouse button when the ScreenTip displays the word *Link* and the Start menu opens. The Woodgrove Info folder is added to the pinned items list, as shown in Figure 7-11. Notice that the original Woodgrove Info folder is still stored in the Documents folder, as well.

Figure 7-11

Pin a folder shortcut to the Start menu

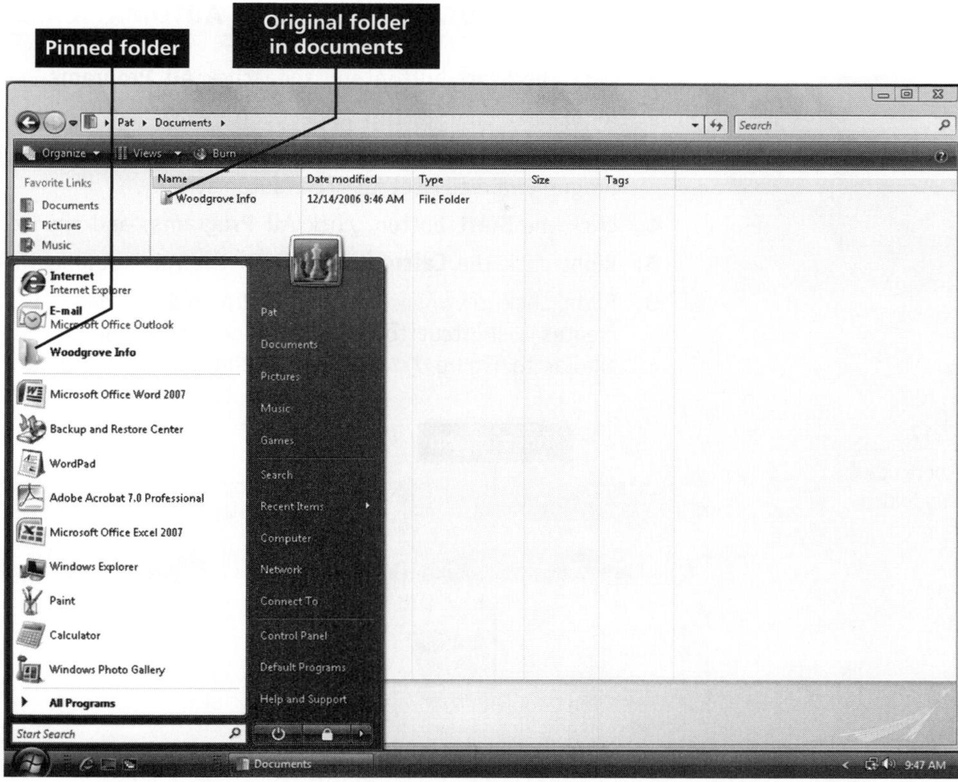

4. At this point, your instructor may ask you to capture an image of the screen. Save it in your Lesson 7 assessment folder as ***Le07_07***.
5. Close the **Documents** folder window.
6. Click the **Start** button to open the Start menu. Then click **Woodgrove Info** on the pinned items list. The Woodgrove Info folder opens.
7. Click the **Start** button, right-click the **Woodgrove Info** icon, and click **Remove from this list** to remove the folder shortcut from the Start menu.
8. From the Woodgrove Info folder window, navigate back to the Documents folder window and then delete the **Woodgrove Info** folder.
9. Close the Documents folder window.

PAUSE. LEAVE your desktop displayed to use in the next exercise.

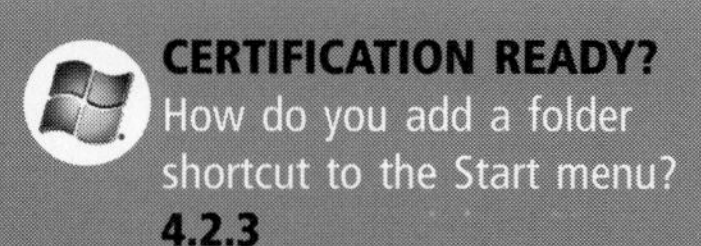
CERTIFICATION READY?
How do you add a folder shortcut to the Start menu?
4.2.3

You can drag any folder, file, or device from its original storage location to the Start menu to add it to the pinned items list. As with programs, the item remains on the Start menu until you select the command to remove it from the list.

Note that you can also create a shortcut to a folder or file in the same location where the original item is stored. Just display the location where the original item is stored, right-click the item, and click Create Shortcut on the shortcut menu. Though it may seem unnecessary to have a shortcut in the same location as the original item, you can then move the shortcut anywhere on your computer system including the desktop, the Quick Launch Toolbar, or the Start menu by using Cut and Paste or drag-and-drop editing.

In the next exercise, you configure a program to start automatically when you start Windows.

Configuring a Program to Start Automatically

If you start the same program or programs every time you start Windows Vista, you can save time by setting the program to start automatically. To do so, simply place a shortcut to the program in the Windows Startup folder.

CONFIGURE A PROGRAM TO START AUTOMATICALLY

TROUBLESHOOTING

You may have to scroll down the All Programs menu to locate the Startup folder.

1. Click the **Start** button and then click **All Programs**.
2. Right-click the **Startup** folder icon.
3. Click **Open** to open the Startup folder window. It may be empty, or there may be programs already set to start automatically.
4. Click the **Start** button, click **All Programs**, and then click **Accessories**.
5. Right-click the **Calculator** icon on the All Programs menu and click **Copy**.
6. Right-click anywhere in the **Startup** folder window and click **Paste**. Windows Vista creates a shortcut to the Calculator program in the Startup folder. It should look similar to Figure 7-12, although the appearance of the icon may vary.

Figure 7-12

Place a shortcut in the Startup folder

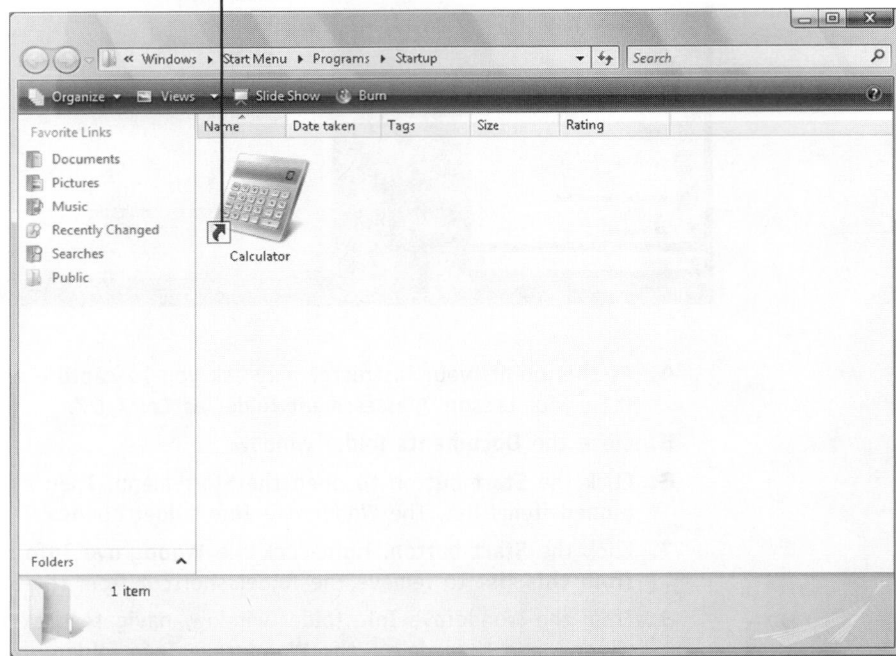

You can drag a shortcut icon from any location into the Startup folder.

7. At this point your instructor may ask you to capture an image of the Startup folder window. Save it in your Lesson 7 assessment folder as ***Le07_08***.
8. Close the Startup folder window and then restart your computer. Log in to your Windows Vista user account. The Calculator program should start automatically and display in its program window on the desktop.
9. Close the Calculator window and all other open windows.
10. Click the **Start** button, click **All Programs**, and then click **Startup**.
11. Right-click **Calculator** in the Startup folder and click **Delete** on the shortcut menu. Click **Yes** in the Delete File dialog box to delete the shortcut from the Startup menu.

PAUSE. LEAVE the desktop open to use in the next exercise.

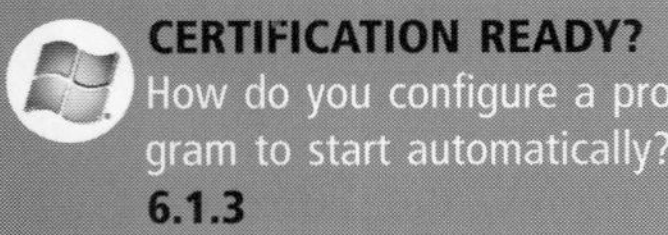

CERTIFICATION READY?
How do you configure a program to start automatically?
6.1.3

You can place a shortcut to any program, folder, or even file into the Startup folder so that it starts automatically when you start Windows Vista. Either copy and paste the item into the Startup folder, or create a shortcut icon for the item and then drag the shortcut into the Startup folder. Windows Defender, a security tool that comes with Windows Vista, may display a notification when you add a program to the Startup folder, and a Windows Defender icon with a question mark may display in the notification area. As long as you are the one who made the change, you do not have to take any action. You learn more about using Windows Defender in Lesson 11, "Monitoring the Windows Vista Environment."

In the next section, you learn how to manage the Windows Sidebar.

■ Managing the Windows Sidebar

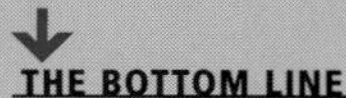

The Windows Sidebar is an area on the desktop where active information displays. ***Active information*** is information that continuously updates, such as the time, or news headlines. You can hide the Sidebar if you want, select where you want it positioned on the desktop, and control whether other windows can cover it. You can also add and remove gadgets, which are the programs that display on the Sidebar.

Hiding and Displaying the Sidebar

By default, the Sidebar displays along the right side of the desktop, where it takes up quite a bit of space. You can hide it at any time, and then display it again when you want.

TROUBLESHOOTING

If the Windows Sidebar is not displayed, click Start>All Programs> Accessories>Windows Sidebar.

HIDE AND DISPLAY THE SIDEBAR

1. Right-click a blank area of the Sidebar to display a shortcut menu.
2. Click **Close Sidebar** on the shortcut menu. The Sidebar is hidden.
3. Open the Start menu, click **All Programs**, click **Accessories**, and then click **Windows Sidebar**. The Sidebar displays.

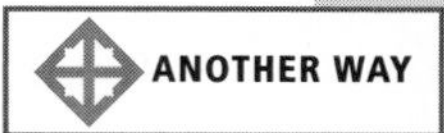

If the Windows Sidebar button icon displays in the notification area, you can use it to open and close the Sidebar. Right-click the icon to display the shortcut menu. Then click Open to display the Sidebar or Close Sidebar to close it. Alternatively, double-click the icon to quickly open the Sidebar.

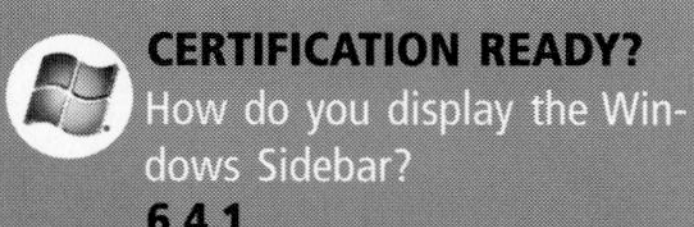

PAUSE. LEAVE the desktop displayed with the Sidebar open to use in the next exercise.

The Windows Sidebar is a feature new to Windows Vista. It lets you place actively updating information on the desktop so you can monitor it while you work without having to change windows.

The items on the Sidebar are called gadgets. By default, three gadgets are displayed—a clock, news headlines, and a picture slideshow.

You can exit the Sidebar, which closes it and removes its icon from the notification area. If you exit the Sidebar and then want to display it again, click Start>All Programs>Accessories> Windows Sidebar, or go to the Customize Windows Sidebar page in Windows Help and Support and click Click to open Windows Sidebar.

In the next section, you select settings to control how the Sidebar displays.

Configuring the Sidebar

You can select options to control the Windows Sidebar, such as where the Sidebar displays on the desktop, and whether it covers other windows.

CONFIGURE THE SIDEBAR

1. Open your personal folder window and maximize it. It hides the Sidebar, because by default, the Sidebar is not set to display on top of other windows.
2. Minimize your personal folder window so you can see the Sidebar.
3. Right-click a blank area of the Sidebar and click **Properties** to display the Windows Sidebar Properties dialog box, as shown in Figure 7-13.

Figure 7-13

Windows Sidebar Properties dialog box

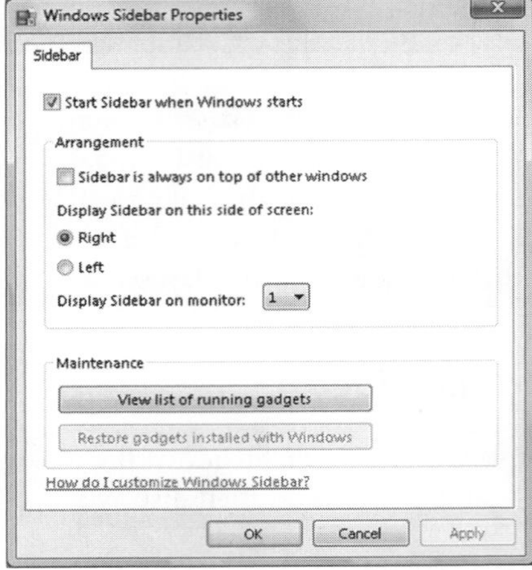

You can also right-click the Windows Sidebar icon in the notification area and click Properties on the shortcut menu to open the Windows Sidebar Properties dialog box.

4. Click to select the **Sidebar is always on top of other windows** checkbox and then click **Apply**.
5. Click your personal folder's Taskbar button to maximize the window. Notice that the Sidebar remains on top.
6. Close your personal folder window.
7. In the Windows Sidebar Properties dialog box, click the **Left** option button and then click **Apply**. The Sidebar moves to the left side of the desktop.
8. In the Windows and Sidebar Properties dialog box, click the **View list of running gadgets** button to display the View Gadgets window. The items in this window are the gadgets that are currently running on your computer.
9. Click the **Close** button to close the window.
10. In the Windows Sidebar Properties dialog box, click to deselect the **Sidebar is always on top of other windows** checkbox, click the **Right** option button, and then click **OK** to apply the changes and close the dialog box.

PAUSE. LEAVE the desktop displayed with the Sidebar open to use in the next exercise.

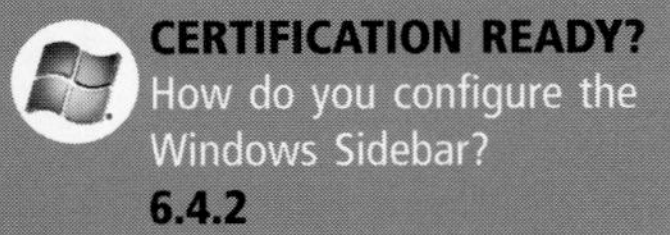

CERTIFICATION READY?
How do you configure the Windows Sidebar?
6.4.2

Other options in the Windows Sidebar Properties dialog box include a checkbox for automatically starting the Sidebar when you start Windows Vista and to display the Sidebar on a secondary monitor. You can also restore gadgets that you may have inadvertently uninstalled.

In the next section, you learn how to add gadgets to the Sidebar.

Adding Gadgets to the Sidebar

Windows Vista comes with a selection of gadgets that you can easily add to the Sidebar. If the Sidebar becomes crowded, you can remove gadgets or drag them off the Sidebar onto the Desktop.

ADD GADGETS TO THE SIDEBAR

1. Right-click a blank area of the Sidebar and click **Add Gadgets. . .** on the shortcut menu to display the Gadget Gallery. It should look similar to Figure 7-14. The ***Gadget Gallery*** displays all of the gadgets installed on your system, including ones that come with Windows Vista and any that you may have downloaded from the Internet.

Figure 7-14

The Gadget Gallery

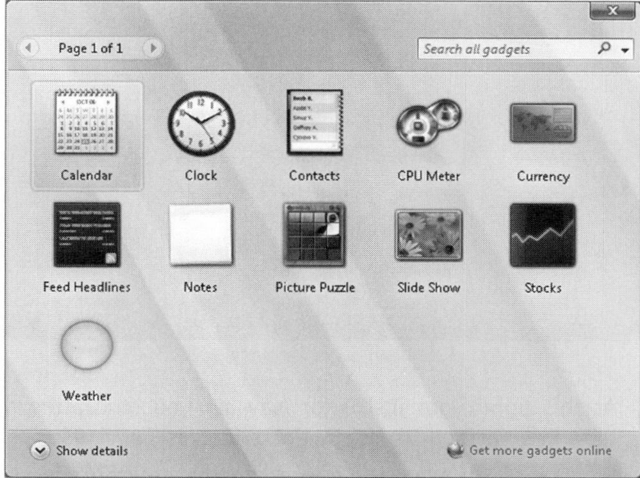

2. Double-click **Calendar** in the Gadget Gallery. It is added to the Sidebar, and the Gadget Gallery remains open.
3. Double-click **Weather** in the Gadget Gallery to add it to the Sidebar.
4. Click the **Close** button in the Gadget Gallery to close the window. You now have at least two gadgets on the Sidebar, and you may have more if some were already there.
5. Right-click the **Weather** gadget in the Sidebar and then click **Options** on the shortcut menu. Each gadget has an options dialog box that you can use to customize the gadget. In this case, you can select the location for which you want the weather, and whether to use Fahrenheit or Celsius.
6. In the search for location box, key **St. Louis, MO** and then click the Start Searching button. If there is more than one location that matches your entry, a menu displays. Click **St. Louis, Missouri** on the menu.

TROUBLESHOOTING You must be connected to the Internet to search for a weather location. If necessary, log on to your Internet service provider.

7. Click the **Fahrenheit** option button, if necessary, and then click **OK.** The temperature in St. Louis, Missouri displays on the Weather gadget.
8. Right-click the **Weather** gadget again and click **Detach from Sidebar.** The gadget moves from the Sidebar to the desktop, as shown in Figure 7-15. You can place any gadget on the desktop so that it displays even if you close the Sidebar, or to make space for additional gadgets on the Sidebar. Notice that the gadget is larger when it is detached from the Sidebar.

Figure 7-15

Move a gadget to the desktop

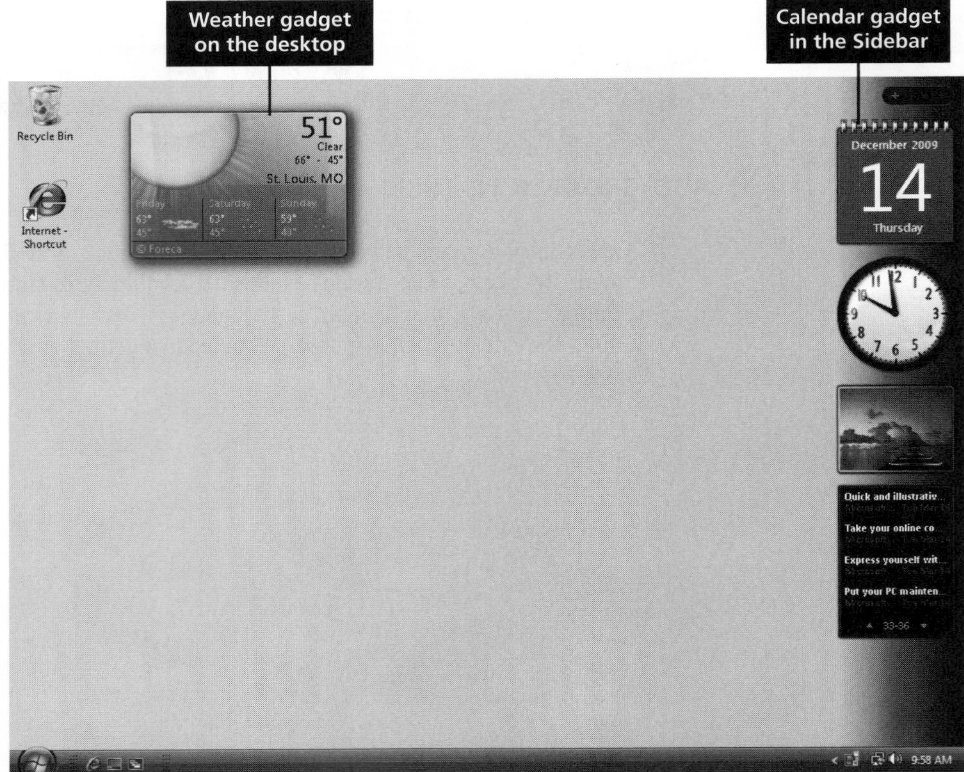

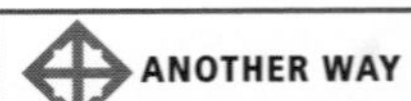

You can simply drag a gadget to the desktop and back to the Sidebar.

9. At this point your instructor may ask you to capture an image of the screen. Save it in your Lesson 7 assessment folder as ***Le07_09***.
10. Right-click the **Weather** gadget on the desktop and click **Opacity**. A menu displays, offering you a choice of percentages that control how opaque or transparent the gadget will be. The default is 100%, which means the gadget is solid and not transparent at all.
11. Click **20%** to make the gadget 20% opaque, or 80% transparent. Move the mouse pointer away from the gadget to see how it displays. It is much less obtrusive on the desktop when it is more transparent. Move the mouse pointer over the gadget to make it 100% opaque.
12. Right-click the **Weather** gadget on the desktop and click **Attach to Sidebar** to move it back on to the Sidebar.
13. Right-click the **Weather** gadget and click **Close Gadget**. If necessary, click Close Gadget in the Windows Sidebar dialog box. The gadget is removed from the Sidebar.

TROUBLESHOOTING

If Windows Vista displays a dialog box asking if you want to close the Sidebar as well, click Close Gadget to continue.

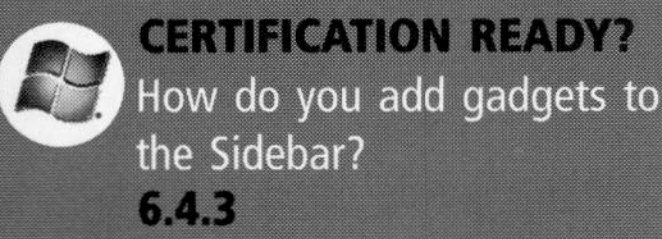

CERTIFICATION READY?
How do you add gadgets to the Sidebar?
6.4.3

14. Right-click the **Calendar** gadget and click **Close Gadget**. It, too, is removed from the Sidebar.

    PAUSE. LEAVE the desktop displayed with the Sidebar open to use in the next exercise.

As mentioned, Windows Vista comes with a selection of gadgets for common tasks, and other gadgets may be available online. To check for gadgets online, display the Gadget Gallery and then click Get more gadgets online. Windows Vista launches your browser and displays a page of gadgets available for download. You learn more about downloading a Sidebar gadget in Lesson 12, "Managing Windows internet Explorer."

You may have noticed that when you rest the mouse pointer on a gadget, a toolbar displays three buttons:

- Close, for closing the gadget and removing it from the Sidebar.
- Options, for displaying the gadget's Options dialog box.
- Handle, for dragging the gadget off the Sidebar.

In addition, an Add Gadgets button at the top of the Sidebar enables you to click to display the Gadget Gallery.

In the next section, you learn how to customize your desktop.

■ Customizing the Desktop

The desktop is your main work area, and you spend a lot of time looking at it. Customizing the desktop is an opportunity to personalize your workspace and to apply settings that you are comfortable having in front of you all day. Most of the options you need to customize the desktop can be accessed from the Appearance and Personalization category of the Control Panel. In this section, you learn how to select a background and colors for your desktop, select and control a screen saver, arrange icons on the desktop, and adjust display settings.

Selecting a Desktop Background

By default, the color of the desktop, windows, the Start menu, and the Taskbar are based on the current ***color scheme***, which is a collection of coordinated colors. The default color scheme for Windows Vista is called Windows Aero. It includes a black desktop. Your system may have been customized already to display a different background. You can easily select a picture or solid color to use as a desktop background.

SELECT A DESKTOP BACKGROUND

1. Click **Start** and then click **Control Panel** to open the Control Panel folder. The Control Panel contains links to the features you use to change the look and settings of Windows Vista.
2. Under Appearance and Personalization, click **Change desktop background.** The Desktop Background folder opens. From this window, you can select the type of background you want to use and then select the specific background.

You can also open the Desktop Background window by right-clicking a blank area of the desktop, clicking Personalize, and then clicking Desktop Background in the Personalization window.

3. Click the **Picture Location** button to drop down a list of available background types and then click **Windows Wallpapers.** (If this option is already selected, you can skip this step.) The available wallpapers display in the window, as shown in Figure 7-16. ***Wallpaper*** is an image or color that displays on your desktop. The Windows Wallpapers are organized into categories. You can scroll through the list to see all available wallpapers.

Figure 7-16

Select a wallpaper for your desktop

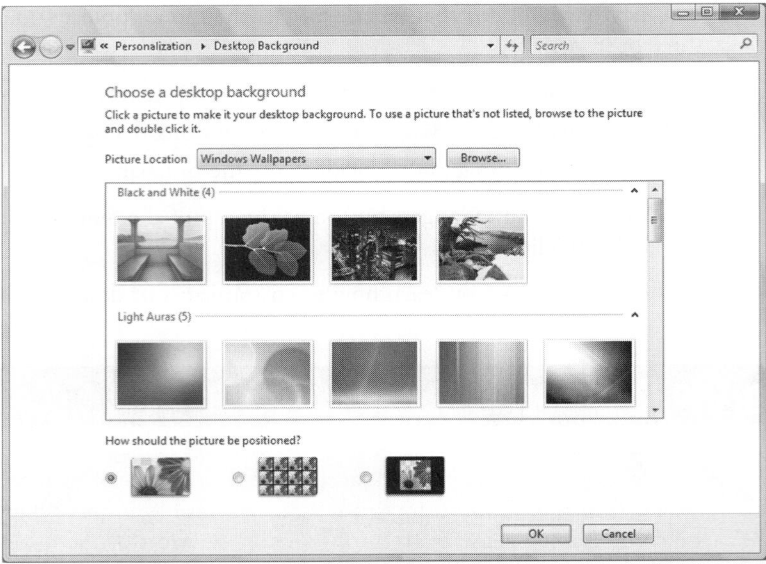

4. Scroll down the list to see all of the available wallpapers. Notice that they are organized into categories, including Black and White images, Light Auras, Paintings, Texture, Vistas, and Widescreen.
5. Click any picture in the Vista category. The picture is applied to your desktop. (You can minimize the Desktop Background window to get a better look.)
6. In the Desktop Background window, click the **Picture Location** button again and then click **Sample Pictures**. The pictures stored in the Sample Pictures folder display.
7. Click the picture of the whale's tail. It is applied to your desktop. (Again, minimize the window to get a better look.)
8. In the Desktop Background window, click the **Picture Location** button and click **Solid Colors**. A list of available colors displays.
9. Click the first color in the list—black. It is applied to the desktop. Click the light gray color that is third from the left in the top row. It is applied to the desktop.
10. Click **OK** to close the Desktop Background window and return to the Control Panel.

PAUSE. LEAVE the Control Panel open to use in the next exercise.

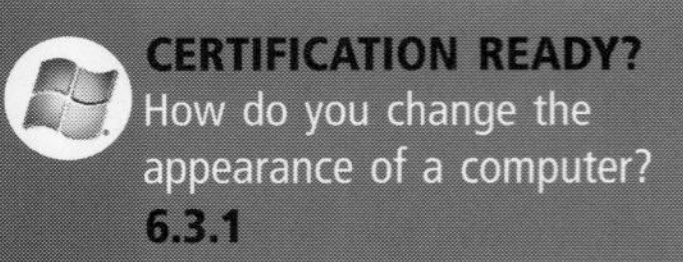

You can use any picture that is stored on your computer as a desktop background. If it does not display in one of the Picture Location categories, click the Browse button and then use Windows navigation tools to locate and select the file. Click Open to display it in the Desktop Background window.

To quickly make any picture the desktop background, open the folder where the picture file is stored, right-click the picture, and then click Set as Desktop Background.

Three positions are available for pictures on the desktop:

- Fit to Screen, which is the default, automatically sizes the picture to fit the screen.
- Tile, which repeats the picture in columns and rows to fill the screen.
- Center, which centers the image in its actual size on the screen. If you center the picture, you can select a background color to display around the edges of the picture.

Note that not all pictures are affected by changing the position. It depends on the original size of the image.

In the next exercise, you learn how to customize the colors of windows.

Customizing Window Colors

As mentioned, the color of windows, the Start menu, and the Taskbar are based on the current color scheme. You can customize the window color and appearance by selecting a different color and by adjusting the transparency and color intensity.

CUSTOMIZE WINDOW COLORS

USE the Control Panel you left open in the previous exercise.

1. In the Control Panel, under Appearance and Personalization, click **Customize Colors**. The Window Color and Appearance window displays.

TROUBLESHOOTING

If the Customize Colors option does not display under Appearance and Personalization, your system may not be set to use the Windows Aero interface. To enable Windows Aero, you must be using the Windows Vista theme and the Windows Aero color scheme. To set the theme, open the Control Panel and click Appearance and Personalization. Under Personalization, click Change the theme. Click the Theme dropdown arrow, click Windows Vista, and then click OK. To set the color scheme, under Personalization, click Change the color scheme. In the Color scheme list, click Windows Aero and then click OK. If the Windows Aero color scheme is not available, your monitor may not support it. Refer to the next section, "Adjusting Display Settings," for more information.

ANOTHER WAY

You can also open the Window Color and Appearance window by right-clicking a blank area of the desktop, clicking Personalize, and then clicking Window Color and Appearance in the Personalization window.

2. Click **Orange**. The color is applied to the window, Taskbar, and Start menu.
3. Click to deselect the **Enable transparency** checkbox. The color becomes opaque.
4. Drag the **Color intensity** slider all the way to the left. The color becomes less intense, fading away to almost gray.
5. Drag the **Color intensity** slider to the middle. The window should look similar to Figure 7-17.

Figure 7-17

Customize desktop colors

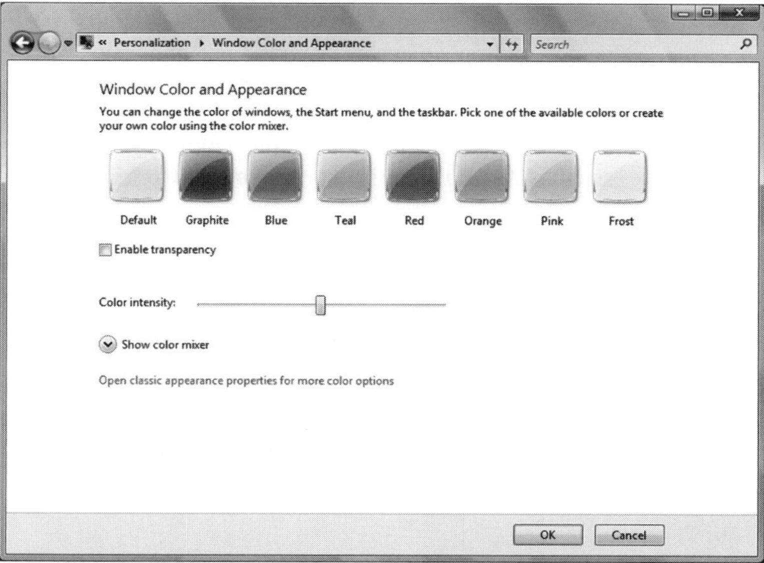

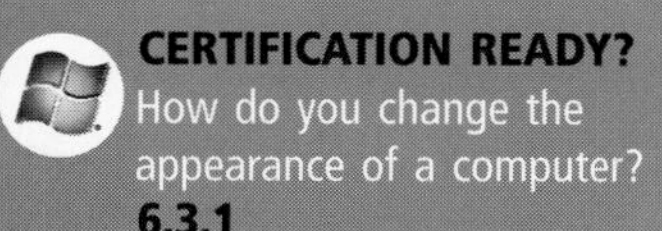

CERTIFICATION READY?
How do you change the appearance of a computer?
6.3.1

6. Click the **Default** color and then click **OK**. The selection is applied to your desktop, and the Control Panel displays.

PAUSE. LEAVE the Control Panel open to use in the next exercise.

If you don't like any of the colors in the Appearance Settings dialog box, you can create a custom color using the Color Mixer. Click the Show color mixer arrow and then adjust the Hue, Saturation, and Brightness sliders to create a color of your choice. As you adjust the sliders, the window color changes so you can preview the selections.

To quickly apply a set of coordinated colors, you can select a color scheme. From the Appearance Settings dialog box, click Open classic appearance properties for more color options. The Appearance Settings dialog box displays. Click a color scheme in the list to preview it in the dialog box. Click OK to apply the selection and close the dialog box. Note that colors in a color scheme override any customized selections you have already made, so you should wait to apply customizations until after you select a color scheme. Also, if you do not use Windows Aero, you may not be able to access some of the visual effects Windows Vista provides, such as transparency.

You can use any picture that is stored on your computer as a desktop background. If it does not display in one of the Picture Location categories, click the Browse button and then use Windows navigation tools to locate and select the file. Click Open to display it in the Desktop Background window.

In the next exercise, you learn how to adjust the settings that control your monitor display.

Adjusting Display Settings

Display settings control the visual clarity of information on your monitor. Windows Vista automatically applies display settings that it believes provide the optimum performance for your system, but you can change the settings if you want. You can adjust the resolution, the refresh rate, and the color depth.

ADJUST DISPLAY SETTINGS

USE the Control Panel you left open in the previous exercise.

1. In the Control Panel, under Appearance and Personalization, click **Adjust screen resolution.** The Display Settings dialog box displays, as shown in Figure 7-18. The options in this dialog box depend on the actual monitor and video card you have installed. A video card is the device that converts electronic information into the content you see on your screen. However, it should have a Resolution slider for adjusting the monitor resolution, a Colors dropdown list for selecting a color depth, and an Advanced Settings button, which opens the dialog box where you can select a refresh rate. ***Resolution*** is the quality or sharpness of an image. It is usually measured in pixels per inch. A ***pixel***, which is short for picture element, is a dot used as a unit of measure. ***Color depth*** is the number of colors used on the screen. ***Refresh rate*** is the frequency that the monitor flickers.

Figure 7-18

Adjust display settings

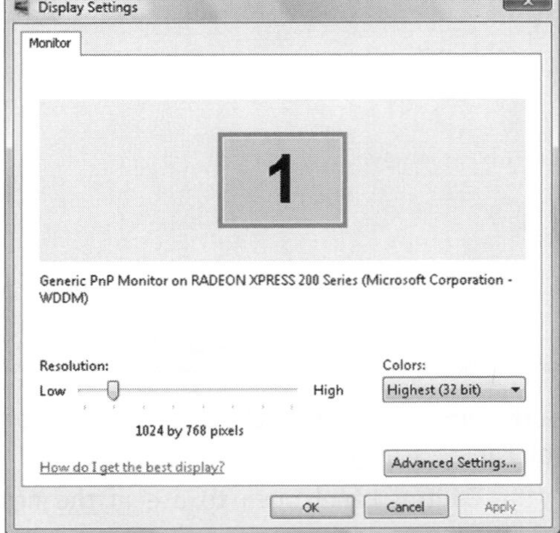

TROUBLESHOOTING The options for adjusting your display settings depend on the monitor and video card you have installed for use with your computer. Some of the options covered in this exercise may be different for your monitor, or they may not be available. For example, if you use a liquid crystal display (LCD) monitor, the maximum refresh rate may be 60. If necessary, consult your instructor, the manual that came with your monitor, or Windows Help and Support for information specific to your monitor.

You should use the highest color depth available to take advantage of the visual effects provided by Windows Vista. If your monitor does not support 32-bit color, you cannot use the Windows Aero interface, so you may not be able to access many of the desktop customization options.

CERTIFICATION READY?
How do you adjust your display resolution?
3.4.1
How do you adjust the display refresh rate?
3.4.2
How do you select the display color depth setting?
3.4.3

2. Drag the **Resolution** slider as far as possible to the left, to the lowest setting. On most systems, this will be 800×600 pixels.
3. Click **Apply**. The change is applied to your monitor. It should make everything larger, and less sharp. A dialog box displays asking if you want to keep the settings. Click **No**.
4. Drag the **Resolution** slider as far as possible to the right, to the highest setting. On most systems, this will be 1280×1024 pixels. Click **Apply** to preview the change. It should make everything smaller and sharper. Click **No** in the dialog box to revert to the previous settings.
5. Click the **Colors** dropdown arrow and click **Medium (16-bit)**. Click **Apply** to preview the change and then click **No** to revert to the previous settings. The higher the color depth, the better the color displays on your monitor. Also, if you do not use 32-bit color, you cannot use the Windows Aero interface.
6. Click the **Advanced Settings** button to display the advanced settings dialog box for your monitor. Then click the **Monitor** tab.
7. Click the Screen refresh rate dropdown arrow and click **75 Hertz**. (If the current setting is 75 Hertz, click a different setting.) The higher the refresh rate, the less the monitor flickers. (If you are using an LCD monitor, skip this step.)
8. Click **Apply** to preview the change and then click **No** to revert to the previous setting.
9. Click **Cancel** to close the dialog box and then click **Cancel** in the Display Settings dialog box.
10. **CLOSE** the Control Panel.

PAUSE. LEAVE the desktop open to use in the next exercise.

As mentioned, Windows Vista automatically applies the display settings that are most appropriate for your particular monitor and video card. You should only change them if they have been already been changed inadvertently, or if you must change them to use with a particular software program or hardware device, or if you notice that the quality of images on your screen is poor. For example, video might be jumpy or grainy, and text might appear rough or jagged. However, you should consult the instructions that came with your monitor before making any changes.

Display settings can affect you, as well as your computer's performance. For example, a low refresh rate might cause headaches or eyestrain for someone who spends a lot of time looking at the screen.

Note that not all resolutions are compatible with all refresh rates, so you may have to adjust the resolution before selecting a different refresh rate.

In the next exercise, you select and configure a screen saver.

Selecting a Screen Saver

A ***screen saver*** is a picture or animation that displays on the monitor when you have not used your system for a set period of time. By default, Windows Vista selects the Windows Logo screen saver set to display after 10 minutes of inactivity. You can select a different screen saver and adjust the delay time, which is length of inactivity that must elapse before the screen saver displays.

SELECT A SCREEN SAVER

1. Right-click a blank area of the desktop and click **Personalize** on the shortcut menu. The Personalization window opens.
2. Click **Screen Saver**. The Screen Saver Settings dialog box displays, as shown in Figure 7-19.

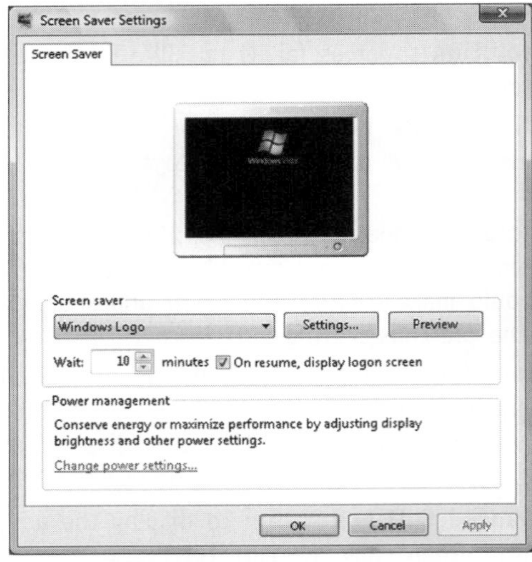

Figure 7-19
Screen Saver Settings dialog box

3. Click the Screen saver dropdown arrow to display the list of available screen savers.
4. Click **Bubbles** and then click **Preview**. You see a preview of the screen saver on your monitor.
5. Move the mouse to cancel the preview and return to the dialog box.
6. Click the **Screen saver** dropdown arrow and click **Ribbons**. Click **Preview** to preview the screen saver on your monitor.
7. Move the mouse to cancel the preview.
8. Click the **Wait** box and then click the **down increment** arrow to set the wait time to 1 minute. This is the amount of time you computer must be idle before the screen saver becomes active.
9. Click **Apply** and then wait 1 minute without touching your mouse or keyboard. After a minute, the Ribbons screen saver should display.
10. Move your mouse to cancel the screen saver. If the logon screen displays, log on to your Windows Vista account. At this point, your instructor may ask you to capture an image of the Screen Saver Settings dialog box. Save it in your Lesson 7 assessment folder as ***Le07_10***.
11. Click the **Screen saver** dropdown arrow and click **Windows Logo**.
12. Click the **Wait** box and click the up increment arrow to set the Wait time back to 10 minutes.
13. Click **OK** to apply the settings.
14. **CLOSE** the Personalization window.

PAUSE. LEAVE the desktop open to use in the next exercise.

CERTIFICATION READY?
How do you change the screen saver?
6.3.4
How do you change the screen saver delay time?
1.4.1

Windows Vista comes with a selection of screen savers. Many screen savers are available on the Internet for free or for a small fee. Be wary of downloading screen savers unless you know and trust the source. They may contain malicious software.

Some screen savers have settings that you can select to control factors such as the speed an image moves, or the colors. To access screen saver options, select the screen saver and then click the Settings button. Select the options you want and then click OK.

In the next exercise, you work with icons on the desktop.

Controlling Desktop Icons

Whether or not you work with many icons on your desktop, you will want to keep the icons organized. You can control icons on the desktop by selecting an icon size, arranging the icons, or even by hiding them completely.

CONTROL DESKTOP ICONS

TROUBLESHOOTING

Recall that a checkmark indicates a command is on, or active. If no checkmarks are next to Auto Arrange and Align to Grid, skip steps 2 and 3.

1. Right-click a blank area of the desktop and point to **View** on the shortcut menu. All of the commands on the shortcut menu let you control your desktop icons.
2. If necessary, click to turn off **Auto Arrange.** Auto Arrange automatically arranges desktop icons neatly starting along the left side on the desktop.
3. Right-click a blank area of the desktop, point to **View**, and click to turn off **Align to Grid.** Align to Grid snaps icons to an invisible grid of columns and rows.
4. Drag the **Recycle Bin** icon to the middle of the desktop.
5. Right-click a blank area of the desktop, point to **View**, and click **Align to Grid**. The icon may shift slightly as it snaps to the imaginary grid.
6. Right-click a blank area of the desktop, point to **View**, and click **Auto Arrange**. The icon moves to the left side of the desktop, along with any other desktop icons.
7. Right-click a blank area of the desktop, point to **View**, and then click **Large Icons** on the shortcut menu. Windows Vista increases the size of the desktop icons, as shown in Figure 7-20. This may be useful if you have trouble seeing the smaller icons. At this point, your instructor may ask you to capture an image of the screen. Save it in your Lesson 7 assessment folder as ***Le07_11***.

Figure 7-20

Customize desktop icons

8. Right-click a blank area of the desktop, point to **View**, and then click **Show Desktop Icons** to deselect it. The icons are hidden. Use this command to hide or show desktop icons.
9. Right-click a blank area of the desktop, point to **View**, and then click **Show Desktop Icons** to select it and display the icons.
10. Right-click a blank area of the desktop, point to **Sort By**, and then click **Type**. Windows Vista rearranges the icons so they are sorted by type. All shortcuts are together, all folders are together, and so on.

CERTIFICATION READY?
How do you arrange desktop icons?
6.3.2
How do you adjust icon size?
3.4.4

11. Right-click a blank area of the desktop, point to **Sort By**, and then click **Size**. Windows Vista rearranges the icons by content size.
12. Right-click a blank area of the desktop, point to **Sort By**, and then click **Name** to arrange the icons alphabetically.
13. Right-click a blank area of the desktop, point to **View**, and then click **Medium icons** to reduce the icon size back to the default Medium.

LOG OFF your Windows Vista user account.

The number and type of icons on your desktop depends on how you customize your system. Many programs automatically place an icon on the desktop during installation. You might create shortcuts to your frequently used files and folders. Arranging the icons can help you find what you need when you need it.

SUMMARY SKILL MATRIX

In This Lesson You Learned	Matrix Skill	Skill Number
To customize the Start menu		
To select Start menu settings	Customize the Start menu	6.1.1
To pin, unpin, and remove Start Menu items	Pin and unpin items from the Start menu; Add a program to the Start menu	6.1.2 6.1.4
To manage the Taskbar		
To move and size the Taskbar	Move the Taskbar to the right side of the screen	6.2.3
To hide the Taskbar	Automatically hide the Taskbar when not in use	6.2.4
To display and hide the Quick Launch Toolbar	Display the Quick Launch toolbar on the Taskbar	6.2.1
To add a toolbar to the Taskbar	Add a toolbar to the Taskbar	6.2.2
To customize the notification area	Customize the notification area	6.2.5
To work with shortcuts		
To add a folder shortcut to the Start menu	Add a folder shortcut to the Start menu	4.2.3
To configure a program to start automatically	Configure a program to start automatically	6.1.3
To manage the Windows Sidebar		
To hide and display the Sidebar	Display the Windows Sidebar	6.4.1
To configure the Sidebar	Configure the Windows Sidebar	6.4.2
To add gadgets to the Sidebar	Add gadgets to the Sidebar	6.4.3
To customize the desktop		
To select a desktop background	Change the appearance of a computer	6.3.1
To customize window colors	Change the appearance of a computer	6.3.1
To adjust display settings	Adjust your display resolution; Adjust the display refresh rate; Adjust the display color depth setting	3.4.1, 3.4.2, 3.4.3
To select a screen saver	Change the screen saver; Change the screen saver delay time	6.3.4 1.4.1
To control desktop icons	Arrange desktop icons; Adjust icon size	6.3.2. 3.4.4

■ Knowledge Assessment

Matching

Match the term in Column 1 to its description in Column 2.

Column 1	Column 2
1. color depth	**a.** pop-up windows that provide information about the status of a program
2. refresh rate	**b.** a thumbnail sized replica of a window; shows the actual window content
3. wallpaper	**c.** a picture or animation that displays on the monitor when you have not used your system for a set period of time
4. notification	**d.** a dot used as a unit of measure
5. screen saver	**e.** not running or in use
6. color scheme	**f.** the frequency that a monitor flickers
7. live preview	**g.** a collection of coordinated colors
8. resolution	**h.** an image or color that displays on your desktop background
9. inactive	**i.** the number of colors used on a screen
10. pixel	**j.** the quality or sharpness of an image

Multiple Choice

Select the best response for the following questions.

1. Which of the following is another term for a shortcut menu?

- **a.** context menu
- **b.** Start menu
- **c.** icon menu
- **d.** link menu

2. What is the name of the area at the top of the left pane of the Start menu?

- **a.** recently used items list
- **b.** pinned items list
- **c.** programs list
- **d.** shortcut list

3. How can you keep the Taskbar from being moved or resized?

- **a.** pin it
- **b.** delete it
- **c.** hide it
- **d.** lock it

4. What are the programs that display on the Sidebar called?

- **a.** calendars
- **b.** gadgets
- **c.** widgets
- **d.** shortcuts

5. What is the name of the default color scheme for Windows Vista?
   a. Windows Ultra
   b. Windows Beta
   c. Windows Aero
   d. Windows Logo
6. Which of the following is *not* a category of Windows Vista wallpapers?
   a. Black and White
   b. Light Auras
   c. Vistas
   d. Prints
7. What is the default Windows Vista screen saver?
   a. Windows Logo
   b. Ribbon
   c. Bubbles
   d. Windows Aero
8. Which of the following might be caused by a low refresh rate?
   a. exhaustion
   b. eyestrain
   c. sneezing
   d. sore throat
9. Which of the following is a system icon that can be displayed in the notification area?
   a. Display
   b. Mouse
   c. Volume
   d. Weather
10. Which of the following options snaps icons into neat columns and rows?
   a. View>Snapshots
   b. View>Sort By
   c. View>Align to Grid
   d. View>Auto Arrange

■ Competency Assessment

Project 7-1: Personalize Your Computer

You recently moved to a new desk and inherited a computer. You want to personalize your computer according to your work habits and needs. In this project, you customize the Start menu and the Taskbar. You also change your desktop background.

GET READY. Before you begin these steps, start your computer and log on to your Windows Vista account. Close all open windows so you can see the desktop.

1. Drag the Taskbar to the top of the desktop.
2. Right-click a blank area of the Taskbar and click **Properties**.

3. On the Taskbar tab, click to select the **Lock the taskbar** checkbox and the **Auto-hide the Taskbar** checkbox. Click to deselect the **Keep the taskbar on top of other windows** checkbox.
4. Click the **Start menu** tab and then click the **Customize** button.
5. Under Computer, click the **Display as a menu** option button.
6. Under Control Panel, click the **Display as a menu** option button.
7. Under Games, click the **Don't display this item** button. (Some editions of Windows Vista may not have the Games options. Skip this step if necessary.)
8. Click to deselect the **Use large icons** checkbox.
9. Set the Number of recent programs to display to **5**.
10. Click **OK** and then click **OK** in the Taskbar and Start Menu Properties dialog box.
11. Move the mouse pointer to the top of the desktop to display the Taskbar. Then click the **Start** button.
12. Rest the mouse pointer on **Control Panel**. It opens as a menu, displaying a list of all options available in the Control Panel. Click **Personalization**.
13. Click **Desktop Background**.
14. Click the **Picture Location** dropdown arrow and then click **Windows Wallpapers**.
15. Scroll down and click the first option under the Textures category.
16. Click **OK.**
17. Click **Display Settings** to open the Display Settings dialog box. Review the display settings for your monitor.
18. Click **OK** and then close the Personalization window.
19. Move the pointer to the top of the desktop to display the Taskbar. Right-click a blank area of the Taskbar, point to **Toolbars**, and then click **Desktop** to add the Desktop toolbar to the Taskbar.
20. At this point, your instructor may ask you to capture an image of the screen with the Start menu displayed. Save it in your Lesson 7 assessment folder as ***Proj07_01***.

PAUSE. LEAVE the Windows Vista desktop displayed to use in the next project.

Project 7-2: Community Fundraiser, Part 1

You have been asked to manage the budget for a community fundraiser. You will often need to use the Calculator, WordPad, and your Documents folder. In this project, you will place a shortcut to the Documents folder on the Start menu, to the WordPad program on the Quick Launch Toolbar, and to the Calculator on the desktop. You will also add the Calendar gadget to the Sidebar and arrange the desktop icons.

1. Move the mouse pointer to the top of the desktop to display the Taskbar.
2. Right-click the Taskbar and click **Properties**. Click to deselect the **Lock the taskbar** and **Auto-hide the taskbar** checkboxes. Then click **OK**.
3. Click the **Start** button and then click your personal folder to open it.
4. Drag the **Documents** folder icon from your personal folder window to the Start button. Release the mouse button when the ScreenTip displays Link, and the Start menu opens. Windows Vista pins a shortcut to the Documents folder to the Start menu.
5. Right-click the Taskbar and click Properties. Click to select the **Lock the taskbar** and **Auto-hide the taskbar** checkboxes. Then click **OK**.
6. Click **All Programs** on the Start menu and then click **Accessories**. Right-click the **WordPad** program icon and click **Add to Quick Launch**. Windows Vista adds a shortcut to the WordPad program to the Quick Launch Toolbar.

7. On the Start menu, under Accessories, right-click the **Calculator** program icon, point to **Send To** on the shortcut menu, and then click **Desktop (create shortcut)**. Windows Vista creates a shortcut to the Calculator on the desktop.
8. Close your personal folder window.
9. Right-click the **Sidebar** icon in the notification area, or a blank area of the Sidebar, and click **Properties**.
10. Click the **Left** option button to set the Sidebar to display on the left side of the desktop and then click **OK**.
11. Right-click the **Sidebar** icon in the notification area, or a blank area of the Sidebar, and click **Properties**. Click the **Right** option button to set the Sidebar to display on the right side of the desktop and then click **OK**.
12. Right-click a blank area of the Sidebar and click **Add Gadgets . . .** to display the Gadget Gallery.
13. Double-click the **Calendar** gadget in the Gadget Gallery to add it to the Sidebar. Then close the Gadget Gallery.
14. Right-click a blank area of the desktop, point to **View**, and then click **Large Icons**.
15. Right-click a blank area of the desktop, point to **Sort by**, and then click **Size**.
16. At this point, your instructor may ask you to capture an image of the desktop. Save it in your Lesson 7 assessment folder as ***Proj07_02***.

PAUSE. LEAVE the desktop open to use in the next project.

■ Proficiency Assessment

Project 7-3: Revert to Default

The new manager of your department has decided she wants everyone to use the same computer settings. In this project, you must revert your Start menu, Taskbar, and desktop back to the default settings.

1. Move the mouse pointer to the top of the desktop to display the Taskbar.
2. Right-click the **Taskbar** and click **Lock the Taskbar** to deselect it.
3. Drag the Taskbar to the bottom of the desktop.
4. Right-click the Taskbar and click **Properties**.
5. On the Taskbar tab, click to deselect the **Auto-hide the taskbar** checkbox. Click to select the **Keep the taskbar on top of other windows** checkbox.
6. Click the **Start menu** tab and then click the **Customize** button.
7. Click the **Use Default Settings** button to revert to the default Start menu settings.
8. Click **OK** and then click **OK** in the Taskbar and Start Menu Properties dialog box.
9. Click the **Start** button and then click **Control Panel** to open the Control Panel window.
10. Under Appearance and Personalization, click **Change desktop background**.
11. Click the **Picture Location** dropdown arrow and then click **Solid Colors**.
12. Click the gray color that is third from the top and second from the left.
13. Click **OK** and then close the Control Panel window.
14. Right-click a blank area of the Taskbar, point to **Toolbars**, and then click **Desktop** to remove the Desktop toolbar from the Taskbar.

PAUSE. LEAVE the desktop displayed to use in the next project.

Project 7-4: Community Fundraiser, Part 2

You have completed your work on the budget for the community fundraiser. You now want to remove the shortcuts you needed for that project from your Start menu, the Quick Launch Toolbar, and your desktop, and remove the Calendar gadget from the Sidebar.

1. Right-click the **WordPad** shortcut icon on the Quick Launch Toolbar and click **Delete.** Click **Yes** in the confirmation dialog box to delete the icon.
2. Right-click the **Calculator** shortcut icon on the desktop and click **Delete**. Click **Yes** in the confirmation dialog box to delete the icon.
3. Click the **Start** button to open the Start menu, right-click the **Documents** folder shortcut in the pinned items list, and then click **Remove from this list.**
4. Right-click the **Calendar** gadget in the Sidebar and then click **Close Gadget.**
5. Right-click a blank area of the desktop, point to **View**, and then click **Medium Icons.**

PAUSE. LEAVE the desktop open to use in the next project.

■ Mastery Assessment

Project 7-5: New Computer

You just purchased a new computer and want to personalize it for your home. In this project, you will customize the Start menu and the Taskbar. You will create shortcuts on the Start menu, the Quick Launch Toolbar, and the Desktop. You will configure the Sidebar, and you will select a desktop background and colors.

1. Customize the Start menu to display Computer, Control Panel, and Personal folder as menus and set the number of recent programs to display to 3.
2. Pin the Calculator, WordPad, and Paint programs to the Start menu.
3. Add a shortcut to the Pictures folder to the Quick Launch Toolbar.
4. Place a shortcut to the Documents folder on the desktop.
5. Set the Sidebar to display on the left side of the desktop.
6. Add the Weather gadget to the Sidebar and customize it to display the temperature in your hometown.
7. Select a Windows Vista wallpaper picture as your desktop background.
8. Customize the window color to red. At this point, your instructor may ask you to capture an image of the screen. Save it in your Lesson 7 assessment folder as ***Proj07_05***.
9. Hide the Quick Launch Toolbar and display the Desktop toolbar on the Taskbar.
10. Select the Bubble screen saver and set the delay time to 15 minutes.
11. Resize the desktop icons to the Classic Icons size and make sure they are automatically arranged and aligned to the grid. Sort them by type.
12. Reverse the steps in this exercise to revert your desktop to its default settings.

PAUSE. LEAVE the desktop displayed to use in the next project.

Project 7-6: Bank Desktop

You have been asked to submit a sample of a customized desktop that would be suitable for all branches of the Woodgrove Bank. In this project, you will use the skills you have learned in this lesson to personalize the Windows Vista workspace.

1. Move the Taskbar to the right side of the desktop and lock it.
2. Move the Sidebar to the left side of the desktop.

3. Set the Taskbar to hide automatically when it is not in use.
4. Customize the Start menu to display only Computer, Documents, Control Panel, Help, and Network on the right pane, and four recently used programs in the left pane.
5. Pin your personal folder and the Notepad program to the Start menu.
6. Place a shortcut to the WordPad program in the Startup folder so that it starts automatically when Windows starts.
7. Place a shortcut to your personal folder on the desktop.
8. Customize the notification area so that all icons display all the time, even when they are inactive.
9. Hide the Quick Launch Toolbar.
10. Add the Calendar and the Weather gadgets to the Sidebar. If necessary, remove the News Headline gadget and the Slide Show.
11. Select a desktop wallpaper picture from the Sample Pictures folder.
12. Change the color of windows to teal, enable transparency, and increase the color intensity as much as possible.
13. Review your display settings to be sure they are set for optimum performance.
14. Select the Mystify screen saver and set the delay time to 5 minutes.
15. Change the desktop icon size to large, disable the Auto Arrange feature, and move the icons around on the desktop. At this point, your instructor may ask you to capture an image of the screen. Save it in your Lesson 7 assessment folder as ***Proj07_06***.
16. Reverse the steps in this exercise to revert your desktop to its default settings.
17. **CLOSE** all open windows.

    LOG OFF your Windows Vista user account.

INTERNET READY

Windows Vista comes with a collection of gadgets that you can add to your Sidebar. Other gadgets are available online. In this exercise, use Internet search tools to locate gadgets online, such as those in the Microsoft Gadget Gallery. Browse through the available gadgets and note the ones that seem interesting, useful, or fun. With your instructor's permission, download a gadget and add it to your Sidebar. Remember that you should only download from a trusted source.

Workplace Ready

Organizing Outlook Items

Nicole Holliday is an instructor at the School of Fine Arts. Every session, a batch of fresh students registers for Nicole's classes. Nicole teaches several classes that require students to submit electronic files. The school doesn't set up mailboxes for each class, so Nicole uses Outlook to organize her messages.

Every session, Nicole sets up a new email folder for each class. She creates rules that sort messages from each student into the correct folder. A few weeks after classes end, Nicole archives the class folders that are no longer needed.

Because Nicole also teaches at a second school, she created a secondary address book to separate the contact information between the two schools. Incorrectly addressing a message to a staff member at the wrong school would be embarrassing.

Getting Help and Support

LESSON SKILL MATRIX

Skills	Matrix Skill	Skill Number
Locating a Help Topic		
Using Windows Help and Support's Table of Contents	Locate information in Windows Help and Support	7.2.1
Searching for a Help Topic	Locate information in Windows Help and Support	7.2.1
Including Windows Online Help Content in a Search	Locate information in Windows Help and Support	7.2.1
Printing a Help Topic		
Getting Help Online		
Using Windows Online Help and How-to Web Site	Locate information in Windows Help and Support	7.2.1
Searching the Microsoft Knowledge Base	Search the Microsoft Knowledge Base from Windows Help and Support	7.2.2
Using Windows Remote Assistance		
Enabling Windows Remote Assistance	Enable Windows Remote Assistance invitations by using Remote Settings; Limit the time that a Remote Assistance invitation is available; Disable WIndows Remote Assistance	7.8.1 7.8.2 2.3.3
Requesting Remote Assistance	Request Remote Assistance through Windows Help and Support ; Disable Remote Assistance invitations	7.8.3 7.8.4

KEY TERMS

AutoComplete
Bandwidth
Frame
Help Experience
Improvement program
Instant messaging
Links bar
Microsoft Knowledge Base
Newsgroup
Offline
Online
Remote Assistance invitation
Remote Assistance

Blue Yonder Airlines, based in Gustavus, Alaska, provides air transportation to commuters and tourists. The business recently installed a new personal computer running the Windows Vista operating system. Because of the airline's remote location, employees rely primarily on the software's built-in Help and Support features as well as online help resources to troubleshoot and solve problems and to find answers to their everyday questions. In this lesson, you will learn how to locate information in Windows Help and Support by using the table of contents and by searching. You will also learn how to access the Microsoft Knowledge Base online and how to use Remote Assistance to get help from someone located elsewhere.

■ Locating a Help Topic

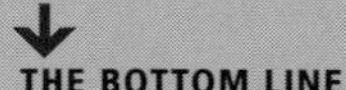

Built-in Help and Support in Windows Vista provides information about every feature in the program. The information is organized into subject categories, such as Windows Basics and Security and Maintenance, which provide access to specific topics. If you are not sure what information you are looking for, you can browse through the subjects by clicking links on one page to go to another page. If you want to go more quickly to specific information, you can start in the Table of Contents, which lists major subject headings that link to help topics, or use the Search box to search for a keyword or phrase. You can even include Windows Online Help content in your search. In this section, you learn how to locate a topic in Windows Help and Support by using the Table of Contents and by searching, and you learn how to include online Help content in your search.

Using Windows Help and Support's Table of Contents

Browsing through all of the information in Windows Vista Help and Support could take a long time. If you are not sure of the exact information you need, but you know the basic subject, you can use the Table of Contents. The Table of Contents lists major subject headings; click a heading to display a list of additional subject headings as well as specific help topics.

USE WINDOWS HELP AND SUPPORT'S TABLE OF CONTENTS

GET READY. Before you begin these steps, start your computer and log on to your Windows Vista account. Close all open windows so you can see the desktop. Create a new folder named Lesson 8 in a storage location specified by your instructor, where you can store assessment files and folders that you create during this lesson.

1. Click the **Start** button and then click **Help and Support** near the bottom of the right pane on the Start menu. The Windows Help and Support home page displays.

X REF For general information on accessing Windows Help and Support and using the home page, see Lesson 1, "Getting Started."

Microsoft updates Windows Help and Support frequently in order to provide you with the most current information. As a result, the links may change. If the specific links used throughout this lesson are not available, use other, similar links.

2. Click **Table of Contents** to display the Contents page. It should look similar to Figure 8-1. Each heading on the page is a link to a list of subheadings and topics. Notice the book icon to the right of each heading.

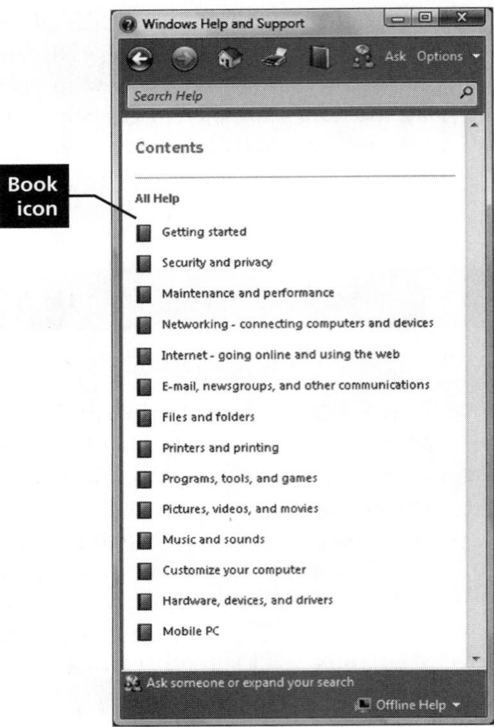

Figure 8-1
Help and Support table of contents

3. Click **Customize your computer**. Windows Vista displays a list similar to the one shown in Figure 8-2. Notice that some items in the list have the book icon, indicating that they are headings, and some items have a question mark, which means they are specific help topics.

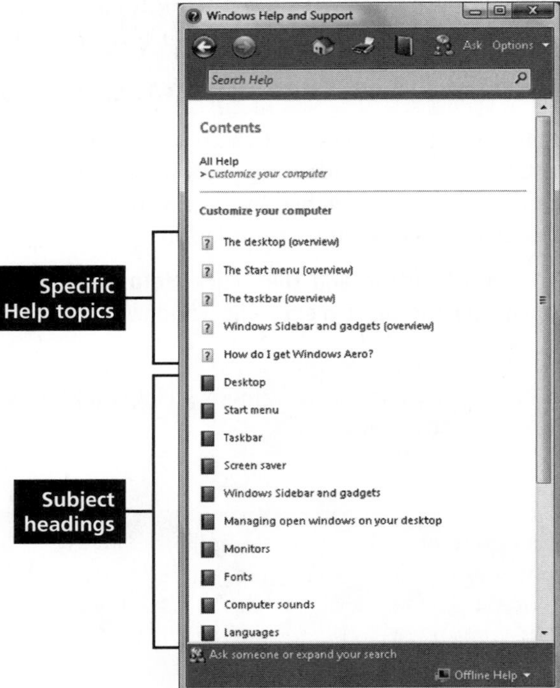

Figure 8-2
Links to information about customizing your computer

4. Click **The desktop (overview)**. The topic displays.
5. Click the **Back** button on the Help and Support toolbar to return to the previous page. Notice that the link you clicked in step 4 now displays in a different color, so you can differentiate between links you have clicked and links you have not clicked.
6. Click **Desktop**. A list of links to information about the desktop displays. Notice that there are links to specific topics, such as *What's new with the Windows desktop?*, and links to headings, such as *Managing the desktop*. Also, notice that the topic *The desktop (overview)* is violet. Even though you clicked the topic from a different page, it displays in a different color here as well.
7. Click **Managing the desktop**. A list of topics about managing the desktop displays. It should look similar to Figure 8-3.

Figure 8-3

Links to information about managing the desktop

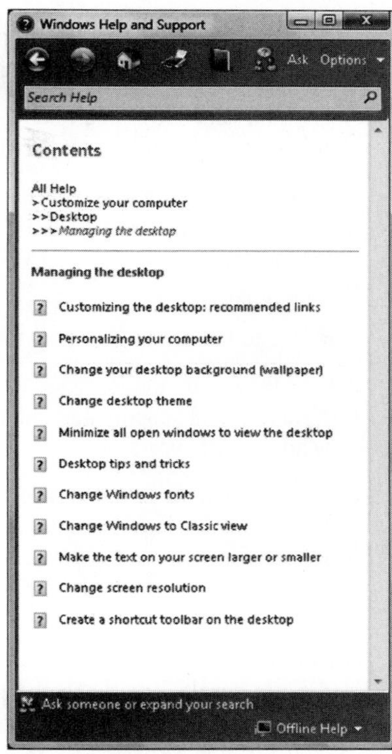

8. Click **Desktop tips and tricks** to display the topic.
9. Click the green text **desktop** in the first sentence on the page. A definition of the term displays in a ScreenTip. To view a definition, you can click any word or phrase that displays in green.
10. Click anywhere outside the ScreenTip to close it.
11. Click **Don't store files on the desktop** under the heading *In this article* in the Help and Support window (look for it in the upper right corner of the window). Windows Vista scrolls to the information about why you should not store files on the desktop, near the end of the current page.
12. At this point, your instructor may ask you to capture an image of the Windows Help and Support window. Save it in your Lesson 8 assessment folder as ***Le08_01***.
13. Click the **Help and Support home** button on the Help and Support toolbar to display the Help and Support home page. (See Table 8-1 for information on the Help and Support home button.)

PAUSE. LEAVE the Help and Support home page displayed to use in the next exercise.

You can also press **Esc** to cancel a ScreenTip.

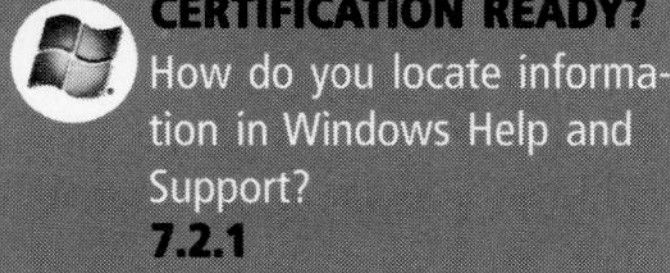

CERTIFICATION READY?
How do you locate information in Windows Help and Support?
7.2.1

As mentioned previously, topic pages in Help and Support use some common elements to help you navigate within a topic and from one topic to another.

- Icons indicate whether a link is to a subject heading (a book icon) or to a specific help topic (a question mark icon).
- The color of linked text indicates whether a link is to additional information (blue), to a definition (green), or if it has already been clicked (violet).
- Use the buttons on the Windows Help and Support toolbar to access features. Table 8-1 describes the buttons.

Table 8-1

Windows Help and Support toolbar buttons

BUTTON	DESCRIPTION
	Click the Back button to display the previously viewed page.
	Click the Forward button to return to the page that was displayed before you clicked the Back button.
	Click the Help and Support home button to display the Windows Help and Support home page.
	Click the Print button to print the current Help and Support page. (You learn more about printing a Help page later in this lesson.)
	Click the Browse Help button to display the Subject page that relates to the currently displayed topic page.
Ask	Click the Ask button to access tools for contacting Microsoft Windows Vista support staff and other knowledgeable Windows Vista users.
Options	Click the Options button to select from a menu of available options and settings for controlling how Windows Help and Support functions and displays.

You might notice that at the top of many help topic pages there is a list of headings under the label *In this article*. Click a heading to scroll directly to the part of the page that discusses that subject. Likewise, at the bottom of most pages, you will find a list of related topics under the heading *See also*. Click an item in the list to go to the Help page that discusses that particular topic.

As mentioned earlier, Microsoft updates the information in Help and Support on a regular basis, so do not be concerned if the information in Help and Support on your computer is not exactly the same as the information displayed in the figures in this lesson. The way Help and Support is organized and the way you use the features to access the information you need should be the same as described.

In the next section, you learn how to search for a help topic.

Searching for a Help Topic

If you know the topic for which you need help, you can enter a keyword or phrase into the Help Search box to display a search results list of related links. The more specific the keyword or phrase, the more likely the link you need will be in the list. In this section, you practice searching for information in Windows Help and Support.

SEARCH FOR A HELP TOPIC

USE the Help and Support home page you left displayed in the previous exercise.

1. Click in the **Search Help** box below the Windows Help and Support window's toolbar.
2. Key **taskbar** and then click the **Search Help** button. The search results display, showing a list of 30 links to pages that relate to the keyword *taskbar*. The list should be similar to the one shown in Figure 8-4. The links are organized based on relevance, which means the pages most likely to be of help are at the top of the list. Notice that unlike searching in Windows Vista for files and folders, you must click the Search Help button to begin searching in Windows Help and Support.

Figure 8-4

Links to items relating to the Taskbar

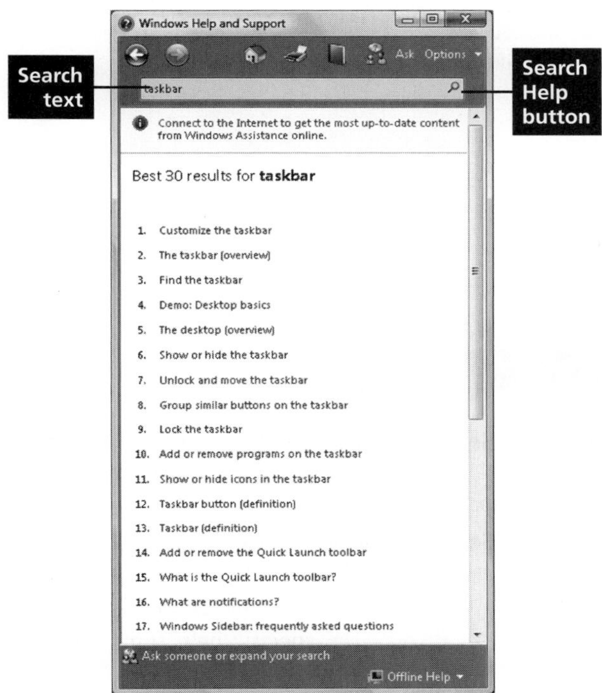

TAKE NOTE* If you are working offline, a message displays at the top of the Help window prompting you to connect so you can include online Help in your search. You learn how to use online Help in the next exercise.

XREF Searching for files and folders is covered in Lesson 6, "Searching for Files and Folders."

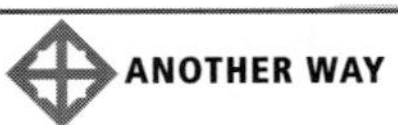

ANOTHER WAY You can press **Enter** instead of clicking the Search Help button to start the search.

3. Click **Find the taskbar** to display the Help topic page. It should look similar to Figure 8-5.

Figure 8-5

Find the Taskbar help page

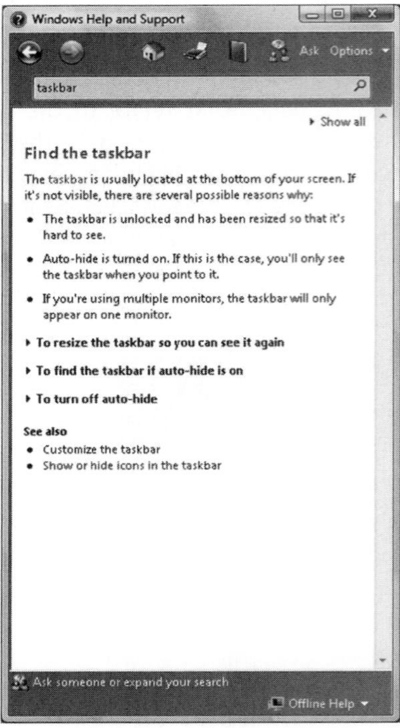

4. Click in the **Search Help** box and delete the keyword *taskbar*. Key **documents** and then click the **Search Help** button. The search results list showing 30 items relating to *documents* displays.
5. Click in the **Search Help** box and change the search text to **documents folder**. Then click the **Search Help** button. The search results list changes so that links relating specifically to the *documents folder* display at the top.
6. Click item 1, to display the specific help topic page.

TAKE NOTE*

If you click a help topic labeled as a Demo, an animated video about the topic displays in Windows Media Player.

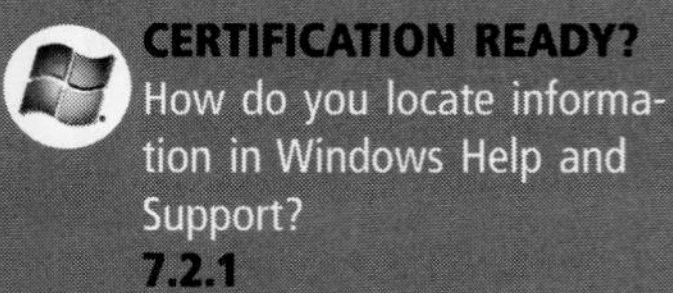

7. At this point, your instructor may ask you to capture an image of the Windows Help and Support window. Save in your Lesson 8 assessment folder as ***Le08_02***.
8. Click the **Help and Support home** button on the Windows Help and Support window's toolbar to return to the Help and Support home page.

PAUSE. LEAVE the Help and Support home page displayed to use in the next exercise.

Some of the items that display in the search results list might not seem very relevant to the search text. Windows Vista includes *all* pages that contain the search text in the list, with the most relevant or useful at the top. That's why the more specific you can be with your search text, the more likely you are to find the help topic you need.

While working through the steps in the previous section, you might have noticed that some links on Help topic pages have a small right-pointing arrowhead next to them (refer to Figure 8-5). When you click the link, collapsed, or hidden, text expands on the page to provide more information or to answer a question. The arrowhead changes to point down, indicating that you can click the link to collapse—or hide—the information. You can click the text *Show all* in the upper right corner of a Help and Support topic page to expand all hidden text on the page. Click *Hide all* to collapse the hidden text.

In the next section, you learn how to include online content when you search for help.

Including Windows Online Help Content in a Search

The very first time you open Windows Help and Support, a dialog box displays asking if you want to access help online. If you select Yes, Windows Vista will automatically include pages stored on the Windows Online Help and How-to Web site in every search results list. If you select No, however, you can later manually change your Help and Support settings to include online information in a search. When you get online Help, you know that you are accessing the most up-to-date information available. In this section, you set Windows Help and Support to include online Help content in search results.

INCLUDE WINDOWS ONLINE HELP CONTENT IN A SEARCH

USE the Help and Support home page you left displayed in the previous exercise.

1. Locate the button in the lower right corner of the Windows Help and Support window that is labeled as either Online Help or Offline Help. ***Offline*** refers to information stored on your local computer, and ***online*** refers to information stored on the Internet or other network. If the button displays Offline Help, continue with step 2. If it displays Online Help, click it and then click **Get Offline Help** on the dropdown menu.
2. Click in the **Search Help** box and delete any text already there. Key **copy files** and then click the **Search Help** button. The search results list displays. It should look similar to Figure 8-6. Only information stored in the offline Help and Support program is included in the search results. A warning message may display above the list informing you that if you want the most up-to-date content you should connect to the Internet.

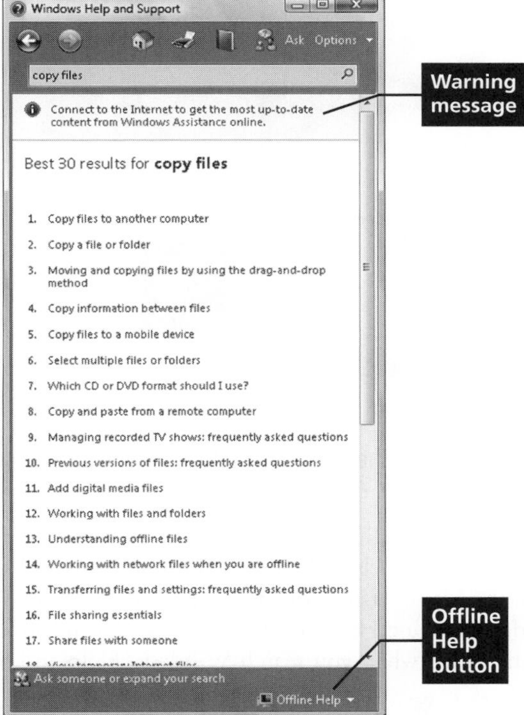

Figure 8-6

Offline search results

3. Click the **Offline Help** button in the lower right corner of the Windows Help and Support window. A menu displays, from which you can select to Get online Help, Get offline Help, or open the Settings dialog box.
4. Click **Get online Help** on the menu. The menu closes, and the Offline Help button changes to the Online Help button.

ANOTHER WAY

You can also enable Windows Online Help by using the Help Settings dialog box. Click the Options button or the Offline Help button and then click Settings. Click to select the Include Windows Online Help and Support when you search for help checkbox, and then click OK.

TROUBLESHOOTING

If you do not have access to the Internet, Windows Vista will display a warning message near the top of the Windows Help and Support window when you enable online Help. Check your connection and then try to connect again, or consult your instructor.

5. Click the **Search Help** button. The search results list changes to include pages stored on the Microsoft Windows Online Help and How-to Web site. It should look similar to Figure 8-7.

Figure 8-7

Search results include online content

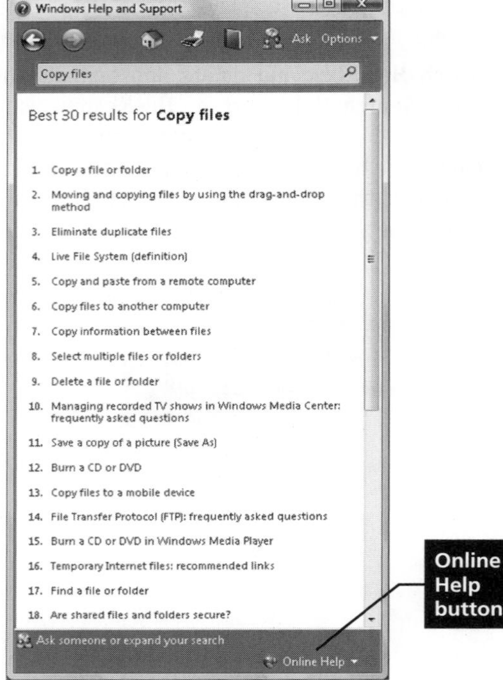

PAUSE. LEAVE the search results for copy files displayed to use in the next exercise.

To disable online help, click the Online Help button and then click Get offline Help on the menu, or deselect the Include Windows Online Help and Support when you search for help checkbox in the Help Settings dialog box. Disabling online help does not mean you cannot access Windows Online Help and How-to just that information from the online support site will not be included when you search Windows Help and Support.

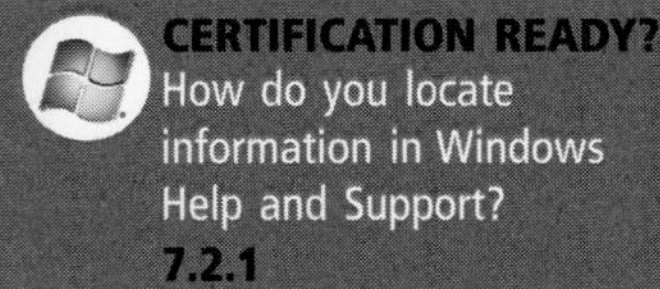

When you include Windows Online Help content in your searches, the question "Was this information helpful?" displays at the bottom of most Help topic pages, along with buttons for Yes, No, and Somewhat. Microsoft uses this feature—called the ***Help Experience Improvement program***—to record your opinion about Windows Help and Support options. If you click Yes, you have the opportunity to enter additional information; if you click No or Somewhat, you can select from a list of options and then enter additional information. If you do not want to contribute to the program, you can ignore it.

Next you learn how to print a help topic.

■ Printing a Help Topic

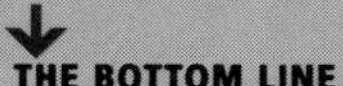

THE BOTTOM LINE

Print a help topic when you need to reference the help information while you work with Windows Vista. For example, if you need to follow the steps for copying files to a CD or for troubleshooting a printer driver, it may be easier to read the printed steps as you perform them instead of switching back to the Windows Help and Support window. All you need is a printer connected to your computer or network. In this section, you learn how to print a help topic.

PRINT A HELP TOPIC

GET READY. Before you begin these steps, make sure you have a printer correctly set up and connected to your computer or network and that it is loaded with paper.

USE the search results for copy files you left displayed in the previous exercise.

1. Click the item **Copy a file or folder** to display the specific Help topic page you will print.
2. Click the **Print** button on Windows Help and Support window's toolbar. The Print dialog box displays, as shown in Figure 8-8.

Figure 8-8

The Print dialog box

ANOTHER WAY

You can also display the Print dialog box by clicking the Options button on the toolbar and then clicking Print.

3. Under Select Printer, click the printer you want to use, if it is not already selected.
4. Click **Print**. The help topic page prints on the selected printer.
5. Click the Help and Support home button on the toolbar.

   PAUSE. LEAVE the Help and Support home page displayed to use in the next exercise.

In addition to printing the current help page, you can select options for printing linked pages as well. Click the Options tab and then click to select or deselect the options you want to use.

- Select the Print all linked documents checkbox if you want to print all pages that are linked to the current page. Keep in mind that this may include a large number of pages.
- Select the Print table of links checkbox if you want to print a list of the linked pages.

If the Help page you are trying to print is an online Web page, options for printing ***frames*** may also be available. A frame is an independent section of a Web page that has its own scroll bar.

- Select the As laid out on screen option to print all frames exactly as they display on your screen.
- Select the Only the selected frame option to print only the frame currently selected.
- Select the All frames individually option to print each frame individually.

In the next section, you learn how to access Windows Help and How-to online.

■ Getting Help Online

THE BOTTOM LINE

Windows Help and Support will usually provide the answers you are looking for. However, when you need additional information, you can look for help online. As long as you have a connection to the Internet, you can access the Windows Online Help and How-to Web site directly, or you can expand your quest for help to online resources such as the Microsoft Knowledge Base. In this section, you learn how to access Windows Online Help and How-to directly and how to search the Microsoft Knowledge Base.

Using Windows Online Help and How-to Web Site

You have seen that you can include information from the Windows Online Help and How-to Web site when you search for help. If you have a connection to the Internet, you can also access the Web site directly and use it in place of Windows Help and Support. In this section, you learn how to use Windows Online Help and How-to.

USE WINDOWS ONLINE HELP AND HOW-TO WEB SITE

GET READY. Before you begin these steps, make sure you have an active connection to the Internet. If you do not, you will not be able to complete these steps.

USE the Windows Help and Support home page you left displayed in the previous exercise.

1. Click **Windows Online Help** under the heading Find an answer near the top of the Windows Help and Support home page. Windows Vista starts your Web browser and displays the Windows Online Help and How-to home page. It should look similar to the one shown in Figure 8-9, but the specific content may be different. Again, that is because Microsoft updates the content frequently. Notice that some of the elements on the page are similar to elements on the Windows Help and Support home page. For example, there are links to general subjects, and there is a Search Help box.

Figure 8-9

Windows Online Help and How-to home page

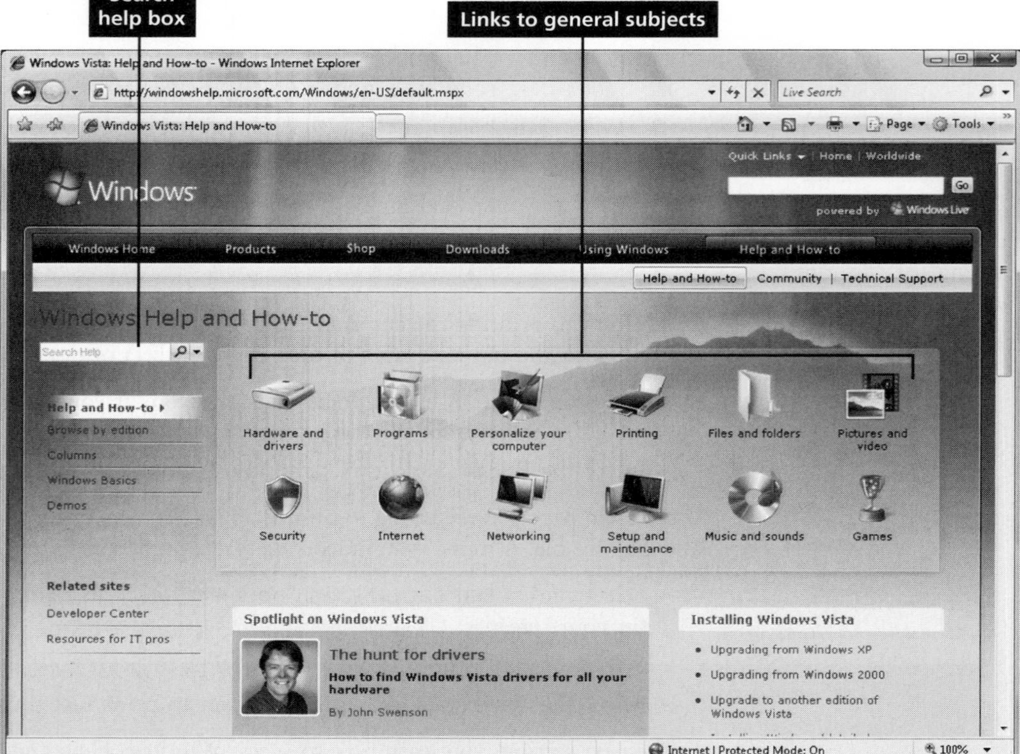

ANOTHER WAY

You can also click the link to Windows Help online near the bottom of the Windows Help and Support home page. Or you can start your browser, key windowshelp.microsoft.com in the address bar, and then press **Enter**.

2. Click the link to **Personalize your computer**. The Personalize your computer Web page displays.
3. Under the heading Windows Sidebar & Taskbar, click **The taskbar (overview)**. The content on the page should be similar to Figure 8-10. It is very similar to the content you accessed from the Windows Help and Support Table of Contents earlier in this lesson. Notice the green text that you can click to display a definition, and the list of headings under In this article.

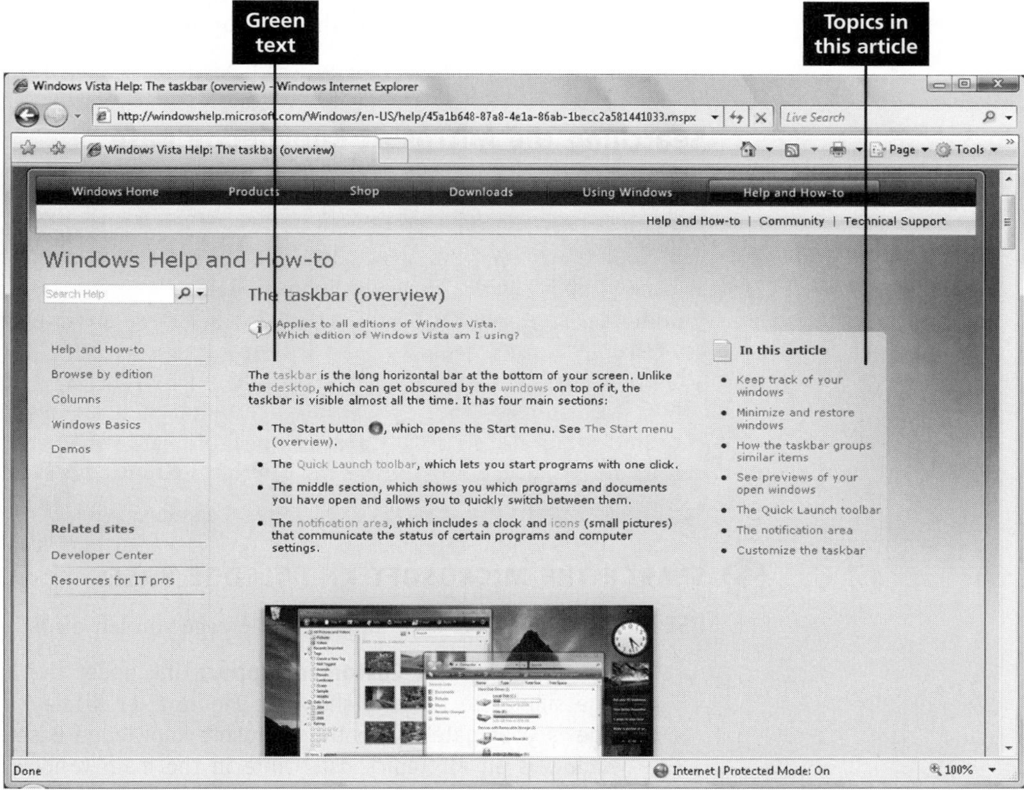

Figure 8-10

The taskbar (overview) page online

4. Click the **Browse** by edition link, which should be on the left side of the Web page, and then click the version of Windows Vista that you are using. (For example, click Ultimate, or click Enterprise.) A list of categories similar to the Table of Contents in Windows Help and Support displays.
5. Click **Maintenance and performance** and then click the topic **Ways to improve your computer's performance**. The Help topic Web page displays.
6. Click in the **Search Help** box, which should be on the left side of the Web page, key **documents folder**, and then click the **Go** button. A search results list displays.

TROUBLESHOOTING

Windows Vista may display a dialog box asking if you want to turn on ***AutoComplete***, a feature that automatically completes words as you type, based on words that you typed previously. Click Yes to turn on the feature, or No to leave it off.

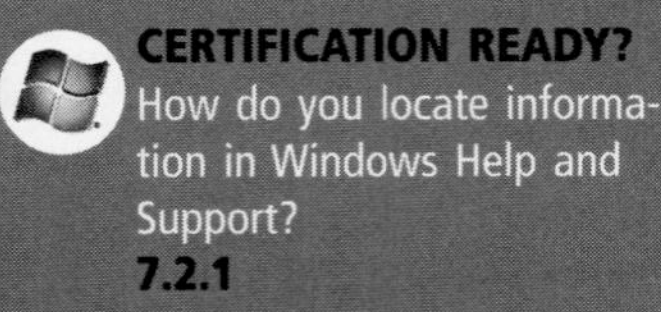

7. Click **Working with the Documents folder** to display the specific Help topic page.
8. At this point your instructor may ask you to capture an image of your browser window. Save it in your Lesson 8 assessment folder as ***Le08_03***.
9. Click the Help and How-to link to return to the Help and How-to home page. You should find the link on the left side of the page, or on a tab near the top of the page.
10. Click your browser's **Close** button to close the window. The Windows Help and Support home page should still be displayed.

PAUSE. LEAVE the Windows Help and Support home page displayed to use in the next exercise.

A lot of the information available in Windows Online Help and How-to is the same as the information available offline in Windows Help and Support. However, if you use Online Help you know you are accessing the most up-to-date information available.

In the next section, you learn how to search Microsoft's Knowledge Base for help information.

Searching the Microsoft Knowledge Base

Windows Help and Support is full of general information and step-by-step instructions about how to use the features and tools in Windows Vista. Most of the time, it will provide the answers you need. But if you have a technical question about a feature, such as how the Malicious Software Removal Tool works, or if you want to know why your audio device stopped working and what you can do about it, you can consult the ***Microsoft Knowledge Base***. The knowledge base is a collection of articles that Microsoft support engineers have written to document solutions to specific problems encountered by real customers. The articles are stored online so you can search them and browse them to find solutions to virtually any technical problem you encounter. In this section, you learn how to access and browse the Microsoft Knowledge Base and how to search it to find the specific article you need.

SEARCH THE MICROSOFT KNOWLEDGE BASE

USE the Windows Help and Support home page you left displayed in the previous exercise.

1. Click the **Microsoft Customer Support** link under the heading Ask someone. A Web page similar to the one shown in Figure 8-11 displays in your Web browser. This page is your gateway to the Microsoft Knowledge Base. Notice on the left of the window is an All Topics list, while in the main window there are links to some of the most current articles. The articles are grouped into three main categories: How-to, Download details, and Troubleshooting. How-to articles provide instructions about how to accomplish a task, or how a feature works. Download details articles describe the programs or files that are available for you to download to use with Windows Vista, and Troubleshooting articles explain problems you might encounter, and if possible, provide information on solving the problems. On the right of the window is a search box and links to access additional tools.

Figure 8-11

Microsoft Windows Vista Solutions Center page

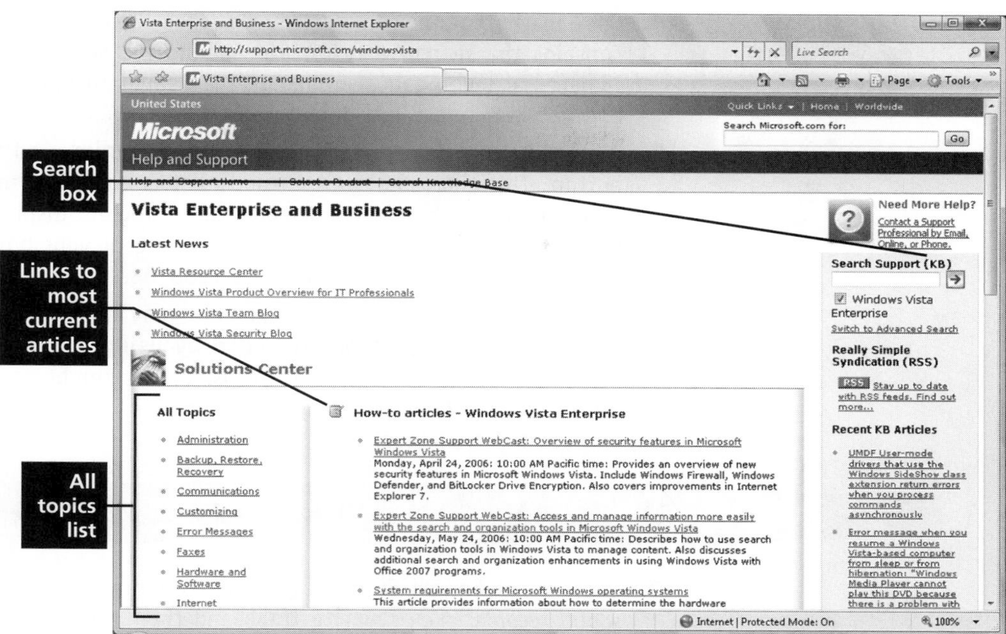

TAKE NOTE*

The articles on the Web page on your screen will probably be different from those in the figure, because Microsoft updates the Web site content frequently.

You can also click More support options on the Windows Help and Support home page and then click Search the online Knowledge Base to access the Microsoft Windows Vista Solutions Center page, or, if you are already browsing the Windows Online Help and Support Web site, click the link to Microsoft Customer Support under the heading Other resources.

2. In the main window, click **More -How-to articles**. A long list of available How-to articles displays. You can browse through the articles, or you can search to find articles related to a specific topic.

3. Click in the **Search Support (KB)** box, key **audio**, and then click the **Run the search** button. A search results page displays, similar to the one in Figure 8-12. The most relevant articles display at the top of the list. As with any search, the more information you can provide, the more focused the search results will be.

Figure 8-12

Knowledge Base search results

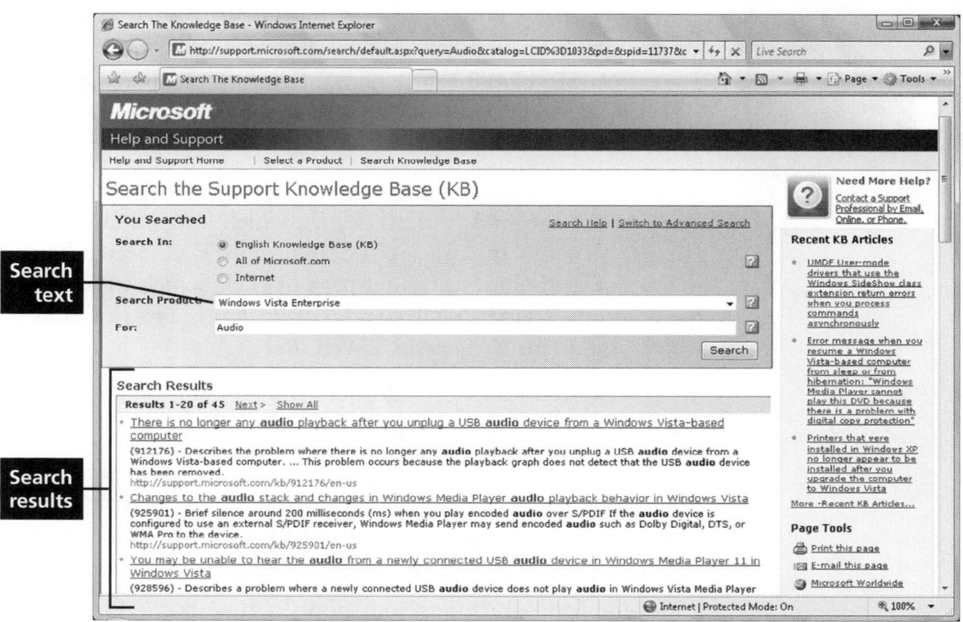

4. Click in the **For:** box in the You Searched area at the top of the window. This box contains the search text. You can modify the search text to change your search. If necessary, you can also change the Search In option to select where to search, and you can select a different Search Product.
5. Delete the search text *audio*, key **sound recorder**, and then click the **Search** button. This time, the search results list is much shorter, because only articles relating to the sound recorder accessory program display. At this point, your instructor may ask you to capture an image of your browser window. Save it in your Lesson 8 assessment folder as Le08_04.
6. Click the link to the article titled "**You may not hear any sound when you play back a recording that was recorded by using the Sound Recorder application in Windows Vista.**" The article displays. It is a troubleshooting article, so it provides information to help you diagnose a problem, understand the cause of the problem, and solve the problem.

TROUBLESHOOTING If the article mentioned in step 6 is not available, click a different article.

7. Click in the **Search Support (KB)** box on the right side of the window and delete *sound recorder*. Key **favorite links** and then click the **Run the search** button. A list of articles relating to favorite links displays.
8. Click the link to the article "**How to customize the Favorites Links list in common file dialog boxes in Windows Explorer in Windows Vista**." The article displays. Because it is a How-to article, it includes information about the Favorites List, how it worked in previous versions of Windows, and technical information about how to permanently customize the list.

TROUBLESHOOTING If the article mentioned in step 8 is not available, click a different article.

TAKE NOTE* The information about customizing the Favorites List is technical information for information technology professionals customizing the Windows Vista environment. It is different from adding and removing Favorite Links items, which you learned to do in Lesson 4, "Customizing Windows Explorer."

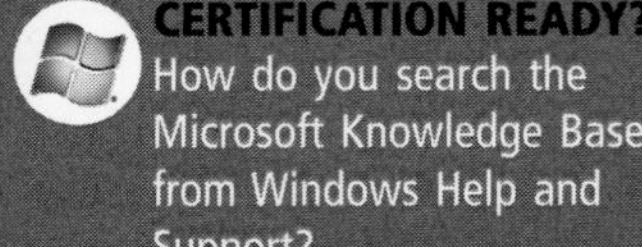

CERTIFICATION READY? How do you search the Microsoft Knowledge Base from Windows Help and Support? **7.2.2**

9. Click your browser's **Close** button to close the window. The Windows Help and Support home page should still be displayed.

PAUSE. LEAVE the Windows Help and Support home page displayed to use in the next exercise.

In the previous exercise, you used a Basic Search to search the Microsoft Knowledge Base. You can also use an Advanced Search, which lets you focus your search by entering additional criteria. To access the Advanced Search tools, click Search Knowledge Base in the Links bar at the top of the Solutions Center page or click Switch to Advanced Search on the right side of the Solutions Center home page. A ***links bar*** is a row of links across the top of a Web page, which you use to navigate in a Web site.

With Advanced Search, in addition to the Search In, Search Product, and For boxes that are available in the Basic Search, you can also select from the following criteria:

- Search Type, which lets you specify whether to search for the search text in the entire article, the title only, the article ID, or in an error message.
- Using, which lets you specify whether to search for all of the words entered in the search text, any of the words entered, the exact search text phrase, or to use a Boolean search.
- Modified, which lets you specify a time frame for when the article was last modified.

- Results, which lets you select how many items will display in the search results list on a single page.
- Include, which lets you select from a series of checkboxes to specify the type of articles you want included in the search results.

If you cannot locate the information you need in the Knowledge Base, you can try contacting other Windows Vista users in a Microsoft Windows Vista newsgroup. A ***newsgroup*** is an online forum for people with common interests. You can read, ask, and respond to questions and comments posted by other people interested in the same topics as you. You can search the newsgroup messages to see if anyone else has had questions or problems similar to yours and to see if anyone has suggested a solution. You can also enter a new message asking for advice or information. Generally, the people who participate in the newsgroups are knowledgeable and helpful and will frequently be able to provide you with the answers you need. To access the newsgroups, on the Windows Help and Support home page, click Windows communities under Ask someone. Select a specific newsgroup on the left page and then browse or search the messages.

Another way to find the information you need is to contact a member of the Microsoft support staff. You may have noticed the Need More Help? link available on many pages in the Windows Online Help site. Click it to contact a Microsoft support professional by phone or email to request assistance. Note that there is almost always a fee for this service, so you should try to find the answers you need on your own first.

In the next section, you learn how to use Windows Remote Assistance.

■ Using Windows Remote Assistance

THE BOTTOM LINE

Windows Remote Assistance is a feature that lets you ask for or provide technical help via a direct connection between two computers. To use the feature, one person issues a ***Remote Assistance invitation***, which is a file that is sent from one person to another to allow a Remote Assistance connection. Once connected, the two people can communicate using ***instant messaging***, which is a method of online communication in which the sender types and sends a message that displays almost immediately on the recipient's screen. In addition, the helper can view the other's desktop so he or she can offer specific advice on what to do next. With permission, the helper can even take control of the other's input device to demonstrate how to perform a task or to fix a problem. When you need help, Remote Assistance may be your best resource, because a trusted friend or technician can show you exactly what you need to do. Likewise, if you have expertise that might benefit someone else, you can provide the assistance directly, even if you are physically far away. In this section, you learn how to use Remote Assistance to ask for help and to provide help.

Enabling Windows Remote Assistance

Before you can issue or accept an invitation to provide Remote Assistance, you must enable the feature on your computer. You can turn Remote Assistance on or off and set a time limit to determine how long an invitation will remain valid. To enable Remote Assistance, you must have an Administrator Account or an administrator's password.

ENABLE WINDOWS REMOTE ASSISTANCE

1. Click the **Start** button and then click **Control Panel**.
2. In the Control Panel, click **System and Maintenance**.
3. Under System, click **Allow remote access**. The User Account Control dialog box displays, verifying that you want to continue the action.

TROUBLESHOOTING

If you do not have an Administrator Account, Windows Vista will prompt you to enter an administrator's password when you select to allow remote access. Ask your instructor for the password, key it in the Password box, and then click OK to display the System Properties dialog box.

4. Click **Continue**, or key an administrator's password and then click OK to display the Remote tab of the System Properties dialog box, as shown in Figure 8-13. The options on the top half of the tab are for Remote Assistance, and the options on the bottom half of the tab are for Remote Desktop.

Figure 8-13

Remote tab of the System Properties dialog box

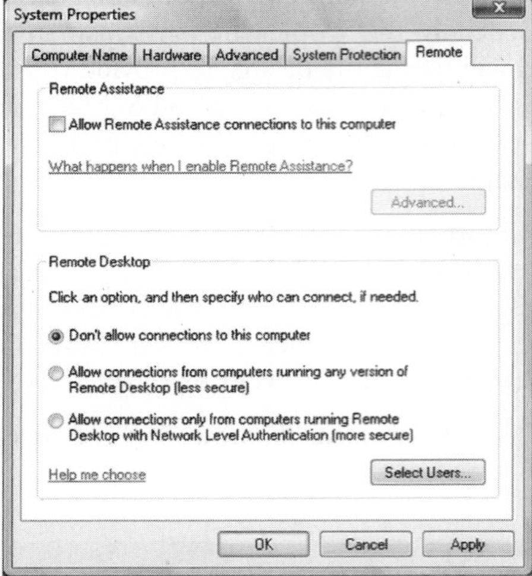

Remote Desktop is a feature of Windows Vista that you use to access programs and files stored on a remote computer. Remote Desktop is covered in Lesson 13, "Managing a Networked Environment."

5. Click to select the **Allow Remote Assistance connections to this computer** checkbox. When the checkbox is selected, the Advanced... button becomes available.
6. Click the **Advanced...** button to display the Remote Assistance Settings dialog box, as shown in Figure 8-14.

Figure 8-14

Remote Assistance Settings dialog box

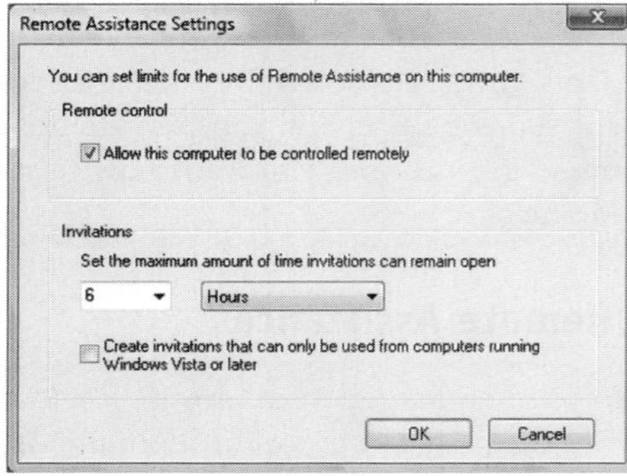

7. Under Invitations, click the number value dropdown arrow and click **90**. Click the time unit dropdown arrow and click **Minutes**. This sets the maximum amount of time that an invitation can remain open to 90 minutes. An invitation must be open for someone to use it to connect to your computer. At this point, your instructor may ask you to capture an image of the Remote Assistance Settings dialog box. Save it in your Lesson 8 assessment folder as ***Le08_05***.
8. Click **OK** to apply the change and close the dialog box.
9. Click the **Advanced...** button again and set the number value to 6 and the time unit to Hours, then click **OK** to restore the default setting.

CERTIFICATION READY?
How do you enable Windows Remote Assistance invitations by using Remote Settings?
7.8.1
How do you limit the time that a Remote Assistance invitation is available?
7.8.2
How to you disable Windows Remote Assistance?
2.3.3

10. Click to deselect the **Allow Remote Assistance connections to this computer** checkbox. This is how you would disable the feature so that no one could connect to your computer directly. You might want to disable the feature if someone else will be using your computer while you are not present.
11. Click to select the **Allow Remote Assistance connections to the computer** checkbox to enable the feature and then click **OK** to close the System Properties dialog box.
12. Click the **Close** button in the Control Panel window to close it. The Windows Help and Support home page should still be displayed.

PAUSE. LEAVE the Windows Help and Support home page displayed to use in the next exercise.

When you set a time limit for an invitation, you can select any value between 1 and 99, and you can select a time unit of Minutes, Hours, or Days. That means that the shortest amount of time an invitation can be valid is 1 minute, and the longest time is 99 days. An invitation must be valid for someone to use Remote Assistance to access your computer.

On the Remote tab of the System Properties dialog box, you can click the What happens when I enable Remote Assistance link to go directly to the relevant Help topic page and learn more about Remote Assistance.

If you do not want to engage in a Remote Assistance session with anyone using a computer that runs a version of Windows prior to Windows Vista, you can select the Create invitations that can only be used from computers running Windows Vista or later checkbox in the Remote Assistance Settings dialog box.

Enabling Remote Assistance and setting a time limit for invitations does not make an invitation available; it just means that your computer is now set up to use Remote Assistance if you want. You learn how to create an invitation in the next section.

Requesting Remote Assistance

Once you have enabled Remote Assistance, you can create an invitation file that you send to the person you want to provide the help. The invitation file can be delivered via email, or on a removable disk or network drive. To create the invitation file, you enter and confirm a password, which you must tell the recipient. He or she opens the invitation file, enters the password, and then connects to your computer. If you know the recipient will receive and respond quickly, you can keep the invitation open while you wait for the response. If you know it will be a while before the recipient is available to respond you can save the invitation to use later. In this section, you create and save an invitation file requesting Remote Assistance, which you save to use later.

REQUEST REMOTE ASSISTANCE

USE the Windows Help and Support home page you left displayed in the previous exercise.

1. Click **Windows Remote Assistance** under Ask someone on the Windows Help and Support home page. The Windows Remote Assistance wizard displays. You can select to invite someone to provide assistance, or you can offer assistance to someone else.
2. Click **Invite someone you trust to help you** to display a page, where you can select to send the invitation via email or save the invitation as a file.

TAKE NOTE* If you have previously created an invitation, it displays in the window so you can use it again. This is useful if you frequently ask the same person for assistance.

3. Click **Save this invitation as a file**. Now you must specify a path and filename for the invitation file and key a password. The default settings store the invitation on the desktop, which is suitable for this exercise. You might edit the path to store it on a removable device so you can deliver it to the other person. You might edit the file name to give it a more descriptive name, indicating either to whom you are issuing the invitation, or even the nature of the problem.
4. Click in the **Password (at least 6 characters):** box and key **yonder29**.
5. Click in the **Confirm the password:** box and key **yonder29**. The window should look similar to Figure 8-15.

Figure 8-15

Creating a Remote Assistance invitation file

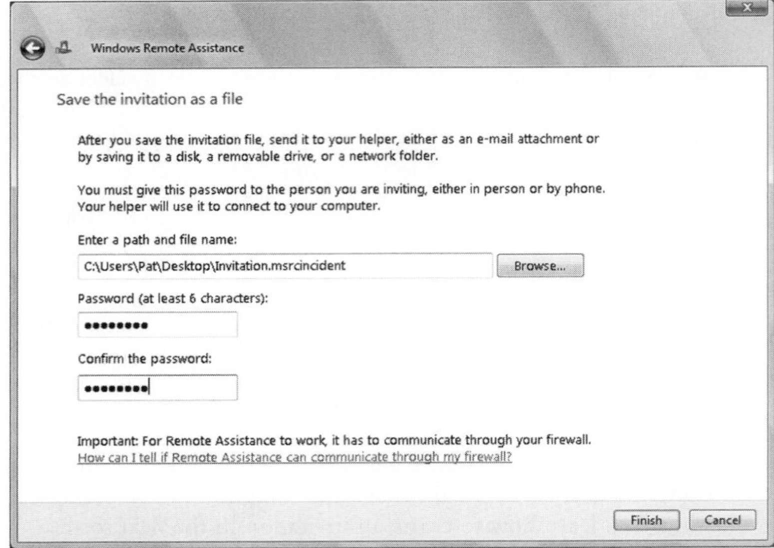

6. Click **Finish** to create and save the file. The Waiting for incoming connection . . . dialog box displays, as shown in Figure 8-16. If you delivered the invitation by e-mail, the recipient will receive it quickly, and may respond quickly. If you are going to deliver the invitation file on a removable device, you may want to close the dialog box and then reopen it later. Closing the Windows Remote Assistance dialog box cancels the current invitation, but saves it so you can use it again later.

Figure 8-16

Waiting for incoming connection dialog box

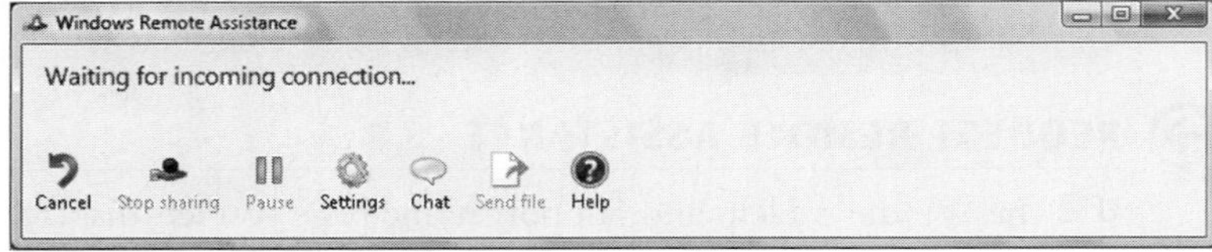

7. Click the **Cancel** button in the Waiting for incoming connection dialog box and then click **Yes** in the Are you sure you want to stop waiting? dialog box. The invitation window remains open, as shown in Figure 8-17. Notice that the invitation you just created is now listed as a previous invitation that you can use again.

Figure 8-17

Reuse an existing invitation file

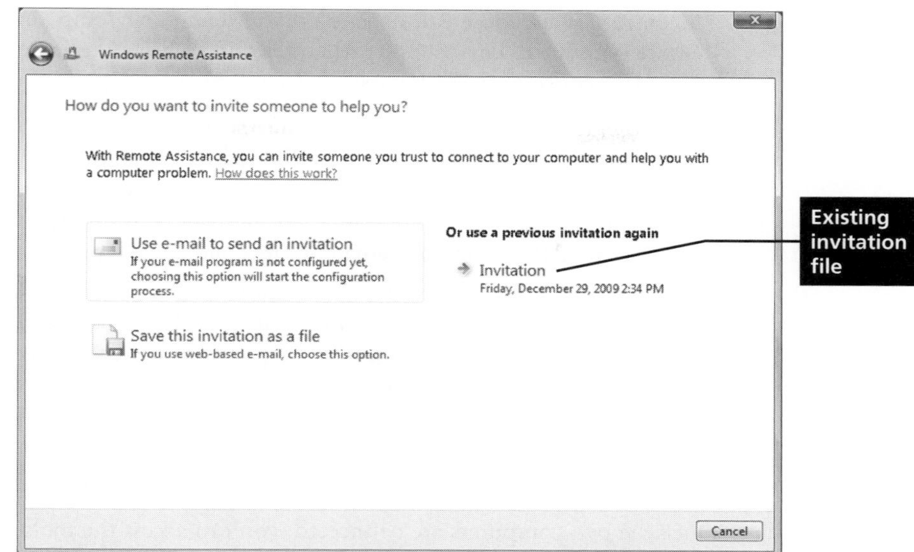

8. Click **Invitation** under Or use a previous invitation again to display the Save the invitation as a file window.
9. Key **yonder29** in the **Password** box**.** Click in the Confirm the password: box and click **yonder29**. Click **Finish** and then click **Yes** in the Do you want to replace the file? dialog box. The Waiting for incoming connection dialog box displays again. If the recipient is trying to connect to your computer, you are ready to begin the Remote Assistance session.

TAKE NOTE* You must communicate the correct password to the recipient so that he or she can use it with the invitation to connect to your computer.

10. Click the **Cancel** button in the Waiting for incoming connection dialog box and then click **Yes** in the Are you sure you want to stop waiting? dialog box. This cancels the invitation. Even if the recipient responds with the correct invitation file and password, he or she cannot gain access to your computer.
11. Click **Cancel** in the Windows Remote Assistance window.
12. Click the **Close** button in Windows Help and Support. You should see the invitation file icon on the desktop.
13. Copy the invitation file to a removable device such as a CD, DVD, or flash drive, or to your Lesson 8 assessment folder, and then delete it from the desktop.

XREF Copying files to a removable device is covered in Lesson 3, "Organizing Files and Folders."

LOG OFF your Windows Vista user account.

CERTIFICATION READY?
How do you request Remote Assistance through Windows Help and Support?
7.8.3
How to you disable Remote Assistance invitations?
7.8.4

You should take a few security measures before initiating a Remote Assistance session. First of all, you should only allow someone you trust to access your computer, so be careful who you send the invitation to, and who you tell the password to. In addition, you should close any files, folders, or programs that you do not want the other person to see.

There are many variables involved when you use Remote Assistance.

- You can issue an invitation for assistance or to provide assistance.
- You can send an invitation by email, or save it in a file.
- You can actively wait for a response right after you issue an invitation, or cancel the session and then at a later time, open an invitation you created previously.

The options you choose will depend on your computer setup and how you plan to use Remote Assistance. For example, when selecting whether to issue an invitation via email or in a file, consider the following:

- To send an invitation by email, you must have an email program such as Microsoft Outlook or Outlook Express configured to work with Windows Vista on your computer. After you enter and confirm the password, Windows Vista starts your email program and creates an email message with an attached invitation file. You enter the recipient's email address and then send the message.
- If you use a Web-based email program such as Hotmail, you can select to save the invitation as a file. You can enter a path and filename for the invitation file—or accept the default—enter and confirm the password, and then save the file. You can then attach the file to an email message or deliver it on a removable disk or network drive.
- With either method, as soon as the recipient receives the file, he or she can open it, enter the password, and gain access to your computer. So if you want an immediate response, you should send the invitation by email or attach it to an email message.

Once the two computers are connected, you can access the tools available to communicate and control the Remote Assistance session. Table 8-2 describes the available tools.

Table 8-2
Remote Assistance tools

Button	Description
Cancel	Click the Cancel button to cancel the session or to cancel an open invitation.
Stop sharing	Click the Stop Sharing button if you want to prevent the other person from controlling your computer. You can also press Esc to stop sharing control.
Pause	Click the Pause button to temporarily suspend the session.
Settings	Click the Settings button to open the Windows Remote Assistance Settings dialog box, where you can select options such as how much bandwidth to use for Remote Assistance, whether to save a log of the session, and whether to use the Esc key to stop sharing control. ***Bandwidth*** is the speed at which data is transferred over a network.
Chat	Click the Chat button to open an instant messaging window that you can use to communicate with your helper.
Send file	Click the Send file button to send a file to the helper.
Help	Click the Help button to go to a relevant Help topic page in Windows Help and Support.

When the Remote Assistance session is finished, remember to end or cancel the session so that the other person does not retain access to your computer.

SUMMARY SKILL MATRIX

In this lesson you learned	Matrix Skill	Skill Number
To locate a Help topic		
To use Windows Help and Support's Table of Contents	Locate information in Windows Help and Support	7.2.1
To search for a Help topic	Locate information in Windows Help and Support	7.2.1
To include Windows Online Help and Support in a search	Locate information in Windows Help and Support	7.2.1
To print a Help topic		
To get help online		
To use Windows Online Help and Support Web site	Locate information in Windows Help and Support	7.2.1
To search the Microsoft Knowledge Base	Search the Microsoft Knowledge Base from Windows Help and Support	7.2.2
To use Windows Remote Assistance		
To enable Windows Remote Assistance	Enable Windows Remote Assistance invitations by using Remote Settings; Limit the time that a Remote Assistance invitation is available; Disable Windows Remote Assistance	7.8.1 7.8.2 2.3.3
To request Remote Assistance	Request Remote Assistance through Windows Help and Support; Disable Remote Assistance invitations	7.8.3 7.8.4

■ Knowledge Assessment

Fill in the Blank

Complete the following sentences by writing the correct word or words in the blanks provided.

1. Windows Help and Support's ______________ lists major subject headings that link to help topics.
2. On a help topic page, ______________ text links to a definition.
3. You can click ______________ in the upper right corner of a Help and Support topic page to expand all hidden text on the page.
4. You must enable ______________ help if you want your help search results to include help topics stored on the Internet.
5. A links ______________ is a row of links across the top of a Web page, you use to navigate in a Web site.
6. Use an ______________ Search in the Microsoft Knowledge Base to focus your search by entering additional criteria.
7. A file that is sent from one person to another to allow a Remote Assistance connection is called a Remote Assistance ______________.
8. During a Remote Assistance session, users can communicate using ______________ messaging.
9. You must tell a Remote Assistance recipient the correct ______________ to use to connect to your computer.
10. The speed at which data is transferred over a network is called ______________.

Multiple Choice

Select the best response for the following questions.

1. Which of the following is an online forum for people with common interests?

a. newsgroup
b. home page
c. Knowledge Base
d. Remote Assistance

2. Which of the following is a feature of Windows Vista that you use to ask for or provide technical help via a direct connection between two computers?

a. newsgroup
b. home page
c. Knowledge Base
d. Remote Assistance

3. What icon displays next to a link to a specific help topic?

a. clock
b. question mark
c. book
d. arrow

4. What icon displays next to a link to a help subject heading?

a. clock
b. question mark
c. book
d. arrow

5. Which of the following is a collection of articles that Microsoft support engineers have written to document solutions to specific problems encountered by real customers?

a. newsgroup
b. home page
c. Knowledge Base
d. Remote Assistance

6. Which type of article explains problems you might encounter while working with Windows Vista?

a. how-to
b. troubleshooting
c. download details
d. news

7. Which type of article provides instructions about how to accomplish a task or how a feature works?

a. how-to
b. troubleshooting
c. download details
d. news

8. Which type of Microsoft Help and Support usually costs a fee?
   a. Remote Assistance
   b. Knowledge Base
   c. phone or email contact
   d. newsgroup
9. In which dialog box can you set a time limit for Remote Assistance invitations?
   a. System Properties
   b. Remote Assistance Settings
   c. System Assistance Settings
   d. Remote Timing Settings
10. Which of the following tools is available for use during a Remote Assistance session?
   a. Stop Sharing
   b. Connect
   c. Print
   d. Ask

■ Competency Assessment

Project 8-1: Learn About Viruses

You manage a florist shop, where you a use a single Windows Vista–based computer to store important data such as billing records, inventory, and contact information. You want to be sure you are doing everything you can to protect your computer from viruses that might damage your files. In this project, you use the Windows Help and Support system to look up and print information about viruses and what you can do to protect your computer.

GET READY. Before you begin these steps, start your computer and log on to your Windows Vista account. Close all open windows so you can see the desktop. Also, make sure you have a printer correctly connected, loaded with paper, and available for use.

1. Click the **Start** button and then click **Help and Support** in the right pane of the Start menu. The Windows Help and Support home page displays.
2. Click **Table of Contents** to display the Contents page, which lists help subject headings.
3. Click **Security and privacy** to display a list of links to help topics and subject headings relating to security and privacy.
4. Click **Understanding security and safe computing** and then read the introductory paragraphs at the top of the page.
5. Click the green text **malicious software** to display a definition and read it.
6. Under In this article, click **Use virus protection** to go to that section of the article. Then read the information. At this point, your instructor may ask you to capture an image of the Windows Help and Support window. Save it in your Lesson 8 assessment folder as ***Proj08_01***.
7. Click the **Browse Help** button on the Windows Help and Support toolbar to return to the Security and privacy links page.
8. Click the subject heading **Helping to protect your computer from viruses** to display a list of links to related help topics.
9. Click the link **How can I help protect my computer from viruses?**
10. Click the **Print** button on the Windows Help and Support toolbar to display the Print dialog box.

11. Click **Print** to use the default settings to print the page, or select Print options and then click Print.
12. Click the **Help and Support home** button on the Windows Help and Support toolbar to display the Windows Help and Support home page.

    PAUSE. LEAVE the Windows Help and Support home page displayed to use in the next project.

Project 8-2: Learn How to Optimize Your Display

A co-worker who is visually impaired needs to use your computer. You know it is possible to optimize the display to make it easier to see, but you are not sure how. In this project, you will choose to include online help in Windows Help and Support and then you will search for and print information about how to make your display more accessible for your co-worker.

1. On the Windows Help and Support home page, click the **Online/Offline Help** button in the lower right corner of the Windows Help and Support window.
2. Click **Get online Help**.
3. Click in the **Search Help** box and delete any text already there.
4. Key **optimize display** and then click the **Search Help** button. The search results list displays related help topics.
5. Locate and click the topic **Make the computer easier to see (optimize visual display)**. The help topic page displays. At this point your instructor may ask you to capture an image of the Windows Help and Support window. Save it your Lesson 8 assessment folder as ***Proj08_02***.
6. Click the **Print** button on the Windows Help and Support toolbar.
7. Click the **Print** button in the Print dialog box to use the default settings to print the topic.
8. Click the **Help and Support home** button on the Windows Help and Support toolbar to display the Windows Help and Support home page.

   PAUSE. LEAVE the Windows Help and Support home page displayed to use in the next project.

■ Proficiency Assessment

Project 8-3: Troubleshoot DVD Recording Problems

At the florist shop, you are having trouble burning more data files to the DVD you use for backing up customer information. Although you should be able to add data to a disc on which you have already recorded information, Windows Vista is not allowing the procedure. In this project, you will search for troubleshooting information in Windows Help and Support. When no information about your specific problem is available, you search the Microsoft Knowledge Base.

GET READY. Before you begin these steps, make sure you have an active connection to the Internet available for use.

1. On the Windows Help and Support home page, click in the **Search Help** box and delete any text already there.
2. Key **add files to dvd** and then click the **Search Help** button.
3. Scan the list of links to see if any relate to problems with burning files to a DVD. Click any link you think might be relevant and read the available information.
4. Click the **Ask** button on the Windows Help and Support toolbar.

5. Under Other resources, click the link to **Knowledge Base**. The Knowledge Base should run a search based on the text in the Search Help box, and display a list of results. (If the Knowledge Base opens without running the search, click in the **Search Support (KB)** box on the right side of the window. Key **add files to dvd** and then click the **Run the search** button.)
6. At this point, your instructor may ask you to capture an image of your browser window. Save it in your Lesson 8 assessment folder as ***Proj08_03***.
7. Scan the list of articles to see if any relate to the problem you are having recording additional files to a DVD.
8. Click the link to **You cannot record more data to a recordable DVD-R Dual Layer disc after you format and then eject the disc in Windows Vista** to display the troubleshooting article.
9. Read the article to determine the problem and the solution.
10. Click your browser's **Close** button to close the window. The Windows Help and Support window should still display.
11. Click the **Help and Support home** button to display the Windows Help and Support home page.

   PAUSE. LEAVE the Windows Help and Support home page displayed to use in the next project.

Project 8-4: Request Remote Assistance

You work for a large university that has a technical support staff available to provide remote assistance to employees located throughout the campus. You are having trouble launching and using a recently installed word processing program. In this project, you will enable Windows Remote Assistance, set a remote assistance invitation time limit of 2 days, and then issue a Remote Assistance invitation to get help with your problem.

1. Click the **Start** button and then click **Control Panel**.
2. Click **System and Maintenance** and then under System, click **Allow remote access**.
3. Click **Continue** in the User Account Control dialog box, or, if you do not have an administrator account, key an administrator's password and press **Enter** to continue.
4. On the Remote tab of the System Properties dialog box, click to select the **Allow Remote Assistance connections to this computer** checkbox, if necessary.
5. Click the **Advanced...** button to display the Remote Assistance Settings dialog box.
6. Under Invitations, click the number value dropdown arrow and click **2**. Click the time unit dropdown arrow and click **Days**.
7. Click **OK** to apply the change and close the dialog box. Then click **OK** to close the System Properties dialog box.
8. Click the **Close** button in the Control Panel window.
9. Under Ask someone on the Windows Help and Support home page, click **Windows Remote Assistance**.
10. Click **Invite someone you trust to help you**.
11. Click **Save this invitation as a file**.
12. In the Enter a path and file name box, replace the file name Invitation.msrcincident with the file name ***Proj08_04.msrcincident***. Then, click in the **Password (at least 6 characters):** box and key **helpme84**. Then click in the **Confirm the password:** box and key **helpme84**.

13. Click **Finish** to create and save the file in the default location, which is the desktop.
14. Copy the invitation file from the desktop to a removable device—such as a CD, DVD or flash drive, and to your Lesson 8 assessment folder. If possible, give the invitation file and the password to someone you trust. (Alternatively, attach the file to an email message and send it to the person you trust.)
15. Have the recipient use the invitation and password to connect to your computer.
16. Establish the connection and conduct a Remote Assistance session. Try the available tools.
17. When you are finished, click the **Cancel** button to cancel the session.
18. Click **Cancel** in the Windows Remote Assistance window to close it. The Windows Help and Support home page should still be displayed.
19. Minimize the Windows Help and Support home page so you can see the desktop.
20. Delete the invitation file from the desktop and then restore the Windows Help and Support window.

    PAUSE. LEAVE the Windows Help and Support home page displayed to use in the next project.

■ Mastery Assessment

Project 8-5: Learn about Wireless Networks

You just purchased a new notebook computer for your home, and you are considering setting up a wireless home network. In this project, you use Windows Help and Support to learn about wireless networks.

1. Make sure that online Help and Support is enabled.
2. Display the Windows Help and Support Table of Contents.
3. Click **Networking - connecting computers and devices**.
4. Display the topic **Wireless networking: frequently asked questions**.
5. Expand all topics to show all of the text on the page.
6. Read the questions and answers and then go back to the Networking - connecting computers and devices links.
7. Display and read the topic **What you need to set up a home network** and then go back to the Networking - connecting computers and devices links.
8. Click the subject **Setting up a network**.
9. Display, read, and print the topic **How is a network at home different from one at work?** and then go back to the Networking - connecting computers and devices links.
10. Display and read the topic **Setting up a home network**. At your instructor's request, capture an image of the Windows Help and Support window. Save it in your Lesson 8 assessment folder as ***Proj08_05***.
11. Return to the Windows Help and Support home page.

    PAUSE. LEAVE the Windows Help and Support home page displayed to use in the next project.

Project 8-6: Get Assistance with an External Hard Drive

At the university where you work, you have been given an external hard drive to use to supplement the local storage space you have on your computer. The drive connects to your PC via a USB device. Unfortunately, Windows Vista has not been able to identify it on your computer system, and you are not sure if you have it connected correctly, if there is a problem with the driver or the USB port, or if you just do not know how to use it. In this project, you will search for assistance in Windows Help and Support and in the Microsoft Knowledge Base. Finally you will issue a Remote Assistance invitation to the university's technical support staff.

1. Search Microsoft Help and Support for information about external drives.
2. Scan the links to see if any relate to problems with Windows Vista identifying external drives.
3. Select to search the **Knowledge Base** for information about the problem.
4. Search the Knowledge Base for information about external drives—specifically troubleshooting articles about problems Windows Vista might have identifying external drives or identifying USB devices
5. Scan the articles to see if any might help.
6. Close your browser and verify that remote access is enabled on your computer.
7. Set a **6 hour** time limit on remote access invitations.
8. Create a remote access invitation file with the name ***Proj08_06***, using the password **exdrive86**.
9. Save the file on the desktop.
10. Deliver the invitation and the password to someone you trust, either on a removable device such as a CD, DVD, flash drive, or floppy drive, or as an email attachment.
11. When the other person attempts to connect to your computer, establish the Remote Assistance session.
12. When you are finished, close the Remote Assistance session, and then disable Remote Assistance on your computer.
13. Copy the invitation file from the desktop to your Lesson 8 assessment folder and then delete it from the desktop.
14. **CLOSE** all open windows.

    LOG OFF your Windows Vista user account.

INTERNET READY

Gustavus is a remote city in southeast Alaska. In this exercise, use Internet search tools to locate information about Gustavus, such as the population, industry, attractions, history, heritage, and weather. You should be able to find pictures as well. Using a word processing program or pen and paper, write a report about Gustavus using the information that you find. Remember to cite your online sources.

Circling Back

The preparations for the series of seminars for high school science teachers are continuing at the Baldwin Museum of Science. For one of the seminars, participants will be using personal computers to complete a project about the weather in Australia. The manager of special events has asked you, her temporary assistant, to develop a consistent desktop environment for all of the PCs that will be in use. Specifically, she has asked you to select a picture to use as a desktop background and to make sure that the programs the teachers will need are easily accessible. To accomplish this, you will need to use the skills you have learned in Lessons 4, 5, 6, 7, and 8 to customize Windows Explorer, work with multimedia files, search for files and folders, personalize the workspace, and get help and support.

Project 1: Prepare Your Windows Explorer Environment

Customize Windows Explorer for your needs by creating a folder where you can store picture files, changing the File list view and the folder window layout, setting folder options, and adding your new folder to the Favorite Links list.

GET READY. Before you begin these steps, turn on your computer and log in to your Windows Vista account. Close all open windows so you have a clear view of the desktop. Create a new folder named CB2 in a storage location specified by your instructor, where you can store assessment files and folders that you create during these projects.

1. Open the Seminars folder you created in Circling Back 1, or create a new folder named **Seminars** in the Documents folder.
2. In the Seminars folder, create a folder named **Desktop Pictures.**
3. Right-click the **Desktop Pictures** folder and click **Properties** on the shortcut menu to display the Desktop Pictures Properties dialog box.
4. Click the **Customize** tab.
5. Click the **Use this folder type as a template:** dropdown arrow and click **Pictures and Videos.**
6. Click **OK** to apply the changes and close the dialog box.
7. Drag the **Desktop Pictures** folder icon from the File list to the Navigation pane to add it to the Favorite Links list. Click **Desktop Pictures** in the Favorite Links list to open the folder.
8. Click the arrow to the right of the Views button on the window's toolbar and then click **Details** to change the File list view.
9. Right-click any column heading in the File list and click to select **Type.**
10. Right-click any column heading and click to select **Dimensions.**
11. Right-click any column heading and click to deselect **Date taken.**
12. Right-click any column heading and click to deselect **Rating.**
13. Right-click any column heading and click to deselect **Size.**
14. Click the **Organize** button, click **Layout**, and then click **Preview Pane** to display the Preview pane.
15. Click the **Organize** button, click **Folder and Search Options**, and then click the **View** tab.
16. Click to select the **Show hidden files and folders** option button and then click **OK.** The Desktop Pictures window should look similar to Figure 1.

Figure 1

Customize the Desktop Pictures window

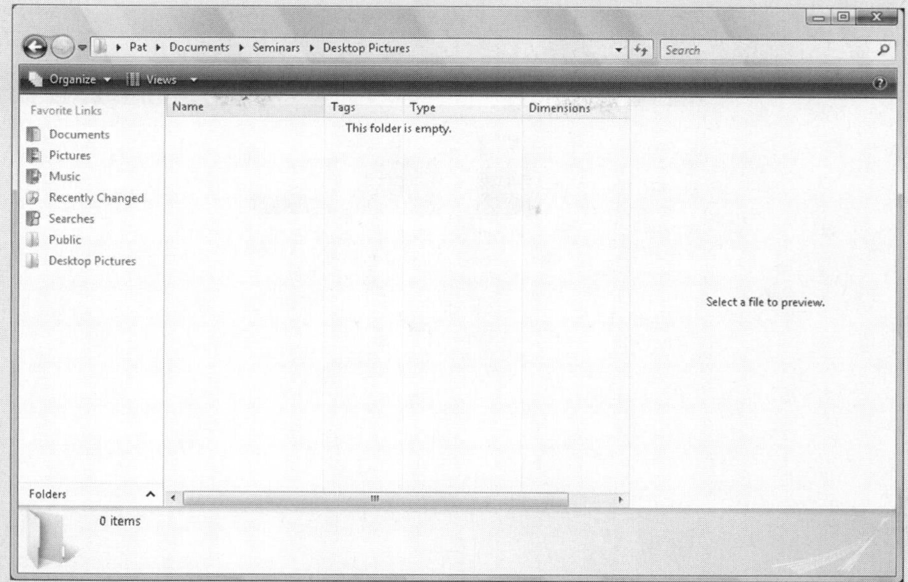

17. At your instructor's request, capture an image of the Desktop Pictures window and save it in your CB2 assessment folder as CB2_01. Close the Desktop Pictures folder window.

    PAUSE. LEAVE the desktop open to use in the next project.

Project 2: Search for Picture Files

The manager of special events provided you with eight picture files, but only three of them are suitable for use as the desktop background for the weather seminar. Locate the suitable picture files by searching for the pictures that are tagged with the keyword Australia. Preview the pictures, print the one you like the best, then copy all of the files to a removable device for safekeeping.

The ***Weather1***, ***Weather2***, ***Weather3***, ***Weather4***, ***Weather5***, ***Weather6***, ***Weather7***, and ***Weather8*** files are available on the companion CD-ROM.

GET READY. Before you begin these steps, make sure your printer is correctly set up for use with your computer, turned on, and loaded with paper. Also, have on hand a blank removable disk such as a CD or DVD, or a device such as a USB Flash drive.

1. Copy the files ***Weather1***, ***Weather2***, ***Weather3***, ***Weather4***, ***Weather5***, ***Weather6***, ***Weather7***, and ***Weather8*** from the data files for this lesson to the Documents folder.
2. Open the **Documents** folder.
3. In the Search box, key **Aus**. As you type, the three pictures that are tagged with the keyword Australia should display in the Search results, which should look similar to Figure 2.

Figure 2

Search results

4. Click ***Weather2***, press and hold [Ctrl], and then click ***Weather3*** and ***Weather8***. All three files should be selected.
5. Right-click the selection and click **Copy** on the shortcut menu.
6. Click **Desktop Pictures** in the Favorites Links list to open the Desktop Pictures folder.
7. Right-click a blank area of the File list and click **Paste** to paste the three pictures into the folder.
8. Click the file ***Weather2*** to preview it.
9. Click the file ***Weather3*** to preview it.
10. Click the file ***Weather8*** to preview it.
11. Right-click ***Weather3*** and click **Print** on the shortcut menu.
12. Click the **Printer:** dropdown arrow and click your printer option.
13. Click the **Paper size:** dropdown arrow and click the size of paper you are using.
14. Click the **Paper type:** dropdown arrow and click the type of paper you are using.
15. In the Layout pane, click the layout that you want to use.
16. Click **Print** to print the picture.
17. When the printing is finished, navigate to the Documents folder.
18. Insert a blank CD or DVD into your recordable drive. Alternatively, if you do not have a CD or DVD drive, you can copy the files to a device such as a USB Flash drive.
19. In the AutoPlay dialog box, click **Burn files to disc**.
20. Key **Backup Pictures** and then click **Next**.
21. Right-click the Taskbar and click **Show Windows Side by Side** so that you can see both the Documents window and the Backup Pictures window.
22. In the Documents window, select all eight of the Weather picture files.
23. Drag the files to the Backup Pictures window. Windows Vista copies the files to the disc.
24. When the copying is finished, eject the disc. Windows Vista closes the disc.
25. Remove the disc from the drive and label it with your name and the current date.
26. At your instructor's request, copy the Desktop Pictures folder to your CB2 assessment folder.

27. **CLOSE** all open windows.

    PAUSE. LEAVE the desktop displayed to use in the next project.

Project 3: Locate Information About Customizing the Desktop

You are almost certain you know how to use any picture as the desktop background, but to be sure, you will use Windows Help and Support to locate the information and print the necessary instructions.

GET READY. Before you begin these steps, make sure your printer is correctly set up for use with your computer, that it is turned on, and that it is loaded with paper.

1. Click **Start** and then click **Help and Support** on the Start menu.
2. If necessary, click the **Offline Help** button in the lower right corner of the window and click **Get online Help** on the popup menu.
3. Click **Table of Contents**.
4. Click **Customize your computer**.
5. Click the link to **The desktop (overview)** to display the Help topic page.
6. Under the heading In this article, click **Picking a desktop background** to jump down to that section of the page. Read the information. At your instructor's request, capture an image of the Windows Help and Support window. Save it in your CB2 assessment folder as CB2_02.
7. Click in the **Search Help** box, key **background**, and then click the **Search Help** button.
8. Click the link to **Change your desktop background (wallpaper)**.
9. Click the **Print** button on the Windows Help and Support toolbar and then click **Print** to print the topic page. (If necessary, select printing options.)
10. When the printing is finished, close the Windows Help and Support window.

    PAUSE. LEAVE the desktop displayed to use in the next project.

Project 4: Customize the Workspace

Now that you have the desktop background picture and information you need, you can develop a prototype of the Windows Vista workspace to use on the personal computers in the seminar. Participants will need to use Calculator, WordPad, and Paint, so in addition to applying the background picture, you will place a shortcut to Calculator on the desktop and a shortcut to Paint on the Quick Launch Toolbar. You will also pin WordPad to the Start menu. In addition, make sure the weather gadget displays the weather for Perth, Australia on the Windows Sidebar.

1. Right-click a blank area of the Taskbar. If a checkmark is to the left of Lock the Taskbar, click it to deselect the option.
2. Drag the Taskbar to the left side of the desktop.
3. Right-click a blank area of the Taskbar and click **Lock the Taskbar** to lock the Taskbar in its current position.
4. Click the **Start** button on the Taskbar and then click Control Panel. Under Appearance and Personalization, click **Change desktop background**.
5. Click the **Picture Location** dropdown arrow and then click **Public Pictures**.
6. Click the **Browse . . .** button and then click **Desktop Pictures** in the Favorite Links list in the Navigation pane.
7. In the Browse window, click the Weather3 picture and then click **Open**.
8. In the Desktop Background window, click the ***Weather3*** picture file (it should be the one in the middle) and then click **OK**.

9. Close the Control Panel window.
10. Click the **Start** button, click in the **Search** box, and key **WordPad**.
11. Right-click the **WordPad** program in the search results list on the Start menu and click **Pin to Start Menu** on the shortcut menu.
12. Click in the **Search** box, delete the text *WordPad*, and key **Paint**.
13. Right-click the Paint program in the search results list on the Start menu and click **Add to Quick Launch**.
14. Click in the **Search** box, delete the text *Paint*, and key **Calculator**.
15. Right-click the **Calculator** program in the search results list, click **Send to**, and then click **Desktop (create shortcut)**.
16. Click a blank area of the desktop to close the Start menu.
17. Right-click a blank area of the desktop, click **Sort By**, and then click **Name** to sort the desktop icons by name.
18. If the Sidebar is not already displayed, click the **Start** button, click **All Programs**, click **Accessories**, and then click **Windows Sidebar**.
19. Right-click a blank area of the **Sidebar** and click **Add Gadgets . . .** to display the Gadget Gallery.
20. Double-click the **Weather** gadget in the Gadget Gallery to add it to the Sidebar. Then close the Gadget Gallery.
21. Right-click the **Weather** gadget and click **Options**. Click in the **Search for location** box; key **Perth, Australia**; and then press Enter. In the list of available locations, click **Perth, Western Australia, Australia**.
22. Click to select the **Celsius** option and then click **OK**.
23. Close all gadgets other than the weather that are currently displayed on the Sidebar. (Right-click the gadget and click Close Gadget.) The desktop should look similar to Figure 3.

Figure 3

Customized desktop

24. At your instructor's request, capture an image of the desktop. Save it in your CB2 assessment folder as CB2_03.

PAUSE. LEAVE the desktop open to use in the next project.

Project 5: Restore the Defaults

Once you complete the prototype and receive approval for your design, you can restore the default settings to your computer.

1. Restore the Sidebar to its previous configuration. For example, if the Sidebar did not display on your desktop prior to step 18 of the previous project, right-click a blank area of the **Sidebar** and then click **Close Sidebar**. If you closed gadgets in step 23 of the previous project, right-click a blank area of the **Sidebar** and click **Add Gadgets . . .** . Then double-click each gadget that you had closed.
2. Right-click the **Calculator** shortcut icon on the desktop, click **Delete**, and then click **Yes** to remove the Calculator shortcut from the desktop.
3. Right-click the **Paint** shortcut icon on the Quick Launch Toolbar, click **Delete**, and then click **Yes** to remove the Paint shortcut from the Quick Launch Toolbar.
4. Click the **Start** button and then right-click WordPad in the Pinned Items list. Click **Unpin from Start Menu** to remove WordPad from the Start menu.
5. Right-click a blank area of the desktop and click **Personalize**.
6. Click **Desktop Background**.
7. Click the **Picture Location** dropdown arrow and then click **Solid Colors**.
8. Click the **light gray color swatch** that is three from the left in the top row and then click **OK**. (If you had a different desktop background prior to the previous exercise, select that background instead.)
9. Close the Personalization window.
10. Right-click a blank area of the **Taskbar** and click **Lock the Taskbar** to unlock it.
11. Drag the Taskbar to the bottom of the desktop.
12. Click **Start** and then click **Documents**.
13. Select and delete all eight Weather picture files.
14. Right-click **Desktop Pictures** in the Favorite Links list, click **Remove Link** on the shortcut menu, and then click **Yes** to remove the link from the list.
15. Click the **Organize** button, click **Layout**, and then click **Preview Pane** to hide the Preview pane.
16. Click the **Organize** button, click **Folder and Search Options**, and then click the **View** tab.
17. Click the **Reset Folders** button and then click **Yes**.
18. Click the **Restore Defaults** button and then click **OK**.
19. Delete the Seminars folder from Documents, and then close the Documents window.

    LOG OFF your Windows Vista user account.

Managing System Resources

LESSON SKILL MATRIX

Skills	Matrix Skill	Skill Number
Locating System Information		
Viewing Basic System Information	Display the amount of installed RAM and the processor speed; Ascertain the system performance rating	7.3.3 7.3.5
Determining Resource Usage	Ascertain the CPU usage of the computer; Ascertain the page file usage of the computer	7.3.1 7.3.2
Using Windows ReadyBoost	Expand memory cache by using Windows ReadyBoost	7.1.1
Managing Power Options		
Selecting a Power Plan	Adjust power options for best performance	7.1.3
Customizing a Power Plan	Configure power settings and options	2.1.1
Changing the Power Button Settings	Place a mobile device in Sleep mode; Place a mobile device in Hibernation mode	2.1.2 2.1.3
Managing Devices and Drivers		
Displaying Installed Devices	Ascertain the hardware and devices installed on a computer	7.3.4
Disabling and Enabling a Device	Enable and disable devices	3.3.1
Working with Drivers	Update or install a device driver; Roll back a driver to a previous version	3.3.2 3.3.3
Safely Removing Hardware	Safely remove PC Cards and USB devices	3.3.4
Installing a Local Printer		
Installing a USB Local Printer	Install a local printer	3.6.1
Installing a Non-USB Local Printer	Install a local printer	3.6.1
Managing Installed Printers		
Setting the Default Printer	Change the default printer	3.6.2
Determining Printer Status	Discover the status of a printer	7.6.1
Managing the Print Queue	Pause, restart, and delete print jobs and queues	7.6.2
Managing Disks		
Determining Free Disk Space	Ascertain the amount of available space on a hard disk	3.2.1
Viewing Partitions	Ascertain whether a hard disk is partitioned	3.2.2
Checking a Disk for Problems	Check a hard disk for problems	3.2.3
Defragmenting a Hard disk	Manually defragment the hard disk	7.1.2

Wide World Importers is an international importer of goods manufactured around the globe. Many employees are telecommuters—which means they work from home offices—and most also travel frequently, relying on notebook computers and other mobile devices to complete tasks and communicate with others. Without access to technical support personnel, it is imperative that employees know how to manage their computer system resources on their own so that they can maintain peak efficiency wherever they are working. With Windows Vista, each person is able to monitor and control system resources, including storage, memory, and devices. In this lesson, you learn how to use Windows Vista to locate system information, set and adjust power options, identify and control devices and drivers, set up a printer, and manage hard disk drives.

KEY TERMS
Basic input/output system (BIOS)
Cache
Central processing unit (CPU)
Device driver
Fragmented
Hibernation
Kernel
Local printer
Logical drive
Offline
Paging file
Partition
PC Card
Primary partition
Print job
Print queue
Random access memory (RAM)
System performance rating
Up time
Virtual memory
Windows ReadyBoost

■ Locating System Information

THE BOTTOM LINE

Understanding the internal components of your PC is imperative if you want to be able to manage and maintain your system resources. System information such as the amount of installed ***random access memory (RAM)***, the speed of the ***central processing unit (CPU)***, the size and usage of the ***paging file***, and the ***system performance rating*** impact the types of programs you can install and run as well as how quickly your computer can process information. Random access memory (RAM)—also called physical memory—is the internal storage area that your computer uses to run programs and store data. The central processing unit (CPU) is the main circuit chip that performs most of the calculations needed to run your computer. The paging file is space on your hard disk that Windows uses for temporarily storing data during processing. It is also called the page file or the swap file. The system performance rating is a score that measures the capability of your computer's hardware and software configuration.

In this section, you will learn how to locate system information so that you can identify the amount of installed RAM, the processor speed, the CPU usage, the page file usage, and the system performance rating. The page file is a hidden file or files on the hard disk that Windows Vista uses to hold parts of programs and data files that do not fit into memory. You will also learn how to use ***Windows ReadyBoost***, a feature of Windows Vista that lets you use storage space on a removable device to increase your system's performance speed.

Viewing Basic System Information

Use the Control Panel to quickly locate basic system information such as the amount of installed RAM, the processor speed, and the system performance rating. You can also view system performance subscores and print all system details. At work and at home, employees of Wide World Importers can use this information when diagnosing performance problems as well as when you want to be sure new software programs or hardware devices will be compatible with your system.

VIEW BASIC SYSTEM INFORMATION

GET READY. Before you begin these steps, start your computer and log on to your Windows Vista account. Close all open windows so you can see the desktop. Make sure you have a printer correctly set up for use with your computer, loaded with paper, and turned on. In addition, create a new folder named Lesson 9 in a storage location specified by your instructor, where you can store assessment files and folders that you create during this lesson.

1. Click the **Start** button and then click **Control Panel**.
2. Click **System and Maintenance**.
3. Under System, click **View amount of RAM and processor speed**. Basic information about your computer displays in the System window. It should look similar to Figure 9-1, although the information will be specific to your PC. Under System, you can see the performance rating, processor speed, and amount of installed RAM.

Figure 9-1

View basic system information

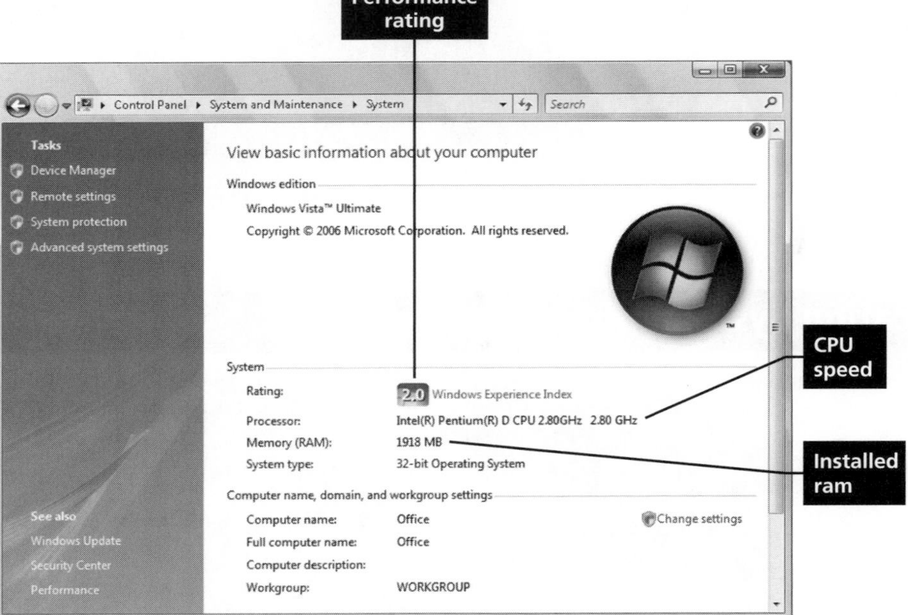

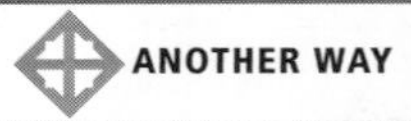

You can also view the amount of installed RAM and the processor speed in the Welcome Center window. Display the Welcome Center and click View computer details. Click Show more details to open the System window.

4. To the right of Rating, click **Windows Experience Index**. The Performance Information and Tools window opens. It should look similar to Figure 9-2. This window displays the individual performance rating subscores for your system components, as well as links for more information. At this point, your instructor may ask you to capture an image of the Performance Information and Tools window. Save it in your Lesson 8 assessment folder as ***Le09_01***.

Figure 9-2

The Performance Information and Tools window

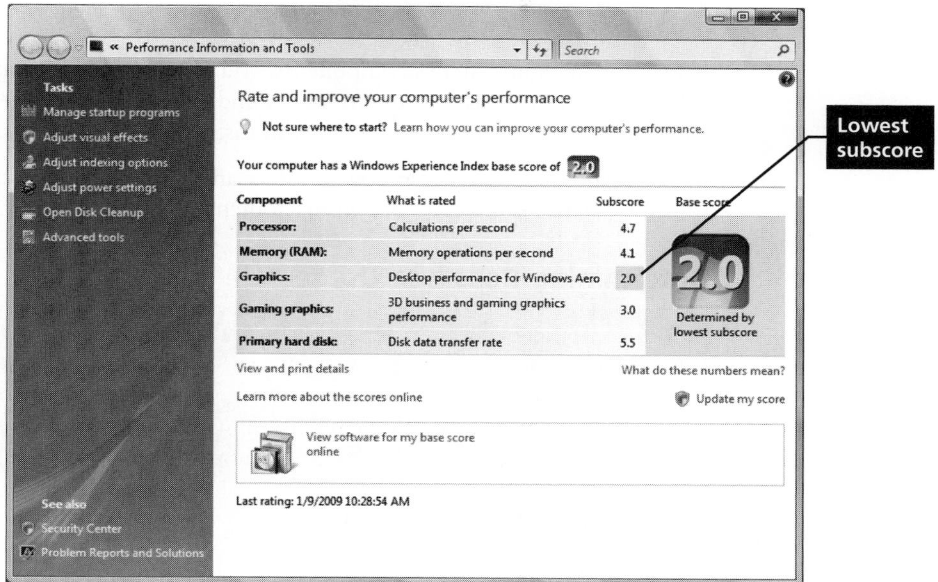

You can also open the Performance Information and Tools window from the Control Panel. Click Start, Control Panel. Then click System and Maintenance. Under System or under Performance Information and Tools, click Check your computer's Windows Experience Index base score.

5. Click **View and print details**. A Performance Information and Tools page suitable for printing displays. In addition to the performance rating subscores, it lists more detailed information about your system, storage, graphics, and networking components.
6. Click **Print this page**, in the top right corner of the window. The Print dialog box displays.
7. Click **Print** to print the page using the default settings, or select different Print options and then click **Print**.
8. When the printing is finished, close the Performance Information and Tools page and then close the Performance Information and Tools window.
9. Close the System window.

PAUSE. LEAVE the desktop displayed to use in the next exercise.

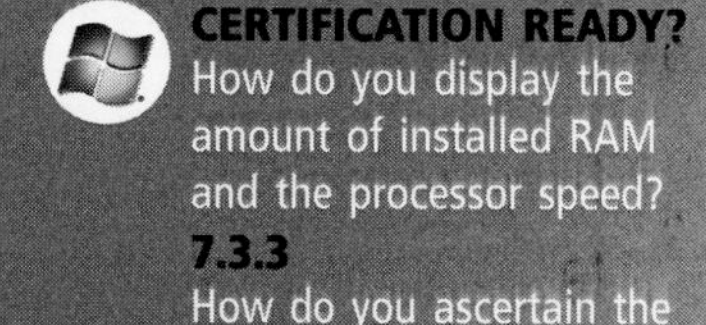

Most software programs have minimum system requirements, which are necessary in order for the program to run correctly. These requirements usually include the amount of RAM and the CPU speed, and may also include the amount of disk storage space and other factors, such as video processor capabilities. You can check the program packaging or online documentation to find out the minimum system requirements before you purchase a program to install.

Many software programs now display a minimum performance rating base score on the packaging. By comparing your system's Windows Experience Index base score to the program's base score, you can determine whether a program will run effectively on your computer.

The base score is a general indication of computer performance. The higher the score, the better and faster your system will perform. To arrive at the base score, Windows Vista evaluates individual components and assigns a subscore to each. The base score is the lowest subscore.

Do not worry if your computer's base score is 2.0. Many of your components may have higher subscores. A 2.0 performance rating indicates that your system can easily perform general computing tasks, such as running Microsoft Office 2007 programs. However, if you plan to use your system for 3-D gaming, or to record and play back high definition video, you may need a rating of 4 or 5.

If you update your system's components, you can click Update my score in the Performance Information and Tools window to have Windows Vista reevaluate the components. (You must have an administrator account or an administrator's password to update the score.)

In the next section, you learn how to locate and display information about how your computer is using system resources at any given moment.

Determining Resource Usage

Your computer is always using resources such as memory and processing power to perform the calculations necessary to accomplish a specific task. You can understand your system's capabilities and limitations by determining resource usage, and then you can use the information to troubleshoot problems and improve system performance. In this section, you will use Windows Task Manager to locate your system's CPU and page file usage.

DETERMINE RESOURCE USAGE

1. Right-click a blank area of the Taskbar and click **Task Manager**. The Windows Task Manager displays. The Task Manager shows programs, processes, and services that are currently running on your computer.

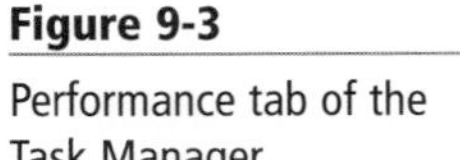

You can also open Task Manager by pressing Ctrl+Alt+Delete and then clicking Task Manager.

2. Click the **Performance** tab. The tab displays information about how your computer is using the CPU and memory resources. Performance graphs show CPU and memory usage in the top half of the window, and performance tables show statistics about system and memory resources in the bottom half of the window. It should look similar to Figure 9-3, although the actual details depend on your system.

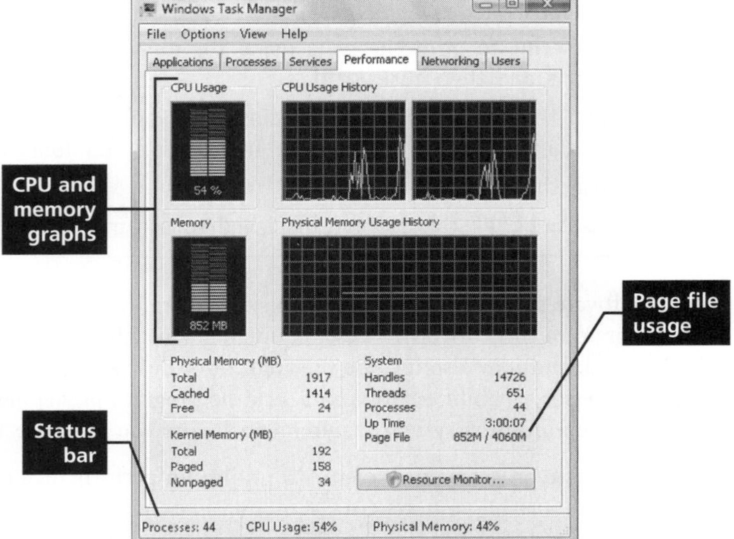

Figure 9-3
Performance tab of the Task Manager

3. Locate the CPU Usage graph. This graph displays the percentage of CPU resources currently in use. (The CPU Usage History graph displays the percentage of CPU resources used in the past few minutes.) The higher the percentage in the graph, the more processing power is being used, and the slower your system will perform.

TAKE NOTE* If the CPU Usage History graph is split, it means your system has multiple CPUs or a dual-core CPU.

4. Locate the Memory graph. This graph displays the amount of RAM currently in use. (The Physical Memory Usage History graph displays the amount of RAM used in the past few minutes.) As with processing power, the more memory being used, the slower the performance will be.
5. Look at the status bar. The percentage of the current CPU Usage, and the current Physical Memory Usage, are displayed on the status bar, along with the number of processes currently running on the system.

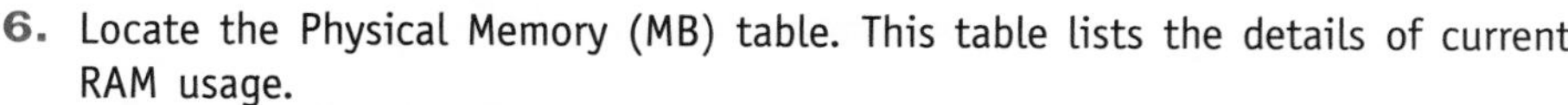

6. Locate the Physical Memory (MB) table. This table lists the details of current RAM usage.
7. Locate the Kernel Memory (MB) table. This table lists the details about the type of memory that the ***kernel***, or core part of the Windows Vista operating system, is currently using.
8. Locate the System table. This table lists details about system processes, including how many processes are currently running, and the ***Up time***, which is how long the computer has been on.
9. In the System table, locate the Page File values. The first number is the total amount of virtual memory currently in use, and the second number is the amount of virtual memory available. ***Virtual memory*** is a combination of the page file and RAM.
10. At this point your instructor may ask you to capture an image of the Performance tab of the Windows Task Manager dialog box. Save it in your Lesson 9 assessment folder as ***Le09_02***.
11. **CLOSE** the Windows Task Manager.

PAUSE. LEAVE the desktop displayed to use in the next exercise.

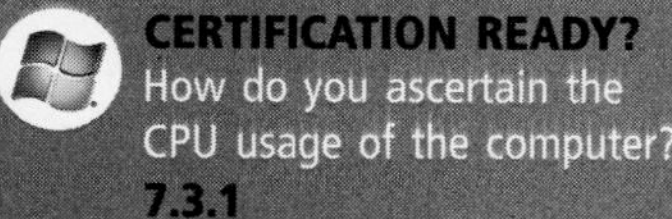

CERTIFICATION READY?
How do you ascertain the CPU usage of the computer?
7.3.1
How do you ascertain the page file usage of the computer?
7.3.2

As mentioned, RAM and the paging file together make up virtual memory. If you ever see a message warning you that your virtual memory is running low, you can increase the minimum size of the paging file. By default, Windows Vista sets the minimum size of the paging file to 300MB more than the amount of installed RAM, and the maximum size to 3 times the amount of installed RAM. If you have an administrator account or password, you can increase the minimum and maximum sizes on the Advanced tab of the System Properties dialog box. Consult Windows Help and Support for more information.

Keep in mind that both RAM and the paging file are temporary storage areas and that they clear when you turn off your computer.

In the next section, you learn how to use Windows ReadyBoost to make more temporary memory available.

Using Windows ReadyBoost

The more memory you have available in your computer, the faster your system can process information. You can make more temporary memory available by using Windows ReadyBoost to access the memory on a removable device, such as a USB flash drive. Wide World Importers employees make use of this feature when they are traveling, to boost the performance of their notebook computers. In this section, you learn how to use Windows ReadyBoost to access memory on a removable device.

USE WINDOWS READYBOOST

GET READY. To complete these steps, you must have a removable device such as a USB flash drive that supports the Windows ReadyBoost feature. If you do not have such a device, skip this exercise.

1. Attach the Windows ReadyBoost-compatible device to your computer. For example, plug a USB flash drive into a USB port. The AutoPlay dialog box displays, as shown in Figure 9-4.

Figure 9-4

Flash drive AutoPlay dialog box

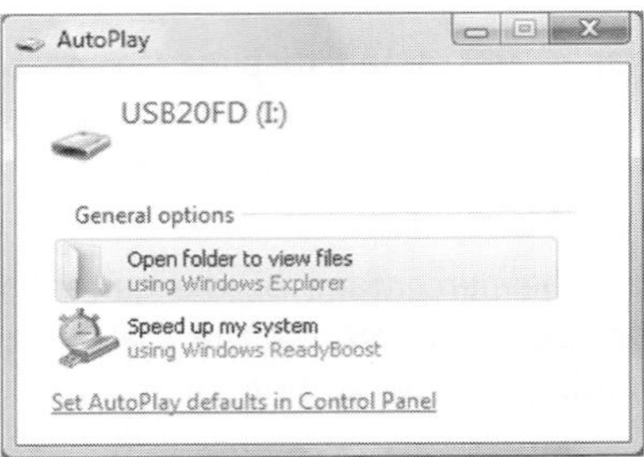

2. Click **Speed up my system using Windows ReadyBoost.** The ReadyBoost tab of the device's Properties dialog box displays so you can specify the amount of memory you want to use.
3. Specify the amount of memory to use and then click **OK.**

TROUBLESHOOTING

Not all removable devices are compatible with Windows ReadyBoost. If the device is not compatible, a message displays on the ReadyBoost tab of the device's Properties dialog box telling you so.

PAUSE. LEAVE the desktop displayed to use in the next exercise.

Microsoft recommends that you allocate between 1 to 3 times the amount of installed RAM for ReadyBoost. That means that if your computer has 1GB of RAM, and you plug in a 4GB flash drive, you will get the best performance boost by allocating between 1GB and 3GB of the drive's memory.

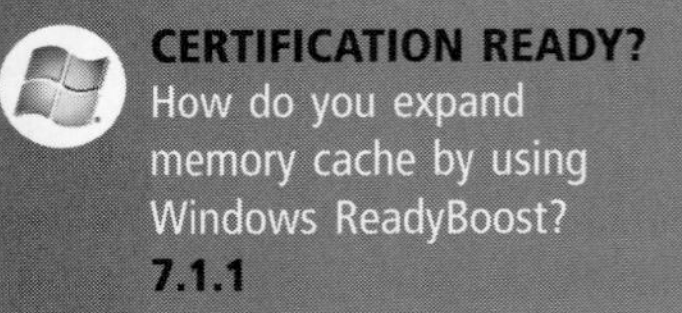

ReadyBoost works by making the fast flash memory that is built into certain storage devices available as a memory cache for Windows Vista. A ***cache*** is a temporary storage area. Not all devices have fast flash memory, so not all devices can be used with ReadyBoost.

Next, you learn how to manage power options.

■ Managing Power Options

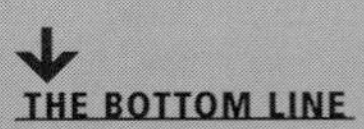

In Windows Vista, you can manage power options to maximize your system performance, to conserve energy, or both. For example, if you use a system that runs on battery power, such as a notebook computer, you can select power options to insure that you do not inadvertently run out of power. Power settings are organized into power plans designed to suit the needs of most people. You can also customize a power plan by selecting options to control such features as the brightness of the display, how long a system is inactive before it goes into sleep mode, and how long the display is inactive before it turns off. In addition, you can change the function of the power button so that instead of turning the system off and on, it starts Sleep mode or Hibernation. In this section, you learn how to select a power plan and how to customize power options for mobile and desktop computers.

Selecting a Power Plan

Windows Vista has three built-in power plans, which suit the needs of most people. One is designed to balance performance with energy consumption, one is designed to minimize energy consumption, and one is designed to maximize performance. In this exercise, you learn how to select a built-in power plan.

SELECT A POWER PLAN

1. Click **Start**, click **Control Panel**, and then click **System and Maintenance**.
2. Click **Power Options** to display the Power Options window, which should look similar to Figure 9-5. The available power plans are listed. Table 9-1 describes the three power plans that come with Windows Vista.

Figure 9-5

Power plans in the Power Options window

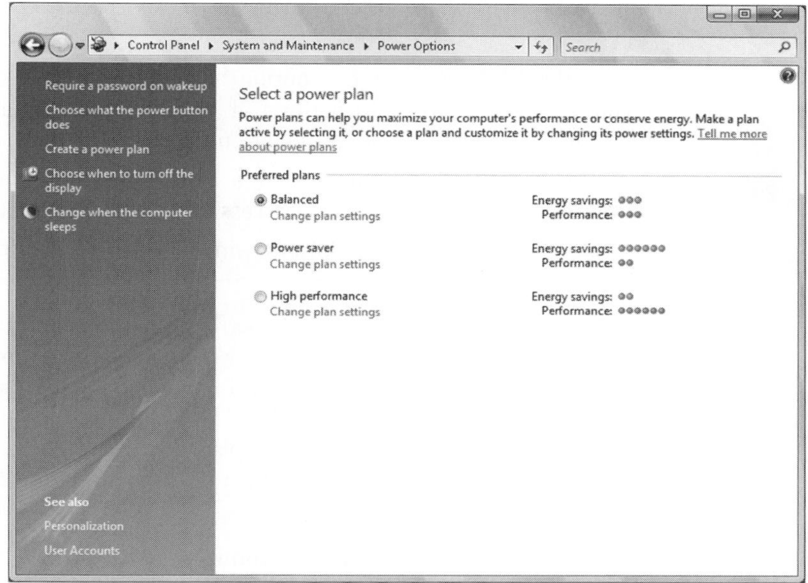

TAKE NOTE*

Notice the blue and purple dots to the right of each power plan. The blue dots indicate the level of energy savings, and the purple dots indicate the level of performance. The more dots, the higher the level.

TROUBLESHOOTING

If you are using a mobile computer, the plans may be listed under the heading Plans shown in the battery meter instead of Preferred plans.

TROUBLESHOOTING

If you have more than three plans on your system, you may have a heading labeled Show additional plans. Click the arrow to expand the list to display all available plans.

Table 9-1

Windows Vista Power Plans

POWER PLAN	DESCRIPTION
Balanced	The Balanced power plan automatically combines performance and energy saving settings. This plan is the default and is suitable for most users.
Power saver	The Power saver plan uses settings that reduce performance in exchange for lower power consumption. This plan may be best if you are working on a mobile device, because it will maximize battery life.
High performance	The High performance power plan maximizes performance but uses a high level of energy. Use this plan if you are not concerned about saving energy, and if you want your system to perform as fast as possible.

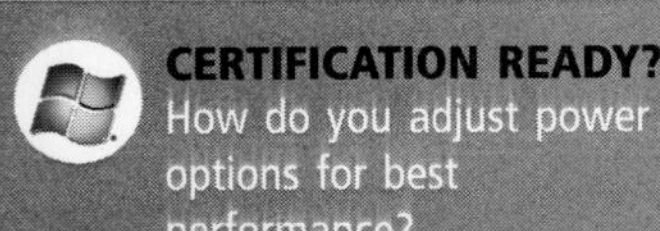
CERTIFICATION READY?
How do you adjust power options for best performance?
7.1.3

3. Click the **High performance** option button. This is the option you should select if you want your system to perform at its best, and if you are not concerned about battery power or energy consumption.
4. At this point, your instructor may ask you to capture an image of the Power Options window. Save it in your Lesson 9 assessment folder as ***Le09_03***.

PAUSE. LEAVE the Power Options window open to use in the next exercise.

In general, processing features that boost performance consume a lot of power. If you are concerned about conserving energy, you may have to sacrifice some performance. On a standard desktop system, you can compromise by selecting the Balanced power plan. If your only concern is fast processing, sharp graphics, and high quality performance, you should select the High performance power plan. If you are using a mobile device, however, you should select the Power saver power plan so that you do not drain your PC's battery too quickly.

In the next section, you learn how to customize a power plan.

Customizing a Power Plan

If none of the built-in power plans suits your needs, you can change the power settings. Basic settings let you select how long the system will remain inactive before the display turns off and how long before the computer enters Sleep mode. If you want to fine-tune the way your system components use power, you can adjust the advanced power settings. In this exercise, you learn how to customize a power plan.

CUSTOMIZE A POWER PLAN

USE the Power Options window you left open in the previous exercise.

1. Click **Change plan settings** under the Power saver power plan. The Edit Plan Settings window displays, showing the current settings for the Power saver plan. It should look similar to Figure 9-6. Note that you can customize the settings for any plan, even if it is not currently the active plan.

Figure 9-6

Default basic Power saver plan settings

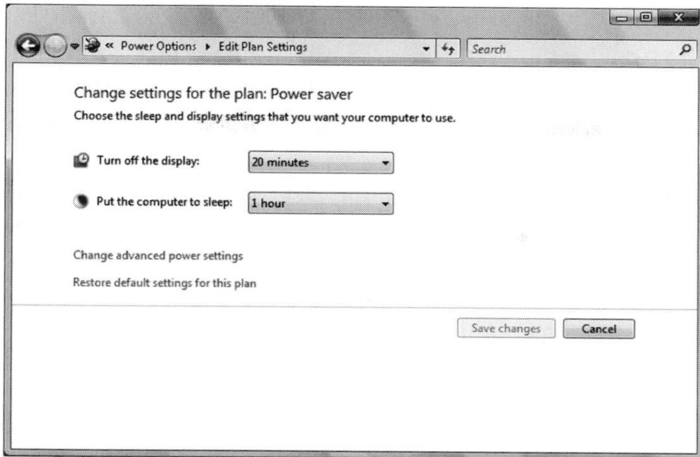

X REF

Sleep mode is also discussed in Lesson 1, "Getting Started."

2. Click the **Turn off the display** dropdown arrow and click **15 minutes**. This sets the length of time the display will remain inactive before Windows Vista turns it off. Turning off the display saves energy and battery power. You can select an interval ranging from 1 minute to Never.
3. Click the **Put the computer to sleep** dropdown arrow and click **20 minutes**. This sets the length of time the computer will remain inactive before Windows Vista puts it into Sleep mode. Putting the computer into Sleep mode also saves energy and battery power.
4. Click the **Save changes** button to apply the changes and close the window.
5. Click **Change plan settings** under the Power Saver power plan to open the Edit Plan Setting window again. At this point, your instructor may ask you to capture an image of the window. Save it in your Lesson 9 assessment folder as ***Le09_04***.
6. Click **Restore default settings for this plan**. A Power Options warning dialog box displays, asking if you are sure you want to make the change.
7. Click **Yes**. The default basic settings for the Power saver plan are restored.
8. Click **Change advanced power settings**. The Power Options dialog box displays, as shown in Figure 9-7. The Power saver plan is currently selected as the plan to modify, but you can modify any available plan by selecting it from the plan dropdown list.

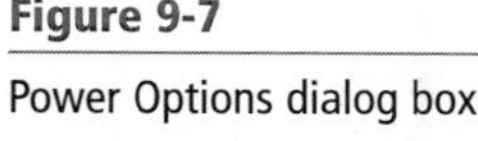

Figure 9-7

Power Options dialog box

9. Click the plan dropdown arrow and click **Balanced**.
10. Click the plus sign to the left of **Hard disk** to expand the list and then click the plus sign to the left of **Turn off hard disk after** to expand it.
11. Click the current setting to make the increment box available and then change the value to **25** minutes.
12. Scroll down and click the plus sign to the left of **Search and Indexing** to expand the list and then click the plus sign to the left of **Power Savings Mode** to expand it (if necessary). Click the current setting to make the dropdown arrow available.
13. Click the dropdown arrow and then click **Balanced**.
14. Click **OK** to apply the changes and close the dialog box. Click **Cancel** to close the Edit Plan Settings window.
15. Click **Change plan settings** under the Balanced power plan. In the Change settings window, click **Restore default settings for this plan**, and then click **Yes** in the Power Options warning dialog box.
16. Click the **Cancel** button to close the window. The Power Options window should still be displayed.

CERTIFICATION READY?
How do you configure power settings and options?
2.1.1

PAUSE. LEAVE the Power Options window open to use in the next exercise.

As you have seen, you can customize a power plan even if it is not the active plan, and you can easily restore the plan's default settings at any time.

You can also create a custom plan based on one of the existing plans. In the left pane of the Power Options window, click Create a power plan and select the plan on which you want to model the new plan. Key a name for your plan and then click Next. By default, it has the same settings as the plan you selected as the model. Select the basic power settings and click Create to add the plan to the list of available plans. You can customize the advanced settings if you want. To delete a custom plan, make any other plan active, click Change plan settings, click Delete this plan, and then click OK.

In the next section, you learn how to change the function of the power button on your computer.

Changing the Power Button Settings

By default, the power button on your computer turns your system off and on, and the power button on the Start menu sends your system into Sleep mode. You can modify the function of the power button so that it sends the computer into Sleep mode or ***hibernation*** instead. Hibernation is a power-saving mode similar to Sleep mode that saves your work to your hard disk. Wide World Importer employees who travel frequently find that changing the power button is particularly useful for their mobile computers because it makes it easy to conserve battery power without turning the system off or accidentally losing work. In this section, you learn how to change the settings of the power button.

CHANGE THE POWER BUTTON SETTINGS

USE the Power Options window you left open in the previous exercise.

1. In the left pane of the window, click **Choose what the power buttons do**. The System Settings window for power options displays, as shown in Figure 9-8.

Figure 9-8

Change the power buttons settings

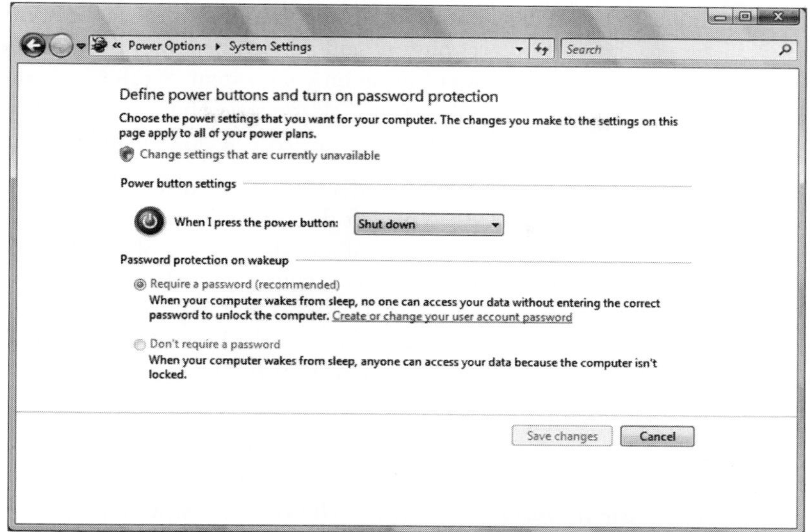

TAKE NOTE*

If you are using a mobile computer, you may have additional options available in the System Settings window. For example, you may be able to select options for what happens when you close the lid of your computer.

2. Click the **When I press the power button:** dropdown arrow to display a list of options.
3. Click **Sleep** to set the power button to send the system into Sleep mode. In Sleep mode, all of your work and information about the programs you are currently using is automatically saved to your hard disk. When you wake up your computer, Windows Vista restores your desktop within seconds so you can get back to work.
4. Click the **When I press the power button:** dropdown arrow and then click **Hibernate** to set the power button to send the system into Hibernation. In Hibernation, all of your work is saved to your hard disk and it is safe to turn off the power to your computer. For example, you could unplug a power cord or remove a battery. At this point, your instructor may ask you to capture an image of the System Settings window. Save it in your Lesson 9 assessment folder as ***Le09_05***.
5. Click the **When I press the power button:** dropdown arrow and then click **Shut down** to set the power button to turn the system off, or select the option that was in effect at the beginning of this exercise.
6. Click **Save changes** to apply the changes and close the window.
7. **CLOSE** the Power options window.

PAUSE. LEAVE the desktop displayed to use in the next exercise.

CERTIFICATION READY?
How do you place a mobile device in Sleep mode?
2.1.1
How do you place a mobile device in Hibernation mode?
2.1.3

Once you apply the power button setting, you simply press the power button on your system to enter the selected mode. For example, if you set the power button to Sleep, when you press the button, the computer goes into Sleep mode. If you set the power button to Hibernate, when you press the button, it goes into Hibernation. To wake your computer, simply press the power button again.

On a mobile device, you can also select options controlling what happens when you close the lid. As with the power button, it can shut down, enter Sleep mode, enter Hibernation, or do nothing. The lid settings are only available if you are using a mobile device.

If you want to apply power button settings to a particular power plan, or if you want to change the settings of the power button on the Start menu, you can use the Advanced settings tab in the Power Options dialog box. From the Power Options window, click Change plan settings and then click Change advanced power settings. In the Power Options dialog box, click the plus sign to the left of power buttons and lid. Set the Power button action to control what happens when you press the power button on your system. Set the Start menu power button action to control what happens when you click the power button on the Start menu. If available, set the Lid option to control what happens when you close the lid on a mobile device.

Earlier versions of Windows used a feature called standby, which saved work to memory instead of to a hard disk. This left the data vulnerable in the event of a power failure. In Windows Vista, Sleep mode combines the features of standby and Hibernation to create a safe power-saving state that protects your data and conserves energy. It also provides a faster waking time so you can get back to work more quickly. Hibernation is still available, but standby is not. In general, sleep mode is the best option for a power-saving state, but you should use Hibernation if you need to turn off the power to the system.

It is possible that you might not be able to put your system into Sleep mode under certain circumstances. For example, the video card in your computer may not support Sleep mode, or your PC's basic input/output system (BIOS) may have power-saving states turned off. The ***basic input/output system (BIOS)*** is the software that controls the start-up functions of your computer, including starting the operating system.

In the next section, you learn how to manage devices and drivers.

■ Managing Devices and Drivers

THE BOTTOM LINE

As mentioned in Lesson 1, a device is any piece of hardware that can be connected to your computer or network, including printers, disk drives, monitors, the keyboard, and the mouse. A ***device driver*** is the software program that lets your computer communicate with the device. It is often called simply a driver. It is important to know how to manage your devices and drivers so that you can keep them working properly, and so you can install new devices when you need them. For example, you can update a driver to make sure the device can access the newest Windows Vista features. If a device stops working, you can disable it so it does not affect the rest of your system and then enable it again once you have it working properly. In this section, you learn how to use Windows Vista to manage devices and drivers. You display a list of all the devices currently installed for use with your computer, enable and disable devices, and learn how to safely remove devices. You also learn how to install, update, and roll back a driver to a previous version.

Displaying Installed Devices

To find out exactly what hardware devices are currently installed for use with your computer, you can use the Windows Vista Device Manager. Device Manager displays a list of categories of components such as disk drives and keyboards. You can expand the list to view the specific device you have installed. In some categories, you are likely to have more than one device. In this section, you open Device Manager to view the devices installed on your computer.

DISPLAY INSTALLED DEVICES

1. Click **Start**, click **Control Panel**, and then click **System and Maintenance**. The System and Maintenance window displays.
2. Click **Device Manager**. If you have an administrator account, the User Account Control dialog box displays. Click **Continue** to open the Device Manager. If you do not have an administrator account, a Device Manager warning dialog box displays, informing you that you cannot make changes to devices and drivers. Click **OK** to display the Device Manager. The Device Manager should look similar to Figure 9-9.

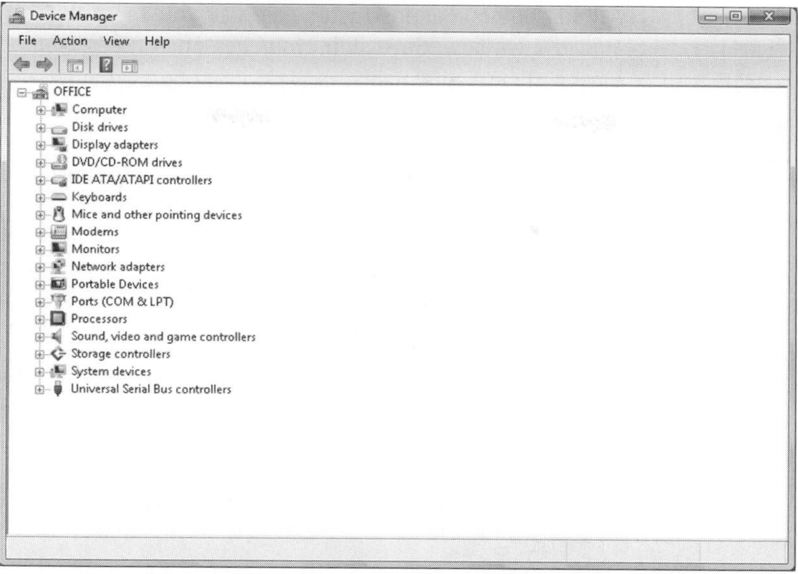

Figure 9-9

Device Manager lists categories of components

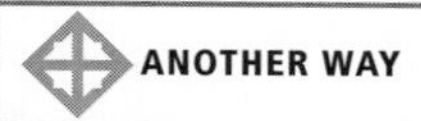

You can also double-click a category to expand it or collapse it.

3. Click the plus sign to the left of the **Computer** device to expand the list. Information about your computer displays.
4. Click the plus sign to the left of **Display adapters** to display information about the display adapters you have installed. The display adapters are the hardware cards that control your display monitor(s).
5. Click the plus sign to the left of **DVD/CD-ROM drives** to display information about the DVD/CD-ROM drives installed in your computer. If the DVD/CD-ROM drives category is not available, skip this step. You may not have a DVD/CD-ROM drive in your computer.
6. Click the plus sign to the left of **Keyboards** to see the keyboard information and then click the minus sign to the left of **Keyboards** to hide the information.
7. Click the plus sign to the left of **Mice and other pointing devices** to see the mouse information.
8. Click the plus sign to the left of **Network Adapters** and then click the plus sign to the left of **Processors**. The Device Manager should look similar to Figure 9-10, although the devices depend on what is installed on your computer.

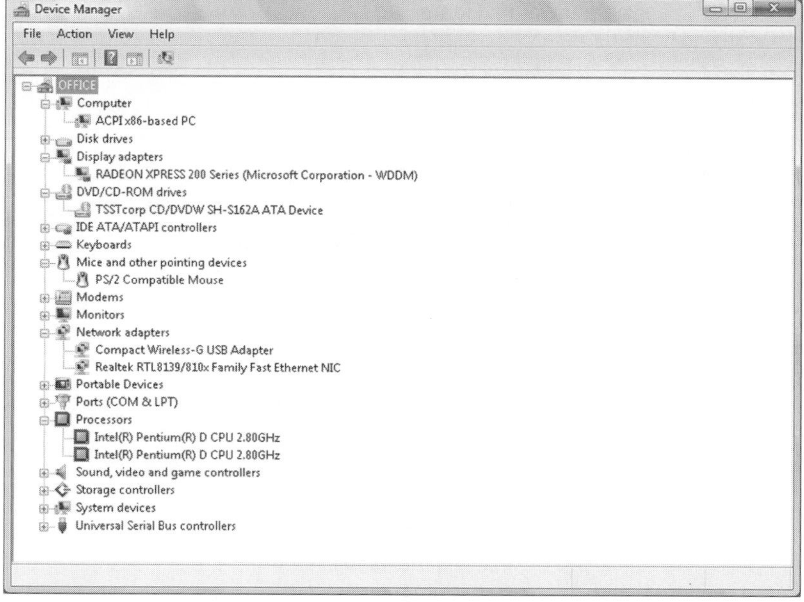

Figure 9-10

All installed devices display in the Device manager window

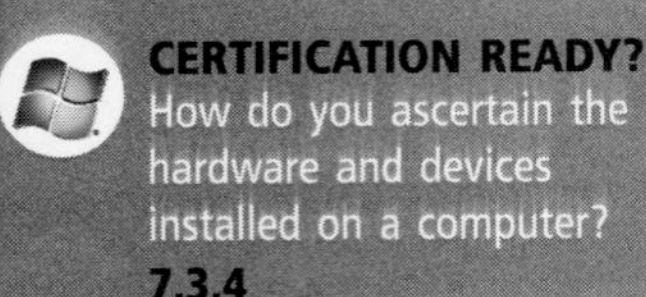

CERTIFICATION READY? How do you ascertain the hardware and devices installed on a computer? **7.3.4**

9. At this point your instructor may ask you to capture an image of the Device Manager window. Save it in your Lesson 9 assessment folder as ***Le09_06***.

   PAUSE. LEAVE the Device Manager window open to use in the next exercise.

TROUBLESHOOTING

If the Disable command does not display on the menu, you are not logged in as an administrator. Log off and log back in using an administrator account.

You can learn a lot about your computer by viewing the installed devices, even if everything is working without problems. If you expect only external devices such as a printer, keyboard, monitor, or mouse, to be listed in Device Manager, you might be in for a surprise. You will find many internal devices, such as disk drives, network adapters, and USB controllers listed as well. To learn about the specific devices you have available, consult the documentation that came with your computer, or check out the manufacturer's Web site.

In the next section, you learn how to use Device Manager to disable and enable a device.

Disabling and Enabling a Device

If a device is not working properly, it may interfere with other devices on your system. If you have an administrator account or password, you can use Device Manager to disable a device. You can enable it again when you have solved the problem. In this exercise, you disable and then enable your DVD or CD-ROM drive. If you do not have a DVD or CD-ROM drive, you can follow the steps to disable a different device, such as a USB port.

DISABLE AND ENABLE A DEVICE

GET READY. Have available for use a DVD or CD that contains data and is compatible with your drive. Alternatively, have a Flash drive or other device that connects to a USB port. You must be logged in using an administrator account to complete this exercise. If you are not, log off and then log back in as an administrator. If you do not have access to an administrator account, you will not be able to complete this exercise or the following exercise.

ANOTHER WAY

You can also disable a device by double-clicking the device to open its Properties dialog box, clicking the Driver tab, and then clicking Disable.

USE the Device Manager window you left open in the previous exercise.

1. Under the category DVD/CD-ROM drives, right-click your DVD or CD drive. A shortcut menu of options displays. Alternatively, expand the Universal Serial Bus controllers category and right-click a USB device.
2. Click **Disable** on the shortcut menu. A device warning dialog box displays, asking you if you are sure you want to disable the device.
3. Click **Yes**. Windows Vista disables the device. Notice an arrow icon now displays on the drive icon in Device Manager, indicating that the device is now disabled, as shown in Figure 9-11.

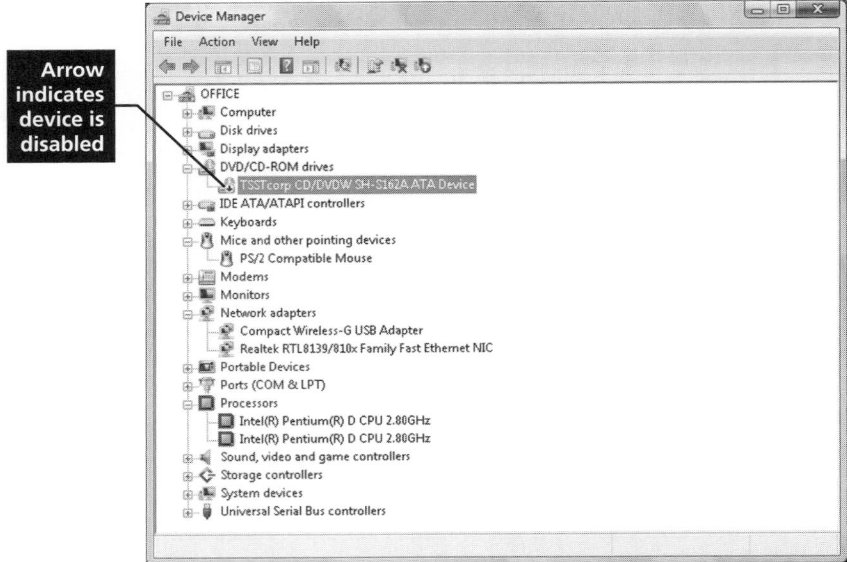

Figure 9-11

The DVD drive is now disabled

4. Insert the DVD or CD into the disabled drive, or attach a device to the USB port. Your computer will not be able to access the drive.
5. Remove the disc from the drive.
6. In Device Manager, right-click the disabled device and click **Enable** on the shortcut menu. Windows Vista enables the device. Notice that the arrow no longer displays on the icon.

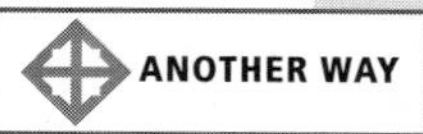

You can also enable a device by double-clicking the device to open its Properties dialog box, clicking the Driver tab, and then clicking Enable.

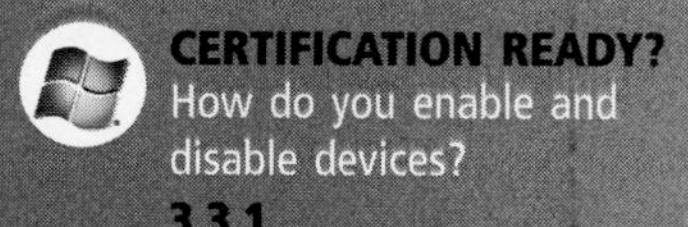

CERTIFICATION READY? How do you enable and disable devices? **3.3.1**

7. Insert the disc into the drive. Your computer accesses the drive and the AutoPlay dialog box displays. Close the dialog box and remove the disc from the drive.

PAUSE. LEAVE the Device Manager window open to use in the next exercise.

Not all devices can be disabled or enabled from the Device Manager. For example, some keyboards and some mice cannot be disabled or enabled, and neither can vital system components such as the processor. The commands simply do not display on the shortcut menu.

Use caution when disabling devices. You may accidentally disable a device that you need to use your computer.

In the next section, you learn how to work with device drivers.

Working with Drivers

To work correctly, all devices require a driver . Windows Vista includes drivers for most devices and installs the driver automatically when you install the device. If not, then the driver is available from the manufacturer on a disk that comes with the device or as a download from a website. Periodically, to fix problems or keep up with changes in Windows Vista, new drivers are made available for existing devices. In that case, you can update the driver. If the device does not work as expected once you update the driver, you can roll it back to the previous version. A buyer for Wide World Importers needs a scanner to scan printed documents into her computer. In this exercise, you install a driver, update a driver, and roll back the driver.

WORK WITH DRIVERS

GET READY. To manually install a new driver, you must have the device and the disk on which the driver is stored. You can use any type of device that is available. In addition, you must be logged on using an administrator's account, or you must have an administrator's password. If you do not have a device driver on a disk, there may be drivers available on a network storage location, or you may be able to download one from a Web site and store it on your computer.

USE the Device Manager window you left open in the previous exercise.

1. Connect the device to your computer. For example, plug it into a USB port. Windows Vista recognizes the device as new and displays the Found New Hardware window, which should look similar to the one in Figure 9-12.

Figure 9-12

Found New Hardware window

TROUBLESHOOTING In Figures 9-12 and 9-13, the device is a scanner. You may be using a different device.

TROUBLESHOOTING If Windows Vista does not recognize the hew hardware, the device may need to be plugged in to a power source and turned on before you connect it to the USB port.

2. Click **Locate and install driver software (recommended)**. If you are logged in as an administrator, the User Account Control dialog box displays. Click **Continue**. If you are not logged in as an administrator, key an administrator password and then click **OK**. Windows Vista will attempt to locate and install a compatible driver. If one is not available, Windows Vista prompts you to insert the disc that came with the device.

TAKE NOTE* Notice the Found New Hardware icon in the Notification area of the Taskbar. ScreenTips may pop up from this icon, informing you of the installation progress.

3. Insert the disc into the compatible drive, or browse to select the location where the driver is stored. Windows Vista searches the disc for the driver software and installs it. When it is finished, a dialog box informs you that the driver installed successfully.

TROUBLESHOOTING Windows Vista always tries to verify the publisher of driver software before installing it. If it cannot verify the publisher, it displays a security warning. If you are certain the driver is from a reliable source, click Install the driver software anyway. If not, click Don't install this driver software and contact the device manufacturer for more information.

4. Click **Close** to close the window. The driver is now installed, and the device is ready for use with your computer.
5. In Device Manager, locate the new device. For example, if you installed a scanner, expand the Imaging devices category to view the scanner device.
6. Double-click the device to open its Properties dialog box and then click the **Driver** tab. It should look similar to Figure 9-13, although you may be using a different device.

Figure 9-13

Driver tab of the device's Properties dialog box

7. Click **Update Driver** to display the Update Driver Software window. You can automatically search for newer driver software in Windows Vista and on the Internet, or you can manually update the driver if you have a new driver file available. For example, you may have downloaded a new driver from a manufacturer's website.

You can also right-click a device in the Device Manager and click Update Driver Software to open the Update Driver Software window.

8. Click **Search automatically for updated driver software**. Windows Vista searches for a newer driver and installs it, if available. Alternatively, click **Browse my computer for driver software**, key or select the location where the driver file is stored, and then click **Next** so Windows Vista can locate and install the driver. When installation is finished, a dialog box informs you that the driver installed successfully.
9. Click **Close**.
10. On the Driver tab of the device's Properties dialog box, click **Roll Back Driver**. The Driver Package rollback window displays, asking if you are sure you want to roll back to the older driver.

TROUBLESHOOTING

The Roll Back Driver button is only available if you recently updated the driver.

CERTIFICATION READY?
How do you update or install a device driver?
3.3.2
How to you roll back a driver to a previous version?
3.3.3

11. Click **Yes**. Windows Vista removes the newer, updated driver and reverts to the previous version of the driver that you had installed.
12. Click **Close** to close the device's Properties dialog box.
13. Close the Device Manager window.
14. Close the Control Panel window.

PAUSE. LEAVE the desktop displayed to use in the next exercise.

Using Windows Update is covered in Lesson 11, "Monitoring the Windows Vista Environment."

In most cases, Windows Vista will automatically install the most up-to-date drivers when you first install a device and then keep it up-to-date using Windows Update. However, if you are having a problem with a device, you may need to manually update or roll back the driver.

Many devices come with software programs as well as drivers. For example, a camera may come with photo editing software. The software may install automatically along with the driver, or you may be able to select whether you want to install it.

In the next section, you learn how to safely remove PC Cards and USB devices that are connected to your computer.

Safely Removing Hardware

When you work with a removable storage device, it is important that you do not disconnect the device while the computer is still writing data on it, or the data may become unreadable. Windows Vista has a feature called Safely Remove Hardware that you can use to identify and close devices such as USB flash drives and PC Cards so that you can disconnect them from your computer without putting the data at risk. A ***PC Card*** is a credit card sized device that is used for data storage. In this exercise, you learn how to use the Safely Remove Hardware tool.

SAFELY REMOVE HARDWARE

GET READY. Have a USB device or PC Card available for use with your computer.

1. Attach the USB device or PC Card to your PC. For example, plug a USB flash drive into a USB port, or insert a PC Card into a PC Card slot.

TAKE NOTE* If you have never attached the device before, Windows Vista may install a device driver for it.

2. Double-click the **Safely Remove Hardware** icon in the notification area of the Taskbar. The Safely Remove Hardware dialog box displays, as shown in Figure 9-14. The items listed in the dialog box are the removable hardware devices currently connected to your computer, so they will be different from those in the figure.

Figure 9-14

Safely Remove Hardware dialog box

TROUBLESHOOTING If the Safely Remove Hardware icon is hidden, click the Show hidden icons arrow to expand the notification area to show hidden icons.

Using the notification area is covered in Lesson 7, "Personalizing the Vista Workspace."

3. Click the device you want to remove.
4. Click **Stop**. The Stop a Hardware device dialog box displays, identifying the device you want to stop. Windows Vista may list more than one name.
5. Click to select the device you want to stop and then click **OK**. Windows Vista verifies that it is safe to remove the device and then displays a Safe to Remove Hardware dialog box.

TROUBLESHOOTING If Windows Vista displays a dialog box informing you that it is not safe to remove the device, wait a few minutes and then try again.

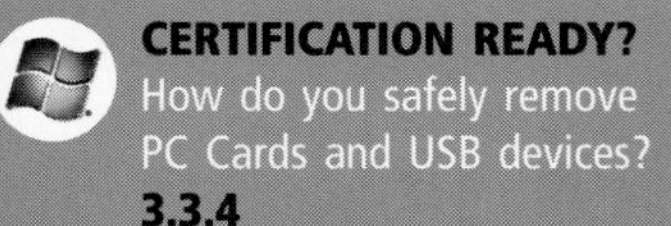

6. Click **OK** and then remove the device.
7. Click **Close** to close the Safely Remove Hardware dialog box.

PAUSE. LEAVE the desktop displayed to use in the next exercise.

Some storage devices have an activity light that indicates when the device is in use. You can usually safely remove the device a few seconds after the light has stopped flashing.

In the next section, you learn how to install and manage a local printer.

■ Installing a Local Printer

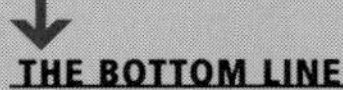

Like any device, for a printer to be usable, it must be connected to your computer and installed using the correct device driver. A printer that is connected directly to your PC via cables is called a ***local printer***. Windows Vista automatically installs a local printer as soon as you plug it into a USB port. If you have a printer that attaches to a different type of port, such as an LPT port or a serial port, you may have to install the device manually. In this section, you install a local USB printer and then you manually install a local printer.

Installing a USB Local Printer

Windows Vista automatically installs a local printer as soon as you plug it into a USB port. In this section, the buyer for Wide World Importers installs a local USB printer using steps similar to those she used to install a scanner earlier in this lesson.

INSTALL A USB LOCAL PRINTER

GET READY. Before you begin these steps, have a printer that connects to a USB port available, along with the USB cable. If necessary, read and follow the printer manufacturer instructions for preparing the printer. For example, you may need to load ink cartridges.

1. Connect the printer's power cord to a power supply and turn the printer on.
2. Connect the printer's USB cable to the printer and to the USB port. Windows Vista should identify the device as new hardware and then search for and install the device driver. When the installation is complete, the Found New Hardware icon in the notification area on the Taskbar displays a ScreenTip informing you that the driver installed successfully and that the device is ready for use.

TROUBLESHOOTING If Windows Vista cannot locate a driver, if may display the Found New Hardware window and prompt you to insert the manufacturer's disk to continue. Refer to the section titled "Working with Drivers" earlier in this lesson for more information on installing a driver.

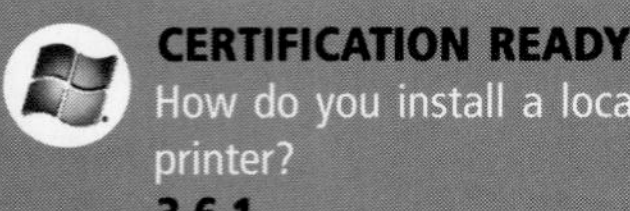

TAKE NOTE
Many printers do not come with a USB cable. You may have to purchase one separately.

PAUSE. LEAVE the desktop displayed to use in the next exercise.

You might notice that printers do not display in the Device Manager. You must use the Printers window to check properties and other device and driver information for your printers.

You do not have to keep a USB printer connected to your computer at all times. Once the printer is installed, you can unplug it without uninstalling the driver. You can plug it in whenever you need to use it. If you want to permanently remove a printer so that is no longer available for use with your computer, right-click it in the Printers window and click Delete.

CERTIFICATION READY?
How do you install a local printer?
3.6.1

Some older printers do not have USB connections. In the next section, you learn how to install a printer that connects to a port other than a USB port.

Installing a Non-USB Local Printer

Some printers may connect to a port other than a USB port. For example, an older printer might connect to an LPT printer port, or a serial printer might connect to a serial port. Windows Vista does not automatically install non-USB printers, so you must manually install the driver software. In this section, you install a printer that connects to a port other than a USB port.

INSTALL A NON-USB LOCAL PRINTER

GET READY. Before you begin these steps, have a printer that connects to a port other than a USB port available, along with the necessary cables. If necessary, read and follow the printer manufacturer instructions for preparing the printer. For example, you may need to load ink cartridges.

1. Connect the printer's power cord to a power supply and turn the printer on.
2. Connect the printer's cable to the appropriate port.
3. Click **Start**, click **Control Panel**, and then click **Hardware and Sound**.
4. Under Printers, click **Add a printer**. The Add Printer Wizard displays the Choose a local or network printer window.
5. Click **Add a local printer** to display the Choose a printer port window.
6. Click the **Use an existing port:** option button, if necessary, and then click the dropdown arrow to display a list of available ports.
7. Click the port to which you attached the printer cable in step 2, and then click **Next**. The Install the printer driver window displays.
8. In the Manufacturer list, click the name of your printer's manufacturer. For example, if you are connecting a Canon printer, click Canon.
9. In the Printers list, click the name of the printer you are connecting. For example, if you are connecting a Canon Inkjet i9950, click Canon Inkjet i9950.

TROUBLESHOOTING
If the manufacturer or printer name is not listed in the Add Printer Wizard, but you have the disk that came with the printer, click Have Disk. Insert the disk and then select the location of the disk and click OK. Windows Vista will install the driver.

10. Click **Next**. If necessary, key a name that will identify the printer on you computer. Click **Next**. Windows Vista will install the driver and make the printer the default.
11. Click **Finish**.

TAKE NOTE
You can print a test page to make sure the printer is working correctly. Before clicking Finish, make sure the printer is loaded with paper and then click the Print a test page button.

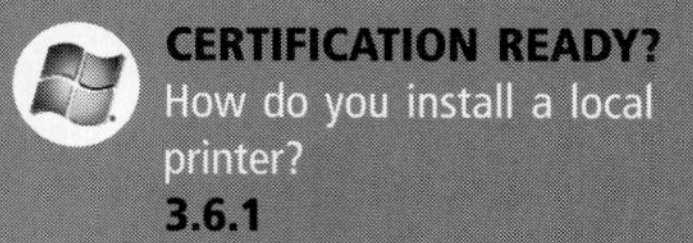

PAUSE. LEAVE the Control Panel's Hardware and Sound window open to use in the next exercise.

In the next section, you learn how to manage installed printers.

■ Managing Installed Printers

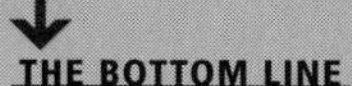

Once you have a printer installed and ready for use, you want to keep it working properly. If you have more than one printer installed, you can select the one you want as the default. For example, you may usually print text documents on a fast black and white printer, but sometimes you want to print a photograph on a color ink jet printer. You can set the black and white printer as the default and then just select the color printer when you need it. To make sure your printer is working properly and efficiently, you can monitor its status as well as the ***print queue***, which is the folder where documents sent to print are temporarily stored while waiting to print. In this section, you learn how to set the default printer and monitor both the printer status and the print queue.

Setting the Default Printer

By default, Windows Vista makes the most recently installed printer the default printer. You can change the default printer at any time. In this exercise, you set the default printer.

SET THE DEFAULT PRINTER

USE the Control Panel's Hardware and Sound window you left open in the previous exercise.

1. Click **Printers** in the Hardware and Sound window. The Printers window opens, displaying all installed printers, as shown in Figure 9-15. The default printer has a green checkmark on its icon.

Figure 9-15

Installed printers display in the Printers window

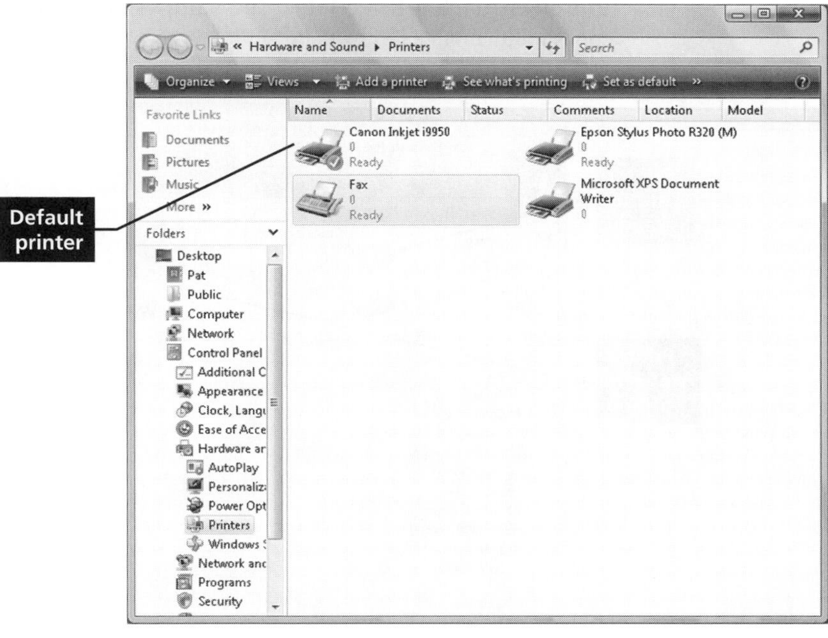

TAKE NOTE*

Even if you only have installed one printer, multiple items may be in the Printers window. For example, if you have an internal fax modem installed, a Fax icon may display. If you have software such as Microsoft Office 2007 installed, the Microsoft XPS Document Writer, which is software that allows you to print to a file, may display. You can use these icons to practice changing the default printer.

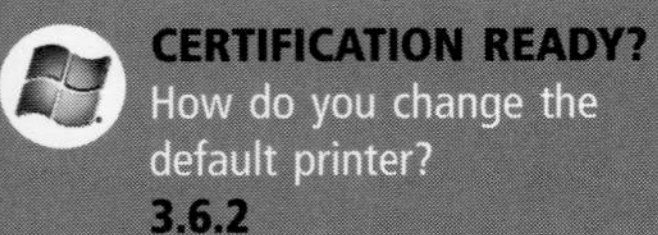

2. Right-click any icon in the window other than the default printer. A shortcut menu displays.
3. Click **Set as Default Printer** on the shortcut menu. The green checkmark moves to the new default printer.
4. Right-click the printer that was the default and click **Set as Default Printer** on the shortcut menu. The green checkmark moves back to the original default printer.
5. At this point, your instructor may ask you to capture an image of the Printers window. Save it in your Lesson 9 assessment folder as ***Le09_07***.

PAUSE. LEAVE the Printers window open to use in the next exercise.

Only one printer can be the default. All documents sent to print will automatically go to the default printer. However, you can usually select a different printer in the Print dialog box before you print a document if you want.

In the next exercise, you learn how to determine printer status.

Determining Printer Status

The status of a printer indicates whether the printer is ready for use, paused, or ***offline***. Offline means that a device is not communicating with the computer and usually indicates that there is a loose cable, a problem with the power source, or the device is simply turned off. If a printer is paused, it is available and working correctly but set to temporarily suspend printing. In this exercise, you determine a printer's status.

DETERMINE PRINTER STATUS

USE the Printers window you left open in the previous exercise.

1. Locate the default printer in the Printers window. Under the printer name is a number, which indicates the number of documents currently waiting to print on that printer, and the printer status. If the printer is working properly, the status is Ready.
2. Turn off or unplug the printer. The status should change to Offline, and the printer icon should dim, as shown in Figure 9-16.

Figure 9-16

View a printer's status

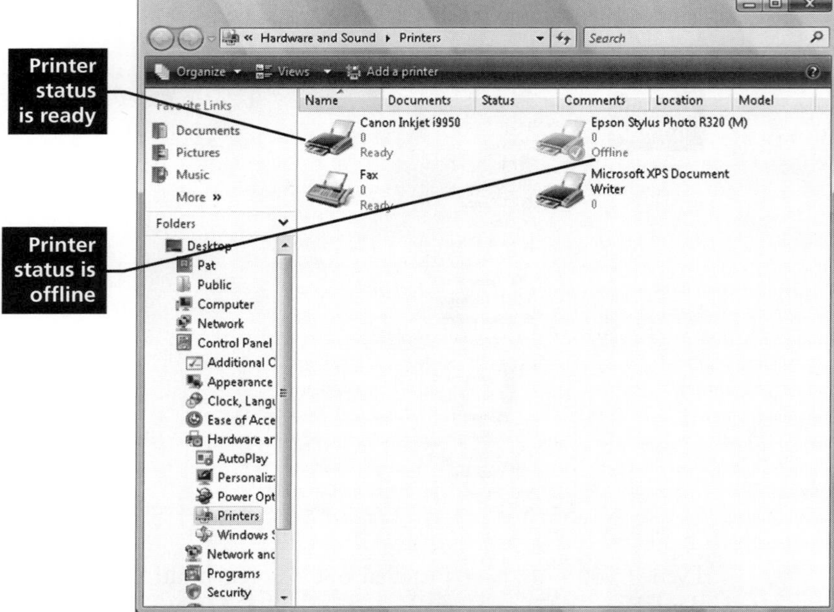

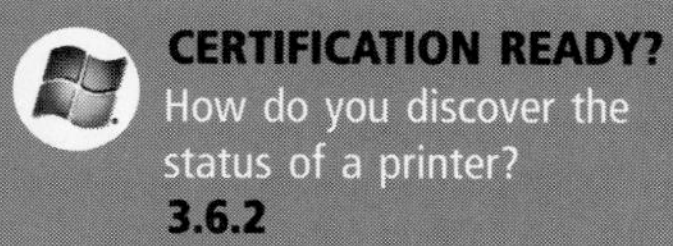

CERTIFICATION READY?
How do you discover the status of a printer?
3.6.2

3. Turn the printer back on, or plug it back in. The status should change to Ready.
4. Right-click the printer icon and click **Pause Printing** on the shortcut menu. The status should change to Paused. (If your instructor asks you to capture an image of the Printers window, save it in your Lesson 9 assessment folder as ***Le09_08***.)
5. Right-click the printer icon and click **Resume Printing** on the shortcut menu. The status should change back to Ready.

PAUSE. LEAVE the Printers window open to use in the next exercise.

You can use the printer status information to start diagnosing problems. If a printer is not working, you can quickly identify whether it is offline or paused. If so, you may be able to fix the problem.

In the next exercise, you learn how to manage the print queue.

Managing the Print Queue

When you select the command to print a document, the file is sent to the print queue, where it waits until the printer is available. If you are printing a single document, it probably will start printing immediately. If you are printing many documents, each must wait in the print queue for its turn to print. You can use the print queue to manage documents that are waiting to print. For example, if you want to change the paper after you send a document to the queue, you can pause a document to temporarily suspend printing. You can also cancel a single document or all documents in the queue. In this exercise, you display the print queue to check the status of documents, and you pause, restart, and delete documents from the print queue.

MANAGE THE PRINT QUEUE

USE the Printers window you left open in the previous exercise.

The ***WWI_Report1***, ***WWI_Report2***, and ***WW1_Letter1*** files are available on the companion CD-ROM.

1. In the Printers window, right-click the default printer and click Pause Printing. While the printer is paused, documents you send to print will sit in the print queue without printing. This will enable you to see and manage the documents, which otherwise might print before you have a chance to see them in the print queue.
2. Click the **Start** button and then click **Documents** to open the Documents folder. Create a new folder named **Importers** and open it.
3. Copy the ***WWI_Report1***, ***WWI_Report2***, and ***WW1_Letter1*** files from the data files for this lesson to the Importers folder.
4. Right-click the ***WWI_Report1*** file and click **Print** on the shortcut menu to send the file to the print queue for your default printer.
5. Right-click the ***WWI_Report2*** file and click **Print** on the shortcut menu to send the file to the print queue for your default printer.
6. Right-click the ***WWI_Letter1*** file and click **Print** on the shortcut menu to send the file to the print queue for your default printer. In the Printers window, notice that three documents are now in the print queue. Each document in the print queue is called a ***print job***.
7. Double-click the icon for your default printer. The print queue window opens. It should look similar to Figure 9-17, although the name of the printer in the title bar depends on the name of the printer you are using. Notice that the printer status—Paused—displays in the title bar. As soon as you set the printer to resume printing, the first file in the queue will begin to print. At this point, your instructor may ask you to capture an image of the Print Queue window. Save it in your Lesson 9 assessment folder as ***Le09_09***.

Figure 9-17

Documents in the print queue

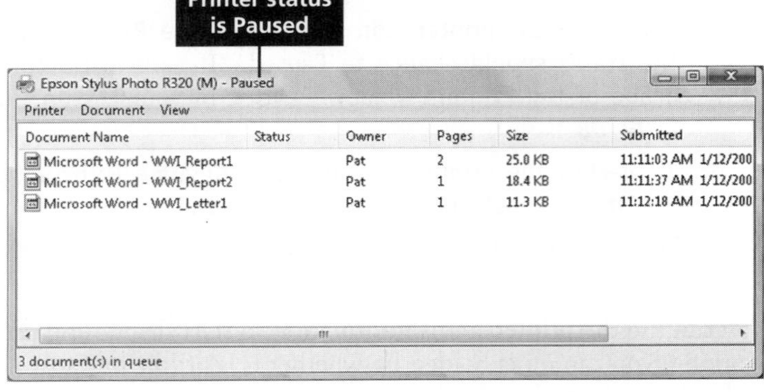

You can also open the print queue by double-clicking the printer icon in the notification area of the Taskbar.

8. Take a moment to look at the print queue. Notice that the three documents are listed in the order in which you sent them to be printed. Each document displays information about the print job, such as the owner, which is the person who sent the file to print; the number of pages; the file size; and the date and time the file was sent to the print queue. There is a column for Status information, but because no files are printing, there is no print status to display.
9. Right-click the second document in the list, ***WWI_Report2***, and click **Pause.** You can control the printing of each item in the print queue independent from the other documents. Now, even when the printer changes from Paused to Ready and starts to print, the ***WWI_Report2*** file will remain paused.
10. Click **Printer** on the window's menu bar and click **Pause Printing.** The printer returns to its Ready status, and printing begins. Notice that the Status of the first document in the queue changes to Printing, while the Status of the second document remains Paused, as shown in Figure 9-18.

Figure 9-18

One document is paused while another prints

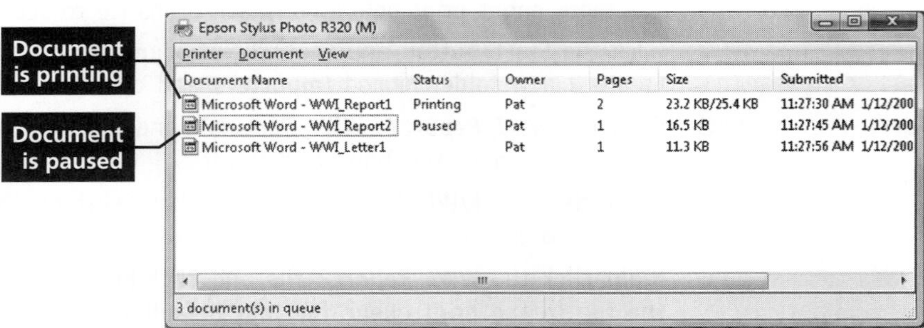

You can also select a document and then use the commands on the Document menu to pause, resume, restart, and cancel printing.

11. Right-click the ***WWI_Letter1*** document and click **Cancel** on the shortcut menu. A dialog box displays, asking if you are sure you want to cancel the document. Click **Yes** to remove the document from the print queue.

12. Right-click the ***WWI_Report2*** document and click **Resume**. It can now print as soon as the first document is finished. When all documents have finished printing, the print queue is empty.

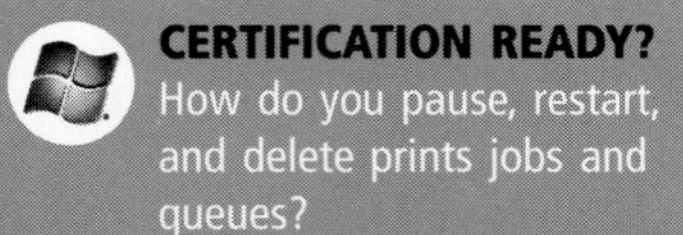

If you do not act quickly enough, the documents may print before you have a chance to pause or cancel them. Simply send them to the print queue again and then continue with the exercise.

13. Click **Printer** on the window's menu bar and click **Pause Printing** to pause the printer. Then send all three documents to the print queue again. For example, select all three in the Importers folder, right-click the selection, and then click **Print** on the shortcut menu.
14. Click **Printer** on the window's menu bar and click **Cancel All Documents.** A dialog box displays, asking if you are sure you want to cancel all documents.
15. Click **Yes.** Windows Vista clears the print queue of all documents.
16. Click **Printer** on the window's menu bar and click **Pause Printing** to return the printer to its Ready status.
17. Close the print queue window.
18. Close the Printers window and then close the Control Panel window.
19. Close the Importers folder and then delete it.
20. Close the Documents folder.

CERTIFICATION READY?
How do you pause, restart, and delete prints jobs and queues?
7.6.2

PAUSE. LEAVE the desktop displayed to use in the next exercise.

As you have seen, you can control the print queue by controlling the printer, or by controlling each individual print job. For example, while the printer is paused, no documents will print. If the printer is not paused, you can pause an individual print job to keep it from printing, while documents that are not paused will print. You can also cancel a single print job, or all print jobs in the queue.

Pausing a printer or a document in the print queue can be helpful if you need to make a change to the printer during printing. For example, you may need to change the paper size or type, or you may need to add ink or toner. Pausing can also be helpful if you need to print a document quickly, but other print jobs are already in the queue. If you pause a print job, the document after it will print first.

You may have noticed that when you pause a print job you have the option of resuming or restarting printing. If you select resume, the printing begins exactly where it left off. If you select restart, the entire print job starts again from the beginning.

In the next section, you learn how to manage disks.

■ Managing Disks

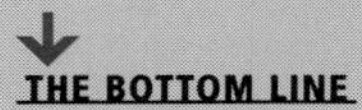

To keep data safe and available for future use, you store it on a hard disk. Therefore, it is vital that you keep your hard disks in good condition and working properly. In this section, you learn how to determine the amount of free space on a disk and how to tell whether a disk is partitioned. You also learn how to check a disk for problems and how to defragment a disk to make more storage space available.

Determining Free Disk Space

Every disk has a storage capacity that tells you how much data it can hold. As data is written to the disk, it takes up space, leaving less free space available. It is important to keep track of the free space so you know whether you still have room to store new data or to install additional programs. In this exercise, you check your local hard disk to see how much space is available.

DETERMINE FREE DISK SPACE

1. Click **Start** and then click **Computer**.
2. Click your local disk. Details about its capacity and free space display in the Details pane of the Computer window, as shown in Figure 9-19.

Figure 9-19

View disk space details in the Computer window

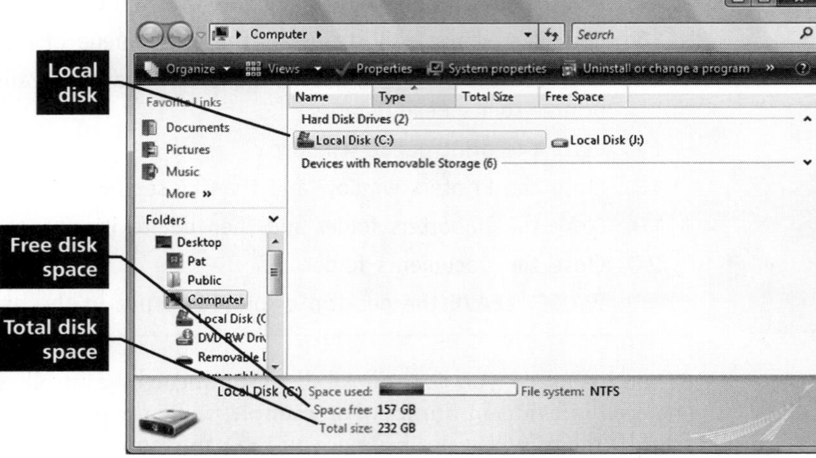

TAKE NOTE*

You can use these steps to check the free space of any disk, even a removable device.

3. Right-click the disk icon and then click **Properties**. The disk's Properties dialog box displays. Information about the disk capacity, used space, and free space displays as a pie chart, as shown in Figure 9-20. If your instructor asks you to capture an image of the Properties dialog box, save it in your Lesson 9 assessment folder as ***Le09_10***.

Figure 9-20

View disk space chart in the Properties dialog box

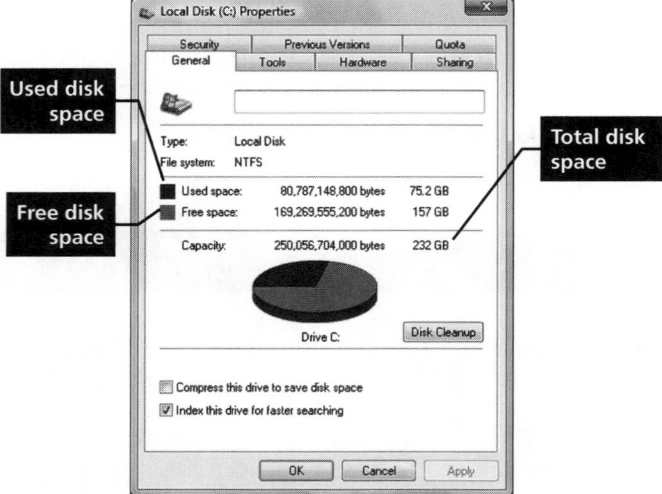

CERTIFICATION READY?
How do you ascertain the amount of available space on a hard disk?
3.2.1

4. Click **OK** to close the dialog box and then close the Computer window.

PAUSE. LEAVE the desktop displayed to use in the next exercise.

In addition to needing free disk space for storing additional data, you may need to know how much free space you have if you are planning to install a new program. Programs take up space on your hard disk, too. Most programs have a minimum free space requirement that you can find on the software box or on the company's website.

In the next section, you learn about hard disk partitions.

Viewing Partitions

A hard disk ***partition*** is an area on a hard disk that functions as if it is a separate disk. Every hard disk must be partitioned and formatted before it can store data. Your hard disk may have a single partition that includes the entire disk, or it may have multiple partitions. Even if your disk is already partitioned, you may be able to create additional partitions. To determine the status of your partitions, you use Windows Vista's Computer Management tool. In this exercise, you view the partitions on your local disk.

VIEWING PARTITIONS

GET READY. You must be logged on as an administrator or have an administrator password to complete this exercise.

1. Click **Start**, click **Control Panel**, and then click **System and Maintenance**.
2. Click **Administrative Tools** and then double-click **Computer Management** in the File list. If you are logged on as an administrator, the User Account Control dialog box displays. Click **Continue**. If not, key the administrator password and then click **OK**. The Computer Management window opens.
3. In the left pane, under Storage, click **Disk Management**. Information about your storage devices displays in the window, as shown in Figure 9-21. Hard disks display in the top half of the window, and all disks display in the bottom half.

Figure 9-21

View partition information

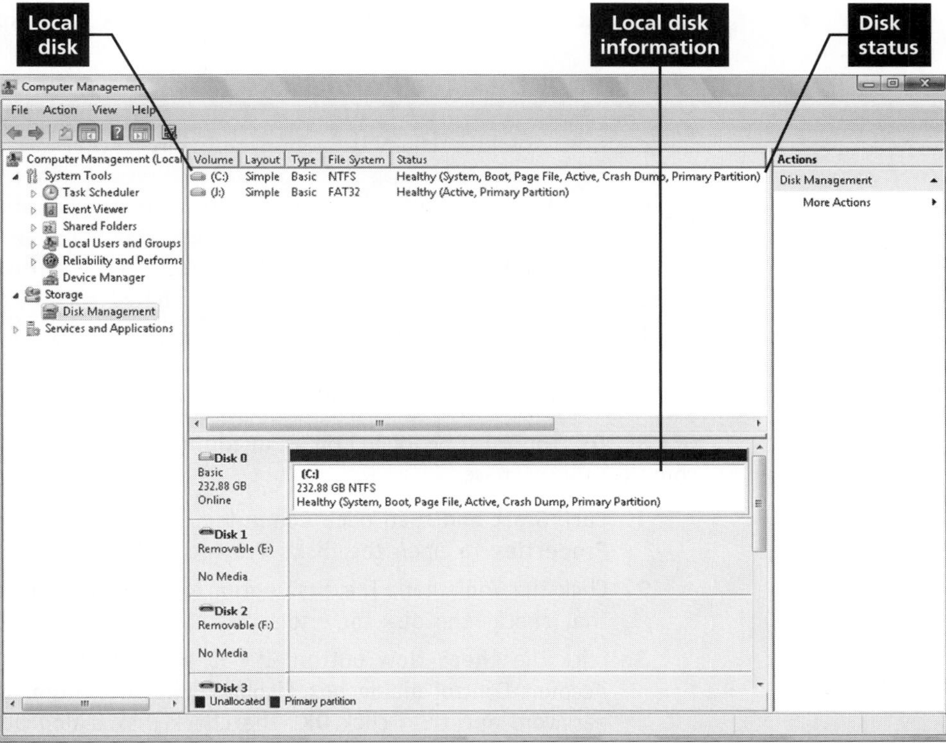

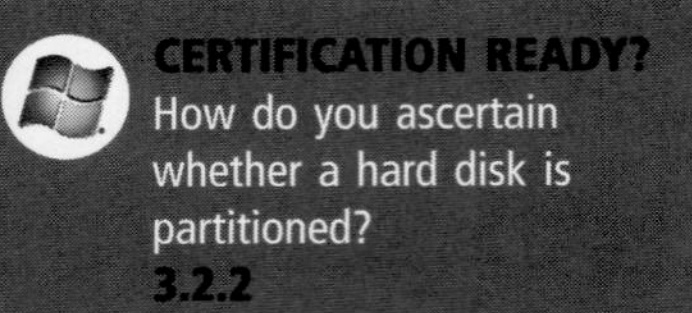

4. Locate the information for your local disk (probably labeled drive C:). Available information includes the type of drive, the file system, and the status. Under Status, you will find information such as the type of partition. Each basic drive may have up to three ***primary partitions***, which are partitions that can be used to start an operating system.
5. If your instructor asks you to capture an image of the Computer Management window, save in your Lesson 9 assessment folder as ***Le09_11***.
6. Close the Computer Management window, close the Administrative Tools window, and then close the Control Panel.

PAUSE. LEAVE the desktop displayed to use in the next exercise.

On a basic disk, which is the most common type of disk used with Windows Vista, you can have up to four partitions. The first three are primary partitions, and the fourth is called an extended partition, which can contain ***logical drives***, which are similar to primary partitions except that they cannot be used to start an operating system. Note that a partition is sometimes referred to as a volume.

You might want to use more than one partition on a disk if you want to keep your programs, data, and operating system files separate. This can be useful for organization and also for keeping your data safe. If you have a problem with one partition, you may be able to repair it without impacting the information stored in the other partitions.

It is possible to create new partitions on a disk that already contains a partition. However, you should be careful not to erase the existing data.

The Administrative Tools folders in Control Panel store tools that system administrators and advanced users can use to control the way Windows Vista runs and how users access Windows Vista features. For example, Computer Management is a tool that lets you monitor system events, configure hard disks, and manage system performance.

In the next section, you learn how to check a hard disk for problems.

Checking a Disk for Problems

You store all of your data and programs on your hard disk, so it is important to monitor the disk for problems. With Windows Vista, you can check a disk for two types of problems. The first is file system errors, which are usually caused when data is written incorrectly on a disk, or if Windows Vista loses track of where data is stored. You can check for and often fix file system errors. The second problem is bad sectors, which are areas on the disk that are damaged. In this exercise, you learn how to check you local disk for both types of problems.

CHECK A DISK FOR PROBLEMS

GET READY. You must be logged on as an administrator or have an administrator password to complete this exercise.

1. Click **Start** and then click **Computer**. Right-click your local disk and click **Properties** to open the disk's Properties dialog box.
2. Click the **Tools** tab. The first option on the tab is Error-checking, which is a tool that checks the disk for errors.
3. Click the **Check Now** button. If you are logged on as an administrator, the User Account Control dialog box displays. Click **Continue**. If not, key the administrator password and then click **OK**. The Check Disk dialog box displays. By default, only the option to check for and fix file system errors is selected.
4. Click to select the **Scan for and attempt recovery of bad sectors** checkbox and then click **Start**. A dialog box displays, stating that you cannot check a disk while it is in use, and prompting you to schedule a check for the next time you start your computer.

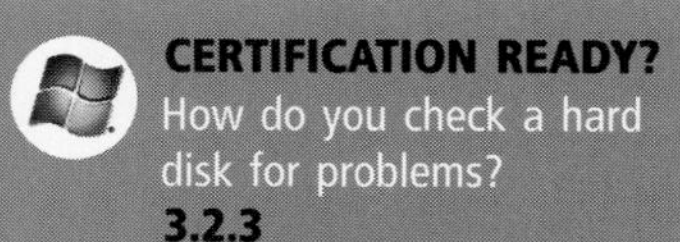
CERTIFICATION READY?
How do you check a hard disk for problems?
3.2.3

5. Click **Schedule disk check**. Windows Vista is now set to check your computer the next time you start your system.
6. Close all open windows and restart your computer. During restart, you will see a message informing you that a disk check has been scheduled and is about to start. You can cancel the check by pressing any key before the check begins. Once the check begins, it may take a while. It thoroughly checks the file system and the physical disk, displaying results as it goes. When the check is complete, a report displays information about problems and fixes, and then your computer restarts.
7. Log in to your Windows Vista user account.

PAUSE. LEAVE the desktop displayed to use in the next exercise.

As mentioned, Windows Vista will attempt to repair any problems that it finds during a disk check. If it cannot fix a problem, you may want to consider replacing the disk drive.

You can use these steps to check other disks for problems as well. For example, you can check an external disk drive.

In the next section, you learn how to defragment a hard disk.

Defragmenting a Hard Disk

Ideally, when you store files on a disk, Windows Vista writes all of the data for one file in consecutive sectors. Over time, as you save, delete, and modify files, the data may become ***fragmented***, which means it is broken up into fragments of data that are spread across non-consecutive sectors. As a result, your computer may slow down as it looks in many locations on the disk to find the data it needs for a single file. You can defragment your disk to rearrange the data into consecutive sectors, which may improve processing speed. Windows Vista automatically defragments your local disk periodically, but you can manually run the defragmenter at any time. In this exercise, you learn how to manually defragment a disk.

DEFRAGMENT A HARD DISK

GET READY. You must be logged on as an administrator or have an administrator password to complete this exercise.

1. Click **Start** and then click **Computer**. Right-click your local disk and click **Properties** to open the disk's Properties dialog box.
2. Click the **Tools** tab. The second option on the tab is Defragmentation, which is the tool that you use to defragment the disk.
3. Click the **Defragment Now** button. If you are logged on as an administrator, the User Account Control dialog box displays. Click **Continue**. If not, key the administrator password and then click **OK**. The Disk Defragmenter window opens. It shows the current schedule that Windows Vista is using for defragmenting.
4. Click **Defragment now**. The defragmenting procedure begins. It may take a while, depending on the size of your hard disk and the amount of fragmentation. When the defragmenting is complete, the Disk Defragmenter window remains open.
5. Click **Close** to close the window.
6. Close all open windows.

LOG OFF your Windows Vista user account.

TROUBLESHOOTING
Click the Cancel defragmentation button in the Disk Defragmenter window to cancel the defragmenting process at any time.

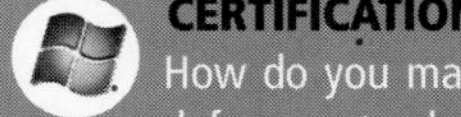
CERTIFICATION READY?
How do you manually defragment a hard disk?
7.1.3

Defragmenting can take a long time. If you need to manually defragment a disk, you should plan it for a time when you do not need your computer. You can continue working during the defragmentation, but if you are writing data to and from the hard disk, it may make the process take even longer.

Before defragmenting a hard disk, you may want to use Windows Vista's Disk Cleanup tool to delete unnecessary files from your hard disk. To use Disk Cleanup, click Start, click Computer, right-click your local disk, and click Properties. On the General tab, click Disk Cleanup. If necessary, select whether you want to clean up your personal files only, or all users' files (you need an administrator account for that). Windows Vista analyzes your disk to determine where you can delete files and then lists the suggestions. For example, it lists files in the Recycle Bin. Select the ones you want to delete and then click OK.

SUMMARY SKILL MATRIX

In this lesson you learned	Matrix Skill	Skill Number
To locate system information		
To view basic system information	Display the amount of installed RAM and the processor speed; Ascertain the system performance rating	7.3.3 7.3.5
To determine resource usage	Ascertain the CPU usage of the computer; Ascertain the page file usage of the computer	7.3.1 7.3.2
To use ReadyBoost	Expand memory cache by using Windows ReadyBoost	7.1.1
To manage power options		
To select a power plan	Adjust power options for best performance	7.1.3
To customize a power plan	Configure power settings and options	2.1.1
To change the power button settings	Place a mobile device in Sleep mode Place a mobile device in Hibernation mode	2.1.2 2.1.3
To manage devices and drivers		
To display installed devices	Ascertain the hardware and devices installed on a computer	7.3.4
To disable and enable a device	Enable and disable devices	3.3.1
To work with drivers	Update or install a device driver; Roll back a driver to a previous version	3.3.2 3.3.3
To safely remove hardware	Safely remove PC Cards and USB devices	3.3.4
To install a local printer		
To install a USB local printer	Install a local printer	3.6.1
To install a non-USB local printer	Install a local printer	3.6.1
To manage installed printers		
To set the default printer	Change the default printer	3.6.2
To determine printer status	Discover the status of a printer	7.6.1
To manage the print queue	Pause, restart, and delete print jobs and queues	7.6.2
To manage disks		
To determine free disk space	Ascertain the amount of available space on a hard disk	3.2.1
To view partitions	Ascertain whether a hard disk is partitioned	3.2.2
To check a disk for problems	Check a hard disk for problems	3.2.3
To defragment a hard disk	Manually defragment the hard disk	7.1.2

■ Knowledge Assessment

Matching

Match the term in Column 1 to its description in Column 2.

Column 1	Column 2
1. print queue	**a.** the software program that lets your computer communicate with a hardware device
2. virtual memory	**b.** the core part of the Windows operating system
3. partition	**c.** the folder where documents sent to print are stored while waiting to print
4. print job	**d.** a feature that lets you use storage space on a USB flash drive to increase the performance speed of your PC
5. driver	**e.** the main circuit chip in your computer
6. ReadyBoost	**f.** the software that controls the start-up functions of your computer, including starting the operating system
7. PC Card	**g.** a combination of the paging file and RAM
8. BIOS	**h.** a document in the print queue
9. kernel	**i.** a credit card sized device that may be used for data storage
10. CPU	**j.** an area on the hard disk that functions as if it is a separate disk

Multiple Choice

Select the best response for the following questions.

1. What type of partition can start an operating system?

- **a.** primary
- **b.** secondary
- **c.** extended
- **d.** logical

2. Which of the following is another name for the paging file?

- **a.** memory file
- **b.** swap file
- **c.** virtual file
- **d.** cache file

3. What is the status of a device that is not communicating with the computer?

- **a.** online
- **b.** ready
- **c.** paused
- **d.** offline

4. What is another name for random access memory?
   a. physical memory
   b. logical memory
   c. device memory
   d. processing memory
5. In what window can you view all devices installed on your computer?
   a. Task Manager
   b. Device Manager
   c. Computer Manager
   d. Driver Manager
6. Which of the following is not one of the power plans built into Windows Vista?
   a. Power Saver
   b. Travel
   c. High Performance
   d. Balanced
7. What is the default setting of the power button on the Start menu?
   a. Standby
   b. Hibernate
   c. Sleep
   d. Shut off
8. Which type of printer will Windows Vista install automatically?
   a. USB
   b. serial
   c. ink jet
   d. laser
9. What symbol displays on the icon of the default printer in the Printers window?
   a. blue triangle
   b. green checkmark
   c. red asterisk
   d. yellow question mark
10. What can you do to temporarily stop a print job from printing?
    a. unplug the printer
    b. pause the print job
    c. cancel the print job
    d. change the default printer

■ Competency Assessment

Project 9-1: Prepare for New Software

You work in an attorney's office and use a desktop PC to prepare documents. You are considering upgrading to a new word processing program, but you need to determine if your computer meets the program's minimum requirements. In this project, you will view basic system information to find out the amount of installed RAM, the speed of your CPU, and your system's performance rating. You will also check the amount of free disk space on your local disk.

GET READY. Before you begin these steps, start your computer and log on to your Windows Vista account. Close all open windows so you can see the desktop. Also, make sure you have a printer correctly connected, loaded with paper, and available for use. You should also have a pen or pencil on hand, or a file or online journal where you can record information.

1. Click the **Start** button and then click **Control Panel**.
2. Click **System and Maintenance**.
3. Under System, click **View amount of RAM and processor speed.** Basic information about your computer displays in the System window. Under System, locate the performance rating, processor speed, and amount of installed RAM.
4. To the right of Rating, click **Windows Experience Index** to open the Performance Information and Tools window.
5. Click **View and print details**.
6. Click **Print this page**, in the top right corner of the window. The Print dialog box displays.
7. Click **Print** to print the page using the default settings, or change the settings and then click **Print**.
8. Close the Performance Information and Tools page, the Performance Information and Tools window, and the System window.
9. Click **Start** and then click **Computer**.
10. Click your local disk and in the Details pane, view the details about its capacity.
11. On the printed page detailing your basic system information, write down the total amount of space on your disk and the amount of free space available. Alternatively, key the information in a file named ***Proj09_01*** in your Lesson 9 assessment folder, or in an online journal.
12. **CLOSE** the Computer window.

PAUSE. LEAVE the desktop displayed to use in the next project.

Project 9-2: Sluggish System

Your computer has been running a bit sluggishly lately. In this project, you will determine your system's resource usage to see if you can identify a problem, and you will try adjusting power settings to see if that improves your system's performance.

GET READY. Before you begin these steps, make sure you have a pen or pencil and a piece of paper available, or a file or online journal where you can record the information.

1. Right-click a blank area of the Taskbar and click **Task Manager** to display the Windows Task Manager.
2. Click the **Performance** tab to see the graphs and tables that display information about how your computer is using the CPU and memory resources.
3. Locate the amount of physical memory and the percentage of physical memory currently in use and record the numbers on a piece of paper, in a file named ***Proj09_02*** in your Lesson 9 assessment folder, or in an online journal.
4. Locate the current CPU usage percentage and record it as well.

5. Locate the Page File usage statistics and record them. Include both the total amount of virtual memory in use and the total amount of memory that is available.
6. Close the Task Manager.
7. Click **Start**, click **Control Panel**, and then click **System and Maintenance**.
8. Click **Power Options** to display the Power Options window.
9. Click the **High Performance** option button.
10. Click **Change plan settings** under the High Performance power plan to open the Change settings window.
11. Click the **Turn off the display** dropdown arrow and click **Never**.
12. Click **Save changes** to apply the changes and close the window.
13. Right-click a blank area of the Taskbar and click **Task Manager** to display the Windows Task Manager again.
14. Click the **Performance** tab.
15. To see if there is any difference, record the current memory and CPU usage information and compare it to the information you recorded before you changed the power plan.
16. Close the Task Manager.
17. In the Power Options window, click **Change plan settings** under the High Performance power plan.
18. Click **Restore default settings for this plan** and then click **Yes** in the Power Options warning dialog box.
19. Click the **Cancel** button to close the window. Then close the Power Options window.

PAUSE. LEAVE the desktop displayed to use in the next project.

■ Proficiency Assessment

Project 9-3: Troubleshoot a Sound Problem

You are a tour guide for a travel agency that specializes in adventure travel tours. You recently returned from a trip to the Amazon, and you want to display the pictures on a computer in your office while playing music through the system's speakers. Unfortunately, no sound is coming from your computer. In this project, you will examine your devices to see if you can identify and fix the speaker problem.

1. Click **Start**, click **Control Panel**, and then click **System and Maintenance**. The System and Maintenance window displays.
2. Click **Device Manager.** If you have an administrator account, the User Account Control dialog box displays. Click **Continue** to open the Device Manager. If you do not have an administrator account, a Device Manager warning dialog box displays, informing you that you cannot make changes to devices and drivers. Click **OK** to display the Device Manager. (With an administrator account, you will not be able to complete all steps in this project.)
3. Click the plus sign to the left of the **Sound, video and game controllers** category to display information about the devices installed on your system.
4. Right-click your sound controller device and click **Disable** on the shortcut menu.
5. To disable the device, click **Yes** in the warning box. If your instructor asks you to capture an image of the Device Manager window, save it in your Lesson 9 assessment folder as ***Proj09_03***.
6. Click **Start**, click **Music**, and double-click the **Sample Music** folder.

7. Double-click any music file to see if you can hear it playing. A message should inform you that your sound device has a problem. Click **OK** to close the message.
8. Make the Device Manager window active.
9. Right-click your sound device and click **Properties**.
10. Click the **Driver** tab and then click **Update Driver**.
11. Click **Search automatically for updated driver software**. If Windows Vista finds a newer driver, it will install it. Otherwise, it displays a message that your driver is up-to-date.
12. Click **Close** to close the Update Driver Software window. Then click **Close** to close the Properties dialog box.
13. Right-click your sound device and click **Enable**.
14. Close the Device Manager window.
15. In the Sample Music folder, double-click any file to see if it will play. When the music is finished, close all open windows.

PAUSE. LEAVE the desktop displayed to use in the next project.

Project 9-4: Printing Help

An attorney at your law office has been having trouble setting up a wireless home network. He has asked you if you would print out some information from Windows Help and Support that he can take home as a reference. Halfway through the printing, he asks you to stop and print a report that must be sent out immediately. In this project, you send three help pages to the print queue. You then pause the printing, send a report to the print queue, and then cancel the remaining help files.

The ***Trial_Report1*** file is available on the companion CD-ROM.

GET READY. Before you begin these steps, copy the ***Trial_Report1*** file from the data files for this lesson to the Documents folder.

1. If necessary, install a printer for use with your computer. Make sure it is on and loaded with paper.
2. Click **Start**, click **Control Panel**, and then click **Hardware and Sound**. Click **Printers** to display the Printers window.
3. Right-click the default printer and click **Pause Printing**.
4. Click **Start** and then click **Help and Support**.
5. Key **wireless network** in the Search Help box and then click the **Search Help** button.
6. Click **Wireless networking: frequently asked questions** and then click the **Print** button on the Windows Help and Support toolbar. Click Print to send the file to the print queue.
7. Click the **Back** button on the Windows Help and Support toolbar, scroll down, and click **What you need to set up a home network**.
8. Click the **Print** button on the Windows Help and Support toolbar and then click **Print** to send the file to the print queue.
9. Scroll to the bottom of the help page and click the link to **Setting up a home network**.
10. Click the **Print** button on the Windows Help and Support toolbar and then click **Print** to send the file to the print queue.
11. Close the Windows Help and Support window.
12. In the Printers window, double-click your default printer icon to open its print queue.
13. Click **Printer** on the window's menu bar and click **Pause Printing** to return the printer to its Ready status. The first print job should begin printing.
14. Right-click the second print job and click **Pause**.

15. Right-click the third print job and click **Pause**.
16. Click **Start** and then click **Documents**. Right-click the ***Trial_Report1*** file and click Print to send it to the print queue. If the first help file is done printing, the report file should print.
17. Make the print queue active. When the ***Trial_Report1*** file is done printing, click **Printer** on the window's menu bar and click **Cancel All Documents**.
18. Click **Yes** in the dialog box. Windows Vista clears the print queue of all documents.
19. Close the print queue window.
20. Close the Printers window and then close the Control Panel window.
21. In Documents, delete the ***Trial_Report1*** file and then close the Documents window.

PAUSE. LEAVE the desktop displayed to use in the next project.

Mastery Assessment

Project 9-5: Notebook Performance

As a buyer for Wide World Importers, you travel frequently. Your notebook computer has been performing slowly and seems to use up battery power too quickly. Someone suggested you adjust power settings and then check the hard disk for problems. You also decide to defragment the disk.

1. Open the **Power Options** window and select the **Power saver** power plan.
2. Customize the power plan settings to turn off the display after **15 minutes** and to put the computer to sleep after **20 minutes**.
3. Set the power button on your computer to put the computer into Sleep mode. If your instructor asks you to capture an image of the System Settings window, save it in your Lesson 9 assessment folder as ***Proj09_05***.
4. If you are using an actual notebook computer, change the settings so that your computer goes into Sleep mode when the notebook lid is closed.
5. Open your local disk's Properties dialog box. Select to check the disk for file system errors the next time you restart your computer.
6. Restart your computer. Watch the screen during the check to see if there are any errors.
7. After the restart, log back in to your Windows Vista user account.
8. Open your local disk's Properties dialog box again and select to defragment the disk manually.
9. Start the defragmentation.
10. When the defragmenting is complete, close the Disk Defragmenter window.
11. Restore the Power Saver power plan to its default settings. Restore the power button to its previous function.
12. **CLOSE** all open windows.

PAUSE. LEAVE the desktop displayed to use in the next project.

Project 9-6: Optimize Performance

You are looking for ways to optimize the performance of your computer. In this project, you will check the amount of installed RAM so you know how much you can allot for Windows ReadyBoost. You attempt to use a USB flash drive with Windows ReadyBoost to provide more processing power. While the drive is available, you will monitor your system resource usage. You will use the Safely Remove Hardware tool when you are ready to remove the drive, and, finally, you will check to see how your hard disk is partitioned.

GET READY. To complete this exercise, you should have a USB flash drive that is compatible with Windows ReadyBoost available.

1. Display basic information about your computer system, including the amount of installed RAM and the CPU speed. Record the information on a piece of paper, in a file stored in your Lesson 9 assessment folder as ***Proj09_06***, or in an online journal.
2. Attach the Windows ReadyBoost-compatible device to your computer.
3. In the AutoPlay dialog box, click **Speed up my system using Windows ReadyBoost.**
4. Allocate two times the amount of installed RAM for use with ReadyBoost.
5. Display the **Task Manager** and check the memory and CPU usage statistics. Record the information in the same location that you used in step 1.
6. Close the Task Manager and the Control Panel if it is still open.
7. Use the **Safely Remove Hardware** tool to stop the flash drive. Then remove it.
8. Open the **Computer Management** window in the Control Panel and select the **Disk Management** tool to display information about your storage devices.
9. Locate the type of partition on your local disk.
10. Close the Computer Management window.
11. Close all open windows.

LOG OFF your Windows Vista user account.

INTERNET READY

Advances in technology have made telecommuting a productive and accepted lifestyle. Many companies not only allow employees to work from home or while traveling, but also encourage it. In this exercise, use Internet search tools to locate information about telecommuting, such as statistics about the number of people who telecommute and the number of businesses that employ telecommuters. You might find information about how and why it has become more popular and accepted in recent years. For example, you might research the technology that makes it possible, such as networking and mobile devices. When you have finished your research, use a word processing program or a pen and paper to write a one-page report about telecommuting.

Managing Software

LESSON SKILL MATRIX

Skills	Matrix Skill	Skill Number
Installing a Program	Install a software program	3.1.2
Changing or Repairing a Program	Repair a software installation	7.5.2
Uninstalling a Program	Uninstall a software program	3.1.3
Configuring an Older Program to Run Under Windows Vista	Configure a program to use a compatibility mode	3.1.5
Shutting Down an Unresponsive Program	Identify and terminate unresponsive programs	7.5.1
Creating a Restore Point	Create a restore point	3.1.1
Using a Restore Point	Restore the computer to a previous point	7.7.2
Scheduling a Backup	Schedule backups	4.7.2
Backing up Data	Back up files and folders	4.7.1
Restoring Files and Folders from a Backup	Restore files and folders from a backup file	4.7.3
Restoring a Previous Version of a File	Restore a previous version of file	4.7.4

Many of the employees of Wide World Importers, an international importer of goods manufactured around the globe, work from offices in their own homes or travel frequently. They must know how to manage the software programs that they rely on for tasks such as preparing documents as well as communicating with customers and coworkers. They must also know how to safeguard their data. Windows Vista provides the tools they need to install programs, diagnose and fix software problems, and back up data. In this lesson, you learn how to use Windows Vista to install, uninstall, or update a software program; identify and repair a program that stops working; and back up and restore data files.

KEY TERMS
Backup file
Install
Installation disk
Registry
Restore point
Restore
Shadow copy
System event
System Restore
Uninstall
Unresponsive program
Update
Upgrade

■ Installing Software

THE BOTTOM LINE

Windows Vista comes with many programs already installed, such as Notepad and Windows Media Player. To use other programs, you must install them. For example, a sales representative for Wide World Importers might need to install a word processing program to write letters, or a spreadsheet program to create an expense report. When you ***install*** a program, you copy the program files from a source location to the hard drive on your computer. The source location may be an installation disk that comes with the software package, a website on the Internet or a network drive or folder. An ***installation disk*** is a CD or DVD that contains the files necessary for installing the program. Programs take up space on your hard drive. Once a program is installed, you may need to change it to add or remove specific features, repair it if it is not working correctly, or, if you no longer use it, uninstall it to remove it from your system. In this section, you will learn how to install, change, repair, and uninstall a program. You will also learn how to install an older program so that it runs on a computer with the Windows Vista operating system.

Installing a Program

Most programs have an Installation or Setup Wizard that prompts you through the process of installing the program. Usually, the installation begins automatically when you insert the installation disk into a drive, or when you select the AutoPlay option to run the installation file. If you are installing from a network location, you may have to open a window for the location and then double-click the installation file. Once the wizard starts, you simply follow the prompts that display on the screen to complete the installation. In this exercise, you install a new software program and then view a list of programs installed on your computer.

INSTALL A PROGRAM

GET READY. Before you begin these steps, start your computer and log on to your Windows Vista account. Close all open windows so you can see the desktop. In addition, you should have the installation disk for a program that is not currently installed on your system, or access to a network location where the program installation file is stored. To complete this exercise, you must be logged on using an administrator account, or you must have an administrator's password. Create a new folder named Lesson 10 in a storage location specified by your instructor where you can store assessment files and folders that you create during this lesson.

1. Insert the installation disk into the appropriate drive in your computer. For example, if the disk is a DVD, insert it into a DVD drive. If the disk is a CD, insert it into a CD drive. Alternatively, open a window for the network location where the installation file is stored and then double-click the installation file. If the AutoPlay dialog box displays, click the option to run the setup program. The specific command depends on the program you are installing, but it should be similar to Run Setup.exe, Run Autorun.exe, or Run Install.exe.

TAKE NOTE*

Most installation files are named setup.exe or install.exe. Some may be named autorun.exe.

TROUBLESHOOTING

If Windows Vista cannot identify the publisher of the program, it will display a User Account Control dialog box informing you that an unidentified program wants to access your computer. This may happen frequently with programs written to run with earlier versions of the Windows operating system. If you are confident that the program is from a reputable source, click Allow. If you are not sure, click Cancel. If you take no action, Windows Vista will cancel the installation automatically. If you are not logged on as an administrator, you must key an administrator's password to continue.

2. The first screen of an installation program or Setup Wizard displays. The information on the screen varies, depending on the program. For example, it might prompt you to select a language to use for the installation, to select a Typical or Custom installation, or it might simply prompt you to click Next to continue. Table 10-1 describes common setup options that you might encounter during an installation. There may be other options specific to your program as well.

TROUBLESHOOTING

If the installation does not begin automatically, you may have to open the Computer window, open the window for the drive where the installation disk is inserted, and then double-click the installation file. Most installation files are named setup.exe or install.exe.

3. Follow the prompts through all of the screens in the installation program or Setup Wizard, using the information provided in Table 10-1 as a guide.

Table 10-1

Common Setup Options

Option	Description
Choose Setup Type	Most programs offer you a choice of a Typical installation or a Custom installation. Select Typical to install the program using the default settings. Select Custom if you want to select the folder where you want to store the program files and select specific features to install.
Run from Installation Disk	Some programs let you choose to install all program files on your hard drive, or install only required files on your hard drive. Installing only the required files takes up much less space on your hard drive, but you must insert the installation disk in your computer to use the program.
Select a Language	Many programs offer you a choice of language to use for the installation.
Create Shortcuts	Most programs ask you to select where you want to place program shortcuts. You may be able to place a shortcut on the desktop, on the Start menu, or on the Quick Launch Toolbar, or you may be able to select not to create any shortcuts at all.
End User License Agreement (EULA)	Most programs require that you read and accept the terms of a EULA before you can install the program.
Product Identification	Most programs require that you enter a product ID, key, or serial number to install the program. The number is usually available on the back of the sleeve or box that the installation disk came in. If you download the software, the vendor may send you the number in an email message.
Select Software	Many installation disks contain more than one program. You may be able to select to install or skip specific programs.
Storage Folder	Most programs will install into a default folder on your hard drive. Some programs offer you the option of accepting the default folder or changing the folder name or location.
Availability	Some programs allow you to select whether the program will be available to all user accounts on the system, or only to your user account.

4. When you have completed all of the screens in the Installation or Setup Wizard, click the **Install** button to install the program. Windows Vista copies the program files to your computer. Usually, a status bar similar to the one in Figure 10-1 displays the progress of the installation.

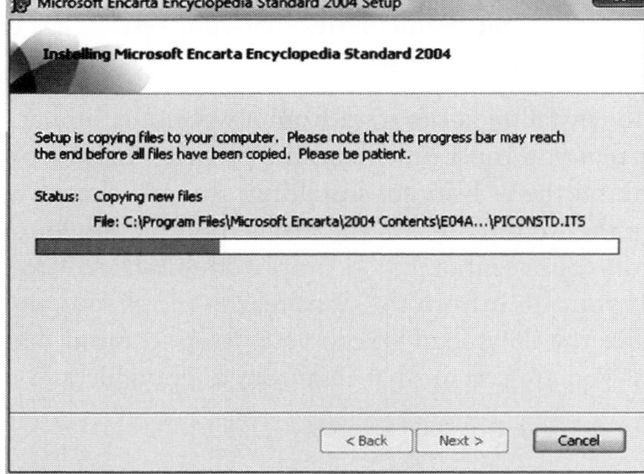

Figure 10-1

View the installation progress

5. When the installation is complete, click **Finish** to close the Installation or Setup Wizard. Some programs may prompt you to restart your computer. Click **Yes** to restart. Then log back in to your Windows Vista account.
6. Click **Start** and then click **Control Panel**. Click **Programs** and then click **Programs and Features**. The Programs and Features window of the Control Panel displays a list of the programs you have installed on your computer. The newly installed program should be included in the list. Although the specific programs on your screen depend on the programs you have installed, this window should look similar to Figure 10-2.

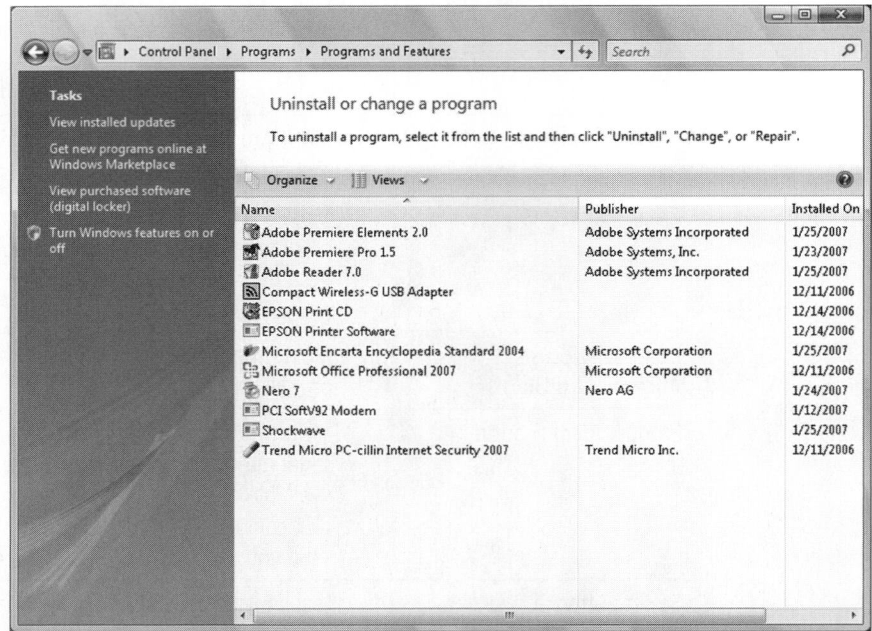

Figure 10-2

Installed programs in the Programs and Features window

You can open the Programs and Features window directly from the Computer window. Click Start>Computer and then click the Uninstall or change a program button on the window's toolbar.

7. At your instructor's request, capture an image of the Programs and Features window. Save it in your Lesson 10 assessment folder as ***Le10_01***.

PAUSE. LEAVE the Programs and Features window open to use in the next exercise.

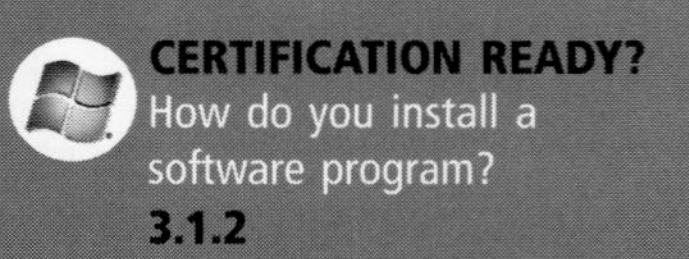

CERTIFICATION READY?
How do you install a software program?
3.1.2

As mentioned in Lesson 9, "Managing System Resources," most software programs have minimum system requirements that are necessary for the program to run correctly. Before you try to install a program, you should verify that your system has enough disk space, RAM, and processing speed to run the program.

The procedure for installing a program from a website is similar to installing from a disk or network, except that you must download the program files before installing. Usually, when you click the link on the website for installing, you can choose whether you want to run the installation from the website or save the installation file on your computer. If you save the installation file on your computer, you simply double-click it to start the Installation or Setup Wizard. If you run it from the website, the Installation or Setup Wizard should start automatically once the download is complete. Keep in mind that you should never download a program unless you are certain that it is from a reputable and trustworthy vendor.

Some programs are ***upgrades***, which means that they are new and improved versions of existing programs. If you have the previous version already installed, you can install the upgrade without installing an entirely new program. It is usually less expensive to purchase an upgrade. If you do not have the previous version, you must install the full version of the new product, which is the complete program. The steps for installing an upgrade are the same as for installing a full, new program. Do not confuse an upgrade with an ***update***, which is usually a small software program that fixes a problem or improves security or performance. You learn about updates in Lesson 11, "Monitoring the Windows Vista Environment."

In the next section, you learn how to change and repair a program.

Changing or Repairing a Program

You can use the tools in the Programs and Features window of the Control Panel to change or repair an installed program. Changing the program lets you add or remove features, or change whether a feature runs from the installation disk or from the hard drive. Repairing lets you reinstall features that may not be working correctly. In this exercise, you will change a program to add or remove a feature, and then you will repair the installation.

CHANGE OR REPAIR A PROGRAM

USE the Programs and Features window that you left open in the previous exercise.

1. Click the name of the program you installed in the previous exercise to select it. Uninstall, Change, and Repair buttons available for that program display on the toolbar. The buttons vary, depending on the options available for the selected program. Table 10-2 describes the buttons.

Table 10-2

Program Uninstall and Change Options

Option	Description
Uninstall/Change	The Uninstall/Change button is available if the same tool is used for uninstalling and changing the program. It may also be used to repair a program.
Uninstall	The Uninstall button is available for uninstalling the program.
Change	The Change button is available if it is possible to change or update the installed program's features. For some programs, the Change button is also used to repair or uninstall a program.
Repair	The Repair button is available if you can repair the installed program. Repairing usually involves reinstalling the program or selected features to fix missing or corrupt files and shortcuts.

2. Click the **Change** button, or the **Uninstall/Change** button, on the window's toolbar. If you are logged in to an administrator account, click **Continue.** If you are not logged in using an administrator account, key an administrator's password and then click **OK** to continue. The same Installation or Setup Wizard that you used to install the program in the previous exercise should start.

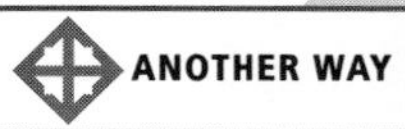

You can also right-click a program in the Programs and Features window and select Change or Uninstall/Change from the shortcut menu.

3. Click **Next** to continue. A Program Maintenance screen similar to the one in Figure 10-3 should display. You can select to modify the installation, repair it, or remove it from your computer. If the program cannot be modified, the Modify option is not available. Skip to step 8.

Figure 10-3

Program Maintenance screen

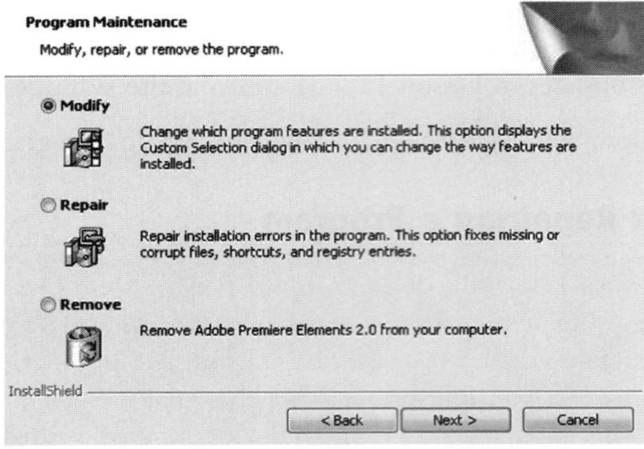

4. Click the **Modify** option button and then click **Next.** A screen listing available components displays. This screen varies depending on the program you are modifying. It may display all available components, with the ones that are installed marked with a checkmark. If so, you can select the components you want to install and deselect those you want to remove. The screen may display only components that are not installed, so you can choose to install them. Some programs let you choose to change an installation to run a component from a disk instead of from the hard drive.
5. If available, click to select a feature that is not currently installed, or to deselect a feature that is currently installed, and then click **Next.** The program may prompt you to insert the installation disk or to select the folder where the setup files are stored. Do so and then click **OK** to continue.
6. When the modification is complete, click **Finish.**
7. Click the **Repair** button on the Programs and Features toolbar, if it is available, or click the **Change** button, or the **Uninstall/Change** button. If you are logged in using an administrator account, a User Account Control dialog box displays. Click **Continue.** If you are not logged in using an administrator account, key an administrator's password and then click **OK** to continue. The Installation or Setup Wizard starts again.
8. Click to select the **Repair** option button and then click **Next.** The program may prompt you to insert the installation disk or to select the folder where the setup files are stored. Do so and then click **OK** to continue. The program checks the installation and then reinstalls components as necessary.
9. When the repair is complete, click **Finish.**

PAUSE. LEAVE the Programs and Features window open to use in the next exercise.

CERTIFICATION READY?
How do you repair a software installation?
7.5.2

Some of the symptoms of a program in need of repair include slow response time, error messages, and unexplained crashes. If one or more of these are occurring, you should try repairing the installation. If that does not help, you may have to uninstall the program and install it again.

In the next exercise, you learn how to uninstall a program.

Uninstalling a Program

When you no longer need a program, you should ***uninstall*** it. Uninstalling removes the program files and other files such as shortcuts from your computer. This frees up disk space for other programs or data files. In this exercise, you will uninstall the program you installed earlier in this lesson.

UNINSTALL A PROGRAM

USE the Programs and Features window that you left open in the previous exercise.

1. Click the name of the program you want to uninstall.
2. Click the **Uninstall** button. If the Uninstall button is not available, click the **Uninstall/Change** button. If you are logged in using an administrator account, a User Account Control dialog box displays. Click **Continue**. If you are not logged in using an administrator account, key an administrator's password and then click **OK** to continue. The next step depends on whether you clicked the Uninstall button or the Uninstall/Change button.

Some programs have an Uninstall command that you can access directly from the Start menu. Click Start, click All Programs, and then expand the folder where the program is stored. If there is an Uninstall command, click it to start the uninstall process.

3. If you clicked the Uninstall button, a Programs and Features dialog box displays, asking if you are sure you want to uninstall the program. Click **Yes**. If necessary, click **Allow** in the User Account Control dialog box. Windows Vista uninstalls the program and removes it from the list of programs in the Programs and Features window.
4. If you clicked the Uninstall/Change button, the Setup program starts and displays a page where you can select to Modify, Repair, or Remove the program. Click the **Remove** option button and then click **Next**. Follow the prompts to select options and start the uninstall process.
5. When the program is uninstalled, click **Finish** to close the Installation or Setup Wizard.
6. **CLOSE** the Programs and Features window.

PAUSE. LEAVE the desktop displayed to use in the next exercise.

CERTIFICATION READY?
How do you uninstall a software program?
3.1.3

Uninstalling is not the same as simply deleting program files or shortcuts. It removes all files copied to the computer during the install procedure and also restores the Windows Vista system files to a configuration that does not include the uninstalled program. Primarily, it removes all references to the program from the system registry.

Some programs share files. For example, the programs in the Microsoft Office suite of applications share common files and folders. During an uninstall, Windows Vista may display a dialog box asking if you want to leave shared files and folders installed to use with other programs. If you are keeping some of the programs that use the shared items installed, you should click Yes so that the shared files and folders remain available.

In the next exercise, you learn how to make an older program work with Windows Vista.

■ Configuring an Older Program to Run Under Windows Vista

THE BOTTOM LINE

When a new operating system becomes available, many software publishers release new, compatible programs that take advantage of the newest features and capabilities. However, not all businesses or individuals want the newer programs. For example, they may not want to spend the money, or learn to use the new program, or they may have systems that rely on the older programs. Most programs written for older versions of the Windows operating system will run under Windows Vista. Some older programs may not run correctly at first or they may not run at all. If you have an older program that you want to install and use with Windows Vista, you can use the Program Compatibility Wizard to start the program in compatibility mode and then automatically change the compatibility settings so that the program will run correctly. In this exercise, you will use the Program Compatibility Wizard to start a program in compatibility mode.

CONFIGURE AN OLDER PROGRAM TO RUN UNDER WINDOWS VISTA

1. Click **Start**, click **Control Panel**, and then click **Programs**.
2. Under Programs and Features, click **Use an older program with this version of Windows**. The Program Compatibility Wizard starts.
3. Click **Next**. At this point, you must use one of three options to identify the program you want to run:
   a. Select **I want to choose from a list of programs** to display a list of programs already installed on your computer. Click **Next** to display the list. Click the program and then click **Next**.
   b. Select **I want to use the program in the CD-ROM drive** if the program is not yet installed, but the installation disk is in your CD-ROM or DVD drive. Click **Next**.
   c. Select **I want to locate the program manually** if you know the path to the program file. For example, it may be on a network drive, external drive, or —if it is very old—on a floppy disk. Click **Next**, key the path, and then click **Next**. Alternatively, you can click Browse to locate and select the program file.
4. Click to select the operating system that is recommended for the program and then click **Next**.
5. Click to select the display settings that are recommended for the program. You may select more than one setting. Click **Next**. You may need to consult the program's documentation to determine the recommended display settings.
6. Click to select the option to run the program as an administrator if the program required administrator privileges under previous versions of Windows. Then click **Next**. A page showing the options you have selected displays. It should look similar to Figure 10-4, with some differences depending on the options you selected. At your instructor's request, capture an image of the window. Save it in your Lesson 10 assessment folder as ***Le10_02***.

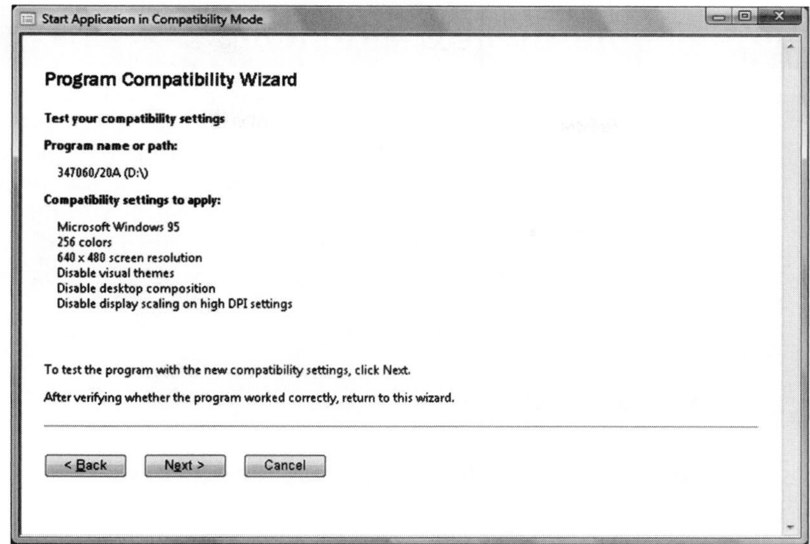

Figure 10-4
Compatibility mode settings

7. Click **Next** to test the settings and return to the Program Compatibility Wizard.
8. At this point, you can take one of three steps:
   a. Click **Yes, set this program to always use these compatibility settings** if the program ran correctly. Click **Next** to continue.
   b. Click **No, try different compatibility settings** if the program did not work and you want to try different settings. The wizard returns to the page where you select the operating system. Repeat from step 4 above.
   c. Click **No, I am finished trying compatibility settings** if you want to stop trying to run the program in compatibility mode. Click **Next** to continue.
9. Click **Yes** to send a program compatibility data report to Microsoft. Click **No** if you do not want to send the data. Then click **Next**.
10. Click **Finish** to close the wizard.
11. **CLOSE** the Control Panel window.

PAUSE. LEAVE the desktop displayed to use in the next exercise.

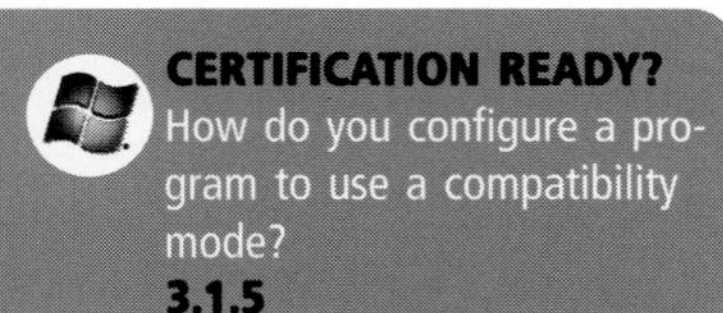

Windows Vista also includes a feature called the Program Compatibility Assistant, which automatically monitors older programs for known compatibility problems. If it detects a problem, it will display a warning message and offer to fix the problem automatically, if possible. You cannot control the Program Compatibility Assistant; it runs automatically.

You can manually configure the compatibility settings for some older programs by using the Compatibility tab in the program's Properties dialog box. Right-click the program icon, click Properties to open the dialog box, and then click the Compatibility tab. Click to select the Run this program in compatibility mode for checkbox and then click the dropdown arrow to select the operating system. Click to select the display setting options and the privilege level options as necessary and then click OK.

Some older programs will not run correctly under Windows Vista, even if you use compatibility mode. If that is the case, you should contact the software publisher to see if a newer version of the program is available.

Microsoft warns users against using program compatibility mode with system utility programs such as older antivirus programs and disk utilities because of the risk of data loss or a security breach.

In the next section, you learn how to shut down a program that has stopped responding.

■ Shutting Down an Unresponsive Program

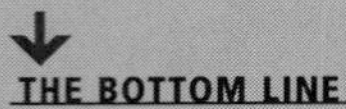

THE BOTTOM LINE

An ***unresponsive program*** is one that is not able to communicate with the user or with the operating system, usually due to a problem in the program itself. As a result, the program runs very slowly, or stops completely. You can identify an unresponsive program because the words *Not Responding* display in parentheses in the program window's title bar. You can wait to see if the problem is temporary, in which case the program will start responding again, or you can use the Task Manager to end the program. In this exercise, you will open a document in Notepad. The document was originally in a non-text format, opened and saved in Notepad, and is quite large. When you attempt to apply formatting, Notepad should stop responding. You will wait to see what happens, and then you will end the program using Task Manager.

SHUT DOWN AN UNRESPONSIVE PROGRAM

CD

The ***File1*** file is available on the companion CD-ROM.

1. Copy the ***File1*** file from the data files for this lesson to your Documents folder.
2. Click **Start** and then click Documents to open the Documents window.
3. Double-click the ***File1*** file to open it. Notepad may stop responding for a moment while trying to open the file. The file contains text characters, some of which appear to be nonsense.
4. Right-click a blank area of the Taskbar and click **Task Manager** on the shortcut menu. The Windows Task Manager dialog box displays.

X REF

For more information on the Task Manager, refer to Lesson 9.

5. Click the **Applications** tab. On the Applications tab, you can see a list of the programs currently running on your system. It should look similar to Figure 10-5. Notice that the status of the Notepad program is Running, which means it is responding to commands.

Figure 10-5

Applications tab of the Windows Task Manager dialog box

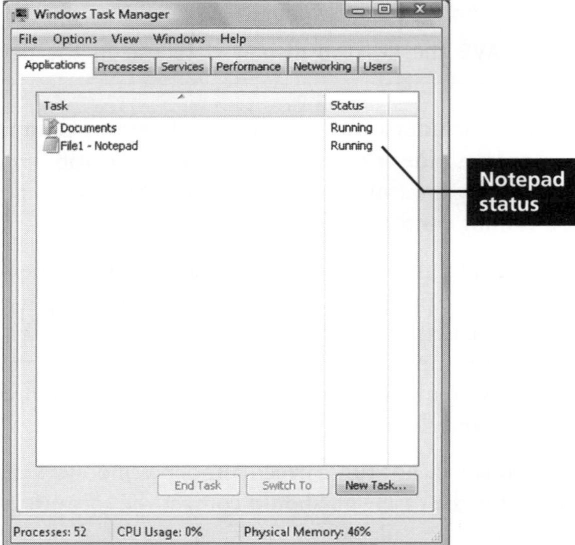

TAKE NOTE*

You can drag the border of the Status column to make it wider if you cannot see the entire contents of the column.

6. Minimize the Task Manager window, but keep it open.
7. In the Notepad window, click **Format** on the menu bar and then click **Word Wrap**. This is the command that instructs Notepad to wrap the lines of text to fit the width of the program window. Notice that the mouse pointer changes to a spinning circle, indicating that Notepad is processing the command. The document window may go blank. After a few moments, (Not Responding) displays in the program's title bar, as shown in Figure 10-6.

Figure 10-6

Unresponsive program

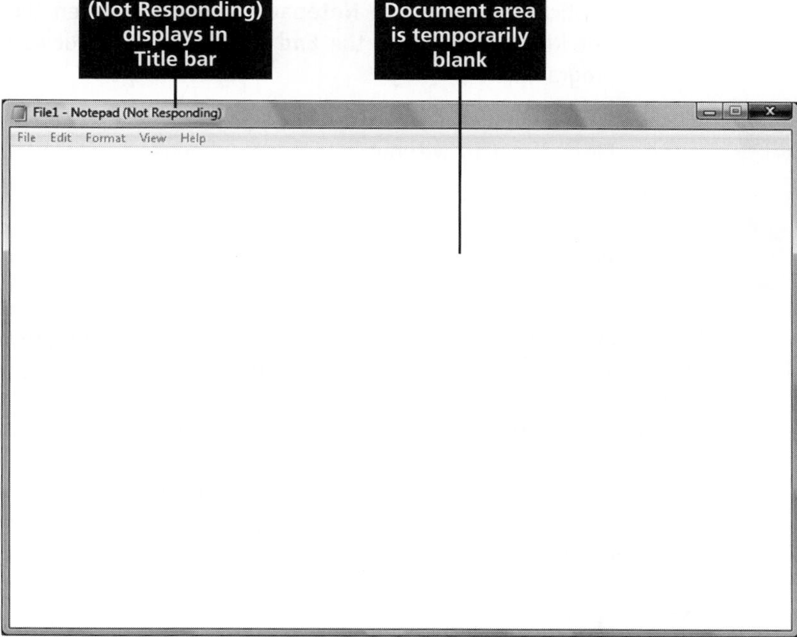

8. Wait to see what happens. Because this is not a serious problem with the software, but rather a slowdown caused by the program trying to execute a command, the program begins responding again. (Not Responding) no longer display in the title bar.
9. Click **Format** on the menu bar and click **Word Wrap** again.
10. Quickly click the **Task Manager** button on the Taskbar to restore the window. Notice that the status of the Notepad program is now Not Responding, as shown in Figure 10-7. When the program starts responding again, the status changes to Running.

Figure 10-7

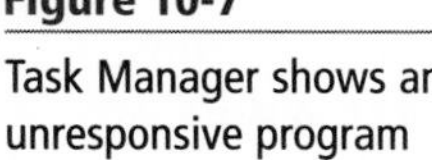

Task Manager shows an unresponsive program

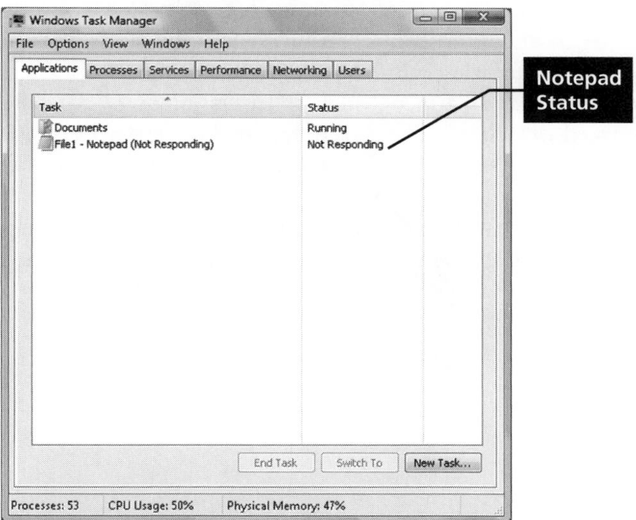

TROUBLESHOOTING

If your system is able to process the commands, you may not see (Not Responding) in the Notepad title bar or in the Task Manager. Try selecting Format>Word Wrap again, or try moving quickly between the Notepad window and the Task Manager window.

11. Minimize the Task Manager again, click **Format** on the Notepad menu bar, and then click **Word Wrap**.
12. Quickly restore the Task Manager window. In the list of programs on the Applications tab, click **Notepad** to select it. When the Notepad status displays Not Responding, click the **End Task** button. Windows Vista ends the unresponsive program.
13. Close the Task Manager.
14. Close Notepad without saving any changes.
15. Delete the *File1* text document from the Documents folder and then close the Documents folder window.

PAUSE. LEAVE the desktop displayed to use in the next exercise.

CERTIFICATION READY?
How do you identify and terminate unresponsive programs?
7.5.1

If Windows Vista determines that a program has been unresponsive for a significant amount of time, it may display a warning dialog box telling you that the program has stopped responding. You may select an option to end the program, or you may choose to continue waiting to see if the program will start responding again. Also, whenever a program stops responding, Windows Vista creates a problem report, which is stored in the Problem Reports and Solutions section under System and Maintenance in the Control Panel. To check for available solutions, you can set your computer to automatically send the problem report to Microsoft via the Internet, or you can manually send the problem report at your convenience. If a solution is available, Windows Vista displays information about the steps you can take to solve the problem.

When you end an unresponsive program you run the risk of losing unsaved data. Because problems can occur at any time, you should develop the habit of saving your data files frequently while you work.

In the next section, you learn how to create and use a restore point.

■ Using System Restore

THE BOTTOM LINE

System Restore is a feature of Windows Vista that lets you restore your computer's system files to an earlier configuration. It lets you undo changes that might be causing a problem or interfering with the way Windows Vista operates. System Restore does not affect data files, so documents such as letters, pictures, databases, and spreadsheets are not damaged or deleted. When the System Protection feature is active, Windows Vista automatically creates restore points at regular intervals and prior to any significant system event, or you can manually create a restore point. A ***restore point*** is a file that contains information about your system configuration at that particular point in time. A ***system event*** is an event that affects the system configuration, such as installing or uninstalling a new program, or updating a device driver. System Protection is active by default. In this section, you learn how to manually create a restore point and how to use a restore point to go back to a previous configuration.

Creating a Restore Point

As mentioned, Windows Vista automatically creates restore points at regularly scheduled intervals as well as prior to any system change, such as installing or uninstalling software. You can use tools on the System Protection tab of the System Properties dialog box to manually create a restore point. For example, a buyer for Wide World Importers might create a restore point before connecting to a vendor's wireless network. In this exercise, you check to be sure System Protection is active and you then create a restore point. You must be logged on to an administrator account or have an administrator account password to create a restore point.

CREATE A RESTORE POINT

1. Click **Start** and then click **Computer**.
2. In the Computer window, click the **System Properties** button on the Computer window toolbar to open the System window in the Control Panel.
3. Under Tasks in the left pane, click **System protection**. If you are logged in to an administrator account, click **Continue**. If not, key an administrator password and then click **OK**. The System Protection tab of the System Properties dialog box displays. It should look similar to Figure 10-8.

Figure 10-8

System Protection tab of the System Properties dialog box

You can also open the System Properties dialog box from the Control Panel. Click Start>Control Panel. Click System and Maintenance. Click Backup and Restore Center. Under Tasks in the left pane, click Create a restore point or change settings.

4. Under the heading Automatic restore points, locate the list of disks. A checkmark next to a disk indicates that System Protection is active. There should be a checkmark next to all available disks. If necessary, click to select the checkboxes next to each disk in the list and then click **Apply**.
5. Click the **Create** button. A System Protection dialog box where you can key a name or description for the restore point displays.
6. Key **Connect to vendor's network** and then click **Create**. Windows Vista creates the restore point, and then displays a dialog box informing you that the restore point was created successfully.
7. Click **OK**.
8. Click **OK** in the System Properties dialog box to close it.
9. **CLOSE** the Control Panel.

PAUSE. LEAVE the desktop displayed to use in the next exercise.

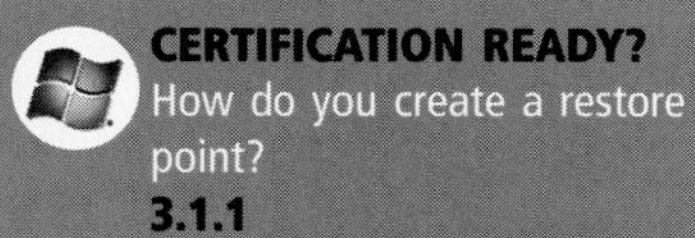

To restore previous versions of operating system files, registry settings, and installed programs, use System Restore. The ***registry*** is a folder where system configuration data is stored. As mentioned, System Restore does not remove or delete data files, even if the files were created after the restore point was created. For example, if you create a report document on Wednesday and then use System Restore to go back to a restore point from Tuesday, the report will remain unchanged in its current storage location.

System Restore cannot run on a hard disk that has a capacity smaller than 1GB. It also requires a minimum of 300MB of free space on your hard disk for storing restore points. Windows Vista will delete older restore points if necessary to free space for newer restore points. If you turn off System Protection, all restore points for that disk are deleted.

In the next exercise, you learn how to use a restore point.

■ Using a Restore Point

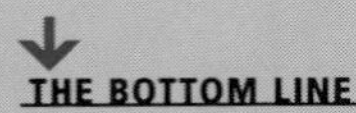

If your system is having trouble processing information, running programs, or communicating with devices, you can revert to a restore point that was created prior to the time you first noticed a problem. Windows Vista maintains a list of restore points. It includes automatically created points, which are labeled with a descriptive name that indicates the system event that prompted the creation of the restore point, as well as the date and time, and manually created points. You can select any restore point in the list and then restore your system to the configuration that was in effect when the restore point was created. You can also undo the restore action if it does not solve the problem, or if it makes the problem worse. In this exercise, you will restore your system to the restore point created when you uninstalled a program earlier in this lesson.

USE A RESTORE POINT

GET READY. During the System Restore, Windows Vista will shut down and restart your computer. Before beginning this exercise, you should save and close all open data files, and close all open programs.

1. Click **Start**, click **Control Panel**, and then click **System and Maintenance**.
2. Click **Backup and Restore Center** and then, under Tasks in the left pane, click **Repair Windows using System Restore**. If you are logged on to an administrator account, click **Continue**. If not, key an administrator password and then click **OK**. The System Restore Wizard displays. It should look similar to Figure 10-9.

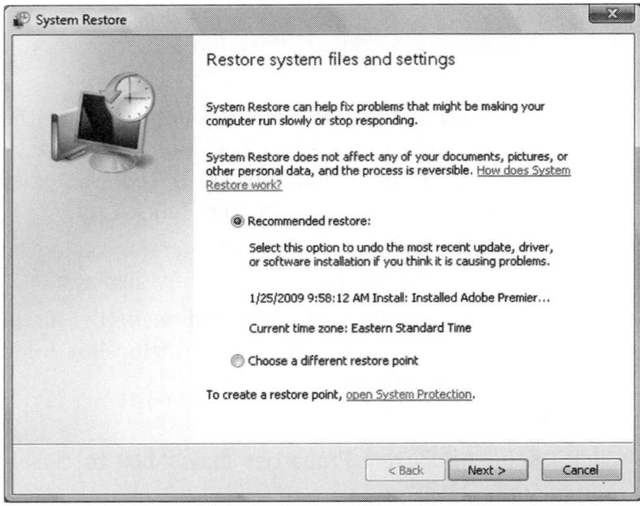

Figure 10-9
System Restore Wizard

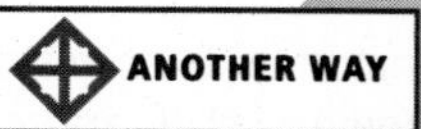

From the System Properties dialog box, click the System Restore button to open the System Restore feature.

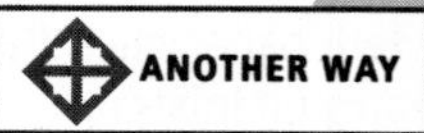

You can open the Backup and Restore Center from the Start menu, click Maintenance, and then click Backup and Restore Center.

3. Click to select the **Choose a different restore point** option button and then click **Next**. Windows Vista displays a list of restore points, similar to the one in Figure 10-10. The first point in the list should be the one you created manually in the previous exercise, named Connect to vendor's network. The others in the list should be automatic points created prior to system events such as installing or uninstalling programs. There may also be points created at regularly scheduled intervals. At your instructor's request, capture an image of the System Restore window. Save it in your Lesson 10 assessment folder as ***Le10_03***.

Figure 10-10

Select a restore point

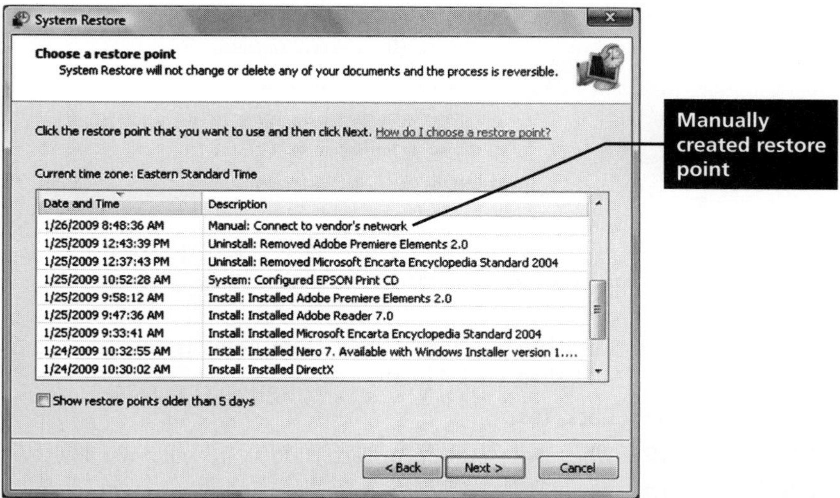

TAKE NOTE

The list of restore points on your computer will not be exactly the same as the one in the figure. It depends on the system events that have occurred on your computer.

4. Click the restore point created when you uninstalled a program previously in this lesson. It may be the second restore point in the list, and it should indicate that it was created because of an Uninstall.
5. Click **Next**. Windows Vista prompts you to confirm that you have selected the restore point you want to use.
6. Click **Finish** and then click **Yes** in the warning dialog box. Windows Vista will begin the System Restore, during which it will shut down and restart your computer.

TAKE NOTE

Although you cannot cancel or undo System Restore during the process, you can undo a System Restore once it is complete.

7. When your system restarts, log in to your Windows Vista user account. It may take longer than usual for the desktop to display, while Windows Vista completes the System Restore. Finally, a dialog box informs you that the System Restore completed successfully.

8. Click **Close** and then close any open windows, such as the Welcome Center. Notice that the program you uninstalled previously in this lesson has now been restored. If there had been shortcuts on the desktop or Quick Launch Toolbar, they are restored; if the program had been listed on the Start menu, it is listed there again.
9. Click **Start**, click **Control Panel**, and then click **System and Maintenance**. Click **Backup and Restore Center** and then, under Tasks in the left pane, click **Repair Windows using System Restore**. If you are logged on to an administrator account, click **Continue.** If not, key an administrator password and then click **OK**. The System Restore Wizard displays. Now, it should look similar to Figure 10-11. Notice that the default option is to Undo the System Restore.

Figure 10-11

Undo a System Restore

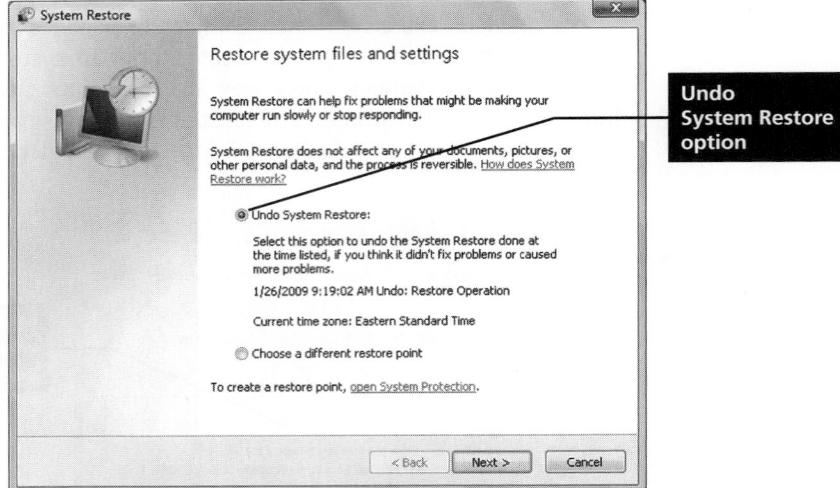

10. Click **Next**, confirm the restore point is to undo the System Restore, and then click **Finish**.
11. Click **Yes**.
12. When your system restarts, log in to your Windows Vista user account.
13. When the System Restore is complete, click **Close** to close the dialog box. Then close any open windows.

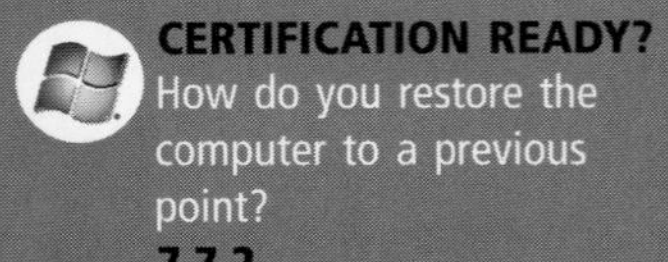

PAUSE. LEAVE the desktop displayed to use in the next exercise.

System Restore is an effective method to use to solve problems that seem to develop suddenly or are linked to a particular system event. You should select a restore point created just prior to the time you first noticed the problems. However, if you use one restore point, and the problems remain, you can undo the restore and try a different restore point.

If the problems cause difficulty with the way Windows Vista starts, System Restore may not help, because it will not be able to restart your computer. Lesson 11 covers troubleshooting startup problems.

Keep in mind that System Restore does not affect data files. That means that you cannot rely on it to recover a data file that has been deleted or damaged. That is why you should create backups of all important files. In the next section, you learn how to backup and restore data files.

■ Backing Up and Restoring Data

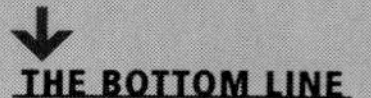

THE BOTTOM LINE

To be certain your data files are safe, you must back them up on a regular basis. Backing up creates a set of copies of the selected files—called a ***backup file*** or backup set—that is stored in a different location. In the event your original data files become damaged or inaccessible, you can ***restore*** the backup to recreate the files. Restoring places a copy of the backed up file into its original location. For example, if your hard disk fails or your notebook computer is stolen, you would not be able to access your data. If you have a backup, you could restore your data files to a new hard disk. Also, if you accidentally delete or replace a file, you could restore it from a backup. Windows Vista comes with the Back Up Files Wizard that you can use to back up and restore your data. You can schedule backups so they occur automatically at regular intervals, or you can start a backup manually at any time. In this section, you learn how to use Windows Vista to schedule backups, back up data, and then restore data from a backup. You also learn how to restore a previous version—or shadow copy—of a file.

Scheduling a Backup

The first time you use the Back Up Files Wizard, it prompts you to select a backup storage location, the types of files you want to back up, and to set a backup schedule. It then performs a full backup, which means that all files of the selected types are backed up. In the future, backups automatically occur at the scheduled time, using the current settings. You can change the settings at any time. Many companies have back up procedures that require employees to back up on a regular basis. Some might want a daily back up, while others might think a weekly back up is fine. In this exercise, you use the Back Up Wizard to select backup settings.

SCHEDULE A BACKUP

1. Click **Start** and then click **Control Panel**. Under System and Maintenance, click **Back up your computer**. The Backup and Restore Center window displays. It should look similar to Figure 10-12. Notice that under Back up files or your entire computer, both the date and time of the most recent backup and the date and time of the next scheduled backup display.

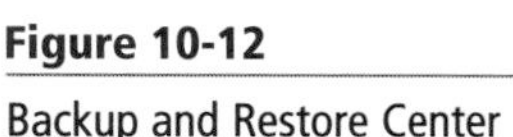

Figure 10-12

Backup and Restore Center

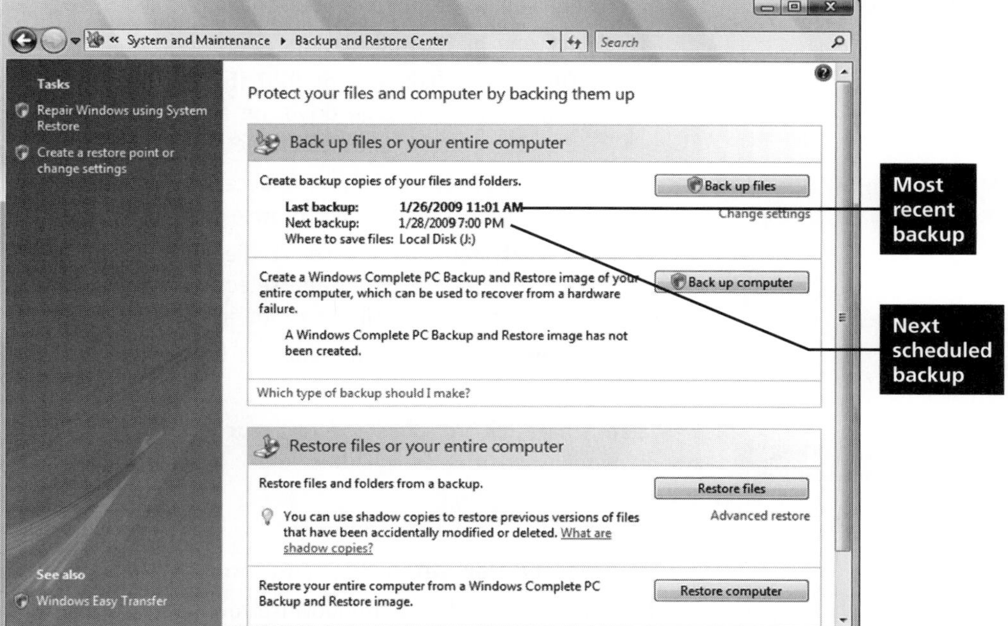

ANOTHER WAY

You can open the Backup and Restore Center from the Start menu. Click Start, click All Programs, click Maintenance and then click Backup and Restore Center.

TROUBLESHOOTING

If you have never used the Back Up Files Wizard to back up data files, there is no recent backup or scheduled backup listed. You must select options and run a full backup before you can change the settings. Click the Back up files button. If you are logged on to an administrator account, click Continue. If not, key an administrator password and then click OK. Skip to step 4 to select backup settings.

2. Click **Change Settings.** The Backup Status and Configuration window opens. It should look similar to Figure 10-13.

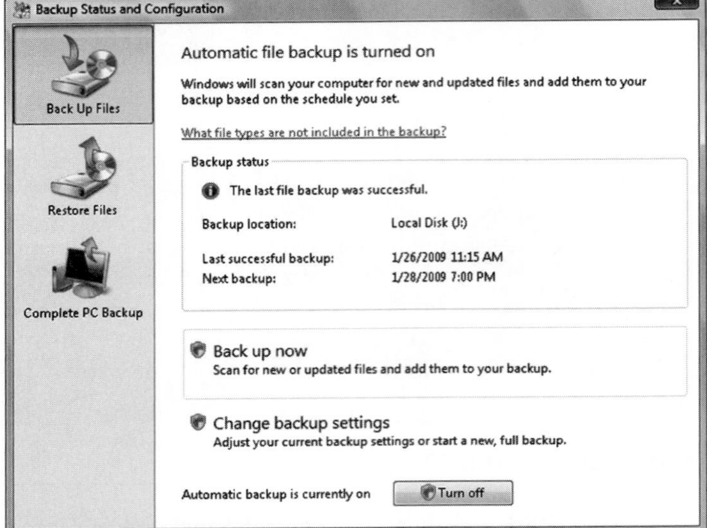

Figure 10-13

Backup Status and Configuration window

TAKE NOTE

You cannot back up to a USB flash drive, or to your local hard disk.

3. Click **Change backup settings.** If you are logged on to an administrator account, click **Continue.** If not, key an administrator password and then click **OK.** Windows Vista starts the Back Up Files Wizard. It searches your system to locate compatible backup devices and then displays a screen where you can select the location where you want to save your backup.
4. Select one of the following:
   a. **On a hard disk, CD, or DVD** if you want to save your backup on a hard drive other than you local drive, on a writable CD, or on a recordable DVD. Click the dropdown arrow and select the specific device.
   b. **On a network** if you have access to a network storage location. Key the path to the location or click Browse and browse to locate and select the location.
5. Click **Next.** You can now select the types of files you want to back up. All common data file types are listed and selected by default. Notice that system files, program files, and temporary files are not included and will not be backed up.
6. Click **Next.** On this page, you set the schedule for automatic backups.

TAKE NOTE

By default, backups are scheduled to occur weekly on Sundays at 1:00 AM. If your system is set to a different schedule, make note of it so you can restore the settings at the end of the exercise.

7. Click the **How often** dropdown arrow and click **Weekly.**
8. Click the **What day** dropdown arrow and click **Friday.**

9. Click the **What time** dropdown arrow and click **5:00 PM**. You have now scheduled automatic backups for every Friday at 5:00 PM. At your instructor's request, capture an image of the window. Save it in your Lesson 10 assessment folder as ***Le10_04***.
10. Click **Save settings and exit** to return to the Backup Status and Configuration window.

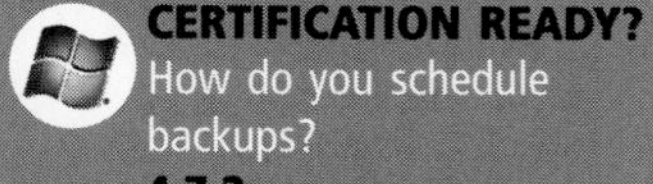

If this is the first time you are using the Back Up Files Wizard, click Finish to start the backup. Windows Vista will perform a new, full backup of the selected file types to the selected storage location. When the backup is complete, click Close and then click Change Settings to display the Backup Status and Configuration window.

11. Click **Change backup settings**. If you are logged on to an administrator account, click **Continue**. If not, key an administrator password and then click **OK**.
12. Click **Next**.
13. Click **Next**.
14. Click the **How often** dropdown arrow and click **Weekly**.
15. Click the **What day** dropdown arrow and click **Sunday**.
16. Click the **What time** dropdown arrow and click **1:00 AM**. You have now scheduled automatic backups for every Sunday at 1:00 AM. (Alternatively, set the schedule that was in place prior to this exercise.)
17. Click **Save settings and exit** to return to the Backup Status and Configuration window.
18. Close the Backup Status and Configuration window. The Backup and Restore Center should still be open.

CERTIFICATION READY?
How do you schedule backups?
4.7.2

PAUSE. LEAVE the Backup and Restore Center open to use in the next exercise.

You cannot schedule backups if you are using Windows Vista Starter or Windows Vista Home Basic.

Once a backup is scheduled, it begins automatically at the scheduled time as long as the computer is on. The backup runs using the current settings for backup location and file types. You can turn off automatic backups from the Backup Status and Configuration window by clicking the Turn off button. The User Account Control dialog box will display.

In the next exercise, you learn how to back up data.

Backing Up Data

As mentioned, scheduled backups run automatically using the current settings, but you can manually start a backup at any time. By default, only new or changed files are added to the backup file set, but you can select to perform a full backup, which includes all files of the selected file types, whether they have been modified or not. Prior to leaving on a business trip to visit clients, for example, a sales representative for Wide World Importers might back up her data files in case her computer is stolen or damaged while traveling. In this exercise, you use the Back Up Wizard to back up data.

BACK UP DATA

GET READY. To back up data files, you must have access to a compatible backup device, such as an external hard drive connected to your system via a USB port, a CD or DVD in a CD or DVD recordable drive, or a storage location on a network drive. If you are using a CD or DVD, have the disc(s) available.

USE the Backup and Restore Center you left open in the previous exercise.

The ***Memo1***, ***Letter1***, and ***Sales1*** files are available on the companion CD-ROM.

1. Open the Documents folder and create a new folder named Wide World Data.
2. Copy the ***Memo1*** and ***Letter1*** files from the data files for this lesson to the Wide World Data folder. Copy the ***Sales1*** file from the data files for this lesson to the Documents folder. Close the folder window.
3. In the Backup and Restore Center, click **Back up files**. If you are logged on to an administrator account, click **Continue**. If not, key an administrator password and then click **OK**. Windows Vista scans your system for new or modified files of the selected file types and adds them to the existing backup file set.

TAKE NOTE* If you are backing up to CD or DVD, Windows Vista will prompt you to insert the discs as necessary.

You can click Back up now in the Backup Status and Configuration window to start a backup of new or modified files.

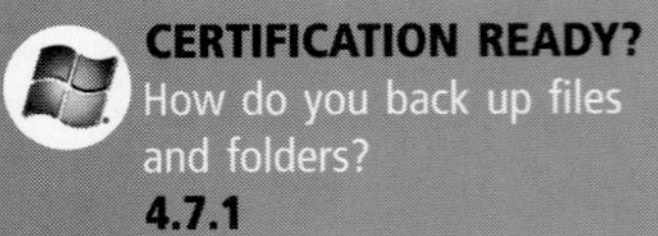

CERTIFICATION READY?
How do you back up files and folders?
4.7.1

4. When the backup is complete, click **Close** to close the Back Up Files window.

PAUSE. LEAVE the Backup and Restore Center open to use in the next exercise.

Backing up may take a long time, depending on the number and size of the files you are backing up. You can continue working with Windows Vista and your programs while the backup takes place. However, you may want to schedule backups for a time when you do not need to use your computer, such as before or after work hours. Your computer must be on for the scheduled backup to take place. If you are using removable media for the backup, you must be available to insert the discs as necessary.

If possible, you should keep the drive or media where the backup files are stored in a safe location away from your computer. For example, you may want to keep backup CDs or DVDs in a fireproof safe.

Backing up is not the same as making a copy of a file. If you have a few files that you want to copy for safekeeping, you can copy them to a removable device. However, backing up is the most efficient method of protecting all of your data files.

As mentioned, by default, Windows Vista adds only files that are new or have changed to the existing backup set. However, you can run a new, full backup at any time if you want. This can be useful if you want to create a second full backup in a different storage location. To perform a full backup, open the Backup and Restore Center. Click Change settings to open the Backup Status and Configuration window and click Change backup settings (the User Account Control dialog box will display). Click Next twice and then click to select the Create a new, full backup now in addition to saving settings checkbox. Then click Save settings and exit.

You can use the Back Up Files Wizard to create a backup of your entire PC. Called a Windows Complete PC Backup and Restore Image, it is an exact replica of the contents and configuration of your system, including program files, registry files, and the operating system files. You can use the Windows Complete PC Backup and Restore image to recreate your entire system if necessary. Microsoft recommends that you create a Windows Complete PC Backup and Restore Image soon after setting up your computer for the first time. To do so, open the Backup and Restore Center and click Back up computer. Follow the prompts to create the image. It may take a while, depending on your system configuration. Also, you must have enough storage space on the backup device.

In the next exercise, you learn how to restore files from a backup.

Restoring Files and Folders from a Backup

Chances are that sooner or later you will need to restore files and folders from a backup. You might accidentally delete a folder containing important files, your hard disk drive might fail, or your computer might be stolen or damaged. If you have maintained regular backups by using the Back Up Files Wizard, you can easily restore a single file, a group of files, or all of the files that you have backed up. In this exercise, you will delete and then restore the Wide World Data folder and the ***Sales1*** file.

RESTORE FILES AND FOLDERS FROM A BACKUP

USE the Backup and Restore Center you left open in the previous exercise.

1. Open the Documents folder and delete the ***Sales1*** file and the Wide World Data folder. Close the Documents folder.
2. In the Backup and Restore Center, under Restore files or your entire computer, click **Restore files**. The Restore Files Wizard opens. You can select to restore files from the latest backup, or from an older backup. The default is to use the latest backup.
3. Click **Next**. You can select to restore any or all files and folders from the backup.

TAKE NOTE If you backed up to removable media such as CD or DVD, Windows Vista may prompt you to insert the disc containing the backup set.

4. Click **Add files**. A folder window listing the files and folders that are in the latest backup file set opens. It should look similar to Figure 10-14. Although the specific folders and files depend on the files you backed up, the Wide World Data folder and the ***Sales1*** file should be displayed. At your instructor's request, capture an image of the window. Save it in your Lesson 10 assessment folder as ***Le10_05***.

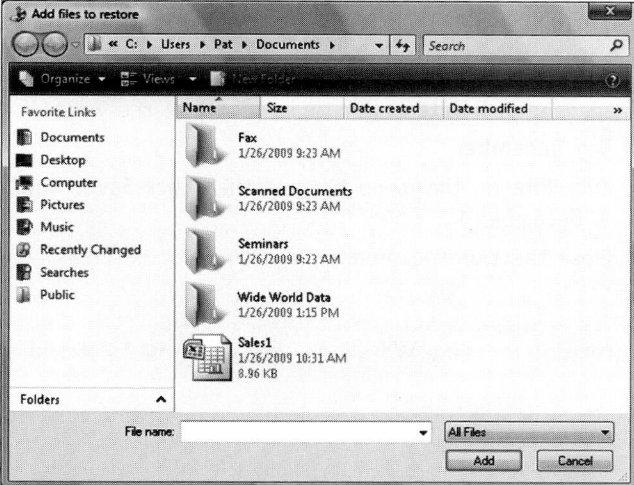

Figure 10-14
Select files to restore

5. Click to select the ***Sales1*** file and then click **Add**. The file is added to the list of files and folders to restore.
6. Click **Add folders**. Click to select the Wide World Data folder and then click Add. The folder is added to the list of files and folders to restore.
7. Click **Next**. You can now select where you want to save the restored files. The default option is in their original location, but you can enter any storage location available on your computer.
8. Click **Start restore**. Windows Vista restores the file and folder.
9. Click **Finish**.

CERTIFICATION READY? How do you restore files and folders from a backup file?
4.7.3

10. Close the Backup and Restore Center window.
11. Open the Documents folder. The Wide World Data folder and the ***Sales1*** file have been restored. Open the Wide World Data folder. The files it contained were restored as well.

PAUSE. LEAVE the Wide World Data folder open to use in the next exercise.

It is possible to restore files by using a backup made on a different computer, as long as you can provide a path to the backup file. For example, if you have a DVD that contains a backup made on a different computer, you can insert the DVD into your DVD drive and use it to restore files. Start from the Backup and Restore Center and then click Advanced restore (the User Account Control dialog box will display). Click Files from a backup made on a different computer and then follow the steps to restore the files.

In the next exercise, you restore a previous version of a file.

Restoring a Previous Version of a File

During a backup, Windows Vista automatically saves a previous version of all files and folders. Likewise, whenever Windows Vista creates a restore point, it saves shadow copies of your files and folders. ***Shadow copies*** are simply versions of a file or folder saved as part of a restore point. You can restore a previous version of a file or folder at any time using options in the item's Properties dialog box. For example, if you accidentally delete files from a folder, you can restore a previous version of the folder. The deleted items will be restored. If you accidentally edit a file without saving a copy, you can restore a version of the file from prior to when you made the edits. In this exercise, you will edit the ***Memo1*** file and save the changes. You will then restore a previous version of the file.

RESTORE A PREVIOUS VERSION OF A FILE

USE the Wide World Data folder you left open in the previous exercise.

1. Open the ***Memo1*** file in WordPad. To do this, you can right-click the file icon, click Open with, and then click WordPad.
2. Click to position the insertion point at the beginning of the word *October* and then press **Delete** seven times to delete the word.
3. Key **December**.
4. Click **File** on the menu bar and then click **Save**. Now, the date of the memo is December 11.
5. Close the WordPad program window.

X REF For information on using WordPad, refer to Lesson 2, "Working with Files and Folders."

6. In the Wide World Data folder, right-click the ***Memo1*** file and then click **Restore previous versions** on the shortcut menu. The Previous Versions tab of the Memo1 Properties dialog box displays, as shown in Figure 10-15. All available previous versions are listed, including shadow copies created with a restore point and backups created during a backup. At your instructor's request, capture an image of the Memo1 Properties dialog box. Save it in your Lesson 10 assessment folder as ***Le10_06***.

Figure 10-15

Previous Versions tab of the Memo1 Properties dialog box

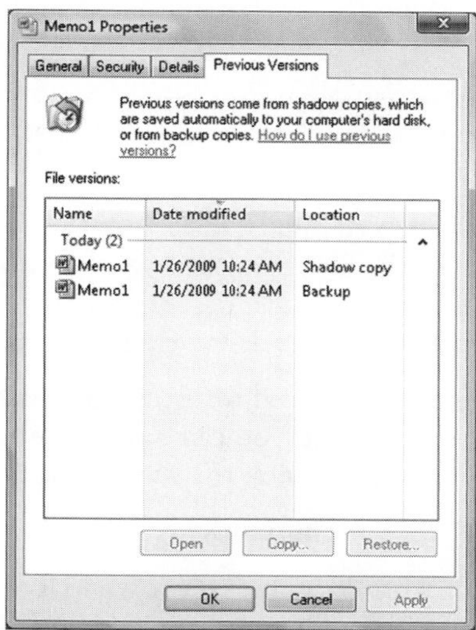

7. Click the version marked as Backup in the list and then click **Restore**.

TAKE NOTE* If the previous version is stored as part of a backup, you may have to insert the backup disc into the appropriate drive.

8. The Restore Files Wizard starts, and a Copy File dialog box displays asking if you want to replace the existing ***Memo1*** file.
9. Click **Copy and Replace**. Windows Vista restores the file. Click **Finish** to close the Restore Files Wizard.
10. Click **OK** to close the Memo1 Properties dialog box.
11. Open the ***Memo1*** file in WordPad. Note that the date is now October 11, which was the date in the previous version of the file, before you made the edits.
12. Close the WordPad window.
13. Navigate to the Documents window. Delete the ***Sales1*** file and the Wide World Data folder.
14. **CLOSE** the Documents folder.

LOG OFF your Windows Vista user account.

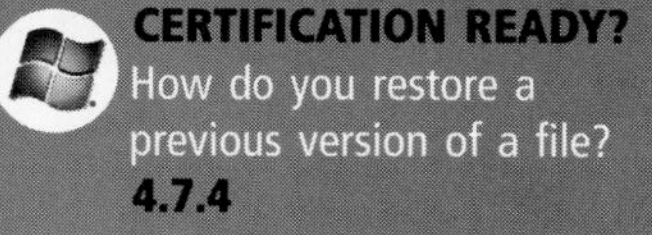

CERTIFICATION READY?
How do you restore a previous version of a file?
4.7.4

You cannot undo the action of restoring a previous version. Therefore, you might want to make a copy of a file or folder before restoring a previous version, or select the option to create a copy during the restore process. That way, you will have a copy of both versions of the file. Use descriptive file names to identify the versions, or store them in different locations.

When you restore a shadow copy of a file, the Restore Files Wizard does not start. Instead, when you select the shadow copy in the properties dialog box and click Restore, a Previous Versions dialog box displays asking you to confirm the operation. Click Restore to restore the file.

✳ Workplace Ready

Have a Backup Plan

You spend two weeks compiling data to create a report for the company president's annual speech to shareholders. On the morning you plan to print the report, the sprinkler system in your building malfunctions, flooding your office. You cannot start your computer, let alone access your hard drive. What now?

If you have a reliable backup system in place, you simply restore the files to a different computer and continue with your work. If you neglected to backup, you might be packing up your desk and revising your resume.

Whether you work alone on a desktop computer, travel using a notebook, or manage a network, a backup plan is vital for protecting the data that keeps your business up and running. Customers do not want to hear that you cannot fill an order because your hard drive failed. Employees want their paychecks, even if the payroll system was destroyed in a fire.

Windows Vista provides all the tools you need to set up and maintain a backup plan. With a little bit of organization and upfront effort, you can have a dependable, secure backup plan in place. In an emergency, you'll be glad you took the time to make it work.

When you create a backup plan for your business, keep these basic rules in mind:

- Start with a full system backup. It might take a while, but it is worth every minute if you ever need it. You can use Windows Complete PC Backup to create a complete backup of all your files, programs, and settings.
- Back up new and modified files daily.
- Test your backup and restore system as often as once a month to be sure it is working.
- Maintain regular restore points so you can use System Restore if your computer experiences problems.
- Store at least one full backup away from your computer in a secure location, such as a waterproof, fireproof safe. If you store the discs in your desk, they can be ruined by the same flood that damages your PC, or stolen by an unauthorized user.

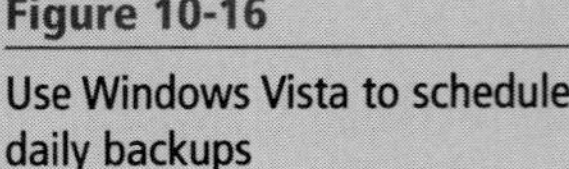

Figure 10-16

Use Windows Vista to schedule daily backups

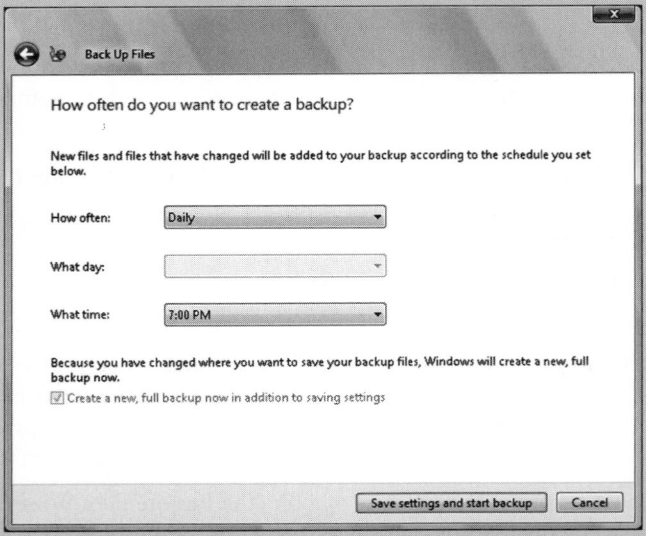

SUMMARY SKILL MATRIX

In this lesson you learned	Matrix Skill	Skill Number
To install a program	Install a software program	3.1.2
To change or repair a program	Repair a software installation	7.5.2
To uninstall a program	Uninstall a software program	3.1.3
To configure an older program to run under Windows Vista	Configure a program to use a compatibility mode	3.1.5
To shut down an unresponsive program	Identify and terminate unresponsive programs	7.5.1
To create a restore point	Create a restore point	3.1.1
To use a restore point	Restore the computer to a previous point	7.7.2
To schedule a backup	Schedule backups	4.7.2
To back up data	Back up files and folders	4.7.1
To restore files and folders from a backup	Restore files and folders from a backup file	4.7.3
To restore a previous version of a file	Restore a previous version of file	4.7.4

■ Knowledge Assessment

Fill in the Blank

Complete the following sentences by writing the correct word or words in the blanks provided.

1. A(n) ______________ file is a set of copies of files or folders created during a backup procedure.
2. A(n) ______________ point is a file that contains information about your system configuration at a particular point in time.
3. A(n) ______________ copy is a version of a file saved as part of a restore point.
4. A(n) ______________ program is not able to communicate with the user or with the operating system.
5. A(n) ______________ is a new and improved version of an existing program.
6. When you ______________ a program, you remove the program files from your computer.
7. The ______________ is a folder where system configuration data is stored.
8. When you ______________ a program, you copy program files from a source location to the hard drive on your computer.
9. A(n) ______________ disk is a CD or DVD that stores the files necessary for installing a program.
10. When you restore a file or folder, you copy a backup or previous version to its ______________ location.

True / False

Circle T if the statement is true or F if the statement is false.

T | F 1. You cannot uninstall a program that you install on your computer.

T | F 2. You can repair a program by reinstalling features that may not be working correctly.

T | F 3. You can run an older program in compatibility mode so that it works with Windows Vista.

T | F 4. The words *(Not Responding)* flash across the window of an unresponsive program.

T | F 5. You can use the Device Manager to end an unresponsive program.

T | F 6. You can undo the changes made during a System Restore.

T | F 7. You cannot manually create a restore point.

T | F 8. Scheduled backups start automatically at the scheduled time as long as the computer is turned on.

T | F 9. By default, files and folders are restored to their original storage locations.

T | F 10. You can undo the changes made when you restore a previous version of a file.

■ Competency Assessment

Project 10-1: Create a Restore Point

You work in the fundraising and development office of a small college. A technician is on his way over to install additional memory and a new DVD recorder in your computer. In case the installation causes problems, you decide to make sure System Protection is active and then to create a restore point. You also check the list of available restore points to make sure the new one is available.

GET READY. Before you begin these steps, start your computer and log on to your Windows Vista account. Close all open windows so you can see the desktop.

1. Click **Start** and then click **Computer**.
2. In the Computer window, click the **System Properties** button on the Computer window toolbar to open the System window in the Control Panel.
3. Under Tasks in the left pane, click **System protection**. If you are logged on to an administrator account, click **Continue**. If not, key an administrator password and then click **OK**.
4. Verify a checkmark is next to your local hard disk drive. If necessary, click to select the checkbox next to the disk.
5. Click the **Create** button.
6. Key **New Memory and DVD** and then click **Create**.
7. Click **OK**.
8. Click **OK** to close the System Properties dialog box.
9. Navigate to the main Control Panel window, if necessary, and then click **System and Maintenance**.
10. Click **Backup and Restore Center** and then, under Tasks in the left pane, click **Repair Windows using System Restore**. If you are logged on to an administrator account, click **Continue**. If not, key an administrator password and then click **OK**.
11. Click to select the **Choose a different restore point** option button and then click **Next**.
12. Locate the new restore point in the list.

13. At your instructor's request, capture an image of the window. Save it in your Lesson 10 assessment folder as ***Proj10_01***.
14. Click **Cancel** to close the System Restore window without making any changes.
15. **CLOSE** the Control Panel window.

    PAUSE. LEAVE the desktop displayed to use in the next project.

Project 10-2: New Software

Your friend Terry has given you some files to look at, but you do not have a compatible program installed. You have purchased a new software program that you can use to open and view the files. Before you install it, you copy Terry's files to your computer and then quickly back up any new or modified files by using the existing backup settings. You then install the program.

GET READY. Before you begin these steps, make sure you have the installation disk for a new software program, or access to the installation files on a network. Also, you must have a compatible backup storage device, such as an external hard drive, writable CD or DVD drive, or access to a network location.

The ***Picture1***, ***Picture2***, and ***Picture3*** files are available on the companion CD-ROM.

1. Open Documents and create a new folder named Terry.
2. Copy the ***Picture1*** and ***Picture2*** files from the data files for this lesson to the Terry folder. Copy the ***Picture3*** file from the data files for this lesson to the Documents folder. Close the folder window. (You will use these files again in Project 10-6.)
3. Click **Start** and then click **Control Panel**. Under System and Maintenance, click **Back up your computer** to open the Backup and Restore Center.
4. Click **Back up files**. If you are logged on to an administrator account, click **Continue**. If not, key an administrator password and then click **OK**.
5. When the backup is complete, click **Close**.
6. Close the Backup and Restore Center.
7. Insert the installation disk for the program you want to install into the appropriate drive in your computer. For example, if the disk is a DVD, insert it into a DVD drive. If the disk is a CD, insert it into a CD drive. Alternatively, open a window for the network location where the installation file is stored and then double-click the installation file.
8. If the AutoPlay dialog box displays, click the option to run the setup program. For example, click Run Setup.exe.
9. If Windows Vista cannot identify the publisher of the program, it will display a User Account Control dialog box. Click **Allow**.
10. In the program's Installation or Setup Wizard, click **Next** and follow the prompts through all of the screens, selecting options and keying data as necessary.
11. When you have completed all of the screens, click the **Install** button to install the program.
12. When the installation is complete, click **Finish**. If necessary, restart your computer and log back in to your Windows Vista account.
13. Click **Start** and then click **Control Panel**. Click **Programs** and then click **Programs and Features**.
14. Locate the newly installed program in the list of programs. At your instructor's request, capture an image of the window. Save it in your Lesson 10 assessment folder as ***Proj10_02***.
15. **CLOSE** the Control Panel window.

    PAUSE. LEAVE the desktop displayed to use in the next project.

■ Proficiency Assessment

Project 10-3: Use System Restore

At your small college, the technician completed installing the memory and the DVD burner, and you are not happy with the system's sluggish performance. You decide to try using System Restore to revert to a previous system configuration. When that does not help, you undo the System Restore.

1. Click **Start**, click **Control Panel**, and then click **System and Maintenance**. The System and Maintenance window displays.
2. Click **Backup and Restore Center** and then, under Tasks in the left pane, click **Repair Windows using System Restore.** If you are logged on to an administrator account, click **Continue.** If not, key an administrator password and then click **OK.**
3. Click to select the **Choose a different restore point** option button and then click **Next.**
4. Select the **New Memory and DVD** restore point you created in Project 10-1.
5. Click **Next.**
6. Click **Finish** and then click **Yes** in the warning dialog box.
7. When your system restarts, log in to your Windows Vista user account.
8. Click Close and then close any open windows.
9. Click **Start**, click **Control Panel**, and then click **System and Maintenance.** Click **Backup and Restore Center** and then, under Tasks in the left pane, click **Repair Windows using System Restore.** If you are logged on to an administrator account, click **Continue.** If not, key an administrator password and then click **OK.**
10. Click **Next**, confirm the restore point is to undo the System Restore, and then click **Finish.**
11. Click **Yes.**
12. When your system restarts, log in to your Windows Vista user account.
13. When the System Restore is complete, click **Close** to close the dialog box. Then close any open windows.

PAUSE. LEAVE the desktop displayed to use in the next project.

Project 10-4: Modify a Software Installation

Some of the features of your new software program are not available or not working correctly. In this project, you try to change the installation and then repair it. When it still does not work, you uninstall it completely.

1. Click **Start** and then click **Control Panel.** Click **Programs** and then click **Programs and Features.**
2. Click the name of the program you installed in Project 10-2 to select it.
3. Click the **Change** button, or the **Uninstall/Change** button, on the window's toolbar. Click **Continue**, or if you are not logged in using an administrator account, key an administrator's password and then click **OK.**
4. Click **Next.**
5. Click the **Modify** option button and then click **Next.**
6. Follow the prompts to select features that are not already installed and then click **Next.** If necessary, insert the installation disk, or select the folder where the setup files are stored, and then click **OK.**
7. When the modification is complete, click **Finish.**

8. Click the **Repair** button on the Programs and Features toolbar, if it is available, or click the **Change** button, or the **Uninstall/Change** button. If you are logged in using an administrator account, click **Continue**. If you are not logged in using an administrator account, key an administrator's password and then click **OK** to continue.
9. Click to select the **Repair** option button and then click **Next**. If necessary, insert the installation disk, or select the folder where the setup files are stored, and then click **OK**.
10. When the repair is complete, click **Finish**.
11. Click the **Uninstall** button. If the Uninstall button is not available, click the **Uninstall/Change** button. If you are logged in using an administrator account, click **Continue**. If you are not logged in using an administrator account, key an administrator's password and then click **OK**.
12. If you clicked the Uninstall button, click **Yes** in the Programs and Features dialog box. If necessary, click **Allow** in the User Account Control dialog box. If you clicked the Uninstall/Change button, click the **Remove** option button and then click **Next**. Follow the prompts to select options and start the uninstall process.
13. When the program is uninstalled, click **Finish** to close the Installation or Setup Wizard.
14. **CLOSE** the Programs and Features window.

PAUSE. LEAVE the desktop displayed to use in the next project.

■ Mastery Assessment

Project 10-5: Test a Software Program

The regional sales manager for Wide World Importers has asked you to test a new software program. In this project, you will change the backup setting and back up new and modified files. You will then install the program. You will use the automatic system event restore point to revert to a configuration prior to installing the program.

1. Open the Backup and Restore Center.
2. Open the Backup Status and Configuration window.
3. Select to change your backup settings.
4. Select the backup storage location, select all file types, and schedule automatic backups for every day at **6:00 PM**. At your instructor's request, capture an image of the Backup Files window. Save it in your Lesson 10 assessment folder as ***Proj10_05***.
5. Save the settings and exit. Then close the Backup Status and Configuration window.
6. **Back up** your new or modified files and then close all open windows.
7. **Install** a new software program and then test it to make sure it starts correctly. Close it.
8. Use System Restore to revert to the restore point prior to when you installed the new software program.
9. Change the automatic backup schedule back to the default Weekly, Sundays, at 1:00 AM, or to whatever the regularly scheduled backup is for your system.
10. **CLOSE** all open windows.

PAUSE. LEAVE the desktop displayed to use in the next project.

Project 10-6: Optimize Performance

You have told your friend Terry that you do not want to reinstall the software program, so you cannot help her with the files. You then delete the files. Terry calls and asks you to send her back the files. You use Restore to restore the files so that you can return them.

1. Open the Documents folder and delete the Terry folder and the ***Picture3*** file.
2. Close the Documents folder.
3. Open the Backup and Restore Center.
4. Select to restore files from the latest backup.
5. Select to restore the Terry folder and the ***Picture3*** file and then restore the file and folder to their original storage location.
6. Check to be sure you have restored the version of the files that Terry sent you originally. If necessary, restore previous versions.
7. Move the ***Picture3*** file into the Terry folder.
8. At your instructor's request, move the Terry folder to a removable device or to your Lesson 10 assessment folder, and then delete it from the Documents folder.
9. **CLOSE** all open windows.

   LOG OFF your Windows Vista user account.

INTERNET READY

In 2007, Microsoft Corp. released Windows Vista, the latest in a long line of Windows operating system products. The product line started in 1985, when Microsoft released Windows 1.0. In this exercise, use Internet search tools to locate information about personal computer operating systems, and Microsoft Windows in particular. For example, you might research the history of personal computers, the evolution of Windows, the technology required to create Windows, or the impact Windows has had on business, home computing, or even on society. When you have finished your research, use a word processing program or a pen and paper to write a report about the Windows operating system.

Monitoring the Windows Vista Environment

LESSON SKILL MATRIX

Skills	Matrix Skill	Skill Number
Setting Up a User Account		
Creating a Password-Protected User Account	Create a standard password-protected local user account	1.6.1
Creating a New Account Using Microsoft Management Console	Require a new user to change his or her password when logging on for the first time	1.6.2
Disabling a User Account	Disable a local user account	1.6.3
Managing Windows Firewall		
Viewing Windows Firewall Status	Display the status of Windows Firewall	1.1.1
Setting Windows Firewall Exceptions	Configure the firewall access for specific programs	1.1.2
Monitoring Your System for Malicious Software		
Viewing the Status of Antispyware and Antivirus Programs	Display the status of spyware-protection and virus-protection programs	1.2.1
Updating and Scanning with Windows Defender	Monitor all programs running on a computer by using Windows Defender; Install a software update	1.2.4 3.1.4
Using Real-Time Protection	Monitor all programs running on a computer by using Windows Defender; Choose not to monitor specific programs; Remove or restore programs blocked by Windows Defender	1.2.4 1.2.5 1.2.2
Using Software Explorer	Remove, enable, or disable programs running on a computer	1.2.3
Using Windows Update		
Customizing Automatic Update Settings	Configure automatic update settings	1.3.1
Manually Updating Windows Vista and Viewing Installed Updates	Manually update Windows Vista; Display a list of installed updates	1.3.2 1.3.3
Troubleshooting Startup Problems		
Using Advanced Startup Options	Use advanced startup options	7.7.1
Repairing the Windows Vista Installation	Repair the Windows Vista installation	7.7.3

Trey Research is a market research company. The nearly 80 employees use Windows Vista–based computers, some standalone systems and some that are networked. It is the responsibility of the system administrator and her assistant to ensure that all systems remain secure. They use Windows Vista's user account management tools to control who has access to files and programs, and they use Windows Vista's Security Center to monitor the status of programs, protect the system from malicious software, and to keep Windows Vista up-to-date. In this lesson, you learn how to use Windows Vista to set up and maintain a user account, to monitor and configure Windows Vista's security tools, and to monitor and maintain the Windows Vista operating system software.

KEY TERMS

Account owner
Administrator account
Boot
Definitions
Firewall
Guest account
Password hint
Password reset disk
Quarantine
Safe mode
Spyware
Standard account
Virus

■ Setting Up a User Account

THE BOTTOM LINE

Every person—or user—who uses a computer running Windows Vista has a user account. As you learned in Lesson 1, "Getting Started," a user account is a collection of information that tells Windows Vista what files and folders a user can access, what changes that user can make to the computer, and that user's personal preferences for his or her desktop settings. User accounts make it possible for multiple people to share access to a system while maintaining their own private data and customized work environment. Only an administrator can create and delete user accounts. The ***account owner***, who is the person assigned to use the account, or an administrator can customize the account at any time. To quickly create or customize a user account, you can use the User Accounts features in the Control Panel. For more advanced options that provide added control, you can use the Microsoft Management Console. In this section, you learn how to use the Control Panel to set up a password-protected user account, customize an account, and delete an account. You also learn how to use the Microsoft Management Console to create and disable an account.

Creating a Password-Protected User Account

Anyone with an administrator account or an administrator's password can create a new user account. An ***administrator account*** provides access to all programs and files on the system. Administrators can make changes that will affect other users, including installing and uninstalling software and hardware, and creating or modifying other user accounts. Most user accounts are ***standard accounts***, which means the user can access most programs and personal data files installed on the system but cannot install or uninstall software and hardware, delete system files, or change settings that affect other users without first keying an administrator's password. When Trey Research hires a new employee, a system administrator sets up a new user account. In this exercise, you create a new standard account and then assign a password to the account.

CREATE A PASSWORD-PROTECTED USER ACCOUNT

GET READY. Before you begin these steps, start your computer and log on to your Windows Vista account. Close all open windows so you can see the desktop. Create a new folder named Lesson 11 in a storage location specified by your instructor, where you can store assessment files and folders that you create during this lesson.

1. Click **Start** and then click **Control Panel**.
2. Under User Accounts and Family Safety, click **Add or remove user accounts**. A User Account Control dialog box displays. If you are logged in to an administrator account, click **Continue**. If you are not logged in using an administrator account, key an administrator's password and then click **OK** to continue. The Manage Accounts window displays. It lists the accounts set up on your system. At least one account is an administrator account, and there may be a guest account as well, although it may not be active. A ***guest account*** is available for people who do not usually use the computer or network. That person can use the guest account to log in to Windows Vista but cannot access data files, install software or hardware, or change settings.
3. In the Manage Accounts window, click **Create a new account** to open the Create New Account window. It should look similar to Figure 11-1. In this window, you name the new account and select the account type.

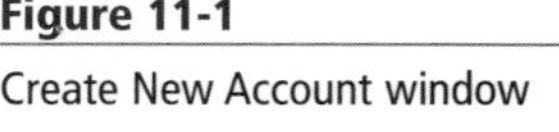

Figure 11-1

Create New Account window

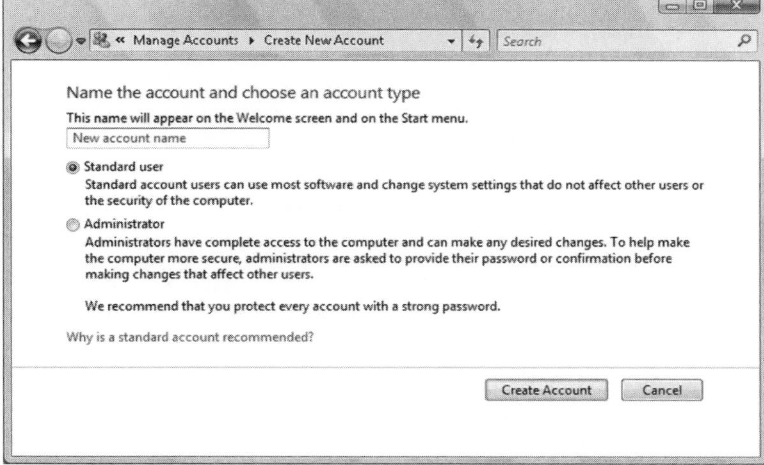

4. In the New account name text box, key **Alice Ciccu**, the employee's name. Verify that the Standard user account option button is selected.
5. Click **Create Account**. Windows Vista creates the account and displays it in the Manage Accounts window. The window should look similar to Figure 11-2, although the specific accounts and pictures depend on the accounts set up on your computer.

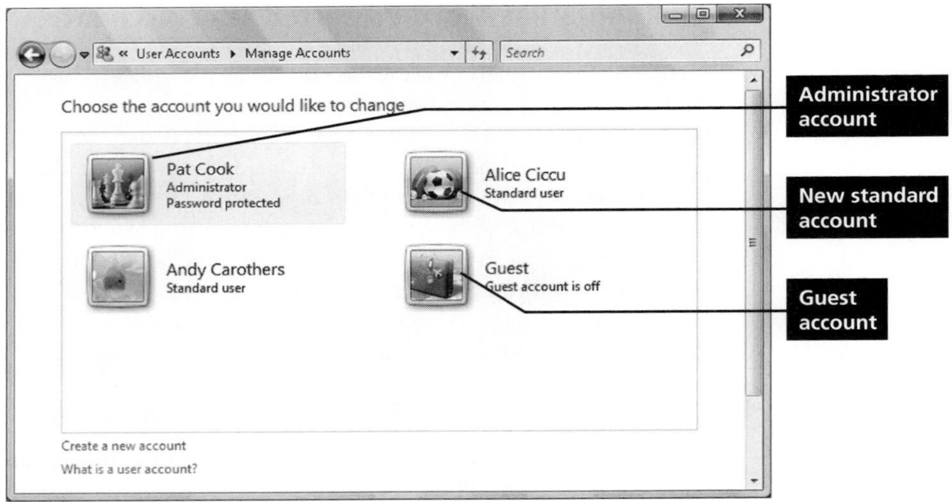

Figure 11-2

Manage Accounts window

TAKE NOTE Pictures are randomly assigned to user accounts. Changing the account picture is covered in the next exercise.

6. Click **Alice Ciccu**. The Change an Account window displays, listing all account aspects that you can change.
7. Click **Create a password** to open the Create Password window, shown in Figure 11-3.

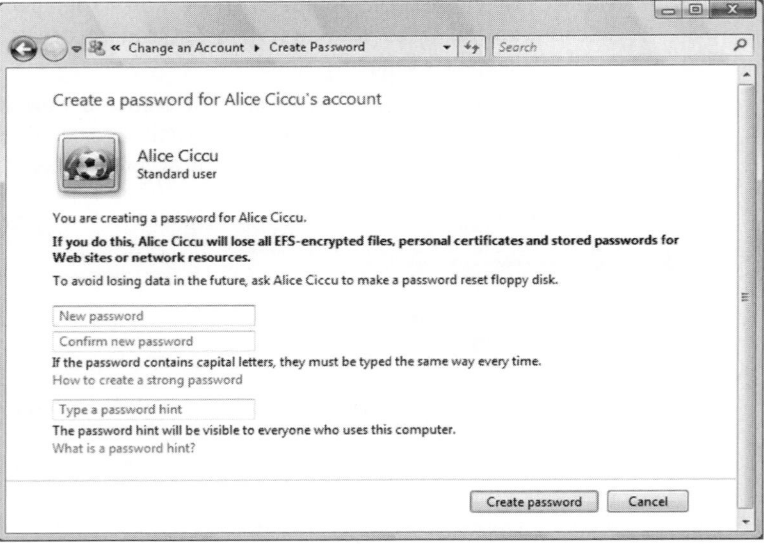

Figure 11-3

Create Password window

8. In the New Password text box, key **AC!hrPW001**. Notice as you type that black dots display in the text box in place of the actual characters. This is a security measure to prevent an unauthorized user from seeing the password.
9. Click in the **Confirm new password** text box and key **AC!hrPW001**. Then click **Create password**. The password is assigned to the user account. To log in to the account, the user must key the password.
10. Close the **Change an Account** window and then log off your Windows Vista user account. The Alice Ciccu account should display on the Welcome page.

TROUBLESHOOTING If you are working on a networked system or a domain, the Welcome screen may not display. If you cannot access the Alice Ciccu account to log in, log back in to your own user account and skip the rest of this exercise.

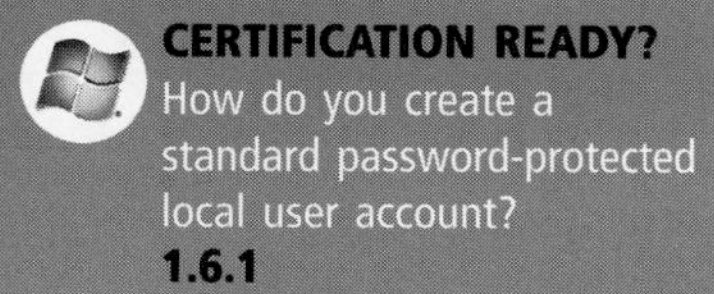

CERTIFICATION READY? How do you create a standard password-protected local user account? **1.6.1**

11. Click the **Alice Ciccu** account. A password text box displays. Key **AC!hrPW001** and then press **Enter** to log on to the new account. Because this is the first time the account is being used, Windows Vista uses the default settings to set up and display the desktop.

PAUSE. Stay logged on to the Alice Ciccu account and leave the desktop displayed to use in the next exercise.

As covered in this exercise, there are three types of user accounts:

- Administrator, which provides access to all programs and files and allows the administrator to make changes that affect all users, including installing and uninstalling hardware and software, as well as creating and managing user accounts.
- Standard, which provides access to most programs and to personal files. Standard users cannot install or uninstall software and hardware, or change settings that affect other users.
- Guest, which provides access to programs. Guest users may create new data files and use Internet connections.

When you set up Windows Vista for the first time, you must create at least one administrator account. Microsoft recommends that you password-protect all accounts, and that you create at least one standard account to use for everyday computing. Note that even while you are using a standard account, you can access features and tools available to administrators by keying an administrator password in the User Account Control dialog box.

A user name does not have to be a person's actual name. It may be a nickname, an alias, or any name the user wants assigned to the account. There are some rules for creating user names and passwords. A user name must be unique, which means there cannot be an identical user name on the computer, or, in a networked environment, on the network. A user name may have up to twenty characters. It can include spaces, but cannot include any of the following sixteen characters: " / \ [ ] : ; | = , + * ? < > @.

A password can have up to fourteen characters, including letters, numbers, symbols, and spaces. It is case sensitive, which means if you create it using lowercase or uppercase letters, you must key those lowercase or uppercase letters when you log in.

In the next section, you learn how to create a password reset disk that you can use to log in to an account even if you do not know the password.

✳ Workplace Ready

Using a Strong Password

A password is a simple yet effective method of preventing unauthorized users from accessing your computer. Unfortunately, most people select a password that is easy to remember, such as a birthday or pet's name. You can bet that if a password is easy to remember, it is also easy for the bad guys to guess.

As an individual, you can do your part to secure your computer system by creating a strong password for your own Windows Vista user account. As a system administrator, you can use Windows Vista's Account Policies feature to establish a password policy that requires all employees to use strong passwords.

According to Microsoft, a strong password follows these rules:

- Has at least eight characters
- Does not include the user name, real name, or company name
- Does not include any complete words
- Contains a combination of uppercase letters, lowercase letters, numbers, and special characters, such as punctuation marks and spaces

With Windows Vista, system administrators can set password policies that include the following:

- Password age requirements that force users to change passwords at regular intervals
- Complexity requirements to ensure that all passwords have at least six characters, including a combination of at least three uppercase letters, lowercase letters, numbers, and special characters
- Password history requirements that prevent users from creating a new password that is the same as an old password.
- Password length requirements that set a minimum number of characters for a password

Creating a Password Reset Disk

You may have noticed in the Create Password window that Windows Vista suggests that all users create a ***password reset disk***, which is a removable device such as a CD or flash drive on which Windows Vista stores information about your password. If you forget your password, you can use the password reset disk to create a new password so you can log in to your user account. It is a good idea to create a password reset disk whenever you create a new password or change your password. You can create a password reset disk for the account to which you are currently logged in. In this exercise, you create a password reset disk for Alice Ciccu.

CREATE A PASSWORD RESET DISK

GET READY. To create a password reset disk, you must have a removable device such as a CD or USB flash drive. Before beginning this exercise, insert the device into the appropriate drive or connect it to the appropriate port. For example, insert a CD in a CD drive or connect a USB flash drive to a USB port. Cancel the AutoPlay dialog box, if necessary.

1. Click **Start** and then click **Control Panel.**
2. Click **User Accounts and Family Safety** and then click **User Accounts.**

3. In the left pane, click **Create a password reset disk.** The Forgotten Password Wizard opens. This wizard will prompt you through the steps for creating a password reset disk.
4. Click **Next.**
5. Click the dropdown arrow and select the location of your removable device. Then click **Next.**
6. Key the password for the current account—**AC!hrPW001**—and then click **Next.** Windows Vista creates the password reset disk.
7. When the progress is 100% complete, click **Next** and then click **Finish.**
8. Remove the device from the drive or the port.
9. Close all open windows.
10. Log off the Alice Ciccu account and log back in to your own user account. Close all open windows.

PAUSE. LEAVE the desktop displayed to use in the next exercise.

You do not have to use a blank device to create a password reset disk. The password information will be added to the device; it will not overwrite existing data.

You should store a password reset disk in a safe place so that if you forget your password, you can use it to log in to your account. Keep in mind that anyone who finds the disk can use it to reset your password and log in to your account. Not only would that put your data at risk, it would jeopardize all data and programs on the computer and possibly keep you from accessing your system.

To reset your password, type an incorrect password when logging in to the account or press Enter without typing any password. In the dialog box that displays, click OK to continue and then click Reset password. Insert or connect your password reset disk and follow the prompts in the Password Reset Wizard to create a new password.

If an administrator resets a password without using a password reset disk, the user may lose access to encrypted files and email messages, as well as stored passwords for websites or network resources. Resetting a password is not the same as changing a password in the Change Password window. You can safely change a password at any time.

In the next exercise, you learn how to customize a user account by changing the password and the picture.

Customizing a User Account

If you have an administrator account, you can customize any user account on the system by changing the password, the account type, or the picture. Without an administrator account, you can customize your own account by changing the password or picture. In this exercise, you change the password and picture assigned to the Alice Ciccu account.

CUSTOMIZE A USER ACCOUNT

1. Click **Start** and then click **Control Panel.**
2. Under User Accounts and Family Safety, click **Add or remove user accounts.** In the User Account Controls dialog box, if you are logged in to an administrator account, click **Continue.** If you are not logged in using an administrator account, key an administrator's password and then click **OK** to continue. The Manage Accounts window displays.
3. Click the **Alice Ciccu** account. This is the account you want to change.

4. In the Change an Account window, click **Change the picture.** The Choose Picture window displays. It lists a selection of pictures that come with Windows Vista, as shown in Figure 11-4.

Figure 11-4

Select a new account picture

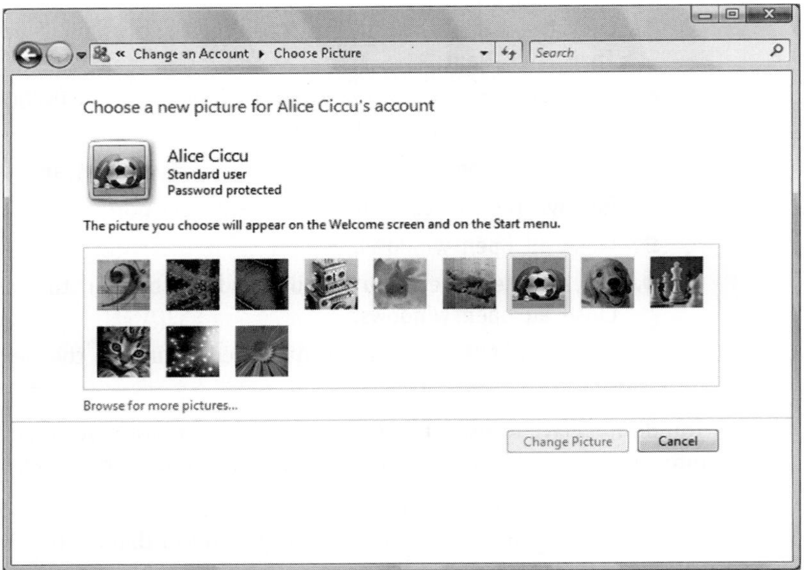

5. Click the orange flower picture and then click **Change Picture** to apply the change and return to the Change an Account window. The selected picture is now assigned to the account.

TAKE NOTE*

You can assign any picture file stored on your computer to an account. In the Change Picture window, click Browse for more pictures, locate and select the picture file, and then click Open.

6. Click **Change the password** to display the Change Password window.
7. In the New password text box, key **AC!hrPW002**.
8. Click in the Confirm new password text box and key **AC!hrPW002** again and then click **Change password.** The new password is now assigned to the Alice Ciccu user account.
9. At this point, your instructor may ask you to capture an image of the Change an Account window. Save it in your Lesson 11 assessment folder as ***Le11_01***.
10. In the Change an Account window, click **Delete the account.** The Delete Account window displays. You have the option of removing or keeping all of the files associated with the account. Keep the files if you want to make the files available for the user on this or a different computer. Delete the files if no one is ever going to use them again.
11. Click **Delete Files** and then click **Delete Account.** The Alice Ciccu account and all associated files are removed from the computer. The Manage Accounts window displays. Notice that the Alice Ciccu account is no longer listed with the other accounts.
12. **CLOSE** the Manage Accounts window.

PAUSE. LEAVE the desktop displayed to use in the next exercise.

You may be wondering why you used a seemingly obscure string of characters as the password for the Alice Ciccu account. A strong password that is difficult for an unauthorized user to guess helps protect your data files and the system files. What seems obscure to you will be obscure to the unauthorized user as well.

You can assign a ***password hint*** to an account to help you remember a password. A password hint is a word or phrase that reminds you of the password, without specifying the password itself. When you create or change a password, key the password hint in the Type a password hint text box before you click the Create password button. A link to the password hint will display on the Welcome or logon screen next to your user account logon information. Keep in mind that anyone can click the link to see the hint.

If you do not want to use a password, you can remove it from the account or simply never create one. To remove a password, open the Change Password window. Leave the New password and Confirm new password text boxes blank and then click the Create password button. Without a password, anyone can log in to the User Account. Microsoft recommends that all accounts be protected by a password to help safeguard your data and programs.

In the next section, you learn how to require a new user to change his or her password and how to temporarily disable a user account without deleting it.

Creating a New Account using Microsoft Management Console

For added control, administrators can use the Microsoft Management Console to create user accounts. The Microsoft Management Console provides options that are not available directly from the Control Panel, such as the ability to require a new user to change a password the first time he or she logs on. In this exercise, you create a new account using the Microsoft Management Console.

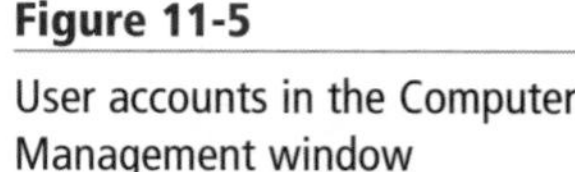

TAKE NOTE User account settings are only available for the Business, Enterprise, and Ultimate editions of Windows Vista. If you are using the Starter, Home Basic, or Home Premium edition, you will not be able to complete this exercise.

CREATE A NEW ACCOUNT USING MICROSOFT MANAGEMENT CONSOLE

1. Click **Start**, click **Control Panel**, click **System and Maintenance**, and then click **Administrative Tools**.
2. In the File list, double-click **Computer Management**. In the User Account Controls dialog box, if you are logged in to an administrator account, click **Continue**. If you are not logged in using an administrator account, key an administrator's password and then click **OK** to continue. The Computer Management window opens.
3. In the Navigation pane of the Computer Management window click the expand arrow to the left of **Local Users and Groups** and then click **Users** in the expanded list. A list of existing accounts displays in the File list. The window should look similar to Figure 11-5, although the actual accounts will be the accounts set up on your system.

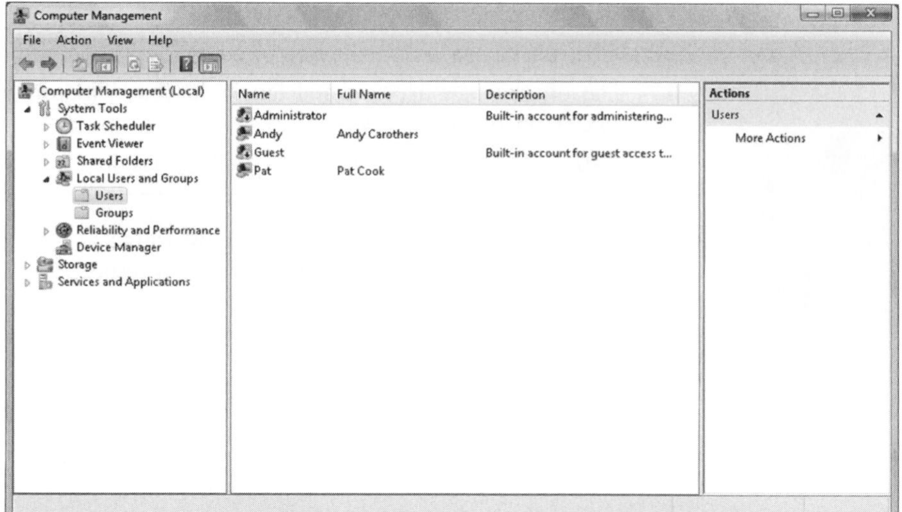

Figure 11-5

User accounts in the Computer Management window

4. Right-click a blank area of the File list and click **New User** on the shortcut menu. The New User dialog box displays, as shown in Figure 11-6. In this dialog box, you can create a new user account by assigning an account name and password. You can also select options for controlling the account.

Figure 11-6

New User dialog box

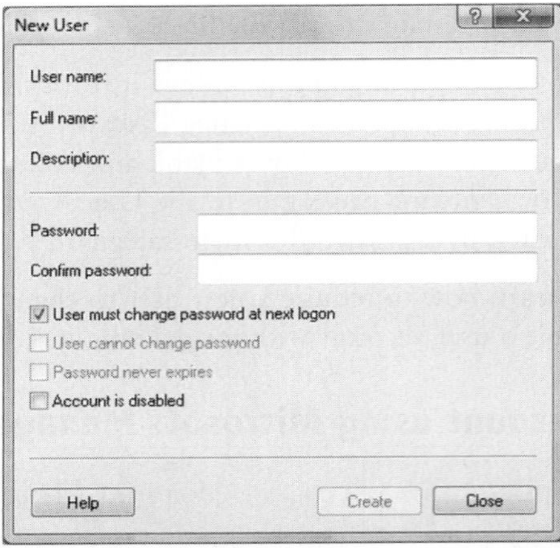

5. In the User Name text box, key **Deb Core.** In the Full name text box, key **Deborah Louise Core.** Leave the Full name text box and in the Description text box key **Marketing Assistant.**
6. In the Password text box, key **CLD?maTR001.**
7. In the Confirm password text box, key **CLD?maTR001.**
8. Verify that the **User must change password at next logon** checkbox is selected. If not, click it to select it. At your instructor's request, capture an image of the dialog box. Save it in your Lesson 11 assessment folder as ***Le11_02***.
9. Click **Create.** Windows Vista creates the account and displays a blank New User dialog box so you can create additional accounts, if necessary.
10. Click **Close** to close the dialog box. Notice that the new account displays in the Computer Management window File list.
11. Close all open windows and log off your Windows Vista user account.
12. From the Welcome or Logon screen, click the **Deb Core** account. In the Password text box, key **CLD?msTR001** and then press **Enter**. Windows Vista displays a message that the user must change the password to log on.
13. Click **OK.**
14. In the New password text box, key **DC!pw002?**
15. In the Confirm password text box, key **DC!pw002?** and then press **Enter**. Windows Vista changes the password.
16. Click **OK** to log on to the new account.
17. Log off the new account and log in to your Windows Vista user account. **CLOSE** all open windows.

PAUSE. LEAVE the desktop displayed to use in the next exercise.

TAKE NOTE*

Windows Vista offers you the option of creating a new password reset disk when you change the password.

CERTIFICATION READY?

How do you require a new user to change his or her password when logging on for the first time?

1.6.2

Requiring a new user to change his or her password is a security measure that is particularly useful in an environment where an administrator is responsible for creating user accounts. The administrator can provide the original password so that the user can access the system, but the user can set a new password to ensure his or her privacy.

Administrators can also help control access to a computer or network by setting rules for the types of passwords that users can create and by setting password expiration dates. Password rules specify the number and type of characters that must be included in a password. Password expiration dates specify how frequently a user must change his or her password.

You select password policy settings using the Local Security Policy feature, which is part of the Microsoft Management Console. Click Start>Control Panel>System and Maintenance>Administrative Tools. In the Administrative Tools window, double-click Local Security Policy. (Click Continue or key an administrator's password and then click OK.) In the Navigation pane, click Account Policies and then double-click Password Policy in the File list. A list of available password policy options displays in the File list. Double-click an option to open its properties dialog box, set a new value, and then click OK. Click the Explain tab to view a description of the option and the recommended setting.

In the next exercise, you disable the Deb Core account.

Disabling a User Account

To temporarily stop access to a user account, you can disable the account. A disabled account is not displayed on the Welcome or Log on Screen, so it cannot be used to log on to the computer. Disabling an account is not the same as deleting it, because the account still exists on the system. When you are ready to allow access again, you can enable the account. In this exercise, you disable and then enable the Deb Core Account. You also delete the account.

DISABLE A USER ACCOUNT

1. Click **Start**, click **Control Panel**, click **System and Maintenance**, and then click **Administrative Tools.**
2. In the File list, double-click **Computer Management.** In the User Account Controls dialog box, if you are logged in to an administrator account, click **Continue.** If you are not logged in using an administrator account, key an administrator's password and then click **OK** to continue. The Computer Management window opens.
3. In the Navigation pane, click **Local Users and Groups** and then double-click |**Users** in the File list. A list of existing accounts displays in the File list.
4. Double-click **Deb Core** in the File list. The Properties dialog box for the selected account displays. In this dialog box, you can modify the full name and description, as well as select options for controlling the account.
5. Click to select the **Account is disabled** checkbox and then click **Apply** to apply the change and leave the dialog box open. At your instructor's request, capture an image of the dialog box. Save it in your Lesson 11 assessment folder as ***Le11_03***.
6. Select to switch user accounts without logging off (click **Start**, click the arrow to the right of the Lock button, and then click **Switch User**). The Welcome or Log on Screen displays. The Deb Core account is not available because it has been disabled.
7. Log back in to your Windows Vista user account.
8. Double-click **Deb Core** in the Computer Management window File list to open its Properties dialog box.
9. Click to deselect the **Account is disabled** checkbox and then click **OK.** This account is enabled again, so it can be used to log in to the system.
10. Close the Computer Management window and the Administrative Tools window. The Control Panel System and Maintenance window should still be open.
11. In the left pane of the Control Panel window, click **User Accounts and Family Safety** and then click **User Accounts.**
12. Click **Manage another account.** If necessary, click **Continue** in the User Account Control dialog box, or key an administrator's password, and then click **OK** to continue. Click the **Deb Core** account. You are going to delete this account.

TROUBLESHOOTING If the Deb Core account is not listed in the Manage Accounts window, it is still disabled. Repeat steps 8 and 9 to enable the account.

CERTIFICATION READY?
How do you disable a local user account?
1.6.3

13. Click **Delete the account.**
14. Click **Delete Files** and then click **Delete Account.** The Deb Core account and all associated files are removed from the computer.
15. **CLOSE** the Manage Accounts window.

PAUSE. LEAVE the desktop displayed to use in the next exercise.

You may need to disable an account if a user will be away from the office for any length of time, such as a vacation, sabbatical, illness, or disability leave, or if you suspect an unauthorized user has been accessing it.

In the next section, you learn how to manage Windows Firewall.

■ Managing Windows Firewall

THE BOTTOM LINE

A ***firewall*** is software that limits access between a computer and a network, or between a network and a different network. It is usually used to protect a computer or network from outside or unauthorized access, and some firewalls can stop a computer from spreading malicious software to a computer on a different network. Windows Vista includes the Windows Firewall security tool. It is active by default, but you can change the settings to allow some programs to communicate through the firewall barrier. At Trey Research, for example, Windows Firewall is always active so that it protects the system from unauthorized access. However, unless the company's instant message program is marked as an exception, the default firewall settings might block it from communicating with users on the Internet. In this section, you learn how to check the status of Windows Firewall and how to configure Windows Firewall to allow access to selected programs.

Viewing Windows Firewall Status

You can view the status of Windows Firewall in the Windows Firewall window in the Control Panel. If Windows Firewall is active, the status is On. If Windows Firewall is not active, the status is Off. You can change the Windows Firewall status in the Windows Firewall Settings dialog box. In this exercise, you check the status in the Windows Firewall window.

VIEW WINDOWS FIREWALL STATUS

1. Click **Start**, click **Control Panel**, and then click **Security**.
2. Click **Windows Firewall.** The Windows Firewall window opens, as shown in Figure 11-7. This window displays the current status of Windows Firewall and provides access to the Windows Firewall Setting dialog box, where you can select options to change the Windows Firewall configuration.

Figure 11-7

Windows Firewall window

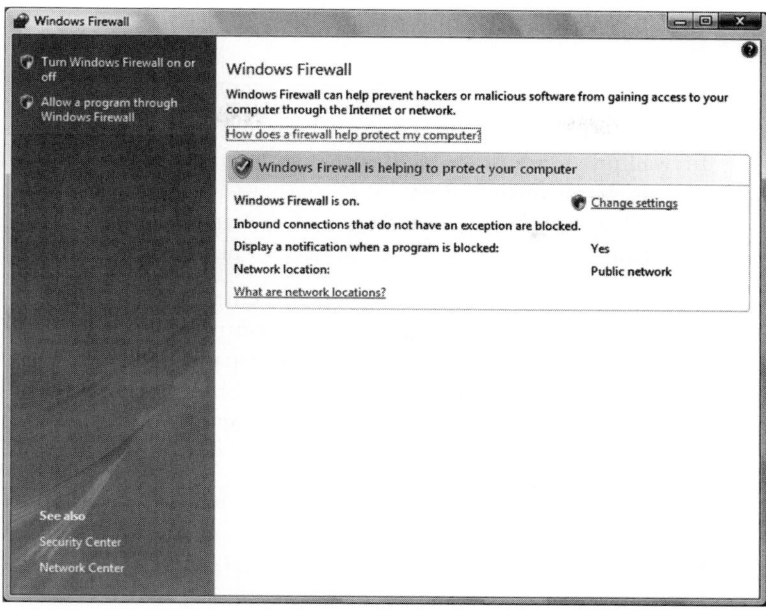

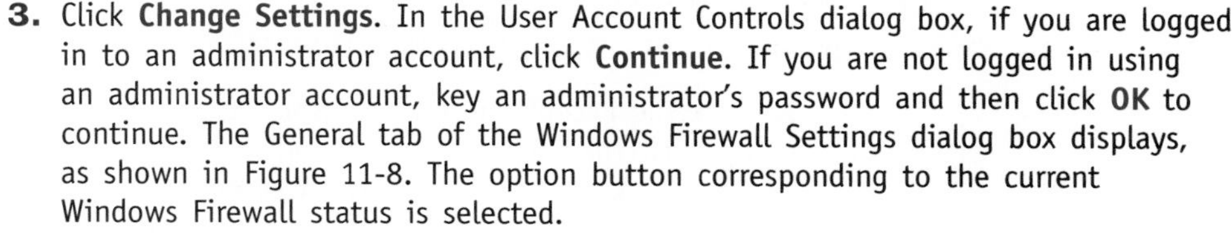

You can also view the status of Windows Firewall in the Security Center. To open the Security Center click Start>Control Panel. Then, under Security, click Check this computer's security status.

TAKE NOTE*

You may have a different firewall program installed and active on your computer. If so, Windows Firewall will be off because only one firewall is required to protect your computer.

3. Click **Change Settings.** In the User Account Controls dialog box, if you are logged in to an administrator account, click **Continue.** If you are not logged in using an administrator account, key an administrator's password and then click **OK** to continue. The General tab of the Windows Firewall Settings dialog box displays, as shown in Figure 11-8. The option button corresponding to the current Windows Firewall status is selected.

Figure 11-8

General tab of the Windows Firewall Settings dialog box

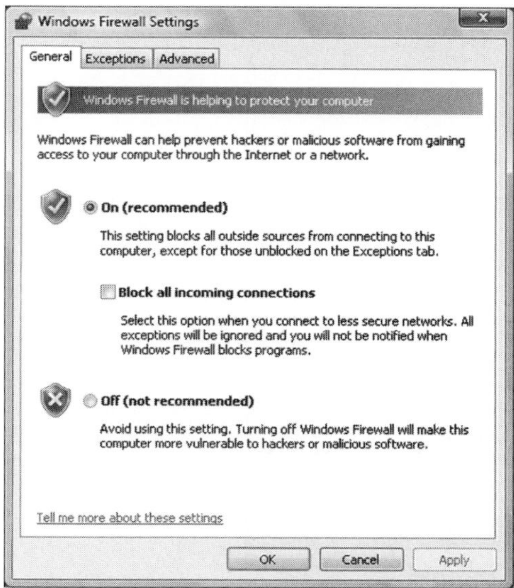

TROUBLESHOOTING

If your computer is part of a domain, which is a group of networked computers that share a common database and security policy, some firewall settings may only be available to the system administrator.

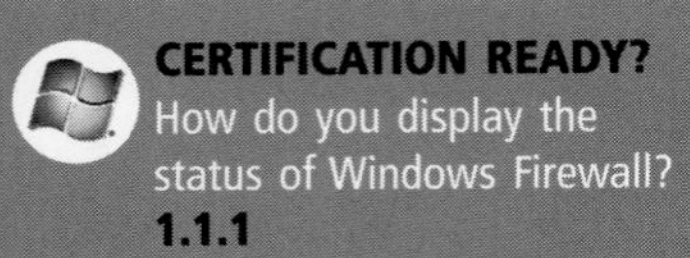

CERTIFICATION READY?
How do you display the status of Windows Firewall?
1.1.1

PAUSE. LEAVE the Windows Firewall Settings dialog box open to use in the next exercise.

Do not be alarmed if the Windows Firewall status is set to Off. You may have an alternative firewall program installed and running on your computer. For example, many virus protection programs include firewalls. If you have a different firewall, you do not need Windows Firewall as well. Two firewalls active at the same time might interfere with each other, causing your computer to run slowly or to have trouble processing certain programs.

You can view all of the firewall programs currently installed on your computer by using the Windows Security Center. Click Start>Control Panel>. Then, under Security, click Check this computer's security status. Click the expand arrow to the right of the Firewall setting to view the firewall options. Click the link to Show me the firewall programs on this computer to view a list of installed firewall programs and their status. Click Close to close the window. Then close the Windows Security Center.

In the next section, you learn how to set Windows Firewall to allow access to certain programs.

Setting Windows Firewall Exceptions

By default, Windows Firewall blocks all unsolicited communication to and from the system. You can create an exception to a particular program so that the program can send and receive information through the firewall. For example, email programs are usually exceptions so that they can communicate through the firewall. You create an exception on the Exceptions tab of the Windows Firewall Settings dialog box.

SET WINDOWS FIREWALL EXCEPTIONS

USE the Windows Firewall Settings dialog box that you left open in the previous exercise.

1. Click the **Exceptions** tab to display the Windows Firewall Settings exceptions options. The tab should look similar to Figure 11-9. Each program that has a checkmark in its checkbox is an exception and can communicate through the firewall. If there is no checkmark, the program is blocked from communicating through the firewall.

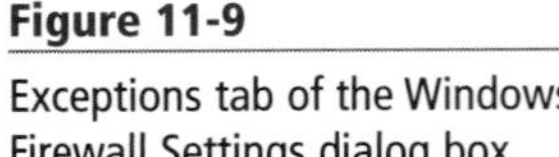

Figure 11-9

Exceptions tab of the Windows Firewall Settings dialog box

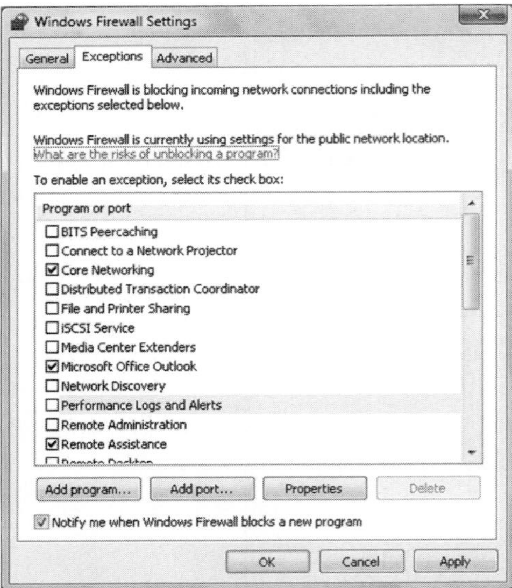

2. Click to select the **Connect to a Network Projector** checkbox. This enables an exception for network projectors. You would select this exception if you planned to use a projector to display a presentation on a network. Without the exception, Windows Firewall would block the presentation program from communicating with the projector on the network.

> **TROUBLESHOOTING**
> If Connect to a Network Projector is already selected, use a different program's checkbox to complete these steps.

3. Click **Apply** to create the exception and keep the dialog box open. At your instructor's request, capture an image of the dialog box. Save it in your Lesson 11 assessment folder as ***Le11_04***.
4. Click to deselect the **Connect to a Network Projector** checkbox. This disables the exception. You should only enable an exception for the length of time you need it. Once the presentation is complete, you would no longer need the exception.
5. Click **OK** to disable the exception and close the dialog box.
6. **CLOSE** the Windows Firewall window. The Security window in the Control Panel should still be open.

To open the Windows Firewall Settings dialog box directly to the Exceptions tab, click Start>Control Panel and then, under Security, click Allow a program through Windows Firewall. (In the User Account Control dialog box, click Continue or key an administrator's password and click OK.)

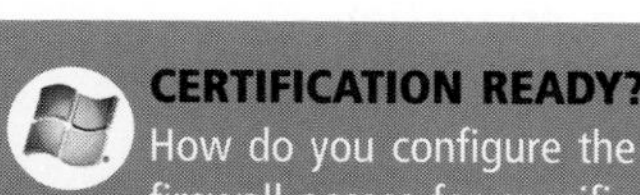

> **CERTIFICATION READY?**
> How do you configure the firewall access for specific programs?
> **1.1.2**

PAUSE. LEAVE the Security window open to use in the next exercise.

If the program for which you want to create an exception is not listed in the Windows Firewall Settings dialog box, you can add it. On the Exceptions tab, click the Add program button to open the Add a Program dialog box. Locate and select the program to add and then click OK. The program is added to the list of programs on the Exceptions tab and is selected by default. To remove a program from the list, select it and then click the Delete button. Click Yes in the Confirmation dialog box.

Keep in mind that when you create an exception, you may be providing malicious software or unauthorized users access to your system. It is a good idea to create exceptions only when necessary and to remove them when you no longer need them.

You might have noticed on the General tab of the Windows Firewall Settings dialog box that you can select a checkbox to block all incoming connections when Windows Firewall is on. Use this option to prohibit all unsolicited communication between an outside network and your computer, including exceptions. For example, if you are using a notebook or mobile device in a public place to connect to a public network, you might want to select this option. It is also useful if there is a known threat such as a software virus or worm spreading through the Internet. Even programs currently enabled on the Exceptions list will be blocked. Windows Firewall will display an alert if a blocked program is trying to communicate through the firewall. You can select to keep blocking or unblock the program.

In the next exercise, you learn how to use the Windows Defender program to protect your system from malicious software.

■ Monitoring Your System for Malicious Software

THE BOTTOM LINE

Malicious software is software designed to harm your computer. You can help protect your system by running antivirus and antispyware programs to monitor and remove harmful software. A ***virus*** is a program that attempts to spread throughout your system and other, networked systems to destroy, change, or manipulate data. ***Spyware*** is a type of malicious software that displays pop-up advertisements, collects information about users, and changes computer settings—all without permission. Windows Vista comes with an antispyware program called Windows Defender, but it does not come with an antivirus program. You must install a separate antivirus program to keep your system safe. In this section, you learn how to check the status of Windows Defender and your antivirus software program. You also learn how to use Windows Defender to protect your computer.

Viewing the Status of Antispyware and Antivirus Programs

In the Windows Security Center, you can view the status of installed antispyware and antivirus programs. In this exercise, you open the Windows Security Center to check the status of both types of programs.

VIEW THE STATUS OF ANTISPYWARE AND ANTIVIRUS PROGRAMS

USE the Control Panel Security window that you left open in the previous exercise.

1. Click **Security Center** in the Security window. The Windows Security Center window opens.

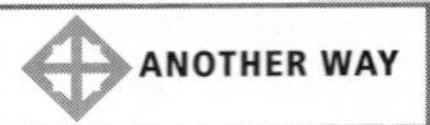

You can open the Security Center directly from the Control Panel. Click Start>Control Panel and then, under Security, click Check this computer's security status.

2. If necessary, click the expand arrow to the right of the **Malware protection** settings to display details about the installed antivirus and antispyware programs. The window should look similar to Figure 11-10, although the specific programs depend on the programs you have installed. For example, you might have a different antivirus program, and the only antispyware program may be Windows Defender.

Figure 11-10

View settings in the Windows Security Center

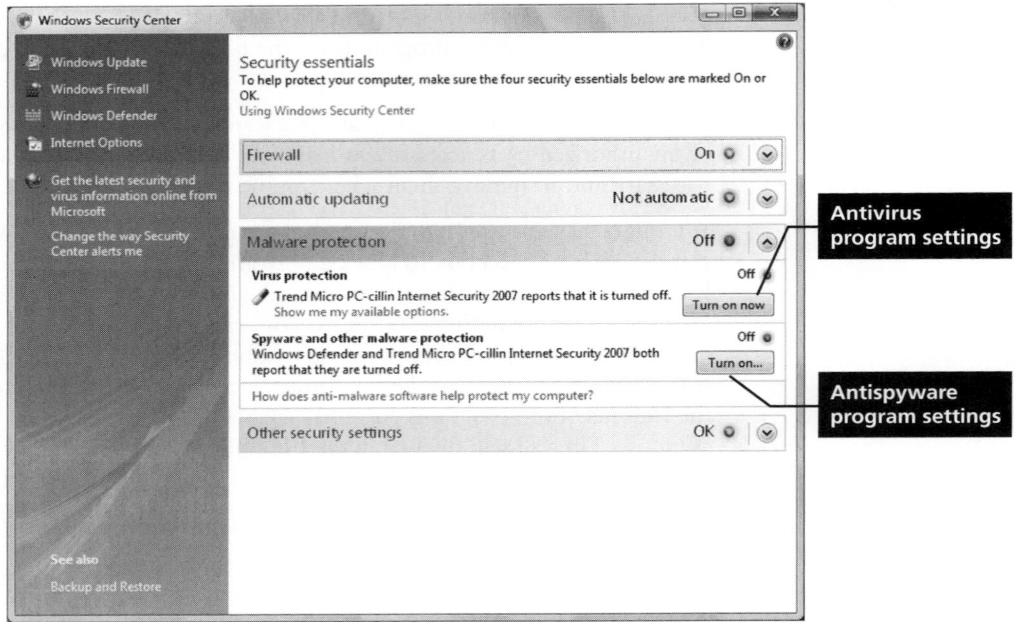

TAKE NOTE

You may have both Windows Defender and another antispyware program running at the same time, because many antivirus programs also come with antispyware programs.

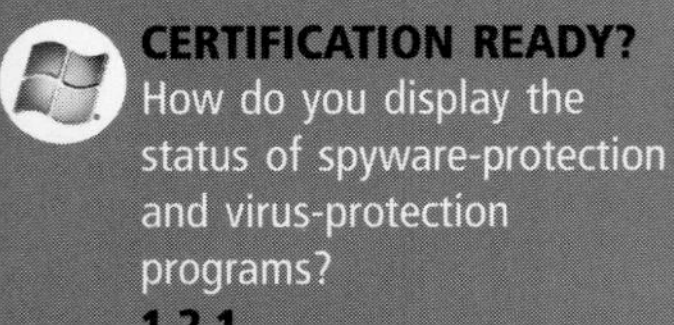

3. At your instructor's request, capture an image of the window. Save it in your Lesson 11 assessment folder as ***Le11_05***.

PAUSE. LEAVE the Windows Security Center open to use in the next exercise.

If you do not have an antivirus program, you should obtain and install one as soon as possible. You can find a list of Windows Vista–compatible programs on the Microsoft website. From the Windows Security Center, click Get the latest security and virus information online from Microsoft to display the Security home page. In the left pane, click Partners and then click Antivirus Partners. Alternatively, go to Microsoft.com and search for antivirus partners.

Note that if you have antivirus and antispyware installed, but they are off or out of date, Windows Vista will display a security alert icon in the Notification area on the Taskbar. Double-click the icon to open the Windows Security Center and then use the buttons in the Malware protection area of the Windows Security Center to turn on the programs.

If you have an antispyware program other than Windows Defender installed and active, the option to display all antispyware programs becomes available in the Malware protection area of the Windows Security Center. Click it to view a list of installed programs and then click Close to close the window.

You might notice that there is an area in the Windows Security Center for Other security settings, which displays the status of Internet security settings and User Account Control. You learn more about Internet security settings in Lesson 12, "Managing Microsoft Internet Explorer." User Account Control is the feature of Windows Vista that protects your computer from unauthorized changes by requiring an administrator's permission for actions that affect other users, such as installing programs or changing system settings.

In the next section, you learn how to use Windows Defender to monitor programs running on your computer.

Updating and Scanning with Windows Defender

By default, Windows Defender is set to automatically protect your system. It regularly checks for, downloads, and installs new ***definitions***, which are files that store information about known spyware and other malicious software, to keep the software up-to-date. It also runs regularly scheduled scans during which it identifies suspicious software. You can manually update definitions or run a scan at any time. For example, if you suspect spyware may have infiltrated your system, you may want to check that you have the most current definitions installed and then run a scan to locate the program. In this exercise, you open the Windows Defender program, check for updated definitions, and run a system scan.

UPDATE AND SCAN WITH WINDOWS DEFENDER

GET READY. You must have a connection to the Internet to check for and download updates.

USE the Windows Security Center window that you left open in the previous exercise.

1. Click **Windows Defender** in the left pane of the Windows Security Center window. The Windows Defender home page opens. It should look similar to Figure 11-11, although the information in the Status area depends on the current status of your computer.

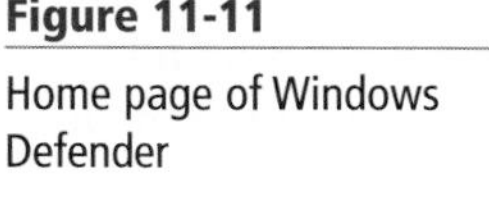

Figure 11-11

Home page of Windows Defender

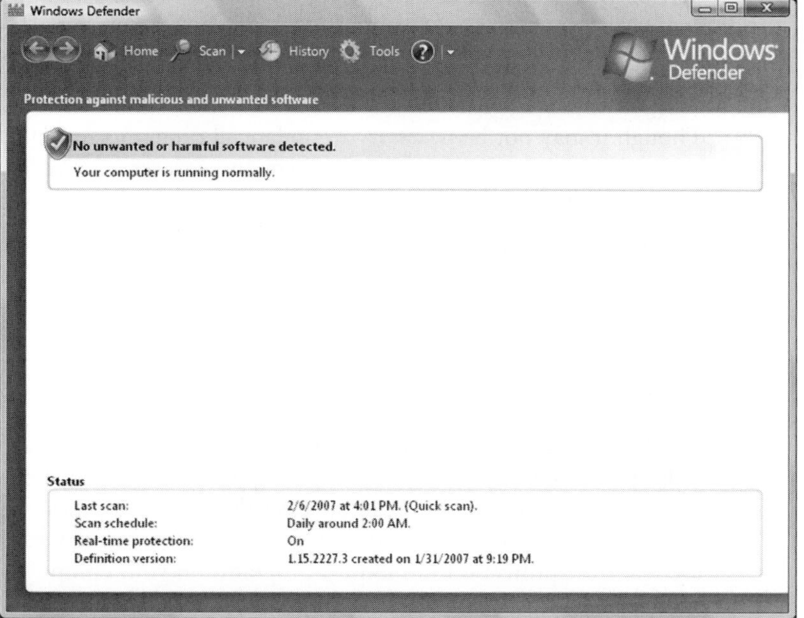

You can open Windows Defender directly from the Start menu. Click Start>All Programs>Windows Defender. If the Windows Defender icon displays in the Notification area of the Taskbar, you can double-click it to open the program.

2. Click the **Windows Defender Help** dropdown arrow on the Windows Defender toolbar and then click **Check for updates.** In the User Account Controls dialog box, if you are logged in to an administrator account, click **Continue.** If you are not logged in using an administrator account, key an administrator's password and then click **OK** to continue. Windows Defender connects to the Internet and checks for new definition files. If there are new definitions, Windows Defender downloads and installs them automatically.

TAKE NOTE*

A ScreenTip in the Notification area indicates the progress while Windows Defender checks for updates.

3. Click the **Scan** button dropdown arrow on the Windows Defender toolbar and then click **Full Scan** to start scanning all files and programs on your computer. Windows Defender begins scanning your system for suspicious software. If it finds anything, it takes the default action or displays an alert so you can select an action.

TROUBLESHOOTING

If the scan is taking a long time, you can click the Stop Scan button to cancel it.

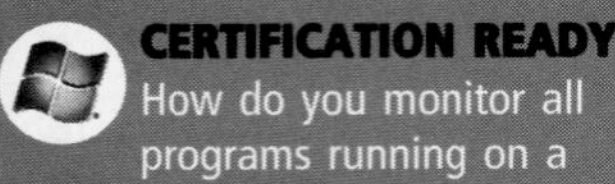

CERTIFICATION READY?
How do you monitor all programs running on a computer by using Windows Defender?
1.2.4
How do you install a software update?
3.1.4

4. When the scan is complete, Windows Defender displays the home page and shows information about the results of the scan.

PAUSE. LEAVE the Windows Defender home page open to use in the next exercise.

Updating Windows Defender with current definitions is a vital part of protecting your system from spyware, because new malicious software is created and released every day. Depending on the settings you have selected for Windows Defender, it may automatically check for updates on a regular basis using the Windows Update feature, which is covered later in this lesson.

Most programs regularly check for updates if there is an Internet connection available. Some may be set to automatically check for, download, and install updates, while others may prompt you when new updates are available. If a prompt displays, you can select to download and install the updates or cancel the process. In most programs you can find the option to schedule updates on a Tools or Options menu. Alternatively, you can manually check for updates.

Though it may not be necessary to update all programs regularly, you should update your antispyware and antivirus programs frequently—even on a daily basis. You learn about updating Windows Vista and other Microsoft programs later in this lesson.

You may have noticed that Windows Defender offers you a choice of three types of scans:

- Quick scan, which scans areas of your computer where spyware is most likely to be found
- Full scan, which scans your entire system
- Custom scan, which scans only selected locations

If you scan your system regularly, once you run a full scan, you can usually use a quick scan to keep your system safe. If you suspect spyware has installed on your computer, however, you may want to run a full scan or select the specific location where you believe the malicious program to be and then scan it with a custom scan. In the next exercise, you learn how to use real-time protection to monitor programs on your computer.

Using Real-Time Protection

Real-time protection is the feature of Windows Defender that continuously watches for and identifies programs that attempt to install on your computer or change Windows Vista system settings without your permission. By default, it monitors all programs and displays an alert whenever it detects anything suspicious so that you can select the action you want to take. For example, if you frequently use a program that you trust, when Windows Defender displays an alert, you can select to add the program to a list of allowed programs so that Windows Defender will not monitor it and will not continue to display alerts about it. In this exercise, you check the status of real-time protection. If possible, you will introduce software that Windows Defender identifies as suspicious so you can take action.

USE REAL-TIME PROTECTION

GET READY. To complete this exercise, you should have a program from a publisher that Windows Vista does not recognize available for installation. If you do not have a program that will trigger a Windows Defender alert, you will not be able to complete the exercise. You can complete the exercise at a different time if Windows Defender identifies a problem and displays an alert.

USE the Windows Defender home page that you left open in the previous exercise.

1. Click the **Tools** button on the Windows Defender toolbar and then click **Options** to display the Windows Defender Options window. It should look similar to Figure 11-12.

Figure 11-12

Windows Defender Options

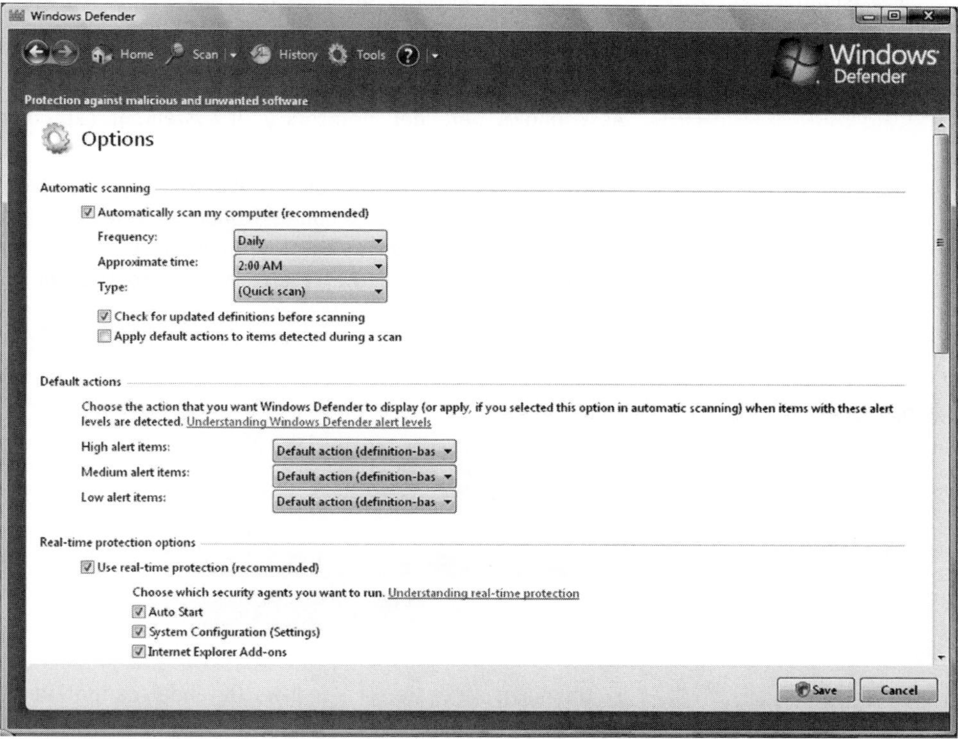

2. Scroll down in the window and note whether the following checkboxes are selected: Automatically scan my computer, Use real-time protection, and Use Windows Defender. These are the three options that control whether Windows Defender is protecting your system.

TAKE NOTE: If the checkboxes are not selected, you may have a different antispyware program running on your system.

3. If necessary, click to select **Use real-time protection** to turn the feature on.
4. Click the **Save** button. In the User Account Controls dialog box, if you are logged in to an administrator account click **Continue**. If you are not logged in using an administrator account, key an administrator's password and then click **OK** to continue. Windows Defender saves the changes and closes the Options window.

TROUBLESHOOTING: If the Save button is not available in the Options window, you did not make any changes. Click Cancel to close the Options window.

5. Begin installing a software program from a publisher that Windows Vista does not recognize. For example, insert an installation disk or begin downloading the program from a website. Windows Defender will monitor the program as it tries to install itself or change system settings. A User Account Control dialog box may display, informing you that an unidentified program wants to access your computer. Click **Allow** to continue.

TROUBLESHOOTING: If Windows Defender recognizes the software—for example, if you have allowed it to be installed on your system at a previous time—it may not display an alert. You will not be able to complete the exercise.

6. As Windows Defender monitors your system, it categorizes programs into one of three groups:
   - Known, legitimate software. If Windows Defender recognizes the software as legitimate, meaning it comes from a known, secure source, it allows it to continue and does not display an alert. It may display a message in the Notification area of the Taskbar similar to the one in Figure 11-13, notifying you of the change.

Figure 11-13

A Windows Defender notification

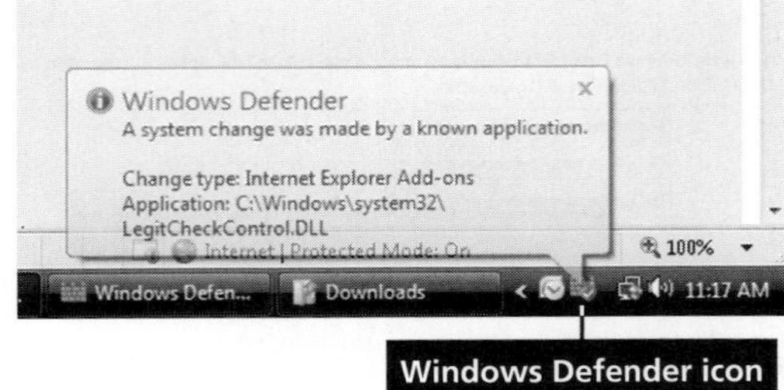

   - Unknown software. If Windows Defender cannot identify the software, it may display an alert where you can select to ignore the alert and continue with the installation; ***quarantine*** or disable the software, which moves it into a separate storage location and temporarily stops it from running; or block the software, which removes it from the system.
   - Known, malicious software. If Windows Defender identifies the software as a known risk, it displays an alert where you can select to ignore the alert, disable the software, or remove the software.
7. If Windows Defender displays an alert, click **Always Allow** to add the program to the list of allowed programs. Windows Defender will consider it safe from now on.

TAKE NOTE If you have a different antispyware program running, or an antivirus program, it might display alerts in place of Windows Defender. The options are probably similar to Windows Defender, but you may need to start the program to view the allowed and quarantined items.

8. If Windows Defender displays another alert, click **Disable** or **Quarantine** to temporarily block the software.
9. When the installation is complete, click the **Tools** button on the Windows Defender toolbar and then click **Allowed items.** The item you specified to Always Allow should display in the list of allowed items.

TAKE NOTE To remove a program from the Allowed items list, select it and then click the Remove From List button. In the User Account Controls dialog box, if you are logged in to an administrator account, click Continue. If you are not logged in using an administrator account, key an administrator's password and then click OK to continue.

10. Click the **Tools** button on the Windows Defender toolbar and then click **Quarantined items.** The item you selected to temporarily block or disable should display in the list, which should look similar to Figure 11-14, although the program(s) listed depend on those quarantined on your system. At your instructor's request, capture an image of the window. Save it in your Lesson 11 assessment folder as ***Le11_06***.

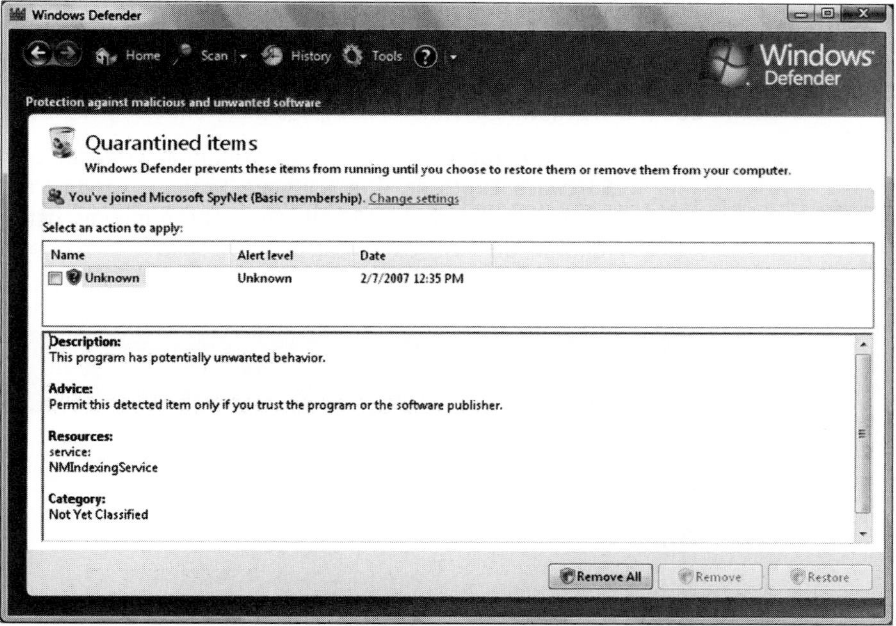

Figure 11-14

Quarantined item in Windows Defender

11. Click to select the checkbox to the left of the item you quarantined in step 8. The Remove All, Remove, and Restore buttons become available.
12. Click **Remove** to remove the item from your computer or, if it is from a trusted source, click **Restore** to restore it to its original location so it can run. Click **Yes** if a warning dialog box displays. In the User Account Controls dialog box, if you are logged in to an administrator account, click **Continue.** If you are not logged in using an administrator account, key an administrator's password and then click **OK** to continue.
13. Click the **Home** button on the Windows Defender toolbar to display the Windows Defender home page.

14. Uninstall the program you installed in steps 5–8.

For information on installing and uninstalling programs, refer to Lesson 10, "Managing Software."

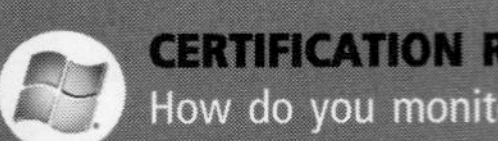

CERTIFICATION READY?
How do you monitor all programs running on a computer by using Windows Defender?
1.2.4
How do you choose not to monitor specific programs?
1.2.5
How do you remove or restore programs blocked by Windows Defender?
1.2.2

PAUSE. LEAVE the Windows Defender home page open to use in the next exercise.

When a program is installing, you might notice the Windows Defender icon in the Notification area of the Taskbar. The icon indicates that Windows Defender is monitoring the program. If there is a problem, it will display an alert.

The Tools and Settings window of Windows Defender has a link to Microsoft SpyNet, which is an online community that identifies spyware. You may elect to join the community and send information about blocked or suspicious programs to Microsoft. Microsoft analyzes the information and can use it to help protect all computers using Windows Defender.

In the next exercise, you use Windows Defender to view and manage programs running on your computer.

Using Software Explorer

Software Explorer is the feature of Windows Defender that lets you monitor installed programs for suspicious behavior. You can also use Software Explorer to remove or disable programs, which can be useful if you suspect a program is malicious or causing your computer to slow down. In this exercise, you use Software Explorer to view installed programs, as well as to disable and enable a program.

USE SOFTWARE EXPLORER

USE the Windows Defender home page that you left open in the previous exercise.

1. Click the **Tools** button on the Windows Defender toolbar and then click **Software Explorer**. The Software Explorer window displays. It should look similar to Figure 11-15, although the programs listed depend on those running on your computer.

Figure 11-15

Software Explorer in Windows Defender

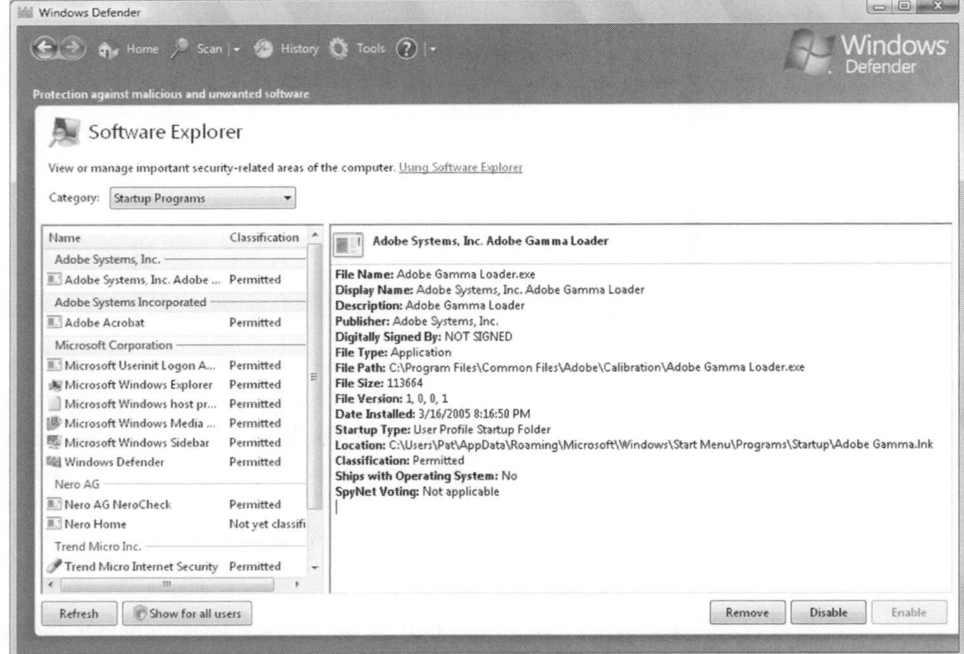

2. Click the **Category** box dropdown arrow and click **Currently Running Programs.** Programs in Software Explorer are organized into four categories:
   - Startup Programs, which are programs that run automatically when you start Windows Vista. You can remove, disable, or enable any program in the Startup Programs category.
   - Currently Running Programs, which are programs that are currently running. You can end any program in the Currently Running Programs category.
   - Network Connected Programs, which are programs or processes that can access a network, or the Internet, thereby allowing communication between your computer and the network. You can end any program in the Network Connected Programs category.
   - Winsock Service Providers, which are Windows Vista system programs that perform low-level networking and communication services. You can end any program in the Winsock Service Providers Programs category.

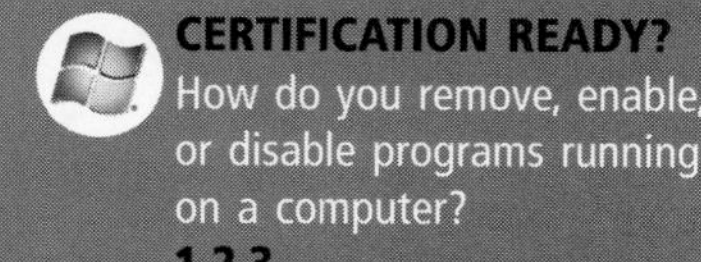

TROUBLESHOOTING

If Microsoft Windows Sidebar is not listed in Startup Programs, select a different program.

3. Click the **Category** box dropdown arrow again and click **Startup Programs.** Malicious software may install itself as a startup program without your knowledge. If an unfamiliar program displays in the Startup Programs category, you may want to disable it until you can verify that it is legitimate.
4. Click to select **Microsoft Windows Sidebar** in the list of programs.
5. Click the **Disable** button and then click **Yes.** Windows Defender disables the program. If it was interfering with Windows Vista, disabling it would give you a chance to identify or fix the problem. If the program was malicious, you could click Remove to remove it from the list of programs that start automatically with Windows Vista.

TAKE NOTE*

If the Remove button is not available when a program is selected, the program cannot be removed from the list of Startup Programs.

CERTIFICATION READY?
How do you remove, enable, or disable programs running on a computer?
1.2.3

6. At your instructor's request, capture an image of the window. Save it in your Lesson 11 assessment folder as ***Le11_07.***
7. Click the **Enable** button and then click **Yes** to enable the program again.
8. Close the Windows Defender window. The Windows Security Center should still be open.

PAUSE. LEAVE the Windows Security Center open to use in the next exercise.

When you select a program in Software Explorer, information about the program displays in the right pane of the window. The information includes the program name, publisher, and version number, and may also include more specific information such as whether it has been certified by a publisher using a digital signature. You can use the information to help determine if a program is legitimate.

You cannot disable or enable programs in any category other than Windows Startup Programs when using Software Explorer. However, you can end a program or process in the Currently Running Programs or Network Connected Programs category by clicking the End Process button. Or you can click the Task Manager button to open the Task Manager window, where you can view and end programs and processes. (For information on using Task Manager to end a program, refer to Lesson 10.) For Network Connected Programs, you may have the option of blocking incoming connections so that users on an outside network cannot access your computer through that program.

In the next exercise, you use Windows Update to check for and install updates to the Windows Vista operating system.

■ Using Windows Update

THE BOTTOM LINE

Windows Update is a feature of Windows Vista that you use to locate, download, and install updates for the Windows Vista operating system. Microsoft distributes three types of updates. Important updates generally affect security and reliability. For example, updates for Windows Defender definitions are important updates. Recommended updates generally affect performance. For example, updates that resolve performance issues affecting Windows Vista are recommended updates. Optional updates provide features and enhancements that do not affect the performance, security, or reliability of the system. For example, updates to games and device drivers might be optional updates. Other updates may also be available, depending on the edition of Windows Vista you are using and whether you have other Microsoft products installed.

By default, Windows Update is set to automatically check for and install important updates on a regular basis. You can customize the automatic update settings, and you can manually check for and install updates at any time. In addition, Windows Update maintains a list of updates that is has installed and that you can display in the Control Panel. In this section, you customize automatic update settings, manually check for updates, and view the list of installed updates.

Customizing Automatic Update Settings

You can view the current automatic update settings in the Windows Security Center, and you can access the Windows Update window to change the settings. For example, you may want to set Windows Update to notify you before it downloads important updates so that you can review the updates and install them on your time. Or you might want to make sure recommended updates are installed automatically. In this exercise, you view and customize the automatic update settings.

CUSTOMIZE AUTOMATIC UPDATE SETTINGS

USE the Windows Security Center that you left open in the previous exercise.

1. In the Windows Security Center, click the expand arrow to the right of the **Automatic updating** settings so you can see details about the current status of automatic updating. Automatic updating may be set to On, Off, Automatic, or Not automatic. If it is set to Off or Not automatic, a Change settings button is available. If it is set to On, there is no Change settings button.
2. Click the **Change settings** button if it is available or click **Windows Update** in the left pane of the Windows Security Center window and then click **Change settings** in the left pane of the Windows Update window. The Windows Update Change Settings window displays, as shown in Figure 11-16. As mentioned previously, you can set Windows Update to automatically check for, download, and install updates; automatically check for and download updates but notify you before installing them; automatically notify you when new updates are available but not download and install them; or you can turn automatic updating off.

Figure 11-16

Select automatic update settings

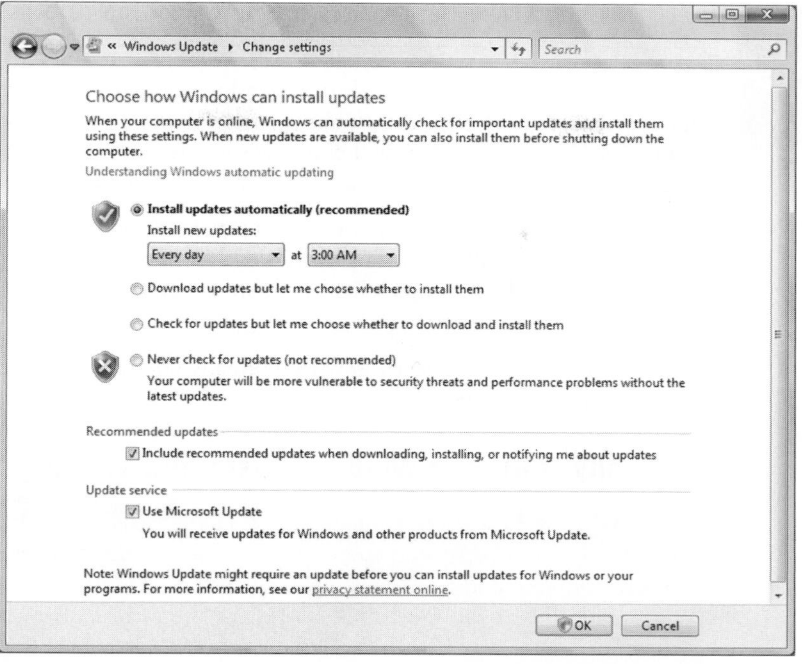

TAKE NOTE

You should not turn automatic updating off. Keeping Windows Vista up-to-date is an important part of maintaining the security and reliability of your computer and data.

3. Click the **Check for updates but let me choose whether to download and install them** option button. This option sets Windows Update to automatically notify you when updates are available so you can decide to download and install them.
4. If necessary, click to select the **Include recommended updates when downloading, installing, or notifying me about updates** checkbox. This ensures that recommended as well as important updates are included.
5. Click **OK** to apply the changes. In the User Account Controls dialog box, if you are logged in to an administrator account, click **Continue**. If you are not logged in using an administrator account, key an administrator's password and then click **OK** to continue. The Windows Update window displays. It should look similar to Figure 11-17, depending on whether new important updates are available. If important updates are available, the Install updates button displays as does a link to view the available updates. If only recommended updates are available, you can select to view the available updates.

Figure 11-17

Set Windows Update to notify you if updates are available

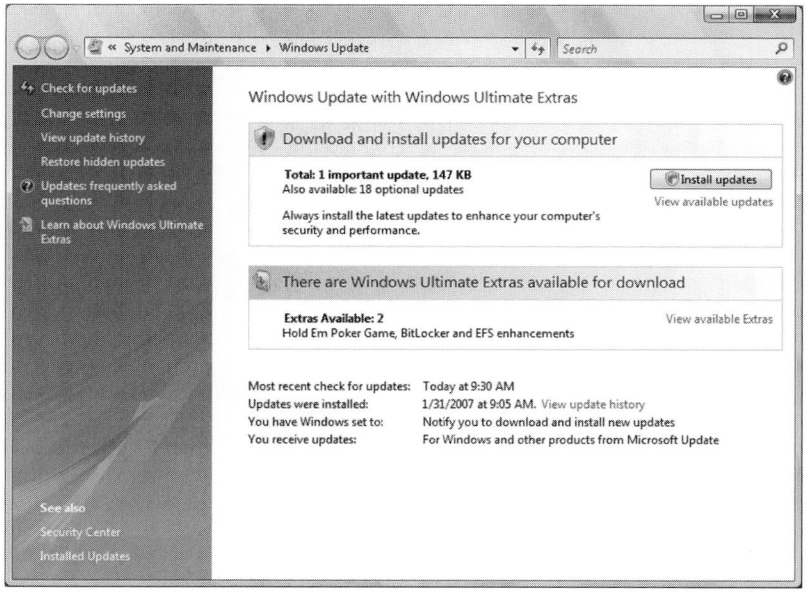

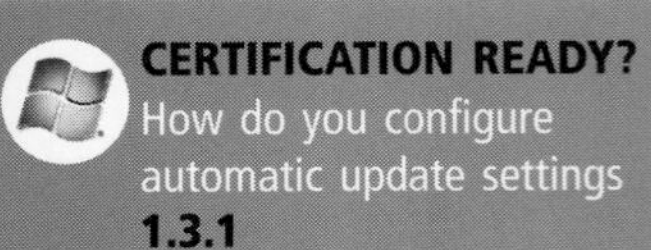
CERTIFICATION READY?
How do you configure automatic update settings
1.3.1

PAUSE. LEAVE the Windows Update window open to use in the next exercise.

By default, if automatic update is on, Windows Update checks for, downloads, and installs updates daily at 3:00 AM without any action on your part. If your system is not on at 3:00 AM, Windows Update will check as soon as you establish a connection to the Internet. You can change the schedule in the Windows Update Change Settings window.

If you set automatic updating to notify you before downloading or installing updates, Windows Update will display an icon in the Notification area of the Taskbar when new updates are available. Double-click the icon to open Windows Update so you can select the updates you want to install.

In the next exercise, you learn how to manually check for updates and view updates that have already been installed.

Manually Updating Windows Vista and Viewing Installed Updates

Even with automatic updating turned on, there may be times when you want to manually check for, download, and install updates. For example, you may want to see if any new optional updates are available. Optional updates are never downloaded and installed automatically, so you must manually check for them and select the ones you want to download and install. In this exercise, you manually check for available updates and view updates that have been installed on your system. You also change the automatic update settings so that updates are downloaded and installed automatically.

MANUALLY UPDATE WINDOWS VISTA AND VIEW INSTALLED UPDATES

GET READY. You must have access to the Internet to update Windows Vista.

1. Click **Check for updates** in the left pane of the Windows Update window. Windows Update connects to the Microsoft Update website, checks to see if any updates that have not already been installed on your system are available, and then displays the Windows Update window again.
2. Click the **View available updates** link. A list of all available updates displays, similar to the one in Figure 11-18. Important updates are selected by default. You can select or clear the updates depending on what you want to install.

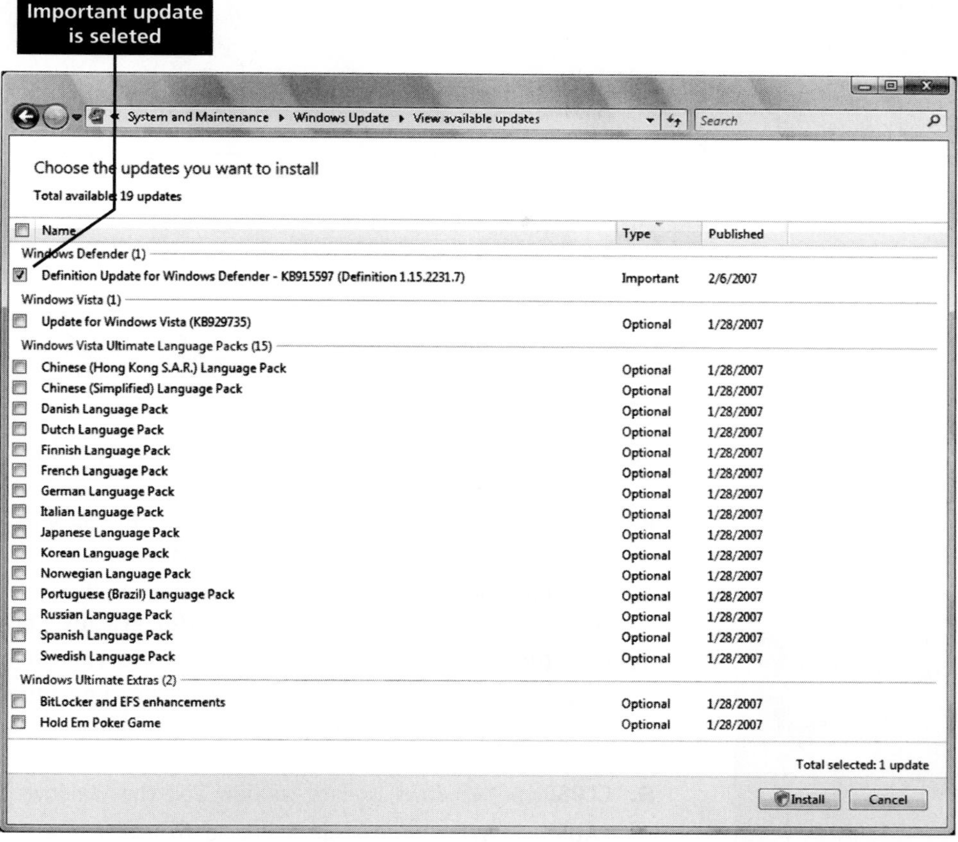

Figure 11-18

Updates available for downloading

TAKE NOTE You can right-click an update and click View details to display information explaining the purpose of the update.

3. If an important update is available and selected, click the **Install** button. Alternatively, select a recommended or optional update and then click the **Install** button. In the User Account Controls dialog box, if you are logged in to an administrator account, click **Continue.** If you are not logged in using an administrator account, key an administrator's password and then click **OK** to continue. Windows downloads and installs the update. When the installation is complete, the Windows Update window displays again.

TAKE NOTE Windows Vista may prompt you to restart your system after installing certain updates. Follow the prompts on your screen to restart, log back in to your Windows Vista user account, and open Windows Update.

4. Click **View update history** in the left pane of the Windows Update window to display a list of updates that have been installed on your system. It should look similar to Figure 11-19, depending on the specific updates that have been installed. At the request of your instructor, capture an image of the window. Save it in your Lesson 11 assessment folder as ***Le11_08***.

Figure 11-19

List of installed updates

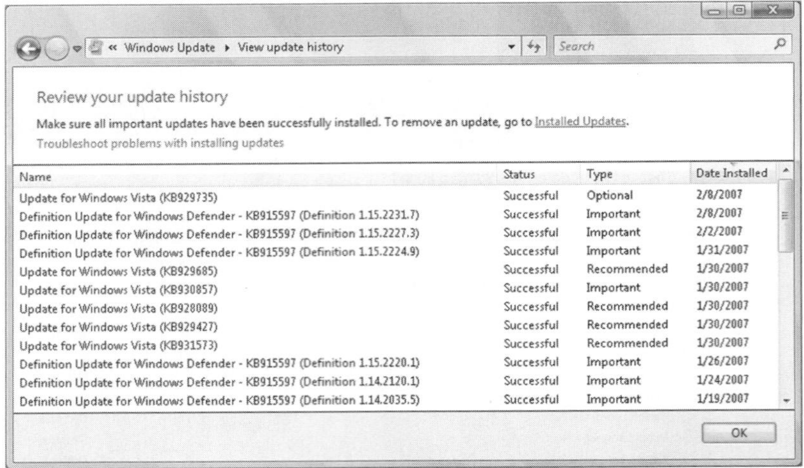

5. Click **Windows Update** in the address bar of the View update history window to return to the Windows Update window.
6. Click **Change settings** in the left pane of the Windows Update window and then click to select the **Install updates automatically** option button.
7. Click **OK** to apply the change. In the User Account Controls dialog box, if you are logged in to an administrator account, click **Continue**. If you are not logged in using an administrator account, key an administrator's password and then click **OK** to continue.
8. **CLOSE** the Windows Update window and the Windows Security Center window.

PAUSE. LEAVE the desktop displayed to use in the next exercise.

CERTIFICATION READY?
How do you manually update Windows Vista?
1.3.2
How to you display a list of installed updates?
1.3.3

Optional updates are never downloaded and installed automatically because they are not required by all users. You can check for optional updates and then determine whether they are necessary for you and your system. For example, a new device driver may become available, but if your device is working properly, you may decide not to install the new driver.

Note that downloading an update is not enough for it to take effect. You must also install the update on your computer. In the next section, you learn how to use advanced startup options to troubleshoot problems with Windows Vista.

■ Troubleshooting Startup Problems

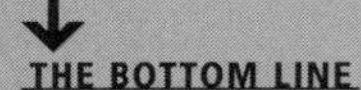

THE BOTTOM LINE

If Windows Vista runs slowly or erratically, you can use System Restore or Device Manager to diagnose and solve the problem. However, if the problem affects the way Windows Vista starts, you may not be able to access the features you need. For example, if an incompatible video device is causing your monitor to stop working, you will not be able to communicate with your system to select commands. Luckily, Windows Vista has advanced startup options and recovery tools that you can use to troubleshoot, diagnose, and possibly solve the problem. In this section, you learn how to display the advanced startup options and how to use the Startup Repair recovery tools to repair startup problems.

Using Advanced Startup Options

Advanced startup options enable you to start your computer with only selected files and drivers, thereby bypassing any device or program that might be interfering with the start-up procedure. They also provide access to diagnostic tools. The advanced startup options are available on the Advanced Boot Options menu. ***Boot*** is a term that refers to starting a computer. To access the menu, press F8 while Windows Vista is starting. From the menu that displays, you can select the option that will best help you diagnose or repair a problem. In this exercise, you display the Advanced Boot Options menu and select an option to start your computer.

USE ADVANCED STARTUP OPTIONS

1. Select to restart your computer. For example, click **Start**, click the arrow to the right of the Lock button, and then click **Restart**.
2. Watch as your system shuts down and restarts. When you see startup information on your monitor, before the Windows Vista logo displays, press **F8**. (You may have to press it multiple times.) The Advanced Boot Options menu displays. It should look similar to Figure 11-20.

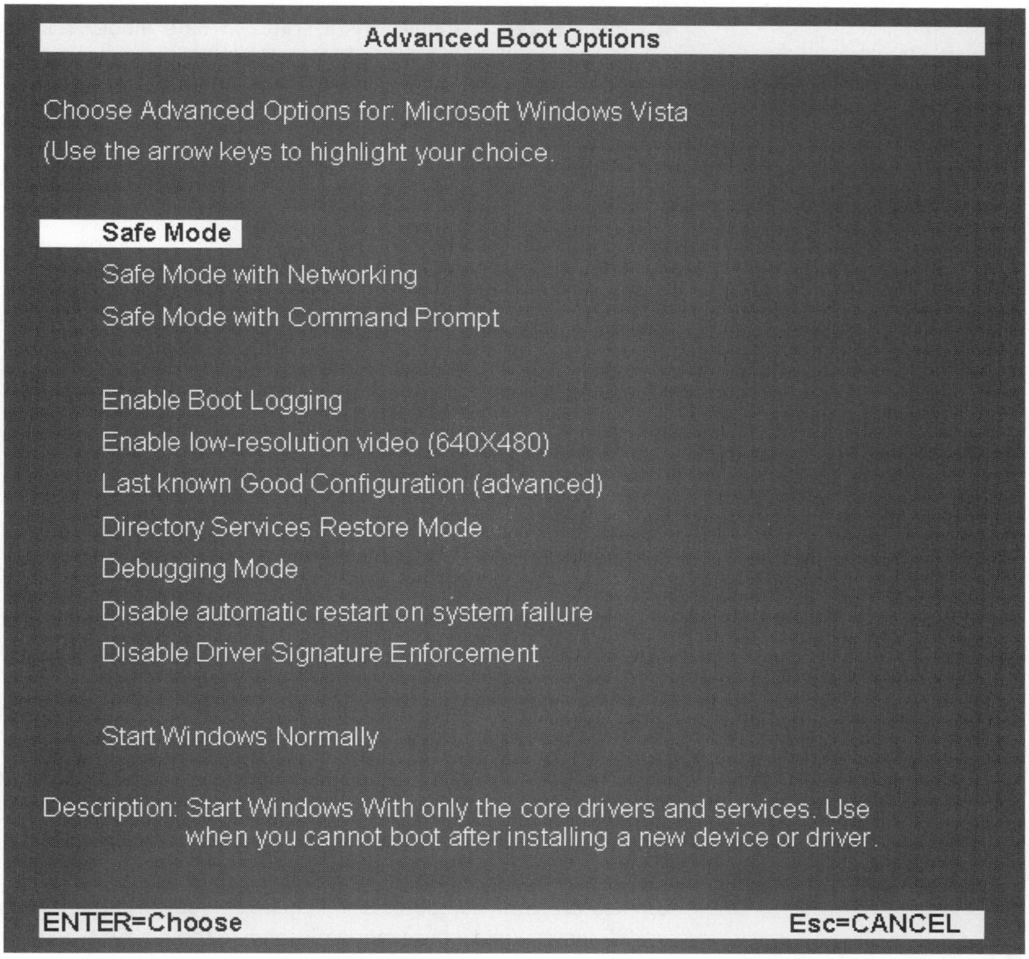

Figure 11-20

Advanced Boot Options menu

Advanced Boot Options

Choose Advanced Options for: Microsoft Windows Vista
(Use the arrow keys to highlight your choice.

Safe Mode
Safe Mode with Networking
Safe Mode with Command Prompt

Enable Boot Logging
Enable low-resolution video (640X480)
Last known Good Configuration (advanced)
Directory Services Restore Mode
Debugging Mode
Disable automatic restart on system failure
Disable Driver Signature Enforcement

Start Windows Normally

Description: Start Windows With only the core drivers and services. Use when you cannot boot after installing a new device or driver.

ENTER=Choose Esc=CANCEL

TROUBLESHOOTING If more than one operating system is installed on your computer, select the operating system and then press F8.

TROUBLESHOOTING If the advanced startup options menu does not display, you did not press F8 in time. You must press it before the Windows Vista logo displays. Restart your computer and try again.

3. Press the **down arrow** key on your keyboard to highlight Safe Mode with Networking. ***Safe mode*** is a troubleshooting option that loads only the basic files and drivers necessary to run Windows Vista. With the networking option, drivers required to access your network or the Internet will be loaded as well so that you can consult online help sources or reinstall programs from a network source.

TAKE NOTE You cannot use your mouse or other pointer device to select an option on the Advanced Boot Options menu because the drivers are not yet loaded.

4. Press **Enter**. Windows Vista starts in Safe mode. Your monitor screen should look similar to Figure 11-21. Notice that your customized display settings are not in effect because only basic files and drivers are available. In addition, the words *Safe Mode* display in all corners of the desktop. Windows Help and Support opens to display information about Safe mode. You can access all of your programs and data files, but most of your devices will not be available. While in Safe mode, you can change system settings or use System Restore to try to repair a problem.

Figure 11-21

Safe mode

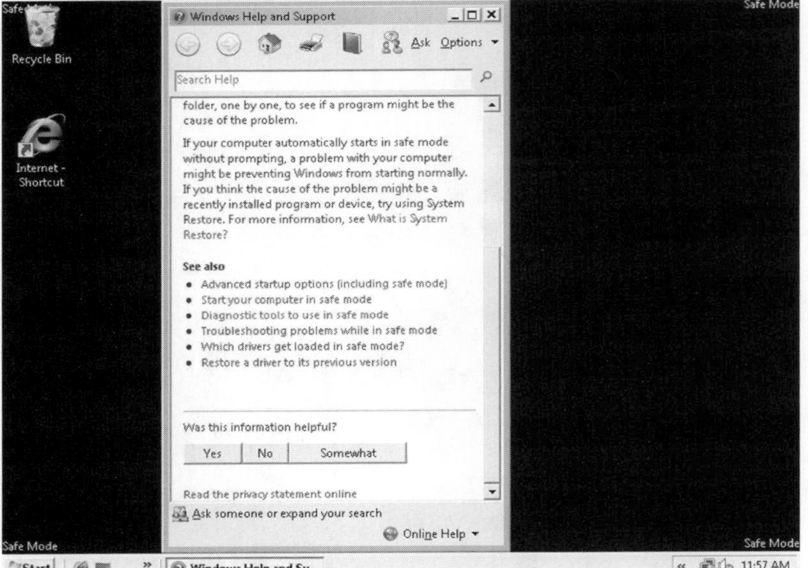

5. Restart your computer and log in to your Windows Vista user account. Windows Vista starts normally and loads all files and drivers.

   PAUSE. LEAVE the desktop displayed to use in the next exercise.

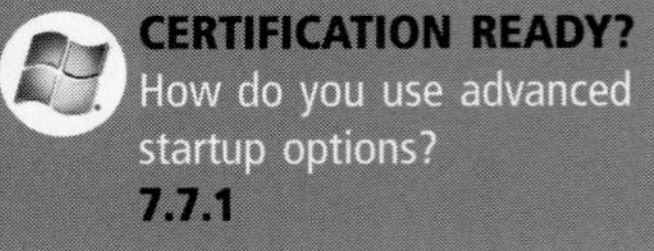
CERTIFICATION READY?
How do you use advanced startup options?
7.7.1

Each option on the Advanced Boot Options menu can be used in a different way to diagnose and solve problems. Table 11-1 describes the available options.

Table 11-1

Advanced Boot Options Menu

Option	Description
Repair Your Computer	Displays a list of system recovery tools that you can use to repair startup problems, run diagnostics, or restore Windows Vista. This option is only available if the recovery tools are installed on your hard disk. Refer to the next exercise for more information.
Safe Mode	Starts with the minimum set of drivers and services required to run Windows Vista.
Safe Mode with Networking	Starts Windows Vista in Safe mode, with the drivers and services required to access the Internet and other network resources.
Safe Mode with Command Prompt	Starts Windows Vista in Safe mode but opens to the command prompt instead of to the Windows Vista desktop. The command prompt is a window that you can use to key command-line instructions.
Enable Boot Logging	Starts Windows Vista normally but creates a file named ntbtlog.txt that lists all the drives installed during startup. You can use the information in the file to troubleshoot problems.
Enable Low Resolution Video (640X480)	Starts Windows Vista using low resolution and refresh rate display settings so that you can diagnose and fix problems with the display.
Last Known Good Configuration (advanced)	Starts Windows Vista using the last registry and driver configuration that worked successfully. This is similar to using System Restore to return to a previous Restore Point.
Directory Services Restore Mode	Starts Windows Domain Controller, which is a service that manages user logon and access to network and shared resources. This enables directory services to be restored. This option is only available for active directory networks and should only be used by information technology (IT) professionals and system administrators.
Debugging Mode	Starts Windows Vista in an advanced troubleshooting mode so that IT professionals or system administrators can use it to diagnose and solve problems.
Disable Automatic Restart on System Failure	Prevents Windows Vista from automatically restarting if an error causes the operating system to fail.
Disable Driver Signature Enforcement	Allows drivers containing improper signatures to be installed.
Start Windows Normally	Starts Windows Vista in Normal mode.

In the next exercise, you learn how to use the Startup Repair utility to repair Windows Vista installation problems.

Repairing the Windows Vista Installation

When you cannot solve startup problems by using System Restore or advanced startup options, you can try using the Startup Repair tool to fix problems such as missing or damaged system files. Startup Repair is one of Windows Vista's system recovery tools. For most systems, you access Startup Repair by using your Windows Vista installation disk. On some systems, the system recovery tools are installed on your hard disk and are available from the Advanced Boot Options menu. In this exercise, you use Startup Repair to repair your Windows Vista installation.

REPAIR THE WINDOWS VISTA INSTALLATION

GET READY. Have your Windows Vista installation CD available for use during this exercise.

If the system recovery tools are installed on your hard disk, restart your computer, pressing F8 before the Windows Vista logo displays to access the Advanced Boot Options menu. Press the down arrow key to select Repair your computer and then press Enter. Select a keyboard layout and then click Next. Select a user name, key a password, and then click OK. Click Startup Repair.

1. Insert your Windows Vista installation disk into the appropriate drive and restart your computer. Click **Next** to select the installation language and display the Install now screen. Then click **Repair your computer**. Windows Vista displays the System Recovery Options dialog box.
2. Click to select the Microsoft Windows Vista installation you want to repair and then click **Next**. A menu of recovery tools displays.
3. Click **Startup Repair**. Windows Vista analyzes your system to determine if a problem with the Windows Vista installation is preventing it from starting correctly. If it identifies a problem, it attempts to reinstall and repair the necessary files. Follow the prompts to complete the repair. You can also view a report listing the diagnostic tests and repair operations that Windows Vista used, or return to the menu of recovery tools to try something else.
4. Click **Finish**, remove the installation disk from the drive, and then click **Restart** to restart your computer normally.

LOG OFF your Windows Vista user account.

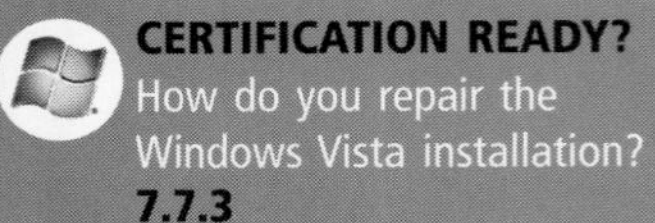

Startup repair cannot fix hardware failures and may not be able to recover from the effects of certain viruses or other malicious software.

In addition to the Startup Repair utility, you can use your Windows Vista installation disk or the Repair Your Computer option on the Advanced Boot Options menu to access the following system recovery tools:

- System Restore. Select this option to use System Restore to restore your Windows Vista installation to an earlier Restore Point.
- Windows Complete PC Restore. Select this option to restore a full backup of your entire computer system. To use the tool, you must have created a complete backup. For information on backing up data, refer to Lesson 10.
- Windows Memory Diagnostic Tool. Select this option to examine your computer's memory hardware for errors.
- Command Prompt. Select this option to open the command prompt window so you can use command-line instructions to communicate with Windows Vista.

SUMMARY SKILL MATRIX

In this lesson you learned	Matrix Skill	Skill Number
To set up a user account		
To create a password-protected user account	Create a standard password-protected local user account	1.6.1
To create a new account using Microsoft Management Console	Require a new user to change his or her password when logging on for the first time	1.6.2
To disable a user account	Disable a local user account	1.6.3
To manage Windows Firewall		
To view Windows Firewall status	Display the status of Windows Firewall	1.1.1
To set Windows Firewall Exceptions	Configure the firewall access for specific programs	1.1.2
To monitor your system for malicious software		
To view the status of antispyware and antivirus programs	Display the status of spyware-protection and virus-protection programs	1.2.1
To update and scan with Windows Defender	Monitor all programs running on a computer by using Windows Defender; Install a software update	1.2.4 3.1.4
To use real-time protection	Monitor all programs running on a computer by using Windows Defender; Choose not to monitor specific programs; Remove or restore programs blocked by Windows Defender	1.2.4 1.2.5 1.2.2
To use Software Explorer	Remove, enable, or disable programs running on a computer	1.2.3
To use Windows Update		
To customize automatic update settings	Configure automatic update settings	1.3.1
To manually update Windows Vista and view installed updates	Manually update Windows Vista; Display a list of installed updates	1.3.2 1.3.3
To troubleshoot startup problems		
To use advanced startup options	Use advanced startup options	7.7.1
To repair a Windows Vista installation	Repair the Windows Vista installation	7.7.3

■ Knowledge Assessment

Multiple Choice

Select the best response for the following questions.

1. What type of user account provides access to all programs and files on the system?
   a. administrator
   b. standard
   c. guest
   d. all access

2. What can you do to temporarily make a user account unavailable?
   a. delete the account
   b. reset the account password
   c. disable the account
   d. block the account
3. Which of the following Windows Vista features limits access between a computer and a network?
   a. Windows Defender
   b. Windows Firewall
   c. Windows Update
   d. Windows Security Center
4. What type of file attempts to spread and destroy, change, or manipulate date?
   a. virus
   b. driver
   c. document
   d. definition
5. What type of file stores information about known spyware so that an antispyware program can use the information to monitor and detect malicious software?
   a. virus
   b. driver
   c. document
   d. definition
6. Which type of scan should you select in Windows Defender to check the area of your computer where spyware is most likely to be found?
   a. full scan
   b. quick scan
   c. custom scan
   d. complete scan
7. Which feature of Windows Defender can you use to disable programs?
   a. Quarantine
   b. Scan
   c. Software Explorer
   d. Microsoft SpyNet
8. Which type of update will never install automatically?
   a. Important
   b. Recommended
   c. Vital
   d. Optional
9. What key do you press to display the Advanced Boot Options menu?
   a. Esc
   b. F8
   c. Ctrl
   d. F10

10. Which of the following is not a Windows Vista system recovery tool?

- **a.** Startup Repair
- **b.** System Restore
- **c.** Windows Complete PC Restore
- **d.** Windows Defender

True / False

Circle T if the statement is true or F if the statement is false.

T | F **1.** When you set up Windows Vista for the first time, you must create at least one administrator account.

T | F **2.** Even while you are using a standard account, you can access features and tools available to administrators by keying an administrator password in the User Account Control dialog box.

T | F **3.** Windows Vista passwords are not case sensitive.

T | F **4.** Windows Firewall may be off if you have an alternative firewall program installed and running on your computer.

T | F **5.** Windows Vista does not include an antivirus program.

T | F **6.** You must download and install updates for them to take effect.

T | F **7.** You cannot use any programs or files while updates are downloading and installing.

T | F **8.** Startup repair cannot fix hardware failures or problems caused by certain viruses.

T | F **9.** When you start Windows Vista in Safe mode, you may not be able to access all of your devices.

T | F **10.** You cannot start Windows Vista normally from the Advanced Boot Options menu.

■ Competency Assessment

Project 11-1: New Employee

You are a system administrator for the financial department at Trey Research, responsible for managing user accounts for everyone in the department. A new accountant is scheduled to start work tomorrow. In this project, you must set up a new user account that the accountant can use to log on and access the Windows Vista–based system. You will set it so that the new accountant must change the password the first time he logs on.

GET READY. Before you begin these steps, start your computer and log on to your Windows Vista account. Close all open windows so you can see the desktop.

1. Click **Start**, click **Control Panel**, click **System and Maintenance**, and then click **Administrative Tools**.
2. In the File list, double-click **Computer Management**. In the User Account Controls dialog box, if you are logged in to an administrator account, click **Continue**. If you are not logged in using an administrator account, key an administrator's password and then click **OK** to continue. The Computer Management window opens.
3. In the Navigation pane, click the expand arrow to the left of **Local Users and Groups** and then click **Users** in the expanded list. A list of existing accounts displays in the File list.
4. Right-click a blank area of the File list and click **New User** on the shortcut menu. The New User dialog box displays.
5. In the User Name text box, key **Greg Weber**. In the Full name text box, key **Gregory Weber**.

6. In the Description text box, key **Accountant, hired 3/15**.
7. In the Password text box, key **!GWacct001!**.
8. In the Confirm password text box, key **!GWacct001!**.
9. Verify that the **User must change password at next logon** checkbox is selected. If not, click it to select it. At your instructor's request, capture an image of the dialog box. Save it in your Lesson 11 assessment folder as ***Proj11_01***.
10. Click **Create**. Windows Vista creates the account and displays a blank New User dialog box so you can create additional accounts, if necessary.
11. Click **Close** to close the dialog box. Notice that the new account displays in the Computer Management window File list.
12. **CLOSE** all open windows.

PAUSE. LEAVE the desktop displayed to use in the next project.

Project 11-2: New Computer

You have recently purchased a new Windows Vista–based computer for use at home. Before you connect to the Internet for the first time, you want to check your security settings to make sure you have a firewall as well as antivirus and antispyware programs installed and running. You also want to make sure that Windows Update is set to automatically download and install updates daily. In this project, you will open the Windows Security Center to check the status of your security programs. You will open each program to customize settings as necessary.

1. Click **Start**, click **Control Panel**, and then, under Security, click **Check this computer's security status**. The Windows Security Center window opens. You can view the status of your firewall, automatic updating, and malware protection programs in the Windows Security Center.
2. In the left pane of the Windows Security Center window, click **Windows Firewall** and then click **Change settings**. In the User Account Controls dialog box, if you are logged in to an administrator account, click **Continue**. If you are not logged in using an administrator account, key an administrator's password and then click **OK** to continue. The General tab of the Windows Firewall Settings dialog box displays.
3. Verify the current settings and then click the **Exceptions** tab to display the Windows Firewall Settings exceptions options.
4. Locate your email program in the list of programs and verify that it is selected. If not, click the checkbox to select it. An item with a checkmark is an exception and can communicate through the firewall.
5. Click **Apply**. If you selected the email program in step 4, click it to deselect it and then click **OK**.
6. Close the Windows Firewall window. The Windows Security Center should still be open.
7. In the left pane, click **Windows Defender** to open the Windows Defender window.
8. Click the **Tools** button on the Windows Defender toolbar and then click **Options** to display the Windows Defender Options window.
9. Scroll down in the window and note the status of the three options that control whether Windows Defender is protecting your system: Automatically scan my computer, Use real-time protection, and Use Windows Defender.
10. Click the **Cancel** button to close the Options window and then close the Windows Defender window. The Windows Security Center should still be displayed.
11. In the left panel, click **Windows Update** to open the Windows Update window.
12. In the left pane, click **Change settings** to open the Change Settings window for Windows Update.

13. Verify that the Install updates automatically option button is selected.
14. Close the Windows Update window. The Windows Security Center should still be displayed.
15. **CLOSE** the Windows Security Center window and the Control Panel.

PAUSE. LEAVE the desktop displayed to use in the next project.

■ Proficiency Assessment

Project 11-3: Log In to a New Account

You are starting a new job as an accountant in the financial department of Trey Research. The system administrator has set up a new user account for you and has given you the password. In this project, you will log in to the account and change the password. You will also create a password reset disk.

GET READY. To create a password reset disk, you must have a removable device such as a CD or USB flash drive. Before beginning this project, insert the device into the appropriate drive or connect it to the appropriate port. For example, insert a CD in a CD drive, or connect a USB flash drive to a USB port. Cancel the AutoPlay dialog box, if necessary.

1. Log off your Windows Vista user account and then restart your computer.
2. At the Welcome or Log in screen, click the **Greg Weber** account.
3. In the Password text box, key **!GWacct001!** and then press Enter. Windows Vista displays a message that the user must change the password to log on.
4. Click **OK**.
5. In the New password text box, key **rebeW23?**.
6. In the Confirm password text box, key **rebeW23?** and then press Enter.
7. Click **Start** and then click **Control Panel**.
8. Click **User Accounts and Family Safety** and then click **User Accounts**.
9. In the left pane, click **Create a password reset disk**. The Forgotten Password Wizard opens. This wizard will prompt you through the steps for creating a password reset disk.
10. Click **Next**.
11. Click the dropdown arrow and select the location of your removable device. Then click **Next**.
12. Key the new password for the current account—**rebeW23?**—and then click **Next**. Windows Vista creates the password reset disk.
13. When the progress is 100% complete, click **Next** and then click **Finish**.
14. Remove the device from the drive or the port.
15. Close all open windows.
16. Log off the Gregory Weber account and log back in to your own user account. Close all open windows.

PAUSE. LEAVE the desktop displayed to use in the next project.

Project 11-4: Suspicious Software

Your new home computer is performing slowly and has shut down unexpectedly on a number of occasions. You suspect that spyware may have installed itself. In this project, you open Windows Defender and disable a program you think might be causing the problem. You then manually update the definitions, run a quick scan, and enable the program again.

GET READY. To check for and download updates, you must have a connection to the Internet.

1. Click **Start**, click **Control Panel**, and then, under Security, click **Check this computer's security status**.
2. Click **Windows Defender** in the left pane of the Windows Security Center window.
3. Click the **Tools** button on the Windows Defender toolbar and then click **Software Explorer**.
4. Click to select any program in the list of programs that is not part of Windows Vista.
5. Click the **Disable** button and then click **Yes**. Windows Defender disables the program.
6. Click the **Help** dropdown arrow on the Windows Defender toolbar and then click **Check for updates**. In the User Account Controls dialog box, if you are logged in to an administrator account, click **Continue**. If you are not logged in using an administrator account, key an administrator's password and then click **OK** to continue. Windows Defender connects to the Internet and checks for new definition files. If new definitions are available, Windows Defender downloads and installs them automatically.
7. Click the **Scan** button dropdown arrow on the Windows Defender toolbar and then click **Quick Scan**. If necessary, in the User Account Controls dialog box, if you are logged in to an administrator account, click **Continue**. If you are not logged in using an administrator account, key an administrator's password and then click **OK** to continue. Windows Defender begins scanning your system for suspicious software. If it finds anything, it takes the default action or displays an alert so you can select an action.
8. When the scan is complete, click the **Tools** button on the Windows Defender toolbar and then click **Software Explorer**.
9. Click to select the disabled program and then click the **Enable** button. Click **Yes** to enable to program again.
10. Close the Windows Defender Window. The Windows Security Center should still be open.
11. Close the Windows Security Center and close the Control Panel.

PAUSE. LEAVE the desktop displayed to use in the next project.

■ Mastery Assessment

Project 11-5: Delete a User Account

The manager of the financial department at Trey Research is concerned because the new accountant did not return after lunch on his first day of work. As the system administrator, it is your responsibility to take the necessary steps to ensure there is not a security breach of the system. In this project, you will disable the user account so that it cannot be used to access the system. You will then delete the account.

1. Open the **Administrative Tools** and open the **Computer Management** window.
2. Display the list of local user accounts.
3. Double-click **Greg Weber** in the File list.
4. Disable the account and then close the dialog box.
5. Close all open windows.
6. Access the list of local user accounts again, enable the Gregory Weber user account, and then close the dialog box and all open windows.
7. Open the **User Accounts** window in **Control Panel** and select to change the **Greg Weber** account.

8. Delete the account, including all files associated with the account.
9. **CLOSE** all open windows.

PAUSE. LEAVE the desktop displayed to use in the next project.

Project 11-6: Troubleshoot Startup Problems

You are still having trouble with your new computer, particularly with startup. In this project, you restart your computer in Safe Mode with Networking. You check Windows Defender for new updates. You will restart your computer and then check Windows Update to see if there are any important updates you have not yet installed. Finally, you will try repairing the installation.

GET READY. To check for and download updates, you must have a connection to the Internet. If the system recovery tools are not installed on your hard disk, you must have your Windows Vista installation CD available to complete this project.

1. Restart your computer and display the Advanced Boot Options menu.
2. Start your computer in **Safe Mode with Networking.**
3. Open Windows Defender.
4. Check for updates and run a Quick Scan.
5. At your instructor's request, capture an image of the desktop. Save it in your Lesson 1 assessment folder as ***Proj11_06***.
6. Restart your system normally. Open the Windows Security Center and Display the Windows Update window. Check for updates. If any new important updates are available, install them.
7. View the list of installed updates to verify that they all installed successfully, and then close Windows Update and the Security Center.
8. Restart your system and access the System Recovery tools. For example, if the tools are installed on your hard disk, restart and access the Advanced Boot Options menu. If the tools are on the installation disk, insert the disk and then restart.
9. Select to use the **Startup Repair** utility.
10. When the Startup Repair utility is complete, start your computer normally.
11. **CLOSE** all open windows.

LOG OFF your Windows Vista user account.

INTERNET READY

Malicious software can wreak havoc on any computer or network. Even if a virus does not destroy data, it can compromise security or cause systems to run so slowly that businesses cannot operate. In this exercise, use Internet search tools to locate information about malicious software. For example, you might look up definitions for different types of malicious software and the type of damage malicious software can cause. When you have finished your research, use a word processing program or a pen and paper, and write a business plan outlining how a company can protect itself from malicious software. You might include a brief explanation of malicious software, how to identify if a system is infected, steps to take to remove the problem, and steps to take to protect the system from future problems.

Circling Back

The Baldwin Museum of Science has been running a series of seminars for high school science teachers. The seminars have been so successful that the museum has decided to hire a full-time employee specifically for organizing educational events. As an assistant system administrator, you are responsible for setting up the desktop computer for the new employee. You will start by creating a restore point, and then you create a standard password-protected user account. You will check the security settings, confirm the hardware configuration, and select power options. Finally, you will troubleshoot problems. To accomplish all of this, you will need to use the skills you have learned in Lessons 9 ("Managing System Resources"), 10 ("Managing Software"), and 11 ("Monitoring the Windows Vista Environment") to manage system resources and software, and to monitor the Windows Vista environment.

Project 1: Set Up a New User Account

Before setting up the computer for the new employee, you will manually create a restore point so that if you run into any problems, you can easily restore the system to its current configuration. You will then create a new standard password-protected user account for the employee that requires him to change the password the first time he logs in.

GET READY. Before you begin these steps, turn on your computer and log in to your Windows Vista user account. Close all open windows so that you have a clear view of the desktop. Create a new folder named CB3 in a storage location specified by your instructor where you can store assessment files that you create during these projects.

1. Click **Start**, click **Computer**, and then click the **System Properties** button on the Computer window toolbar.
2. Under Tasks in the left pane, click **System protection**. If you are logged on to an administrator account, click **Continue**. If not, key an administrator password and then click **OK**.
3. Verify a checkmark is next to your local hard disk drive. If necessary, click to select the checkbox next to the disk.
4. Click the **Create** button to create a new restore point.
5. Key **BMS Ed** and then click **Create**.
6. Click **OK** to create the restore point.
7. When the restore point is complete, click **OK**, and then click **OK** to close the System Properties dialog box.
8. From the System page of the Control Panel, navigate to the System and Maintenance window. For example, click **System and Maintenance** in the Address bar, and then click **Administrative Tools**.
9. In the File list, double-click **Computer Management**. If you are logged on to an administrator account, click **Continue**. If not, key an administrator password and then click **OK**.
10. In the Navigation pane, click **Local Users and Groups** and then double-click **Users** in the File list.
11. Right-click a blank area of the File list and click **New User** on the shortcut menu. The New User dialog box displays.
12. In the User Name text box, key **Peter**. In the Full name text box, key **Peter Houston**.
13. In the Description text box, key **Educational Programs Manager, hired 9/6**.
14. In the Password text box, key **admin!NW_01**.
15. In the Confirm password text box, key **admin!NW_01**.
16. Verify that the **User must change password at next logon** checkbox is selected. If not, click it to select it. At this point, your instructor may ask you to capture an image of the New User dialog box. Save it in your CB3 assessment folder as ***CB3_01***.
17. Click **Create** and then click **Close** to close the New User dialog box.
18. **CLOSE** all open windows.

    PAUSE. LEAVE the Windows Vista desktop displayed to use in the next project.

Project 2: Monitor and Set Security Options

Before connecting the new system to the museum's network, you must verify that the new system is safe from malicious software. In this project, you will open the Windows Security Center and check the settings for the firewall, malware protection, and Windows Update. You will scan the computer for malicious software. After connecting to the Internet, you will check for and install important updates. Finally, you will schedule regular backups.

1. Click **Start**, click **Control Panel**, and then, under Security, click **Check this computer's security status**.
2. Verify the status of the firewall, automatic updating, and malware protection.
3. If one of the Windows Vista security features is not on, verify that a different program is installed and protecting the system. For example, if Windows Firewall is not on, confirm that a different firewall program is on. Also check that an antivirus program is running.
4. In the left pane of the Windows Security Center, click **Windows Defender**.
5. Click the **Tools** button on the Windows Defender toolbar and then click **Options**.
6. Scroll down in the window and note the status of the three options that control whether Windows Defender is protecting your system: Automatically scan my computer, Use real-time protection, and Use Windows Defender.
7. Click the **Scan** button dropdown arrow on the Windows Defender toolbar and then click **Full Scan** to start scanning all files and programs on the computer.
   If necessary, in the User Account Controls dialog box, if you are logged in to an administrator account click **Continue**. If you are not logged in using an administrator account, key an administrator's password and then click **OK** to continue.
   If Windows Defender finds suspicious software and displays an alert, select the appropriate option to either remove, quarantine, or allow the software.
8. When the scan is complete, close the Windows Defender window.
9. If necessary, establish a connection to the Internet.
10. In the left pane of the Windows Security Center, click **Windows Update** and then, in the left pane, click **Check for updates**.
11. Click the **View available updates** link. If an important update is available and selected, click the **Install** button. Alternatively, select a recommended or optional update and then click the **Install** button. In the User Account Controls dialog box, if you are logged in to an administrator account, click **Continue**. If you are not logged in using an administrator account, key an administrator's password and then click **OK** to continue.
12. When the installation is complete, click **View update history** in the left pane of the Windows Update window.
13. Close the View Update History window.
14. Close the Windows Security Center window.
15. Navigate to the Control Panel, and then, Under System and Maintenance, click **Back up your computer**.
16. Click **Change Settings** and then click **Change backup settings**. If you are logged on to an administrator account, click **Continue**. If not, key an administrator password and then click **OK**.
17. Select the location where you want to save your backups and then click **Next**.
18. Select the types of files you want to back up and then click **Next**.
19. Click the **How often** dropdown arrow and click **Daily**.
20. Click the **What time** dropdown arrow and click **7:00 PM**. At this point, your instructor may ask you to capture an image of the Back Up Files wizard page. Save it in your CB3 assessment folder as *CB3_02*.
21. Click **Save settings and exit**.
22. **CLOSE** all open windows.

PAUSE. LEAVE the Windows Vista desktop displayed to use in the next project.

Project 3: Monitor and Set Hardware Resource Options

Before you can install new hardware and software, you must check the available resources on the computer and set power options. In this project, you will locate, display, and print information about the amount of installed random access memory (RAM) and the processor speed, as well as other resource information. You will locate information about the amount of available disk space, and you will set power options for maximum performance.

GET READY. Make sure you have a printer correctly connected, loaded with paper, and available for use. You should also have available a method for recording information you find during this project. For example, you may have a pen or pencil on hand, or you may have a text or document file or an online journal.

1. Click **Start** and then click **Control Panel**.
2. Click **System and Maintenance**.
3. Under System, click **View amount of RAM and processor speed**.
4. To the right of Rating, click **Windows Experience Index** to open the Performance Information and Tools window.
5. Click **View and print details**.
6. Click **Print this page**, in the top right corner of the window, and then click **Print** in the Print dialog box.
7. Close all open windows.
8. Click **Start** and then click **Computer**.
9. Click your local disk and view the details about its capacity that display to the right of the disk icon.
10. On the printed page detailing your basic system information, write down the total amount of space on your disk and the amount of free space available. Alternatively, record the information in an electronic file or online journal.
11. Close the Computer window.
12. Click **Start**, click **Control Panel**, and then click **System and Maintenance**.
13. Click **Power Options** to display the Power Options window.
14. Click the **High performance** option button. At your instructor's request, capture an image of the Power Options window. Save it in your CB3 assessment folder as ***CB3_03***, and then close the Control Panel window.

    PAUSE. LEAVE the desktop displayed and keep the pen or pencil available to use in the next project.

Project 4: Troubleshoot Problems

The computer you are setting up seems to be having trouble processing certain information, and you suspect it might be due to a problem with the DVD drive. (If you do not have a DVD drive in your computer, your instructor may ask you to use a different device to complete this project.) In this project, you use the Device Manager to see if disabling or updating the driver solves the problem. You then start the computer in Safe Mode and check the Task Manager for performance statistics. Finally, you check your hard disk for errors.

1. Click **Start**, click **Control Panel**, and then click **System and Maintenance**. The System and Maintenance window displays.
2. Click **Device Manager**. If you are logged on to an administrator account, click **Continue**. If not, key an administrator password and then click **OK**.
3. Click the plus sign to the left of the **DVD/CD-ROM drives** category.
4. Right-click your DVD device and click **Disable** on the shortcut menu. Then click **Yes** in the warning box.
5. Right-click your sound device and click **Properties**. Click the **Driver** tab and then click **Update Driver...**.
6. Click **Search automatically for updated driver software**. If Windows Vista finds a newer driver, it will install it. Otherwise, it displays a message that your driver is up-to-date.

7. Click **Close** to close the Update Driver Software window and then click **Close** to close the Properties dialog box.
8. Right-click your DVD device and click **Enable.**
9. Close all open windows.
10. Restart your computer and press F8 during startup to display the Advanced Boot Options menu.
11. Select to start your computer in **Safe Mode with Networking** and then press Enter.
12. Log in to your Windows Vista user account.
13. Close the Windows Help and Support window. Then right-click a blank area of the Taskbar and click **Task Manager** to display the Windows Task Manager.
14. Click the **Performance** tab to see the graphs and tables that display information about how your computer is using the CPU and memory resources. At your instructor's request, capture an image of the Performance tab of the Task Manager dialog box. Save it in you CB3 assessment folder as ***CB3_04***.
15. Locate the amount of physical memory and the percentage of physical memory currently in use, the current CPU usage percentage, and the Page File usage statistics and write down the information. Alternatively, record the information in an electronic file or online journal.
16. Close the Task Manager.
17. Click **Start** and then click **Computer**. Right-click your local disk and then click **Properties**.
18. Click the **Tools** tab and then Click the **Check Now...** button. If you are logged on as an administrator, the User Account Control dialog box displays. Click **Continue**. If not, key the administrator password and then click **OK**.
19. Click **Start** and then click **Schedule disk check.**
20. Close all open windows and restart your computer. Watch to see if Windows Vista identifies any errors.
21. After the restart, log back in to your Windows Vista user account.

PAUSE. LEAVE the desktop displayed to use in the next project.

Project 5: Repair and Restore Windows Vista

The computer is still not running smoothly. In this project, you will try to repair the Windows Vista installation, and then you will use the restore point you created in Project 1 to restore a previous configuration.

1. Restart your system and access the System Recovery tools. For example, if the tools are installed on your hard disk, restart and press F8 to access the Advanced Boot Options menu. If the tools are on the installation disk, insert the disk and then restart the computer.
2. Select to use the **Startup Repair** utility.
3. When the Startup Repair utility is complete, restart your computer normally and log in to your Windows Vista user account. Close all open windows.
4. Click **Start**, click **Control Panel**, and then click **System and Maintenance**.
5. Click **Backup and Restore Center** and then, under Tasks in the left pane, click **Repair Windows using System Restore**. If you are logged on to an administrator account, click **Continue**. If not, key an administrator password and then click **OK**.
6. Click to select the **Choose a different restore point** option and then click **Next**.
7. Select the **BMS Ed** restore point you created in Project 1.
8. Click **Next.** At your instructor's request, capture an image of the System Restore wizard window. Save it in you CB3 assessment folder as ***CB3_05***.
9. Click **Finish** and then click **Yes** in the warning dialog box.
10. When your system restarts, log in to your Windows Vista user account.
11. Take a few minutes to check the system changes you made in Projects 1–4. Notice that they are no longer in effect, because the system has been restored to an earlier configuration. Even the new user account you set up in Project 1 no longer exists.

LOG OFF your Windows Vista user account.

Managing Windows Internet Explorer

LESSON SKILL MATRIX

Skills	Matrix Skill	Skill Number
Setting Windows Internet Explorer Security Levels	Configure Windows Internet Explorer security settings	1.5.1
Setting Windows Internet Explorer Privacy Levels		
Managing Cookies	Configure privacy settings	1.5.4
Using Windows Internet Explorer's Pop-up Blocker	Allow selected pop-up windows	1.5.5
Using Windows Internet Explorer's Phishing Filter	Use the Phishing filter	1.5.2
Selecting Temporary Internet Files and History Settings	Configure history and temporary Internet files settings	1.5.3
Using Windows Internet Explorer		
Downloading a Sidebar Gadget	Download a gadget from the Internet	6.4.4

KEY TERMS

Browser tabs
Cookie
First-party cookie
Information bar
Intranet
Phishing
Pop-up
Protected Mode
Search provider
Security level
Security zone
Temporary Internet files
Third-party cookie
Web browser

Adventure Works is an international travel agency. Employees use their computers to access and store data about destinations, lodging, restaurants, employees, and customers. They rely on the Internet and the Windows Internet Explorer web browser for research and communication. For example, they use these tools to book flights and hotel rooms, and to take reservations from customers. The office manager, who is also responsible for system administration, knows that any web browser can be a risk to the security of individual computers or a network. Unauthorized users might be able to exploit a web browser connection to send malicious software into the system via a web page or an email message. In addition, any action that involves the exchange of personal or financial information can be a risk to privacy. For example, unauthorized users may be able to acquire information such as credit card or bank account numbers and use it for illegal purposes such as identify theft and fraud. As a result, the office manager makes sure all employees are trained in selecting and applying Windows Internet Explorer security settings for their desktop and notebook computers. In this lesson, you learn how to select Windows Internet Security settings and how to use Windows Internet Explorer to locate information on the Internet.

■ Setting Windows Internet Explorer Security Levels

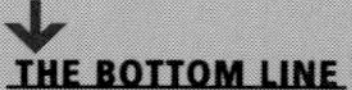

Windows Vista comes with the Windows Internet Explorer ***web browser***, which is a program that you can use to locate and view pages on the Internet, an intranet, or the World Wide Web (web). Although the Internet is a wonderful resource for information on virtually every topic, it can also provide access to potentially harmful or malicious programs. Many websites are designed specifically to infiltrate your system with spyware and other malicious software. These sites attempt to save files or install programs on your computer when you access a site or click a link. Windows Internet Explorer security settings help you protect your computer by identifying and monitoring potentially harmful websites, and by displaying warnings if a website attempts to run or install a program. In this section, you learn how to start Windows Internet Explorer and configure security settings.

SET WINDOWS INTERNET EXPLORER SECURITY LEVELS

GET READY. Before you begin these steps, start your computer and log on to your Windows Vista account. Close all open windows so that you can see the desktop. Create a new folder named Lesson 12 in a storage location specified by your instructor where you can store assessment files and folders that you create during this lesson. You must be logged on using an administrator account, or you must have an administrator's password to complete this exercise.

1. Click **Start** and then, at the top of the left pane of the Start menu, click **Internet Explorer**. The default home page opens in Windows Internet Explorer.

You can also start Windows Internet Explorer by clicking the Internet Explorer icon on the Quick Launch Toolbar.

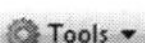

2. Click the **Tools** button on the Windows Internet Explorer toolbar and then click **Internet Options** to open the Internet Options dialog box.
3. Click the **Security** tab to display the Security settings. The dialog box should look similar to Figure 12-1 with the settings for the Internet security zone displayed. A ***security zone*** is a category that Windows Internet Explorer uses to identify websites based on the level of risk they pose. The Internet zone is one of the security zones. It includes all websites that are not manually designated as Trusted or Restricted. The default security level for the Internet zone is Medium-high, and Protected Mode is enabled. A ***security level*** is a pre-selected group of

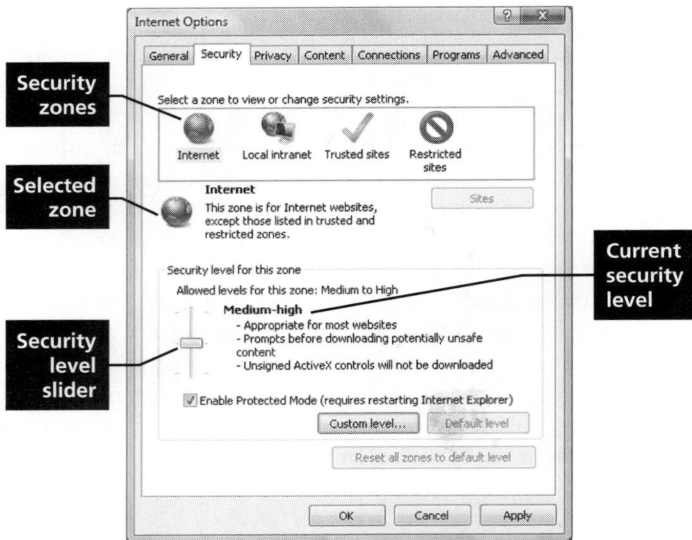

Figure 12-1

Security tab of the Internet Options dialog box

security settings that can be applied to a security zone. ***Protected Mode*** is a feature that enables Windows Internet Explorer to display a warning whenever a website tries to install or run a program or file on your computer so that you have the opportunity to cancel or allow the installation.

TAKE NOTE* While you browse the Internet, the zone of the current web page and the status of Protected Mode display on the Status bar in the Windows Internet Explorer window.

4. Click the **Local intranet** zone to view its security settings. The Local intranet zone includes all sites on your local intranet. An ***intranet*** is a corporate network that uses Internet technologies but can only be accessed by employees and other authorized users. The default security level is Medium-low, because there should be less risk from sites on your intranet than from sites on the Internet.
5. Click the **Trusted sites** zone. The Trusted sites zone includes sites that you manually designate as safe. Its default security level is Medium. Notice that Protected Mode is not enabled in the Trusted sites zone.
6. Click the **Restricted sites** zone. This zone includes sites that you manually designate as high risk. The default security level is High.
7. Click the **Internet** zone and then drag the **Security level slider** down as far as it will go. This sets the security level to Medium, as shown in Figure 12-2. You cannot set the security level for the Internet zone lower than Medium, because it would pose too much of a risk to your computer. Notice that when you change the level, buttons for resetting the zone or all zones to the default level become available.

Figure 12-2

Change the security level

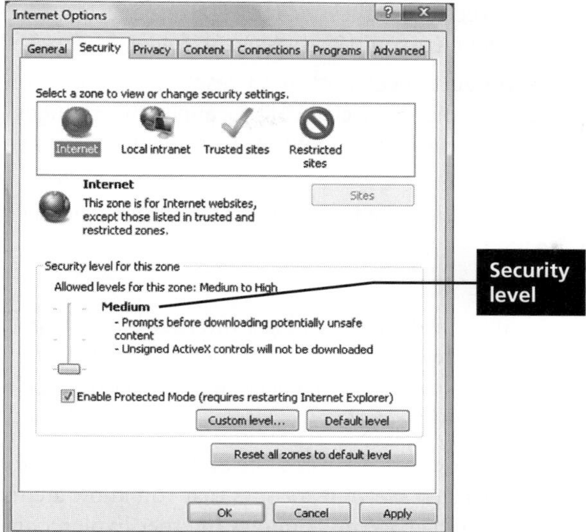

8. Click the **Custom level** button to display the Security Settings dialog box, as shown in Figure 12-3. This dialog box lists all available security settings so that you can select or deselect the specific options you want to use. Scroll down the list and note which options are enabled, which are disabled, and which are set to display a prompt.

Figure 12-3

Select custom security settings

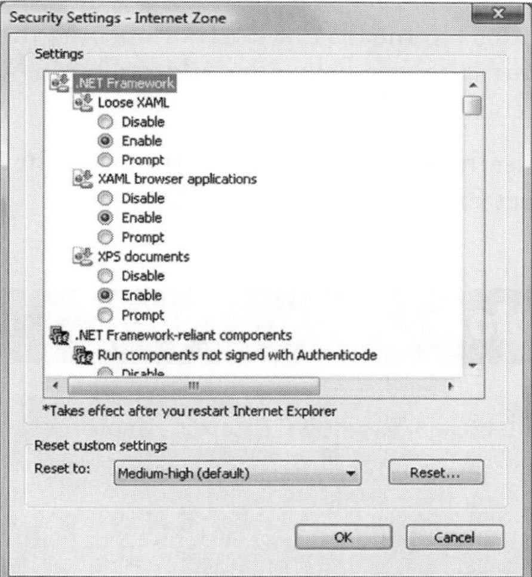

TAKE NOTE*

You can select custom security settings for each security zone.

9. Under Downloads in the list of security settings, click to select **Enable** under the option Automatic prompting for file downloads and then click **OK**. Click **Yes** in the Warning dialog box to return to the Security tab of the Internet Options dialog box. Notice that the security level is now set to Custom.
10. Click to clear the **Enable Protected Mode** checkbox. This disables Protected Mode so that Windows Internet Explorer will not prompt you if a website tries to install or run a program or file on your computer.
11. Click **Apply**. A warning displays, as shown in Figure 12-4, notifying you that the current settings put your computer at risk. Click **OK** to apply the changes and keep the Internet Options dialog box open.

Figure 12-4

Warning dialog box

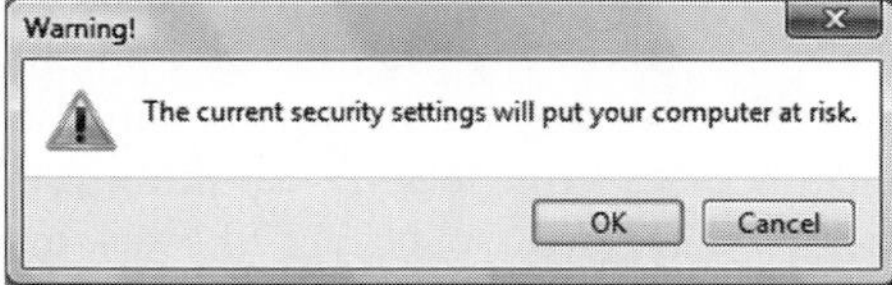

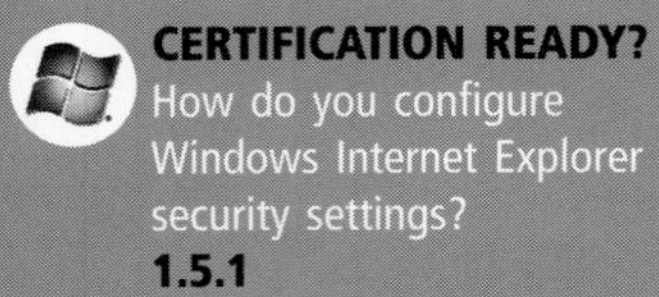

12. At your instructor's request, capture an image of the Internet Options dialog box. Save it in your Lesson 12 assessment folder as ***Le12_01***.
13. Click the **Default level** button to reset the security level for the Internet zone to its default and then click **OK** to apply the changes and close the dialog box. The default home page should still be displayed in the Windows Internet Explorer browser window.

PAUSE. LEAVE the Windows Internet Explorer window open to use in the next exercise.

In this exercise, you learned that Windows Internet Explorer places every website into one of four security zones and sets security levels for each zone ranging from Low to High. You can adjust the security level for a zone or select custom security options. You can reset the security level to the default at any time.

By default, no websites are in the Trusted site and Restricted site zones. You can add sites that you know are safe to the Trusted site zone, or sites that you know are risky to the Restricted site zone. To add a site, browse to the page in Windows Internet Explorer and then display the Security tab of the Internet Options dialog box to select the desired zone. Click the Sites button to display a list of sites in the zone and then click Add. To remove a site, select it in the list of sites and then click Remove. Click Close to close the dialog box. (To add a site to the Trusted sites zone, you may have to deselect the Require server verification (https://) for all sites in this zone checkbox.)

If you use Windows Internet Explorer with settings that might put your computer at risk, the Information bar at the top of the Windows Internet Explorer window displays the message *Your security setting level puts your computer at risk.* Click the Information bar to display options for fixing the settings to the default levels or opening the Internet Options dialog box. The ***Information bar*** is an area below the Address bar in Windows Internet Explorer where messages about security display.

In the next section, you learn how to set privacy settings for the Internet zone and how to manage Windows Internet Explorer's pop-up blocker.

■ Setting Windows Internet Explorer Privacy Levels

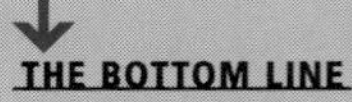

The privacy settings available in Windows Internet Explorer are designed to help protect your personal information from unauthorized access. Specifically, you can manage the way Windows Internet Explorer handles cookies, and you can control pop-ups by configuring Windows Internet Explorer's Pop-up Blocker feature. ***Cookies*** are small files that a website creates and stores on your computer. A cookie contains information that identifies you to the website, such as your user name and email address. It may also contain information such as passwords and account numbers. ***Pop-ups*** are browser windows that display over the web page you are currently viewing. They are usually advertisements that display without your permission. In this section, you learn how to select privacy settings to control the way cookies are stored on your computer and how to manage Windows Internet Explorer's Pop-up Blocker feature.

Managing Cookies

Most websites that you visit create and store a cookie on your computer. Cookies can be helpful because they make it easier to visit a trusted site more than once without having to log in each time or reenter information. Unfortunately, some websites use cookies without your permission to record personal information such as which websites you visit, what items you search for, and even what products you purchase online. You can adjust general privacy settings to block or allow cookies. You can also set Windows Internet Explorer to block or allow cookies from specific websites. In this exercise, you learn how to use Windows Internet Explorer privacy settings to block or allow cookies.

MANAGE COOKIES

USE the Windows Internet Explorer window you left open in the previous exercise.

1. Click the **Tools** button on the Windows Internet Explorer window toolbar and then click **Internet Options**.
2. Click the **Privacy** tab to display the Privacy settings. The tab should look similar to Figure 12-5. Like a security level, you can set a privacy level for all sites in the Internet zone to control which cookies are blocked and which are allowed. The default privacy level is Medium, which blocks cookies from many websites that do not meet specific privacy policy guidelines.

Figure 12-5

Select custom privacy settings

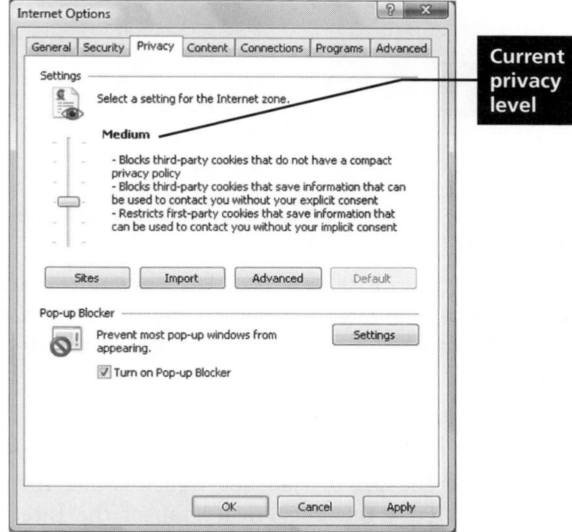

3. Drag the slider as far up as it will go. This sets the privacy level for all sites in the Internet zone to block all new cookies and to prohibit websites from reading cookies already stored on your computer.
4. Drag the slider as far down as it will go. This allows all cookies from websites in the Internet zone.
5. Click the **Default** button to restore the default Medium settings. Now, try managing cookies for a specific website.
6. Click the **Sites** button to open the Per Site Privacy Actions dialog box. In this dialog box, you can select to block or allow cookies for specific websites.
7. In the Address of website text box, key **www.microsoft.com** and then click **Allow**. The site is added to the list of Managed websites, as shown in Figure 12-6. Note that the setting is Always Allow, which means Windows Internet Explorer will always allow cookies from this website.

Figure 12-6

Set privacy actions for specific sites

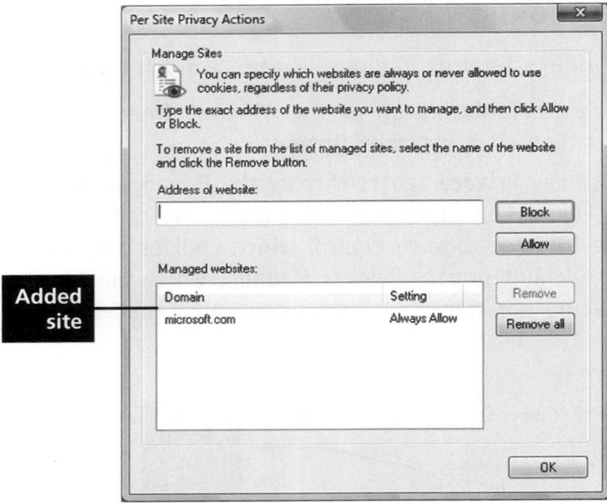

8. Click the site in the list of Managed websites and then click **Remove** to remove it from the list.
9. In the Address of website text box, key **www.microsoft.com** again and then click **Block**. This time, the site is added to the list of Managed websites and is set to Always Block. Internet Explorer will not allow the site to install any cookies on your computer.
10. At your instructor's request, capture an image of the Internet Options dialog box. Save it in your Lesson 12 assessment folder as ***Le12_02***.
11. Click the site in the list of Managed websites and then click **Remove** to remove it from the list. Click **OK**. The Privacy tab of the Internet Options dialog box should still be displayed.

PAUSE. LEAVE the Internet Options dialog box open to use in the next exercise.

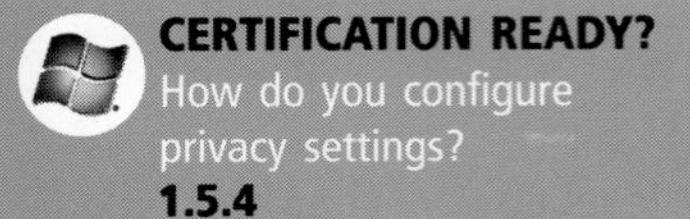

CERTIFICATION READY?
How do you configure privacy settings?
1.5.4

As you have learned, you can adjust general privacy settings to block or allow cookies, and you can select specific sites for which you want to block or allow cookies. Windows Internet Explorer bases the general privacy settings on whether a website adheres to certain privacy policy guidelines. For example, some sites have policies that guarantee they will not collect or share personal information without your consent, whereas other sites have no such policies.

In addition, cookies may be identified as First-party cookies or Third-party cookies. A ***First-party cookie*** is created by the website you are currently viewing and is usually used to store information that will identify you to the site. A ***Third-party cookie*** is created by a website other than the one you are currently viewing, such as an advertiser. It might be used to track your browsing and shopping habits so that the advertiser can target you with pop-up and email solicitations.

Also, cookies may be temporary or persistent. Temporary cookies are not actually stored on your computer, and they are removed as soon as you end the current Windows Internet Explorer session. Persistent cookies are stored on your computer even after you close Windows Internet Explorer so that they can be used whenever you visit the website that placed the cookie on your computer.

You can delete all cookies from your computer if you want. In Windows Internet Explorer, click the Tools button and then click Internet Options. On the General tab, under Browsing history click Delete, click the Delete Cookies button, and then click Yes. Click Close, and then click OK. Be aware that deleting cookies may cause problems when you try to browse some websites.

In the next exercise, you learn how to manage Windows Internet Explorer's Pop-up Blocker.

Using Windows Internet Explorer's Pop-up Blocker

Pop-ups can be annoying and distracting, but they can also be dangerous. Some are designed so that when you click them, they direct you to a fraudulent website, or they install malicious software. By default, Windows Internet Explorer is set to block most pop-up windows. You can turn the Pop-up Blocker off if you want to allow pop-ups, or you can selectively allow pop-ups from some websites. In this exercise, you learn how to manage pop-ups using Windows Internet Explorer's Pop-up Blocker feature.

USE WINDOWS INTERNET EXPLORER'S POP-UP BLOCKER

USE the Internet Options dialog box you left open in the previous exercise.

1. On the Privacy tab of the Internet Options dialog box, click to deselect the **Turn on Pop-up Blocker** checkbox. This turns off the Pop-up Blocker, allowing pop-up windows to display.
2. Click to select the **Turn on Pop-up Blocker** checkbox to turn the Pop-up Blocker on. When the Pop-up Blocker is on, most pop-up windows will not display.

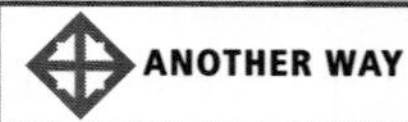

You can also turn the Pop-up Blocker off or on from the Internet Explorer Tools menu. To turn the Pop-up Blocker off, click the Tools button, point to Pop-up Blocker, and then click Turn Off Pop-up Blocker. To turn it on, click the Tools button, point to Pop-up Blocker, and then click Turn On Pop-up Blocker.

3. Click the **Settings** button to display the Pop-up Blocker Settings dialog box. It should look similar to Figure 12-7. In this dialog box, you can specify sites on which you want to allow pop-ups. You can also adjust the Notifications and filter level settings for pop-ups.

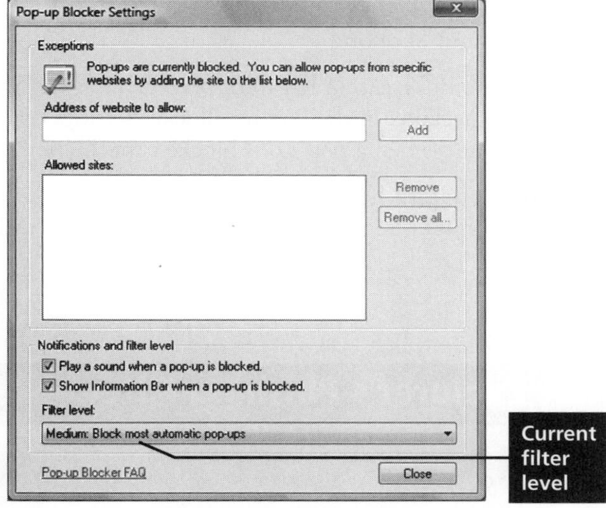

Figure 12-7
Pop-up Blocker Settings dialog box

TROUBLESHOOTING

If the Settings button is not available on the Privacy tab of the Internet Options dialog box, the Pop-up Blocker is off. Click to select the Turn on Pop-up Blocker checkbox.

To open the Pop-up Blocker Settings dialog box from the Internet Explorer Tools menu, click the Tools button and then click Pop-up Blocker Settings.

4. Click the **Filter level** dropdown arrow and click **High: Block all pop-ups**. This setting blocks all pop-ups.
5. Click the **Filter level** dropdown arrow and click **Low: Allow pop-ups from secure sites**. This setting allows pop-ups from secure sites, but blocks pop-ups on all other sites.

6. Click the **Filter level** dropdown arrow and click **Medium: Block most automatic pop-ups** to return to the default setting.
7. In the Address of website to allow text box, key **www.microsoft.com** and then click **Add.** The site is added to the list of Allowed sites. When you are viewing that site, Windows Internet Explorer will allow it to display pop-ups.
8. At your instructor's request, capture an image of the Pop-up Blocker Settings dialog box. Save it in your Lesson 12 assessment folder as ***Le12_03***.
9. Click the site in the list of Allowed sites and then click **Remove.**
10. Click **Close** to close the dialog box and then click **OK** to close the Internet Options dialog box.

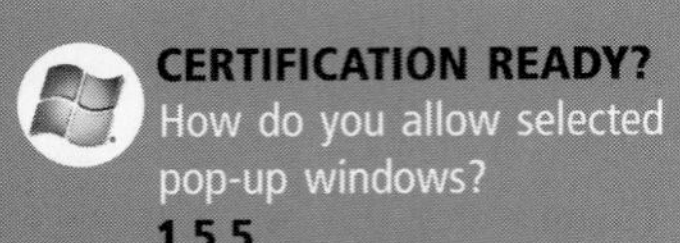
CERTIFICATION READY? How do you allow selected pop-up windows? **1.5.5**

PAUSE. LEAVE the Windows Internet Explorer browser open to use in the next exercise.

Keep in mind that not all pop-up windows are advertisements. Many websites are designed to display links in a new, separate browser window, leaving the original window open as well. When pop-ups are blocked, you can display these types of pop-up windows by pressing Ctrl+Alt when you click a link to a pop-up window.

By default, when Windows Internet Explorer blocks a pop-up, a message displays in the Information bar (and a sound plays). When you click the Information bar, a menu displays the following options:

- Temporarily Allow Pop-ups. Click this option to allow pop-ups during the current session.
- Always Allow Pop-ups from This Site. Click this option to add the current page to the list of Allowed Sites.
- Settings. Click this option to turn the Pop-up Blocker off, to show or hide the Information bar, or to open the Pop-up Blocker Settings dialog box.
- More Information. Click this option to display the relevant information in Windows Help and Support.

If you do not want the Information bar to display, deselect the Show Information Bar when a pop-up is blocked checkbox in the Pop-up Blocker settings dialog box. Likewise, you can deselect the Play a sound when a pop-up is blocked checkbox.

In the next section, you learn how to use Windows Internet Explorer's Phishing Filter to identify websites that might be trying to collect your personal or financial information.

■ Using Windows Internet Explorer's Phishing Filter

THE BOTTOM LINE

Phishing is the act of trying to collect personal or financial information without permission through an email message or website. Phishing scams usually involve misdirecting a browser to a fraudulent website where the user enters the information, believing that the website is legitimate. Windows Internet Explorer includes a Phishing Filter that helps detect phishing websites while you browse the web. By default, the Phishing Filter compares sites you visit to a list of legitimate websites that is stored on your computer, and it looks for characteristics that are commonly found on phishing websites. In addition, you can set the Phishing Filter to automatically send the addresses of certain sites you visit to Microsoft, where they can be checked against a list of known phishing sites. And you can manually check a website at any time. In this section, you learn how to turn on automatic checking, how to manually check a website, and how to report a site that you suspect is a phishing website.

 USE WINDOWS INTERNET EXPLORER'S PHISHING FILTER

USE the Windows Internet Explorer window you left open in the previous exercise.

1. Click the **Tools** button on the Windows Internet Explorer window toolbar, point to **Phishing Filter**, and then click **Turn on Automatic Website Checking.** The Microsoft Phishing Filter dialog box displays, as shown in Figure 12-8.

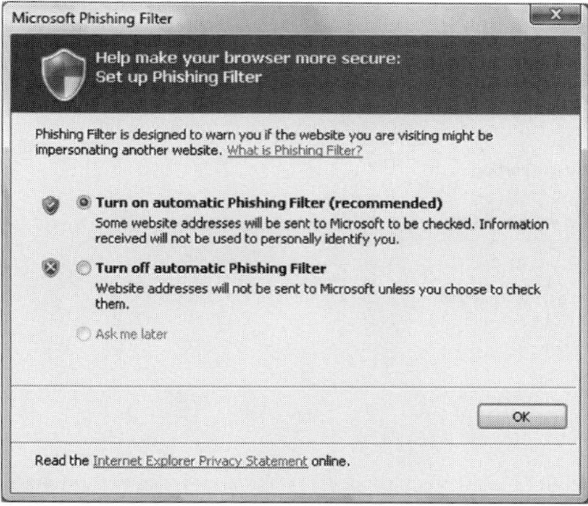

Figure 12-8

Microsoft Phishing Filter dialog box

TROUBLESHOOTING

If automatic checking is already on, to display the dialog box, click Turn off Automatic Website Checking.

2. If necessary, click to select the **Turn on automatic Phishing Filter (recommended)** option button and then click **OK**. The Phishing Filter is now set to automatically send information about certain sites to Microsoft to see if they are on the list of known phishing sites.

TAKE NOTE*

If the Phishing Filter identifies a site as a possible phishing site, it displays a message in the Information bar notifying you that it might be a phishing site. If it identifies a site as a known phishing site, it blocks the site, displays a web page providing more information, and the Information bar turns red.

3. Click the **Tools** button on the Windows Internet Explorer window toolbar, point to **Phishing Filter**, and then click **Check this site**. A Phishing Filter warning dialog box should display.

TAKE NOTE*

The warning dialog box may not display if it has already been disabled. For example, if someone has selected the Don't show this again checkbox, it will not display.

4. Click **OK** to check the current website against the list Microsoft maintains of known phishing sites. After the check, a message in the dialog box lets you know whether the site is a known phishing site. Click **OK** to close the dialog box.
5. Click the **Tools** button on the Windows Internet Explorer window toolbar, point to **Phishing Filter**, and then click **Report this Website**. Internet Explorer displays the Microsoft Phishing Filter Report a website page. It should look similar to Figure 12-9. (If you suspect the current site is a phishing site, you would click to select the I think this is a phishing website checkbox and then click Submit. Microsoft will investigate the site, and, if necessary, add it to the list of known phishing sites to help protect others.)

Figure 12-9

Microsoft Phishing Filter Report a website page

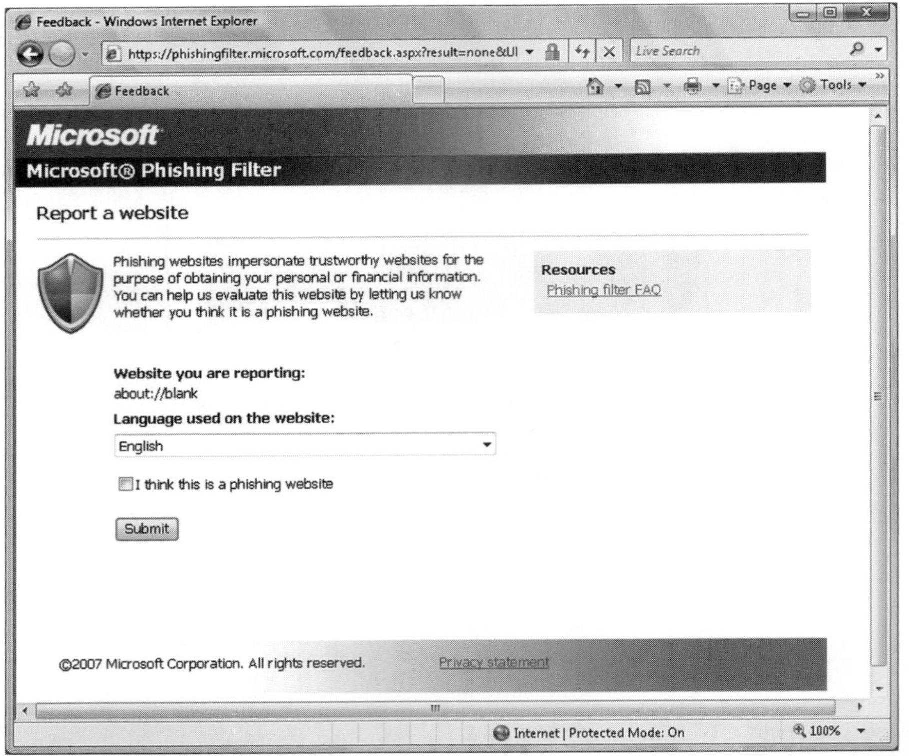

6. At your instructor's request, capture an image of the Report a website page. Save it in your Lesson 12 assessment folder as ***Le12_04***.
7. Close the web page without selecting the I think this is a phishing website checkbox. Your Windows Internet Explorer window should still be open to your default home page.

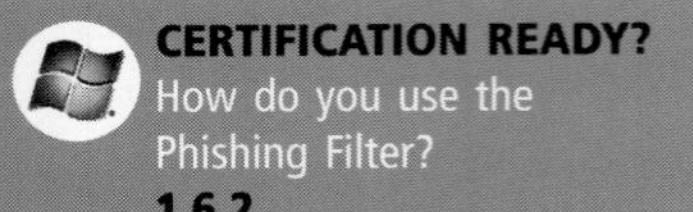

CERTIFICATION READY?
How do you use the Phishing Filter?
1.6.2

PAUSE. LEAVE the Windows Internet Explorer window open to use in the next exercise.

If the Phishing Filter flags a site as a possible phishing site, but you know it is a legitimate site, you can report the site to Microsoft as a legitimate site. Display the site in Windows Internet Explorer, click the Tools button, click Phishing Filter, and then click Report This Website. On the Report a website page, click to select the I think this is not a phishing website checkbox and then click Submit. To keep a site from being checked automatically by the Phishing Filter, you can add it to the Trusted Sites zone.

Although it is not recommended, you can turn off the Phishing Filter completely. Open Windows Internet Explorer, click the Tools button, click Phishing Filter, and then click Phishing Filter Settings. Scroll down to the Phishing Filter settings, near the bottom of the list; click to select the Disable Phishing Filter option button; and then click OK.

In the next exercise, you learn how to configure the history and temporary Internet file settings to control how Windows Internet Explorer stores information about sites you have visited.

■ Selecting Temporary Internet Files and History Settings

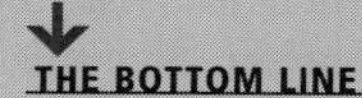

Windows Internet Explorer stores on your computer two categories of information about websites that you visit. First, it stores ***temporary Internet files***, which are copies of web pages, images, and media that you view on the Internet. Keeping these files stored on your computer makes it possible to display the page more quickly if you visit it again later. Second, it keeps a History list of the websites you have visited. You can use the list to quickly select a site that you want to view again. You can configure the temporary Internet files to specify how frequently Windows Internet Explorer checks for newer versions of the stored pages as well as how much disk space to use for storing these files. You can configure the History settings to specify how long Windows Internet Explorer should store the list. In this exercise, you learn how to configure the temporary Internet files and History settings.

SELECT TEMPORARY INTERNET FILES AND HISTORY SETTINGS

USE the Windows Internet Explorer window you left open in the previous exercise.

1. Click the **Tools** button on the Windows Internet Explorer window toolbar and then click **Internet Options**.
2. On the General tab, under Browsing history, click **Settings** to open the Temporary Internet Files and History Settings dialog box, as shown in Figure 12-10.

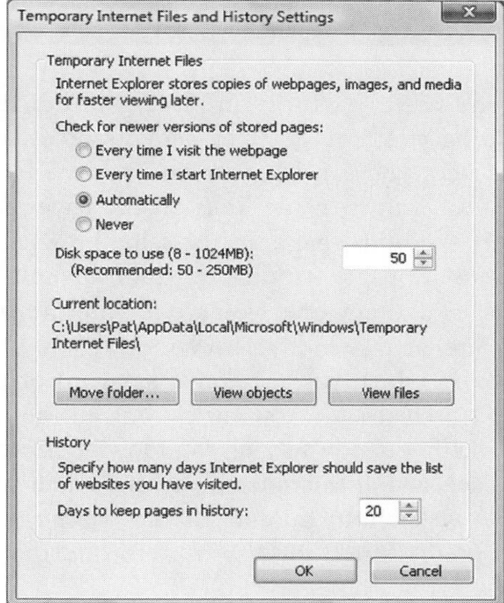

Figure 12-10

Temporary Internet Files and History Settings dialog box

3. In the Temporary Internet Files area, click to select the **Every time I visit the webpage** option. This sets Internet Explorer to check for a new version of a web page whenever you visit the page and to update the copy stored on your computer, if necessary.
4. Locate the amount of disk space currently allocated for storing temporary Internet files. If it is more than 250MB or less than 50MB, change the **Disk space to use** value to fall within that recommended range.
5. In the History area, check the **Days to keep pages in history** value to see how many days Windows Internet Explorer is currently set to store the History list. If it is not set to 20 days, change the setting to **20**.

CERTIFICATION READY?
How do you configure history and temporary Internet files settings?
1.5.3

6. At your instructor's request, capture an image of the Temporary Internet Files and History Settings dialog box. Save it in your Lesson 12 assessment folder as ***Le12_05***.
7. Click **OK** to apply the changes and close the dialog box. Then click **OK** to close the Internet Options dialog box.

PAUSE. LEAVE the Windows Internet Explorer window open to use in the next exercise.

Temporary Internet files may make it quicker to display web pages when you visit them again, but they also take up disk space. If you find yourself running low on disk space, you can delete the files. In Windows Internet Explorer, click the Tools button and then click Delete browsing history to open the Delete Browsing History dialog box. Click Delete files and then click Yes. Click Close to close the dialog box.

If you want to delete the items in the History list, open the Delete Browsing History dialog box, click Delete history, and then click Yes. Click Close to close the dialog box.

While browsing the web, if you notice that web pages you have visited before display old or out-of-date information, you might have Windows Internet Explorer set to never check for newer versions of files. You can click the Refresh button to the right of the Address bar to update the page.

In the next section, you learn how to use Windows Internet Explorer to locate and view information on the Internet.

■ Using Windows Internet Explorer

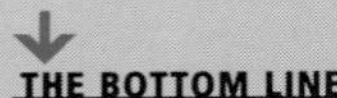

THE BOTTOM LINE

Once you have appropriate security settings in place, you can feel comfortable browsing the Internet without putting your computer or network at risk. If you know the address of the page you want to view, you can key it in the Address bar and press Enter to quickly display the page. You can then use links on the page to display other, related pages. You can even open additional pages in the same browser window by using browser tabs. ***Browser tabs*** are pages within the window, similar to tabs in a dialog box. If you do not know a page's address, or if you are looking for general information, you can search the Internet. Similar to windows in Windows Vista, Windows Internet Explorer has a Search box in which you can key a keyword or phrase and then press Enter to display a list of search results. You click a link in the list to display that page. Agents at Adventure Works frequently rely on Windows Internet Explorer to locate information for clients, such as information on museums and galleries in New York and Washington, D.C. for a traveler from Europe. In this section, you use Internet Explorer to browse a website and then sssearch for a website to find the information.

USE WINDOWS INTERNET EXPLORER

GET READY. To complete this exercise, you must be connected to the Internet.

USE the Windows Internet Explorer window you left open in the previous exercise.

1. Click in the Address bar at the top of the Windows Internet Explorer window. If necessary, select the text already in the Address bar and then key **www.metmuseum.org**. This is the web address of the Metropolitan Museum of Art in New York City.
2. Press Enter. Windows Internet Explorer locates and displays the welcome page for the Metropolitan Museum's website. The content changes daily, but the page contains links to the site's home page and other locations.

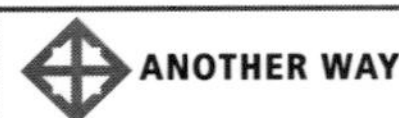

You can click the Go button to the right of the Address bar instead of pressing Enter.

3. Click the text **Welcome to the Met. Enter here.** Windows Internet Explorer displays the site's home page. Although the content depends on the current exhibits, the page should look similar to Figure 12-11. It has many links to different areas of the museum's site.

Figure 12-11

The Metropolitan Museum of Art's home page

4. In the index on the left side of the page, under Works of Art, click **Permanent Collection** to display the Works of Art Permanent Collection page. You can continue using links on the pages to browse through the site. The painting of George Washington that is the link to American Paintings and Sculpture looks like it was painted by the artist Gilbert Stuart.
5. You can search the Internet to locate information about Gilbert Stuart. Move the pointer up to the blank tab to the right of the The Metropolitan Museum of Art tab on the window's toolbar. The New tab icon should display.

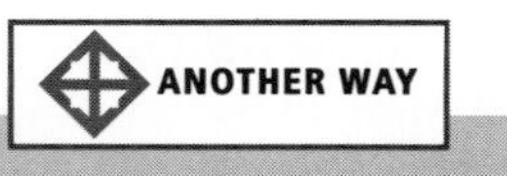

You can press Ctrl+C to open a new tab.

6. Click the **New Tab** icon to open a new browser tab.
7. Click in the **Live Search** box in the upper right corner of the window, key **painter Gilbert Stuart**, and then press **Enter**. Windows Internet Explorer searches for websites relating to the painter Gilbert Stuart and displays the search results on the new tab.
8. Scroll down and click the link to **National Gallery of Art–Gilbert Stuart: Introduction**. Internet Explorer displays the page. It should look similar to Figure 12-12.

Figure 12-12

National Gallery of Art web page

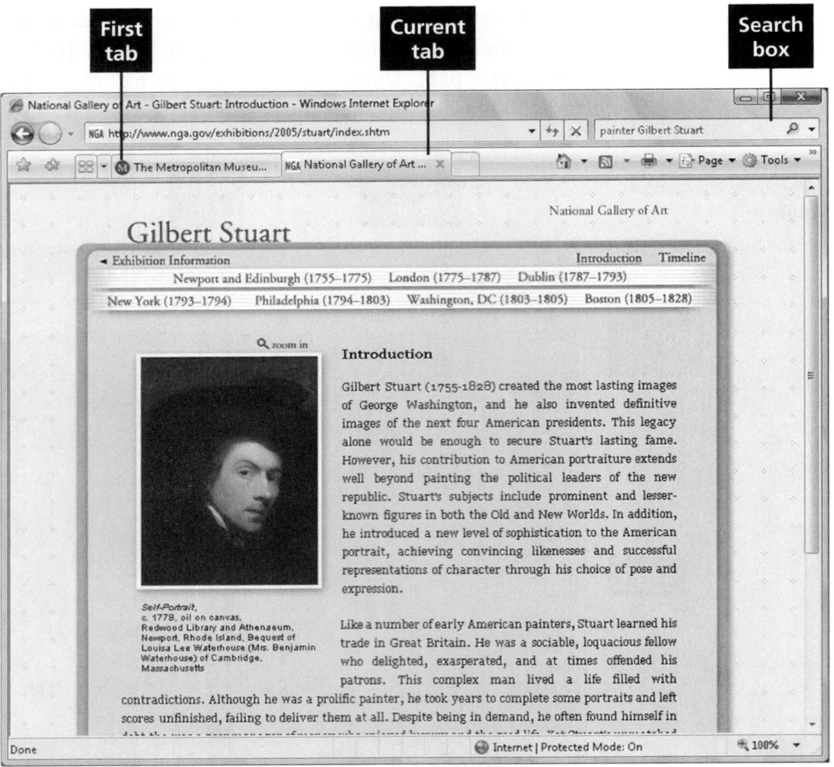

You can press Ctrl+W to close the current tab.

9. At your instructor's request, capture an image of the browser window. Save it in your Lesson 12 assessment folder as ***Le12_06***.
10. Click the **The Metropolitan Museum of Art** tab to make it active and then click the **Close Tab** button. Now, only the National Gallery of Art page remains open in Internet Explorer.
11. **CLOSE** the Windows Internet Explorer window.

PAUSE. LEAVE the desktop displayed to use in the next exercise.

The default search provider for Windows Internet Explorer is Live Search, but you can select a different provider if you prefer. A ***search provider*** is a website designed to search the Internet. Some common search providers include Google, Yahoo!, Lycos, and Ask.com. To use a provider other than Live Search, click the Search dropdown arrow to the right of the Search box in the Windows Internet Explorer window and click Find More Providers. The Add Search Providers to Internet Explorer Web page displays. To display the Add Search Provider dialog box, click a provider to add. If you want to make the new provider the default, click to select the Make this my default search provider checkbox. Click Add Provider. The provider is added to the Search dropdown list.

Rather than using the Search box, you can use a search provider's website to search the Internet. Key the website address in the Address bar and press Enter to display the site. Then key the search text in the search box and press Enter. For example, to use Google, key www.google.com in the Address bar and press Enter. On the Google home page, key the search text in the Search box and then press Enter.

In the next section, you learn how to locate and download a Sidebar gadget on the Internet.

■ Downloading a Sidebar Gadget

THE BOTTOM LINE

As you learned in Lesson 7, "Personalizing the Windows Vista Workspace," Windows Vista comes with a collection of useful Sidebar gadgets. In addition, Microsoft makes gadgets available for download from the Windows Live Gallery website, which is a website from which you can download different types of programs and files for use with Windows Vista. The number of gadgets in the gallery increases as new gadgets become available. In this exercise, you use Windows Internet Explorer to locate and download a new gadget from the online gadget gallery.

XREF For more information about the Windows Sidebar, refer to Lesson 7.

DOWNLOADING A SIDEBAR GADGET

TROUBLESHOOTING

If the Sidebar is not displayed, click Start>All Programs> Accessories>Windows Sidebar.

1. Right-click any blank area of the Sidebar on your desktop and click **Add Gadgets**. The Gadget Gallery window displays.
2. Click **Get more gadgets online**. Windows Internet Explorer starts and displays the Personalize Windows Vista Sidebar page.
3. Click the **See all gadgets** button to display the Windows Live Gallery Gadgets page. All gadgets are displayed by default, and you can scroll through the pages to locate the gadget you want. To narrow the list of available gadgets, you can select a category in the left pane of the page.

TAKE NOTE*

You can change the gadget gallery view to text only, text and thumbnails, or thumbnails only by clicking a Display views icon near the upper right corner of the page.

4. Click the **Tools and utilities** category. The page should look similar to Figure 12-13, although the content might change as new gadgets become available. Notice that the description of each gadget includes useful information such as a rating, the user name of the person who created the gadget, and the date the gadget was last updated.

Figure 12-13

Gadgets in the Tools and utilities category

TAKE NOTE

If a third-party—someone other than Microsoft—created a gadget, a message warning you that you should only download files if you know and trust the source displays when you click the Download button.

5. Locate the Traffic by Live Search Maps gadget and click its **Download** button. (You may have to scroll to the next page to locate the gadget.) A File Download dialog box displays, as shown in Figure 12-14. You can open the file directly from the website or save it on your computer.

Figure 12-14

File Download dialog box

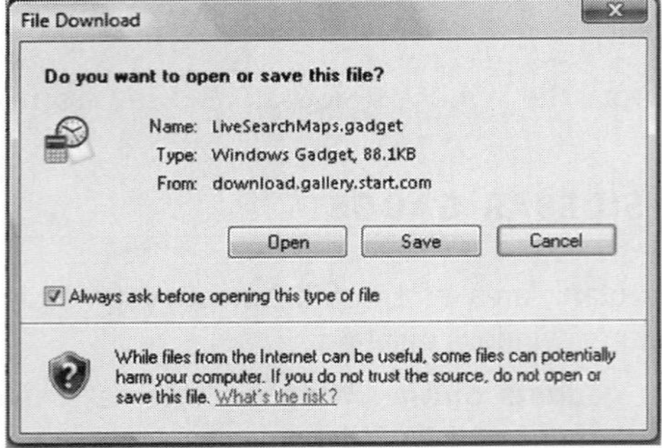

6. Click **Open**. A Windows Sidebar Security warning dialog box displays, as shown in Figure 12-15. Notice that the name of the gadget and the publisher display in the dialog box so you can verify that it is the item you want. Because the publisher is Microsoft Windows, you can feel safe allowing the content. If you do not know the publisher, you might not want to allow the content on your computer.

Figure 12-15

Internet Explorer Security dialog box

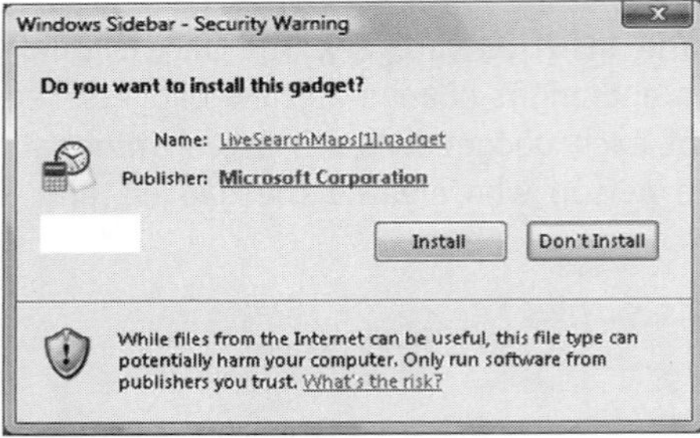

TAKE NOTE

If you choose to save the file instead of opening it, it is downloaded to the Downloads folder in your Personal folder. Double-click it to install it on the Sidebar.

7. Click **Install**. The gadget is installed and displays on your Sidebar.
8. Close Internet Explorer and close the Gadget Gallery window.
9. On the Traffic by Live Search Maps gadget, click any city. The traffic map for that city displays. Your Sidebar should look similar to Figure 12-16.

Figure 12-16

Traffic by Live Search Maps gadget on the Sidebar

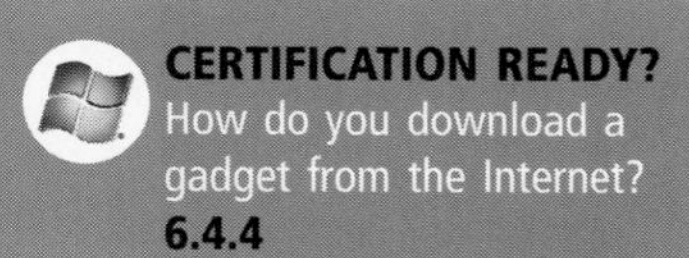

CERTIFICATION READY?
How do you download a gadget from the Internet?
6.4.4

10. At your instructor's request, capture an image of your desktop. Save it in your Lesson 12 assessment folder as ***Le12_07***.
11. Right-click the gadget and click **Close Gadget** to remove it from the Sidebar. **LOG OFF** your Windows Vista user account.

When you download a file, there is always a risk that the file might contain a virus or other malicious software. Windows Vista will use all available tools to monitor the download to prevent a problem, which is why you might see multiple warnings. Each warning gives you an opportunity to cancel the download if you are not sure of the source. You can always try again in the future if you verify that the source is legitimate.

SUMMARY SKILL MATRIX

In This Lesson You Learned	Matrix Skill	Skill Number
To set Windows Internet Explorer security levels	Configure Windows Internet Explorer security settings	1.5.1
To set Windows Internet Explorer privacy levels		
To manage cookies	Configure privacy settings	1.5.4
To use Windows Internet Explorer's Pop-up Blocker	Allow selected pop-up windows	1.5.5
To use Windows Internet Explorer's Phishing Filter	Use the Phishing filter	1.5.2
To select temporary Internet files and history settings	Configure history and temporary Internet files settings	1.5.3
To use Windows Internet Explorer		
To download a Sidebar gadget	Download a gadget from the Internet	6.4.4

■ Knowledge Assessment

Multiple Choice

Select the best response for the following questions.

1. Which security zone includes all websites that are not manually designated as part of a different zone?
   a. Internet
   b. Local intranet
   c. Trusted sites
   d. Restricted sites
2. What is the default security level for the Restricted zone?
   a. Medium-high
   b. Medium-low
   c. Low
   d. High
3. What is the subject of messages that display in the Information bar?
   a. help
   b. security
   c. available downloads
   d. search results
4. Which of the following is part of Windows Internet Explorer's privacy settings?
   a. security zone
   b. Pop-up Blocker
   c. Protected Mode
   d. History
5. Which type of cookie is created by the website you are currently viewing?
   a. First-party cookie
   b. Second-party cookie
   c. Third-party cookie
   d. Fourth-party cookie
6. Which type of cookie is created by a website other than the one you are currently viewing?
   a. First-party cookie
   b. Second-party cookie
   c. Third-party cookie
   d. Fourth-party cookie
7. To which zone should you add a website if you want to keep it from being checked automatically by the Phishing Filter?
   a. Internet
   b. Local intranet
   c. Trusted sites
   d. Restricted sites

8. Which feature of Windows Internet Explorer lets you open multiple web pages in a single browser window?
   a. Phishing Filter
   b. Pop-up Blocker
   c. Live Search
   d. Browser tabs
9. Which Microsoft website has gadgets available for download?
   a. Windows Help and Support Online
   b. Sidebar Gallery
   c. Windows Live Gallery
   d. Live Search
10. Which feature of Internet Explorer displays a warning whenever a website tries to install or run a program or file on your computer?
    a. Phishing Filter
    b. Pop-up Blocker
    c. Protected Mode
    d. Browser tabs

Fill in the Blank

Complete the following sentences by writing the correct word or words in the blanks provided.

1. A(n) ______________ is a small file containing information about you that a website creates and stores on your computer.
2. A(n) ______________ is a browser window that displays over the web page you are currently viewing.
3. A security ______________ is a category that Internet Explorer uses to identify websites based on the level of risk they pose.
4. ______________ is the act of trying to collect personal or financial information without permission through an email message or website.
5. A(n) ______________ is a corporate network that uses Internet technologies but can only be accessed by employees and other authorized users.
6. The ______________ settings available in Windows Internet Explorer are designed to help protect your personal information from unauthorized access.
7. Internet Explorer stores ______________ Internet files—copies of web pages, images, and media that you view on the Internet—on your computer.
8. A ______________ is a website designed to search the Internet.
9. The default security level for the Trusted sites zone is ______________.
10. If you use Internet Explorer with settings that might put your computer at risk, a warning message displays in the ______________.

■ Competency Assessment

Project 12-1: Security on the Road

An agent for Adventure Works plans to use her notebook computer to communicate with the main office while traveling to review potential hotels and resorts. If the Windows Internet Explorer security settings are not set properly, the notebook could be vulnerable to malicious software and could put the company's network at risk. In this project, you will check the security levels on the notebook and add the default home page to the Trusted sites security zone.

GET READY. Before you begin these steps, start your computer and log on to your Windows Vista account. Close all open windows so that you can see the desktop.

1. Click **Start** and then, at the top of the left pane of the Start menu, click **Internet Explorer**. The default home page opens in Windows Internet Explorer.
2. Click the **Tools** button on the Windows Internet Explorer toolbar and then click **Internet Options** to open the Internet Options dialog box.
3. Click the **Security** tab to display the Security settings. Confirm that the settings for the Internet zone are set to the default security level and that Protected Mode is on.
4. Click the **Local intranet** zone to view its security settings. Confirm that the settings for the zone are set to the default security level and that Protected Mode is on.
5. Click the **Trusted sites** zone and confirm that the default settings are in effect.
6. Click the **Restricted sites** zone and confirm that the default settings are in effect and that Protected Mode is on.
7. Now, add your default Internet Explorer home page to the Trusted sites zone by clicking the **Trusted sites** zone. Then click the **Sites** button to display a list of sites in the zone. The address of the current page should display in the Add this website to the zone text box.
8. Click to deselect the **Require server verification (https://) for all sites in this zone** checkbox.
9. Click **Add** to add the site to the Trusted sites zone. If requested by your instructor, capture an image of the Trusted sites dialog box. Save it in your Lesson 12 assessment folder as ***Proj12_01***. Then click **Close** to close the dialog box.
10. Click **OK** to close the Internet Options dialog box.

    PAUSE. LEAVE the Windows Internet Explorer window open to use in the next project.

Project 12-2: Security at Home

You recently received an email message that you suspect came from a phishing website. In this project, you check the privacy and phishing settings on your computer to make sure you have the maximum level of protection in place.

USE the Internet Explorer window you left open in the previous exercise.

1. Click the **Tools** button on the Windows Internet Explorer window toolbar and then click **Internet Options**.
2. Click the **Privacy** tab to display the Privacy settings.
3. Drag the slider up so the setting is Medium High. At your instructor's request, capture an image of the dialog box. Save it in your Lesson 12 assessment folder as ***Proj12_2a***.
4. If necessary, click to select the **Turn on Pop-up Blocker** checkbox.

5. Click the **Settings** button to display the Pop-up Blocker Settings dialog box.
6. Click the **Filter level** dropdown arrow and click **High: Block all pop-ups**. At your instructor's request, capture an image of the dialog box. Save it in your Lesson 12 assessment folder as ***Proj12_2b***.
7. Click **Close** to close the dialog box and then click **OK** to close the Internet Options dialog box.
8. Click the **Tools** button on the Windows Internet Explorer window toolbar and point to **Phishing Filter**.
9. If the command **Turn on Automatic Website Checking** displays, click it. Otherwise, skip to step 11.
10. In the Microsoft Phishing Filter dialog box, confirm that **Turn on automatic Phishing Filter (recommended)** is selected and then click **OK** to enable the feature.
11. Click the **Tools** button on the Windows Internet Explorer window toolbar and then click **Internet Options**.
12. On the General tab, under Browsing history, click **Settings** to open the Temporary Internet Files and History Settings dialog box.
13. In the Temporary Internet Files area, click to select the **Every time I start Internet Explorer** option button. This sets Windows Internet Explorer to check for a new version of a page and update the stored copy every time you start Windows Internet Explorer.
14. Confirm that the Disk space to use value is set within the recommended range of 50MB to 250MB.
15. In the History area, set the Days to keep pages in history value to **15**. At your instructor's request, capture an image of the dialog box. Save it in your Lesson 12 assessment folder as ***Proj12_2c***.
16. Click **OK** to apply the changes and close the dialog box, and then click **OK** to close the Internet Options dialog box.

PAUSE. LEAVE the Windows Internet Explorer window open to use in the next exercise.

■ Proficiency Assessment

Project 12-3: Phishing Protection

An Adventure Works employee is gathering information about resorts in Belize, a country in Central America. He wants to make sure that web pages he visits using Windows Internet Explorer are legitimate. In this project, you use Windows Internet Explorer to navigate to websites featuring information about travel to Belize. You then manually use the Phishing Filter to check two pages.

USE the Windows Internet Explorer window you left open in the previous exercise.

1. In the Internet Explorer Address bar, key **www.belizenet.com** and then press Enter. The site's home page displays.
2. On the left side of the page, under Belize Information, click **General Info**.
3. Click the **New Tab** icon to open a new browser tab.
4. In the **Live Search** box in the upper right corner of the window, key **Belize resorts** and then press Enter. Windows Internet Explorer displays the search results list.
5. Click the link to **All Inclusive Belize Resorts at Kanantik**. (If you cannot locate the link, key **www.kanantik.com** in the Address bar and press Enter.)

6. Click the **Tools** button on the Internet Explorer window toolbar, point to **Phishing Filter**, and then click **Check this Website**.
7. In the Phishing Filter dialog box, click **OK**.
8. Click the **Close Tab** button to close the Kanantik web page.
9. With the Belizenet page displayed, click the **Tools** button on the Windows Internet Explorer window toolbar, point to **Phishing Filter**, and then click **Check this Website**.
10. In the Phishing Filter dialog box, click **OK**.
11. **CLOSE** the Windows Internet Explorer window.

PAUSE. LEAVE the desktop displayed to use in the next project.

Project 12-4: Shopping Security

You are considering buying the newest Xbox game system. In this project, you use Windows Internet Explorer to locate information about the Xbox online and to see if there any Xbox-related Sidebar gadgets are available. You use the Phishing Filter to manually check a web page, and you download a gadget to the Sidebar.

1. Click **Start** and then click **Internet Explorer**.
2. In the Address bar, key **www.xbox.com** and then press Enter. The site's home page displays. (The Information bar may display a message that the site wants to install an add-on. Ignore it.)
3. In the links bar across the top of the page, click **Catalog**.
4. Click the **Tools** button on the Windows Internet Explorer window toolbar, point to **Phishing Filter**, and then click **Check this Website**.
5. In the Phishing Filter dialog box, click **OK**.
6. Click the **New Tab** icon to open a new browser tab.
7. In the Address bar, key **www.gallery.live.com** and then press Enter to display the Windows Live Gallery website.
8. Locate and click the link to Sidebar gadgets.
9. In the Search box at the top of the page, key **Xbox** and then click **Search Gallery**. The page displays all gadgets related to the Xbox.
10. Under Sidebar gadgets, locate the Xbox Gamertag gadget and click its **Download** button. If you cannot locate the Xbox Gamertag gadget, select a different gadget to download, instead. Click Open in the File Download dialog box.
11. With your instructor's permission, click **Install**. Alternatively, click **Don't install**. Close all Windows Internet Explorer tabs and skip the remaining steps in this project.
12. When the download is complete, close all Windows Internet Explorer tabs.
13. Right-click the new gadget on the Sidebar and click **Close Gadget** to remove it from the Sidebar.

PAUSE. LEAVE the desktop displayed to use in the next project.

■ Mastery Assessment

Project 12-5: Secure Research

Adventure Works has hired a research assistant to research new destinations around the world. She will be spending a lot of time using the Internet to locate information and communicate with contacts. In this project, you check and set all Windows Internet Explorer security settings on her computer.

1. Start **Internet Explorer** and display the **Internet Options** dialog box.
2. Apply the default security levels to all four security zones.
3. Remove the default home page from the **Trusted sites** zone.
4. Apply the default privacy setting for cookies.
5. Turn off the **Pop-up Blocker** and then turn it back on.
6. Set the Pop-up Blocker filter level to **Medium**.
7. Turn off the automatic **Phishing Filter** and then turn it back on.
8. Set Internet Explorer to automatically check for newer versions of temporary Internet files.
9. Set the amount of disk space to use for storing temporary Internet files to **50MB**.
10. Set the days to keep pages in history value to **20**.
11. **CLOSE** all open dialog boxes.

PAUSE. LEAVE the desktop displayed to use in the next project.

Project 12-6: Dual Core Information

You have a computer with a dual core processor, but you are not sure what that means. In this project, you will use the Internet to find information about dual core processors. You will then download a dual core meter gadget for your Windows Sidebar.

1. Start **Internet Explorer** and search for information about **dual core processors.**
2. Click a link that provides information, not one that directs you to vendor or sales pages.
3. Read the page. If it does not provide the information you need to learn about dual core processors, go back to the Search results list and try a different page.
4. Check the page manually with the **Phishing Filter**.
5. Display the Windows Live Gallery website. (You can do this by keying **www.gallery.live.com** in the Address bar, or by opening the Gadget Gallery on your computer and clicking **Get more gadgets online**.)
6. Locate the **Multi Meter (Dual Core) monitor** gadget, which displays information about your processor's resource usage. If it is not available, select a similar gadget.
7. With your instructor's permission, download the gadget to your Windows Sidebar. Capture an image of your desktop with the gadget installed. Save it in your Lesson 12 assessment folder as ***Proj12_6***.
8. Close Windows Internet Explorer and any other open windows.
9. If you downloaded a gadget, remove it from the Sidebar.

LOG OFF your Windows Vista user account.

INTERNET READY

The more you know about the dangers of Internet fraud and identity theft, the more you will be able to protect yourself from the risks. In this project, use Internet search tools to locate information about how you can minimize the risk of becoming a victim. Use legitimate websites to provide source information. For example, your state's attorney general's office might provide information about current scams and phishing sites. When you have completed your research, create a document that lists the potential threats and provides suggestions for how to prevent or counteract an attack.

Managing Network Connections

LESSON SKILL MATRIX

Skills	Matrix Skill	Skill Number
Connecting to a Network	Choose a network connection from the Network Center Find and connect to an available wireless network Check the status of a wireless network connection	2.2.1 2.2.2 2.2.3
Troubleshooting a Network Connection		
Locating Your Computer's IP Address	Locate the IP configuration of the computer	7.4.1
Using the Ping Command	Ping another computer to ascertain connectivity status	7.4.2
Disabling and Enabling a Network Connection	Enable and disable a network connection	7.4.3
Connecting to a Workplace Network from a Remote Location	Remotely connect to a network at your workplace	2.2.4
Using Remote Desktop Connection		
Enabling Remote Desktop Connection on Your Computer	Allow remote desktop connections to your computer	2.3.1
Authorizing Remote Desktop Users	Specify who can connect to your computer by using Remote Desktop Connection	2.3.2
Connecting to a Remote Computer	Connect to another computer by using Remote Desktop Connection	2.4.1

KEY TERMS

Command Prompt
Gateway
IP address
Network
Network adapter
Network Level Authentication (NLA)
Physical connection
Ping
Protocol
Remote Desktop Connection
Router
Terminal Services (TS) Gateway
Virtual private network (VPN)
Wireless connection

The School of Fine Art, which offers classes in the visual and performing arts to people of all ages, provides campus-wide Internet access through a combination of wired and wireless networks. Public networks give students, employees, and visitors access to the Internet in common areas, such as the library, theater lobbies, and cafeterias. Secure networks are available within departments so that authorized users can access the school's intranet as well as the Internet from their desktop systems, or using notebook computers. Employees and students receive training in how to use Windows Vista to connect to the networks and to troubleshoot connection-related problems. In this lesson, you learn how to use Windows Vista to identify and connect to a network, and to troubleshoot problems with a network connection. You also learn how to connect remotely from one computer to another using a virtual private network (VPN) and Windows Remote Desktop Connection.

■ Connecting to a Network

THE BOTTOM LINE

A ***network*** is a group of computers and devices that are connected so that they can communicate with one another. The network may use a ***physical connection***, which means actual cables run from one computer or device to another. Or it may use a ***wireless connection***, which means the connection is via radio signals instead of wires or cables. Most Windows Vista–based computers come equipped to identify and connect to both physical and wireless networks. By default, when you install a network adapter in your computer, Windows Vista creates a network connection for it. A ***network adapter*** is a device that enables your computer to connect to a network. You can view, manage, and select a network connection by using the Network and Internet group in the Control Panel. In this section, you learn how to use the Network Center to view available network connections, connect to a network, and check the status of a network.

CONNECT TO A NETWORK

GET READY. Before you begin these steps, start your computer and log on to your Windows Vista account. Close all open windows so that you can see the desktop. Create a new folder named Lesson 13 in a storage location specified by your instructor where you can store assessment files and folders that you create during this lesson. To complete this exercise, you must have at least one network adapter (preferably wireless) installed in your computer and set up to work with a network.

1. Click **Start** and then click **Control Panel.**
2. Click **Network and Internet** to display the Network and Internet home page in the Control Panel and then click **Network and Sharing Center.** The Network and Sharing Center window displays, listing information about the networks that are currently enabled on your computer. It should look similar to Figure 13-1, although the specific networks, status, and other settings depend on the networks available on your system.

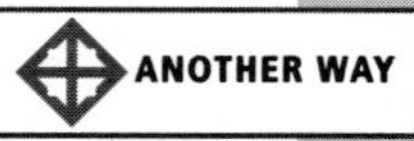

You can open the Network and Sharing Center directly from the Control Panel window. Click Start>Control Panel, and then click View network status and tasks under Network and Internet.

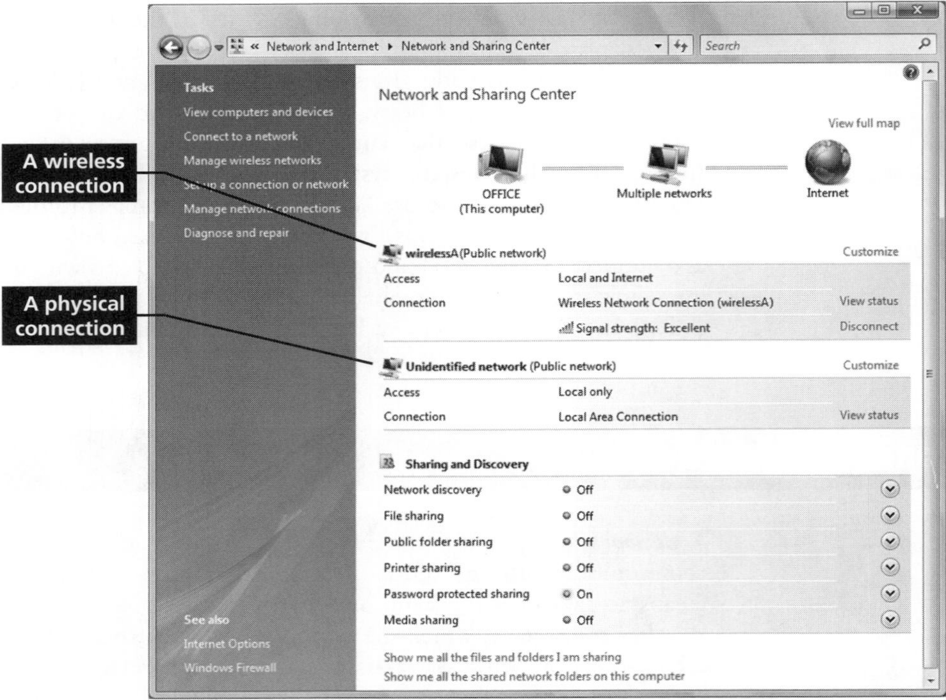

Figure 13-1

Network and Sharing Center

TROUBLESHOOTING If no networks are listed in the Network and Sharing Center, it means that none are currently enabled. Continue with step 3 to connect to a network.

TAKE NOTE* To see all computers and devices currently connected to your network, click View full map in the top right of the Network and Sharing Center window.

3. Under Tasks in the left pane of the window, click **Connect to a network.** The Connect to a network dialog box displays, as shown in Figure 13-2. Again, the networks listed depend on those installed on your computer. If a network is already connected, you can select to disconnect it and use a different connection. If it is not connected, you can select to connect to it.

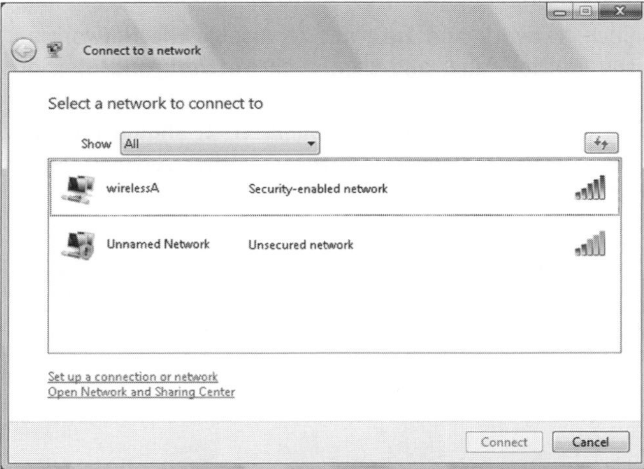

Figure 13-2

Connect to a network

4. Click the wireless network to which you want to connect and then click the **Connect** button. Windows Vista establishes the network connection and then displays a dialog box indicating that the connection was successful.

TROUBLESHOOTING If Windows Vista is unable to connect to the network, it will give you the option of trying to connect to a different network or trying to diagnose the problem.

5. Click **Close** to close the dialog box and display the Network and Sharing Center window.
6. To the right of the connected network, click **View status**. The Wireless Network Connection Status dialog box displays, as shown in Figure 13-3. You can view information about the connection, including the strength of the signal, the connection speed, and how long the connection has been active.

Figure 13-3

Wireless Network Connection Status dialog box

7. Click **Close** to close the dialog box. The Network and Sharing Center should still be displayed.

PAUSE. LEAVE the Network and Sharing Center window open to use in the next exercise.

CERTIFICATION READY?
How do you choose a network connection from the Network Center?
2.2.1
How do you find and connect to an available wireless network?
2.2.2
How do you check the status of a wireless network connection?
2.2.3

In this exercise, you learned that Windows Vista automatically creates a network connection for any installed network adapter, and that you can view available connections in the Network and Sharing Center. You can also connect to a network and view its status.

By default, a Network icon displays in the Notification area on the Taskbar. If the network is connected, a globe displays on the icon. If the network is not connected, a red X displays on the icon. Click the icon to view information about the connection, such as the connection name and signal strength. Right-click the icon to display a menu of options for connecting and disconnecting and accessing other networking features.

In the next section, you learn how to troubleshoot network connection problems.

■ Troubleshooting a Network Connection

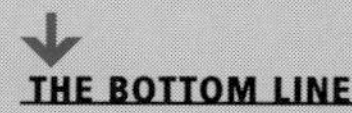

If you are having problems accessing a network, your network connection may have a problem. You may be able to solve the problem yourself by disabling and enabling the connection. If not, you can take steps to determine what is causing the problem so that when you request technical assistance, you can provide the information necessary to solve the problem. In this section, you learn how to identify the IP address of your computer. The ***IP address***, or Internet Protocol address, is a unique series of numbers that identifies your computer to other computers on a network or on the Internet. You also learn how to check the connectivity status by using Ping, and how to enable and disable a network connection. ***Ping*** is a command that you can use to check whether a particular IP address is available on the network.

Locating Your Computer's IP Address

You need an IP address to set up an Internet connection, allow other computers to connect to your computer via the Internet, and to troubleshoot network problems. In this exercise, you learn how to locate your computer's IP address by using the Network Connection Status dialog box and Windows Vista's ***Command Prompt*** feature. Command Promptenables you to input certain computer commands by keying the commands on a command line.

LOCATE YOUR COMPUTER'S IP ADDRESS

USE the Network and Sharing Center window you left open in the previous exercise.

1. Click **View status** to the right of your network connection to display the Network Connection Status dialog box.
2. Click the **Details** button to display the Network Connection Details dialog box. It should look similar to Figure 13-4, although the specific information depends on your computer and network settings. The IP address is the fifth property from the top.

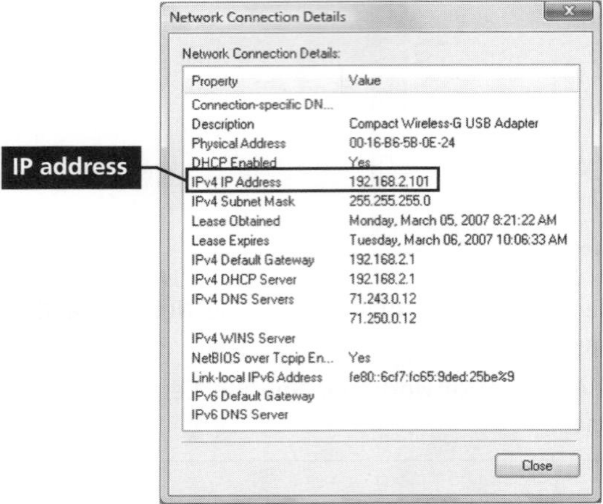

Figure 13-4
Network Connection Details dialog box

3. Click **Close** to close the Network Connection Details dialog box. Then click **Close** to close the Network Connection Status dialog box.
4. Close the Network and Sharing Center window.
5. Click **Start**, click **All Programs**, and then click **Accessories**.
6. Under Accessories, click **Command Prompt** to open the Command Prompt window. It should look similar to Figure 13-5.

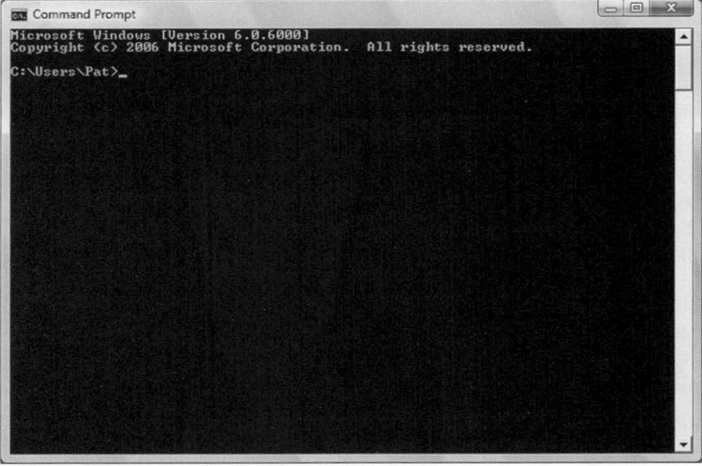

Figure 13-5
Command Prompt window

You can also open the Command Prompt window by keying Command Prompt in the Search box on the Start menu and then double-clicking Command Prompt under Programs in the Search Results list.

7. Key **ipconfig** and then press **Enter**. Windows Vista displays information about all of the network connections on your computer, including the IP address. It should look similar to Figure 13-6, although the specific information depends on your computer and network settings.

Figure 13-6

Use Command Prompt to find an IP address

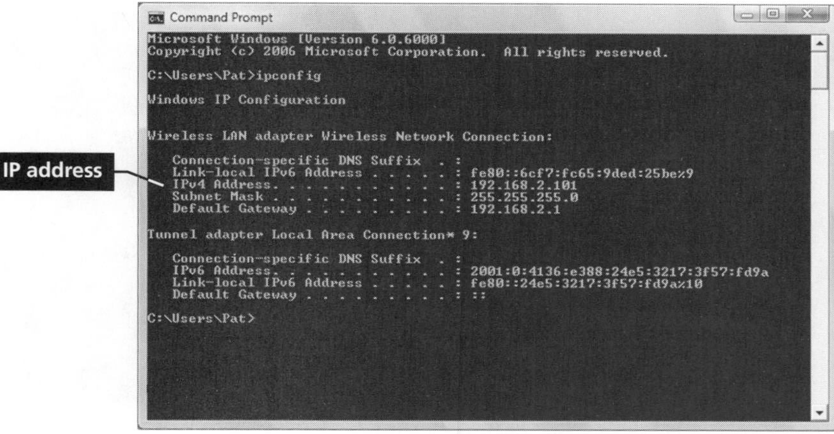

8. At the request of your instructor, capture an image of the Command Prompt window. Save it in your Lesson 13 assessment folder as ***Le13_01***.

PAUSE. LEAVE the Command Prompt window open to use in the next exercise.

CERTIFICATION READY?
How do you locate the IP configuration of the computer?
7.4.1

An IP address is usually a series of four groups of numbers separated by periods. Each computer on a network must have a unique IP address. If two computers try to use the same IP address, there will be an IP address conflict. Windows Vista will display an error message, and you will have to fix the problem. You can use the Windows Network Diagnostics tool to identify and solve the conflict. To start the Windows Network Diagnostics tool, open the Network and Sharing Center and then click Diagnose and repair in the left pane, under Tasks.

In the next exercise, you learn how to use the Ping command to verify whether an IP address is accessible.

Using the Ping Command

Using the Ping command, you can check to see if a computer is accessible on the network by sending a message to the IP address and waiting for a response. It is useful for diagnosing network or router problems because it bypasses the network hardware on your system to directly contact the other computer. If the IP address responds to the ping, you know that the connection is valid and the other computer is working, so the problem must be with a different part of the network, such as a setting on your computer or router. A ***router*** is a device that sends information between two networks. In this exercise, you look up the IP address for a website and then use Ping to check the connection.

USE THE PING COMMAND

USE the Command Prompt window you left open in the previous exercise.

1. Key **nslookup microsoft.com** and press **Enter**. The command prompt returns information about the microsoft.com website, including the IP address. Now that you know the IP address, you can use Ping to check the connection status.

TROUBLESHOOTING If nslookup does not work, make sure you left a space between the command and the website address.

2. Key **ping 207.46.197.32** and then press **Enter**. Ping sends four messages to the IP address. If the IP address responds, the responses are listed in the Command Prompt window, along with statistics, as shown in Figure 13-7. If the IP address does not respond, the message *Request timed out* displays in the Command prompt window instead.

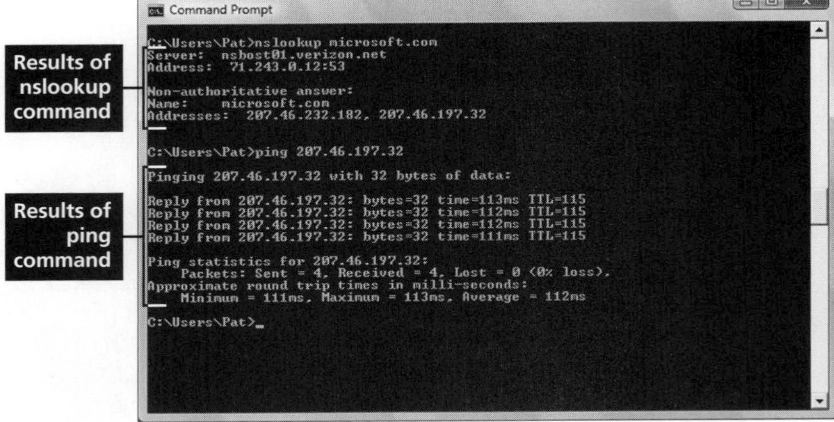

Figure 13-7
Results of the Ping command

TROUBLESHOOTING If the IP address does not respond to the Ping command, the IP address provided may not be valid. Look at the results of the nslookup command from step 1 to see if the IP address is different, and use the different address instead.

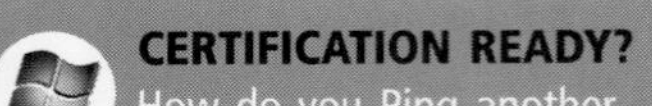

CERTIFICATION READY?
How do you Ping another computer to ascertain connectivity status?
7.4.2

3. Close the Command Prompt window.

   PAUSE. LEAVE the Windows Vista desktop displayed to use in the next exercise.

As you have seen, using the Ping command can help you identify whether an IP address is available on the network. However, if you do not receive a response to a ping, you cannot immediately know why not. Some possible reasons include the following:

- The IP address is for a server that is currently not working.
- The IP address is not valid.
- The transmission equipment between your computer and the IP address may have a problem. For example, the cable may be damaged, or there may be interference.

Likewise, if the IP address responds to the ping, but you still cannot connect to your network, you must continue trying to diagnose the problem. You may have a problem with your router, or there may be an incorrect setting somewhere in your network setup.

You can use the Ping command with a website address if you do not know the IP address. For example, you could ping the microsoft.com website by keying ping microsoft.com at the command prompt.

In addition to simply identifying whether a computer responds to a ping, you can also learn something about how far the signals have to travel by looking at the Ping statistics that display in the Command Prompt window. The statistics include the number of pings—or packets of information—that were sent and received, and how long it took to send the ping and receive a reply. The length of time helps indicate how far the packets traveled, as well as how fast the connection is functioning.

In the next exercise, you learn how enable and disable a network connection.

Disabling and Enabling a Network Connection

Sometimes the easiest way to fix a network connection problem is to disable the network adapter and then enable it again. You also might want to disable a network connection so that you can use a different connection. For example, you might usually use a particular connection on your notebook when you are home, but you might need to use a different connection when you are traveling. In this exercise, you disable and then enable your network connection.

DISABLE AND ENABLE A NETWORK CONNECTION

1. Click **Start**, click **Control Panel**, and then click **View network status and tasks** under Network and Internet. This will open the Network and Sharing Center window.
2. In the left pane, under Tasks, click **Manage network connections.** The Network Connections window displays. It lists all network connections on your computer. It should look similar to Figure 13-8, although the specific network connections depend on the network adapters available on your computer.

Figure 13-8

Network Connections window

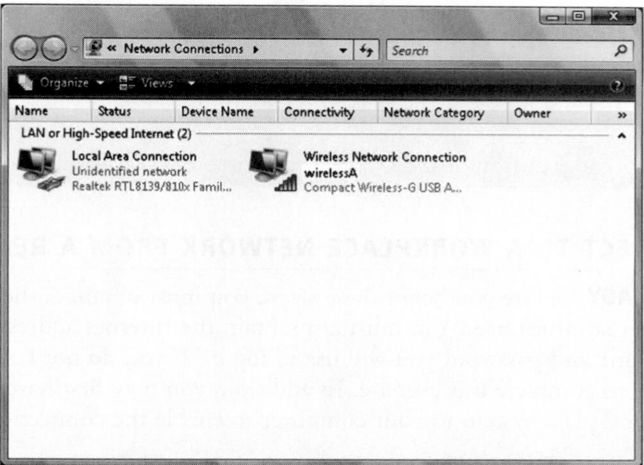

3. Right-click the connection you want to disable and click **Disable** on the shortcut menu. If you are logged on as an administrator, click **Continue** in the User Account Control dialog box. Alternatively, key an administrator's password and then click **OK**. Windows Vista disables the connection.
4. Right-click the connection and click **Enable** on the shortcut menu. If you are logged on as an administrator, click **Continue** in the User Account Control dialog box. Alternatively, key an administrator's password and then click **OK**. Windows Vista enables the connection. Depending on your network connection settings, Windows Vista may automatically connect to the network.
5. Close the Network Connections window.

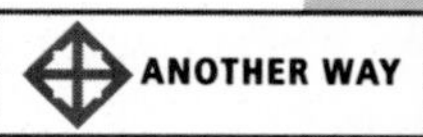

You can also use the Disable this network device button and the Enable this network device button on the Network Connections window toolbar to disable and enable a connection. Click the connection to select it and then click the button on the toolbar.

TROUBLESHOOTING

If Windows Vista does not automatically reestablish the network connection when you enable it, click Connect to a network in the Network and Sharing Center, select the network, and click Connect.

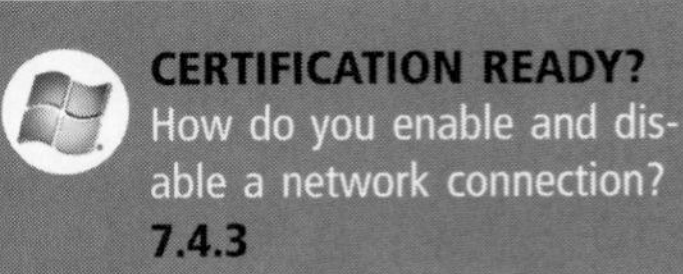
CERTIFICATION READY?
How do you enable and disable a network connection?
7.4.3

PAUSE. LEAVE the Network and Sharing Center window displayed to use in the next exercise.

Disabling a connection is not the same as disconnecting from a network. Disabling temporarily makes the network adapter unavailable for use. When you enable the connection again, it should automatically reestablish the previous connection.

In the next section you learn how to connect to a workplace network from a remote location by using a virtual private network.

■ Connecting to a Workplace Network from a Remote Location

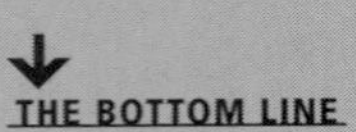
THE BOTTOM LINE

Most workplace networks are protected by many layers of security so that unauthorized users cannot gain access to the company's files. If you have authorization, you can use Windows Vista tools to connect to your workplace network from any remote location by setting up a ***virtual private network (VPN).*** A ***VPN*** is an encrypted network that connects one or more computers to a large network via the Internet. A VPN makes it possible to use the resources of your workplace network no matter where you are. You might be at home, at a customer's office, or even in a coffee shop, but if you have authorization to use a VPN, you can connect to your company's network. In this exercise, you learn how to use Windows Vista's Connect to a Workplace Wizard so that you can use VPN to connect from a remote location to your workplace network over the Internet.

CONNECT TO A WORKPLACE NETWORK FROM A REMOTE LOCATION

GET READY. Before you begin these steps, you must obtain authorization from your workplace network administrator. You must also obtain the Internet address of the VPN, as well as the user name and password you will use to log in. If you do not have authorization, you will not be able to complete this exercise. In addition, you may first have to download software from your workplace system to your computer to enable the connection.

USE the Network and Sharing Center window you left open in the previous exercise.

1. Under Tasks in the left pane, click **Set up a connection or network.** The Set up a connection or network wizard displays.
2. Click **Connect to a workplace** and then click **Next.** The How do you want to connect? window displays, as shown in Figure 13-9.

Figure 13-9

Use a VPN to connect to a workplace

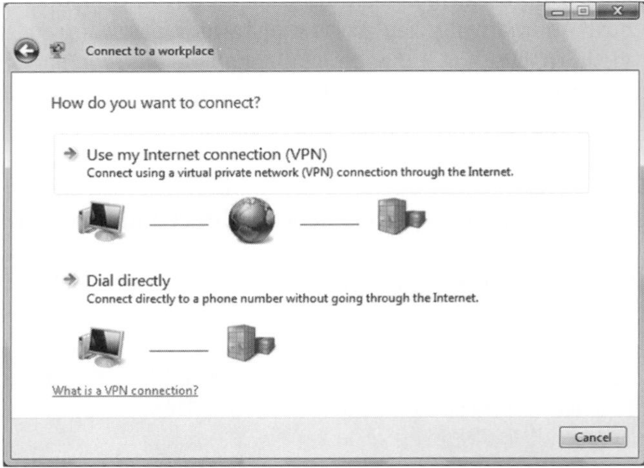

3. Click **Use my Internet connection (VPN)**. The Type the Internet address to connect to window displays, as shown in Figure 13-10.

Figure 13-10

Specify the Internet address of the VPN

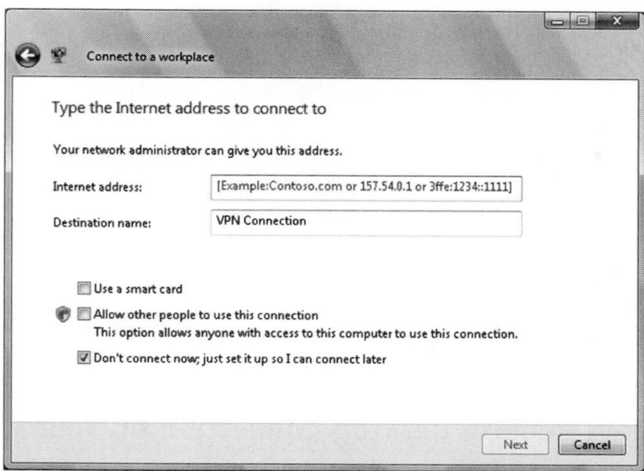

4. Key the **Internet address** of the VPN. You can enter the IP address or the domain name, as specified by your network administrator. Click **Next**. The Type your user name and password window displays.
5. Key the user name supplied by your network administrator, click in the Password box, and key your password. Click **Connect**. Windows Vista sets up the connection and connects to the workplace network. You can access your account, files, and programs.

TROUBLESHOOTING

Some VPNs may have different procedures. If you experience difficulty setting up and connecting to your workplace by using a VPN, contact your network administrator for assistance.

6. When you are finished using the VPN, disconnect as instructed by your network administrator.
7. Navigate to the Network and Sharing Center window.
8. Click **Manage network connections** under Tasks in the left pane. At this point, your instructor may ask you to capture an image of the Network Connections window, showing the VPN connection. Save it in your Lesson 13 assessment folder as ***Le13_02***.
9. Right-click the **VPN connection** and then click **Delete** on the shortcut menu.
10. Click **Yes** to delete the VPN connection from your computer.
11. Close the Network Connections window.
12. Close the Network and Sharing Center window.

PAUSE. LEAVE the Windows Vista desktop displayed to use in the next exercise.

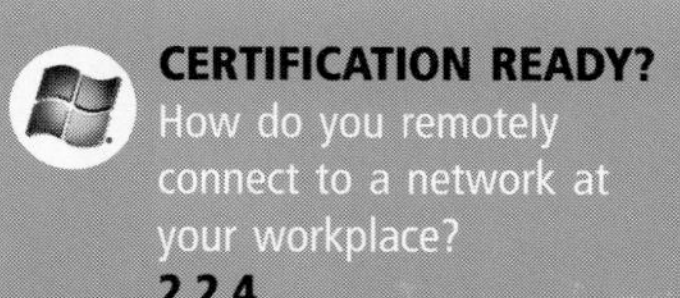

Do not delete the VPN connection if you plan to use it again in the future to access your workplace network. It will remain listed as an available connection so that you can use the steps described in the previous exercise to connect to your workplace network at any time, without having to set up the VPN connection again.

In the next section, you learn how to use Remote Desktop Connection to communicate with a remote computer.

■ Using Remote Desktop Connection

THE BOTTOM LINE

Remote Desktop Connection is a feature of Windows Vista that lets you access a computer running Windows Vista or some other versions of the Windows operating system from another computer running Windows Vista. The computers must be connected to the same network or to the Internet for the connection to work, and you must have a user account and password on the remote computer to gain access. Once the connection is established, you can access all files, programs, and resources on the remote computer just as if you were working directly on that system. In this section, you learn how to enable Remote Desktop Connection on your computer so that you can access it from another location. You also learn how to authorize a user to access your computer remotely. Finally, you learn how to connect your computer to another computer using Remote Desktop Connection.

Enabling Remote Desktop Connection on Your Computer

Remote Desktop Connection is installed as part of Windows Vista, but it is not active by default. To allow remote access, you must first enable remote connections. In this exercise, you learn how to enable Remote Desktop Connection.

ENABLE REMOTE DESKTOP CONNECTION ON YOUR COMPUTER

1. Click **Start**, click **Control Panel**, and then click **System and Maintenance.**
2. Under System, click **Allow remote access.** If you are logged on as an administrator, click **Continue** in the User Account Control dialog box, or key an administrator password and click **OK.** The Remote tab of the System Properties dialog box displays, as shown in Figure 13-11. Notice that the Remote Desktop settings are in the lower half of the dialog box.

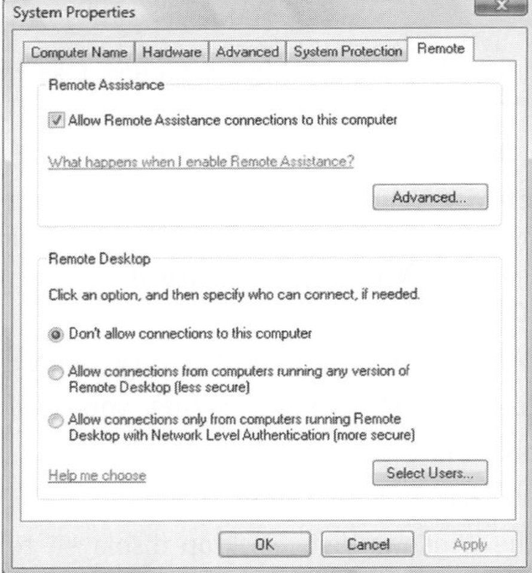

Figure 13-11

Remote tab of the System Properties dialog box

X REF

Remote Desktop is not the same feature as Remote Assistance. For information on using Remote Assistance, refer to Lesson 8, "Getting Help and Support."

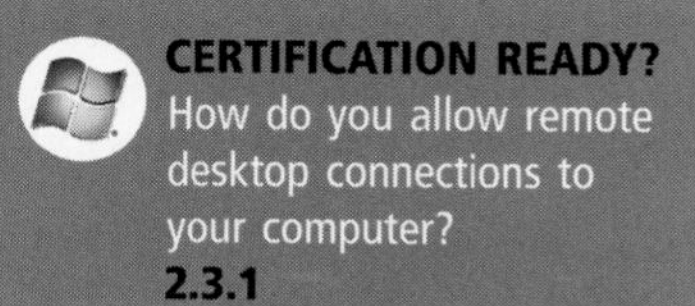

3. Click to select the **Allow connections from computers running any version of Remote Desktop** option. This setting lets computers running Windows Vista as well as some earlier versions of Windows, such as Windows XP Professional, connect to your computer.
4. Click **Apply** to apply the change and leave the dialog box open.

   PAUSE. LEAVE the Remote tab of the System Properties dialog box open to use in the next exercise.

In Windows Vista, Remote Desktop Connection uses ***Network Level Authentication (NLA)***, which is a method of checking the identity of a user before allowing remote access to a computer. It provides a more secure operating environment, but it must be available on both computers. If you are certain it is available on both computers, you can select the Allow connections from computers running Remote Desktop with Network Level Authentication option. If both computers are not running Windows Vista, or if you are not sure, you should use the Allow connections from computers running any version of Remote Desktop option.

Note that you cannot use Remote Desktop Connection to connect to computers running Windows Vista Starter, Windows Vista Home Basic, Windows Vista Home Basic N, or Windows Vista Home Premium. You can, however, create outgoing connections from computers running those editions of Windows Vista. You cannot use Remote Desktop Connection with computers running Windows XP Home version.

If a Windows Firewall exception for Remote Desktop is not set on your computer, Windows Vista will prompt you to set one. Open Windows Firewall from the Control Panel and, in the left pane of the Windows Firewall window, click Allow a program through Windows Firewall. Click Continue in the User Account Control dialog box or key an administrator password and click OK. Click to select the Remote Desktop checkbox and then click OK. For more information about setting Firewall exceptions, see Lesson 11, "Monitoring the Windows Vista Environment."

In the next exercise, you learn how to provide authorization to specify which users can access your computer remotely.

Authorizing Remote Desktop Users

Once you enable Remote Desktop Connection, you must specify which users are allowed to access the computer remotely. By default, the system administrator account has access, and you can add other users who have password-protected accounts on the computer. In this exercise, you learn how to select users who you want to allow remote access to your computer.

AUTHORIZE REMOTE DESKTOP USERS

USE the Remote tab of the System Properties dialog box you left open in the previous exercise.

1. Click the **Select Users** button to open the Remote Desktop Users dialog box. Notice that the administrator account is already authorized to remotely access the computer.
2. Click **Add** to open the Select Users dialog box. It should look similar to Figure 13-12.

Figure 13-12

Select Users dialog box

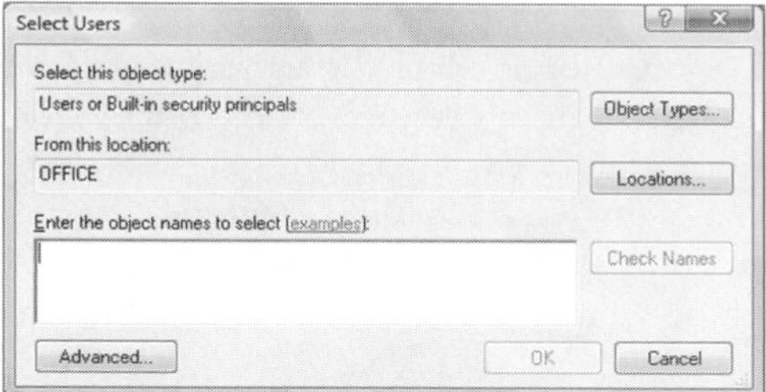

3. In the Enter the object names to select text box, key your user name or the user name of the person you want to authorize. Then click **OK**. The name is added to the list of Remote Desktop Users who are authorized to access the computer, as shown in Figure 13-13.

Figure 13-13
Remote Desktop Users dialog box

TAKE NOTE*

If the name you key is not a name associated with a user account on the computer, Windows Vista will not be able to locate it and add it to the Remote Desktop Users list.

4. At this point, your instructor may ask you to capture an image of the Select Users dialog box. Save it in your Lesson 13 assessment folder as ***Le13_03***.
5. Click **OK** to close the Remote Desktop Users dialog box and then click **OK** to close the System Properties dialog box.
6. **CLOSE** the Control Panel.

TROUBLESHOOTING

If the user you authorize does not have a password-protected account, he or she will not be able to log in from a remote location. Change the account to add password protection. For more information on adding a password, refer to Lesson 11.

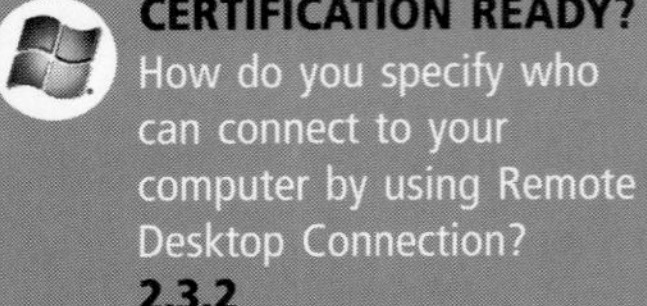

CERTIFICATION READY?
How do you specify who can connect to your computer by using Remote Desktop Connection?
2.3.2

PAUSE. LEAVE the Windows Vista desktop open to use in the next exercise.

As you learned in this exercise, to be authorized as a Remote Desktop User, you must have a password-protected user account on the computer you wish to access. You will enter the user name and password to log in remotely. For example, if you want to be able to access your work computer when you are home, you must enable Remote Desktop Connection on your work computer and add your user name to the Remote Desktop Users list. Then, you can use Remote Desktop Connection on your home computer to log in to your work computer. You will be prompted to enter your work computer user account name and password to gain access.

Be careful when authorizing users for Remote Desktop Connection. If a user can log in remotely, they have access to all of the files and programs stored on the computer. This can leave your computer vulnerable to hackers or others who may delete or damage your data.

In the next section, you learn how to use Remote Desktop Connection to connect your computer to a remote computer.

Connecting to a Remote Computer

If Remote Desktop Connection is enabled on a remote computer, and you are an authorized Remote Desktop user, you can connect from your Windows Vista computer to the remote computer. Once connected, you can use all files, programs, and resources on the remote computer from your Windows Vista computer desktop. In this exercise, you learn how to connect to a remote computer by using Remote Desktop Connection. You also disable Remote Desktop Connection and remove an authorized user from the Remote Desktop Users list.

CONNECT TO A REMOTE COMPUTER

GET READY. To connect to a remote computer, Remote Desktop Connection must be enabled on the remote computer, and you must have a user account and password on the remote computer. In addition, you must know the remote computer's name or IP address.

1. Click **Start**, click **All Programs**, and then click **Accessories.**
2. Under Accessories, click **Remote Desktop Connection.** The Remote Desktop Connection window displays, as shown in Figure 13-14.

Figure 13-14

Remote Desktop Connection window

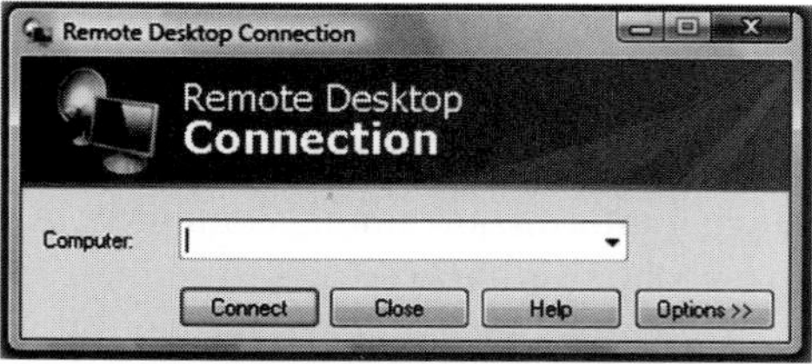

3. In the Computer text box, key the name of the remote computer, or the IP address, and then click **Connect.** A Windows Security dialog box displays, in which you provide your user name and password.

TAKE NOTE If you have entered the information in the Computer text box before, Windows Vista will fill it in as you type, or you can click the dropdown arrow and select it from the list.

4. In the user name text box, key your user name for the remote computer.
5. In the password text box, key your password for the remote computer.
6. Click **OK.** Windows Vista will establish the Remote Desktop Connection and display the remote computer's desktop on your Windows Vista computer. You can use all features, files, and programs as if you were sitting at the remote computer.

TROUBLESHOOTING If the remote computer is not using NLA, or is running a version of Windows prior to Windows Vista, your computer may display a warning dialog box before establishing the connection. Click Yes to establish the remote connection. Or click No to cancel the connection.

7. To end the Remote Desktop Connection, click the **Close** button on the Remote Desktop tab at the top of your screen and then click **Yes** in the dialog box that displays.
8. Click **Start**, click **Control Panel**, and then click **System and Maintenance.**
9. Under System, click **Allow remote access.** If you are logged on as an administrator, click **Continue** in the User Account Control dialog box, or key an administrator password and click **OK.**
10. Click to select the **Don't allow connections to this computer** option and then click **Apply.**
11. Click the **Select Users** button to open the Remote Desktop Users dialog box.
12. Click the name of the user you added earlier in this lesson and then click the **Remove** button. Click **OK** to close the dialog box.
13. Click **OK** to close the System Properties dialog box.
14. **CLOSE** all open windows.

LOG OFF your Windows Vista user account.

CERTIFICATION READY?
How do you connect to another computer by using Remote Desktop Connection?
2.4.1

Note that if Remote Desktop Connection is using NLA, to establish the connection, you must enter the full computer name of the remote computer in the Remote Desktop Connection dialog box. The full computer name includes the complete path to the computer, including the computer name, the domain name, and any higher level domains, each separated by a period. Alternatively, you can enter the IP address.

You may have problems establishing a remote connection if your computer does not have enough memory to support running both your local computer and the remote session. If the error message *Not enough memory* displays, try closing some programs on your local computer before establishing the Remote Desktop Connection.

Some networks—particularly corporate or other workplace networks—may have a Terminal Services (TS) Gateway server installed to enable Remote Desktop Connections. A ***gateway*** is a computer connecting two networks that use different protocols. A ***protocol*** is the set of standards used for exchanging information among computers. A ***Terminal Services (TS) Gateway*** is a gateway that enables authorized users to connect to a remote computer on a corporate network without having to set up a VPN connection. If you are trying to use Remote Desktop Connection to connect to a computer on a network that uses a TS Gateway server, you must specify the server name and settings in the Remote Desktop Connection dialog box.

First, ask your network administrator if you need to specify a TS Gateway server, and if so, what name and settings you should use. Then, open the Remote Desktop Connection dialog box, click the Options button, click the Advanced tab, and then, under Connect from anywhere, click Settings. Select the Use these TS Gateway server settings and then enter the information as instructed by your network administrator.

SUMMARY SKILL MATRIX

In This Lesson You Learned	Matrix Skill	Skill Number
To connect to a network	Choose a network connection from the Network Center Find and connect to an available wireless network Check the status of a wireless network connection	2.2.1 2.2.2 2.2.3
To troubleshoot a network connection		
To locate your computer's IP address	Locate the IP configuration of the computer	7.4.1
To use the Ping command	Ping another computer to ascertain connectivity status	7.4.2
To disable and enable a network connection	Enable and disable a network connection	7.4.3
To connect to a workplace network from a remote location	Remotely connect to a network at your workplace	2.2.4
To use Remote Desktop Connection		
To enable Remote Desktop Connection on your computer	Allow remote desktop connections to your computer	2.3.1
To authorize remote desktop users	Specify who can connect to your computer by using Remote Desktop Connection	2.3.2
To connect to a remote computer	Connect to another computer by using Remote Desktop Connection	2.4.1

Matching

Match the term in Column 1 to its description in Column 2.

Column 1	Column 2
1. IP address	**a.** a feature used for inputting commands on a command line
2. protocol	**b.** a device that sends information between two networks
3. virtual private network	**c.** a command you can use with the Command Prompt to find out the IP address of a website
4. gateway	**d.** a unique number that identifies your computer to other computers on a network or on the Internet
5. network adapter	**e.** a computer connecting two networks that use different protocols
6. router	**f.** a command used to check whether a particular IP address is available on a network or the Internet
7. Command Prompt	**g.** a set of standard rules that allow the exchange of information among computers
8. Ping	**h.** a command you can use with the Command Prompt to identify the IP address of your computer
9. ipconfig	**i.** an encrypted network that connects one or more computers to a large network via the Internet
10. nslookup	**j.** a device that enables a computer to connect to a network

True / False

Circle T if the statement is true or F if the statement is false.

T | F **1.** When you install a network adapter in your computer, Windows Vista creates a network connection for it.

T | F **2.** A physical network connection uses radio signals to enable communication between computers.

T | F **3.** If you know a website's address, you can find its IP address.

T | F **4.** No response to a Ping command means that the connection to the network or Internet is not valid.

T | F **5.** A virtual private network lets anyone connect to the Internet if they are in a public area and are using a wireless connection.

T | F **6.** You must have a user account and password on the remote computer to gain access using Remote Desktop Connection.

T | F **7.** Remote Desktop Connection is active by default.

T | F **8.** When you enable Remote Assistance on your computer, you also enable Remote Desktop Connection.

T | F **9.** To use Network Level Authentication with Remote Desktop Connection, NLA must be available on both the local and the remote computers.

T | F **10.** System administrator accounts have Remote Desktop authorization by default.

■ Competency Assessment

Project 13-1: Wireless at the Coffee Shop

You are meeting a friend at a coffee shop that offers free Internet access via a wireless network. You arrive early, so you have time to turn on your notebook computer, log on to the Internet, and check your e-mail. You disconnect when your friend arrives. In this project, you identify available network connections. You then connect to an available wireless network and check the status of the network.

GET READY. Before you begin these steps, start your computer and log on to your Windows Vista account. Close all open windows so that you can see the desktop. You must have an available network connection to complete these steps.

1. Click **Start** and then click **Control Panel**.
2. Click **Network and Internet** and then click **Network and Sharing Center** to open the Network and Sharing Center window.
3. In the left pane, under Tasks, click **Connect to a network**.
4. Click the network to which you want to connect and then click the **Connect** button.
5. Click **Close** to close the dialog box and display the Network and Sharing Center window.
6. To the right of the connected network, click **View status**. The Connection Status dialog box displays.
7. In the Connection Status dialog box, locate the amount of the time the connection has been active.
8. Locate the speed at which the network is operating.
9. Note the current signal quality.
10. At your instructor's request, capture an image of the Connection Status dialog box. Save it in your Lesson 13 assessment folder as ***Proj13_01***. Click the **Close** button to close the Connection Status dialog box.
11. In the left pane, under Tasks, click **Connect to a network**.
12. Click the network that you want to disconnect and then click the **Disconnect** button.
13. Click Disconnect in the dialog box and then click **Close** to close the dialog box and display the Network and Sharing Center window.

    PAUSE. LEAVE the Network and Sharing Center window open to use in the next project.

Project 13-2: Solve Connection Problems

You are a network technician at the School of Fine Art. An instructor has been having trouble using his notebook computer to connect to the campus-wide wireless network. In this project, you connect the network and then work to diagnose and fix the problem. You use the Command Prompt to check the computer's IP address and the Ping command to make sure the connection is functioning. You then try disabling and enabling the connection.

GET READY. Have a pen or pencil and a piece of paper on hand so that you can write down the IP addresses that you identify during this project. Alternatively, create a text or word processing file where you can record the information. Save it in your Lesson 13 assessment folder as ***Proj13_02a***.

USE the Network and Sharing Center window you left open in the previous exercise.

1. In the left pane, under Tasks, click **Connect to a network**.
2. Click the network to which you want to connect and then click the **Connect** button.
3. Click **Close** to close the dialog box and display the Network and Sharing Center window.
4. Close the Network and Sharing Center window.
5. Click **Start**, click **All Programs**, and then click **Accessories**.

6. Under Accessories, click **Command Prompt** to open the Command Prompt window.
7. In the Command Prompt window, key **ipconfig** and then press **Enter**.
8. Locate the IP address listed under your wireless connection, or for a different connection, and write it down on your piece of paper or record it in the Proj13_02a file. Recall that an IP address is usually four sets of numbers, separated by periods.
9. In the Command Prompt window, key **ping**, press the **spacebar**, and then key the IP address you wrote down in step 8.
10. Press **Enter**. Watch in the Command Prompt window to see if your computer replies to the ping, and how long it takes. Record the approximate round trip time statistics.
11. In the Command Prompt window, key **nslookup umass.edu** and press **Enter**. This is the web address of the University of Massachusetts. (You may use a different university if you want, such as the state university where you live or study.)
12. Record the IP address for the university website.
13. In the Command Prompt window, key **ping**, press the **spacebar**, and then key the IP address you wrote down in step 12.
14. Press **Enter**. Locate and then record the approximate round trip time statistics. Compare the time to the time you recorded in step 10. The university ping reply should have taken longer, because the website server is further away than your own computer.
15. At your instructor's request, capture an image of the Command Prompt window. Save it in your Lesson 13 assessment folder as ***Proj13_02b***. Close the Command Prompt window.
16. Click **Start**, click **Control Panel**, and then click **View network status and tasks** to open the Network and Sharing Center window.
17. In the left pane, under Tasks, click **Manage network connections** to open the Network Connections window.
18. Right-click an enabled connection and click **Disable** on the shortcut menu. If you are logged on as an administrator, click **Continue** in the User Account Control dialog box. Alternatively, key an administrator's password and then click **OK**. Windows Vista disables the connection.
19. Right-click the connection and click **Enable** on the shortcut menu. If you are logged on as an administrator, click **Continue** in the User Account Control dialog box. Alternatively, key an administrator's password and then click **OK**. Windows Vista enables the connection.
20. If necessary, close the Network Connections window and click **Connect to a network** under Tasks in the left pane of the Network and Sharing Center window.
21. Click the network to which you want to connect and then click **Connect**.
22. Click **Close** to close the dialog box.
23. **CLOSE** the Network and Sharing Center window.

PAUSE. LEAVE the Windows Vista desktop displayed and keep the pen or pencil and paper or the electronic file on hand to use in the next project.

■ Proficiency Assessment

Project 13-3: Upstairs Downstairs

At home, you have a desktop computer upstairs in a spare bedroom, and you use a notebook computer for work and when traveling. On occasion you would like to be able to access the files and programs that are on the desktop computer while you are using your notebook computer. In this project, you set up Remote Desktop Connection so that you can access the desktop computer from the notebook computer. You then disable the connection.

GET READY. To complete this project, you should have access to two separate computers. If you do not, you can enable Remote Desktop Connection and authorize users, but you will not be able to use Remote Desktop Connection to access a remote system.

1. On the computer that you want to access remotely, click **Start**, click **Control Panel**, and then click **System and Maintenance**.
2. Under System, click **Allow remote access**. If you are logged on as an administrator, click **Continue** in the User Account Control dialog box, or key an administrator password and click **OK**.
3. Click to select the **Allow connections from computers running any version of Remote Desktop** option and then click **Apply** to apply the change and leave the dialog box open.
4. Click the **Select Users** button to open the Remote Desktop Users dialog box.
5. Click **Add** to open the Select Users dialog box.
6. In the Enter the object names to select text box, key your user name or the user name of the person you want to authorize and then click **OK**. Recall that the user must have a password-protected account on the computer.
7. Click **OK** to close the Remote Desktop Users dialog box and then click **OK** to close the System Properties dialog box.
8. If you do not already know the IP address of the computer you wish to access remotely, click **Start**, click **All Programs**, click **Accessories**, and then click **Command Prompt**. Key **ipconfig** and then press Enter. Locate the IP address listed under your wireless connection, or for a different connection, and record it on paper. Alternatively, enter it in a text or word processing file. Save the file in your Lesson 13 assessment folder as ***Proj13_03a***. Then close the Command Prompt window.
9. On the computer that you want to use to access the remote computer, click **Start**, click **All Programs**, and then click **Accessories**.
10. Under Accessories, click **Remote Desktop Connection**.
11. In the Computer text box, key the IP address of the remote computer and then click **Connect**.
12. In the user name text box, key your user name for the remote computer.
13. In the password text box, key your password for the remote computer.
14. Click **OK**. If the remote computer is not using NLA, or is running a version of Windows prior to Windows Vista, your computer may display a warning dialog box before establishing the connection. Click **Yes** to establish the remote connection.
15. To end the Remote Desktop Connection, click the **Close** button on the Remote Desktop tab at the top of your screen and then click **Yes** in the dialog box that displays.
16. On the computer that you accessed remotely, click **Start**, click **Control Panel**, and then click **System and Maintenance**. Under System, click **Allow remote access**. If you are logged on as an administrator, click **Continue** in the User Account Control dialog box, or key an administrator password and click **OK**.
17. At your instructor's request, capture an image of the dialog box. Save it in your Lesson 13 assessment folder as ***Proj13_03b***. Then, click to select the **Don't allow connections to this computer** option and then click **Apply**.
18. Click the **Select Users** button. Click the name of the user you added earlier in this project and then click the **Remove** button. Click **OK** to close the dialog box.
19. Click **OK** to close the System Properties dialog box and then **CLOSE** the Control Panel.

PAUSE. LEAVE the Windows Vista desktop displayed to use in the next project.

Project 13-4: Remote Connection

As an alumni coordinator for the School of Fine Art, you travel to speak to alumni groups on a regular basis. The school's network administrator recently gave you authorization to use a virtual private network to log in to the school's network from any location at which you can access the Internet. In this project, you set up the VPN on your computer and use it to log in to the school's network.

GET READY. Before you begin these steps, you must obtain authorization from your network administrator. You must also obtain the Internet address of the VPN, as well as the user name and password you will use to log in. If you do not have authorization, you will not be able to complete this exercise.

1. Click **Start**, click **Control Panel**, and then click **View network status and tasks**.
2. Under Tasks in the left pane, click **Set up a connection or network**.
3. Click **Connect to a workplace** and then click **Next**.
4. Click **Use my Internet connection (VPN)**.
5. Key the Internet address of the VPN. You can enter the IP address or the domain name, as specified by your network administrator. At the request of your instructor, capture an image of the window and save it in your Lesson 13 assessment folder as ***Proj13_04a***.
6. Click **Next**.
7. Key the user name supplied by your network administrator.
8. Click in the Password box and key your password.
9. Click **Create**.
10. Log in to the network, using the necessary login procedure.
11. When you are finished using the VPN, disconnect as instructed by your network administrator.
12. Navigate to the Network and Sharing Center window.
13. Click **Manage network connections** under Tasks in the left pane. If requested by your instructor, capture an image of the window. Save it in your Lesson 13 assessment folder as ***Proj13_04b***.
14. Right-click the **VPN connection** and then click **Delete** on the shortcut menu.
15. Click **Yes** to delete the VPN connection from your computer.
16. Close the Network Connections window.
17. Close the Network and Sharing Center window.

PAUSE. LEAVE the Windows Vista desktop displayed to use in the next project.

■ Mastery Assessment

Project 13-5: Internet Access at the Airport

You are waiting to meet someone at the airport and want to take advantage of the free wireless network for accessing the Internet. Unfortunately, although you are able to establish the connection, it does not seem to be working properly. In this project, you display available network connections and connect to the wireless network. You then try to identify the source of the problem. Finally, you disable and then enable the connection.

GET READY. Have a pen or pencil and a piece of paper on hand or create a text or word processing file so that you can record the IP addresses that you identify during this project. Save the file in your Lesson 13 assessment folder as ***Proj13_05a***.

1. Open the Network and Sharing Center window and select **Connect to a network**.
2. View the available networks and then connect to an available wireless network.
3. Open the **Command Prompt** window and use the **ipconfig** command to determine the IP address of your computer. Record the IP address.
4. Use the **Ping** command to test the connection to your computer's IP address.
5. Use the **nslookup** command to find the IP address of a website you use frequently.
6. Use the **Ping** command to test the connection to the website's IP address. If requested by your instructor, capture an image of the Command Prompt window. Save it in your Lesson 13 assessment folder as ***Proj13_05b***.

7. Navigate to the Network and Sharing Center window.
8. Open the Network Connections window.
9. Disable the wireless network connection. At your instructor's request, capture an image of the Network Connections window. Save it in your Lesson 13 assessment folder as ***Proj13_05c***.
10. Enable the wireless network connection.
11. If necessary, reconnect to the wireless network.
12. **CLOSE** all open windows.

PAUSE. LEAVE the desktop displayed to use in the next project.

Project 13-6: Workplace Files at Home

You are an assistant to the dean of the School of Fine Art, responsible for community outreach. You are going to be out of the office for a week recovering from foot surgery, but the dean has agreed that you can easily work from home using Remote Desktop Connection to access your files. In this project, you enable Remote Desktop Connection and make sure you are an authorized user. You use Remote Desktop Connection to access a remote computer. Finally, you disable the connection.

GET READY. To complete this project, you should have access to two separate computers. If you do not, you can enable Remote Desktop Connection and authorize users, but you will not be able to use Remote Desktop Connection to access a remote system.

1. On the computer that you want to access remotely, open the Remote tab of the System Properties dialog box and enable Remote Desktop access.
2. Click the **Select Users** button and add your user name to the list of Remote Desktop Users. If requested by your instructor, capture an image of the dialog box. Save it in your Lesson 13 assessment folder as ***Proj13_06***.
3. If you do not already know the IP address of the computer you wish to access remotely, use the **ipconfig** command to locate it.
4. On the computer that you want to use to access the remote computer, open the Remote Desktop Connection window and connect to the remote computer.
5. Enter your user name and password to log in.
6. When you have completed the Remote Desktop Connection session, log out.
7. Disable Remote Desktop Connection on the remote computer.
8. Remove your user name from the list of authorized users.
9. **CLOSE** all open windows.

LOG OFF your Windows Vista user account.

INTERNET READY

Before the Windows operating system, there was MS DOS and the Command Prompt. To communicate with a personal computer, you typed a command on a command line, pressed Enter, and waited for the results. You could type DIR to display a list of the contents of a folder—called a directory back then—or type CD to change to a different folder. You could use hundreds of commands to control your system. In this project, use Internet search tools to locate information about MS DOS, the Command Prompt, and command line commands. For example, you can look for information about how the command line was used, and how and why it gave way to Windows. Look for a list of commands and what they did. When you have completed your research, create a spreadsheet document and list at least ten MS DOS command line commands, along with the equivalent Windows Vista steps you need to accomplish the same thing.

Collaborating with Others

LESSON SKILL MATRIX

Skills	Matrix Skill	Skill Number
Sharing Folders and Files		
Using the Public Folder	Share a folder on a hard disk	4.3.1
Sharing a Folder with Selected Users	Secure a share by adding permissions for specific users	4.3.2
Configuring NTFS Permissions	Configure NTFS permissions on a folder so that different users have different permissions	4.2.5
Sharing Resources on a Network		
Enabling File and Printer Sharing on a Network	Share a printer that is connected to your computer	3.6.4
Customizing a Printer Share	Make drivers available for other operating systems	3.6.5
Browsing Your Network	Connect to another computer by browsing a network Connect to another computer by accessing shared folders	2.4.3 2.4.4
Mapping a Network Drive	Connect to another computer by mapping a drive to a network share	2.4.2
Using a Network Printer	Locate and install a network printer	3.6.3
Using Network Files Offline		
Enabling Offline Files	Set up your computer to use offline files	2.5.1
Making Files and Folders Available Offline	Make a file or folder available offline	2.5.2
Synchronizing Offline Files and Folders Manually	Synchronize folders between computers	2.5.4
Resolving Synchronization Conflicts	Resolve synchronization conflicts	2.5.3
Making a Web Page Available Offline	Make the content of a favorite website available offline	2.5.6
Using Windows Meeting Space		
Starting a Meeting	Start a local collaboration session	5.1.2
Joining a Meeting	Join an existing local collaboration session	5.1.3
Signing In to People Near Me	Sign in to a local collaboration network	5.1.1

A. Datum Corporation is a market research company. Teams work closely to identify target markets and gather data for clients. Team members rely on the company's network and the Internet to enable them to communicate and share information easily whether they are in the same building, visiting clients, or traveling. They use their Windows Vista–based computers to access shared files, folders, and printers. They also meet in small, online collaboration groups to brainstorm and keep each other up-to-date by sharing information. Network administrators help protect the privacy of employees by controlling the level of access different users have to data and resources. In this lesson, you will learn how to use Windows Vista to collaborate with others by sharing data and devices, setting access control, and using local collaboration networks.

KEY TERMS

Ad hoc network
Local collaboration program
Local collaboration network
Map
NTFS permissions
Offline files
Peer-to-peer network
Permissions
Private network
Public folder
Public network
RSS feed
Share
Share permissions
Sync conflict
Sync partnership
Synchronize

■ Sharing Files and Folders

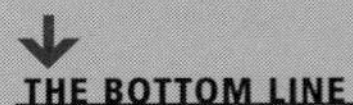

When different people share the same computer, it is important to provide security by limiting the amount of access a user has to someone else's data. By default, those who have administrator accounts can access any object—such as a file or folder—stored on a computer, whereas those with standard user accounts can access only their own files and folders. You can use Windows Vista to make files, folders, and other objects available to share. ***Share*** means to provide access to other users. It can also refer to the object that is being shared. You can also configure different levels of access to specific files or folders. For example, to make files and folders available to everyone, you can store them in the Public folder. To make a specific file or folder available, you can identify it as a shared resource. In this section, you learn how to use Windows Vista to share files and folders.

Using the Public Folder

The ***Public folder*** is a folder that is set up automatically when you set up Windows Vista, in which you can store files and folders that you want to share with others. When you store a file or folder in the Public folder, it immediately becomes available to everyone who has a user account on the computer. In this exercise, you create a file in the Public folder. You then create a new user account, log in using the new account, and access the file in the Public folder.

USE THE PUBLIC FOLDER

GET READY. Before you begin these steps, start your computer and log on to your Windows Vista account. Close all open windows so that you can see the desktop. Create a new folder named Lesson 14 in a storage location specified by your instructor where you can store assessment files and folders that you create during this lesson.

1. Click **Start** and then click **Documents.**
2. In the Favorite Links list in the Navigation pane, click **Public.** The Public folder opens. It should look similar to Figure 14-1, although the Public folder on your computer may contain other files or folders, or the folder view may be different.

Figure 14-1

The Public folder

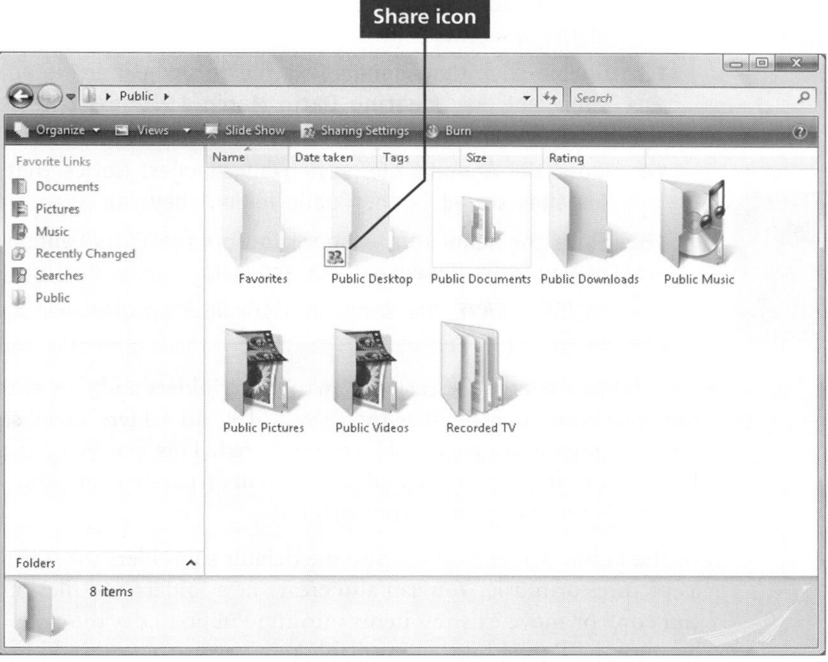

X REF

For more information on creating folders and files, refer to Lesson 2, "Working with Files and Folders."

3. Right-click a blank area of the Public folder window, click **New** and then click **Folder.** Key **Team Info** and then press **Enter** to rename the folder. Double-click the **Team Info** folder to open it.
4. Right-click a blank area of the File list, click **New** and then click **Text Document.** Key **Agenda** and then press **Enter** to rename the file.
5. Close the **Team Info** window.
6. Click **Start**, click **Control Panel** and then click **Add or remove user accounts** (under User Accounts and Family Safety). If you have an administrator account, click **Continue** in the User Account Control dialog box. Otherwise, key an administrator's password and then click **OK.**

X REF For more information on setting up a user account, refer to Lesson 11, "Monitoring the Windows Vista Environment."

7. Click **Create a new account** to display the Create New Account window.
8. Key **Chris Cannon**, verify that the Standard user option is selected and then click **Create Account**.
9. Repeat steps 7 and 8 to create a second new Standard user account with the user name **Bob Gage**.
10. Log off your Windows Vista user account and log in to the new Chris Cannon account.

TAKE NOTE* To log in as Chris Cannon without actually logging off your own account, you can use the Switch User command. Click Start, point to the arrow to the right of the Lock this computer icon, and then click Switch User.

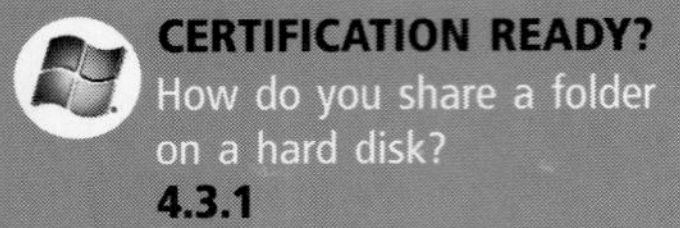

For more information on setting up a user account, refer to Lesson 1, "Getting Started."

CERTIFICATION READY? How do you share a folder on a hard disk? 4.3.1

11. Click **Start** and then click **Documents**. Click **Public** in the Favorites list. Notice that the Team Info folder displays in the window.
12. Double-click **Team Info** to open it. The Agenda text document should display in the window.
13. Double-click the **Agenda** text file to open it in Notepad. On the first line of the document, key **Meeting Date: March 15**. Press Enter and key **Discuss banking focus group. (Chris Cannon)**.
14. Close the **Agenda** file, saving all changes. Notice that other users can not only see files stored in the Public folder, they can open and edit them as well.
15. Close the Team Info window, log off the Chris Cannon account, and log back in to your own Windows Vista account.

PAUSE. LEAVE the Windows Vista desktop displayed to use in the next exercise.

The Public folder is the easiest way to share folders and files with other people who use the same computer. Because the shared files and folders are all stored in the same location, you can quickly see which objects are shared. This makes it easier to control shared access. In addition, it lets you keep all shared items separate from your own personal files and folders, helping to protect your privacy.

In the Public folder, you can use the default subfolders for storing specific types of files, such as pictures or music. You can also create new folders and files in the Public folder, or you can copy or move existing items into the Public folder to make them accessible. Of course, because the Public folder is available to everyone, you should be careful that you never store anything in the Public folder that you do not want everyone to be able to access.

As you learned in this exercise, not only can others view the items stored in the Public folder, but they can also open and edit them. They can rename, copy, move, and even delete them. This puts every item in the Public folder at risk. You may want to maintain copies of items you store in the Public folder in a different location, as well.

Another way to share files is to send them via email to someone else. You can also copy them to a removable device and give the device to the other person.

In the next exercise, you learn how to share a folder that is not in the Public folder.

Sharing a Folder with Selected Users

You can share a folder with individual users or a group of users without making it available to everyone who has access to the Public folder. When you share a folder, its contents are shared as well. By default, when you share a folder outside the Public folder, it is available with a Reader permission level, which means other users can read it but cannot modify it in any way. ***Permissions*** are the rules that control access to shared resources. You can change the ***share permissions*** for an object to allow different levels of access. In this exercise, you move the Team Info folder out of the Public folder and select to share it with two different users. You assign different share permissions to each user.

SHARE A FOLDER WITH SELECTED USERS

1. Click **Start**, click **Documents** and then click **Public** in the Favorite Links list.
2. Right-click the **Team Info** folder and click **Cut** on the shortcut menu. Close the Public folder window. Right-click a blank area of the desktop and click **Paste** on the shortcut menu to paste the Team Info folder on the desktop.

For more information on moving folders and files, refer to Lesson 3, "Organizing Files and Folders."

3. Right-click the **Team Info** folder and click **Share...** on the shortcut menu. The File Sharing window displays. Names in the list are those users who can access the current folder. In this case, only your—the account owner—and any administrator accounts should be listed. The window should look similar to Figure 14-2, although the names of users depend on those available on your computer.

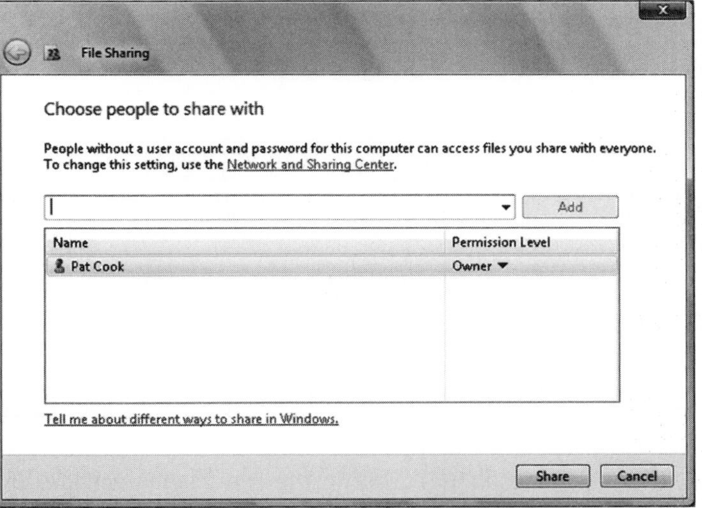

Figure 14-2
File Sharing window

TROUBLESHOOTING

If the sentence under the heading *Choose people to share with* states that only people with user accounts and passwords can access shared files, do the following: Click Network and Sharing Center to open the Network and Sharing Center window. Under Sharing and Discovery, click the expand arrow to the right of Password protect sharing. Click the Turn off password protected sharing button and then click Apply. If you are using an administrator account, click Continue. Otherwise, key an administrator's password in the User Account Control dialog box and then click OK. You learn more about setting Sharing and Discovery options later in this lesson.

You can also access the File Sharing window through the file or folder's Properties dialog box. Right-click the item, click Properties and then click the Sharing tab. Click the Share... button to open the File Sharing window. If the folder is already shared, click Change sharing permissions.

4. Click the dropdown arrow above the list of names to display a list of user accounts on your computer.

TAKE NOTE* In addition to selecting individual users, you can select Everyone, or you can create a new user account.

5. Click **Chris Cannon** in the dropdown list of user accounts and then click the **Add** button. Windows Vista adds Chris Cannon to the list of people authorized to access the current folder, with the default permission level Reader.
6. Click the dropdown arrow above the list of names, click **Bob Gage** and then click the **Add** button. Now, both Bob Gage and Chris Cannon are authorized to share the folder.
7. Click the Permission Level dropdown arrow to the right of Bob Gage to display the available permission options. Click **Co-owner** to change the permission level so that Bob Gage has full access. The window should look similar to Figure 14-3. At your instructor's request, capture an image of the window and save it in your Lesson 14 assessment folder as ***Le14_01***.

Figure 14-3

Assign different permissions to different users

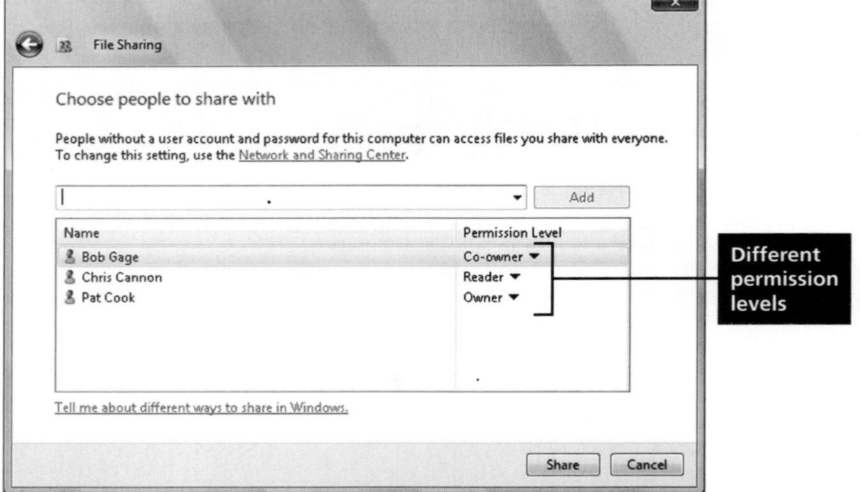

8. Click the **Share** button in the File Sharing window. If you have an administrator account, click **Continue** in the User Account Control dialog box. Otherwise, key an administrator's password and then click **OK**. Windows Vista configures your system to enable sharing. When the configuration is complete, the File Sharing window displays the message "Your folder is shared." Note that when you share a folder, all items stored in the folder are shared as well.

TAKE NOTE* You can use the links in the File Sharing window to send an email to the authorized users with a link to the shared item. The users can click the link to access the item.

9. Click **Done** to close the window. Notice that a share icon displays on the Team Info folder. The share icon lets you know at a glance that the folder is shared.
10. Log off your Windows Vista user account and log in using the Chris Cannon account. Alternatively, use the Switch User command to switch user accounts without logging off.
11. Click **Start** and then click **Computer**. In the Search box in the Computer folder window, key **Team Info**. The shared Team Info folder should display in the Search Results list, as shown in Figure 14-4.

Figure 14-4

Search for the shared folder

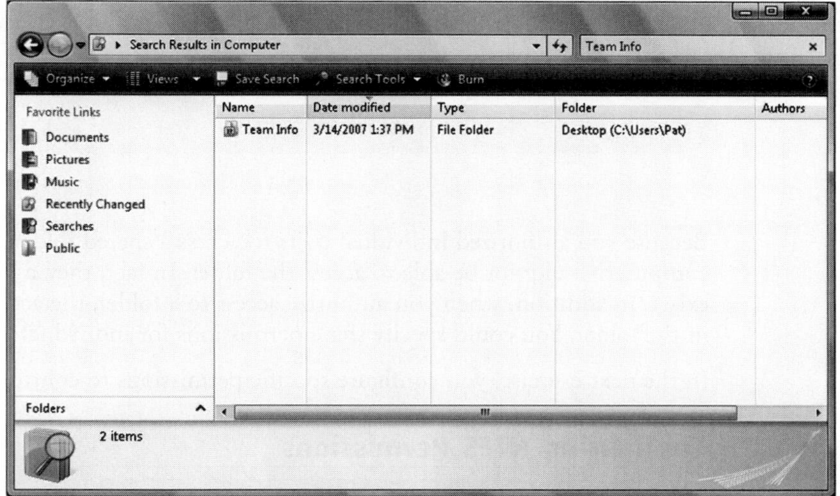

12. Double-click the **Team Info** folder in the list and then double-click the **Agenda** file to open it in Notepad. Click at the end of the second line of text and press Enter. Key **Outline client report.**
13. Click **File** on the menu bar and then click **Save**. Notepad displays a message that it cannot create the file. Click **OK**. Notepad displays the Save As dialog box so that you can save the file with a new name. Key **Edited Agenda** and then click **OK**. Notepad displays a message that you are not authorized to save a file in the Team Info folder.
14. Close the file without saving and close the **Team Info** folder window.
15. Log off the Chris Cannon account and log in using the Bob Gage account. Click **Start** and then click **Computer**. In the Search box in the Computer folder window, key **Team Info**.
16. Double-click the **Team Info** folder in the list and then double-click the **Agenda** file to open it in Notepad. Click at the end of the second line of text and press Enter. Key **Outline client report. (Bob Gage)**.
17. Click **File** on the menu bar and then click **Save**. Notepad saves the file because Bob Gage has full access to view and edit the shared items.
18. Close the file and close the Team Info folder window.
19. Log off the Bob Gage account and log in to your own Windows Vista user account.

PAUSE. LEAVE the Windows Vista desktop displayed to use in the next exercise.

CERTIFICATION READY?
How do you secure a share by adding permissions for specific users?
4.3.2

In this exercise, you learned that sharing a folder with specific users provides more control over access than simply storing the item in the Public folder. When you selectively share a folder, you can not only select the person or people who can access the item, you can control the level of access each user has. Table 14-1 describes the four share Permission Level options you can select in the File Sharing window.

Table 14-1
Permission Level

Level	Description
Reader	The Reader level restricts the user to only viewing shared items. He or she cannot edit, save, delete, rename, or otherwise modify the file or folder in any way.
Contributor	The Contributor level enables the user to view shared folders, and to store new items in the shared folder. This level is not available for shared files.
Co-owner	The Co-owner level provides full access to all shared items. The user can view, edit, rename, and even delete the items.
Remove	Select this option to remove all sharing permissions from the selected user.

Because you authorized individual users to access a shared folder, the other users on the computer would not be able to access the folder. In fact, they might not even know the folder exists. In addition, when you authorize access to a folder, the access extends to all items stored in the folder. You could specify share permissions for individual files, if necessary.

In the next exercise, you configure specific permissions to control access to a folder.

Configuring NTFS Permissions

The four share permission levels you learned about in the previous exercise provide basic control over who can read and edit shared objects. You can obtain even more access control by customizing the ***NTFS permissions*** by using the options on the Security tab of the object's Properties dialog box. NTFS stands for NT file system. It is the system Windows Vista uses to store and retrieve files on a hard disk. NTFS permissions are similar to the share permissions, but they offer more options, and you can apply them to individual files as well as folders. In this exercise you learn how to configure NTFS permissions for a folder.

CONFIGURE NTFS PERMISSIONS

1. Right-click the **Team Info** folder on your desktop and click **Properties** to display the folder's Properties dialog box. Click the **Security** tab. The tab displays information about the current user permissions for the Team Info folder.
2. In the list of Group or user names, click **Bob Gage**. The permissions for Bob Gage display in the lower half of the dialog box, as shown in Figure 14-5. Because Bob Gage has Co-owner permission, all permissions are set to Allow.

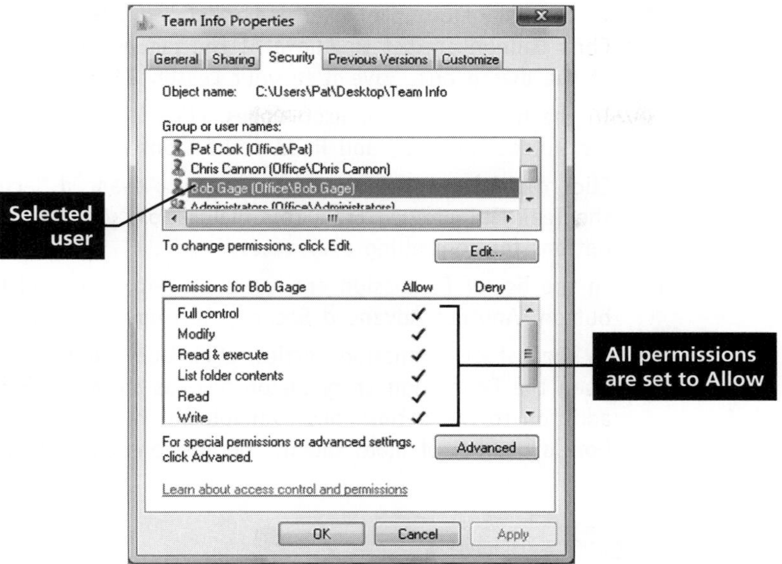

Figure 14-5

Security tab of Team Info Properties dialog box

3. In the list of Group or user names, click **Chris Cannon**. The permissions for Chris Cannon display. Because Chris Cannon has Reader permissions, only Read & execute, List folder contents, and Read permissions are allowed.
4. Click the **Edit...** button to open the Permissions for Team Info dialog box.
5. In the list of Group or user names, click **Bob Gage**. The permission checkboxes in the lower half of the dialog box become available, as shown in Figure 14-6. You can select to Allow or Deny specific permissions to control Bob Gage's access to the Team Info folder.

Figure 14-6

Edit permissions in the Permissions dialog box

6. Click to deselect the **Allow** checkbox to the right of the Write permission (you may have to scroll down the list of permissions). Deselecting the Write permission prevents the user from saving changes to a file. Notice that as soon as you deselect the checkbox, the Allow checkboxes for the Full control and Modify permissions are cleared as well, because the user no longer has full access.
7. In the list of Group or user names, click **Chris Cannon** and then click the **Allow** checkbox to the right of the Full control permission. Now, Chris Cannon has full access to items in the Team Info folder.
8. Click **OK** to apply the changes and close the dialog box. The Security tab of the Team Info Properties dialog box is still displayed.

9. In the list of Group or user names, click **Chris Cannon**. Now, all permissions for Chris Cannon are set to Allow. At the request of your instructor, capture an image of the dialog box. Save it in your Lesson 14 assessment folder as ***Le14_02***.
10. In the list of Group or user names, click **Bob Gage**. Now, only Read & execute, List folder contents, and Read permissions are set to Allow.
11. Click the **Advanced** button to open the Advanced Security Settings dialog box for the Team Info folder. From this dialog box, you can select special permissions options for controlling user access.
12. In the list of Permission entries, click **Bob Gage** and then click the **Edit...** button. Another Advanced Security Settings dialog box displays.
13. In the list of Permission entries, click **Bob Gage** and then click **Edit...** to open the Permission Entry dialog box, as shown in Figure 14-7. Notice that in addition to the permissions available in the Permissions for Team Info dialog box, a number of more specific permissions options are available here.

Figure 14-7

Permission Entry dialog box

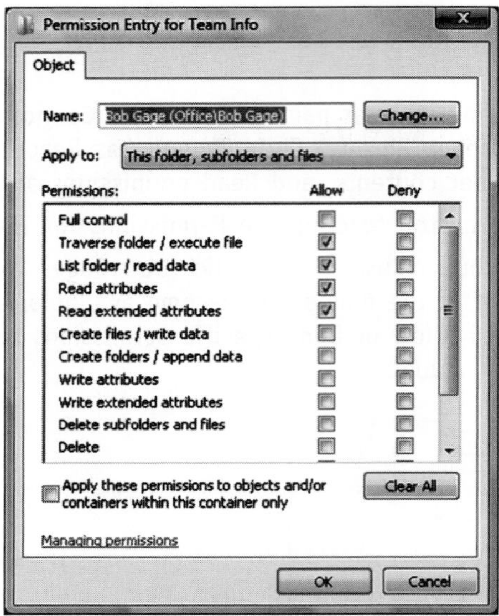

14. Click to select the **Deny** checkbox to the right of the Delete permission. At the request of your instructor, capture an image of the dialog box. Save it in your Lesson 14 assessment folder as ***Le14_03***. Then click **OK** to close the dialog box.
15. In the Advanced Security Settings for Team Info dialog box, click **OK**. Windows Security displays a message confirming that you want to set a Deny permission. Click **Yes**.
16. Click **OK** to close the dialog box. The Security tab of the Team Info Properties dialog box is still displayed.
17. In the list of Group or user names, click **Bob Gage** and then scroll down to the bottom of the list of Permissions in the lower half of the dialog box. Notice that a checkmark is in the Deny column, to the right of Special permissions, as shown in Figure 14-8.

Figure 14-8

Modified NTFS permissions

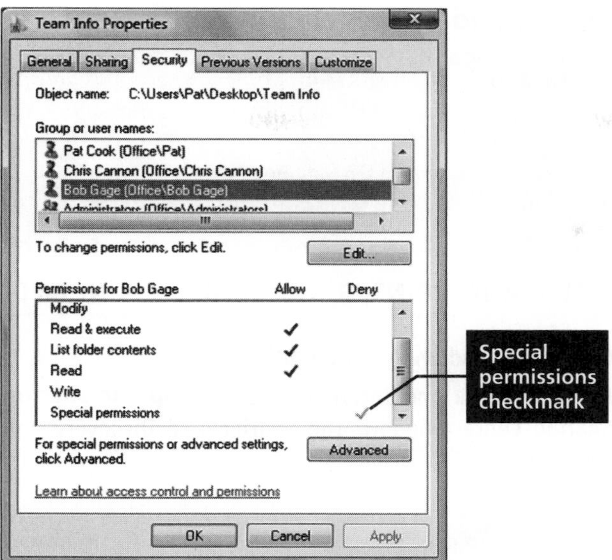

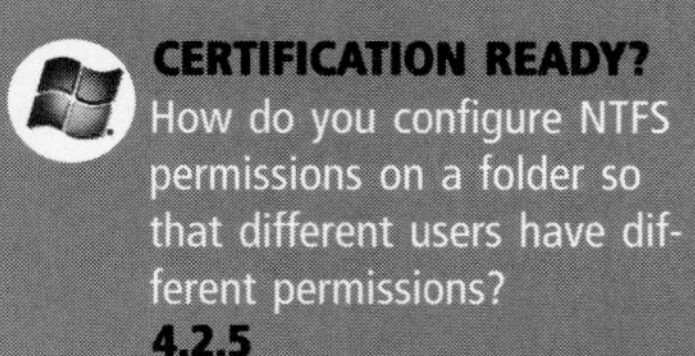

18. At your instructor's request, capture an image of the dialog box. Save it in your Lesson 14 assessment folder as ***Le14_04***.
19. Click **OK** to apply the changes and close the dialog box.

PAUSE. LEAVE the Windows Vista desktop displayed to use in the next exercise.

As you can see, you can apply many levels of NTFS permissions to individual users or groups of users to control access to objects on a computer. You can apply share permissions, NTFS permissions, or both. If both types of permissions are set, Windows Vista will apply the more restrictive settings.

Permissions are an important level of security on a shared system, whether the system is a standalone desktop computer or part of a large network or domain. For example, you can use permissions to ensure that only human resources employees can access employee records, or to keep temporary employees from editing files.

You can also use Windows Vista's Computer Management feature to view shares and modify shared object settings. To open the Computer Management tool, click Control Panel>System and Maintenance>Administrative Tools and then double-click Computer Management in the File list. If you have an administrator account, click Continue in the User Account Control dialog box. Otherwise, key an administrator password and then click OK. In the left pane, click Shared Folders and then double-click Shares in the File list. You can right-click a folder to display available commands, such as removing all share permissions or opening the Properties dialog box to access the Share Permissions and Security options.

In the next section, you learn how to share resources on a network.

■ Sharing Resources on a Network

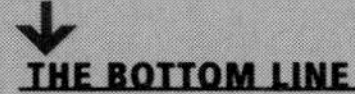

Most computers now are connected to some type of network, whether it is a corporate intranet, a wireless home network, or the Internet. You can easily set Windows Vista options so that you can access and share resources such as files, folders, printers, and backup drives on a network. Once you enable sharing on the network, Windows Vista offers different methods for locating and accessing network resources. You can ***map*** a network drive or shared folder, which means creating a shortcut to the drive or folder in your Computer folder. You can also browse the network to see all available resources, including shared folders and printers. In this section, you learn how to enable sharing on a network, and how to access and use network resources.

Enabling File and Printer Sharing on a Network

As you learned earlier in this lesson, you can share files and folder on your computer with other users on your computer simply by storing the items in the Public folder or specifying a share. If you want to share resources over a network, you must enable network File sharing. When you enable File sharing, Printer sharing is enabled as well. You use options in the Network and Sharing Center to turn File sharing off or on. In this exercise, you enable File sharing on a network.

ENABLE FILE AND PRINTER SHARING ON A NETWORK

1. Click **Start** and then click **Control Panel**.
2. Under Network and Internet, click **Set up file sharing** to display the Network and Sharing Center window. The Sharing and Discovery options are in the lower half of the window.

For more information on the Network and Sharing Center, refer to Lesson 13, "Managing Network Connections."

3. Click the **Network discovery** expand arrow to display the Network discovery options, as shown in Figure 14-9. Network discovery is a setting that enables your computer to see and be seen by other computers and devices on your network. If this setting is Off, your computer cannot communicate on the network.

Figure 14-9

Display the Network discovery options

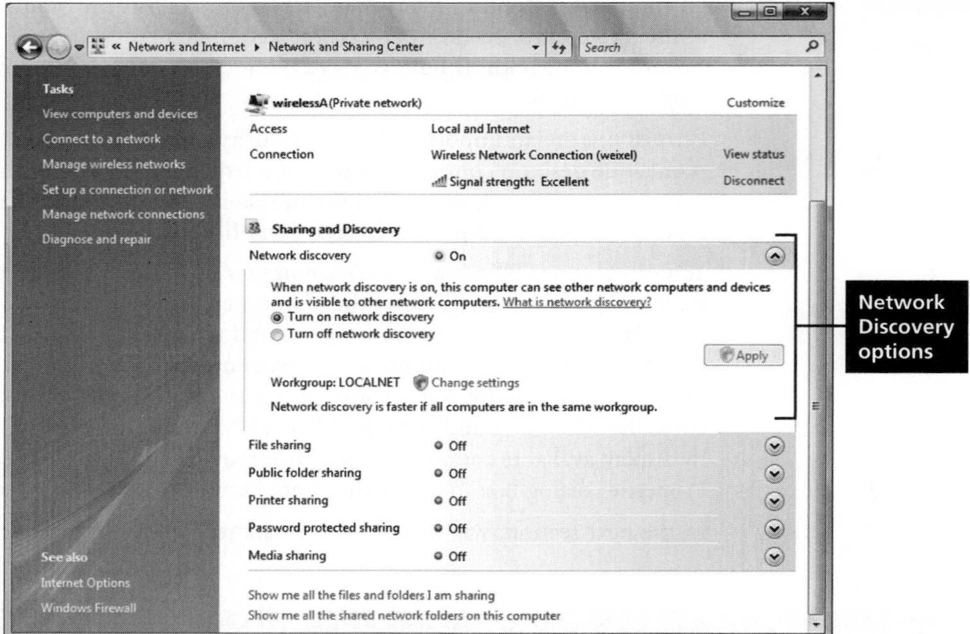

4. If necessary, click to select the **Turn on network discovery** option and then click the **Apply** button. If you are using an administrator account, click **Continue**. Otherwise, key an administrator password and then click **OK**.
5. Click the **Network discovery** collapse arrow to hide the options and then click the **File sharing** expand arrow to display the File sharing options. File sharing makes shared files and folders on your computer available to users on the network.
6. If necessary, click to select the **Turn on file sharing** option and then click the **Apply** button. If you are using an administrator account, click **Continue**. Otherwise, key an administrator password and then click **OK**. Notice that when File sharing is

TAKE NOTE

You can turn off Printer sharing even if File sharing is on.

TROUBLESHOOTING

If no printers are installed, Printer sharing is off by default.

TAKE NOTE

If you change the File list to Details view, the Shared with column displays by default. It lists the users who can access each shared object.

on, Public folder and Printer sharing are turned on as well. By default, all printers connected to your computer become available to network users. However, the default access level for the Public folder on the network is read only, so that network users can read items in the Public folder but not edit them.

7. Click the **File sharing** collapse arrow to hide the options and then click the **Public folder sharing** expand arrow.
8. Click to select the **Turn on sharing so anyone with network access can open, change, and create files** option and then click the **Apply** button. If you are using an administrator account, click **Continue**. Otherwise, key an administrator password and then click **OK**. Now, network users can read and edit items in the Public folder.
9. Click the **Show me all the files and folders I am sharing** link below the Sharing and Discovery options. A Shared by Me search results window opens to display all of the shared folders you own and have made available as shares. It should include the Team Info folder, and there may be other folders as well.
10. Close the Shared by Me window and then click the **Show me all the shared network folders on this computer** link. A window opens to display all shared folders on the computer. The Team Info folder should be here as well as the Public folder, and possibly a Printers folder, as shown in Figure 14-10. Again, there may be other folders and printers. These are the folders and printers that other users on the network will see when they browse the shared objects on your computer.

Figure 14-10

Shared network folders on your computer

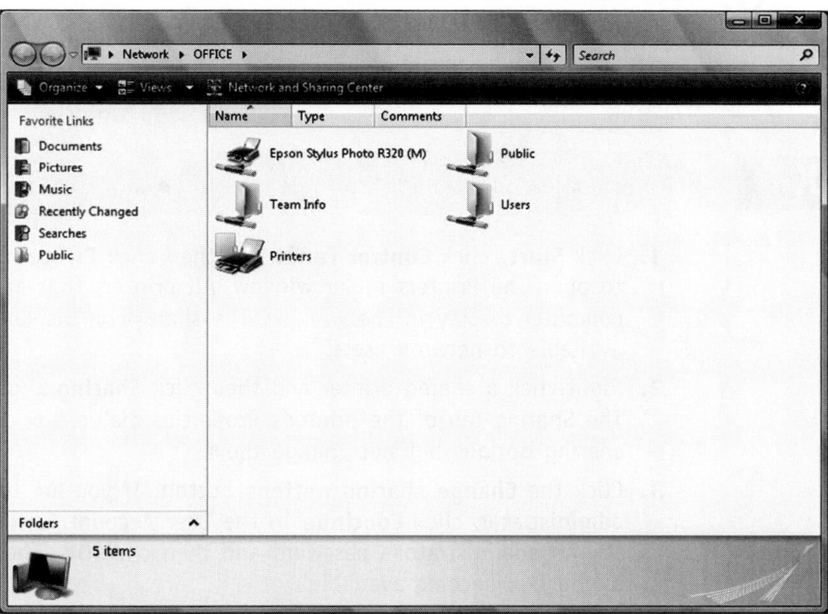

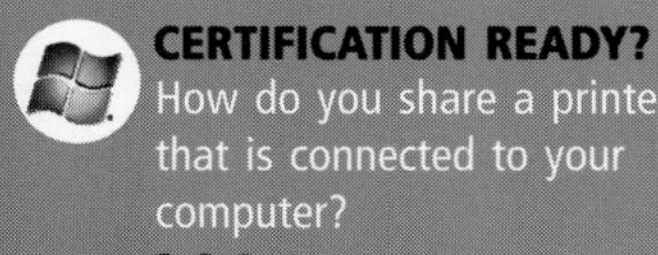

CERTIFICATION READY?
How do you share a printer that is connected to your computer?
3.6.4

11. At your instructor's request, capture an image of the window. Save it in your Lesson 14 assessment folder as ***Le14_05***.
12. Close the window and then close the Network and Sharing Center window.

PAUSE. LEAVE the Windows Vista desktop displayed to use in the next exercise.

Even when network File sharing is on, users on the network can only access shared objects. They may not access your private files and folders. As noted, you can disable Printer sharing even if you want to enable File sharing. Simply click the expand arrow to the right of Printer sharing in the Network and Sharing Center window, click to select the Turn off printer sharing option and then click Apply. Click Continue in the User Account Control dialog box, or key an administrator password and then click OK. Note that shared printers are not available on the network when the computer to which the printer is connected is in Sleep Mode.

The Sharing and Discovery area of the Network and Sharing Center has two additional categories that you can use to control access to your computer on the network:

- Password protected sharing lets you limit access on the network to users who have password-protected accounts on your computer. This option is useful for allowing remote access to those who usually use the computer, including yourself.
- Media sharing lets you provide access to media files such as music and video stored on your computer. You may need to enable this option to provide media sharing if you are using a ***public network***. A public network is one that is available to many different users, such as a network in a public place. A ***private network*** is one that is limited to authorized users.

In the next exercise, you learn how to add printer drivers for different operating systems to a shared printer.

Customizing a Printer Share

A network user running a different version of the Windows operating system than you are may have trouble using a printer connected to your computer. You can make it easier by installing drivers for other operating systems. That way, network users will not have to find the printer driver when they need to use the printer. In this exercise, you install additional printer drivers.

CUSTOMIZE A PRINTER SHARE

GET READY. To complete this exercise, you should have a printer installed, connected, and available for use. In addition, you must have the driver available on a disk or on a network storage location.

X REF For information on installing a printer, refer to Lesson 9, "Managing System Resources."

1. Click **Start**, click **Control Panel** and then click **Printer** under Hardware and Sound to open the Printers folder window. All printers that are installed for use on your computer display in the window. The share icon displays on any printer that is available to network users.
2. Right-click a shared printer and then click **Sharing...** on the shortcut menu. The Sharing tab of the printer's Properties dialog box displays. You can view the sharing options but not change them.
3. Click the **Change sharing options** button. If you are logged on as an administrator, click **Continue** in the User Account Control dialog box. Otherwise, key an administrator's password and then click **OK**. The sharing options in the dialog box become available.
4. Click the **Additional Drivers...** button. The Additional Drivers dialog box displays. The different operating systems for which drivers available are listed in the dialog box.
5. Click to select the checkbox next to the operating systems for which you want to make drivers available and then click **OK**.
6. Click the **Browse** button and browse to the location where the printer driver file is stored. For example, if the driver is on a CD, browse to the CD drive. If necessary, click the driver file and then click **Open**. Windows Vista installs the printer driver.
7. Click **OK** and then click **Close**.
8. **CLOSE** all open windows.

PAUSE. LEAVE the Windows Vista desktop displayed to use in the next exercise.

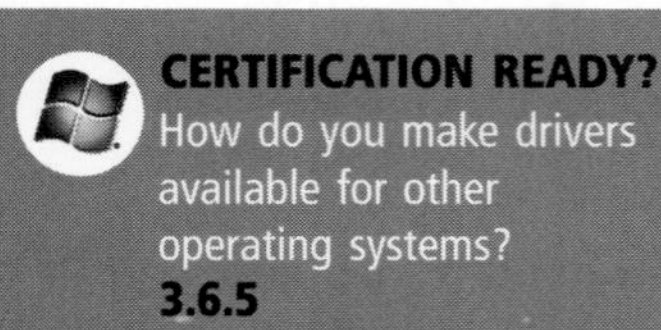

Although a printer is available to all users of the computer to which the printer is connected, and a shared printer is available to all network users, you can set permissions for a printer to control user access. Printer permissions are similar to NTFS permissions you set for a file or folder. You access printer permissions through the Security tab in the printer's Properties dialog box. Right-click the printer in the Printers folder and click Properties. Then click the Security tab. You can add or remove users and select permissions for a user or group. Specifically, you can allow or deny the following permissions:

- Print. This permission gives the user access to use the printer to print.
- Manage printers. This permission gives the user access to select printer tasks, such as setting the default printer or disabling the printer.
- Manage documents. This permission gives the user access to the print queue.
- Special permissions. Click the Advanced button to access additional permissions such as the ability to change permissions for the printer or to take ownership of the printer.

In the next exercise, you learn how to browse the network to connect to another computer.

Browsing Your Network

On the network map, you can view all computers and devices on your network. In the Network window, you can browse through available network objects. If you are authorized to access an object on the network, such as a folder or printer, you can open it from the Network window just as if it were stored locally on your computer. In this exercise, you view and browse computers on the network.

BROWSE YOUR NETWORK

1. Click **Start**, click **Control Panel** and then, under Network and Internet, click **Set up file sharing** to display the Network and Sharing Center window. Click the **View full map** link in the upper right corner of the Network and Sharing Center window.
   The Network Map window displays, showing a map of your network components. Solid lines indicate a physical connection, and dashed lines indicate a wireless connection. The example in Figure 14-11 shows a wireless network with three computers, a router, and an Internet connection. Your network map shows your network configuration, which may have more computers and devices.

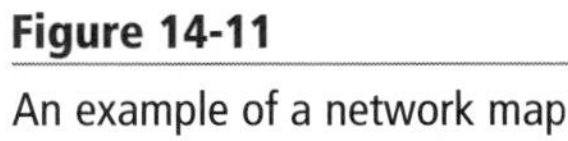

Figure 14-11

An example of a network map

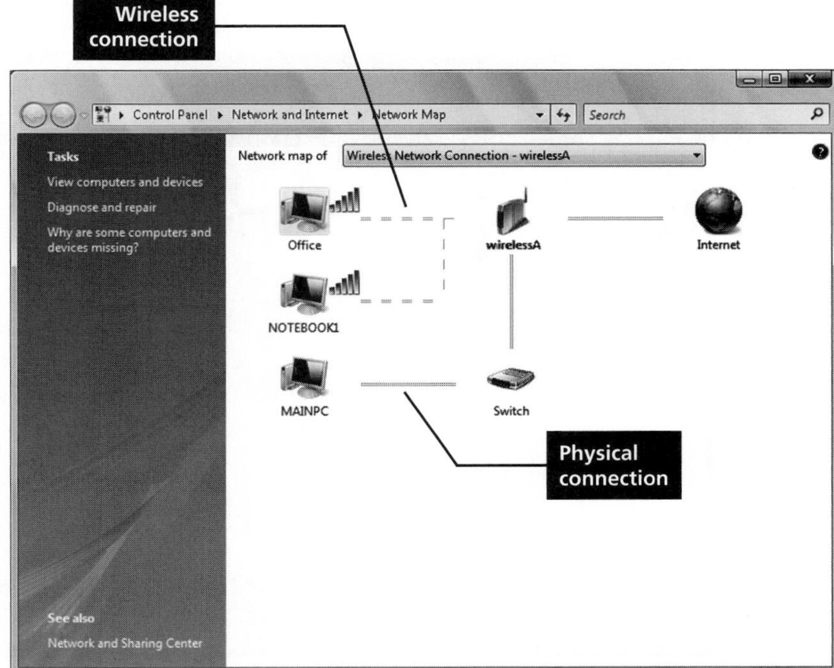

2. Under Tasks in the left pane, click **View computers and devices**. The Network window opens, showing the computers and devices in your network. The example in Figure 14-12 shows the computers in the network that are displayed in Figure 14-11. In the Network window, you do not see the connections—just the computers.

Figure 14-12

An example of computers in the Network window

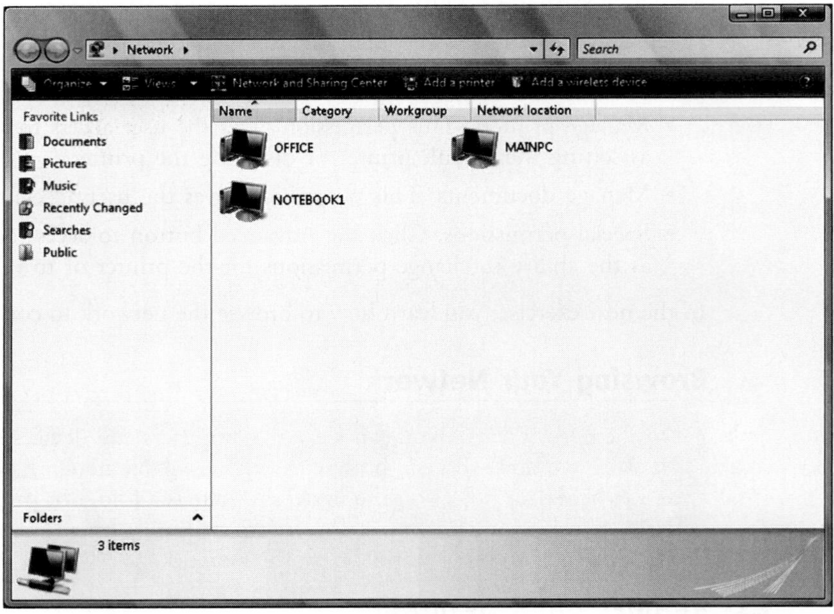

You can also click Start and then click Network in the right pane of the Start menu to open the Network window.

3. In the Network window, double-click any computer that is not the one you are currently working on. A window showing the objects available to you on that computer displays. The example in Figure 14-13 shows the shared contents on the NOTEBOOK1 computer: a Public folder, a printer, and the Printers folder. If requested by your instructor, capture an image of the window. Save it in your Lesson 14 assessment folder as ***Le14_06***.

Figure 14-13

The shared objects on a network computer

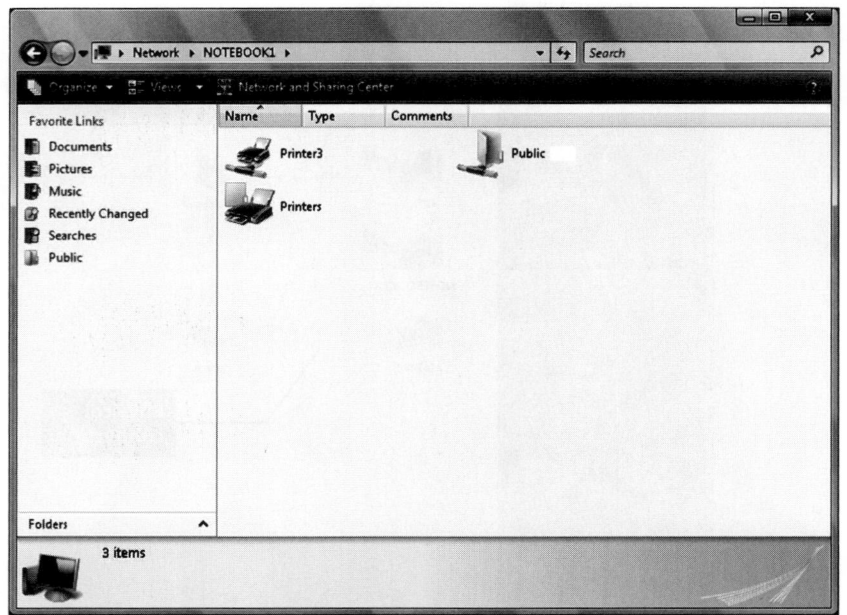

TAKE NOTE

If you double-click your own computer in the Network window, you see the same window that displays when you click the Show me all the shared network folders on this computer link in the Network and Sharing Center window (Figure 14-10).

TAKE NOTE

You may have to enter a user name and password to access a different computer on the network.

CERTIFICATION READY?
How do you connect to another computer by browsing a network?
2.4.3
How do you connect to another computer by accessing shared folders?
2.4.4

4. Double-click a shared folder, such as the Public folder. The contents of the folder display, just as if the folder were stored directly on your computer. If you have permission, you can double-click an item in the File list to open it on your computer.
5. **CLOSE** all open windows.

PAUSE. LEAVE the Windows Vista desktop displayed to use in the next exercise.

Viewing the full network map can be useful for visually identifying connections between computers and devices. You can easily see which connections are physical and which are wireless. In addition, you can immediately identify if there is a problem, because a big red X will display along the connection lines.

In the next exercise, you learn how to map a network drive so that you can access a shared network resource quickly.

Mapping a Network Drive

If you frequently use the same network resource, you can map it on your computer. Mapping creates a shortcut to the resource—appearing in your Computer window—so you can quickly access the resource at any time. In this exercise, you map a shared network folder.

MAP A NETWORK DRIVE

1. To open the Computer window, click **Start** and then click **Computer** in the right pane of the Start menu.
2. On the Computer window toolbar, click the **Map Network Drive** button. The Map Network Drive window displays, as shown in Figure 14-14. In this window, you give the resource a drive letter and browse to select the resource you want to map. The default drive letter is *Z*. If no other resource is using the letter *Z*, you can use it for this map.

TROUBLESHOOTING

If *Z* is already assigned to a drive, select any letter that is not in use.

Figure 14-14
The Map Network Drive window

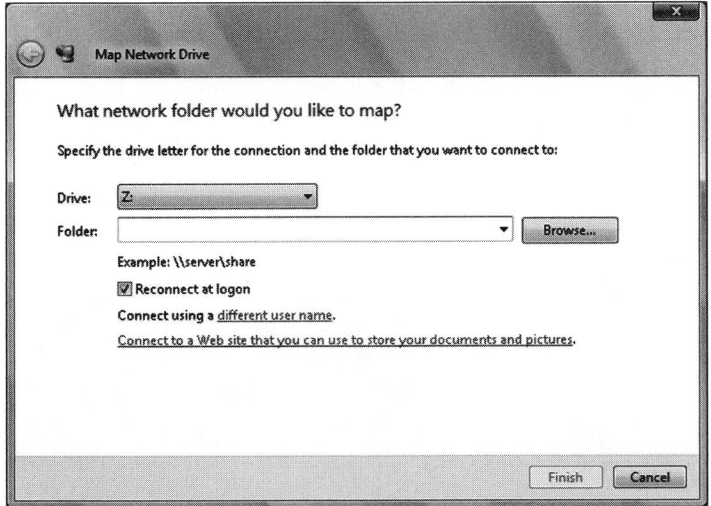

3. Click the **Browse...** button to display the Browse for Folder dialog box. The available network computers display. You can select a computer or select a specific object stored on the computer.
4. Click the arrow to the left of the network computer on which the shared folder is stored. For example, select the computer you used in step 3 of the previous exercise. The list expands to display the available shared network folders.
5. Click the shared folder you want to map. For example, click the Public folder. The list may expand to show the contents of the folder. Click **OK**. The path to the shared folder is entered in the Map Network Drive window.
6. Click **Finish**. Windows Vista maps the network resource and opens it in a new window.
7. Close the window. The Computer window should still be displayed. The mapped resource should display under Network Location, as shown in Figure 14-15.

Figure 14-15

The mapped drive in the Computer window

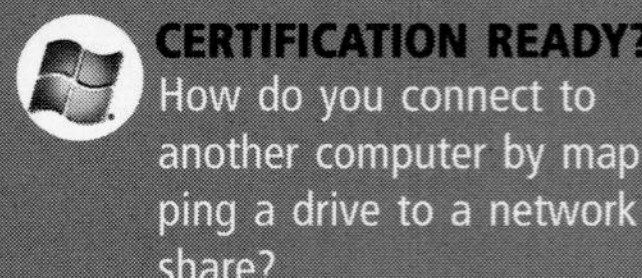

CERTIFICATION READY?
How do you connect to another computer by mapping a drive to a network share?
2.4.2

8. Double-click the shared network folder in the Computer window. The shared folder window opens.
9. **CLOSE** the window.

PAUSE. LEAVE the Windows Vista desktop displayed to use in the next exercise.

The term *mapping a network drive* may be confusing, because you can map any network resource, not just a drive. The term is used because when you map the resource, you assign it a drive letter for identification. You can assign it any drive letter that is not currently in use.

In the next exercise, you learn how to use a network printer.

Using a Network Printer

To use a printer connected to your network, but not directly to your computer, you must locate it on the network and then install it for use. Once the driver is installed, the printer displays in the Printers folder on your computer, and you can use it to print any document, as long as the network printer is available for use. In this exercise, you locate and install a network printer.

USE A NETWORK PRINTER

GET READY. To complete this exercise, a shared printer should be installed on your network and turned on.

1. Click the Start menu and then click Network in the right pane to open the Network window. Double-click the network computer to which the printer you want to use is attached. The available shared resources are listed in the window.

You can search for the network computer from the Start menu if you know its name. Click Start, click in the Search box and then key // followed by the computer name. Double-click the computer in the search results list to open its network folder window.

2. Double-click the **Printers** folder to open the Printers window on the network computer. Printers installed and connected to that network computer are listed in the window, as shown in Figure 14-16.

Figure 14-16

Printers available on the network computer

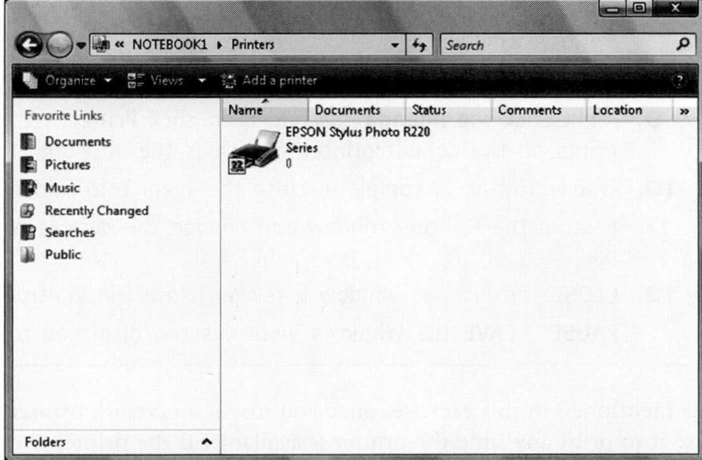

3. Double-click the icon of the printer you want to use. Windows Vista starts the installation process. It displays a warning message asking you to confirm that you want to install the driver.

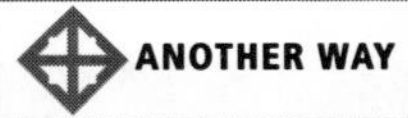

You can right-click the printer icon and click Connect on the shortcut menu to install the network printer for use with your computer.

4. Click **Install Driver**. If you are logged on as an administrator, click **Continue** in the User Account Control dialog box. If not, key an administrator's password and then click **OK**. Windows Vista installs the driver and sets up the printer for use with your computer. It may open a printer window for the printer as well.
5. Close the printer window, if necessary and then close the network computer's Printers window.
6. Click **Start**, click **Control Panel** and then click **Printer** under Hardware and Sound to open the Printer window for your computer. The newly installed printer should display, as shown in Figure 14-17.

Figure 14-17

Network printer in your Printers folder

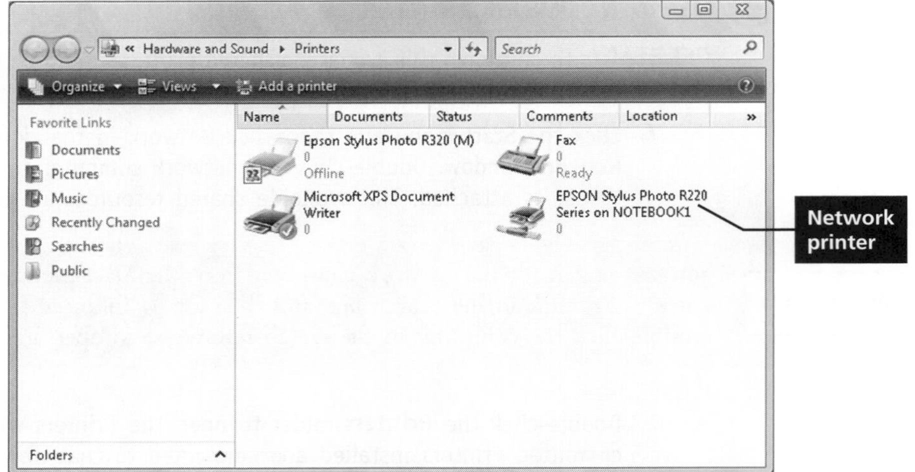

7. Right-click the network printer and click **Set as Default Printer**. Minimize the Printers window.
8. Double-click the **Team Info** folder on your desktop to open it.
9. Right-click the **Agenda** file and then click **Print** on the shortcut menu. The file prints on the default printer—which is the network printer you just installed.
10. When printing is complete, close the Team Info folder window.
11. Restore the Printers window and change the default printer back to its previous setting.
12. **CLOSE** the Printers window and then close the Control Panel.

PAUSE. LEAVE the Windows Vista desktop displayed to use in the next exercise.

CERTIFICATION READY?
How do you locate and install a network printer?
3.6.3

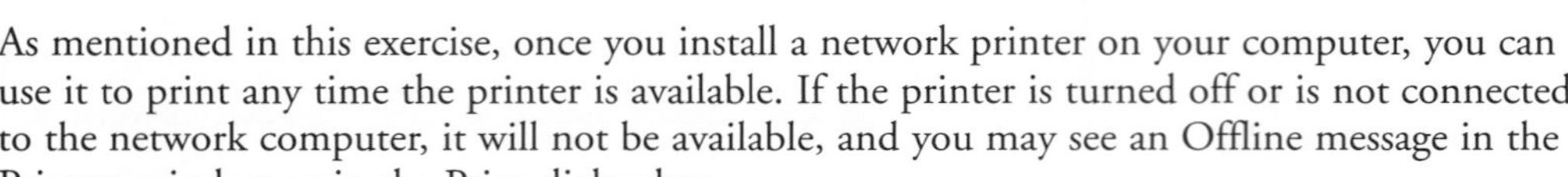

As mentioned in this exercise, once you install a network printer on your computer, you can use it to print any time the printer is available. If the printer is turned off or is not connected to the network computer, it will not be available, and you may see an Offline message in the Printers window or in the Print dialog box.

In the next section, you learn how to work with network files even if you are not currently connected to the network.

■ Using Network Files Offline

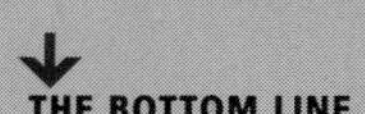

THE BOTTOM LINE

Accessing resources on network computers makes it easy to share data. However, what happens if the network is unavailable, or the computer where the data is stored is not turned on? To be able to work with network files even if the network is not available, you can make network folders available offline. Windows Vista creates ***offline files***, which are copies of the network files stored locally on your computer. It uses the network files when the network is available but uses the offline files when the network is not available. Windows Vista automatically ***synchronizes*** the files in both locations as soon as the network becomes available again, so you can be sure that both sets are up-to-date. To synchronize means to compare the files and save the most recent version in both locations. In this section, you learn how to set up your computer to use offline files, how to make a file or folder available offline, and how to manage synchronization. You also learn how to make the content of a website available offline.

Enabling Offline Files

The first step in making network files available offline is to enable offline files on your computer. In this exercise, you check to see if offline files are enabled and then enable them, if necessary.

ENABLE OFFLINE FILES

1. Click **Start**, click **Control Panel** and then click **Network and Internet.**
2. Click **Offline Files**. The Offline Files dialog box displays. The default setting for offline files is enabled. If your setting is enabled, skip the rest of the steps in this exercise.
3. If your setting is disabled, as shown in Figure 14-18, click **Enable Offline Files**. If you are logged in as an administrator, click **Continue** in the User Account Control dialog box. If not, key an administrator's password and then click **OK**. Windows Vista enables offline files, but you must restart your computer for the change to take effect.

Figure 14-18

Offline Files dialog box

4. Click **OK** and then click **Yes** to restart your computer.
5. When your computer restarts, log in to your Windows Vista user account.
6. Click **Start**, click **Control Panel** and then click Network and Internet.
7. Click **Offline Files**. Offline files should be enabled.

TAKE NOTE*

When you disable offline files, you must restart your computer for the change to take effect.

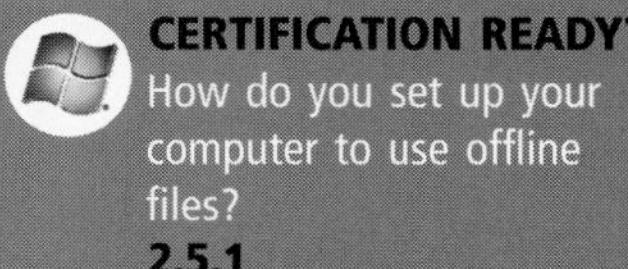

CERTIFICATION READY?
How do you set up your computer to use offline files?
2.5.1

8. Click the **Disk Usage** tab in the Offline Files dialog box. On this tab, you can see how much disk space is allocated for storing offline files, and you can change the limits if necessary.
9. Click **OK** to close the dialog box.
10. **CLOSE** the Control Panel.

PAUSE. LEAVE the Windows Vista desktop displayed to use in the next exercise.

The amount of disk space required for offline files depends on the number and size of the files. The default settings are based on a percentage of disk space. You might need to increase the limit if you use many or large offline files, or you might need to decrease the limit if you find you are running out of storage space for other files and programs.

You can choose to encrypt offline files if you are concerned about unauthorized users accessing your data. Encrypting affects only the offline files on your computer, not the original network files. Windows Vista automatically decrypts the encrypted files for synchronization or when you need to work with them. To encrypt offline files, open the Offline Files dialog box and click the Encryption tab. Click the Encrypt button and then click OK. To stop encrypting, click the Unencrypt button on the Encrypt tab in the Offline Files dialog box.

If you are working on a network that has a slow connection, you can use offline files so that you do not have to wait for your computer to process the network communications. To automatically set Windows Vista to use offline files when a network is slow, open the Offline Files dialog box and click the Network tab. Click to select On slow connections, automatically work offline. You can then set a length of time that Windows Vista should wait before checking for a slow connection and switching to offline files, if necessary. Click OK to apply the change. Click to clear the checkbox on the Network tab of the Offline Files dialog box to cancel the setting.

In the next section, you learn how to make a file or folder available for use offline.

Making Files and Folders Available Offline

To create offline files, you must locate the file or folder on the network and select the option to make it available offline. In this section, you move the Team Info folder to a shared network folder and then make it available offline. You then work with a file offline.

MAKE FILES AND FOLDERS AVAILABLE OFFLINE

1. Right-click the **Team Info** folder on the desktop and click **Cut**. Windows Vista may display a Sharing message informing you that if you delete the folder, it will no longer be shared. Click **Continue**. If you are using an administrator account, click **Continue** in the User Account Control dialog box. Otherwise, key an administrator's password and click **OK**.
2. Click **Start**, click **Computer** and then double-click the mapped network folder under Network Location. The shared folder window opens.
3. Right-click a blank area of the File list and click **Paste** to paste the Team Info folder into the shared network folder. Now, the Team Info folder is stored on a network resource, not locally on your computer.
4. In the shared network folder window, right-click the **Team Info** folder and click **Always Available Offline** on the shortcut menu. Windows Vista copies the folder to your hard disk and synchronizes the copy with the original so that the folder is available offline. Notice that a Sync Center icon displays on the Team Info folder, as shown in Figure 14-19. A Sync Center icon also displays in the Notification area on the Taskbar.

Figure 14-19

An icon indicates the folder is available offline

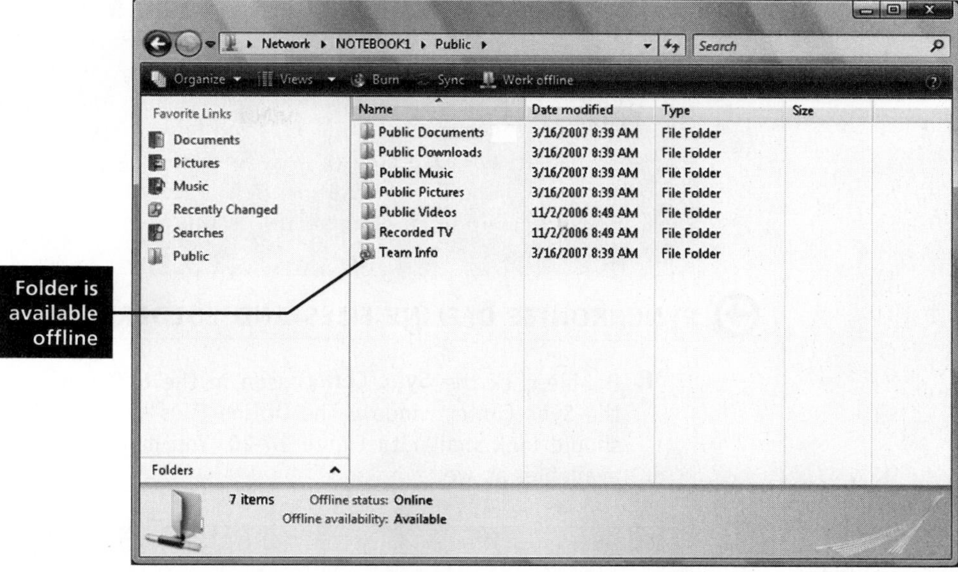

5. Double-click the **Team Info** folder to open it.

6. Click to select the **Agenda** file in the File list and then click the **Work offline** button on the window's toolbar. Windows Vista disconnects from the network. Despite the fact that you are no longer connected to the network, you can open and edit the file.

TAKE NOTE When you select to work offline, files and folders that are not available offline display with a gray X over their folder icons in the File list.

7. Double-click the **Agenda** file to open it. Click at the end of the last line, press [Enter], and key **Plan new account presentation.**
8. Click **File** on the menu bar and then click **Save.** Close the Notepad window.

9. In the Team Info window, click the **Work online** button on the toolbar to reconnect to the network. Windows Vista automatically syncs the files as soon as the connection is established.
10. **CLOSE** the Team Info window, close the shared folder window and then close the Computer window.

PAUSE. LEAVE the Windows Vista desktop displayed to use in the next exercise.

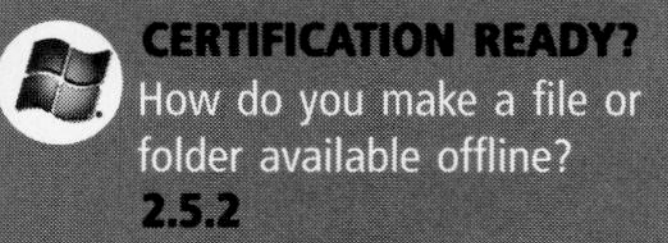

In this exercise, you made an entire folder available offline. You can use the same steps to set up individual offline files. Note that if the network connection is lost while you are working online with files that are available offline, Windows Vista automatically switches you to working offline.

When you make files or folders stored on another computer or device available offline, you create a ***sync partnership***, which is a profile in Windows Vista's Sync Center that defines how and when files will be synchronized between the two locations. You can also set up sync partnerships between your computer and other devices, such as a personal digital assistant (PDA), mobile phone, or music player.

The ability to sync with folders and files on a network is not available in Windows Vista Starter, Windows Vista Home Basic, or Windows Vista Home Premium.

In the next exercise, you learn how to synchronize offline files and folders manually.

Synchronizing Offline Files and Folders Manually

When Windows Vista synchronizes offline files and folders, it identifies the version of the item that is most recent and updates other versions to match. Although Windows Vista automatically synchronizes offline files and folders, sometimes you may want to manually perform a sync. For example, you may want to make sure you have the most-up-to-date files on your notebook computer before you leave on a business trip. You can sync a specific partnership or all partnerships. In this exercise, you manually synchronize offline files and folders.

SYNCHRONIZE OFFLINE FILES AND FOLDERS MANUALLY

1. Double-click the **Sync Center** icon in the Notification area on the Taskbar to open the Sync Center window. The Offline Files sync partnership is listed. The window should look similar to Figure 14-20. You may have other sync partnerships available, as well.

Figure 14-20

The Sync Center window

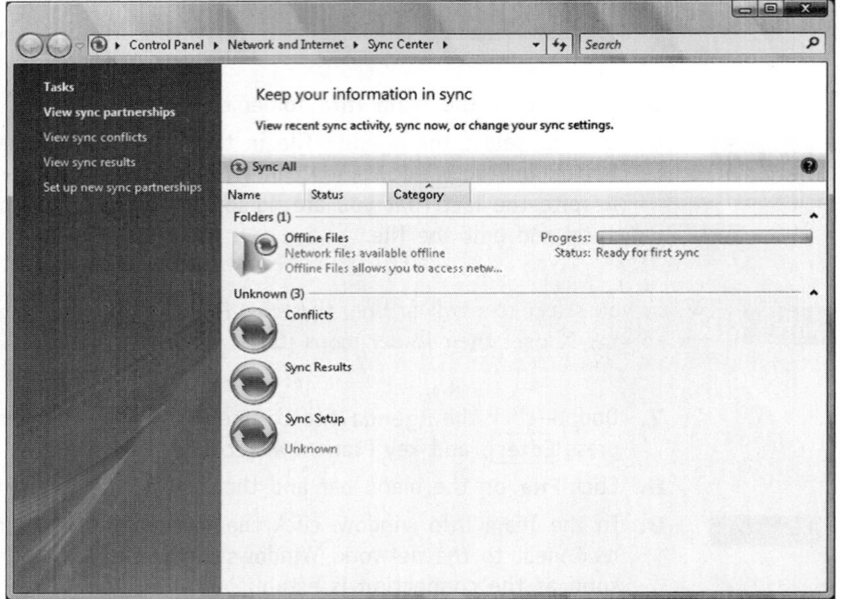

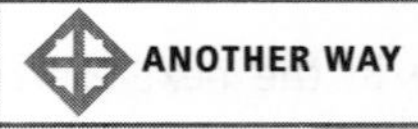

ANOTHER WAY You can also open the Sync Center from the Control Panel. Click Start>Control Panel>Network and Internet. Then click Sync Center.

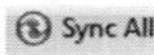

2. Click the **Sync All** button. Windows Vista synchronizes all partnerships. You can view the progress in the Progress bar to the right of each partnership.
3. Click the **Offline Files** partnership to select it.

4. Click the **Sync** button. Windows Vista synchronizes only the selected partnership.

TAKE NOTE* To synchronize the contents of a folder, open the folder and then click the Sync button on the window's toolbar. To synchronize a file, right-click the file in the File list and then click Sync on the shortcut menu.

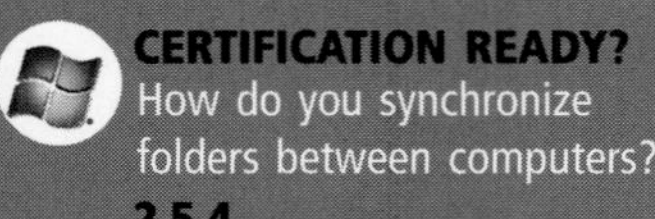

CERTIFICATION READY? How do you synchronize folders between computers? **2.5.4**

PAUSE. LEAVE the Sync Center window open to use in the next exercise.

Synchronization can be one-way or two-way.

- In a two-way synch, when you modify a file in either location, the data is updated in the other location. This option is commonly used to sync network folders and files.
- In a one-way synch, when you modify data stored in one location, the data is updated in the other location. This option is commonly used to sync a mobile device with a computer.

In the next exercise, you learn how to view and resolve synchronization conflicts.

Resolving Synchronization Conflicts

If Windows Vista is unable to synchronize offline files, a ***sync conflict*** occurs. A sync conflict indicates that differences between a file stored in one location and a version of the same file in another location cannot be reconciled. A sync conflict might occur if you edit a document on your desktop computer and then edit the same document on your notebook computer. When Windows Vista goes to sync the offline lines, it will encounter two different edited versions of the file, and it will not know which version is the most up-to-date. Therefore, Windows Vista will not be able to determine which version to save. Windows Vista will prompt you to select a version to save, thereby resolving the conflict. In this exercise, you create a synchronization conflict and then resolve it.

RESOLVE SYNCHRONIZATION CONFLICTS

GET READY. To complete this exercise, you must have access to a computer on which you can work offline with the Agenda file, as well as access to the network computer on which the Team Info folder is currently stored.

1. On your computer, click **Start**, click **Computer** and then double-click the mapped network folder under Network Location to open the shared folder window.
2. Double-click the **Team Info** folder to open it and then click to select the **Agenda** file in the File list. Click the **Work offline** button on the window's toolbar.
3. Double-click the **Agenda** file to open it and then change the meeting date from March 15 to **March 22**. Close the file, saving all changes. Continue to work offline so that the offline Agenda file does not sync with the original network file.
4. On the second computer, navigate to the shared folder where the Team Info folder is stored.
5. Open the **Team Info** folder and then open the **Agenda** file in Notepad. Notice that the date is still March 15, because the files have not yet been synchronized.
6. Edit the meeting date from March 15 to **March 31** and then close the file, saving all changes. Close the Team Info window.
7. Return to your own computer and click the **Work online** button in the Team Info window. Once the network connection is established, click the **Sync** button on the window's toolbar.
8. Close the Team Info window and then close the shared documents window.
   In the Sync Center window, a link under the Progress bar indicates that there is 1 conflict, as shown in Figure 14-21.

Figure 14-21

The conflict is noted in the Sync Center window

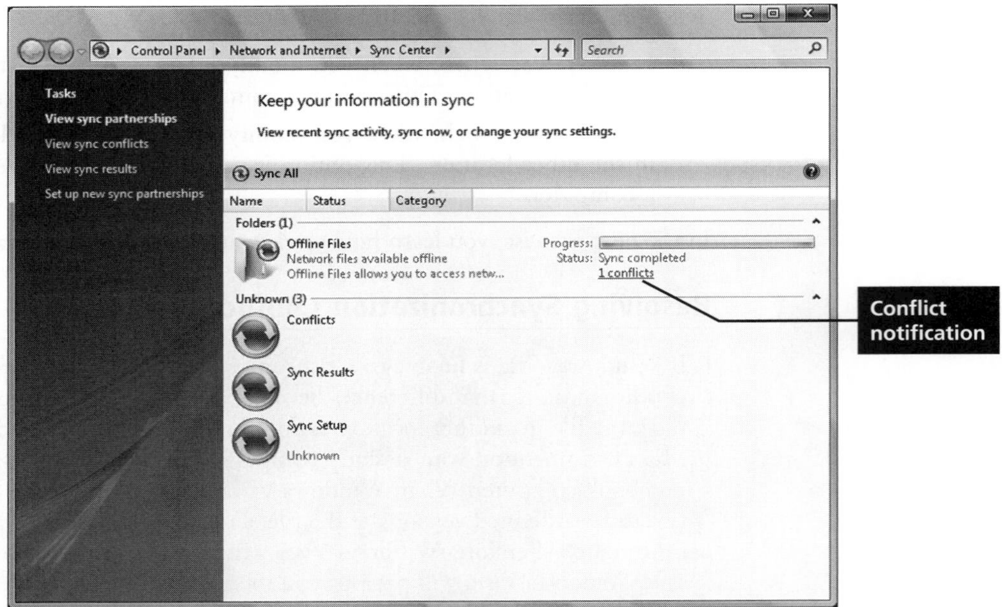

TAKE NOTE*

A warning icon displays on the Sync Center icon in the Notification area when there is a sync conflict.

9. In the left pane under Tasks, click **View sync conflicts** to display the Conflicts window. Unresolved sync conflicts are listed, as shown in Figure 14-22.

Figure 14-22

The Conflicts window

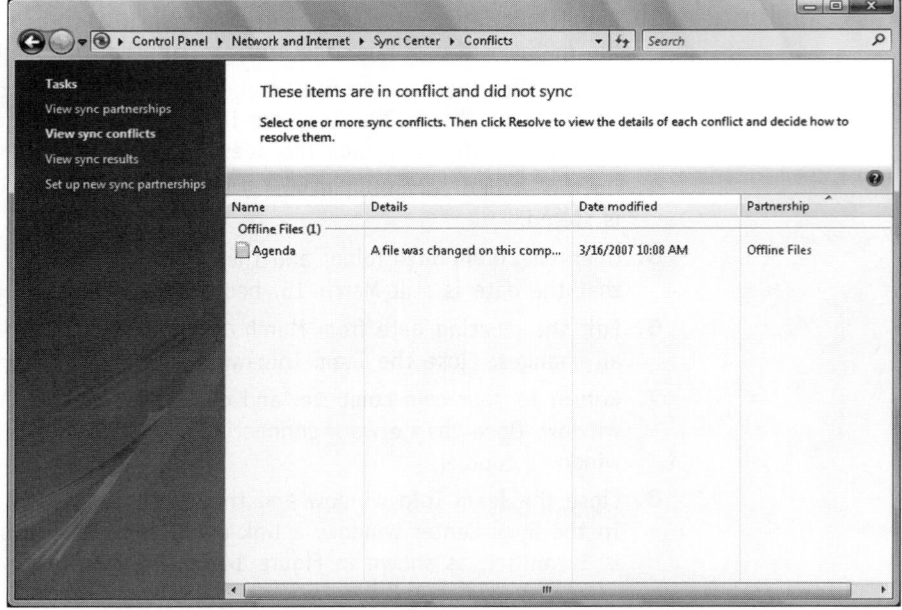

ANOTHER WAY

You can click the conflict link under the message bar to display the Conflicts window.

10. Click the **Agenda** file to select it. A Resolve button becomes available.
11. Click the **Resolve** button. A Resolve Conflict dialog box displays. In this dialog box, you can select the version of the file you want to keep.
12. Click to select the newer version of the file. Windows Vista resolves the conflict and synchronizes the files.

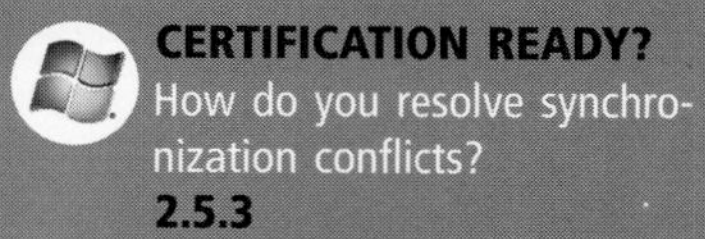

CERTIFICATION READY?
How do you resolve synchronization conflicts?
2.5.3

13. **CLOSE** the Sync Center window.

PAUSE. LEAVE the Windows Vista desktop displayed to use in the next exercise.

Most sync conflicts can be resolved easily by selecting the file you want to keep. If you are not sure which file to keep, you can select to keep them both. Windows Vista will rename one version of the file and save both versions of the file in both locations.

In addition to conflicts that arise from editing different versions of the file on different computers, you might encounter a conflict if you delete a version of the file while working offline. You can resolve the conflict by confirming that you want to delete the file or saving the version that was not deleted.

It is possible to ignore a sync conflict instead of resolving it. In the Conflicts window, right-click the conflict and click Ignore on the shortcut menu. Windows Vista will not try to sync the conflicted files until you resolve the conflict.

In the next exercise, you learn how to make a web page available offline.

Making a Web Page Available Offline

You can work offline in Windows Internet Explorer, which may be useful if you lose your Internet connection or are unable to connect to the Internet. Pages that you visited recently will remain available offline. However, to be sure you can view a page when you do not have an Internet connection, you should save the page locally. For example, you may want to ensure a page with directions to a client's office will be available even if you cannot connect to the Internet. In any case, you will not be able to browse to new pages until you are connected to the Internet again. In this exercise, you save a web page locally and open it in Internet Explorer.

MAKE A WEB PAGE AVAILABLE OFFLINE

1. Click **Start** and then click **Internet Explorer** to open the Internet Explorer browser to your home page.
2. In the Address bar, key **www.metmuseum.org** and then press **Enter** to display the Metropolitan Museum of Art website.
3. Click the **Enter here** link. In the left pane of the home page, click **Visitor Information**. This page displays information such as the museum address and hours of operation.
4. Click the **Page** button on the window's toolbar and then click **Save As...** A Save as dialog box displays. The default file type is Web Archive, single file (*.mht).
5. If necessary, navigate to the Desktop by clicking **Desktop** in the list of Favorite Links.

TROUBLESHOOTING If Desktop does not display in the list of Favorite Links, click the Folders arrow to display the list of folders and then click Desktop.

TAKE NOTE*

When you open a file in Internet Explorer, you are viewing the file, not the actual web page.

6. Click **Save**. Windows Vista saves the file on your desktop.
7. Close the Internet Explorer window.
8. Double-click the **The Metropolitan Museum of Art – Visitor Information** file icon on your desktop. The file opens in Internet Explorer.
9. Close Internet Explorer.
10. Copy the The Metropolitan Museum of Art – Visitor Information file to your Lesson 14 assessment folder, and then delete it from your desktop.

PAUSE. LEAVE the Windows Vista desktop displayed to use in the next exercise.

CERTIFICATION READY?
How do you make the content of a favorite website available offline?
2.5.6

Although you can open a saved web page in Internet Explorer, you will not be able to browse to new pages until you are connected to the Internet again. To set Internet Explorer to work offline, click the Tools button on the window's toolbar and then click Work Offline. The text (Working Offline) will display in the Internet Explorer window's title bar. If you try to access a page that is not available offline, a message displays asking if you want to work online again.

You may also be able to make ***RSS feed*** content available offline. RSS feed is web content that is updated frequently, such as breaking news. RSS feed content can usually be downloaded and read even when you are working offline. Internet Explorer automatically looks for available feeds when you visit a web page. Click the Feeds button on the Internet Explorer toolbar to see a list of available feeds and then click the feed you want to see. If you subscribe to a feed, the content is downloaded to your desktop automatically. To subscribe to a feed, display the feed in Internet Explorer, click the Subscribe to the Feed button on the toolbar, and then click Subscribe to this Feed. Key a name for the feed, select the folder where you want to store the feed, and then click Subscribe.

In the next section, you learn how to use Windows Meeting Space to collaborate in real time.

■ Using Windows Meeting Space

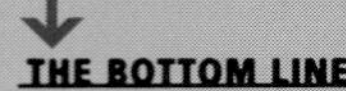

Windows Meeting Space is a local collaboration program included with Windows Vista. A ***local collaboration program*** lets you use a peer-to-peer network to communicate in real time with up to ten other people. A ***peer-to-peer network*** is one that connects computers directly, without using a network server. It can make use of an existing network or the Internet, or you can set up an ***ad hoc network***, which is a temporary network that enables direct computer-to-computer communication. You can exchange messages; view programs and documents on each other's desktops; and deliver documents, called handouts, to everyone in the meeting. To use Windows Meeting Space, you must set it up for use on your computer and sign in to the People Near Me ***local collaboration network***. A local collaboration network stores information about users to identify them to others signed in to the same network. In this section, you enable Windows Meeting Space and learn how to start a session and join an existing session. You also learn how to sign in to People Near Me.

Starting a Meeting

The first time you use Windows Meeting Space, you must set it up for use on your computer. Windows Vista automatically modifies your computer to enable local collaboration, but you must select settings for People Near Me. Once you set up Windows Meeting Space, you can start a new meeting. In this exercise, you set up Windows Meeting Space and start a new meeting.

START A MEETING

1. Click **Start**, click **All Programs** and then click **Windows Meeting Space**. If this is the first time you are using the program, a window displays prompting you to start the setup process. If Windows Meeting Space is already set up on your computer, skip steps 2 and 3.
2. Click **Yes, continue setting up Windows Meeting Space**. If you are logged on as an administrator, click **Continue** in the User Account Control dialog box. Otherwise, key an administrator password and then click **OK**. Windows Vista displays the People Near Me dialog box so that you can enable the feature. It should look similar to Figure 14-23, although your user name should display in the Your display name text box. The default settings sign you in automatically when Windows Vista starts and allow for invitations from anyone who is also signed in.

Figure 14-23

The People Near Me dialog box

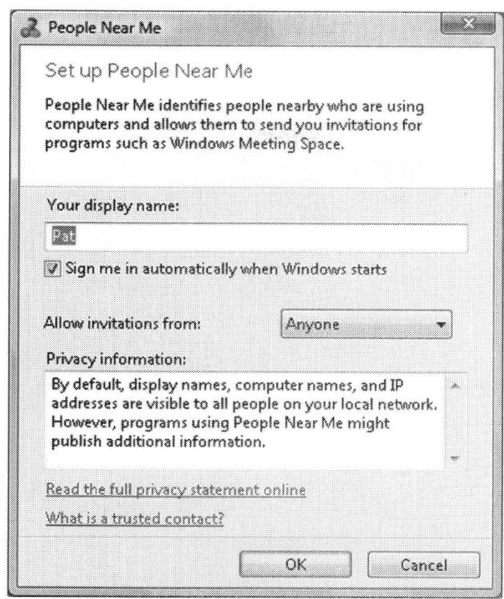

3. Click **OK** to use the default settings. Windows Vista completes the setup and displays the Windows Meeting Space program window. It should look similar to Figure 14-24.

Figure 14-24

Windows Meeting Space

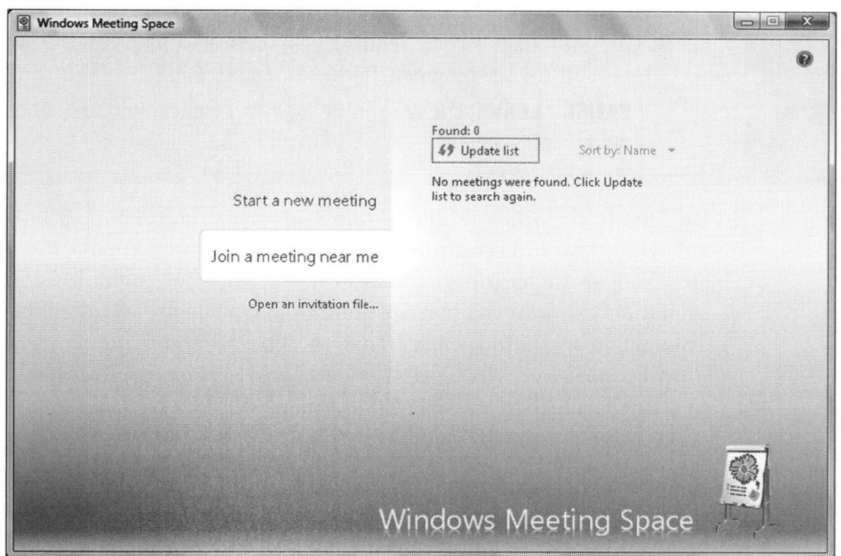

TAKE NOTE*

When you start Windows Meeting Space, if Windows Vista detects meetings already in progress, it displays the number of meetings and the session names.

TAKE NOTE*

You must tell others the password so that they can join the meeting.

4. Click **Start a new meeting**. On the right side of the window, text boxes for entering a meeting name and password display.
5. Click in the Meeting name text box and key **Team Info**.
6. Click in the Password text box and key **team212A**. Other people joining the meeting will have to enter this password in order to gain access.

7. Press **Enter**. Windows Vista starts the meeting and displays the meeting window. It should look similar to Figure 14-25.

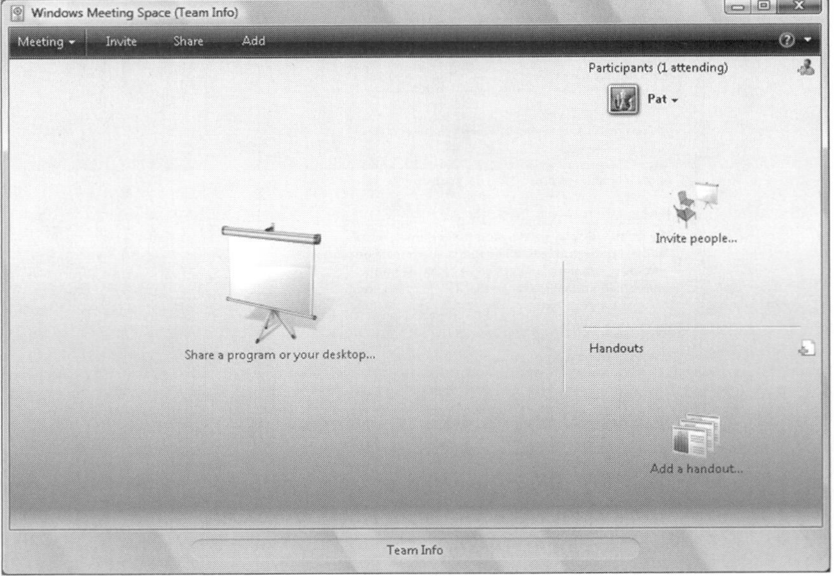

Figure 14-25
Team Info Meeting window

8. At your instructor's request, capture an image of the window. Save it in your Lesson 14 assessment folder as ***Le14_07***.

PAUSE. LEAVE the Windows Meeting Space window open to use in the next exercise.

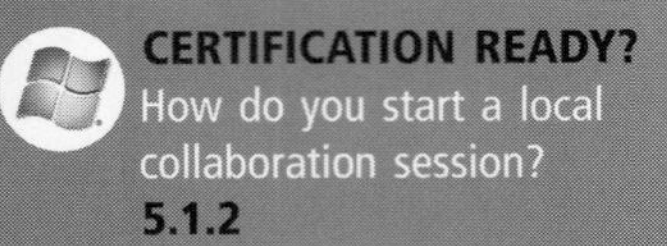
CERTIFICATION READY?
How do you start a local collaboration session?
5.1.2

By default, for other people to join your meeting, they must know the meeting name and password. You can send them the information in an email or tell them personally. You can also issue an invitation to the meeting. If you issue invitations, only those who receive an invitation can join the meeting, and you can specify whether they have to enter a password. To issue an invitation, click Invite people in the meeting window to see a list of people signed in to People Near Me. Select the people to invite, select or deselect the Require participants to type the meeting password checkbox, and then click Send invitations. You can also create an invitation from the main Windows Meeting Space window.

Windows Meeting Space comes with Windows Vista and is a convenient tool for collaborating with a group in real time. Other local collaboration programs are available, and you may have a different one installed on your computer. The features are probably similar to those of Windows Meeting Space.

In the next exercise, you learn how to join an existing Windows Meeting Space meeting.

Joining a Meeting

You can join an existing meeting by using the Windows Meeting Space window. If the meeting is open to anyone, you simply select it in the Windows Meeting Space window, and enter your user name and password to join. In this exercise, you join an existing meeting.

JOIN A MEETING

GET READY. If you have other people nearby who are signed in to Windows Meeting Space and People Near Me, you can work together to join each other's meetings. If not, you can complete this exercise by switching user accounts on your own computer.

1. Click **Start**, point to the arrow to the right of the Lock this computer icon, and then click **Switch User**. Log in to the Chris Cannon user account you created earlier in this lesson.

2. Click **Start**, click **All Programs**, and then click **Windows Meeting Space**.
3. Click **Yes, continue setting up Windows Meeting Space.** If you are logged on as an administrator, click **Continue** in the User Account Control dialog box. Otherwise, key an administrator password and then click **OK**. Windows Vista displays the People Near Me dialog box so that you can enable the feature.
4. Click **OK** to use the default settings. Windows Vista completes the setup and displays the Windows Meeting Space program window. The Team Info meeting should be listed as an available meeting.
5. Click the **Team Info** meeting. Key **team212A** in the password box and then press Enter. The Team Info meeting window displays. In the list of attendees, you can see that there are now two participants, as shown in Figure 14-26. At your instructor's request, capture an image of the window. Save it in your Lesson 14 assessment folder as ***Le14_08***.

Figure 14-26

Two people participating in the Team Info meeting

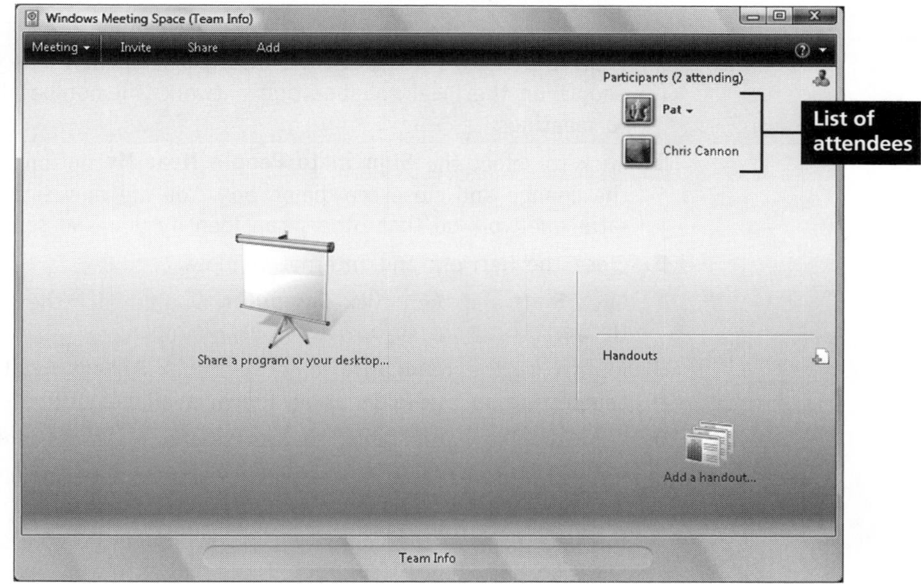

6. Click **Meeting** on the window's menu bar and then click **Leave Meeting**. Chris Cannon is no longer part of the Team Info meeting.
7. Close the Windows Meeting Space window, log off the Chris Cannon account, and log back in to your own Windows Vista user account. The Team Info meeting window should still be open.
8. Click **Meeting** on the menu bar and then click **Exit**. The meeting ends.
9. If necessary, close the Windows Meeting Space window.

PAUSE. LEAVE the Windows Vista desktop displayed to use in the next exercise.

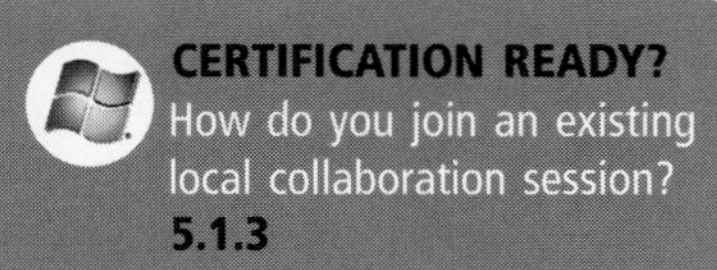
CERTIFICATION READY?
How do you join an existing local collaboration session?
5.1.3

If you receive an invitation to a meeting, you will see a Taskbar button labeled Invitation Details. Click the button to display the Invitation Details dialog box and then click Accept to open Windows Meeting Space, Decline to decline the invitation, or Cancel to close the dialog box without responding to the invitation. If necessary, key the meeting password and then click the Go button or press Enter to join the meeting.

Note that to sign in to a Windows Meeting Space session, users must be on a computer using the Windows Vista operating system and must be signed in to People Near Me. You cannot use different operating systems in the same session.

In the next exercise, you learn how to manage your People Near Me settings.

Signing In to People Near Me

Once you set up Windows Meeting Space, you are automatically part of the People Near Me local collaboration network. Depending on your settings, you may be signed in whenever Windows Vista starts, or you can manually sign in. In either case, you are signed in automatically whenever you start Windows Meeting Space. In this exercise, you learn how to manually sign in to People Near Me. You also remove settings and shares you have applied throughout this lesson.

SIGN IN TO PEOPLE NEAR ME

1. Click **Start**, click **Control Panel**, and then click **Network and Internet**.
2. In the Network and Internet window, click **People Near Me**. The Settings tab of the People Near Me dialog box displays.
3. Click the **Sign in** tab.
4. Click to select the **Sign out of People Near Me** option and then click **Apply** to apply the change and keep the dialog box open. When you are signed out, other people on the local collaboration network will not be able to send you invitations to meetings.
5. Click to select the **Sign in to People Near Me** option and then click **OK** to apply the change and close the dialog box. You are now signed in to the local collaboration network so that others can identify you and send you meeting invitations.
6. Close the Network and Internet window.
7. Click **Start** and then click **Computer**. Double-click the mapped network drive under Network Locations to open the shared folder.
8. Right-click the **Team Info** folder and click **Always Available Offline**. This changes the setting so the folder is no longer available offline.
9. Copy the Team Info folder to your Lesson 14 assessment folder. Then, right-click the **Team Info** folder in the shared network folder and click **Delete**. Click **Yes** in the confirmation dialog box to delete the folder and its contents.
10. Navigate back to the Computer window. Right-click the shared folder under Network Location and click **Disconnect**. This removes the mapped drive. Close the Computer window.
11. Click **Start**, click **Control Panel**, and then click **Add or remove user accounts** under User Accounts and Family Safety. If you are using an administrator account, click **Continue** in the User Account Control dialog box. Otherwise, key an administrator password and then click **OK**.
12. Click the **Bob Gage** account and then click **Delete the account**. Click **Delete Files** and then click **Delete Account**.
13. Click the **Chris Cannon** account and then click **Delete the account**. Click **Delete Files** and then click **Delete Account**.
14. Navigate to the Control Panel window and click **Printer** under Hardware and Sound to open the Printers window.
15. Right-click the network printer and click **Delete** on the shortcut menu.
16. Navigate to the Control Panel window and click **Set up file sharing** under Network and Internet to open the Network and Sharing Center.
17. Under Sharing and Discovery, click the **Expand** arrow to the right of File sharing. Click to select the **Turn off file sharing** option and then click the **Apply** button. If you are using an administrator account, click **Continue** in the User Account Control dialog box. Otherwise, key an administrator's password and then click **OK**.
18. **CLOSE** the Network and Sharing Center window.

LOG OFF your Windows Vista user account.

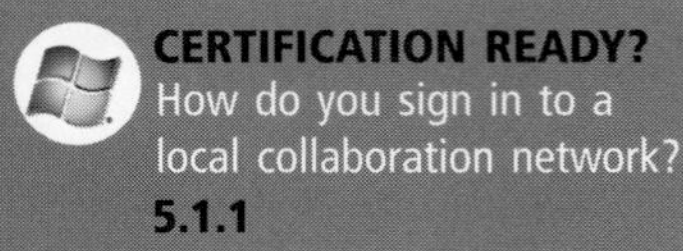

People Near Me is the local collaboration network that comes with Windows Vista. You may have a different local collaboration network available on your system, or you may be able to set up and use an independent ad hoc network. In addition, People Near Me can be used with peer-to-peer networking programs other than Windows Meeting Space. Peer-to-peer programs use peer-to-peer technology, which enables computers to communicate directly with each other without the need for a server.

Workplace Ready

Virtual Meeting Management

Teamwork and collaboration are key principles in most businesses, but if a meeting is not well planned and well managed, it can take up valuable time without producing effective results. Meetings that take place in local collaboration networks such as Windows Meeting Space require the same type of planning as face-to-face meetings, and they also bring new issues to the virtual table.

When you plan a meeting—virtual or personal—consider the following:

- Who to invite
- When to meet
- How long the meeting should last

You should set an agenda, decide who will speak, and make supplemental materials such as handouts available.

When you plan a virtual meeting, you should also consider the following:

- Do all participants have the necessary hardware and software installed and available for use?
- Are security measures in place to protect the privacy of all participants and their data?
- Is there a backup plan if the technology fails?

Finally, do not forget that a virtual meeting brings up unique etiquette issues that might not occur during a face-to-face meeting. Participants cannot see each other, and communication may be written rather than spoken. This can lead to misunderstandings and miscommunication. Some basic rules of courtesy for a local collaboration network meeting include:

- All participants should be fully engaged, not distracted by other tasks that might be on their desks at the moment.
- If the meeting is at meal time, agree beforehand on whether participants should feel free to eat.
- Take turns! If everyone tries to communicate at once, it will be confusing, and the network may have trouble processing the information.

Whether your meeting is face-to-face or on a local collaboration network, a little planning can go a long way toward ensuring successful communication, positive feedback, and strong productivity.

SUMMARY SKILL MATRIX

In this lesson you learned	Matrix Skill	Skill Number
To share folders and files		
To use the public folder	Share a folder on a hard disk	4.3.1
To share a folder with selected users	Secure a share by adding permissions for specific users	4.3.2
To configure NTFS permissions	Configure NTFS permissions on a folder so that different users have different permissions	4.2.5
To share resources on a network		
To enable File and Printer sharing on a network	Share a printer that is connected to your computer	3.6.4
To customize a printer share	Make drivers available for other operating systems	3.6.5
To browse your network	Connect to another computer by browsing a network Connect to another computer by accessing shared folders	2.4.3 2.4.4
To map a network drive	Connect to another computer by mapping a drive to a network share	2.4.2
To use a network printer	Locate and install a network printer	3.6.3
To use network files offline		
To enable offline files	Set up your computer to use offline files	2.5.1
To make files and folders available offline	Make a file or folder available offline	2.5.2
To synchronize offline files and folders manually	Synchronize folders between computers	2.5.4
To resolve synchronization conflicts	Resolve synchronization conflicts	2.5.3
To make a web page available offline	Make the content of a favorite website available offline	2.5.6
To use Windows Meeting Space		
To start a meeting	Start a local collaboration session	5.1.2
To join a meeting	Join an existing local collaboration session	5.1.3
To sign in to People Near Me	Sign in to a local collaboration network	5.1.1

■ Knowledge Assessment

Multiple Choice

Select the best response for the following questions.

1. Which permission level enables the user to view shared folders and store new items in the shared folder?
   a. Reader
   b. Contributor
   c. Co-owner
   d. Writer

2. Which permission level restricts the user to viewing shared items only?
   a. Reader
   b. Contributor
   c. Co-owner
   d. Writer
3. If both share and NTFS permissions are in effect, which settings will Windows Vista apply?
   a. share permissions
   b. NTFS permissions
   c. printer permissions
   d. the more restrictive settings
4. In which of the following windows can you see a visual representation of which network connections are physical and which are wireless?
   a. Network and Sharing Center
   b. Network Map
   c. Network
   d. Public
5. Which of the following letters is never available for a mapped network drive?
   a. Z
   b. X
   c. W
   d. C
6. What is the name of a profile that defines how and when files will be synchronized between two locations?
   a. sync profile
   b. sync pair
   c. sync partnership
   d. sync collaboration
7. Which type of synchronization is commonly used to sync network folders and files?
   a. one-way synch
   b. two-way synch
   c. three-way synch
   d. four-way synch
8. Which type of program lets you communicate in real time with up to ten other people by using a peer-to-peer network?
   a. synchronization program
   b. ad hoc program
   c. File sharing program
   d. local collaboration program
9. What is the name of the local collaboration network that comes with Windows Vista?
   a. Nearby Computers
   b. Online Meetings
   c. People Near Me
   d. My Network Computers

10. Which type of network temporarily enables direct computer-to-computer communication?
    a. local collaboration network
    b. peer-to-peer network
    c. ad hoc network
    d. public network

Fill in the Blank

Complete the following sentences by writing the correct word or words in the blanks provided.

1. ______________ are rules that control access to shared resources.
2. An easy way to share a file with others is to store it in the ______________ folder.
3. By default, someone with a(n) ______________ user account can access only his or her own files and folders.
4. When you ______________ a network driver, you create a shortcut in your Computer folder to the drive.
5. You can make it easier for people to use a network printer by installing ______________ for other operating systems.
6. To be able to work with network files even if the network is not available, you can make network folders available ______________.
7. When Windows Vista ______________ offline files, it identifies the version of the file that is most recent and updates other versions of the file to match.
8. A(n) ______________ might occur if you edit a document on your desktop computer and then edit the same document on your notebook computer.
9. To restrict access to a local collaboration session, issue ______________ to the people you want to join.
10. By default, when you share a folder outside the Public folder, it is available with a(n) ______________ permission level.

■ Competency Assessment

Project 14-1: Collaborating on a Presentation Cover

You are part of a team at the A. Datum Corporation working on a market research report for a travel company. You have two photos you think would be suitable for the report cover, but you want your team members to help you pick the best one. You are going out of town, so you have asked someone else in the team to make sure the files are available to everyone. In this project, you set up two new user accounts. You then place the picture files in a folder on your desktop. You move the folder to the Public folder where your co-workers can access them. Finally, you log in using one of the new user accounts and view the photos.

GET READY. Before you begin these steps, start your computer and log on to your Windows Vista account. Close all open windows so that you can see the desktop. To complete these steps, you must have an available network connection.

1. Click **Start**, click **Control Panel**, and then click **Add or remove user accounts** under User Accounts and Family Safety. If you have an administrator account, click **Continue** in the User Account Control dialog box. Otherwise, key an administrator's password and then click **OK**.

2. Click **Create a new account** to display the Create New Account window.
3. Key **Amy Rusko**, verify that the Standard user button is selected, and then click **Create Account**.
4. Create a second new Standard user account with the user name **Keith Harris**. Close the Control Panel window.
5. Right-click a blank area of the desktop, click **New**, and then click **Folder**. Key **Report Cover** and then press Enter to rename the folder. Double-click the **Report Cover** folder to open it.

The ***Cover1*** and ***Cover2*** files are available on the companion CD-ROM.

6. Copy the files ***Cover1*** and ***Cover2*** from the data files for this lesson to the Report Cover folder, then close the Report Cover folder window.
7. Right-click the **Report Cover** folder icon and click **Cut** on the shortcut menu.
8. Click **Start** and then click **Documents**.
9. In the Favorites list in the left pane, click **Public**. The Public folder opens.
10. Right-click a blank area in the File list and click **Paste** on the shortcut menu.
11. Close the **Public** folder window.
12. Log off your Windows Vista user account and log in to the new Amy Rusko account. Alternatively, use the Switch User command to switch user accounts without logging off.
13. Click **Start** and then click **Documents**. Click **Public** in the Favorite Links list.
14. Double-click the **Report Cover** folder to open it. The two photo files display.
15. If necessary, click the **Views** button dropdown arrow on the Report Cover window toolbar and then click **Extra Large** icons so that you can get a good look at the pictures.
16. Close the **Report Cover** folder window.
17. Log off the **Amy Rusko** account and log back in to your own Windows Vista account. Alternatively, use the Switch User command to switch user accounts without logging off.

PAUSE. LEAVE the Windows Vista desktop displayed to use in the next project.

Project 14-2: Home Networking

You have recently purchased a notebook computer, and you have set up a wireless network so that you can access the Internet through your desktop PC at home. You would like to be able to access files stored on the desktop PC while you are working on the notebook, and you would also like to be able to use the printer that is connected to the desktop PC. In this project, you enable File and Printer sharing, view the network, and install the network printer for use.

GET READY. To complete these steps, you should have access to a network with at least two computers—the one on which you are currently working as well as a remote computer on the network. A printer should be connected to and installed on the remote computer, and the printer should be turned on.

1. Click **Start** and then click **Control Panel**.
2. Under Network and Internet, click **Set up file sharing** to display the Network and Sharing Center window.
3. Click the **Network discovery** expand arrow to display the Network discovery options.
4. If necessary, click to select the **Turn on network discovery** option and then click the **Apply** button. If you are using an administrator account, click **Continue**. Otherwise, key an administrator password and then click **OK**.
5. Click the **Network discovery** collapse arrow to hide the options and then click the **File sharing** expand arrow to display the File sharing options.

6. Click to select the **Turn on file sharing** option and then click the **Apply** button. If you are using an administrator account, click **Continue**. Otherwise, key an administrator password and then click **OK**. File sharing, Public folder sharing, and Printer sharing are all turned on.
7. If necessary, click the **File sharing** collapse arrow to hide the options and then click the **Public folder sharing** expand arrow.
8. Click to select the **Turn on sharing so anyone with network access can open, change, and create files** option and then click the **Apply** button. If you are using an administrator account, click **Continue**. Otherwise, key an administrator password and then click **OK**. Now, network users can read and edit items in the Public folder.
9. Click the **Show me all the files and folders I am sharing** link below the Sharing and Discovery options. A Shared by Me search results window opens to display all of the shared folders you own and have made available as shares.
10. Close the Shared by Me window and then click the **Show me all the shared network folders on this computer** link. A window opens to display all shared folders on the computer. At your instructor's request, capture an image of the window. Save it in your Lesson 14 assessment folder as ***Proj14_02***.
11. Close the window.
12. Click the **View full map** link in the upper right corner of the Network and Sharing Center window to view a map of your network components.
13. Under Tasks in the left pane, click **View computers and devices**. The Network window opens, showing the computers and devices in your network.
14. Double-click the network computer to which the printer you want to use is attached. The available shared resources are listed in the window.
15. Double-click the **Printers** folder to open the Printers window on the network computer. Printers installed and connected to that network computer are listed in the window.
16. Double-click the icon of the printer you want to use. Windows Vista starts the installation process. It displays a warning message asking you to confirm that you want to install the driver.
17. Click **Install Driver**. If you are logged on as an administrator, click **Continue** in the User Account Control dialog box. If not, key an administrator's password and then click **OK**. Windows Vista installs the driver and sets up the printer for use with your computer. It may open a printer window for the printer as well.
18. Close the printer window, if necessary, and then close the network computer's Printers window. The network printer is now installed and ready for use.
19. **CLOSE** all open windows.

PAUSE. LEAVE the Windows Vista desktop displayed to use in the next project.

■ Proficiency Assessment

Project 14-3: Travel Report

The A. Datum Corporation team is finalizing the market research report for the travel company. Amy Rusko, a team member, has selected the best photo for the cover and wants to make it available for you to send to the printer. She does not want anyone else to be able to edit or delete the files. In this project, you log in to the Amy Rusko user account and move the Report Cover folder out of the Public folder to the desktop. You set it up to share with the Keith Harris account as a Reader and with your own user account as a Co-owner. You then log in to your own user account, move the folder to your own desktop, and configure the NTFS permissions for the folder to limit Amy Rusko's access. Finally, you open the folder and delete the photo that is not going to be used.

1. Log off your Windows Vista user account and log in using the Amy Rusko account. Alternatively, use the Switch User command to switch user accounts without logging off.
2. Click **Start**, click **Documents**, and then click **Public** in the Favorite Links list.
3. Right-click the **Report Cover** folder and click **Cut** on the shortcut menu. Close the Public folder window. Right-click a blank area of the desktop and click **Paste** on the shortcut menu.
4. Right-click the **Report Cover** folder and click **Share...** on the shortcut menu.
5. Click the dropdown arrow above the list of names to display a list of user accounts.
6. Click **Keith Harris** in the dropdown list of user accounts and then click the **Add** button.
7. Click the dropdown arrow above the list of names, click your own user account name, and then click the **Add** button.
8. Click the **Permission Level** dropdown arrow to the right of your user account name and click **Co-owner**. At your instructor's request, capture an image of the window. Save it in your Lesson 14 assessment folder as ***Proj14_03***.
9. Click the **Share** button.
10. Click **Done** to close the window.
11. Log off the Amy Rusko account and log back in to your own user account. Alternatively, use the Switch User command to switch user accounts without logging off.
12. Click **Start** and then click **Computer**. In the Search box in the Computer folder window, key **Report Cover**.
13. Right-click the **Report Cover** folder in the Search results list and click **Cut**. Click **Yes** to continue.
14. Close the Search Results window, right-click your desktop, and click **Paste**.
15. Right-click the **Report Cover** folder on the desktop and click **Properties**. Click the **Security** tab.
16. Click the **Edit...** button.
17. In the list of Group or user names, click **Amy Rusko**.
18. Click to deselect the **Allow** checkbox to the right of the Modify permission and then click **OK**.
19. Click **OK** to close the Properties dialog box.
20. Double-click the **Report Cover** folder to open it.
21. Right-click the ***Cover1*** file and click **Delete**. Click **Yes** to delete the file.
22. **CLOSE** all open windows.

PAUSE. LEAVE the Windows Vista desktop displayed to use in the next project.

Project 14-4: Vacation Pictures

You have vacation photos stored on your home desktop PC in a Public folder. You want to be able to display them on your notebook PC so that guests can view them in any room of the house. You also want to make sure the photos will be available even if the network connection is unavailable. In this project, you map a network drive to make the folder where the photos are stored available in your Computer folder. You make the folder available offline and then, if possible, you disconnect the remote computer from the network and access the folder offline.

GET READY. To complete these steps, you should have access to a network with at least two computers—the one on which you are currently working and a remote computer on the network. The remote computer should have a shared or Public folder, which should contain a Shared Pictures or Public Pictures folder.

1. Click **Start** and then click **Computer**.
2. On the Computer window toolbar, click the **Map Network Drive** button.
3. Click the **Browse...** button.
4. Click the arrow to the left of the network computer on which the shared folder is stored.
5. Click to select the folder you want to map. For example, click the Public folder.
6. Click **OK** and then click **Finish**.
7. Close the folder window.
8. Double-click the shared network folder in the Computer window to open it.
9. Click **Start**, click **Control Panel**, and then click **Network and Internet**.
10. Click **Offline Files**. The Offline Files dialog box displays. If Offline Files is currently enabled, skip to step 11. If Offline Files is disabled click **Enable Offline Files**. If you are logged in as an administrator, click **Continue** in the User Account Control dialog box. If not, key an administrator's password and then click **OK**. Click **OK** and then click **Yes** to restart your computer. Log back in to your Windows Vista user account.
11. Click **Start** and click **Computer**.
12. Double-click the mapped network folder under Network Location to open its window.
13. In the shared network folder window, right-click the folder you want to make available offline. For example, right-click the Public Pictures folder.
14. Click **Always Available Offline** on the shortcut menu.
15. Close the shared folder window.
16. If possible, turn off the remote computer or disconnect it from the network.
17. Click **Start** and click **Computer**.
18. Double-click the mapped network folder under Network Location to open its window.
19. Navigate to the folder that is available offline and view its contents. At the request of your instructor, capture an image of the folder window. Save it in your Lesson 14 assessment folder as ***Proj14_04***.
20. Close all open windows.
21. Turn the remote computer back on or reconnect it to the network.
22. Click the **Sync Center** icon in the Notification area to open the Sync Center.
23. Click **Sync All** to manually synchronize all sync partnerships.
24. Close the Sync Center window.
25. Click **Start**, click **Computer**, and then right-click the mapped network drive and click **Disconnect**.

PAUSE. LEAVE the Windows Vista desktop displayed to use in the next project.

Project 14-5: Team Meeting

The A. Datum Corporation team members want to plan a visit to the travel company client. In this project, you will start Windows Meeting Space and set up a meeting. You will then log in to the Keith Harris account and set up Windows Meeting Space and People Near Me for use. Keith Harris will then join the existing meeting.

1. Click **Start**, click **All Programs**, and then click **Windows Meeting Space**.
2. In the Windows Meeting Space window, click **Start a new meeting**.
3. Click in the Meeting name text box and key **Vacation Team**.
4. Click in the Password text box and key **datumteam1**.
5. Press Enter to start the meeting.

6. Click **Start**, point to the arrow to the right of the Lock this computer icon, and then click **Switch User**. Log in to the Keith Harris user account you created in Project 14-1.
7. Click **Start**, click **All Programs**, and then click **Windows Meeting Space**.
8. Click **Yes, continue setting up Windows Meeting Space**. If you are logged on as an administrator, click **Continue** in the User Account Control dialog box. Otherwise, key an administrator password and then click **OK**.
9. Click **OK** to set up People Near Me using the default settings.
10. In the Windows Meeting Space window, click the **Vacation Team** meeting.
11. Key **datumteam1** in the password box and then press **Enter**. (Once in the meeting, you may want to take the time to experiment with some of the Windows Meeting Space features.) At your instructor's request, capture an image of the meeting window. Save it in your Lesson 14 assessment folder as ***Proj14_05***.
12. Click **Meeting** on the window's menu bar and then click **Leave Meeting**.
13. Close the Windows Meeting Space window, log off the Keith Harris account, and log back in to your own Windows Vista user account.
14. In the Windows Meeting Space window, click **Meeting** on the menu bar and then click **Exit**. The meeting ends, and the Windows Meeting Space window closes.

PAUSE. LEAVE the Windows Vista desktop displayed to use in the next project.

■ Mastery Assessment

Project 14-6: New Client

Your A. Datum Corporation team has been assigned to a new account—Tailspin Toys. You are setting up a shared folder where everyone can store related files. You then start a local collaboration session so that you can review the files and discuss the approach you all want to take.

1. Create a new folder on your desktop named **Tailspin Account**.
2. Share the folder with Keith Harris and Amy Rusko, assigning Co-owner permissions to both.
3. Log off your user account and log in to the Keith Harris account. Alternatively, use the Switch User command to switch user accounts without logging off.
4. Locate and open the **Tailspin Account** folder.
5. Create a new text document named **First Thoughts** in the Tailspin Account folder and open it in Notepad. Key **Plan focus group**, press **Enter**, and key **Visit client**. Then close the file, saving all changes.
6. Log off the Keith Harris account and log in to the Amy Rusko account. Alternatively, use the Switch User command to switch user accounts without logging off.
7. Locate and open the **Tailspin Account** folder and open the **First Thoughts** file.
8. Move the insertion point to the end of the last line and press **Enter**. Key **Design a questionnaire** and then close the file, saving all changes.
9. Log off the Amy Rusko account and log in to your own Windows Vista user account.
10. Open the **Tailspin Account** folder and open the **First Thoughts** file. Move the insertion point to the end of the last line and press **Enter**. Key **Plan collaboration meeting**. Close the file, saving all changes.
11. Start Windows Meeting Space and set up a new meeting, named **Tailspin Launch**, with the password **datumteam2**.
12. Switch users and log in to the Keith Harris account.

13. Start **Windows Meeting Space** and join the **Tailspin Launch** meeting.
14. Switch users and log in to the Amy Rusko account.
15. Set up Windows Meeting Space and People Near Me and then join the **Tailspin Launch** meeting. At your instructor's request, capture an image of the meeting window. Save it in your Lesson 14 assessment folder as ***Proj14_06***.
16. Leave the meeting and log off the **Amy Rusko** account.
17. Log in to the Keith Harris account, leave the meeting, and log off the account.
18. Log in to your own Windows Vista user account and end the meeting.
19. **CLOSE** all open windows.

PAUSE. LEAVE the Windows Vista desktop displayed to use in the next project.

Project 14-7: Expand the Home Network

Your brother has come to live with you, and has brought his computer, which is using your home wireless network. He wants to be able to use your printer, and he wants you to be able to access his music files. In this project, you will make older printer drivers available for his computer, and you will map a network drive so that you can access his music files in a shared folder. You will also make the music files available offline, test the offline files, and sync the files manually. Finally, you will reverse all the changes you have made in Projects 14-1 through 14-7.

GET READY. To complete this project, you should have access to a network with at least two computers—the one on which you are currently working and a remote computer on the network. The remote computer should have a shared or Public folder, which should contain a Shared Music or Public Music folder. You should also have a printer installed, connected, and available for use. In addition, you should have the driver for an older operating system available on a disk or on a network storage location.

1. Open the **Printers** window and identify the shared printer that you want to make available to users with older operating systems.
2. Right-click the printer and click **Sharing...** and then click the **Change sharing** button. (Click **Continue** or key an administrator's password and click **OK**.)
3. Select to install additional drivers and then select the operating systems.
4. Install the drivers.
5. Close all open windows.
6. Open the **Computer** window on your computer and map a network drive to the folder where the shared music files are stored.
7. Make the shared music files available offline. At your instructor's request, capture an image of the Computer window showing the mapped drive. Save it in your Lesson 14 assessment folder as ***Proj14_07***.
8. To test the offline files, disconnect the remote computer from the network or turn it off.
9. Locate and open the shared music folder and double-click a file to play it.
10. Close all open windows.
11. Reconnect the remote computer or turn it back on.
12. Manually sync all sync partnerships.
13. Close all open windows.
14. Disconnect the mapped network drive.
15. Delete the network printer from your Printers folder.
16. Delete the **Keith Harris** and **Amy Rusko** user accounts.
17. Copy the Tailspin Account folder to your Lesson 14 assessment folder, and then delete it from your desktop.

18. Copy the Report Cover folder to your Lesson 14 assessment folder and then delete it from your desktop.
19. Turn off File and Printer sharing.
20. **CLOSE** all open windows.

    LOG OFF your Windows Vista user account.

INTERNET READY

Collaborating with co-workers can be a wonderful way to brainstorm ideas, share knowledge and skills, and quickly accomplish tasks that would take one person alone a long time to complete. In this project, use Internet search tools to research some effective collaboration tools and techniques for the workplace. You might try to find information about communication tools, meeting and scheduling tools, and even etiquette techniques that facilitate collaboration. Look for common problems as well as solutions. When you have completed your research, open a new word processing document and write a report about the information you have learned.

Customizing Your Computing Environment

LESSON SKILL MATRIX

Skills	Matrix Skill	Skill Number
Changing the Sound Settings		
Setting the Volume	Change the sound settings	6.3.3
Changing the Sound Scheme	Change the sound settings	6.3.3
Customizing the Mouse		
Customizing the Mouse Buttons	Change the mouse settings	6.3.5
Customizing the Mouse Pointers	Change the mouse settings	6.3.5
Using Multiple Monitors		
Connecting a Second Monitor	Extend the desktop onto a second monitor Display information on an external display device	3.5.2 5.2.2
Configuring Secondary Monitors	Adjust the resolution of a secondary monitor Select the primary monitor	3.5.1 3.5.3
Using a Computer to Present Information		
Preparing a Computer for a Presentation	Prepare your computer for presenting information	5.2.1
Connecting to a Network Projector	Connect to a network projector	5.2.3

KEY TERMS

Event sound
Extended desktop
Extended Display Identification Data (EDID)
Mirrored desktop
Mute
Network projector
Pointer scheme
Pointer trails
Presentation settings
Primary monitor
Primary mouse button
Secondary monitor
Secondary mouse button
Sound scheme

The Graphic Design Institute is a not-for-profit association of graphic design professionals. It sponsors meetings and conferences at which members can share ideas and network with others; sets standards; and fosters communication between designers, businesses, and the community. The 20 employees at the national office use their Windows Vista–based computers to plan events, track membership, and to provide marketing and professional development support to an international network of local groups. As design professionals themselves, they value their individuality and appreciate the flexibility provided by Windows Vista when it comes to customizing their computing environment. In this lesson, you will learn how to customize the Windows Vista environment by changing the sound and mouse settings. You will also learn how to use multiple monitors with a single computer, and how to use an external device to display presentation information.

■ Changing the Sound Settings

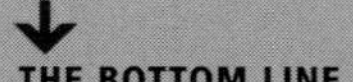

If your computer is equipped with a sound card and speakers, it can play sound. Using a program such as Windows Media Player, it can play music or narration, as covered in Lesson 5, "Working with Multimedia Files." It can also play ***event sounds***, which are sounds associated with a specific program event, such as starting or exiting Windows Vista. The default Windows ***sound scheme*** assigns certain sounds to certain events. A sound scheme is a set of coordinated sounds. For example, one sound plays when you connect a new device, and a different sound plays when you disconnect the device. You can customize the sound scheme by changing the sound associated with an event or by adding a sound to an event that does not have one. You can save your modified scheme as a new scheme so that you can revert to it if you—or someone else—modifies the sounds on your system. You can also adjust the sound volume. In this section, you will start by learning how to adjust the volume, and you will then modify and save a sound scheme.

Setting the Volume

You can adjust the volume to control how loudly sound plays. In this exercise, you adjust the volume to be certain you will be able to hear the sounds your computer makes.

SET THE VOLUME

GET READY. Before you begin these steps, start your computer and log on to your Windows Vista account. Close all open windows so that you can see the desktop. Create a new folder named Lesson 15 in a storage location specified by your instructor where you can store assessment files and folders that you create during this lesson. You must have a sound card and speakers installed and set up to work with your computer in order to hear the sounds in the exercise.

For more information on installing devices and device drivers, consult Lesson 9, "Managing System Resources."

1. Click **Start**, click **Control Panel**, and then click **Hardware and Sound**.
2. Under Sound, click **Adjust system volume**. The Volume Mixer window opens. It should look similar to Figure 15-1, although your Volume Mixer may display additional devices, depending on your system configuration.

Figure 15-1
Volume Mixer

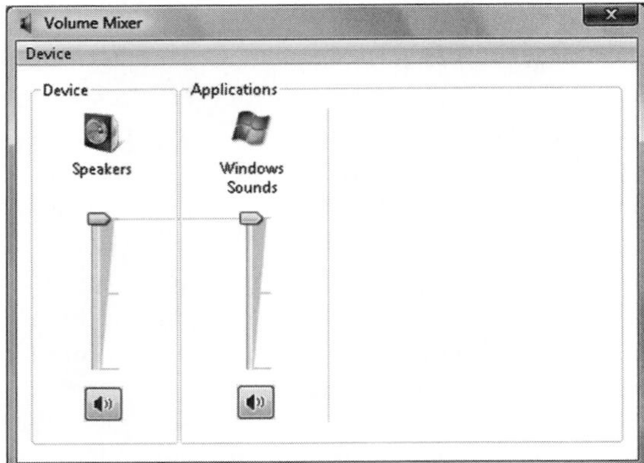

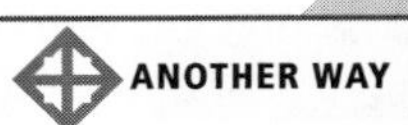

You can also open the Volume Mixer by right-clicking the Volume icon in the Notification area on the Taskbar and then clicking Mixer.

3. Drag the **Applications slider** up or down. As you drag, a ScreenTip indicates the current volume, on a range of 0 (the lowest) to 100 (the highest).
4. Drag the slider up to the top and release the mouse button. When you release the mouse button, a sound plays at the loudest volume.

TROUBLESHOOTING

If you do not hear any sound, check to make sure your speakers are correctly attached and turned on, and that the sound card is installed with the correct driver.

TAKE NOTE*

When the volume is muted, a red circle with a line through it displays on the Mute icon.

5. Drag the slider down to **25**. When you release the mouse button, a sound plays at a lower volume.
6. Click the **Mute** button below the slider. ***Mute*** means to turn the sound off temporarily. When mute is on, no sound emanates from the speakers. At your instructor's request, capture an image of the dialog box. Save it in your Lesson 15 assessment folder as ***Le15_01***.
7. Drag the slider about 3/4 of the way up—the ScreenTip will display 75. At this volume, you should be able to hear the sounds.
8. **CLOSE** the **Volume Mixer** window.

PAUSE. LEAVE the Control Panel window open to use in the next exercise.

CERTIFICATION READY?
How do you change the sound settings?
6.3.3

Some sound cards and speakers may have more options available for controlling sound. For example, you may be able to adjust the volume of each speaker independently, or you may have options for controlling the bass and treble as well as the volume.

You should consider your work environment when you set the volume on your computer, as well as how much sound you listen to. If you work where others can hear your computer, you should keep the volume low or use headphones. On the other hand, if you work alone, or in an office with a door you can close, you might want to keep the volume higher.

In the next exercise, you learn how to change the sound scheme.

Changing the Sound Scheme

The built-in Windows Vista default sound scheme controls the sounds associated with typical program events, such as logging on or off Windows Vista. You can customize your system by changing the sounds or adding new sounds. In this exercise, you modify the sound scheme and save it as a new scheme.

CHANGE THE SOUND SCHEME

USE the Control Panel window you left open in the previous exercise.

1. Under Sound, click **Change system sounds**. The Sounds tab of the Sound dialog box displays, as shown in Figure 15-2. Program events that can be associated with a sound display in the Program list. A speaker icon to the left of an event means that a sound is currently associated with the event.

Figure 15-2

The Sounds tab of the Sound dialog box

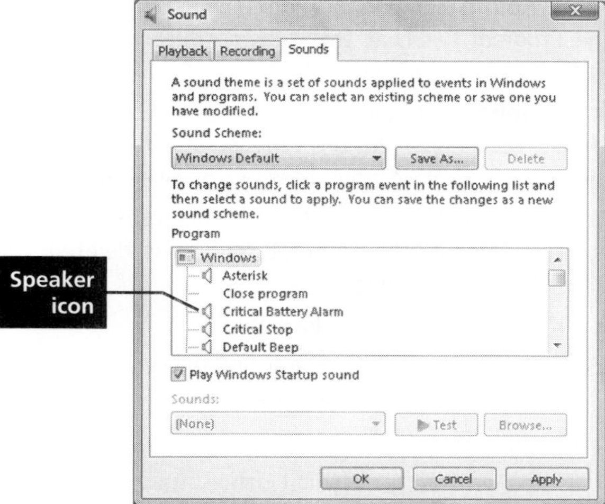

TROUBLESHOOTING If Windows Default does not display on the Sound Scheme button on the Sounds tab of the Sound dialog box, click the Sound Scheme dropdown arrow and click Windows Default. If prompted, click No to change the scheme without saving the current settings.

ANOTHER WAY If the Volume icon displays in the Notification area on the Taskbar, right-click it and click Sounds to display the Sounds tab of the Sound dialog box.

2. In the Program list, click **Device Connect**. The name of the sound file associated with the event—Windows Hardware Insert.wav—displays on the Sounds button.

3. Click the **Test** button. The sound plays.

TAKE NOTE* The .wav file extension indicates that the file is in WAVE form audio format, which is a common, high-quality audio file type.

4. In the Program list, click **Device Disconnect** and then click the **Test** button. The sound that indicates that a device has been disconnected plays.
5. Scroll down the Program list and click **Maximize**. This event—which indicates that a window has been maximized—does not have a sound.
6. Click the **Sounds** button dropdown arrow to display a list of available sound files and then click **chimes.wav**. This assigns the chimes.wav sound to the Maximize event. Click the **Test** button to hear the sound.
7. Click **Minimize** in the Program list, click the **Sounds** button dropdown arrow, and click **chord.wav**. Click the **Test** button to hear the sound.
8. Click **Apply** to apply the changes without closing the Sound dialog box.
9. Make the Control Panel window active and then minimize it. The chord sound should play.

TROUBLESHOOTING

If the Control Panel is already maximized, restore it down and then maximize it.

10. Restore the Control Panel and then maximize it. The chimes sound should play.
11. Make the Sound dialog box active again. Notice that the Sound Scheme is now called Windows Default (modified), because you have changed the default scheme. You can save it with a new name to add it to the list of available schemes.
12. Click the **Save As...** button to open the Save Scheme As, key **Sounds1**, and then click **OK**. Windows Vista saves the sound scheme. Its name displays in the Sound Scheme box.
13. Click the **Sound Scheme** box dropdown arrow and click **Windows Default.** Notice in the Program list that this scheme does not have sounds associated with the Maximize and Minimize events.
14. Click the **Sound Scheme** button dropdown arrow and click **Sounds1** to make it the active scheme. At the request of your instructor, capture an image of the dialog box. Save it in your Lesson 15 assessment folder as ***Le15_02***.
15. Click the **Delete** button. In the Scheme confirmation dialog box, click **Yes** to delete the scheme. The Sounds1 scheme is deleted, and the sound scheme reverts back to Windows Default.
16. Click **OK** to close the Sounds dialog box.

PAUSE. LEAVE the Control Panel window open to use in the next exercise.

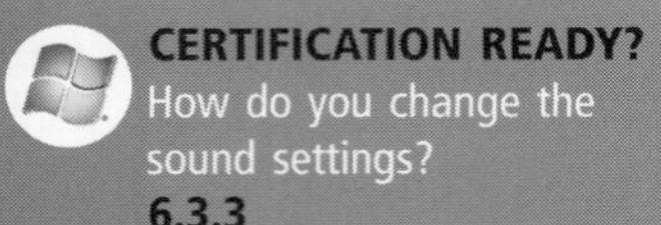
CERTIFICATION READY?
How do you change the sound settings?
6.3.3

As you learned in this exercise, you can add sounds to events that do not already have sounds. You can also use the same steps to change the sound assigned to an event. Simply select the event, select a new sound file, and then click OK or Apply.

The list of available sound files includes the .wav sound files stored in the Media folder, which is in the Windows folder installed when you set up Windows Vista. If you have other .wav sound files stored in a different location, you can use them as well. Select the event on the Sounds tab of the Sound dialog box, click the Browse button, and then navigate to the location where the .wav files is stored. Click the file to select it and then click Open.

In the next section, you learn how to customize the mouse.

■ Customizing the Mouse

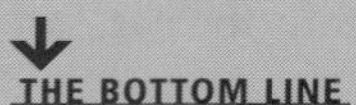
THE BOTTOM LINE

The mouse is the main input device you use to communicate with Windows Vista. At a minimum, most mouse devices have a left and right button. Some have more buttons and a scroll wheel. You can customize the mouse to suit your needs. For example, you can swap the functions of the buttons, set the double-click speed, and change the way the pointers look on the screen. Customizing the mouse can make it easier to use your computer and also make it more personal. In this section, you learn how to swap the mouse button functions, change the mouse pointer scheme, and customize the way the pointer moves on the screen.

Customizing the Mouse Buttons

A mouse device comes set up for use in your right hand, which means that the ***primary mouse button*** is on the left. You use it for primary tasks such as clicking and dragging. The ***secondary mouse button*** is on the right. You use it for secondary tasks such as right-clicking. If you are left handed, or if you have an injured or disabled right hand, it can be difficult to use your mouse effectively. Luckily, you can swap the mouse button functions to optimize it for use in your left hand. You can also adjust the double-click speed, which is the rate at which you must click for the computer to register two clicks as a single double-click.

CUSTOMIZE THE MOUSE BUTTONS

Use the Control Panel window you left open in the previous exercise.

1. Under Hardware and Sound, click **Mouse.** The Buttons tab of the Mouse Properties dialog box displays. It should look similar to Figure 15-3, although some mice might have additional options available.

Figure 15-3

Buttons tab of the Mouse Properties dialog box

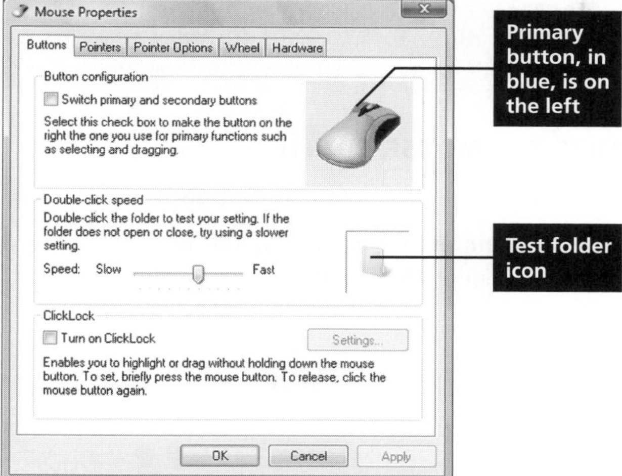

2. Under Button configuration, click to select the **Switch primary and secondary buttons** checkbox. This setting swaps the functions of the left and right buttons, making the right button primary and the left button secondary. You would find this useful if you are left handed or cannot use your right hand for any reason.
3. Move the mouse pointer to the **Switch primary and secondary buttons** checkbox, and click the right mouse button to clear it. You must use the right mouse button because you switched the buttons. If you click with the left mouse button, nothing will happen!
4. Click **Apply** to apply the change and keep the dialog box open.
5. Drag the **Double-click speed** slider to Fast. This slider sets the rate at which Windows Vista will respond to a double-click. If the setting is Fast, you must double-click fast for it to register as a double-click and not as two separate single clicks. If the setting is Slow, you can double-click more slowly.
6. Double-click on the folder icon to the right of the slider to test the setting. The folder opens or closes if Windows Vista registers the double-click. If nothing happens, try double-clicking faster.
7. Drag the **Double-click speed** slider to Slow and then double-click the test folder. You can click much more slowly and still have the double-click register.
8. Drag the **Double-click speed** slider to the middle, or to a setting that is comfortable for you, and then click **Apply** to apply the change and keep the dialog box open.

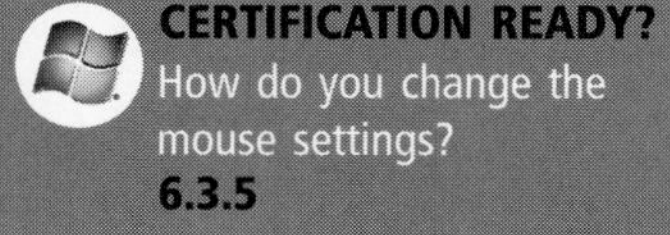
CERTIFICATION READY?
How do you change the mouse settings?
6.3.5

PAUSE. LEAVE the Mouse Properties dialog box open to use in the next exercise.

Some mouse devices have a feature called ClickLock that lets you select and drag items without holding down the mouse button. When ClickLock is on, you press the mouse button to lock the click in place. You can then drag without holding down the button. When you want to stop dragging, you click the button again. To enable the feature, select the Turn on ClickLock checkbox. Click the Settings... button and drag the slider to set the length of time you must hold down the mouse button before the click is locked. Click OK.

In the next exercise, you customize the mouse pointer scheme.

Customizing the Mouse Pointers

A mouse ***pointer scheme*** is a collection of coordinated pointer shapes that you can assign to different actions. For example, in the Windows Aero pointer scheme, the pointer that displays when Windows Vista is busy executing a command is a rotating circle. In the Windows Standard pointer scheme, it is an hourglass. The default scheme depends on the Windows Vista Theme you are using. You can select a different pointer scheme to make the pointers easier to see or just for fun. You can also customize pointer options to control the way the pointer moves on the screen. In this exercise, you learn how to change the pointer scheme and customize pointer options.

CUSTOMIZE THE MOUSE POINTERS

USE the Mouse Properties dialog box you left open in the previous exercise.

1. Click the **Pointers** tab to display the pointer scheme options. It should look similar to Figure 15-4, although you might have a different pointer scheme selected. Take note of the default scheme on your system.

Figure 15-4

Pointers tab of the Mouse Properties dialog box

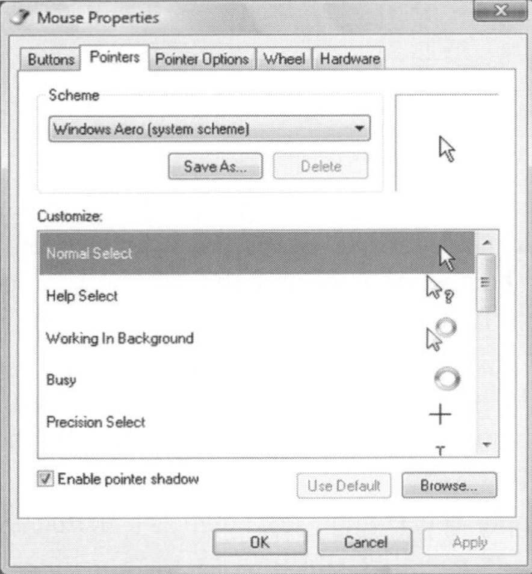

2. Click the **Scheme** dropdown arrow to display a list of available pointer schemes and click **3D-Bronze (system scheme)**. The pointers in the 3D-Bronze scheme display in the Customize list.
3. Click **Apply** to apply the change and keep the dialog box open. The 3D-Bronze (system scheme) is now active.
4. Move the mouse pointer to the Buttons tab of the dialog box. Notice that the pointer is now a yellow arrow.
5. Click the **Scheme** dropdown arrow, click **Conductor**, and then click **Apply** to change the scheme from 3D-Bronze to Conductor. This scheme has some pointers designed for music lovers, such as a metronome and a drum. At your instructor's request, capture an image of the dialog box. Save it in your Lesson 15 assessment folder as ***Le15_03***.
6. Click the **Scheme** dropdown arrow and click the default scheme that was in place in step 1.
7. Keep your eye on the mouse pointer and click **Apply**. Notice that the metronome pointer displays while Windows Vista is making the change.
8. Click the **Pointer Options** tab in the Mouse Properties dialog box. The Pointer Options tab should look similar to Figure 15-5. On this tab, you can select options to control the way the pointer moves on the screen.

Figure 15-5

Pointer Options tab of the Mouse Properties dialog box

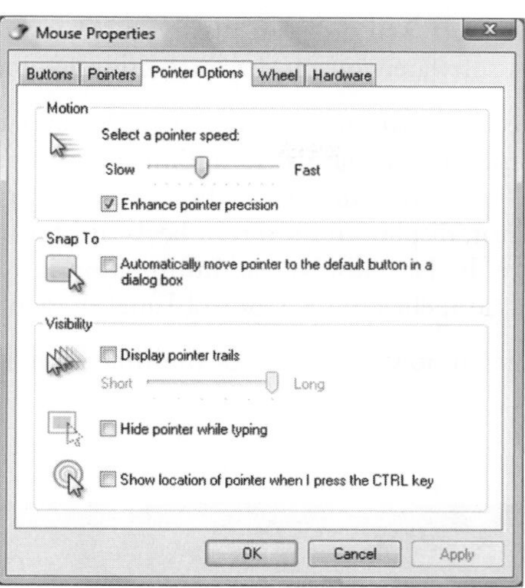

9. Drag the **Select a pointer speed** slider to **Slow** and then move the mouse pointer around your desktop. It should move slowly. Drag the slider to **Fast** and move the mouse pointer. It should move quickly. Drag the slider to the middle to set a mouse speed that you find comfortable.
10. Click to select the **Automatically move pointer to the default button in a dialog box** checkbox. This option sets Windows Vista so that the default button, which is the button that is in effect if you press Enter or click OK, is highlighted whenever you open a dialog box.
11. Click to select the **Display pointer trails** checkbox and then move the mouse pointer around. The ***pointer trails***—which are images of the pointer repeated behind the it as it moves—display on the screen. You might like this setting if you have trouble seeing the pointer moving on the screen.
12. Click to select the **Hide pointer while typing** checkbox. (If it is already selected, click to deselect it.) This option sets Windows Vista to hide the mouse pointer when you are using the keyboard. Turn this setting on if you spend a lot of time typing, and you do not want the mouse pointer obscuring the data on your screen.
13. Click to select the **Show location of pointer when I press the CTRL key** checkbox and then press **Ctrl** on your keyboard. A diminishing circle displays around the pointer, helping you locate the pointer on the screen. At your instructor's request, capture an image of the dialog box. Save it in your Lesson 15 assessment folder as ***Le15_04***.
14. Click to clear the checkboxes you selected in steps 10–13 and then click **OK** to apply changes and close the dialog box.
15. **CLOSE** the Control Panel.

PAUSE. LEAVE the Windows Vista desktop displayed to use in the next exercise.

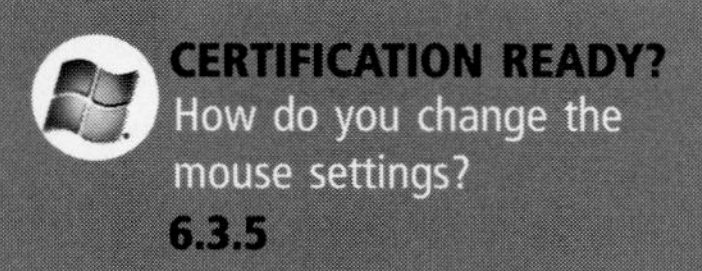
CERTIFICATION READY?
How do you change the mouse settings?
6.3.5

You can create a custom mouse pointer scheme by selecting a pointer for each task. Click the task you want to customize and then click Browse. The available pointers stored in the Cursor folder display. Click the pointer you want to apply and then click Open. You can save your customized scheme by clicking the Save As... button, typing a scheme name, and then clicking OK. You can delete a custom scheme by selecting it from the Scheme dropdown list, clicking the Delete button, and then clicking Yes.

Depending on the type of input device you have installed, you may have other tabs in your Mouse Properties dialog box. If your mouse has a scroll wheel, you can customize the wheel to change the number of lines that scroll at a time. If there is a Hardware tab, it displays information about the device, including whether it is working properly.

Some mouse devices have their own programs that you can use to customize properties. If your mouse came with software, consult the instruction manual for more information.

By customizing the mouse, you can make your computer easier to use. Windows Vista also has Ease of Access options that you can use to optimize your system for use by people with disabilities. For example, you can optimize the display to use high contrast to make images easier to see on the monitor, display an on-screen keyboard for use by someone who has trouble typing, or activate the Narrator to read information instead of displaying it on the screen. For more information, click Start>Control Panel>Ease of Access.

In the next section, you learn how to work with multiple monitors.

■ Using Multiple Monitors

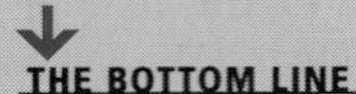

Windows Vista supports the use of more than one monitor, which means you can connect multiple monitors to a single computer running Windows Vista. With multiple monitors, you can effectively increase the size of your desktop, making it easier to work with multiple programs and windows at the same time. You can also use a large wall mounted display or projector to share documents or presentations with an audience. Using multiple monitors is particularly useful when you work on mobile devices, such as notebooks or laptop computers, which typically have smaller displays. It is also useful if you work with large pictures, edit videos, or work with large documents such as spreadsheets. In this section, you learn how to work with multiple monitors.

Connecting a Second Monitor

When you connect a second monitor to your computer, Windows Vista automatically detects the additional monitor—called a ***secondary monitor***—and installs the necessary drivers to set it up to work with your system. The main monitor is called the ***primary monitor***. The first time you connect the second monitor, you can select options to control how you want the desktop displayed. In this exercise, you learn how to connect a second monitor to your computer.

CONNECT A SECOND MONITOR

GET READY. To complete this exercise, you must have a computer set up to support multiple monitors using either a single video card with multiple ports or multiple, compatible video cards. If you have connected the second monitor before, skip this exercise.

1. Connect the second monitor to your computer by plugging the monitor cable into the second video port and plugging the monitor's alternating current (AC) adapter into an electrical power source. Turn the monitor on. Windows Vista will detect the device.
2. If this is the first time you have connected the second monitor, Windows Vista will install the device driver, automatically detect the second monitor, and then display the New Display Detected dialog box so that you can select display options. Icons represent the two monitors: 1 is the primary monitor, and 2 is the secondary monitor. The options in the dialog box depend on your monitors, video card(s), and system configuration.

X REF For information on installing devices, refer to Lesson 9.

TROUBLESHOOTING If Windows Vista does not automatically detect the second display, you must manually configure it using the steps in the next exercise, Configuring Secondary Monitors.

3. Click to select the display option you want to use:
   - **Mirrored.** A ***mirrored desktop*** duplicates the primary monitor desktop on the secondary monitor(s). In effect, this gives you access to multiple desktops. You can display different information on each monitor, but you cannot move a window from one monitor to another. You should use this option if you plan to use your computer to deliver a presentation on a projector, large wall mounted display, or a TV monitor.
   - **Extended.** An ***extended desktop*** spans all monitors connected to the computer. In effect, this option increases the size of your display monitor. You can display large images or large documents across all monitors or open and move windows from one monitor to another. You should use this option if you plan to use additional monitors to give yourself more space on the desktop for working with programs, files, and folders.
   - **External display only.** This option lets you display your desktop on a secondary monitor only. It is particularly useful on a mobile device that you are using with a large external monitor to display information to an audience or to view video, because you can turn off the mobile device display while you use the external display, thus saving battery power.

TROUBLESHOOTING

If the Mirrored or External display only options are not available, your video card or display driver may not support them.

CERTIFICATION READY?
How do you extend the desktop onto a second monitor?
3.5.2
How do you display information on an external display device?
5.2.2

4. Click **OK** to apply the changes and close the dialog box. If necessary, click **Yes** to confirm your selection. Your second monitor is set up for use.

   PAUSE. LEAVE the Windows Vista desktop displayed to use in the next exercise.

Windows Vista automatically detects and configures monitors by using ***Extended Display Identification Data (EDID)***, which is a standard video data format available on newer displays. EDID contains basic information about a display's capabilities, such as the maximum screen size and resolution. If you are connecting a monitor that does not support EDID, you must configure it manually.

If you are trying to connect an additional monitor to a mobile device, and Windows Vista does not detect the monitor, you must open the New Display Detected dialog box manually. Your mobile device may have a keyboard shortcut to turn on an additional monitor, such as FN+F5. Alternatively, use the Control Panel to access the Windows Mobility Center, click the External Display tab, and then click Connect display.

Windows Vista will only automatically detect the second monitor that you connect. The first time you connect a third—or more—monitor, you must manually configure it using the options in the Display Settings dialog box. After the first time, Windows Vista will recognize the monitor and apply the previously configured options.

Using multiple monitors may take some practice. You might have trouble identifying the location of the pointer across the different monitors and moving the pointer from one monitor to another. For example, if you have the desktop extended, you can drag windows and icons to another monitor, but you may run out of room to move the mouse or other pointing device.

In the next exercise, you learn how to configure display options for multiple monitors.

Configuring Secondary Monitors

If Windows Vista does not automatically detect an additional monitor, or if you want to change the configuration of additional monitors, you can use the options in the Display Settings dialog box. For example, you can change the resolution of a secondary monitor, change the way the desktop is configured, and even change the primary monitor. In this section, you configure a second monitor attached to your computer.

CONFIGURE SECONDARY MONITORS

GET READY. To complete this exercise, you must have a computer set up to support multiple monitors using either a single video card with multiple ports or multiple, compatible video cards, and you must have a second monitor connected and ready for use.

TROUBLESHOOTING: If there is no Monitor tab, click the Settings tab.

1. Right-click a blank area of the desktop and click **Personalize** to open the Personalization window.
2. Click **Display Settings** to open the Display Settings dialog box. If necessary, click the **Monitor** tab.

ANOTHER WAY: You can also click Start, click Control Panel, and then, under Appearance and Personalization, click Adjust screen resolution to open the Display Settings dialog box.

3. Click the **Identify Monitors** button. Windows Vista displays a number 1 on the primary monitor display and a number 2 on the secondary monitor display. (Additional monitors are numbered consecutively.) The icons should look similar to Figure 15-6.

Figure 15-6

Monitor icons

4. In the dialog box, click the icon representing the monitor you want to configure.
5. To make the selected monitor the primary monitor, click to select the **This is my main monitor** checkbox.
6. To change the resolution for the selected monitor, drag the **Resolution** slider to the desired position.
7. To change the color depth, click the **Colors** dropdown arrow and click the desired setting.

X REF: For more information on selecting display settings, refer to Lesson 7, "Personalizing the Windows Workspace."

8. To change the desktop options, click to select the option you want to use:
   - **Mirrored**

TROUBLESHOOTING: If Mirrored or External display only are not available, your video card or display driver may not support these options.

   - **Extend the desktop on to this monitor**
   - **External display only**

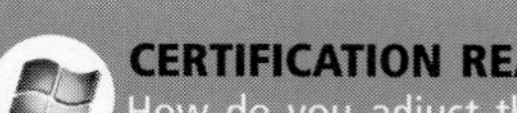

CERTIFICATION READY?
How do you adjust the resolution of a secondary monitor?
3.5.1
How do you select the primary monitor?
3.5.3

9. Repeat steps 4–8 to configure additional monitors.
10. Click **OK** to apply the changes and close the dialog box. If necessary, click **Yes** to confirm the changes.
11. Disconnect the secondary monitor from the power source and from your computer.
12. **CLOSE** all open windows.

PAUSE. LEAVE the Windows Vista desktop displayed to use in the next exercise.

If you are having trouble dragging a window to an extended desktop, make sure the window is not maximized. You cannot move a maximized window. You may need to change the arrangement of multiple monitors to match the physical arrangement of the monitors on your desk. By default, Windows Vista assumes each additional monitor is positioned to the right of the primary monitor. That means you drag windows to the right on the primary monitor desktop on to an extended desktop. If you have the secondary monitor physically positioned in a different location relative to the primary monitor, you can change the relationship in the Display Properties dialog box to match the physical setup. In the Display Properties dialog box, simply drag the icon representing the secondary monitor to position it relative to the primary monitor.

In the next section, you learn how to present information on an external display device.

■ Using a Computer to Present Information

THE BOTTOM LINE

Sharing information with co-workers, clients, or the community is vital in many businesses today. Slideshow presentations are used in a variety of situations for diverse tasks such as developing marketing plans, selling ideas or commodities, or educating. You can create and edit videos and then present them to an audience for entertainment or education. Windows Vista provides the tools you need to use your computer to present information to an audience. As you learned earlier in this lesson, you can connect your computer to a secondary monitor that is large enough to be viewed by an audience in a meeting room or to a projector. You can also use a ***network projector*** to present information over a network to an audience. A network projector is a projector that is connected to a network through a wired or wireless connection. In this section, you learn how to prepare your computer to present information and then how to connect to a network projector.

Preparing a Computer for a Presentation

Before you start a presentation, you should take steps to prepare your computer. For example, if you forget to turn off your screen saver, it may start halfway through your presentation. You can customize power options as well as other settings to make sure your computer is ready. In this section, you learn how to prepare your computer for a presentation.

PREPARE A COMPUTER FOR A PRESENTATION

1. Click **Start**, click **Control Panel**, and click **Hardware and Sound**. The Hardware and Sound window displays. From this window, you can access most settings that might interfere with a presentation.
2. Click **Power Options** to display the Power Options settings.

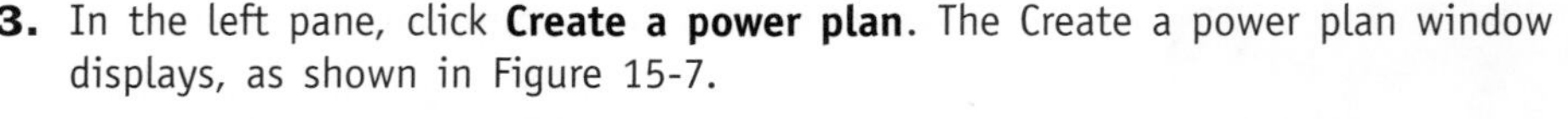

3. In the left pane, click **Create a power plan**. The Create a power plan window displays, as shown in Figure 15-7.

Figure 15-7

Create a power plan for presenting information

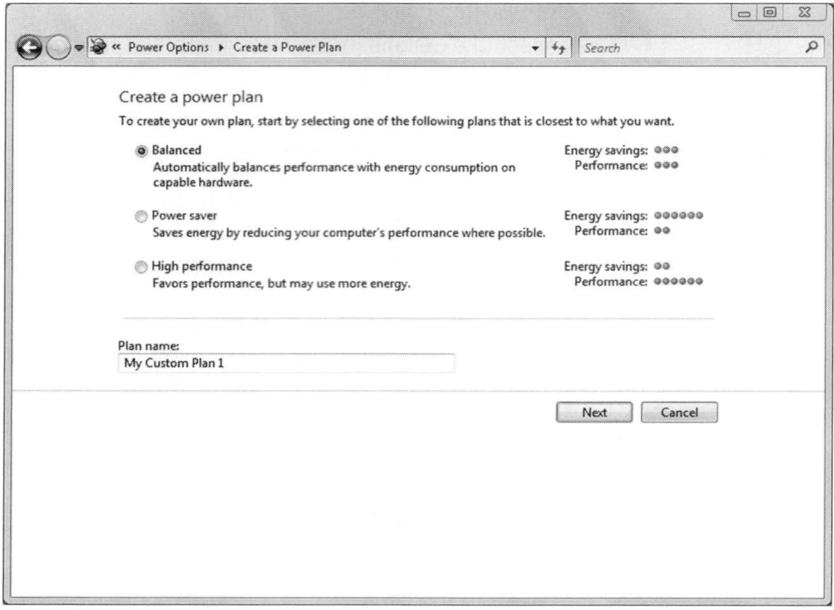

4. Click in the Plan name text box and key **Presentations**. Click **Next**.
5. Click the **Turn off the display** dropdown arrow and click **Never**. With this option set to Never, you do not have to worry about the display turning off in the middle of a presentation.
6. Click the **Put the computer to sleep** dropdown arrow and click **Never**. With this option set to Never, you do not have to worry about the computer going into Sleep Mode in the middle of a presentation.
7. Click **Create**. The plan is added to your list of preferred plans so that you can select it before any presentation.
8. Click the option button for the power plan you usually use.
9. Under the Presentation power plan, click **Change plan settings**. Click **Delete this plan** and then click **OK**.
10. Navigate back to the Control Panel. Click **Appearance and Personalization** and then click **Personalization**.
11. Click **Screen Saver**. The Screen Saver Settings dialog box displays, as shown in Figure 15-8.

X REF

For more information on power plans, refer to Lesson 9.

Figure 15-8

Do not use screen savers while presenting information

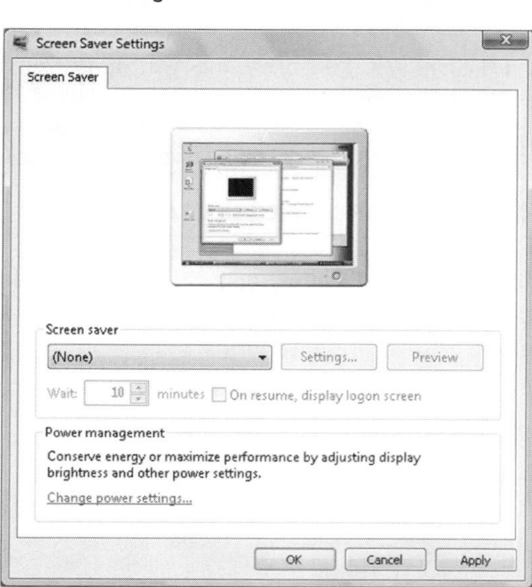

12. Click the **Screen saver** dropdown arrow and click **None**.
13. Click **Apply** to apply the change.
14. Select the Screen Saver settings you usually use.
15. Click **OK** to apply the changes and close the dialog box.
16. **CLOSE** the Control Panel window.

PAUSE. LEAVE the Windows Vista desktop displayed to use in the next exercise.

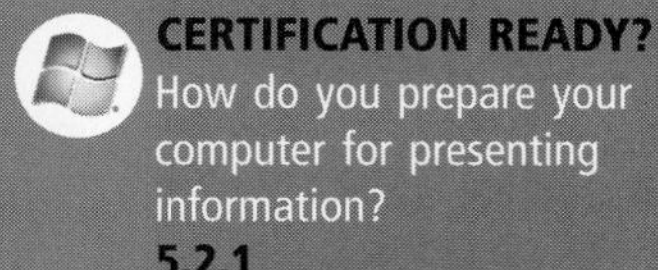

For more information on screen savers, refer to Lesson 7.

CERTIFICATION READY? How do you prepare your computer for presenting information? **5.2.1**

Your computer may be configured with other settings that might interfere with a presentation. The best way to determine if the presentation will proceed as planned is to practice. Then, you can identify and fix problems before you present to an audience. For example, you might find that the color or picture on your desktop interferes with the presentation material, or you might want to adjust the system volume.

In addition, before presenting information, you should make sure you have the necessary hardware to connect to the external display device, such as cables and video cards. If you are traveling to a new location to deliver the presentation, such as client's office or a convention center, you should find out in advance the type of facility they have available to make sure it is compatible with your computer. If you are using the equipment available at the facility, make sure you know how to use it before you have to deliver the presentation.

If you are using a mobile device to deliver a presentation, you can use the Windows Mobility Center to set and apply ***presentation settings***, which are a collection of settings that optimize a mobile computer for delivering a presentation. Open the Windows Mobility Center and click Presentation Settings. Select the settings you want to use and then click OK. The settings are saved so that you can apply them all at once when you are going to present information. Before delivering a presentation, open the Windows Mobility Center and click the Turn on button to turn on the presentation settings. When the presentation is finished, click the Turn off button to turn off the presentation settings and revert to your normal operating settings.

In the next exercise, you learn how to use a network projector.

Connecting to a Network Projector

If you have access to a network projector, you can use it to deliver a presentation to an audience. You can connect to the projector remotely so that you can deliver a presentation from any location that has network access. In this exercise, you learn how to connect to a network projector so that you can deliver a presentation.

 CONNECT TO A NETWORK PROJECTOR

GET READY. To complete this exercise, you must have access to a network to which a network projector is connected. It can be a wired or wireless network. The network projector must be turned on. You may also need a password to connect to the projector. It can probably be obtained from your system administrator.

1. Click **Start**, click **all Programs**, click **Accessories**, and then click **Connect to a Network Projector**. The Connect to a Network Projector Wizard starts, as shown in Figure 15-9. You have the option of searching for projectors that are connected to your local area network or entering the projector address.

Figure 15-9

Connect to a Network Projector Wizard

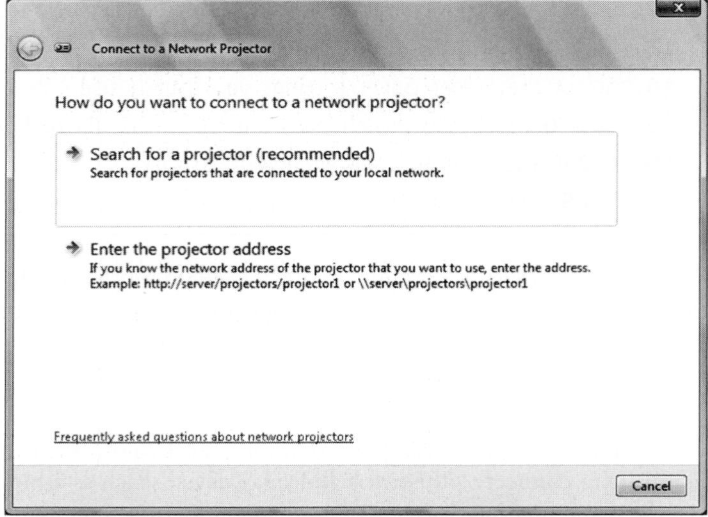

TAKE NOTE*

If you know the network projector's address and the password for the network projector, click Enter the projector address, key the address in the Network address text box, key the Projector password in the Projector password box, and then click Connect.

2. Click **Search for a projector**. Windows Vista begins searching the network and lists all available projectors.
3. In the Available projectors list, click the projector you want to use. If necessary, key the projector password and then click **Connect**. When the connection is established, the Network Presentation dialog box displays as a button on the Windows Taskbar.

TROUBLESHOOTING

If Windows Vista cannot locate the projector, it may not be turned on. If you are searching, the projector may not be in the same network segment that your computer is in. You may have to identify the network projector's address and try to connect using that option.

4. If the presentation starts automatically, click the **Network Presentation** button on the Taskbar and click the **Pause** button to pause the presentation until you are ready to begin. Click the **Resume** button to begin the presentation.
5. When the presentation is finished, click the **Disconnect** button to end the presentation and disconnect from the projector.
6. **CLOSE** all open windows.

   LOG OFF your Windows Vista user account.

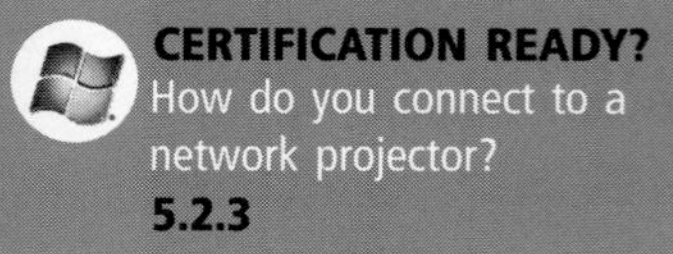

CERTIFICATION READY?
How do you connect to a network projector?
5.2.3

When you use a network projector, the audience must be in the same room as the projector to view the presentation material. However, you can connect to multiple network projectors at the same time to deliver a presentation to more than one audience.

Only one person can use a particular network projector at a time. If you have trouble connecting, the projector may already be in use.

SUMMARY SKILL MATRIX

In This Lesson You Learned	Matrix Skill	Skill Number
To change the sound settings		
To set the volume	Change the sound settings	6.3.3
To change the sound scheme	Change the sound settings	6.3.3
To customize the mouse		
To customize the mouse buttons	Change the mouse settings	6.3.5
To customize the mouse pointers	Change the mouse settings	6.3.5
To use multiple monitors		
To connect to a second monitor	Extend the desktop onto a second monitor Display information on an external display device	3.5.2 5.2.2
To configure secondary monitors	Adjust the resolution of a secondary monitor Select the primary monitor	3.5.1 3.5.3
To use a computer to present information		
To prepare a computer for a presentation	Prepare your computer for presenting information	5.2.1
To connect to a network projector	Connect to a network projector	5.2.3

■ Knowledge Assessment

Matching

Match the term in Column 1 to its description in Column 2.

Column 1	Column 2
1. network projector	**a.** a multiple monitor configuration that duplicates the primary monitor desktop on the secondary monitor(s)
2. event sound	**b.** a collection of coordinated mouse point shapes assigned to different actions
3. extended desktop	**c.** turn off sound temporarily
4. mirrored desktop	**d.** repeated images of the mouse pointer that display when the pointer moves
5. extended display identification data	**e.** a device that is connected to a network and is used to deliver presentation information to an audience
6. mute	**f.** the main monitor connected to your computer
7. pointer trails	**g.** a collection of settings used to optimize a mobile device for delivering a presentation
8. pointer scheme	**h.** a multiple monitor configuration that expands the desktop across all available monitors
9. primary monitor	**i.** a sound associated with a program event
10. presentation settings	**j.** a standard video data format that contains basic information about a display's capabilities

Fill in the Blank

Complete the following sentences by writing the correct word or words in the blanks provided.

1. Use the ______________ desktop option if you plan to use your computer to deliver a presentation on a projector, large wall mounted display, or a TV monitor.
2. In a multiple monitor configuration, any monitor that is not the main monitor is called a(n) ______________ monitor.
3. The ______________ mouse button is used for tasks such as clicking and dragging.
4. The ______________ mouse button is used for tasks such as opening a shortcut menu.
5. You can adjust speaker volume by using sliders in the Volume ______________ window.
6. Sound files used in a sound scheme are in ______________ file format.
7. If you are using a mobile device to deliver a presentation, use the Windows ______________ Center to set and turn on presentation settings.
8. If a(n) ______________ icon displays next to an event in the Program list on the Sounds tab of the Sound dialog box, it means a sound is associated with the event.
9. The default mouse pointer scheme depends on the Windows Vista ______________ you are currently using.
10. To connect multiple monitors, you must have a video card with multiple ______________ or multiple, compatible video cards.

■ Competency Assessment

Project 15-1: Customizing for a Left-Handed Employee

The new director of special events for the Graphic Design Institute is left handed. In this project, you customize the mouse on her computer so it is easier for her to use. She can then modify other mouse settings on her own.

GET READY. Before you begin these steps, start your computer and log on to your Windows Vista account. Close all open windows so that you can see the desktop.

1. Click **Start** and then click **Control Panel**. Under Hardware and Sound, click **Mouse**.
2. Under Button configuration, click to select the **Switch primary and secondary buttons** checkbox.
3. Click **Apply** to apply the change and keep the dialog box open.
4. Using the right mouse button as the primary mouse button, drag the **Double-click speed** slider to Fast.
5. Using the right mouse button, double-click on the **folder icon** to the right of the slider to test the setting.
6. Using the right mouse button, drag the **Double-click speed** slider to Slow and then double-click the test folder.
7. Using the right mouse button, drag the **Double-click speed** slider to the middle, or to a setting that is comfortable for you, and then click **Apply** to apply the change and keep the dialog box open.

8. Using the right mouse button, click the **Pointers** tab to display the pointer scheme options. Note the current scheme on the Schemes dropdown button.
9. Using the right mouse button, click the **Scheme** dropdown arrow to display a list of available pointer schemes and click **Windows Standard (large) (system scheme)**.
10. Using the right mouse button, click **Apply** to apply the change and keep the dialog box open.
11. Using the right mouse button, click the **Pointer Options** tab in the Mouse Properties dialog box.
12. Using the right mouse button, drag the **Select a pointer speed** slider to **Slow** and then move the mouse pointer around your desktop. It should move slowly. Drag the slider to **Fast** and move the mouse pointer. It should move quickly. Drag the slider to the middle to set a mouse speed that you find comfortable.
13. Using the right mouse button, click the **Pointers** tab.
14. Using the right mouse button, click the **Scheme** dropdown arrow and click the default scheme that was in place in step 8.
15. Using the right mouse button, click the **Buttons** tab. At your instructor's request, capture an image of the dialog box. Save it in your Lesson 15 assessment folder as ***Proj15_01***.
16. Using the right mouse button, click to deselect the **Switch primary and secondary buttons** checkbox
17. Click **OK** to apply the changes and close the dialog box.

PAUSE. LEAVE the Control Panel window open to use in the next project.

Project 15-2: Sound Settings

You recently purchased new speakers for your home computer. In this project, you will adjust the volume and create a customized sound scheme.

GET READY. To hear the sounds in the exercise, you must have a sound card and speakers installed and set up to work with your computer.

USE the Control Panel window you left open in the previous exercise.

1. Click **Hardware and Sound.**
2. Under Sound, click **Adjust system volume** to open the Volume Mixer window.
3. Drag the **Applications slider** down to 25 and release the mouse button.
4. You want the volume louder than 25! Drag the slider up to the top and release the mouse button.
5. Close the **Volume Mixer** window.
6. In the Control Panel, under Sound, click **Change system sounds** to display the Sounds tab of the Sound dialog box
7. In the Program list, click **Device Connect**.
8. Click the **Sounds** button dropdown arrow to display a list of available sound files and click **tada.wav**. Click the **Test** button to hear the sound.
9. In the Program list, click **Device Disconnect**.
10. Click the **Sounds** button dropdown arrow to display a list of available sound files and then click **tada.wav**. This assigns the same sound you applied to the Device Connect event to the Device Disconnect event.
11. In the Program list, click **Maximize**. Click the **Sounds** button dropdown arrow and click **Windows Exclamation.wav**. Click the **Test** button to hear the sound.
12. Click **Minimize** in the Program list, click the **Sounds** button dropdown arrow, and click **notify.wav**. Click the **Test** button to hear the sound.
13. Click **Apply** to apply the changes without closing the Sound dialog box.

14. Make the Control Panel window active and then minimize it. The notify.wav sound should play.
15. Restore the Control Panel and then maximize it. The windows Exclamation.wav sound should play.
16. If you have a device such as a USB flash drive, plug it in to a USB port. When you connect the device, the tada.wav sound that you applied to the Device Connect event should play.
17. Disconnect the device. The tada.wav sound that you applied to the Device Disconnect event should play.
18. Make the Sound dialog box active again and click the **Save As...** button to open the Save Scheme As dialog box. Key **MySounds1** and then click **OK** to save the sound scheme. At your instructor's request, capture an image of the dialog box. Save it in your Lesson 15 assessment folder as ***Proj15_02***.
19. Click the **Sound Scheme** button dropdown arrow, click **Windows Default** and then click the **Apply** button.
20. Minimize the Control Panel window. No sound should play.
21. Click the **Sound Scheme** button dropdown arrow and click **MySounds1.** Click the **Delete** button. In the Scheme confirmation dialog box, click **Yes** to delete the scheme.
22. Click **OK** to close the Sounds dialog box.

PAUSE. LEAVE the Control Panel open to use in the next project.

Project 15-3: Membership Presentation

As the membership director at the Graphic Design Institute, you frequently visit local groups to deliver a presentation about the benefits of membership. In this project, you prepare your computer to display the presentation, connect it to an external monitor, and configure the secondary monitor for use.

GET READY. To complete this exercise, you must have a computer set up to support multiple monitors using either a single video card with multiple ports or multiple, compatible video cards.

USE the Control Panel window you left open in the previous exercise.

1. Click **Hardware and Sound** to open the Hardware and Sound window.
2. Click **Power Options** to display the Power Options settings.
3. In the left pane, click **Create a power plan**.
4. Click in the Plan name text box and key **Present**. Click **Next**.
5. Click the **Turn off the display** dropdown arrow and click **Never**.
6. Click the **Put the computer to sleep** dropdown arrow and click **Never**. At your instructor's request, capture an image of the window. Save it in your Lesson 15 assessment folder as ***Proj15_03a***.
7. Click **Create**. The plan is added to your list of preferred plans, so you can select it before any presentation.
8. Navigate back to the Control Panel. Click **Appearance and Personalization** and then click **Personalization**.
9. Click **Screen Saver** to open the Screen Saver Settings dialog box.
10. Click the **Screen saver** dropdown arrow, click **None**. At your instructor's request, capture an image of the dialog box. Save it in your Lesson 15 assessment folder as ***Proj15_02b***. Then, click **OK** to apply the change and close the dialog box.
11. Close the Control Panel window.

12. Connect a second monitor to your computer by plugging the monitor cable into the second video port and plugging the monitor's AC adapter into an electrical power source. Turn the monitor on. Windows Vista will detect the device. If the New Display Detected dialog box displays, click **Cancel** and skip to step 15.
13. Right-click a blank area of the desktop and click **Personalize** to open the Personalization window.
14. Click **Display Setting**s to open the Display Settings dialog box. If necessary, click the **Monitor** tab.
15. Click the **Identify Monitors** button to see which display is the primary and which is the secondary.
16. In the dialog box, click the icon representing the secondary monitor.
17. Click to select the **This is my main monitor** checkbox.
18. Drag the **Resolution** slider to the desired position.
19. Click to select the **Mirrored** option. If Mirrored is not available, select the **Extend the desktop to this monitor** checkbox. If requested by your instructor, capture an image of the dialog box. Save it in your Lesson 15 assessment folder as *Proj15_03c*.
20. Click **OK** to apply the changes and close the dialog box. If necessary, click **Yes** to confirm the changes.
21. Disconnect the secondary monitor from the power source and from your computer.

PAUSE. LEAVE the Windows Vista desktop displayed to use in the next project.

■ Proficiency Assessment

Project 15-4: Making the Mouse Easier to See

A marketing assistant at the Graphic Design Institute has been having trouble seeing the mouse on the screen and hearing sounds from his computer. In this project, you customize the mouse to make it easier to locate. You also adjust the speaker volume.

1. Click **Start** and then click **Control Panel**. Under Hardware and Sound, click **Mouse**.
2. Click the **Pointers** tab to display the pointer scheme options.
3. Click the **Scheme** dropdown arrow to display a list of available pointer schemes and click **Windows Aero (extra large) (system scheme)**. If your system does not support Windows Aero, **click Windows Standard (extra large) (system scheme)**.
4. Click **Apply**. At your instructor's request, capture an image of the dialog box. Save it in your Lesson 15 assessment folder as ***Proj15_04***.
5. Click the **Pointer Options** tab in the Mouse Properties dialog box.
6. Click to select the **Automatically move pointer to the default button in a dialog box** checkbox.
7. Click to select the **Display pointer trails** checkbox.
8. Click to select the **Show location of pointer when I press the CTRL key** checkbox.
9. Click **OK** to apply the changes and close the dialog box.
10. Press **Ctrl** on your keyboard. A diminishing circle displays around the pointer, helping you locate the pointer on the screen.
11. In the Control Panel, click **Hardware and Sound**.
12. Under Sound, click **Adjust system volume** to open the Volume Mixer window.
13. Drag the **Applications slider** down to 50 and release the mouse button.
14. Close the **Volume Mixer** window.

15. In the Hardware and Sound window, under Mouse, click **Change pointer appearance**. If necessary, click the Pointers tab.
16. Click the **Scheme** dropdown arrow and click the default scheme for your computer.
17. Click the Pointer Options tab, click to clear the checkboxes you selected in steps 6–8, and then click **OK** to apply changes and close the dialog box.
18. **CLOSE** the Control Panel window.

PAUSE. LEAVE the Windows Vista desktop displayed to use in the next project.

Project 15-5: Network Projector

Before using a network projector to deliver a presentation to an audience, you want to make sure the projector is available and that you know how to find it and use it. In this project, practice connecting to a network projector.

GET READY. To complete this exercise, you must have access to a network to which a network projector is connected. It can be a wired or wireless network. The network projector must be turned on. You may also need a password to connect to the projector. It can probably be obtained from your system administrator.

1. Click **Start**, click **all Programs**, click **Accessories**, and then click **Connect to a Network Projector** to start the Connect to a Network Projector Wizard.
2. Click **Search for a projector**.
3. In the Available projectors list, click the projector you want to use. If necessary, key the projector password.
4. Click **Connect**. When the connection is established, the Network Presentation dialog box displays as a button on the Windows Taskbar.
5. If the presentation starts automatically, click the **Network Presentation** button on the Taskbar and click the **Pause** button to pause the presentation until you are ready to begin.
6. Click the **Resume** button to begin the presentation. If requested by your instructor, capture an image of the window. Save it in your Lesson 15 assessment folder as ***Proj15_05***.
7. When the presentation is finished, click the **Disconnect** button to end the presentation and disconnect from the projector.
8. **CLOSE** all open windows.

PAUSE. LEAVE the Windows Vista desktop displayed to use in the next project.

■ Mastery Assessment

Project 15-6: Customize the Mouse and System Sounds

At home, you share your computer with other family members. You want to be able to express your individuality through your computing environment. In this project, you customize the sound scheme and the pointer scheme.

1. **OPEN** the **Sound** dialog box and make the Sounds tab active.
2. Customize the **Sound Scheme** by adding sounds to events that do not have them and by changing the sounds currently associated with events. If you have .wav files stored on your computer other than those in the Windows Media folder, try using them as event sounds.
3. Save the sound scheme as **MySounds**. At your instructor's request, capture an image of the Sounds tab of the Sound dialog box. Save it in your Lesson 15 assessment folder as ***Proj15_06a***.

4. Test the sound scheme by performing actions to trigger the associated events. For example, start or exit a program or log off and then on to your Windows Vista user account.
5. Open the **Mouse Properties** dialog box and make the **Pointers** tab active.
6. Select a pointer scheme and then try customizing it. For example, change the **Normal Select** pointer or change the **Link Select** pointer.
7. Save the pointer scheme as **MyPointers**. At your instructor's request, capture an image of the Pointers tab of the Mouse Properties dialog box. Save it in your Lesson 15 assessment folder as ***Proj15_06b***.
8. Test the pointer scheme by performing standard tasks, such as navigating in the Control Panel.
9. Delete the MySounds sound scheme.
10. Delete the MyPointers pointer scheme.
11. **CLOSE** all open windows.

PAUSE. LEAVE the Windows Vista desktop displayed to use in the next project.

Project 15-7: Displaying a Large Image

A member of the Graphic Design Institute has asked if you can review a photograph that he will send to you. The picture is quite large, and you will need to use multiple monitors to view it in its entirety. In this project, add a secondary monitor to your computer and extend the desktop so that it is large enough to view the picture.

GET READY. To complete this exercise, you must have a computer set up to support multiple monitors using either a single video card with multiple ports or multiple, compatible video cards.

The ***Skyline*** file is available on the companion CD-ROM.

1. **Connect a second monitor to your computer.**
2. Extend your desktop onto the secondary monitor.
3. Copy the ***Skyline*** file from the data files for this lesson to your desktop.
4. Open the ***Skyline*** file in a picture viewing and editing program, such as Windows Photo gallery.
5. Display the picture at its actual size, using the desktop on both the primary and secondary monitors.
6. Close the picture viewing and editing program.
7. Disconnect the secondary monitor from the power source and from your computer.
8. **CLOSE** all open windows.

LOG OFF your Windows Vista user account.

INTERNET READY

As you learned in this lesson, event sounds are .wav format files. This is one of many types of sound files your computer can play. In this project, use Internet search tools to locate information about the different types of sound files that are compatible with your computer. Learn the names of the different sound file types, the file extension associated with each file type, the differences between the file types, and which are most appropriate for which applications. You might also want to know which use newer technology and which have been around for a long time. When you have completed your research, create a spreadsheet document and list the types of sound files and the information you have learned about each file type. If you locate any free sound file samples during your research, ask your instructor if you may download them and play them on your computer.

Circling Back

The Educational Events Director at the Baldwin Museum of Science is organizing a summer symposium with the help of a team of volunteers. One volunteer is acting as project manager. Most of the time he will be working at home using a notebook computer with wireless Internet access, but on occasion he will use his computer in an office at the museum. In the following projects, you will set up a password-protected user account for the volunteer so that he will be able to access the museum's network, and you will customize the mouse and sound settings for the account. You will also check the Internet Explorer security settings so that he can safely use the Internet without putting the museum's network at risk. You will check the status of network connections, make sure the computer can communicate with the Internet, enable remote access, and set up a virtual private network (VPN) for home use. Finally, you will make sure team members can collaborate with each other by sharing files, folders, and network resources—including external monitors and projectors—and Windows Meeting Space. To accomplish all of this, you will need to use the skills you have learned in Lessons 12, 13, and 14.

Project 1: Customize Mouse and Sound Settings for a New Account

In this project, you will create a new user account and then check the mouse settings to make sure the mouse is easy to use. Because the computer will be in a busy area, you will customize system sounds to make very little noise.

GET READY. Before you begin these steps, turn on your computer and log in to your Windows Vista user account. Close all open windows so that you have a clear view of the desktop. Create a new folder named CB4 in a storage location specified by your instructor where you can store assessment files that you create during these projects.

1. Click **Start**, click **Control Panel**, and then click **Add or remove user accounts** under User Accounts and Family Safety. If you have an administrator account, click **Continue** in the User Account Control dialog box. Alternatively, key an administrator's password and then click **OK**.
2. Click **Create a new account** to display the Create New Account window.
3. Key **Frank Lee**, verify that the Standard user option is selected, and then click **Create Account**. Click the **Frank Lee** account and then click **Create a password**. Key **!franKie?**, click in the **Confirm new password** box, key **!franKie?**, and then click **Create password**. At your instructor's request, capture an image of the Change an Account window. Save it in your CB4 assessment folder as ***CB4_01***. Close the Change an Account window.
4. Log off your Windows Vista user account and log in to the new Frank Lee account, using the password **!franKie?**. Alternatively, use the Switch User command to switch user accounts without logging off.
5. Click **Start** and then click **Control Panel**. Under Hardware and Sound, click **Mouse**.
6. Under Button configuration, click to select the **Switch primary and secondary buttons** checkbox.
7. Using the right mouse button, drag the **Double-click speed** slider to Fast. At your instructor's request, capture an image of the Mouse Properties dialog box. Save it in your CB4 assessment folder as ***CB4_02***.
8. Using the right mouse button, to test the setting, double-click on the folder icon to the right of the slider.
9. Using the right mouse button, drag the **Double-click** speed slider to the middle, or to a setting that is comfortable for you.
10. Using the right mouse button, click to deselect the **Switch primary and secondary buttons** checkbox and then click **Apply** to apply the change and keep the dialog box open.

11. Using the right mouse button, click the **Pointers** tab to display the pointer scheme options. Note the current scheme on the Schemes dropdown button.
12. Click the **Scheme** dropdown arrow to display a list of available pointer schemes and click **Windows Standard (large) (system scheme)**.
13. Click **Apply** to apply the change and keep the dialog box open.
14. Click the **Pointer Options** tab in the Mouse Properties dialog box.
15. Drag the **Select a pointer speed** slider to **Slow** and then move the mouse pointer around your desktop. It should move slowly. Drag the slider to the middle to set a mouse speed that you find comfortable.
16. Click the **Pointers** tab.
17. Click the **Scheme** dropdown arrow and click the default scheme that was in place in step 11.
18. Click **OK** to apply the changes and close the dialog box.
19. In the Control Panel, click **Hardware and Sound**. Under Sound, click **Adjust system volume** to open the Volume Mixer window.
20. Drag the **Applications** slider down to 20 and release the mouse button.
21. Close the Volume Mixer window.
22. In the Control Panel, under Sound, click **Change system sounds** to display the Sounds tab of the Sound dialog box.
23. In the Program list, click **Device Connect**.
24. Click the Sounds button dropdown arrow and click **(None)**.
25. In the Program list, click **New Mail Notification**, click the **Sounds** button dropdown arrow, and click **(None)**.
26. In the Program list, click **Blocked Pop-up Window**, click the **Sounds** button dropdown arrow, and click **(None)**.
27. Click the **Save As...** button to open the Save Scheme As dialog box, key **Quiet**, and then click **OK** to save the sound scheme.
28. Click the **Delete** button and then click **Yes** to delete the Quiet sound scheme.
29. Click **OK** to close the Sounds dialog box.
30. **CLOSE** the Control Panel window.

PAUSE. LEAVE the Windows Vista desktop displayed to use in the next project.

Project 2: Secure the Account for Windows Internet Access

You must make sure that the Windows Internet Explorer settings for the new account are secure so that the volunteer can access the Internet without putting the museum's network at risk. In this project, you will set the security settings and privacy levels, and you will verify that the Pop-up Blocker and Phishing filter are active. You will also configure the History and Temporary Internet file settings.

1. Click **Start** and then, at the top of the left pane of the Start menu, click **Internet Explorer**.
2. Click the **Tools** button on the Internet Explorer toolbar and then click **Internet Options** to open the Internet Options dialog box.
3. Click the **Security** tab to display the Security settings. Confirm that the settings for the Internet zone are set to the default security level and that Protected Mode is on.
4. Click the **Local intranet** zone to view its security settings. Confirm that the settings for the zone are set to the default security level and that Protected Mode is on.

5. Click the **Trusted sites** zone and confirm that the default settings are in effect.
6. Click the **Restricted sites** zone and confirm that the default settings are in effect and that Protected Mode is on.
7. Click the **Trusted sites** zone and click the Sites button to display a list of sites in the zone. The address of the current page should display in the Add this website to the zone text box.
8. Click to deselect the **Require server verification (https://) for all sites in this zone** checkbox if necessary.
9. Click **Add** to add the site to the Trusted sites zone and then click **Close** to close the dialog box.
10. Click **Apply** to apply the changes and leave the Internet Options dialog box open.
11. Click the **Privacy** tab to display the Privacy settings.
12. Drag the slider up so that the setting is Medium High.
13. If necessary, click to select the **Turn on Pop-up Blocker** checkbox.
14. Click the **Settings** button to display the Pop-up Blocker Settings dialog box.
15. Click the **Filter level** dropdown arrow and click **High: Block all pop-ups** if it is not already selected.
16. Click **Close** to close the dialog box. At your instructor's request, capture an image of the Privacy tab of the Internet Options dialog box. Save it in your CB4 assessment folder as *CB4_03*, and then click **OK** to close the Internet Options dialog box.
17. Click the **Tools** button on the Internet Explorer window toolbar and point to **Phishing Filter**.
18. If the command **Turn on Automatic Website Checking** displays, click it.
19. In the Microsoft Phishing Filter dialog box, confirm that the **Turn on automatic Phishing Filter (recommended)** option is selected and then click **OK** to enable the feature.
20. Click the **Tools** button on the Internet Explorer window toolbar and then click **Internet Options**.
21. On the General tab, under Browsing history, click **Settings** to open the Temporary Internet Files and History Settings dialog box.
22. In the Temporary Internet Files area, click to select the **Every time I start Internet Explorer** option. This sets Internet Explorer to check for a new version of a page and update the stored copy every time you start Internet Explorer.
23. Confirm that the Disk space to use value is set within the recommended range of 50MB to 250MB.
24. In the History area, set the Days to keep pages in history value to **15**. At your instructor's request, capture an image of the Temporary Internet Files and History dialog box. Save it in your CB4 assessment folder as *CB4_04*.
25. Click **OK** to apply the changes and close the dialog box, and then click **OK** to close the Internet Options dialog box.
26. **CLOSE** all open windows.

PAUSE. LEAVE the Windows Vista desktop displayed to use in the next project.

Project 3: Preparing Network Connections

Now that the new user account is ready for use, you want to test to make sure it can use its wireless connection to access the network at the museum. In this project, you will display available network connections and connect to the network. You then check the status of the connection and identify the IP address so that you can check the connection. Finally, you disable the connection and enable it again.

GET READY. Have a pen or pencil and a piece of paper on hand to use to write down information you locate during this project. Alternatively, you can record the information in a text or document file, or in an online journal. You must have an available network connection to complete these steps.

1. Click **Start** and then click **Control Panel**.
2. Click **Network and Internet** and then click **Network and Sharing Center** to open the Network and Sharing Center window.
3. In the left pane, under Tasks, click **Connect to a network.**
4. Click the network to which you want to connect and then click the **Connect** button.
5. Click **Close** to close the dialog box and display the Network and Sharing Center window.
6. To the right of the connected network, click **View status**. The Connection Status dialog box displays.
7. In the Connection Status dialog box, locate the amount of the time the connection has been active, the speed at which the network is operating, and the current signal quality. Write the information on a piece of paper or record it in an electronic file or online journal. At your instructor's request, capture an image of the dialog box. Save it in your CB4 assessment folder as ***CB4_05***.
8. Click the **Close** button to close the Connection Status dialog box and then close the Network and Sharing Center window.
9. Click **Start**, click **All Programs**, and then click **Accessories**.
10. Under Accessories, click **Command Prompt** to open the Command Prompt window.
11. In the Command Prompt window, key **ipconfig** and then press **Enter**.
12. Locate the IP address listed under your wireless connection, or for a different connection, and write it down on your piece of paper. Alternatively, record it in an electronic file or online journal.
13. In the Command Prompt window, key **ping**, press the **spacebar**, and then key the IP address you recorded in step 12.
14. Press **Enter**. Watch in the Command Prompt window to see if your computer replies to the ping, and how long it takes. Record the approximate round trip time statistics.
15. In the Command Prompt window, key **nslookup metmuseum.org** and press **Enter**. This is the Web address of the Metropolitan Museum of Art.
16. Record the IP address for the museum's Web site.
17. In the Command Prompt window, key **ping**, press the **spacebar**, and then key the IP address you recorded in step 16.
18. Press **Enter**. Locate and then record the approximate round trip time statistics. Compare the time to the time you recorded in step 14. The museum ping reply should have taken longer, because the Web site server is further away than your own computer.
19. Close the Command Prompt window.
20. Click **Start**, click **Control Panel**, and then click **View network status and tasks** under Network and Internet to open the Network and Sharing Center window.
21. In the left pane, under Tasks, click **Manage network connections** to open the Network Connections window
22. Right-click an enabled connection and click **Disable** on the shortcut menu. If you are logged on as an administrator, click **Continue** in the User Account Control dialog box. Alternatively, key an administrator's password and then click **OK.** Windows Vista disables the connection.

23. Right-click the connection and click **Enable** on the shortcut menu. If you are logged on as an administrator, click **Continue** in the User Account Control dialog box. Alternatively, key an administrator's password and then click **OK**. Windows Vista enables the connection.
24. If necessary, close the Network Connections window and click **Connect to a network** under Tasks in the left pane of the Network and Sharing Center window.
25. Click the network to which you want to connect and then click **Connect**.
26. Click **Close** to close the dialog box.
27. **CLOSE** the Network and Sharing Center window.

PAUSE. LEAVE the Windows Vista desktop displayed and keep the pen or pencil and paper or electronic file available to use in the next project.

Project 4: Set Up a VPN Network

You want the volunteer to be able to log in to the museum's network from home using a VPN. In this project, you set up the VPN.

GET READY. Before you begin these steps, you must obtain authorization from your network administrator. You must get the Internet address of the VPN to which you want to connect, as well as the user name and password you will use to log in. If you do not have authorization, you will not be able to complete this exercise.

1. Click **Start**, click **Control Panel**, and then click **View network status and tasks** under Network and Internet.
2. Under Tasks in the left pane, click **Set up a connection or network**.
3. Click **Connect to a workplace** and then click **Next**.
4. Click **Use my Internet connection (VPN)**.
5. Key the Internet address of the VPN. You can enter the IP address or the domain name, as specified by your network administrator.
6. Click **Next**.
7. Key the user name supplied by your network administrator.
8. Click in the Password box and key your password.
9. Click **Connect**.
10. Log in to the network, using the necessary login procedure.
11. When you are finished using the VPN, disconnect as instructed by your network administrator.
12. Navigate to the Network and Sharing Center window.
13. Click **Manage network connections** under Tasks in the left pane.
14. Right-click the **VPN connection** and then click **Delete** on the shortcut menu.
15. Click **Yes** to delete the VPN connection from your computer.
16. **CLOSE** the Network Connections window.
17. **CLOSE** the Network and Sharing Center window.
18. Log off the Frank Lee user account and log in to your own Windows Vista user account.

PAUSE. LEAVE the Windows Vista desktop displayed to use in the next project.

Project 5: Enable Remote Access

In this project, you set up a Remote Desktop Connection so that the volunteer can check files and folders on a desktop computer from his laptop.

GET READY. To complete this project, you should have access to two separate computers that are connected to the same network. If you do not, you can enable Remote Desktop Connection and authorize users, but you will not be able to use Remote Desktop Connection to access a remote system.

1. On the computer that you want to access remotely, click **Start**, click **Control Panel**, and then click **System and Maintenance**.
2. Under System, click **Allow remote access**. If you are logged on as an administrator, click **Continue** in the User Account Control dialog box. Alternatively, key an administrator password and click **OK**.
3. Click to select the **Allow connections from computers running any version of Remote Desktop** option and then click **Apply** to apply the change and leave the dialog box open.
4. Click the **Select Users** button to open the Remote Desktop Users dialog box.
5. Click **Add** to open the Select Users dialog box.
6. In the Enter the object names to select text box, key **Frank Lee** and then click **OK**. Recall that the user must have a password-protected account on the computer. At your instructor's request, capture an image of the Remote Desktop Users dialog box. Save it in your CB4 assessment folder as ***CB4_06***.
7. Click **OK** to close the Remote Desktop Users dialog box and then click **OK** to close the System Properties dialog box.
8. If you do not already know the IP address of the computer you wish to access remotely, click **Start**, click **All Programs**, click **Accessories**, and then click **Command Prompt**. Key **ipconfig** and then press Enter. Locate the IP address listed under your wireless connection, or for a different connection, and write it down on your piece of paper. Then close the Command Prompt window.
9. On the computer that you want to use to access the remote computer, click **Start**, click **All Programs**, and then click **Accessories**.
10. Under Accessories, click **Remote Desktop Connection**.
11. In the Computer text box, key the IP address of the remote computer and then click **Connect**.
12. In the user name text box, key **Frank Lee**.
13. In the password text box, key **!franKie?**.
14. Click **OK**. If the remote computer is not using network level authentication (NLA), or is running a version of Windows prior to Windows Vista, your computer may display a warning dialog box before establishing the connection. Click **Yes** to establish the remote connection.
15. To end the Remote Desktop Connection, click the **Close** button on the Remote Desktop tab at the top of your screen and then click **Yes** in the dialog box that displays.
16. On the computer that you accessed remotely, click **Start**, click **Control Panel**, and then click **System and Maintenance**. Under System, click **Allow remote access**. If you are logged on as an administrator, click **Continue** in the User Account Control dialog box. Alternatively, key an administrator password and click **OK**.
17. Click to select the **Don't allow connections to this computer** option, and then click **Apply**.
18. Click the **Select Users** button. Click **Frank Lee** and then click the **Remove** button. Click **OK** to close the dialog box.
19. Click **OK** to close the System Properties dialog box. Then close the Control Panel.

PAUSE. LEAVE the Windows Vista desktop displayed to use in the next project.

Project 6: Enable Shared Resources

Frank Lee and the museum's education director have agreed that team members should be able to access Frank's computer when he is in the museum so that they can share files, folders, and network resources. In this project, you will enable file and printer sharing, view the network, and install a network printer for use.

GET READY. To complete this project, you should have access to two separate computers that are connected to the same network. The remote computer should have a shared or Public folder. You should also have access to a network printer. If you do not have access to two separate computers, you can use two separate user accounts on the same computer, but you will not be able to view and access network features.

1. On the local computer, click **Start** and then click **Control Panel**.
2. Under Network and Internet, click **Set up file sharing** to display the Network and Sharing Center window.
3. Click the **Network discovery** expand arrow to display the Network discovery options.
4. If necessary, click to select the **Turn on network discovery** option and then click the **Apply** button. If you are using an administrator account, click **Continue**. Alternatively, key an administrator password and then click **OK**.
5. Click the **Network discovery** collapse arrow to hide the options and then click the File sharing expand arrow to display the **File sharing** options.
6. Click to select the **Turn on file sharing** option and then click the **Apply** button. If you are using an administrator account, click **Continue**. Alternatively, key an administrator password and then click **OK**. File sharing, Public folder sharing, and Printer sharing are all turned on.
7. If necessary, click the **File sharing** collapse arrow to hide the options and then click the **Public folder sharing** expand arrow.
8. Click to select the **Turn on sharing so anyone with network access can open, change, and create files** option and then click the **Apply** button. If you are using an administrator account, click **Continue**. Alternatively, key an administrator password and then click **OK**. Now, network users can read and edit items in the Public folder.
9. Click the **Show me all the files and folders I am sharing** link below the Sharing and Discovery options. A Shared by Me search results window opens to display all of the shared folders you own and have made available as shared.
10. Close the Shared by Me window and then click the **Show me all the shared network folders on this computer** link. A window opens to display all shared folders on the computer.
11. Close the window and then repeat steps 1–10 to enable file and printer sharing on the remote computer.
12. On the local computer, click the **View full map** link in the upper right corner of the Network and Sharing Center window to view a map of your network components.
13. Under Tasks in the left pane, click **View computers and devices**. The Network window opens, showing the computers and devices in your network.
14. Double-click the network computer to which the printer you want to use is attached. The available shared resources are listed in the window.
15. Double-click the **Printers** folder to open the Printers window on the network computer. Printers installed and connected to that network computer are listed in the window.
16. Double-click the icon of the printer you want to use. Windows Vista starts the installation process. It displays a warning message asking you to confirm that you want to install the driver.

17. Click **Install Driver**. If you are logged on as an administrator, click **Continue** in the User Account Control dialog box. If not, key an administrator's password and then click **OK**. Windows Vista installs the driver and sets up the printer for use with your computer. It may open a printer window for the printer as well.
18. **CLOSE** the printer window, if necessary, and then **CLOSE** the network computer's Printers window. The network printer is now installed and ready for use.
19. **CLOSE** all open windows.

PAUSE. LEAVE the Windows Vista desktop displayed to use in the next project.

Project 7: Access Shared Resources

Frank Lee wants everyone on the team to view and comment on two picture files he is considering for use in a presentation. You will start this project by enabling offline files. Then, you will make the pictures available in the Public folder on a remote computer. You will map the Public folder on the remote computer so that you can access it from your Computer folder, and you will make the files available offline.

GET READY. To complete this project, you should have access to two separate computers that are connected to the same network. The remote computer should have a shared or Public folder. You should also have access to a network printer that has been set up for use with your computer. If you do not have access to two separate computers, you can use two separate user accounts on the same computer, but you will not be able to view and access network features.

1. On the local computer, click **Start**, click **Control Panel**, and then click **Network and Internet**.
2. Click **Offline Files**. The Offline Files dialog box displays. If your setting is enabled, skip to step 3. If your setting is disabled, click **Enable Offline Files**. If you are logged in as an administrator, click **Continue** in the User Account Control dialog box. If not, key an administrator's password and then click **OK**. Click **OK** and then click **Yes** to restart your computer. Log back in to your Windows Vista user account.
3. On the remote computer, click **Start** and then click **Documents**. Click **Public** in the Favorites list.
4. Right-click a blank area of the File list, click **New**, and then click **Folder**. Key **Photos** and then press Enter to rename the folder. Double-click the **Photos** folder to open it.

The ***Picture1*** and ***Picture2*** files are available on the companion CD-ROM.

5. Copy the files *Picture1* and *Picture2* from the data files for this lesson to the Photos folder and then close the Photos folder window.
6. On the local computer, click **Start** and then click **Computer**.
7. On the Computer window toolbar, click the **Map Network Drive** button.
8. Click the **Browse...** button.
9. Click the arrow to the left of the network computer on which the shared folder is stored.
10. Click to select the **Public** folder.
11. Click **OK** and then click **Finish**.
12. Close the folder window.
13. Double-click the mapped **Public** folder under Network Location in the Computer window to open it.
14. In the shared network folder window, right-click the **Photos** folder.
15. Click **Always Available Offline** on the shortcut menu.
16. Close the shared folder window.
17. If possible, turn off the remote computer or disconnect it from the network.
18. On the local computer, click **Start** and click **Computer**.
19. Double-click the mapped **Public** folder under Network Location to open its window.

20. Double-click the Photos folder and then double-click the ***Picture1*** file. It should open in Windows Photo Gallery.
21. Close the Windows Photo Gallery window.
22. Turn the remote computer back on or reconnect it to the network.
23. Click the **Sync Center** icon in the Notification area to open the Sync Center.
24. Click **Sync All** to manually synchronize all sync partnerships.
25. Close the Sync Center window.
26. Navigate to the mapped Public folder window and open the Photos folder. Right-click the ***Picture2*** file in the File list and click Print. Select print options to print the picture on the network printer.
27. When printing is complete, close the Photos folder window.
28. In your Computer window, right-click the mapped network drive and click **Disconnect**.

PAUSE. LEAVE the Windows Vista desktop displayed to use in the next project.

Project 8: Restricting Access

Frank Lee has been asked to work on a different project temporarily, and the education director does not want him to be able to access symposium files until he rejoins the team. You will start this project by creating a new user account for another team member. Then, on your desktop, you will create a folder where you can store symposium files. You will set up the folder to share with one user account as a Reader and with Frank Lee as a Co-owner. Then, you will configure the NTFS permissions for the folder to limit Frank Lee's access.

1. Click **Start**, click **Control Panel**, and then click **Add or remove user accounts** under User Accounts and Family Safety. If you have an administrator account, click **Continue** in the User Account Control dialog box. Alternatively, key an administrator's password and then click **OK**.
2. Click **Create a new account** to display the Create New Account window.
3. Key **Katie Jordan**, verify that the Standard user option is selected, and then click **Create Account**. Close the Manage Accounts window.
4. Right-click a blank area of the desktop, click **New**, and then click **Folder**. Key **Symposium** and then press **Enter** to rename the folder.
5. Right-click the **Symposium** folder and click **Share** on the shortcut menu.
6. Click the dropdown arrow above the list of names to display a list of user accounts.
7. Click **Katie Jordan** in the dropdown list of user accounts and then click the **Add** button.
8. Click the dropdown arrow above the list of names, click **Frank Lee**, and then click the **Add** button.
9. Click the **Permission Level** dropdown arrow to the right of Frank Lee's name and click **Co-owner**. At your instructor's request, capture an image of the File Sharing window. Save it in your CB4 assessment folder as *CB4_07*.
10. Click the **Share** button.
11. Click **Done** to close the window.
12. Right-click the **Symposium** folder on the desktop and click **Properties.** Click the **Security** tab.
13. Click the **Edit** button.
14. In the list of Group or user names, click **Frank Lee**.
15. Click to deselect the Allow checkbox to the right of the Modify permission. At your instructor's request, capture an image of the Permissions for Symposium dialog box. Save it in your CB4 assessment folder as ***CB4_08,*** and then click **OK**.

16. Click **OK** to close the Properties dialog box.

PAUSE. LEAVE the Windows Vista desktop displayed to use in the next project.

Project 9: Meeting as a Team

Frank Lee is back to work on the symposium and wants to use the Windows Meeting Space local collaboration network to catch up with what other team members have been doing. In this project, you will log in to the Frank Lee account, set up Windows Meeting Space and People Near Me for use, and set up a meeting. You will then log in to the Katie Jordan account and set up Windows Meeting Space and People Near Me for use, and then join the existing meeting.

1. Log off your Windows Vista user account and log in to the **Frank Lee** user account using the password **!franKie?**.
2. Click **Start**, click **All Programs**, and then click **Windows Meeting Space**.
3. Click **Yes, continue setting up Windows Meeting Space**. If you are logged on as an administrator, click **Continue** in the User Account Control dialog box. Otherwise, key an administrator password and then click **OK**.
4. Click **OK** to set up People Near Me using the default settings.
5. In the Windows Meeting Space window, click **Start a new meeting**.
6. Click in the **Meeting name** text box and key **Symposium Team**.
7. Click in the Password text box and key **LeeMeeting1**.
8. Press **Enter** to start the meeting.
9. Click **Start**, point to the arrow to the right of the Lock this computer icon, and then click **Switch User**. Log in to the Katie Jordan user account.
10. Click **Start**, click **All Programs**, and then click **Windows Meeting Space**.
11. Click **Yes, continue setting up Windows Meeting Space**. If you are logged on as an administrator, click **Continue** in the User Account Control dialog box. Otherwise, key an administrator password and then click **OK**.
12. Click **OK** to set up People Near Me using the default settings.
13. In the Windows Meeting Space window, click the Symposium Team meeting.
14. Key **LeeMeeting1** in the password box and then press **Enter**. At your instructor's request, capture an image of the Meeting Space window. Save it in your CB4 assessment folder as ***CB4_09***. (If necessary, store the file in the Public folder so you can access it when you log in to your own user account, and then move it into your CB4 folder.)
15. Click **Meeting** on the window's menu bar and then click **Leave Meeting**.
16. Close the Windows Meeting Space window, log off the Katie Jordan account, and log back in to the Frank Lee user account.
17. In the Windows Meeting Space window, click **Meeting** on the menu bar and then click **Exit**. The meeting ends, and the Windows Meeting Space window closes.
18. Log off the Frank Lee user account and in to your own Windows Vista user account.

PAUSE. LEAVE the Windows Vista desktop displayed to use in the next project.

Project 10: Prepare a Presentation

The education director has a presentation to deliver to the team members. In this project, you prepare your computer to display a presentation, connect it to an external monitor, and configure the secondary monitor for use.

GET READY. To complete this exercise, you must have a computer set up to support multiple monitors using either a single video card with multiple ports or multiple, compatible video cards.

1. Click **Start**, click **Control Panel**, and then click **Hardware and Sound** to open the Hardware and Sound window.
2. Click Power Options to display the Power Options settings.
3. In the left pane, click **Create a power plan**.
4. Click in the Plan name text box and key **Presentation**. Click **Next**.
5. Click the **Turn off the display** dropdown arrow and click **Never**.
6. Click the **Put the computer to sleep** dropdown arrow and click **Never**.
7. Click **Create**.
8. Navigate back to the Control Panel. Click **Appearance and Personalization** and then click **Personalization**.
9. Click **Screen Saver** to open the Screen Saver Settings dialog box.
10. Click the Screen saver dropdown arrow and click **(None)**. Then click **OK** to apply the change and close the dialog box.
11. Close the Control Panel window.
12. Connect a second monitor to your computer by plugging the monitor cable into the second video port and plugging the monitor AC adapter into an electrical power source. Turn the monitor on. Windows Vista will detect the device. If the New Display Detected dialog box displays, click **Cancel** and skip to step 15.
13. Right-click a blank area of the desktop and click **Personalize** to open the Personalization window.
14. Click **Display Settings** to open the Display Settings dialog box. If necessary, click the **Monitor** tab.
15. Click the **Identify Monitors** button to see which display is the primary and which is the secondary.
16. In the dialog box, click the icon representing the secondary monitor.
17. Click to select the **This is my main monitor** checkbox.
18. Drag the **Resolution** slider to the desired position.
19. Click to select the **Mirrored** option. If Mirrored is not available, select the **Extend the desktop to this monitor** checkbox.
20. Click **OK** to apply the changes and close the dialog box. If necessary, click **Yes** to confirm the changes.
21. Disconnect the secondary monitor from the power source and from your computer.
22. Delete the Frank Lee and Katie Jordan user accounts.
23. Delete the Symposium folder from your desktop.

LOG OFF your Windows Vista user account and shut down Windows Vista.

Appendix A
Microsoft Certified Application Specialist (MCAS) Skills

MATRIX SKILL	SKILL NUMBER	LESSON NUMBER
Display the status of Windows Firewall	1.1.1	11
Configure the firewall access for specific programs	1.1.2	11
Display the status of spyware-protection and virus-protection programs	1.2.1	11
Remove or restore programs blocked by Windows Defender	1.2.2	11
Remove, enable, or disable programs running on a computer	1.2.3	11
Monitor all programs running on a computer by using Windows Defender	1.2.4	11
Choose not to monitor specific programs	1.2.5	11
Configure automatic update settings	1.3.1	11
Manually update Windows Vista	1.3.2	11
Display a list of installed updates	1.3.3	11
Change the screen saver delay time	1.4.1	7
Manually lock a computer	1.4.2	1
Configure Windows Internet Explorer security settings	1.5.1	12
Use the Phishing filter	1.5.2	12
Configure history and temporary Internet files settings	1.5.3	12
Configure privacy settings	1.5.4	12
Allow selected pop-up windows	1.5.5	12
Create a standard password-protected local user account	1.6.1	11
Require a new user to change his or her password when logging on for the first time	1.6.2	11
Disable a local user account	1.6.3	11
Configure power settings and options	2.1.1	9
Place a mobile device in Sleep mode	2.1.2	9
Place a mobile device in Hibernation mode	2.1.3	9
Choose a network connection	2.2.1	13
Find and connect to an available wireless network	2.2.2	13
Check the status of a wireless network connection	2.2.3	13
Remotely connect to a network at your workplace	2.2.4	13
Allow remote desktop connections to your computer	2.3.1	13
Specify who can connect to your computer by using Remote Desktop Connection	2.3.2	13
Disable Windows Remote Assistance	2.3.3	8
Connect to another computer by using Remote Desktop Connection	2.4.1	13
Connect to another computer by mapping a drive to a network share	2.4.2	14
Connect to another computer by browsing a network	2.4.3	14
Connect to another computer by accessing shared folders	2.4.4	14
Set up your computer to use offline files	2.5.1	14
Make a file or folder available offline	2.5.2	14

continued

Matrix Skill	Skill Number	Lesson Number
Resolve synchronization conflicts	2.5.3	14
Synchronize folders between computers	2.5.4	14
Make the content of a favorite website available offline	2.5.6	14
Create a restore point	3.1.1	10
Install a software program	3.1.2	10
Uninstall a software program	3.1.3	10
Install a software update	3.1.4	11
Configure a program to use Compatibility mode	3.1.5	10
Ascertain the amount of available space on a hard disk	3.2.1	9
Ascertain whether a hard disk is partitioned	3.2.2	9
Check a hard disk for problems	3.2.3	9
Enable and disable devices	3.3.1	9
Update or install a device driver	3.3.2	9
Roll back a driver to a previous version	3.3.3	9
Safely remove PC Cards and USB devices	3.3.4	9
Adjust your display resolution	3.4.1	7
Adjust the display refresh rate	3.4.2	7
Select the display color depth setting	3.4.3	7
Adjust icon size	3.4.4	7
Adjust the resolution of a secondary monitor	3.5.1	15
Extend the desktop onto a second monitor	3.5.2	15
Select the primary monitor	3.5.3	15
Install a local printer	3.6.1	9
Change the default printer	3.6.2	9
Locate and install a network printer	3.6.3	14
Share a printer that is connected to your computer	3.6.4	14
Make drivers available for other operating systems	3.6.5	14
Show and hide file extensions	4.1.1	4
Show and hide protected operating system files	4.1.2	4
Show hidden files and folders	4.1.3	4
Configure Windows Explorer layouts	4.1.4	4
Create a folder	4.2.1	2
Rename a folder	4.2.2	2
Add a folder shortcut to the Start menu	4.2.3	7
Add folders to the Favorite Links list	4.2.4	4
Configure NTFS permissions on a folder so that different users have different permissions	4.2.5	14
Set the folder type	4.2.6	5
Share a folder on a hard disk	4.3.1	14
Secure a share by adding permissions for specific users	4.3.2	14
Specify whether a folder should be indexed	4.4.1	6
Search by using a virtual folder	4.4.2	6
Search by using wildcards	4.4.3	6

continued

Matrix Skill	Skill Number	Lesson Number
Search by using keywords	4.4.4	6
Redisplay the results of a previous search	4.4.5	6
Filter results of a search	4.4.6	6
Change the way files are displayed within folders	4.5.1	4
Display or hide file and folder details	4.5.2	4
Group files by details	4.5.3	4
Sort files by details	4.5.4	4
Stack files by details	4.5.5	4
Add metadata to a file	4.6.1	3
Remove properties and personal information from a file	4.6.2	3
Create, delete, rename, and move files	4.6.3	2, 3
Copy data files to a CD or DVD	4.6.4	3, 5
Back up files and folders	4.7.1	10
Schedule backups	4.7.2	10
Restore files and folders from a backup file	4.7.3	10
Restore a previous version of file	4.7.4	10
Sign in to a local collaboration network	5.1.1	14
Start a local collaboration session	5.1.2	14
Join an existing local collaboration session	5.1.3	14
Prepare your computer for presenting information	5.2.1	15
Display information on an external display device	5.2.2	15
Connect to a network projector	5.2.3	15
Customize the Start menu	6.1.1	7
Pin and unpin items from the Start menu	6.1.2	7
Configure a program to start automatically	6.1.3	7
Add a program to the Start menu	6.1.4	7
Display the Quick Launch bar on the Taskbar	6.2.1	7
Add a toolbar to the Taskbar	6.2.2	7
Move the Taskbar to the right side of the screen	6.2.3	7
Automatically hide the Taskbar when not in use	6.2.4	7
Customize the notification area	6.2.5	7
Change the appearance of a computer	6.3.1	7
Arrange desktop icons	6.3.2	7
Change the sound settings	6.3.3	15
Change the screen saver	6.3.4	7
Change the Mouse settings	6.3.5	15
Display the Windows Sidebar	6.4.1	7
Configure the Windows Sidebar	6.4.2	7
Add gadgets to the Windows Sidebar	6.4.3	7
Download a gadget from the Internet	6.4.4	12
Expand memory cache by using Windows ReadyBoost	7.1.1	9
Manually defragment a hard disk	7.1.2	9
Adjust power options for best performance	7.1.3	9
Locate information in Windows Help and Support	7.2.1	1, 8

continued

Matrix Skill	Skill Number	Lesson Number
Search the Microsoft Knowledge Base from Windows Help and Support	7.2.2	8
Ascertain the CPU usage of the computer	7.3.1	9
Ascertain the page file usage of the computer	7.3.2	9
Display the amount of installed RAM and the processor speed	7.3.3	9
Ascertain the hardware and devices installed on a computer	7.3.4	9
Ascertain the system performance rating	7.3.5	9
Ascertain the IP configuration of the computer	7.4.1	13
Ping another computer to ascertain connectivity status	7.4.2	13
Enable and disable a network connection	7.4.3	13
Identify and terminate unresponsive programs	7.5.1	10
Repair a software installation	7.5.2	10
Discover the status of a printer	7.6.1	9
Pause, restart, and delete print jobs and queues	7.6.2	9
Use advanced startup options	7.7.1	11
Restore the computer to a previous point	7.7.2	10
Repair the Windows Vista installation	7.7.3	11
Enable Windows Remote Assistance invitations by using Remote Settings	7.8.1	8
Limit the time that a Remote Assistance invitation is available	7.8.2	8
Request Remote Assistance through Windows Help and Support	7.8.3	8
Disable Remote Assistance invitations	7.8.4	8

Appendix B
Microsoft Office Professional 2007

TO USE MICROSOFT OFFICE PROFESSIONAL 2007, YOU WILL NEED:

COMPONENT	REQUIREMENT
Computer and processor	500 megahertz (MHz) processor or higher[1]
Memory	256 megabyte (MB) RAM or higher[1, 2]
Hard disk	2 gigabyte (GB); a portion of this disk space will be freed after installation if the original download package is removed from the hard drive.
Drive	CD-ROM or DVD drive
Display	1024x768 or higher resolution monitor
Operating system	Microsoft Windows XP with Service Pack (SP) 2, Windows Server 2003 with SP1, or later operating system[3]
Other	Certain inking features require running Microsoft Windows XP Tablet PC Edition or later. Speech recognition functionality requires a close-talk microphone and audio output device. Information Rights Management features require access to a Windows 2003 Server with SP1 or later running Windows Rights Management Services. Connectivity to Microsoft Exchange Server 2000 or later is required for certain advanced functionality in Outlook 2007. Instant Search requires Microsoft Windows Desktop Search 3.0. Dynamic Calendars require server connectivity. Connectivity to Microsoft Windows Server 2003 with SP1 or later running Microsoft Windows SharePoint Services is required for certain advanced collaboration functionality. Microsoft Office SharePoint Server 2007 is required for certain advanced functionality. PowerPoint Slide Library requires Office SharePoint Server 2007. To share data among multiple computers, the host computer must be running Windows Server 2003 with SP1, Windows XP Professional with SP2, or later. Internet Explorer 6.0 or later, 32 bit browser only. Internet functionality requires Internet access (fees may apply).
Additional	Actual requirements and product functionality may vary based on your system configuration and operating system.

[1] 1 gigahertz (GHz) processor or higher and 512 MB RAM or higher recommended for Business Contact Manager. Business Contact Manager not available in all languages.

[2] 512 MB RAM or higher recommended for Outlook Instant Search. Grammar and contextual spelling in Word is not turned on unless the machine has 1 GB memory.

[3] Office Clean-up wizard not available on 64 bit OS.

Glossary

A

account A collection of settings that defines user rights and permissions. Also called user account.

account owner The person assigned to a user account.

active The item that the next command or action will affect. Also, current.

active information Information that continuously updates, such as the time or news headlines.

ad hoc network A temporary network that enables direct computer-to-computer communication.

administrator account A type of Windows Vista user account that provides access to all programs and files on the system. Administrators can make changes that will affect other users, including installing and uninstalling software and hardware, and creating or modifying other user accounts.

archive Back up.

ascending order Sorted alphabetically from A to Z, numerically from 0 to 9, or chronologically from oldest to newest.

attribute A setting that determines how a file or folder can be viewed or edited.

AutoComplete A feature that automatically completes words as you type, based on words that you typed previously.

AutoPlay A feature of Windows Vista that you use to select a program or action to use whenever you work with digital media.

B

back up To create a copy of data for safekeeping.

background The empty area of the desktop where windows open and display content.

backup file A set of copies of files or folders created during a backup procedure. Also called a backup set.

bandwidth The speed at which data is transferred over a network.

basic input/output system (BIOS) The software that controls the start-up functions of your computer, including starting the operating system.

Boolean filter A filter that uses common logical phrases, such as AND, OR, and NOT to combine words.

boot To start a computer.

browser tabs Pages within a web browser window that you use to open multiple web pages in a single window. They are similar to tabs in a dialog box.

burn Copy files to a CD or DVD

button An element you can click to select a command or action.

byte A unit of data representing one character.

C

cache A temporary storage area for data.

cascade Arrange windows to overlap one another in an orderly fashion, starting in the upper left corner of the desktop. The active window, which is on top, displays in its entirety, whereas only the top and left portions of the other windows are visible.

CD drive A drive that reads data on a compact disk. If the drive is a CD burner, it can also write data on a CD.

central processing unit (CPU) The main circuit chip in your computer, responsible for performing most of the calculations needed to run the computer.

chronologically By date.

click The action of pressing and releasing the left mouse button.

click-and-drag The action of pressing and holding the left mouse button and dragging the mouse to a different location. Also called drag.

Clipboard A temporary storage area that can hold one item at a time. Use to copy and move files, folders, and selected data.

collapse Hide the contents of a folder in a list or menu.

color depth The number of colors used on a screen.

color scheme A collection of coordinated colors.

Command Prompt A feature used for inputting certain commands by keying the commands on a command line. Also, the angle bracket character (>) that indicates the location of the command line.

compatible program Any program that reads a particular file type.

compress Reduce in size.

context menu A shortcut menu that displays when you right-click an item.

controller toolbar A toolbar that has buttons for playing, pausing, stopping, and sometimes rewinding or fast-forwarding a media file.

cookie A small file that a website creates and stores on your computer. A cookie contains information that identifies you to the website, such as your user name and email address. It may also contain information such as passwords and account numbers.

current The item that the next command or action will affect. Also, active.

D

definitions Files that store information about known spyware, viruses, and other malicious software. The files are used to monitor, block, and remove the suspicious software.

descending order Sorted alphabetically from Z to A, numerically from 9 to 0, or chronologically from newest to oldest.

desktop The main word area that displays when Windows Vista is running.

destination location A new storage location for a moved or copied file. Also, target.

details Specific information about an item, similar to properties.

device driver The software program that lets your computer communicate with a hardware device. Sometimes called a driver.

device Any piece of equipment that can be attached to a computer or network.

dialog box A window in which you select options or enter data to control the way a program executes a command.

digital camera A camera that records and stores pictures in digital format.

digital video camcorder A video camcorder that records and stores video in digital format.

double-click The action of pressing and releasing the left mouse button twice in rapid succession.

drag-and-drop The combination of dragging and dropping an item with a mouse to move the item to a different location.

drag The action of pressing and holding the left mouse button and dragging the mouse to a different location. Also called click and drag.

drive A device that reads and writes data on storage media.

drop The action of releasing the left mouse button after a drag. Usually used to move an item to a different location. When combined with a drag it may be called Drag-and-drop.

DVD drive A drive that reads data on digital video disks (DVDs) or compact disks (CDs). If the drive is a DVD burner, it can also write data on the disk.

E

encrypt Scramble so as to be indecipherable without an encryption key.

encryption key Code used to unscramble encrypted data.

event sound A sound associated with a specific program event, such as starting a program.

expand Display the contents of a folder in a list or menu. Also, to open, or increase in size to display content that would otherwise be hidden.

extended desktop A multiple monitor configuration that expands the desktop across all available monitors, effectively increasing the size of your display.

Extended Display Identification Data (EDID) A standard video data format that contains basic information about a display's capabilities, such as the maximum screen size and resolution.

extended partition A partition that can contain a logical drive.

F

file A set of information stored with a single name.

filename extension A set of characters added to the end of a filename to identify the file type.

file properties Details that identify a file. Also called metadata.

file type The way a file is saved. Sometimes called file format, the file type determines which programs will be able to read and edit the file.

filter To find items that meet certain criteria while excluding items that do not meet the criteria. Also, the criteria used in a search.

firewall Software that limits access between a computer and a network or between a network and a different network.

first-party cookie A cookie created by the website you are currently viewing.

flash drive A small storage device that plugs into a Universal Serial Bus (USB) port on a computer.

folder A place where you can store items such as files and other folders.

format To apply features to change the appearance of data in a file. Also, the way data is stored.

fragmented Broken into fragments of data that are spread across non-consecutive sectors.

frame A single image in a video. Also, an independent section of a web page that has its own scroll bar.

G

gadget gallery A menu of all the gadgets installed on your computer system.

gadget A program or tool usually displayed on the Sidebar, designed to provide information at a glance.

gateway A computer that connects two networks that use different protocols.

gigabyte A unit of data equal to about 1 billion bytes.

guest account A type of Windows Vista user account that is available for people who do not usually use the computer or network. Guest account users can log in to Windows Vista and use programs, but they cannot access personal data files, install software or hardware, or change settings.

H

hard disk A device that contains one or more inflexible platters coated with material in which data can be recorded magnetically.

hard disk drive A device that reads data from and writes data to a hard disk.

Help Experience Improvement program A feature designed to record users' opinions about Windows Help and Support options.

hibernation A power-saving mode similar to sleep mode that saves your work to your hard disk.

hidden An attribute that keeps a file from being displayed in a file list.

I

icon A small picture that represents an item or command.

inactive A program that is not running or a feature that is not in use.

index A collection of information about items stored on a computer, used to increase the speed and accuracy of a search.

indexed location A location that is included in the Windows Vista index.

information bar An area below the Address bar in Internet Explorer where messages about security and other activities display.

insertion point A blinking vertical bar that indicates the location where text will be inserted.

install Copy program files from a source location to the hard drive on your computer.

installation disk A CD or DVD that stores the files necessary for installing a program.

instant messaging A method of online communication in which the sender types and sends a message that displays almost immediately on the recipient's screen.

intranet A corporate network that uses Internet technologies but can only be accessed by employees and other authorized users.

IP address Internet Protocol address, which is the unique number that identifies your computer to other computers on a network or on the Internet.

J

jpg A graphics file type often used for photos. It is short for joint photographic experts group.

K

kernel The core part of the Windows operating system.

keyword A word that relates to a particular topic.

kilobyte A unit of data equal to 1,024 bytes.

L

link Text or graphics that you click to go to a new destination.

links bar A row of links across the top of a web page that you use to navigate in a website.

Live File System A format for CDs or DVDs that enables you to copy files to the disc at any time instead of all at once.

live preview A thumbnail-sized replica of a window that shows the actual window content. Live previews are only available if you are using the Aero version of Windows Vista.

local collaboration network A network that stores information about users to identify them to others signed in to the same network.

local collaboration program A program that lets you communicate in real time with up to ten other people on a peer-to-peer network.
local printer A printer connected directly to your PC via cables.
logical drive A partition that cannot be used to start an operating system.
loop Display continuously from beginning to end and back to the beginning again, without stopping.

M

map Create a shortcut to a network resource.
mastered A format for CDs or DVDs that requires you to burn all files to a disc at the same time.
maximize To expand a window to fill the desktop.
megabyte A unit of data equal to about 1 million bytes.
menu A list of choices.
metadata Data about data. Another term for file properties.
Microsoft Knowledge Base A collection of articles that Microsoft support engineers have written to document solutions to specific problems encountered by real customers.
minimize To reduce a window to a button on the taskbar.
mirrored desktop A multiple monitor configuration that duplicates the primary monitor desktop on the secondary monitor(s), effectively giving you access to multiple desktops.
mouse An input device commonly used to select features and command.
multimedia Files that store audio, graphics, animation, and video in digital format.
mute Turn the sound off temporarily.

N

network A group of computers and/or devices that communicate with each other using a wireless or physical connection.
network adapter A device that enables a computer to connect to a network.
network drive Any type of drive that is connected to a network and that can be accessed by users on the network.
network level authentication (NLA) A method of checking the identity of a user before allowing remote access to a computer.
network projector A device that is connected to a network through a wired or wireless connection and is used to deliver presentation information to an audience.
newsgroup An online forum for people with common interests, where you can read, ask, and respond to questions and comments posted by other people.
notifications Pop-up windows in the notification area that provide information about the status of a program, or prompt you to take action.
NTFS permissions Detailed permissions you can apply to files, folders, and other resources.

O

Offline The status of a device that is not communicating with the computer.
offline files Copies of network files stored locally on your computer.
online Information stored on the Internet or other network.

P

paging file Space on the hard disk that Windows Vista uses for storing data temporarily during processing. Also called the page file, or the swap file.
pane A section of an area on the screen, such as a section of a window.
partition An area on the hard disk that functions as if it is a separate disk. Also called a volume.
password hint A word or phrase that reminds the user of a password, without specifying the password itself.
password reset disk A removable device such as a CD or flash drive on which Windows Vista stores information about a user account, including the password. It can be used to change the password to access the account.
password A string of characters, such as a word or phrase, that protects an account from unauthorized access.
path The route Windows Vista takes from a storage device through folders and subfolders to a specific destination.
PC Card A credit card sized device that may be used for data storage.
peer-to-peer network A network that lets computers communicate directly with each other without using a network server.
permissions Rules that control access to shared resources.
phishing The act of trying to collect personal or financial information without permission through an email message or website.
physical connection A connection between computers or devices that is created using cables.
physical memory Random access memory (RAM).
pin To place a shortcut in the pinned items list at the top of the left pane of the Start menu.
ping A command used to check whether a particular IP address is available on a network or the Internet.
pixel A dot used as a unit of measure. Short for picture element.
playlist A group of audio or video files stored together for convenient playback.
pointer The icon that moves on the screen in response to the movement of the mouse or other input device.
pointer scheme A collection of coordinated mouse pointer shapes assigned to different actions.
pointer trails Repeated images of the mouse pointer that display when the pointer moves.
pop-up A browser window that displays over the web page you are currently viewing.
presentation settings A collection of settings that optimizes a mobile computer for delivering a presentation.
primary monitor The main monitor connected to your computer.
primary mouse button The mouse button used for primary tasks, such as clicking and dragging.
primary partition A partition that can be used to start an operating system.
print job A document in the print queue.
print queue The folder where documents sent to print are stored while waiting to print.
private network A network that is limited to authorized users.
program A set of instructions that a computer uses to perform a task, such as word processing or photo editing. Sometimes called an application.
properties Details or characteristics about an item.
property label The name of a property.
property value The variable property data that is specific to a file.
protected mode A feature that displays a warning whenever a website tries to install or run a program or file on your computer.
protocol A set of standards used for exchanging information among computers.
Public folder A folder that is set up when you set up Windows Vista, in which you can store files and folders that you want to share with others.
public network A network that is available to many different users, such as a network in a public place.

Q

quarantine Move a suspicious file to an isolated storage location and temporarily stop it from running.

Quick Launch Toolbar An area of the taskbar that displays shortcuts to frequently used programs.

R

random access memory (RAM) The internal storage area that your computer uses to run programs and store data. Also called physical memory.

read-only An attribute that enables a file to be read or copied but not changed or saved.

Recycle Bin A place where deleted items are stored until they are removed permanently or restored to their original location.

redo To reverse the previous Undo action.

refresh rate The frequency that a monitor flickers.

Registry A folder where system configuration data is stored.

Remote Assistance A feature of Windows Vista that lets you ask for or provide technical help via a direct connection between two computers.

Remote Assistance invitation A file that is sent from one person to another to allow a Remote Access connection.

Remote Desktop Connection A feature of Windows Vista that enables access from a computer running Windows Vista to another computer running Windows Vista or some other version of the Windows operating system.

resolution The quality or sharpness of an image.

restore Copy a backup or previous version of a file or folder back to its original location.

restore down To return a window to its previous size and position on the desktop.

restore point A file that contains information about your system configuration at a particular point in time.

right-click The action of pressing and releasing the right mouse button.

router A device that sends information between two networks.

RSS feed Web content that is updated frequently and downloaded.

S

Safe mode A troubleshooting option that loads only the basic files and drivers necessary to run Windows Vista.

scanner A device that converts a printed image to a digital file.

screen saver A picture or animation that displays on the monitor when you have not used your system for a set period of time.

ScreenTip A pop-up balloon that displays information about the current item.

scrollbar A tool used to scroll the display to show items that do not fit within the current window.

scroll To shift a display up, down, left, or right.

scroll box A box on the scroll bar that you can drag to quickly scroll the window.

search box An area where you can key search text.

search folder A virtual folder designed specifically for searching.

search provider A website designed to search the Internet.

search results The items that match the specified criteria.

search text The text that Windows Vista will look for to locate programs, files, and folders stored on your computer.

secondary monitor Any additional monitor connected to your computer that is not the main, or primary, monitory.

secondary mouse button The mouse button used for secondary tasks, such as opening a shortcut menu.

security level A pre-selected group of security settings that can be applied to a security zone.

security zone A category that Internet Explorer uses to identify websites based on the level of risk they pose.

select To mark an item to indicate that it will be affected by the next action or command.

shadow copy A version of a file saved as part of a restore point.

share To provide access to other users. Also, the object that is being shared.

share permissions Four levels of permissions you can apply to folders.

shortcut A link to a program, feature, or command.

shortcut menu A list of commands or options relevant to the current task that displays when you right-click an item.

shuffle Display in random order.

Sidebar A vertical bar usually located along the right side of the desktop where gadgets can be displayed.

Sleep mode A state of low power consumption.

sound card A hardware device installed inside your computer that lets your computer input, process, and output sound.

sound scheme A set of coordinated sounds assigned to different program events.

source location The location where an item is originally stored.

spyware A type of malicious software that displays pop-up advertisements, collects information about users, and changes computer settings, all without permission.

stack A collection of related files displayed as a single icon that looks like a pile of items. Also, to tile windows horizontally so that they display one above the other without overlapping.

standard account A type of Windows Vista user account that provides access to most programs and to personal data files. Standard users cannot install or uninstall software or hardware, delete system files, or change settings that affect other users without first keying an administrator's password.

Start button A round button with the Microsoft Windows logo on it that you click to open the Start menu.

Start menu A menu that provides access to all the programs, files, and folders stored on your computer.

subfolder A folder stored within another folder.

submenu A menu that opens off of another menu.

swap file Another name for the paging file.

sync conflict When differences between a file stored in one location and a version of the same file in another location cannot be reconciled; therefore, the files cannot be synchronized.

Sync Partnership A profile in Windows Vista that defines how and when files will be synchronized between two locations.

synchronize To compare offline and online files and save the most recent version. Sometimes abbreviated to sync.

syntax The way words are arranged.

system event An event that affects the system configuration, such as installing or uninstalling a new program.

system performance rating A score that measures the capability of your computer's hardware and software configuration.

System Restore A feature that lets you restore your computer's system files to an earlier configuration.

T

tag A custom property that you can add to provide specific information not included in any other property.

taskbar A row, usually across the bottom of the desktop, that displays icons that let you access frequently used features, programs, and commands.

template A model that has certain characteristics or features you may want to recreate.

temporary Internet files Copies of web pages, images, and media that you view on the Internet, that Internet Explorer stores on your computer.

Terminal Services (TS) gateway A gateway that enables authorized users to connect to a remote computer on a corporate network without having to set up a VPN connection.

text editor A program that you can use to create and edit text-based files.

third-party cookie A cookie created by a website other than the one you are currently viewing, such as an advertiser.

tile Arrange windows so that they display without overlapping. Tile horizontally to stack windows one above the other. Tile vertically to arrange windows side by side.

tiles Medium-sized icons with a label displaying the item name and type to the right.

toolbar sizing handle A screen element at one end of a taskbar toolbar, consisting of three columns of dots. Drag the handle to change the width of the toolbar.

U

undo To reverse the previous action or command.

uninstall Remove the program files and other files, such as shortcuts associated with the program from your computer.

unresponsive program A program that is not able to communicate with the user or with the operating system, usually due to a problem in the program itself.

up time The length of time a computer has been running.

update A software program that fixes a problem or improves security or performance.

upgrade A new and improved version of an existing program. Or, to install an upgrade.

user rights Tasks that a user may perform.

user A person who is authorized to use a computer and who has a user account.

V

virtual folder A temporary location used to store the results of a search.

virtual memory A combination of the paging file and RAM.

virtual private network (VPN) An encrypted network that connects one or more computers to a large network via the Internet.

virus A program that attempts to spread throughout a system and other networked systems to destroy, change, or manipulate data.

W

wallpaper An image or color that displays on your desktop.

web browser A program that you can use to locate and view pages on the Internet, an intranet, or the World Wide Web (web).

wildcard characters Characters that substitute for one or more actual characters.

Windows ReadyBoost A feature of Windows Vista that lets you use storage space on some removable media devices, such as USB flash drives, to increase the performance speed of your PC.

wireless connection A connection between computers or devices that is created using radio signals.

wma Windows Media Audio, a file format commonly used for audio that will play on a Windows-based computer.

wmf A graphics file type often used for drawings. It is short for Windows media file.

wmv Windows Media Video, a file format commonly used for video that will play on a Windows-based computer.

Index

Photo Credits

Lesson 1
Purestock/Superstock

Lesson 2
"PhotoDisc, Inc./Getty Images Inc."

Lesson 3
Corbis Digital Stock

Lesson 4
Corbis Digital Stock

Lesson 5
Corbis Digital Stock

Lesson 6
"PhotoDisc, Inc./Getty Images Inc."

Lesson 7
"PhotoDisc, Inc."

Lesson 8
Corbis Digital Stock

Lesson 9
Purestock

Lesson 10
Digital Vision

Lesson 11
Purestock

Lesson 12
Digital Vision

Lesson 13
Purestock

Lesson 14
© IT Stock

Lesson 15
Purestock

▪ System Requirements

Microsoft Office Ultimate 2007

To use Microsoft Office Ultimate 2007, you will need:

Component	Requirement
Computer and processor	500 megahertz (MHz) processor or higher[1]
Memory	256 megabyte (MB) RAM or higher[1, 2, 3]
Hard disk	3 gigabyte (GB); a portion of this disk space will be freed after installation if the original download package is removed from the hard drive.
Drive	CD-ROM or DVD drive
Display	1024x768 or higher resolution monitor
Operating system	Microsoft Windows(R) XP with Service Pack (SP) 2, Windows Server(R) 2003 with SP1, or later operating system[4]
Other	Certain inking features require running Microsoft Windows XP Tablet PC Edition or later. Speech recognition functionality requires a close-talk microphone and audio output device. Information Rights Management features require access to a Windows 2003 Server with SP1 or later running Windows Rights Management Services. Connectivity to Microsoft Exchange Server 2000 or later is required for certain advanced functionality in Outlook 2007. Instant Search requires Microsoft Windows Desktop Search 3.0. Dynamic Calendars require server connectivity. Connectivity to Microsoft Windows Server 2003 with SP1 or later running Microsoft Windows SharePoint Services or Office SharePoint Server 2007 is required for certain advanced collaboration functionality. PowerPoint Slide Library requires Office SharePoint Server 2007. Connectivity to Office SharePoint Server 2007 required for browser-enabled InfoPath forms and additional collaboration functionality. Groove Messenger integration requires Windows Messenger 5.1 or later or Communicator 1.0 or later. Includes a 5 year subscription to the Groove relay service. Some features require Microsoft Windows Desktop Search 3.0, Microsoft Windows Media Player 9.0, Microsoft DirectX 9.0b, Microsoft Active Sync 4.1, microphone[1], audio output device, video recording device (such as a webcam), TWAIN-compatible digital camera or scanner, Windows Mobile 2003 powered Smartphone or Windows Mobile 5 powered Smartphone or Pocket PC, or a router that supports Universal Plug and Play (UPnP). Sharing notebooks requires users to be on the same network. Internet Explorer 6.0 or later, 32 bit browser only. Internet functionality requires Internet access (fees may apply).
Additional	Actual requirements and product functionality may vary based on your system configuration and operating system.

[1] 2 gigahertz (GHz) processor or higher and 1 GB RAM or higher recommended for **OneNote Audio Search**. Close-talking microphone required. Audio Search not available in all languages.

[2] 1 gigahertz (GHz) processor or higher and 512 MB RAM or higher recommended for **Business Contact Manager**. Business Contact Manager not available in all languages.

[3] 512 MB RAM or higher recommended for **Outlook Instant Search**. Grammar and contextual spelling in *Word* is not turned on unless the machine has 1 GB memory.

[4] Send to **OneNote 2007** print driver not available on a 64 bit operating system. Groove Folder **Synchronization** not available on 64 bit operating system. Office Clean-up wizard not available on 64 bit OS.